FOUNDATION PRESS

DEATH PENALTY STORIES

Edited By

JOHN H. BLUME

Cornell Law School

and

JORDAN M. STEIKER

University of Texas
School of Law

FOUNDATION PRESS

2009

THOMSON REUTERS

© 2009 By THOMSON REUTERS/FOUNDATION PRESS

195 Broadway, 9th Floor
New York, NY 10007
Phone Toll Free 1–877–888–1330
Fax (212) 367–6799
foundation–press.com

Printed in the United States of America
ISBN 978–1–59941–343–3

TEXT IS PRINTED ON 10% POST
CONSUMER RECYCLED PAPER

for Drucy, Hank and Casey — JB

for Eliza, Blake and Aaron — JS

*

DEATH PENALTY STORIES

FOUNDATION PRESS

DEATH PENALTY STORIES

*

Introduction

John Blume and Jordan Steiker

The American death penalty has had an unusual history. Capital punishment was an ordinary part of colonial criminal justice, and the death penalty was available in all states at the time of the founding (indeed, two liberty-protecting clauses of the Bill of Rights in the U.S. Constitution clearly anticipate capital prosecutions—the provision for a grand jury in cases involving "capital" or otherwise infamous crimes, and the guarantee that no person shall be "deprived of life" without due process of law). But the enlightenment philosophy that animated the American experiment with democratic self-rule also led to unprecedented efforts to cabin the reach of the death penalty. In the 1790s, Pennsylvania became the first jurisdiction to limit the availability of the death penalty for certain murders, and its effort to divide murders into "degrees"—and to withhold the death penalty for "lesser" murders—became a blueprint for the reform of capital punishment.

Over the next half-century, the death penalty in at least some American jurisdictions was on the path of reform. In the 1830s, several states brought executions behind penitentiary walls because of the perceived coarsening effect of public executions. With the advent of penitentiaries also came the first sustained political efforts to abolish the death penalty, and Michigan became the first state to abolish the death penalty in 1846 (for all crimes other than treason)—a decision it has never reversed. Those states that retained the death penalty rejected its mandatory application, and even in cases of first degree murder, juries gradually and then universally were afforded the choice to reject the ultimate punishment. Over the next century, death penalty reform waxed and waned, with a sustained abolitionist moment in the period before the First World War (nine states). The Red Scare and the Depression reinvigorated capital punishment, with executions reaching their all-time high in absolute numbers in the mid–1930s.[1]

---

[1] *See generally* William J. Bowers, Executions in America 5–9, 22 (1974).

The American death penalty was notable in two divergent respects during its first sesquicentennial: contrary to its current standing, the American death penalty was more exceptional for its ameliorations (and in some cases abolition) than it was for its severity, and at the same time its administration was virtually unregulated by federal authorities (including the federal courts). Capital prosecutions and executions were overwhelmingly local events, and defendants had little recourse to federal law as a means of challenging their convictions and sentences. Capital trials were in many cases summary affairs, judicial review was minimal (even at the state level), and the most promising form of "review" could be had via executive clemency. The time between the pronouncement of sentence and execution was measured in weeks or months rather than years. For these reasons, there are few "landmark" capital cases before the Second World War (and none in this volume).

Two of the most famous constitutional cases involving the death penalty during the pre-War period, in which state death-row inmates alleged that their sentences were the product of "mob-dominated" trials, reflect the minimalism of federal constitutional regulation of the death penalty throughout much of our constitutional history. In the case of Leo Frank, in 1915, the U.S. Supreme Court rejected his habeas challenge to his conviction notwithstanding the presence of a hostile and dangerous crowd at his trial (Frank and his attorneys were not present at the verdict for fear of being lynched).[2] Because the various protections afforded criminal defendants via the Bill of Rights had not yet been extended to the States, Frank claimed a generalized denial of "due process," which the Court rejected on the theory that he was afforded an opportunity for review of his claims within the state courts. Justice Holmes, in dissent, lamented that "[m]ob law does not become due process of law by securing the assent of a terrorized jury."[3] Frank ultimately received a commutation of his death sentence from Georgia's Governor John Slaton, only to be lynched by a mob less than two months later (Governor Slaton himself was threatened with mob violence because of his decision). In the other case, numerous African–Americans were charged with murder and sentenced to death based on events stemming from a 1919 race riot in Phillips County, Arkansas.[4] The defendants were threatened with lynching, but the mob dispersed on assurances that the defendants would be convicted and executed through "law." The Court, over two dissents, reversed the denial of federal habeas relief, concluding that "if the whole proceeding is a mask—that counsel, jury and judge were swept to the fatal end by an irresistible

---

[2] Frank v. Mangum, 237 U.S. 309 (1915).

[3] *Id*. at 347 (Holmes, J., dissenting).

[4] Moore v. Dempsey, 261 U.S. 86 (1923).

wave of public passion, and that the State Courts failed to correct the wrong," the requirements of due process were violated.[5]

The grant of relief to these defendants reflected the extreme circumstances required for federal courts to upset the judgments of state courts in criminal justice matters—including ones involving the death penalty. Together with the Frank case, the Arkansas case also reflected quite literally the close and complicated relationship between lynching and state-sponsored executions during the first part of the twentieth century. The national anti-lynching sentiment exerted pressure to channel violence through courts, and the countervailing demands for swift and sure punishment produced trials that were often quick, non-adversarial, and designed to ratify a pre-existing societal verdict.

The litigation stemming from the "Scottsboro Boys" cases in the 1930s provided the first hint that federal constitutional law might play a distinctive role in state capital trials. Nine African–American males, ranging in age from 13 to 30, were charged with raping two white females on a train as it passed through Scottsboro, Alabama. Despite the victims' inconsistent accounts of the alleged sexual assault and the absence of any physical evidence of rape, the cases were called for trial twelve days after the defendants' arrest. Observers estimated that five to ten thousand people waited outside the courthouse, and the National Guard was summoned to make sure the defendants were not lynched. The trial judge appointed the entire county bar as counsel for the defendants, but not a single lawyer showed for trial. The judge then appointed a Tennessee lawyer who had been sent by the defendants' families to observe the proceedings. Despite the lawyer's objection that he knew nothing about the case or Alabama law, and despite the fact that he appeared to be drunk, the trial judge pressed forward with the trial after allowing counsel less than half an hour to meet with his "clients." All nine defendants were found guilty and eight were sentenced to death in three trials, none of which lasted more than a few hours. The refusal of the state authorities to provide meaningful representation to the defendants in those cases led the Court, in *Powell v. Alabama*,[6] to recognize a right to counsel for state defendants facing the death penalty, a right that would not be fully extended to state non-capital cases for almost three decades. *Powell*, then, stands as a notable exception to the extraordinarily deferential posture of federal courts to state capital procedures and judgments in the years before the modern era.

Both the summary features of state criminal trials (particularly in the South) and the limited nature of federal constitutional review are

---

[5] *Id.* at 91.

[6] 287 U.S. 45 (1932).

reflected in the first story in this volume—Deborah Denno's extraordinary account of the 1947 botched execution of Willie Francis. The *Francis* case[7] has always represented the fragility and contradictions of American capital punishment—the desire to tame the death penalty by making it less gruesome and more humane and the conflicting determination to impose the ultimate sanction at all costs and without regard to circumstance. Denno's thick description of the Francis trial in St. Martinville, the small city in Louisiana where Francis was ultimately executed after the first effort to electrocute him failed, provides a portrait of the old regime of Southern justice. The proceedings were characterized by questionable evidence, inadequate representation, and fifteen minutes of jury deliberation. Denno brings to her account an unusual array of primary materials, including Francis' correspondence and Denno's interviews with Francis family members and residents of St. Martinville. Denno also reflects on the significance of the *Francis* litigation for contemporary constitutional debates regarding the permissible modes and protocols for the "execution" of executions.

After the Second World War, the death penalty began a significant decline, both in the numbers of defendants sentenced to death and the number of executions. In addition, a confluence of social, political, and legal developments led to unprecedented national circumspection regarding capital punishment. The Civil Rights movement linked the death penalty to racial injustice, especially in light of the disproportionate application of the penalty in the South and in cases involving African–American defendants (particularly for the crime of rape). The war in Vietnam undermined confidence in governmental actors and faith in the benign administration of justice. By the mid–1960s, the Gallup Poll found for the first (and only time) that opponents outnumbered supporters of capital punishment.[8]

On the legal side, the Warren Court effected a sea-change in the federal supervision of state criminal systems by extending virtually all of the federal constitutional protections in criminal trials to state proceedings (including the Fourth Amendment exclusionary rule, the Fifth Amendment protections against self-incrimination (most notably the prophylactic *Miranda* warnings), and the Sixth Amendment right to counsel). Two cases in particular foreshadowed extensive federal regulation of the states' administration of the death penalty: the decision in 1962 to incorporate and apply against the states the Eighth Amend-

---

[7] Louisiana ex rel. Francis v. Resweber, 329 U.S. 459 (1947).

[8] Jeffrey M. Jones, "Support for the Death Penalty 30 Years After the Supreme Court Ruling," Gallup News Service, 6/30/2006, http://www.gallup.com/poll/23548/Support–Death–Penalty–Years–After–Supreme–Court–Ruling.aspx ("The year 1966 marked the only time more Americans said they were against the death penalty (47%) than said they were for it (42%).").

ment's prohibition of cruel and unusual punishments,[9] and Justice Goldberg's 1963 dissent from the denial of certiorari in *Rudolph v. Alabama*,[10] joined by Justices Brennan and Douglas, making clear that at least three members of the Court believed that the death penalty might be disproportionate when imposed for the crime of rape.

These developments inspired the "moratorium" strategy of the NAACP Legal Defense Fund to bring executions in the U.S. to a halt, a strategy that succeeded by 1967, inaugurating the longest period without executions (almost ten years) in American history.[11] The LDF challenges to the death penalty culminated in the U.S. Supreme Court's decision in *Furman v. Georgia*,[12] which invalidated virtually all existing capital statutes and might well have wrought the end of the American death penalty. Carol Steiker's engaging chapter on *Furman* describes the events and strategies that culminated in the momentous decision, including the other cases—*Witherspoon v. Illinois*,[13] *Boykin v. Alabama*,[14] *Maxwell v. Bishop*,[15] and *McGautha v. California*[16]—that might have emerged (but did not) as the "landmark" capital cases of that era. Steiker explores the backlash to *Furman* and the resulting reinvigoration of the American death penalty, suggesting that its robust reemergence since the 1970s might have been partly because of, and not merely in spite of, the Court's intervention and continuing supervision. Steiker also closely examines the various grounds of decision embodied in the five separate opinions supporting the Court's judgment and traces their impact on contemporary jurisprudence. She concludes that the conventional account of *Furman*—which emphasizes its concern with standardless discretion—fails to appreciate the extent to which prevailing constitutional regulation subordinates that concern to other powerful doctrines traceable to *Furman*, particularly the importance of individualized sentencing and proportionality.

The states' rapid response to *Furman*—thirty five states enacted new capital statutes in the wake of the decision—assured that the constitutionality of the death penalty would return to the Supreme Court, particularly in light of the large numbers of inmates sentenced to

---

[9] Robinson v. California, 370 U.S. 660 (1962).

[10] 375 U.S. 889 (1963).

[11] *See* Death Penalty Info. Cntr., Executions in the U.S. 1609–2002: The Espy File, Executions by Date, http://www.deathpenaltyinfo.org/executions-us-1608-2002-espy-file (last visited Feb. 9, 2009), at 238.

[12] 408 U.S. 238 (1972).

[13] 391 U.S. 510 (1968).

[14] 395 U.S. 238 (1969).

[15] 398 U.S. 262 (1970).

[16] 402 U.S. 183 (1970).

death following *Furman* and the dramatic shift in popular support for the punishment. Hugo Bedau's chapter on *Gregg v. Georgia*,[17] one of the five cases before the Court in 1976, traces what in retrospect appears to be the inevitable path to constitutional reexamination. Bedau explores the intricacies of the Georgia scheme that the Court upheld and compares it to the other state statutes (Florida, Texas, North Carolina, and Louisiana) that the Court simultaneously reviewed.[18] He also closely analyzes and critiques the retentionist arguments embraced by the two plurality opinions in *Gregg*. With a detailed account of Solicitor General Robert Bork's arguments to the Court in support of the constitutionality of capital punishment, Bedau reminds us of the important role that the federal government played in sustaining the death penalty.

Gregg and its companion cases established the rough framework for the ongoing project of federal constitutional regulation of the death penalty. In the year following *Gregg*, the Court reviewed another Georgia case that would generate perhaps the most significant line of attack against the American death penalty—that its use in particular cases violates prevailing standards of decency. Sheri Lynn Johnson's chapter on *Coker v. Georgia*[19] recounts the Court's invalidation of the death penalty for the crime of raping an adult woman. Johnson laments the astonishing absence of any discussion of race in the Court's decision. In Johnson's view, the Court's deliberate decision to choose a white defendant-white victim case (even though the petitions of African–American defendants sentenced to death for rape arrived at the Court before Coker's), and its refusal to confront the demonstrably discriminatory use of the death penalty to punish African–American defendants accused of raping white victims, made it more difficult for the Court to confront racial discrimination as a distinct claim when the Court revisited Georgia's death penalty system in *McCleskey v. Kemp*[20] (discussed below). Although Johnson applauds the Court's recent decision in *Kennedy v. Louisiana*[21] extending *Coker*'s proportionality analysis to all ordinary crimes that do not result in death (including the rape of a child), Johnson regards *Coker* as an abdication of the Court's responsibility to weave historical context and contemporary reality into its Eighth Amendment decisionmaking.

The Court's 1976 decisions paved the way for the resumption of executions in the United States. John Blume's chapter on *Gilmore v.*

---

[17] 428 U.S. 153 (1976).

[18] Proffitt v. Florida, 428 U.S. 242 (1976); Jurek v. Texas, 428 U.S. 262 (1976); Woodson v. North Carolina, 428 U.S. 280 (1976); Roberts v. Louisiana, 428 U.S. 325 (1976).

[19] 433 U.S. 584 (1977).

[20] 481 U.S. 279 (1987).

[21] 128 S. Ct. 2641 (2008).

Utah[22] offers an account of the events that culminated in Gary Gilmore's execution in 1977, including Gilmore's background, crime, and truncated appeals. The most significant aspect of Gilmore's case—apart from ending the nationwide moratorium on executions—was Gilmore's status as a "volunteer." Gilmore had waived his appeals, and the state and federal courts had to decide whether and under what circumstances an inmate could speed his own execution. Blume recounts the extraordinary determination of state actors to carry out Gilmore's execution, and examines the difficult legal and moral questions surrounding what Justice Marshall deemed "state-administered suicide."[23] Ultimately, Gilmore's execution became a symbol of the renewed American death penalty, and established a significant feature of contemporary death penalty practice, the ability of death-sentenced inmates to bypass lengthy appellate and postconviction review. "Volunteers" have accounted for a substantial number of post-*Furman* executions (over 10% of the 1145 executions carried out in the modern era[24]), particularly in states (such as Utah) with few executions. If the current trend toward fewer overall executions continues, perhaps reflecting greater national circumspection about the value of capital punishment, "volunteers" might well play a significant role in creating the appearance of a more robust American death penalty.

The American death penalty stabilized in the decade following Gilmore's execution. The varied state capital statutes were subject to extensive litigation, and the broad parameters of federal constitutional regulation began to emerge. State death-row populations, as well as executions, climbed substantially. Looming on the horizon, though, was a broad and potentially crippling attack against the implementation of the death penalty. The NAACP LDF, which had been instrumental in challenging the arbitrary and discriminatory use of the death penalty in the 1960s, sought to demonstrate that race discrimination continued to plague the death penalty notwithstanding the post-*Furman* modifications of state capital practices. Their efforts culminated in an unprecedented, sophisticated, empirical test of Georgia's capital charging and sentencing decisions. The resulting study, which found very powerful race-of-the-victim effects in capital cases, raised a fundamental question: given that *Furman* had invalidated state capital schemes based on the *fear* of arbitrary and perhaps discriminatory decisionmaking, would empirical *demonstration* of significant race-based discrimination require the abandonment (or severe curtailment) of capital punishment? David

---

[22] 429 U.S. 1012 (1976).

[23] *See* Godfrey v. Georgia, 446 U.S. 420, 439 (1980) (Marshall, J., concurring in the judgment).

[24] *See* Death Penalty Info. Cntr., Execution Database, http://deathpenaltyinfo.org/execu tions (last viewed Feb. 10th, 2009) (compare search of "Factors: Volunteers," "Year: Search All Years," with search of "Factors: All Factors," "Year: Search All Years").

Baldus, George Woodworth, and Charles Pulaski, the authors of the Georgia study (which came to be known as the "Baldus Study"), together with Jack Boger, the principal LDF lawyer who litigated the race discrimination claim to the Supreme Court, provide their own insightful account of the research and litigation that culminated in *McCleskey v. Kemp*.[25] They offer a thorough guide to the methodology underlying their research and a nuanced review of the jurisprudential theories underlying McCleskey's claims. The Court's denial of relief in *McCleskey* was ultimately instrumental in sustaining the American death penalty, and the authors critically engage the Court's decision at this pivotal point in modern capital history. Their story neither conceals their own disappointment and disagreement with the Court's resolution, nor obscures the genuine complexity surrounding the global challenge to capital punishment that the Baldus Study represented.

With the *McCleskey* challenge swept aside, the American death penalty reached its height in death sentences and executions over the ensuing decade. As the U.S. became the symbol of the resurgent death penalty, Texas emerged as the American death penalty capital, accounting for well over a third of the executions conducted nationwide over the past thirty years. Jordan Steiker's account of *Penry v. Lynaugh*[26] explains how the unusual Texas capital statute managed to secure provisional approval in 1976 as a "guided discretion" statute, in part because of the strategic challenges presented by the LDF's effort to litigate on behalf of death-row inmates sentenced under divergent state schemes. When the Court subsequently found the Texas statute inadequate to facilitate consideration of Penry's mental retardation and childhood abuse in 1989, it threatened to derail the Texas death penalty. But the extraordinary resistance to *Penry* by the Texas and federal courts allowed Texas to carry out scores of executions during the 1990s—even in cases of demonstrable constitutional error. In a strange twist of fate, it was Penry's own case, returning to the Court after a retrial, which finally prompted the Court to police its original *Penry* decision,[27] belatedly enforcing a broad principle of individualized sentencing in capital cases. Steiker also addresses the "other" half of *Penry*—the defendant's claim that his mental retardation precluded his execution altogether. Penry's "loss" on this issue ultimately led states to statutorily bar the practice, and these political developments eventually caused the Court to revisit the issue and ban the execution of persons with mental retardation.[28] One central lesson of *Penry*, Steiker argues, is that both victories

---

[25] 481 U.S. 279 (1987).

[26] 492 U.S. 302 (1989).

[27] Penry v. Johnson, 532 U.S. 782 (2001).

[28] Atkins v. Virginia, 536 U.S. 304 (2002).

and defeats in the courts can be fleeting, and the end point of constitutional regulation of the death penalty might turn out to be quite different from what even informed observers would predict.

The emergence of a robust American death penalty is also traceable in part to a relatively recent social movement valorizing the claims of victims of crime. In his careful study of *Payne v. Tennessee*,[29] Austin Sarat examines the concrete doctrinal manifestation of the victims' rights movement in capital cases—the Court's about-face on the admissibility of "victim impact" evidence in capital prosecutions. After fashioning a bright-line protection against such evidence in two decisions issued in the late 1980s,[30] the Court reconsidered and overruled those precedents just a few years later in *Payne*. Sarat explores the various political interests and events that shaped the victims' right movement in the U.S. and offers a detailed view of the conflicting constitutional arguments implicated by the use of such evidence in capital cases. As supporters of the death penalty have shifted the weight of their arguments from deterrence to retribution, cases like *Payne* reveal the divergent strands of retributive justification for punishment, and Sarat critically engages the judicial effort to police the line between social justice and private vengeance.

Over the past ten years, death-sentencing rates (both in absolute numbers and in relation to homicides) have declined enormously, and some would argue that we have entered a new era of restriction and perhaps even abolition of the American death penalty. In the mid–1990s, over three hundred defendants were sentenced to death nationwide each year (with a modern era high of 328 in 1994), whereas fewer than 150 defendants were sentenced to death in each of the past five years (with a modern era low of 115 in 2007).[31] Nationwide executions have dropped as well, from a high of 98 in 1999 to a decade low of 37 in 2008[32] (attributable in part to a brief moratorium on executions caused by litigation surrounding state lethal injection protocols).

The precipitous nationwide decline in the use of the death penalty, reflected in these numbers, stems from a variety of factors. The discovery in Illinois of numerous wrongful convictions in capital cases led to the most striking mass commutation of capital sentences in American history (167 inmates), as Republican Governor George Ryan publicly

---

[29] 501 U.S. 808, 822 (1991).

[30] South Carolina v. Gathers, 490 U.S. 805 (1989); Booth v. Maryland, 482 U.S. 496 (1987).

[31] *See* Death Penalty Info. Cntr., Death Sentences By Year, http://www.deathpenalty info.org/death-sentences-year–1977–2008 (last visited Feb. 9, 2009).

[32] *See* Death Penalty Info. Cntr., Execution Database, http://deathpenaltyinfo.org/execu tions (last visited Feb. 9, 2009).

campaigned to reform and indeed abolish the ultimate punishment. Concerns about wrongful convictions also prompted nationwide soul-searching about the prevailing safeguards in capital (and non-capital) cases, and numerous states have sought to study and amend existing practices; one state, New Jersey, concluded its study with the decision to abolish capital punishment in 2007, the first state to secure legislative abolition since 1976. The prospect of wrongful convictions has undoubtedly contributed to the decline in death-sentencing and executions, as concerns about factual error have had greater traction in public discourse about the death penalty than the more amorphous, *Furman*-era concerns about its distribution, fairness, and fundamental justice.

In addition, the past twenty years have seen the widespread adoption of life-without-possibility-of-parole (LWOP) as a sentencing alternative to the death penalty, and many district attorneys have chosen to forego capital prosecutions because of the comparative costs associated with capital prosecutions and the newly-available option of lifetime incapacitation. Public opinion polls have long revealed a significant decline in support for the death penalty when the question is framed in terms of the choice between capital punishment versus life-without-possibility-of-parole.

The expectations for capital defense practice have also changed significantly over the past twenty years, and it is has become less common (and less acceptable) for capital defense lawyers to devote their energies primarily or exclusively to the guilt-innocence phase of capital trials. Capital trial lawyers are more aware of the importance of developing and presenting mitigating evidence and of the need to embrace trial strategies that weave the defense mitigation theory into the guilt-innocence phase of the proceedings. The emergence of "mitigation specialists" as a distinct class of capital trial participants, who coordinate the investigation and presentation of a defendant's family, social, psychological and psychiatric history, represents a marked departure from capital litigation in the immediate post-*Furman* era; during that period, "generalist" criminal defense lawyers would try capital cases without sufficient attention to the distinctive need to focus their energies toward the fundamental *moral* question of life-or-death rather than merely to challenge the state's burden of proof on the underlying offense. The changes in expectations regarding the duties of capital trial counsel are reflected in the Court's recent decisions finding ineffective assistance of counsel in three capital cases where state courts had found either no deficiency in representation or no prejudice to the defendant[33] (even

[33] Rompilla v. Beard, 545 U.S. 374 (2005); Wiggins v. Smith, 539 U.S. 510 (2003); T. Williams v. Taylor, 529 U.S. 362 (2000).

though all three cases came to the Court via federal habeas corpus, which requires broad deference to state court decisionmaking).

Lastly, the Court's recent proportionality decisions have narrowed the net of death eligibility, with the constitutional exclusion of juveniles,[34] persons with mental retardation,[35] and defendants convicted of ordinary, non-homicidal offenses.[36] The Court's decisions mandating these exclusions rested on the Court's conclusion in each case that "evolving standards of decency" no longer tolerated the challenged application of the death penalty. More striking than the specific results in these cases is the Court's newly-articulated means of discerning prevailing standards of decency. Whereas the Court's prior jurisprudence focused almost entirely on the number of jurisdictions that forbade a given practice (and perhaps the willingness of jurors to return capital verdicts in such circumstances), its more recent approach privileges the Court's own assessment of proportionality and other, non-statutory gauges of prevailing opinion, including professional and elite views, opinion polls, and international norms and practices. The Court's refinement of its proportionality analysis significantly enhances the prospects for further, more encompassing constitutional regulation of the death penalty, including the possibility of judicial abolition. It also comes at a time when several members of the current Court, in a variety of majority, concurring, and dissenting opinions, have expressed serious doubts about the contemporary administration of the American death penalty.[37]

The last four chapters of the volume involve cases at the heart of these emerging issues—the interaction between death and LWOP, proportionality limits on the death penalty, the constitutional floor for representation in capital cases, and the significance of the possibility of error—or innocence—in capital litigation. In his chapter on *Simmons v. South Carolina*,[38] David Bruck offers a vivid account of the struggle over

---

[34] Roper v. Simmons, 543 U.S. 551 (2005).

[35] Atkins v. Virginia, 536 U.S. 304 (2002).

[36] Kennedy v. Louisiana, 128 S. Ct. 2641 (2008).

[37] Kennedy, 128 S. Ct., at 2661 ("[T]he resulting imprecision and the tension between evaluating the individual circumstances and consistency of treatment have been tolerated where the victim dies. It should not be introduced into our justice system, though, where death has not occurred."); Baze v. Rees, 128 S. Ct. 1520, 1551 (2008) (Stevens, J., concurring) (finding the death penalty "patently excessive and cruel and unusual punishment") (internal quotations omitted); Ring v. Arizona, 536 U.S. 584, 616–618 (2002) (Breyer, J., concurring) (cataloging deficiencies in the contemporary administration of the death penalty including, among other things, its potentially discriminatory and arbitrary implementation); Kansas v. Marsh, 548 U.S. 163, 208–210 (2006) (Souter, J., dissenting) (noting the high risk of wrongful conviction in capital cases).

[38] 512 U.S. 154 (1994).

what jurors should be told about the possibility or impossibility of parole in capital cases. Bruck details South Carolina's decision to adopt LWOP as a sentencing alternative coupled with its determined effort to conceal from juries the fact and significance of the change. Bruck served as Simmons' counsel on appeal and in the Supreme Court, and he sheds light on the extraordinary twists and turns that culminated in the reversal of Simmons' death sentence. The Court ultimately held that defendants must be permitted to rebut a prosecutor's claim of dangerousness with accurate information about the impossibility of parole. Bruck argues that heightened reliability in capital cases requires a broader rule, given the extent to which jurors frequently rely on inaccurate perceptions of "future dangerousness" in their decisions to impose death. The near-universal adoption of LWOP in the years following *Simmons*, coupled with the much greater transparency of the LWOP alternative, lends support to Bruck's conclusion, given the radical decline in capital sentencing that these developments have arguably produced.

As the Supreme Court constitutionalized death penalty law in *Furman* and the 1976 cases, it repeatedly insisted that the uniqueness of capital punishment—its severity and irrevocability—required heightened safeguards. But in the two decades that followed, the "death-is-different" principle became more of a slogan than a significant doctrinal imperative. The refusal of the Court to mandate significantly enhanced protections in capital cases was most apparent in the context of Sixth Amendment claims of ineffective assistance of counsel. When the Court framed its approach to resolving such claims (in the context of a death-sentenced inmate who asserted inadequate representation), it adopted a unitary rule applicable to both capital and non-capital proceedings.[39] Most significantly, the Court's approach insisted that judges broadly defer to decisions of trial counsel and not second-guess litigation "strategy." David Dow's chapter on *Bell v. Cone*[40] illustrates the Court's consistently deferential posture toward trial counsel's decisions in the two decades following *Furman*. Such a posture led the Court to sustain Cone's death sentence even though his jury was not aware of extensive mitigating evidence, including mental illness and personal trauma, which could have been, but was not, discovered and presented at sentencing. Dow also discusses one of the infamous "sleeping lawyer" cases out of Texas, and how the Court's laissez-faire approach led a panel of the Fifth Circuit Court of Appeals to deny relief because the defendant could not establish whether anything particularly important was transpiring during the lawyer's naps.[41] Overall, Dow draws attention to the Court's

---

[39] Strickland v. Washington, 466 U.S. 668 (1984).

[40] 543 U.S. 447 (2005).

[41] Burdine v. Johnson, 231 F.3d 950 (5th Cir. 2000).

missed opportunity in failing to recognize the uniquely demanding aspects of punishment-phase advocacy—the responsibility of capital trial lawyers to zealously present a compelling moral narrative which would support their clients' right to live. Dow chronicles the Court's more recent decisions finding Sixth Amendment error in capital cases, but laments the arbitrariness wrought by the twin lotteries in capital litigation—the first in who is appointed to represent the defendant, and the second in the perspective brought to bear by the court that happens to review trial counsel's performance.

As much as the U.S. is increasingly an outlier in its retention of the death penalty, no aspect of its practices was more reflective of its exceptionalism than its willingness to execute juvenile defendants. In 1989, when the Court first upheld the constitutionality of executing offenders who were 16 or 17 at the time of their crimes,[42] few nations around the world authorized or engaged in the practice. Sixteen years later, when the issue returned to the Supreme Court, the U.S . was literally alone among all nations in claiming the power to execute juveniles. Scott Howe's detailed story of *Roper v. Simmons*[43] offers a broad perspective on the challenged practice, recounting some of the more famous capital prosecutions involving juveniles (including the Leopold and Loeb case from the 1920s and the case of Willie Francis discussed above). Howe traces the *Simmons* litigation through the Missouri courts, including the unusual decision of the Missouri Supreme Court to reject on federal constitutional grounds a practice that the U.S. Supreme Court had recently and explicitly endorsed. Howe's analysis of the subsequent decision by the U.S. Supreme Court affirming the Missouri judgment focuses on the apparent gravitational pull exerted by international norms in Justice Kennedy's majority opinion. Howe also reflects on the potentially wider jurisprudential implications of the Court's reasoning—the extent to which the Court's newly emerging proportionality methodology enhances the prospects for judicial abolition of the death penalty altogether.

The concern about executing innocents has always been an important part of the death penalty debate. Throughout much of our history, the primary—indeed, almost exclusive—safeguards against wrongful convictions and executions were procedural protections at trial (e.g., the right to counsel, evidentiary rules such as those prohibiting the use of coerced confessions, and the requirement of proof beyond a reasonable doubt). The relative swiftness of judgment in capital cases, in which executions were carried out within weeks or months of capital verdicts, made it difficult and rare for defendants to mount challenges to their

---

[42] Stanford v. Kentucky, 492 U.S. 361 (1989).

[43] 543 U.S. 551 (2005).

convictions based on claims of actual innocence. For this reason, when the Supreme Court first addressed in 1993 whether the Constitution requires a post-conviction judicial forum for claims of actual innocence, Chief Justice Rehnquist's opinion announcing the judgment of the Court strongly suggested that defendants have no such right.[44] Instead, Chief Justice Rehnquist argued, executive clemency has long served—at the State's discretion—as the appropriate means of preventing grave miscarriages of justice. More provocatively put, the Court refused to conclude that the Constitution forbids the execution of the actually innocent. The public reaction to the Court's decision was perhaps surprisingly muted, and the state and lower federal courts continued to express skepticism whenever inmates challenged their convictions on factual grounds of innocence rather than by asserting a distinct constitutional violation (such as undisclosed exculpatory evidence or ineffective assistance of counsel).

Subsequent events have pushed the issue of innocence to the forefront of the death penalty controversy. The experience in Illinois, with the discovery of numerous innocents on death row, has increased the pressure on the legal system to provide post-conviction remedies for inmates wrongfully sentenced to death. Joseph Hoffmann's chapter on *House v. Bell*[45] offers an illuminating account of the difficulties courts have had in confronting post-trial claims of factual error. Hoffmann describes the procedural maze through which such claims are channeled, and the remarkable resistance in some cases for responsible actors (prosecutors and judges) to acknowledge and remedy the troubling possibility that the wrong person has been condemned. In House's own case, the Supreme Court held that there was sufficient doubt about his guilt to overlook procedural barriers to his constitutional claims (concerning ineffective representation and prosecutorial misconduct), but not enough proof to grant relief based on his innocence alone. The disconnect between the mounting public concern about human fallibility in capital cases and the judicial reticence to recognize factual innocence as a constitutional basis for relief seems unstable, and Hoffmann explores the possible means of closing the divide.

* * *

For most of our history, stories about the death penalty did not involve much "law." But the gradual constitutional expansion of protections in all criminal cases inevitably transformed the debate over capital punishment into a constitutional one. One of the Court's central projects over the past thirty five years has been to mediate the tensions between generalized commitments to equality, fairness, and accuracy, on the one

---

[44] Herrera v. Collins, 506 U.S. 390 (1993).

[45] 547 U.S. 518 (2006).

hand, and the country's increasingly isolated practice of executing offenders on the other. This volume collects many of the landmark cases
during this period and looks beneath the Court's opinions to the individual actors, social movements, and larger legal context that led to each
constitutional judgment. In many respects, this volume is the story of
the modern American death penalty, a story of extraordinary drama and
complexity, with a final chapter yet to be written.

*

1

Deborah W. Denno*

When Willie Francis Died: The "Disturbing" Story Behind One of the Eighth Amendment's Most Enduring Standards of Risk**

I reckon dying is black.
Some folks say it's gold.
Some say it's white as hominy-grits.
I been mighty close.
I reckon it's black.

Willie Francis, 1946***

* I am grateful to the many people who contributed to this Chapter, most particularly the relatives of Willie Francis who so caringly shared their memories and mementoes: Joseph Davis, Jr., Allen Francis, MaEsther Francis, Hilda Henry, and Keith Landry. Longtime residents of St. Martinville graciously opened their doors to interviews that provided invaluable information and perspective: James Akers, Allan Durand, Edmond Guidrey, Jr., Velma Johnson, Winfield Ledet, Thomas Nelson, Nary Smith, and Leo Thomas. Allan Durand was extraordinarily generous with his loan of a cache of original court documents, notes, and letters from Bertrand de Blanc's case files. For insightful comments I would also like to thank Robert Bloom, Jeffrey Bowman, Gilbert King, Barrett Prettyman, Jr., Daniel Rinaldi, and Julie Salwen—as well as faculty at the law schools of Boston College, Fordham University, and the University of Texas. In addition, I give special thanks to a treasure trove of dedicated research assistants: Jennifer Daly, Brandy Ellis, Marianna Gebhardt, Eileen McNerney, Justin Nematzadeh, Daniel Rinaldi, Julie Salwen, Kristina Scotto, and Lisa–Sheri Torrence. As always, Juan Fernandez, Karin Johnsrud, and Todd Melnick volunteered terrific assistance from the Fordham Law Library.

** James Marlow, *Francis Gets the Details of His Case*, RALEIGH TIMES, Jan. 16, 1947, at 5 (noting that Justice Felix Frankfurter stated that Willie's "whole situation was very 'disturbing.' "). For purposes of clarity, this Chapter generally refers to Willie and his numerous family members by their first names only because most share the same last name.

*** Elliott Chaze, *'Plumb Mizzuble' Covers Willie Francis' Idea of Electric Chair*, DAILY ADVERTISER (Lafayette, La.), July 1, 1946, at 1.

INTRODUCTION

On May 3, 1946, in St. Martinville, Louisiana, Willie Francis, a black youth of seventeen years, sat in the state's electric chair, strapped in, ready to die. Willie was just like many convicted murderers throughout the country awaiting their punishments—poor minority teenagers stuck in a criminal justice system offering few of the legal protections available today. Like Willie, some of the condemned would have been only fifteen at the time of their purported crimes.[1] Yet in a matter of minutes Willie would be plucked from the masses. He would survive the electrocution in a way no one else had—an event that would take him from the front of the execution line to front-page news. In a country just recovering from the Second World War, time and again, Willie's experience would be called a "miracle," a "blessing from God," or "divine intervention" by layperson and lawyer alike.

Whatever role the "hand of God" played in saving Willie that day, eventually it would withdraw. Immediately after the attempted execution, the State sent Willie back to jail, thereby prompting a year-long personal and legal battle concerning Willie's fate. That struggle would go all the way up to the United States Supreme Court with *Louisiana* ex rel. *Francis v. Resweber*,[2] and then right back down to St. Martinville again after the Court affirmed the State of Louisiana's decision to execute Willie rather than give him life imprisonment. On May 9, 1947, the State finally did execute Willie for the murder of Andrew Thomas, St. Martinville's popular white pharmacist.

There are many stories to tell in the course of examining both the life and death of Willie Francis—stories about racism that look small-town and southern but are really nationwide in scope; stories about the risks of penal and technological debacles that appear antiquated but in fact have troubling parallels to the potential for botched electrocutions and lethal injections decades later. And, of course, there are the intimate stories about religious faith and the people surrounding Willie and his family.

The following pages bring together Willie's life narrative—often framed by the themes of race, risk, and religion—based on correspon-

---

[1] *See* DAVID C. BALDUS, GEORGE G. WOODWORTH & CHARLES A. PULASKI, JR., EQUAL JUSTICE AND THE DEATH PENALTY: A LEGAL AND EMPIRICAL ANALYSIS 249–53 (1990); Death Penalty Information Center, Executions in the U.S. 1608–2002: The Espy File, http://www.deathpenalty info.org/executions-us–1608–2002–espy-file (last visited Jan. 9, 2009).

[2] 329 U.S. 459 (1947).

dence, interviews, and accounts that have never been revealed elsewhere, as well as court documents, case law, and interdisciplinary literature.[3] Particularly compelling are numerous letters that people from all over the country wrote Willie while he was waiting in jail. These writers discussed many topics, including their reflections on racial injustice in America and the need for religious redemption, not only for Willie but also for his judgers and this country. Yet a number of letters were deeper, more private. Willie, it seems, was not only an imprint of the social and legal times, but also a projected muse of sorts to whom individuals could confide their heartfelt thoughts and wishes—about God, death, health, hopes, family, even romance. Indeed, many of the personal and legal bits of Willie's experiences are intertwined far too tightly to extricate. Willie's life and execution are as much an account about him and society at that time as they are depictions of where this legal system has been and how the precedent of *Resweber* prompts where the legal system is going.

The precedential aspects of *Resweber* are critical to consider in context. As the facts of Willie's alleged crime and first attempted execution unfold, some modern lawyers may be astonished that Willie was ever destined for the death penalty. While Willie confessed to Andrew's murder and, from all told, never recanted, those acts were viewed far more definitively in 1947 Louisiana than they would ever be today. New scientific research, for example, can explain the behavior of some of the most ardent, yet factually innocent, confessors of crime. In addition, the Court decided *Resweber* fifteen years before it held that the Eighth Amendment's Cruel and Unusual Punishments Clause applied to the states.[4] Attempting to operate under such constitutional constraints, the *Resweber* Court based its conclusion about Willie on a guideline developed prior to the incorporation of the Eighth Amendment into the Fourteenth Amendment's Due Process Clause. As a result, the Court only hastily assumed the Eighth Amendment's applicability—primarily to ensure that the Court's plurality opinion received sufficient votes. Even more significant in retrospect is the Court's 2005 holding in *Roper v. Simmons* that offenders can no longer be executed for crimes committed when they were juveniles under age eighteen.[5] Because of Willie's youth at the time of Andrew's murder, he could not be executed today. In sum, the passage of six decades has heralded these developments and other massive changes in criminal law and procedure that cast a troubling light on the use of *Resweber* as modern guidance.

This Chapter explores *Resweber*'s history and force over the years with a particular focus on the defendant at the core of such a key case.

---

[3] The following two works in particular were very helpful in terms of their storytelling, research, and resources: Gilbert King, The Execution of Willie Francis: Race, Murder, and the Search for Justice in the American South (2008) and Arthur S. Miller & Jeffrey H. Bowman, Death by Installments: The Ordeal of Willie Francis (1988).

[4] *See* Robinson v. California, 370 U.S. 660, 666–67 (1962).

[5] 543 U.S. 551, 578 (2005).

The discussion begins with an overview of Willie's life in St. Martinville, including what is known of his childhood, family, and personality, to provide perspective for examining the social and racial underpinnings of Willie's legal foray—from his arrest, trial, and conviction up to his death sentence. But it is the electric chair's transcendent botch that momentarily saves Willie and leads his lawyers into an Eighth Amendment wilderness. While Willie perished, *Resweber* lives on, hampered by an outmoded pre-incorporation standard: a burning reminder that Supreme Court case law can emanate from the very societal ills this country perpetually struggles to discard.

I. WILLIE'S LIFE AND TIMES

A. St. Martinville, Louisiana

The small city of St. Martinville, where Willie lived, is located in southwestern Louisiana in St. Martin Parish, the middle of Acadian (Cajun) country.[6] Founded in the eighteenth century as the military Poste des Attakapas, the city lies along the Bayou Teche, a slow-moving, "once-vital" waterway that earlier catalyzed agricultural commerce. Although impoverished today, St. Martinville is rich in history.

During the 1700s and 1800s, St. Martinville became the destination for many French-speaking immigrants. A large number of these settlers were exiled Acadians, Roman Catholic peasants, who, by 1632, became the dominant cultural group in the French colony of Acadia, a territory in northeastern North America encompassing what is now known as Nova Scotia. Others included Royalists fleeing the French Revolution and, later on, adherents of Napoleon. In its prime, the city was referred to as "le Petit Paris." St. Martinville featured opera, theater, and luxurious hotels for its renowned visitors who affirmed and escalated the city's lush existence. Over the years, however, the French and other groups in St. Martinville assumed social superiority over the Acadians, who never seemed to lose their peasant status. Eventually this social hierarchy would change. Paralleling developments throughout the United States involving other immigrant groups, the status of the Acadians

---

[6] The historical discussion that follows draws from the following sources: Interview with Thomas Nelson, Mayor, St. Martinville, La., in St. Martinville, La. (June 12, 2007); Interview with James Akers, Historian and Tour Guide, Acadian Memorial, in St. Martinville, La. (June 12, 2007); Interview with Nary Smith, Assistant Chief of Police, St. Martinville Police Department, in St. Martinville, La. (June 13, 2007); LAWRENCE CAPUDER, 1896 IN LE PETIT PARIS: TURNING THE CENTURY IN SOUTHWEST LOUISIANA 18, 20 (1999); CHARLES LARROQUE, MEMORIES OF ST. MARTINVILLE 2 (1999); CARL A. BRASSEAUX, ACADIAN TO CAJUN: TRANSFORMATION OF A PEOPLE, 1803–1877, at 4 (1992); CARL A. BRASSEAUX, THE FOUNDING OF NEW ACADIA: THE BEGINNINGS OF ACADIAN LIFE IN LOUISIANA, 1765–1803, at 2–5, 91, 150–52, 167, 192–93 (1987); WILLIAM FAULKNER RUSHTON, THE CAJUNS: FROM ACADIA TO LOUISIANA 127–29 (1979); BONA ARSENAULT, HISTORY OF THE ACADIANS 11, 189 (1978); and LEONA MARTIN GUIRARD, ST. MARTINVILLE: THE LAND OF EVANGELINE IN PICTURE STORY 4 (1950).

would eventually rise due to the arrival of African slaves who would come to occupy the bottom rung of society.

In the middle of the nineteenth century, disease and natural disasters greatly diminished St. Martinville's prosperity; whatever chance the town had for recovery was destroyed by the Civil War and its aftermath. The culture of le Petit Paris would never exist again. Yet a number of St. Martinville residents have claimed over the years that there were additional reasons for the decline, specifically, that a wrongful lynching of a black man long ago had put a "curse" on the city—a hex of sorts that Willie Francis's own unjust execution simply perpetuated.[7]

During the 1940s, St. Martinville showed little evidence of overcoming the fate to which it had fallen.[8] The city's population of about 4,000 residents (roughly two thirds of whom were white), was poor economically and educationally relative to both the United States as a whole and the state of Louisiana, which itself was deprived. According to data from the 1940 census, for example, Louisiana had the lowest literacy rate in the United States, and St. Martin Parish (which houses St. Martinville) had the lowest literacy rate in Louisiana. Blacks especially suffered. This was the era of Jim Crow laws and de jure segregation that preceded *Brown v. Board of Education*[9] and the Civil Rights Laws of 1964.[10]

While the entire country was rethinking race relations, a focus on St. Martinville provides background on the cultural influences that encompassed Willie's life and case.[11] As Willie noted in his own personal

---

[7] According to Gilbert King's research and interview with James Akers, who is considered St. Martinville's historian, the curse went into effect in the 1890s, when Louis Michel, a black man, was wrongly accused of killing a white mother and her daughter in St. Martinville. KING, *supra* note 3, at xii-xiv. Moments before Michel was hung, he proclaimed his innocence and put a curse on the city so that it would not flourish. *Id.* at xiii. The real killer was eventually found and convicted, thereby confirming Michel's assertions. *Id.* Willie's case revived talk of the curse among the city's residents. *Id.* at 166. Many today still believe it exists. *Id.* at 288.

[8] The statistical information referred to in this paragraph can be found in LOUISIANA ALMANAC: 2006–2007 EDITION 245 (Milburn Calhoun & Jeanne Frois eds., 2006); U.S. DEP'T OF COMMERCE, BUREAU OF THE CENSUS, COUNTY AND CITY DATA BOOK 1952: A STATISTICAL ABSTRACT SUPPLEMENT 210–11 (1953); U.S. DEP'T OF COMMERCE, BUREAU OF THE CENSUS, STATISTICAL ABSTRACT OF THE UNITED STATES 1951, at 112, 271 (1951); U.S. DEP'T OF COMMERCE, BUREAU OF THE CENSUS, COUNTY DATA BOOK: A SUPPLEMENT TO THE STATISTICAL ABSTRACT OF THE UNITED STATES 186 (1947); Paul C. Young, *Can They Read?*, WKLY. MESSENGER (St. Martinville, La.), Aug. 10, 1945, at 3; and *20,000 Children Do Not Attend School in Louisiana*, WKLY. MESSENGER (St. Martinville, La.), Aug. 3, 1945, at 2.

[9] 347 U.S. 483 (1954).

[10] Civil Rights Act of 1964, Pub. L. No. 88–352, 78 Stat. 241 (codified as amended in scattered sections of 5, 28, and 42 U.S.C.).

[11] The following discussion of race in St. Martinville draws from, among other sources, WILLIE FRANCIS AS TOLD TO SAM MONTGOMERY, MY TRIP TO THE CHAIR (1947); GUIRARD, *supra* note 6, at 34; Tom Gillen, Jr., *Around the Capitol*, WKLY. MESSENGER (St. Martinville, La.), Nov.

story, St. Martinville in 1947 was "just a little town where everybody knows everybody else." But, the city had "two sections, one for the white people and the other for the colored.... The white tend to their own business and the colored tend to theirs." By law, "any person of either sex of the white race who shall habitually loiter around or frequent or reside in private or public places owned by negroes or frequented by negroes" was guilty of vagrancy.

Racial issues were prominent in the city's newspaper, *The Weekly Messenger*. Founded in 1886, the *Messenger*'s coverage of whites and blacks was usually physically segregated, even including separate announcements for white and "negro" inductions into the armed services. Marcel "Blackie" Bienvenu, the editor and manager, seemed to go out of his way to insert the word "nigger" into the paper, frequently referring to one regular contributor as the paper's "Nigger–French columnist" and even describing slingshots as "nigger shooters." Bienvenu used his *This & That* column to insult African Americans, suggesting, for example, that they do not want to work, and stating that racial animus existed throughout the country, not just the south.

Reported differences in the education of whites and blacks were striking. The St. Martin Parish School Board noted, matter-of-factly, without apology, that there were no high schools for blacks and that white teachers were paid roughly twice as much as "negro" teachers. Veiled references to school segregation and the surrounding political controversy were not uncommon. Indeed, an occasional *Messenger* column discussing Louisiana state political news frequently focused (along

---

22, 1946, at 3; *In the News at the Capitol*, WKLY. MESSENGER (St. Martinville, La.), Nov. 15, 1946, at 4; *Capitol Highlights*, WKLY. MESSENGER (St. Martinville, La.), Nov. 15, 1946, at 3; Tom Gillen, Jr., *Around the Capitol*, WKLY. MESSENGER (St. Martinville, La.), Nov. 1, 1946, at 3; Tom Gillen, Jr., *Around the Capitol*, WKLY. MESSENGER (St. Martinville, La.), Oct. 11, 1946, at 1; Tom Gillen, Jr., *Around the Capitol*, WKLY. MESSENGER (St. Martinville, La.), Sept. 27, 1946, at 9; "Blackie," Editorial, *This & That*, WKLY. MESSENGER (St. Martinville, La.), Sept. 6, 1946, at 1; "Blackie," Editorial, *This & That*, WKLY. MESSENGER (St. Martinville, La.), Sept. 7, 1945, at 1; *Proceedings of the St. Martin Parish School Board*, WKLY. MESSENGER (St. Martinville, La.), Aug. 24, 1945, at 3; "Blackie," Editorial, *This & That*, WKLY. MESSENGER (St. Martinville, La.), May 18, 1945, at 1; *5 Colored Men Inducted in Service Wednesday*, WKLY. MESSENGER (St. Martinville, La.), Mar. 2, 1945, at 1; *9 From Parish Inducted Into Armed Services*, WKLY. MESSENGER (St. Martinville, La.), Mar. 2, 1945, at 1; "Blackie," Editorial, *This & That*, WKLY. MESSENGER (St. Martinville, La.), Nov. 17, 1944, at 1; Political Advertisement, *Help Elect Louis J. Michot*, WKLY. MESSENGER (St. Martinville, La.), Sept. 8, 1944, at 3; Political Advertisement, *Keep Politics Out of Schools!*, WKLY. MESSENGER (St. Martinville, La.), Sept. 1, 1944, at 6; *Proceedings of the St. Martin Parish School Board*, WKLY. MESSENGER (St. Martinville, La.), Aug. 18, 1944, at 3; *Coxe Summarizes School Legislation*, WKLY. MESSENGER (St. Martinville, La.), July 21, 1944, at 4; *Proceedings of the St. Martin Parish Police Jury*, WKLY. MESSENGER (St. Martinville, La.), May 26, 1944, at 3; and *Proceedings of the St. Martin Parish School Board*, WKLY. MESSENGER (St. Martinville, La.), Jan. 14, 1944, at 2.

with other such columns) on the case of a young "negress" applying to Louisiana State University Medical School in New Orleans—at one point heralding "the suggestion ... that Louisiana could solve all of its problems—and suits—concerning higher education by placing Southern University under LSU [Louisiana Southern University], as a 'colored' division."

The *Messenger*'s content during 1944–1947, however despicable by today's standards, had power in 1940s St. Martinville. These were the years encompassing Willie's trial and punishment. Those reading and writing in the *Messenger* constituted Willie's judge and jury. They determined if he would live or die.

B. Willie's Childhood

Key components of Willie's story are his personal experiences and perspectives on life, particularly with his family. Unfortunately, little is known of either. Willie was, after all, just a teenager when he was executed. As Willie himself explained from his jail cell, "A lot of people write to me and ask me to tell them something about what I did when I was young. I am only eighteen now, so I guess they mean when I was very young." What is available about Willie is derived primarily from books, letters, newspaper articles, interviews, and especially Willie's own brief account in a pamphlet entitled, *My Trip to the Chair* (*"The Chair"*).[12] *The Chair* was written in the spring of 1947 when Willie and a local resident, Sam Montgomery, collaborated to document Willie's experiences during the first attempted electrocution. The effort was also designed to garner sales to help fund Willie's Supreme Court appeal. Willie made clear that he agreed to write *The Chair* story on the condition that he not be expected to discuss Andrew Thomas's murder. While a reader can get some sense of Willie's personality from the pamphlet, the writing appears edited and formalized by his collaborator, so the extent of Willie's voice is unclear. But the facts of Willie's life speak for themselves.

Willie was born on January 12, 1929, to Frederick Francis and Louise Taylor Francis. Baptized a month later as "Willie Francis" at St. Martin Catholic Church, he became the youngest in a family of thirteen

---

[12] This Section draws mainly from Willie's pamphlet, FRANCIS AS TOLD TO MONTGOMERY, *supra* note 11. Other sources include Certificate of Baptism of Willie Francis, St. Martin Catholic Church, St. Martinville, La. (Aug. 7, 1945) (available at St. Martin Parish Courthouse, St. Martinville, La.); Funeral Services Program for Junius (Blue) A. Francis, Notre Dame Catholic Church (July 31, 1993) (copy on file with author); Interview with Keith Landry, Willie Francis's grandnephew, in St. Martinville, La. (June 10, 2007); Interview with Thomas Nelson, *supra* note 6; KING, *supra* note 3, at 265, 286; MILLER & BOWMAN, *supra* note 3, at 149 & n.1; Elliott Chaze, *Willie is Ready; Mother Isn't*, TIMES-PICAYUNE (New Orleans, La.), May 9, 1947, at 2; and Jessyl Taylor, *Was This an Act of God?*, WORLD'S MESSENGER, July 1946, at 5, 20.

children, six boys and seven girls.[13] The Francis household resided "in the colored section" of St. Martinville at 800 Washington Street. Their "little house" was filled with children "running through it all the time." Despite their numbers, they were "happy" and "got along fine together because [they] had to." Willie "was pretty much the family pet until he got in trouble with the law."

Like most St. Martinville residents, Frederick, Louise, and their children were devout Roman Catholics. They all regularly attended services at Notre Dame de Perpetual Secours Church, a place of worship for the city's blacks. Religion was a dominant force in the family's life. Frederick was employed in a sugar cane factory during the caning season and performed "odd jobs," making enough to feed the family. In an already poor city, the Francis family was poorer still. Louise was a housewife whom Willie depicted as being immaculately well organized and efficient, running "everything." "I don't know how she did it," Willie commented, although "things got better and mother had more rest" as the children grew older and could help at home.

According to Willie's personal account, he "used to like to play jokes" and make people laugh; "my friends used to tell me I could make almost anyone laugh when I said or did something." He and "a bunch of kids who went around together a lot" would spend much of their time at the bayou, either fishing or swimming or eating watermelon and figs. Occasionally, the group would play marbles, a game at which Willie was "pretty good," and at other times a "little baseball" using "a broomstick for a bat." Periodically, the group would engage in mischief— "snitch[ing]" the figs they so enjoyed eating, for instance, or spending the day swimming in the bayou without anyone's knowledge, acts for which Willie would get "spanked" when he got home. "It's something to laugh at now," he explained in his jail cell, "but we didn't like the whipping at the time."

Willie's life was not just school and play, however. He also worked for Andrew Thomas and others in town. His employment with Andrew was not "steady." On occasion Willie would deliver packages or sweep the floor in Andrew's drugstore or rake and clean Andrew's yard. Years later, another employee at Andrew's store would describe Willie as a " 'nice boy.' " Indeed, most people depicted Willie as pleasant and "co-operative."

---

[13] The six boys were Junius (Blue) Francis, Early Francis, Joseph Francis, Wilbert Francis, Adam Francis, and Willie Francis; the seven girls were (using their married names) Emily Branch, Amelia Washington, Marie Neal, Scerita McCauley, Beulah Fuzee, Mae Ella Landry, and Cecile Gage. Funeral Services Program for Junius (Blue) A. Francis, *supra* note 12. Emily Branch and Amelia Washington, the oldest of the siblings, were twins. Interview with Keith Landry, *supra* note 12.

C. Willie's Mental Aptitude

Willie's mental aptitude was characterized in vastly different ways depending on who was doing the describing and when.[14] His intellect became a focus in attempts to explain why he may have killed Andrew or, alternatively, why he may have consistently confessed to a crime he never committed at all. Depictions of Willie's abilities ranged along a continuum, all the way from "mentally deficient," the characterization provided by James Akers, an historian and tour guide for St. Martinville's Acadian Memorial, to not "bright," in the eyes of Willie's loyal pastor, Father Maurice Rousseve, to "normal" based on the arresting sheriff's testimony, up to "intelligent," the account given by a journalist writing for a black newspaper who interviewed Willie while he was in jail. Indeed, Willie's press quotes describing his first attempted electrocution so greatly impressed the executive secretary of the National Association for the Advancement of Colored People ("NAACP") that he wrote about it in his column: "What a miracle that a virtually illiterate (but far from ignorant or untalented) boy should think in imagery as deeply moving and beautiful as any contemporary poet."

Willie did have a serious stutter that may have affected the way that others perceived his capabilities. According to one St. Martinville resident, for example, Willie "walked kind of funny and didn't seem very bright by the way he talked." Willie was also described as a bit of a light-hearted prankster who acted younger than his age, an image he projects in *The Chair*. At the same time, Willie avidly corresponded with a myriad of people while he was in prison, demonstrating an ability to both read and write that defied St. Martinville's illiteracy rate.

On May 8, 1947, the evening before Willie's execution, Associated Press reporter Elliott Chaze provided a particularly intimate view of Willie through the eyes of his mother. Chaze described Louise Francis as

---

[14] The discussion in this Section draws from the following sources: Transcript of Hearing Before Louisiana Board of Pardons, Testimony of Gilbert Ozenne, Sheriff, New Iberia (May 31, 1946) (copy on file with author) [*hereinafter* Pardons Board Testimony of Gilbert Ozenne]; Transcript of Hearing Before Louisiana Board of Pardons, Testimony of E.L. Resweber, Sheriff, St. Martin Parish (May 31, 1946) (copy on file with author) [*hereinafter* Pardons Board Testimony of E.L. Resweber]; Interview with James Akers, *supra* note 6; Interview by Jeffrey Bowman with Bertrand de Blanc, Esq., in Lafayette, La. (Sept. 25, 1982); Letter from Doris McClain, Houston, Tex., to Willie Francis (May 10, 1946) (copy on file with author); KING, *supra* note 3, at 145, 265; RICHARD A. LEO, POLICE INTERROGATION AND AMERICAN JUSTICE 233–34 (2008); Chaze, *Willie is Ready; Mother Isn't*, *supra* note 12; Walter White, *How It Feels*, CHI. DEFENDER, Aug. 31, 1946, at 15; Taylor, *supra* note 12, at 20; Fred Atwater, *Louisianans See Hand of God in Francis Execution Failure*, CHI. DEFENDER, June 8, 1946, at 9; *Willie Francis Gets Second Reprieve; Case to Supreme Court Now*, LA. WKLY. (New Orleans, La.), June 8, 1946, at 1; and "Scoop" Jones, *Mystery and Intrigue Surround Youth Who Survived the Electric Chair; Believe Francis to be Insane*, LA. WKLY. (New Orleans, La.), May 18, 1946, at 9.

"a gentle, gray-haired Negro woman," unable to comprehend the impending execution of her youngest child the next day in a jail just five blocks away from the Francis family's home. " 'I used to walk by that jail,' " Louise explained. " 'Never thought my baby'd be going there to die.' " " 'My Willie was always kind. He used to play with little children, even when he was a big boy he used to play with 'em. There wasn't no bad in him. I just don't understand.' "

Willie had a gift for entertaining himself. " 'You know, Willie was a funny boy. Times he'd sit here on the floor and play with clothes pins, rubbin' 'em and stackin' 'em on top of one t'other. He'd make little fences and pig styes with 'em, and he smiled a lot when he was doin' it.' " Louise was clearly amused by Willie's playthings. " 'Sometimes I'd get wonderin' how Willie could have himself such a time with those old clothes pins. I believe his mind would run off places. Not bad places, but places.' "

Louise also stressed how much Willie differed from other children, especially boys. Oddly, her account varied substantially from what Willie writes about himself in *The Chair*. " 'He didn't like no baseball or football. Didn't even shoot marbles. Most times he was around the house when he wasn't in school, and he was the Lord's own blessing when it come to helping his mama.' " Indeed, Louise's account makes it seem as though Willie eschewed a masculine role. " 'That child could cook and make a bed as good as women folks.' "

In any family, no matter how close, it is never clear how well the parents know their children. In one of many letters Willie received while in jail, for example, the writer, Doris McClain from Houston, Texas, consoled Willie about the fact he had not heard from his girlfriend. Mrs. McClain explained that "maybe she [the girlfriend] is sick or something like that." Putting herself in the place of the girlfriend, Mrs. McClain empathetically insisted, "I wouldn't stop writing you just because you were in jail, I really would stick closer than every thin [sic]." "After all you schould [sic] know her better than I," Mrs. McClain continued. In all the accounts of Willie so far, this letter is the first to mention that Willie had a girlfriend. Perhaps she was known to his family, perhaps not. Like anyone else, Willie had his own private moments.

Closer to the time of Willie's execution, stories seemed to exaggerate Willie's purported oddities, perhaps in an effort to provide the kind of defense he never had. One article concluded, for example, that Willie demonstrated "indications of insanity" based on two pieces of evidence— Frederick and Louise's admissions that Willie "never had the tendencies of a normal child" as well as accounts by "[n]eighbors, friends and other members of the community" of Willie's "harmless pranks that he has played from childhood." Another story also questioned Willie's mental acuity—saying many believed Willie was "mentally subnormal." Willie's own sister, Emily Branch, had stated that Willie " 'is not quite normal.' " Indeed, there were statements that Willie "never seemed actually aware that he was on trial for his life" and "appeared to be cocky and acting like a kid who was playing a game." One newspaper reported that the NAACP was considering filing a brief on Willie's behalf before the State Lunacy Board, although it appears the NAACP did not follow through. Of course, without more evidence available regarding Willie's mental abilities, such random descriptions do not seem to support an argument for insanity; yet they were able to feed a journalist's conclusion that "Willie Francis should have never been sentenced to die." And they would raise concerns that a conscientious modern attorney would investigate.

Despite all the disparate depictions of Willie, however, two clear and consistent traits emerge—his extraordinarily low level of emotional maturity, even for his young age, as well as his desperate need to please everyone and anyone no matter what the cost, personally or legally. Time and again Willie proved to be highly suggestible and compliant to others—whether it was the pastor who insisted, the first time around, that the electric chair would only "tickle" when in fact it really caused acute pain, the stranger writing to ask Willie to donate his eyes for her blind brother until Willie's family insisted no, or the sheriff who wanted Willie to confess to a murder and then die for it. It seemed, to a self-sacrificing fault, that Willie wanted to gratify them all.

Not surprisingly, Willie's attributes epitomize the three general characteristics of juvenile offenders that the Supreme Court targeted in *Roper v. Simmons*[15] to demonstrate that juveniles have diminished culpability and that consequently they "cannot with reliability be classified among the worst offenders." Relative to adults, juveniles are (1) more immature and irresponsible, (2) vulnerable to negative pressures from their peers and environment, and (3) fragile and unstable in their identities. These differences not only heighten the likelihood that juveniles will engage in impulsive thinking and conduct, they also provide an explanation of why the crimes of juveniles, however heinous, may be less indicative of the offender's character or intent. Research also shows that the same kind of vulnerability and immaturity make it far more likely for juveniles to confess to crimes they never committed.[16] With far fewer

---

[15] 543 U.S. 551 (2005).

[16] In an interview with Jeffrey Bowman in September of 1982, de Blanc acknowledged having thought of the possibility that Willie's age and immaturity had something to do with his agreeing to sign two confessions:

> Q. I guess that's what I was thinking with Willie. I mean, you've got a 15 or 16–year-old black kid, gets arrested, they find a wallet on him, and then, I'm not sure how they

legal protections sixty years ago, Willie faced an even greater risk of injustice.

It is unlikely that Willie knew the lore of St. Martinville's curse that had seemingly so befallen the city. He did, however, feel that he had a jinx of his own. "I guess from the first minute I was born I gave people something to worry about." Willie's misfortune centered on the number thirteen. "Maybe you will think I am superstitious," he commented. "I guess I am because I have a lot of reasons to be." Willie was the thirteenth child in his family, he was convicted of murder on September 13, 1945, and the Supreme Court denied his appeal on January 13, 1947. Yet Willie would end up suffering from another scourge far more powerful than the number thirteen—that of an incompetent criminal justice system. That system also gave people something to worry about. It still does.

II. THE MURDER OF ANDREW THOMAS

Curse aside, St. Martinville was rarely a place that created excitement.[17] But as much as Andrew Thomas's murder caused great sadness in the community, it also brought gossip and intrigue.

---

arrive at the confession, but scared, wondering what's going to happen. I mean uh not to bring up, you know, racial tensions, but a 15 or 16–year-old black kid with the white sheriffs around him that's pretty scary and plus A. Oh yeah it is scary I tell you it is scary. Q. Plus, the second confession apparently was given on the two-hour ride back to St. Martinville. You know, black kid surrounded by these you know the white sheriffs, "Did you do it, Willie?" "Yeah, let me sign on the dotted line." I don't you know, I'm just thinking aloud here. It's ... A. It's conjective. I don't know. But then ... I thought about all those things, but then I said, "Don't leave the main thing. Get busy on that. No man should go to the chair twice." Of course, you can talk to people about a confession, all the evidence being circumstantial. Maybe he didn't confess; maybe it was forced, but....

Interview by Jeffrey Bowman with Bertrand de Blanc, *supra* note 14.

[17] The discussion that follows regarding Andrew Thomas and his murder draws from the following sources: Francis as told to Montgomery, *supra* note 11; Transcript of Coroner's Inquest Held Before Dr. S.D. Yongue, Coroner of St. Martin Parish, La., Re: Death of Andrew I. Thomas (Nov. 8, 1944) (copy on file with author); Pardons Board Testimony of E.L. Resweber, *supra* note 14; Interview with James Akers, *supra* note 6; Interview with Allan Durand, Attorney, Perrin, Landry, de Launay & Durand, in Lafayette, La. (June 13, 2007); Interview with Thomas Nelson, *supra* note 6; Interview with Velma Johnson, Tour Guide, St. Martinville Cultural Heritage Center, in St. Martinville, La. (June 12, 2007); Interview with Edmond L. Guidry, Jr., Retired Chief Judge, Louisiana Court of Appeals, in St. Martinville, La. (June 12, 2007); Certificate of Baptism of André Isidore Thomas, Church of St. Martin de Tours, St. Martinville, La. (Aug. 25, 2008) (copy on file with author); Indictment, State v. Francis, No. 2161 (16th Jud. Dist. Ct. La. Sept. 5, 1945), *reprinted in* Transcript of Record at 1–2, Louisiana *ex rel.* Francis v. Resweber, 329 U.S. 459 (1947) (No. 142); King, *supra* note 3, at 63, 66–67, 264–65; Bob Hamm, *The Man Who Cheated the Chair ... for Awhile*, Daily Advertiser (Lafayette, La.), Apr. 25, 1993, at D1; *Negro Murderer to Die Here Today*, Wkly. Messenger (St. Martinville, La.), May 3,

Andrew was the fifty-three-year-old white Cajun owner of Thomas Drugstore, St. Martinville's primary pharmacy in 1944, located in the heart of the city on Main Street. Like many of St. Martinville's stores today, the building is abandoned, having housed a number of businesses after Andrew's death. In the 1940s, however, Thomas Drugstore was a popular "hang out" for young people. Andrew himself, "a handsome, educated bachelor with his own successful business," was "well loved in [the] community by all who knew him." "Besides enjoying a host of friends and relatives he was loved by all the children and youths of the community who affectionately called him 'Drew.'" As the *Messenger* emphasized, "no one can think of an enemy that he ever had."

Andrew never married, but he did have five brothers and two sisters. The Thomas family was prominent in the city, and two of his brothers held significant positions of power: Claude Thomas was Chief of Police and R.L. ("Zie") Thomas was Secretary–Treasurer of the St. Martin Parish Police Jury, which helped govern St. Martin Parish. "[E]verybody . . . want[ed] to know who" killed Claude and Zie's brother.

A.   The Murder

Testimony indicated that Andrew was murdered at his home late on the night of November 7, 1944. He was found the next morning by Zie, and by his sister-in-law, Mrs. R.L. Thomas, informally known as "Mrs. Zie." A local storeowner, Lucien Bienvenu, had noticed that the normally punctual Andrew had not yet arrived to open his drugstore by 8:45 a.m. After calling Andrew at his home and getting no answer, Bienvenu called Mrs. Zie, suggesting she investigate. Mrs. Zie then picked up her husband before driving to Andrew's home.

When Zie and Mrs. Zie arrived at Andrew's address, located on the edge of the city, they saw Andrew's dead body splayed on the ground "about half way between the garage and the steps" of his home. After a doctor from the hospital had examined the body, Dr. S.D. Yongue, the Coroner of St. Martin Parish, and a coroner's jury convened to determine officially the cause of Andrew's death.

During the inquest, Alvin and Ida Van Brocklin, Andrew's neighbors and the only witnesses to the murder, testified. According to the Van Brocklins, on November 7, between 11:30 p.m. and midnight, both were awakened by gunshots, "fast one after the other." Thinking that the shots were coming from Evangeline State Park, directly across the

---

1946, at 1; *No Arrest Made Yet in Thomas Murder Case*, WKLY. MESSENGER (St. Martinville, La.), Nov. 17, 1944, at 1; *Andrew Thomas Killed at His Home Here Tuesday Night*, WKLY. MESSENGER (St. Martinville, La.), Nov. 10, 1944, at 1; and "Blackie," Editorial, *This & That*, WKLY. MESSENGER (St. Martinville, La.), Nov. 10, 1944, at 1.

street, Alvin walked out onto his porch while Ida stayed in bed and looked out the window toward Andrew's house. According to Ida, a car was parked in front of Andrew's house with its lights on; but, feeling afraid, she stopped looking and therefore did not know how long the car stayed or any other information.

Evidence later revealed that Andrew had been dining that evening with nearby friends. Andrew arrived home, parked his car in the garage, and started toward his house when somebody jumped him. According to the *Messenger*, Andrew had been shot five times after "a terrific struggle." The coroner's jury concluded that two shots were on his left side, two entered his back, while the fifth penetrated his right eye socket. The weapon was a .38 caliber pistol or rifle, and any of the shots that hit Andrew would have caused death. His pockets had been emptied, leading the police to believe the motive was robbery.

B.   The Murder's Aftermath

Andrew's murder was more than just a mystery; for the city of St. Martinville it was "one of the most tragic crimes [the] community ever had." The residents of St. Martinville reacted to the murder with shock and terror: the killer was unknown. After Andrew's November 9 funeral at Saint Martin de Tours Catholic Church, however, fear was accompanied by gossip about the murderer's identity. Long before the shooting, Andrew was known as a "ladies' man." Speculation in the town grew that perhaps Andrew was not robbed but rather killed by a jealous husband or boyfriend. Alvin Van Brocklin testified before the coroner's jury about such rumors and confirmed that he had seen Andrew's car parked in front of two women's homes: Bea (Mrs. Louis) Nassans and Henrietta (Mrs. Homer) Duplantis. Both Bea and Henrietta lived with their families in Pine Grove, a separate St. Martinville neighborhood located directly across the Bayou Teche, which divides the city. And both women's husbands were away for long periods of time because they worked in the oil industry.

Alvin's testimony helped little. Interviews with the two women's husbands, Louis Nassans and Homer Duplantis, revealed no evidence of a revenge killing much less any credible tie to Andrew's death. Besides, the Parish's sheriff, Leonard (E.L.) Resweber, had never handled a murder case before and had no training in homicide investigations. Nor did he have any viable leads. Although Police Chief Thomas and Sheriff Resweber had found bullets at the scene of the crime, they discovered no murder weapon, fingerprints, or witnesses other than the Van Brocklins.

For seven months—from November 24, 1944, through June 8, 1945—each issue of the *Messenger* ran a reward notice of $500.00 sponsored by Sheriff Resweber and the Thomas family for "information leading to the arrest and conviction" of Andrew's murderer.[18] As the months went by and no other murders or violent robberies occurred, the city's rumors again increasingly centered on the belief that romantic revenge had caused Andrew's demise.

During my 2007 visit to St. Martinville, James Akers told me that the continuing rumors greatly affected the reputations of Bea Nassans and Henrietta Duplantis. He said that shortly after the murder, Henrietta had written a letter to the *Messenger*, apparently never published, "thanking" the community for "ruining her life" by gossiping she was an adulteress. Henrietta also told Akers that Andrew was gay, and that it was ridiculous that people suspected Andrew was having affairs with women. She explained that some of the mothers in St. Martinville invited Andrew to dinner to show their gratitude for allowing them to acquire their medicine on credit from his store—an enormous gift to them during the World War II years when many drugs had restricted availability.

Henrietta's daughter, Genevieve, who was sixteen at the time of Andrew's murder and had worked in Andrew's store, further confirmed years later that Andrew and Henrietta were not lovers. According to Genevieve, Andrew was " 'a family friend' " who would often attend baseball games in New Iberia with her and her parents. Because Bea and Henrietta had a lot of flexible time, they would spend many an afternoon talking and drinking sodas at Andrew's drugstore. Indeed, Andrew's amorous reputation was fueled in part by his enthusiasm over seemingly innocuous activities, such as instructing women on how to use the popular facial creams sold in his store.

While Akers' account is, of course, hearsay, it emboldened me to ask a few of the people I interviewed if they had heard Andrew was gay. Nobody contradicted that interpretation. Allan Durand, an attorney and lifelong St. Martinville resident, informed me that homosexuality was not a topic that was openly discussed at the time Andrew was alive; indeed, many members of the community would not have understood the meaning of the concept. After learning more about Andrew, it becomes clear that his relationship with Willie was one of a number of unaddressed matters that could have been potentially relevant to Willie's defense.

---

[18] WKLY. MESSENGER (St. Martinville, La.), Nov. 24, 1944, at 6; Dec. 1, 1944, at 3; Dec. 8, 1944, at 3; Dec. 15, 1945, at 2; Dec. 22, 1944, at 8; Dec. 29, 1944, at 2; Jan. 12, 1945, at 2; Jan. 19, 1945, at 2; Jan. 26, 1945, at 2; Feb. 2, 1945, at 2; Feb. 9, 1945, at 2; Feb. 16, 1945, at 2; Feb. 23, 1945, at 2; Mar. 2, 1945, at 2; Mar. 9, 1945, at 14; Mar. 16, 1945, at 2; Mar. 23, 1945, at 2; Mar. 30, 1945, at 2; Apr. 6, 1945, at 2; Apr. 13, 1945, at 2; Apr. 20, 1945, at 2; Apr. 27, 1945, at 2; May 4, 1945, at 2; May 11, 1945, at 2; May 18, 1945, at 2; May 25, 1945, at 2; June 1, 1945, at 2; June 8, 1945, at 2.

III. WILLIE'S ARREST AND DETENTION
A. The Arrest

In July of 1945, several months after Andrew's murder, Sheriff
Resweber had so exhausted any leads on the case that he started to turn
elsewhere.[19] Resweber asked Claude W. Goldsmith, the Chief of Police of
Port Arthur, Texas—an industrial city less than two hundred miles west
of St. Martinville—if Goldsmith's force could detain "any man" from St.
Martin Parish who appeared in Port Arthur.

On the evening of August 3, 1945, Police Chief Goldsmith and
another officer were at the Port Arthur train station expecting to
apprehend a suspected drug dealer. When a questionable-looking man
with a suitcase got off the train, the two policemen pursued him. At just
that time, Willie, who was visiting his sister's home close by, took a pre-
dinner stroll around the block. When Willie saw the two white officers
running his way, he attempted to hide, only to be taken into custody on
the presumption that he was the suspected drug dealer's accomplice.

When questioned back at the police station, Willie appeared nervous
and began to stutter. (It would later become known that Willie stuttered
habitually.) His interrogators quickly determined that Willie was from
St. Martin Parish, not Port Arthur, and discovered that Willie was in
possession of a wallet and an identification card belonging to Andrew
Thomas. Willie was apparently able to convince the officers that he was
not involved with the suspected drug dealer they had chased earlier, but
within "two or three or five minutes," the officers obtained Willie's
written confession to Andrew's murder. They also managed to extract
Willie's confession to another, unrelated crime—the robbery and assault
of an elderly man in Port Arthur.

Willie's police interrogation occurred twenty years before *Miranda v.
Arizona*,[20] a decision requiring police to inform suspects questioned while

---

[19] The following discussion draws from the following sources: FRANCIS AS TOLD TO
MONTGOMERY, *supra* note 11; Transcript of Hearing Before Louisiana Board of Pardons,
Address of L.O. Pecot, District Attorney, Iberia, St. Mary, and St. Martin Parishes (May 31,
1946) (copy on file with author) [*hereinafter* Pardons Board Address of L.O. Pecot];
Pardons Board Testimony of E.L. Resweber, *supra* note 14; Pardons Board Testimony of
Gilbert Ozenne, *supra* note 14; Voluntary Statement While in Custody by Willie Francis
(Aug. 5, 1945) (on file with St. Martin Parish Courthouse, St. Martinville, La.); Undated
Confession by Willie Francis to the Murder of Andrew Thomas (on file with St. Martin
Parish Courthouse, St. Martinville, La.); Minutes, State v. Francis, No. 2161 (16th Jud.
Dist. Ct. La. Sept. 6, 1945); Letter from E.L. Resweber, Sheriff, St. Martin Parish, to M.E.
Culligan, Assistant Attorney General (Oct. 25, 1946) (copy on file with author); Indictment,
supra note 17; KING, *supra* note 3, at 68–69, 73, 78; NICHOLAS LEMANN, OUT OF THE FORTIES 93
(1983); *Andrew Thomas' Murderer Found*, WKLY. MESSENGER (St. Martinville, La.), Aug. 10,
1945, at 1; and *9–Month-Old St. Martinville Slaying Mystery is Cleared by Arrest Here*,
PORT ARTHUR NEWS (Port Arthur, Tex.), Aug. 6, 1945, at 1.

[20] 384 U.S. 436 (1966).

in custody of their rights to counsel and silence before attempting to acquire confessions. Sixteen-year-old Willie faced his inquisitors alone, without the advice and support of a lawyer, a family member, or a friend. In another case decided three years after Willie's arrest,[21] the Supreme Court reversed a murder conviction based on a fifteen-year-old defendant's confession garnered during five hours of questioning while the defendant was alone with the police. As the Court recognized,

> [t]hat which would leave a man cold and unimpressed can overawe and overwhelm a lad in his early teens. This is the period of great instability which the crisis of adolescence produces.... [W]e cannot believe that a lad of tender years is a match for the police in such a contest. He needs counsel and support if he is not to become the victim first of fear, then of panic. He needs someone on whom to lean lest the overpowering presence of the law, as he knows it, crush him.

The Court no longer holds that a juvenile is entitled to special protections during questioning because the requirements of *Miranda* apply to both children and adults.[22] Willie, of course, was not so shielded.

B. Willie's Confessions

Willie's Port Arthur confession of August 5, 1945 ("first confession") was one sheet. The top third of that sheet consisted of a typed statement provided by Police Chief Goldsmith asserting that the Port Arthur police did not coerce Willie to confess.[23] The bottom two thirds in Willie's handwritten scrawl stated:

> I Willie Francis now 16 years old I stole the gun from Mr. Ogise at St. Martinville La. and kill Andrew Thomas November 9, 1944 or about the time at St. Martinville La it was a secret about me and him. I took a black purse with card 1280182 in it four dollars in it. I all so took a watch on him and sell it in new Iberia La. That all I am said I throw gun away .38 Pistol

---

[21] Haley v. Ohio, 332 U.S. 596 (1948).

[22] *See* Yarborough v. Alvarado, 541 U.S. 652, 666 (2004) ("Our Court has not stated that a suspect's age or experience is relevant to the *Miranda* custody analysis...."){.}

[23] The statement provided by Goldsmith reads as follows:

I, Willie Francis, being in the custody of Claude W. Goldsmith, Chief of Police of the City of Port Arthur, Jefferson County, Texas and having been warned by E. L. Canada, Justice of the Peace, Jefferson County, Texas, the person to whom the hereinafter set out statement is by me made, that I do not have to make any statement at all, and that any statement made by me may be used in evidence against me on my trial for the offense concerning which this statement is made, do here make the following voluntary statement in writing to the said, E. L. Canada, towit [sic]:

Voluntary Statement While in Custody by Willie Francis, *supra* note 19.

Willie Francis

[Witnesses to the statement: E. L. Canada, Justice of the Peace, Jefferson County, Texas; Claude W. Goldsmith, Chief of Police, Port Arthur, Texas]

"Mr. Ogise," one of the names Willie referred to in his first confession, was the phonetic spelling for "Mr. August," the first name of August Fuselier, the deputy sheriff of St. Martinville whose gun Willie allegedly stole. Purportedly, in September 1944, two months before Andrew's murder, Fuselier had reported his Smith & Wesson .38 caliber gun missing from his car; yet there was no evidence of such a report other than the district attorney's memory.

Willie would write another confession ("second confession") the next day, August 6, 1945, while being transported back to St. Martinville by Sheriff Resweber. This time, the confession was far less formal, penciled on a small piece of filmy white paper with no date and no typed paragraph assuring its voluntariness. This confession, again in Willie's scrawl, read as follows:

Yes Willie Francis confess that he kill Andrew Thmas on November 8, 1944 i went to his house about 11:30 PM i hide backing his garage about a half hour, When he came out the garage i shot him five times. That all i remember A short story

Sinarely Willie Francis

Both confessions have perplexing content. Some of the language resembles stilted legalese that another person seemingly provided for Willie. The first confession's phrases, "I Willie Francis now 16 years old" and "or about the time," seem unlikely to have come from an untutored Willie. In the second confession Willie mixes up pronouns. He starts with the phrase, "Yes Willie Francis confess that *he* kill Andrew Thomas" but later writes, "*i* shot him." This confusion may be due to Willie's own ambiguous accounts. Initially, he said he had two accomplices to the crime, but he later recanted and said that he acted alone. There is an additional discrepancy concerning the date of the crime: the first confession indicates Andrew was killed on November 9, 1944, while the second confession gives the date as November 8. Andrew was actually killed either during the late evening of November 7 or the very early morning of November 8.

C.   Willie's Pre–Trial Incarceration

Willie's arrest generated "widespread attention." As a result, a decision was made to incarcerate him immediately nine miles away, in the Iberia Parish jail, because Willie would not be safe in the St. Martinville jail. The two men in charge of the New Iberia Parish jail,

Sheriff Gilbert Ozenne and Deputy Gus Walker, had such a reputation for treating blacks violently that FBI Director J. Edgar Hoover had ordered a civil rights investigation of them by the Department of Justice. While Willie would be protected from the possible mayhem of uncontrolled St. Martinville residents, ironically, he faced a potentially more daunting threat of injury by those now in authority.

Willie was interrogated repeatedly in the Iberia Parish jail during the months preceding his trial—all the while being described as an accommodating inmate, an account he confirmed. It was during several investigatory trips at this time that Willie provided the evidence that District Attorney L.O. Pecot stated was sufficient to convict him. According to Sheriff Resweber, on one trip to St. Martinville, Willie supposedly took law enforcement officers to an area near the railroad tracks a couple of blocks north of Andrew Thomas's house where Willie said he had dumped the murder weapon. Apparently, a town resident had found a .38 caliber pistol in the same spot soon after Andrew's death, and someone else had discovered a gun holster close by that matched August Fuselier's description. On a different trip to New Iberia, Resweber said that Willie led him and his deputies to the Rivere Jewelry Store, where Willie informed the owner, Mr. Rivere, that he had sold him a particular watchcase with initials on it for $5.00. Although Rivere claimed he did not remember Willie, his records documented the purchase. While Resweber stated that Willie confessed to having two "colored boys" as accomplices to the murder, Resweber concluded that their names were fictitious and that Willie had acted alone.

At no time was Willie represented by an attorney during his confessions or the investigation conducted during his pre-trial incarceration. Willie could not afford a lawyer or bail, nor was Willie eligible for court-appointed counsel during this period because Sheriff Resweber did not have him indicted until a month after his arrest. This strategy was no accident. "Detentions such as Willie's were in direct violation of a state statute, but they were 'the custom throughout Louisiana for generation upon generation.'" Although Willie had been jailed uncharged since August 6, 1945, he never met with a lawyer until September 6, 1945, less than a week before his trial for first degree murder.

IV. WILLIE'S TRIAL

Willie was tried at the St. Martin Parish courthouse in St. Martinville.[24] Because no transcribed record of the trial was taken,[25] knowledge

---

[24] The discussion of Willie's trial and possible motive draws from Brief in Behalf of Petitioner at 9, Louisiana *ex rel.* Francis v. Resweber, 329 U.S. 459 (1947) (No. 142); Brief in Opposition to the Writ Granted at 26, 30–31, Louisiana *ex rel.* Francis v. Resweber, 329 U.S. 459 (1947) (No. 142); Minutes, State v. Francis, No. 2161 (16th Jud. Dist. Ct. La. Sept. 6, 12–14, 1945); Affidavit of L. Charles Willis, Clerk of Court, St. Martin Parish, State v.

of what occurred is based on a few limited sources, including journalists'
accounts and, in particular, the terse minutes taken by the deputy clerk
of court. These sources alone, however, show the disturbing nature of
what took place.

A.   Troubling Proceedings

On September 6, 1945, Willie's judge, James Dudley Simon, appointed James Randlett Parkerson and Otto J. Mestayer, two lawyers with
well regarded reputations, to represent Willie. Yet the lawyers' efforts
were inept on every level. They never questioned the indictment, nor did
they make a motion for change of venue, despite the widespread publicity about the murder of a beloved white member of a small community by
a black youth. Even worse, defense counsel's first move was to request
permission to withdraw Willie's original plea of not guilty—a strategy
that would have ensured a quick death for Willie under Louisiana's then
mandatory death penalty provision for convicted murderers.[26] Ultimately, Willie's plea was not changed, but there was more legal irresponsibili-
ty to come. Counsel did not object to Willie's September 12 trial date,
even though it allowed them less than six days to prepare. Nor did they
preserve any exceptions at trial.

On September 12, at the suggestion of defense counsel, Judge Simon
ordered the sheriff to summon forty men to be considered for jury
service. All forty of the potential jurors were white—a perturbing outcome given that five years earlier the Supreme Court had decried such a
practice:[27] "If there has been discrimination [resulting in a totally white
jury pool], whether accomplished ingeniously or ingenuously, the conviction cannot stand." Regardless, twelve white men were selected to be

Francis, No. 2161 (16th Jud. Dist. Ct. La., Received & Filed Apr. 4, 1946); Pardons Board
Address of L.O. Pecot, *supra* note 19; KING, *supra* note 3, at 82–86, 90–91, 94, 153, 156,
266–67, 282–83; LEMANN, *supra* note 19, at 93; Taylor, *supra* note 12, at 5–6; *Negro Lives to
Tell Death Chair Story*, WKLY. IBERIAN (New Iberia, La.), May 7, 1946, at 1; and *Jury Finds
Murderer of Andrew Thomas Guilty*, WKLY. MESSENGER (St. Martinville, La.), Sept. 14, 1945,
at 1.

[25] The matter of there being no trial transcript was later raised on appeal to the U.S.
Supreme Court. In arguing that the Supreme Court of Louisiana had erred in holding that
Willie was not denied due process of law, Willie's attorneys noted that the U.S. Supreme
Court could "never know the full story of the trial of Willie Francis because *no stenographic record was taken at the trial*." Brief in Behalf of Petitioner, *supra* note 24, at 9. It
appears, however, that the practice of creating a verbatim record of trial proceedings was
not common in Louisiana. According to the respondents, "in thousands of criminal cases in
Louisiana, no stenographic notes of the testimony of witnesses is [sic] taken for the legal
reason, and no other, that under the Constitution of Louisiana, ... there can be no appeal
on the facts." Brief in Opposition to the Writ Granted, *supra* note 24, at 26.

[26] LA. CODE CRIM. L. & PROC. ANN. art. 740–30(2) (1943).

[27] Smith v. Texas, 311 U.S. 128 (1940).

Willie's jury after the attorneys entered challenges (the details of the challenges are not known). Despite District Attorney Pecot's claim that no juror came from St. Martin Parish, Gilbert King's research shows that at least three were from St. Martinville, and that a number of the other jurors were from a neighboring town in St. Martin Parish. In addition, nine jurors "bore surnames that appeared on Judge Simon's family tree."

Willie's trial was just two days long. The gun supposedly used in the murder, and the bullets recovered from the crime scene, were never introduced as evidence. They had been lost—reportedly on the way to the FBI for analysis. As King suggests,

> Perhaps the intent was, in fact, to lose the ballistics evidence at the behest of someone in St. Martinville who had the ability, motivation, and opportunity to arrange its disappearance, thus leaving a poor, uneducated black youth and his hapless (or worse, complicit) public defenders in the awkward position of having to convince twelve white jurors and Judge Simon that the law enforcement officials in their town were corrupt and incompetent.

Moreover, there was no evidence of fingerprints taken from the gun and no clear proof that the bullet wounds in Andrew Thomas's body had actually derived from a .38 caliber bullet, much less the Smith & Wesson stolen from August Fuselier. In addition, the owner of Rivere's Jewelry Store was not present to testify that Willie had sold Andrew's watch to the store. "Without the alleged murder weapon, bullets, fingerprints, or the wristwatch as evidence, the bulk of [the district attorney's] case rested exclusively on confessions obtained by police while the teenaged Willie Francis was in custody and without legal counsel."

After District Attorney Pecot introduced the State's case against Willie by reading the grand jury indictment and presenting his opening statement, defense counsel "waived the right of their opening statement but reserved the privilege of making such statement at the conclusion of the State's case." Counsel never did present such a statement in defense of Willie nor did they call a single witness. When the State rested its case, the defense informed the court that it "had no evidence to offer on behalf of the accused and rested its case." Therefore, the jury was never informed that: (1) the murder weapon and crime scene bullets no longer existed, having been lost in the mail; (2) Willie's fingerprints were never found on the gun because the police never checked for fingerprints; (3) there were inconsistencies in the dates and other aspects of Willie's confessions; (4) rumors abounded that someone's husband or lover may have killed Andrew given his reputation for being a bachelor-around-town and visiting married women; and (5) Andrew's neighbor, Ida Van Brocklin, had testified before the coroner's jury that she saw a car parked in front of Andrew's house with its lights on after she heard the gunshots, thereby refuting Willie's account that Andrew's car was in the garage at the time of the killing and supporting the suspicion that others were involved. Nor did the jury hear the suggestion that the State's evidence was planted and Willie's confessions were coerced.

There were other unanswered questions. How did Willie succeed in stealing a gun from a sheriff's deputy much less use it with the extraordinary precision that would have been required of the shooter? Willie had never owned a gun nor learned how to fire one. Shy stammering Willie, who had no record of violence, did not strike residents as a killer who had the ability to engage in a "terrific struggle" with Andrew. The town talk was that Willie had been framed and his confessions forced. Nevertheless, his attorneys never investigated the possibility that Willie's statements, made without a lawyer or family member present, were involuntary despite heavily documented, nationwide evidence of police force being used against minorities.

It appears from the trial minutes that defense counsel presented a closing argument, but there is no record of what that may have been. Regardless, the jury reached their verdict the very same day (September 13, 1945): Willie Francis was guilty. He was sentenced to death the next day. According to the *Messenger*, "Throughout the trial the negro was uninterested and showed very little emotion." With all that had been bungled during the trial, perhaps even Willie, a non-lawyer, could sense his fate. He may not have shown emotion but surely he must have felt it—terror perhaps, depression most certainly, and then, resignation.

B. Motive

Among the trial's unanswered questions was one of the most intriguing: Willie's alleged motive for murdering Andrew. In an interview after the attempted electrocution, Willie stated that he considered Andrew a " 'pretty good boss' " and a " 'swell guy' ": he "didn't have a grudge against him nor was he after money." In *The Chair*, Willie described Andrew as "a very fine fellow." As Gilbert King notes, if the motive was robbery, then the timing seemed odd. During the two months following Willie's alleged theft of August Fuselier's gun, there were no reported instances of robbery at gunpoint in St. Martinville. Further, Willie had other nonviolent opportunities to steal from Andrew, either by breaking into his home or his store.

There was talk that at some point an "altercation" had taken place between Willie and Andrew. Additional speculation was that a "white person," presumably August Fuselier, had learned of the altercation and then given Willie his gun to use. After all, according to Father Rousseve, Fuselier himself had once threatened to kill Andrew, warning him to stay away from his wife or there would be repercussions. Although married, Fuselier was also said to have had girlfriends; therefore, his threat to Andrew may actually have pertained to a purported consort, Lena Foti, who managed a saloon that Fuslier frequented. Fuselier's gun was reported to have been stolen from his car while it was parked in front of the saloon.

Recent interviews by Gilbert King uncovered another possible motive. Before Andrew's murder, one of his employees, Stella Vincent, abruptly and inexplicably quit her job, insisting to her sisters that she no longer wanted to work for Andrew. Soon thereafter, she moved to Florida. Thirty years later, on her deathbed, Stella told her sister Edith why she had left. Stella explained that she "had witnessed something at the [Thomas] drugstore that had so disturbed her she could not bear to return." In one of the rooms in the back of the store, Stella had seen " 'an incident' " between Andrew and fifteen-year-old Willie that ended with Andrew "yelling and lashing out at the boy." Stella had been so affected by what she saw that she kept her experience a secret for decades.

Perhaps this "incident" helps explain the most mysterious phrase in Willie's first confession—"it was a secret about me and him." It is not certain, however, which "him" Willie was referencing—Andrew Thomas or August Fuselier ("Mr. Ogise"). Any secret between Willie and Andrew supports the idea that the two may have had a sexual relationship, coerced or not. As far as can be determined from my interviews and those of Gilbert King, this possibility was raised only decades after the crime, not before, when Willie was on trial or awaiting execution. The alternative theory—that the secret was between Willie and Fuselier— suggests that Willie had conspirators and that Fuselier was one of them.

Regardless, what becomes clear is that there were a number of potential theories in this case that were never fully investigated. Willie's attorneys, for example, could have pointed inculpatory fingers at other residents of St. Martinville, based on the jealousies aroused by Thomas's roving reputation. Or his attorneys could have introduced mitigating evidence or a provocation defense that might have resulted in a manslaughter rather than a murder conviction. As it turns out, Willie's attorneys never presented any evidence whatsoever to the jury. Willie's guilt would remain the only focus of the investigation.

C.   The Post–Trial Period

After Willie's conviction, there is no documentation that his lawyers ever contacted him, much less attempted to appeal either his verdict or his death sentence.[28] Legal help may have been offered by another

---

[28] The discussion in this Section draws from Francis as told to Montgomery, *supra* note 11; Affidavit of L. Charles Willis, *supra* note 24; Letter from Michel A. Maroun, Wilson &

source, however. On November 9, 1945, an attorney from a law firm in Shreveport, Louisiana, wrote Sheriff Resweber explaining that the firm had "been employed to represent [Willie] in his petition to the Pardon Board for commutation of sentence," and asked for an account of Willie's behavior in prison. Likewise, Willie mentioned learning about the possibility of a second trial in a February 15, 1946, letter to Resweber. However, there is no verification that a second trial was attempted or that anything more was done on Willie's behalf during the six-month period after Judge Simon sentenced Willie to death but before Willie received his execution date.

At the same time, the contents of Willie's February 15, 1946, letter to Resweber are disturbing. Willie's basic purpose was to satisfy Resweber's execution goals, so much so that he told Resweber that he did not want a second trial and that he was willing to die. Willie's desire to accommodate, as well as the racial differences between him and Andrew, were foremost in Willie's mind:

I'm a negro, I killed A white man.

I know that you are trying to give me a death penalty.

I don't mind at all.

After a few months in jail, then, Willie seemed to have become a death penalty volunteer, possibly offering to forego any further trials or appeals on his behalf. If there was little-to-no movement on Willie's case at this time, it may have been due, in whole or in part, to Willie's lack of interest. Hopelessness and despair are common feelings among death row inmates. Although Willie was visited by family and friends who brought books and magazines for him to read, Willie's position must have been disheartening.

Willie's account in *The Chair* gives some perspective on his state of mind when he was returned to the New Iberia Parish jail. Although he was told that the "the death cell [was] bigger and more comfortable" than a comparable cell in St. Martinville, to Willie, "[i]t didn't make much difference." "They hadn't said when they were going to kill me, so I didn't care where they put me." It was probably during this period that, according to Sheriff Resweber, Willie threatened suicide with a safety razor. No matter, Willie's time would soon come. In early April,

---

Abramson, to Sheriff, St. Martin Parish (Nov. 9, 1945) (copy on file with author); Unsigned Letter from Willie Francis to E.L. Resweber (Feb. 15, 1946) (on file at St. Martin Parish Courthouse, St. Martinville, La.); Letter from L.O. Pecot, District Attorney, 16th Judicial District of Louisiana, to E.L. Resweber, Sheriff, St. Martin Parish (Apr. 5, 1946) (copy on file with author); Death Warrant, Executive Department, State of Louisiana (Mar. 29, 1946) (copy on file with author); John H. Blume, *Killing the Willing: "Volunteers," Suicide and Competency*, 103 MICH. L. REV. 939, 963 (2005); and *Willie Francis Shows Little Interest in Fate*, DUNKIRK EVENING OBSERVER (Dunkirk, N.Y.), Jan. 14, 1947, at 1.

Willie received the final word: the State issued a death warrant, establishing May 3, 1946, as his execution date.

V. THE EXECUTION FAILS

Apart from his family and friends, the person who was perhaps
closest to Willie during this period was Father Charles Hannigan, a fifty-
nine-year-old Irish Catholic and a member of a religious order called the
Holy Ghost Fathers.[29] Father Hannigan had visited Willie in the New
Iberia jail throughout Willie's incarceration and was particularly helpful
on May 2, 1946, the morning preceding Willie's attempted execution.
Father Hannigan explained that in many ways Willie was "lucky"
because, unlike most people, he knew when he was going to die and he
could "prepare" for his fate. Also, the electric chair would only "tickle"
for a short time. Father Hannigan encouraged Willie to show that he
"was able to die like a man," because, in Father Hannigan's view, "[i]t
is one of the hardest things to make yourself learn how to die right."
One of Willie's greatest concerns was that he not act like a "cry-baby"
on his execution day. At the same time, he wondered "why the chair was
called the 'hot seat' " if it would only " 'tickle' " him.

---

[29] The following discussion of Willie's execution and executioners draws from FRANCIS AS
TOLD TO MONTGOMERY, *supra* note 11; Transcript of Hearing Before Louisiana Board of
Pardons, Testimony of Captain E. Foster (May 31, 1946) (copy on file with author)
[*hereinafter* Pardons Board Testimony of E. Foster]; Transcript of Hearing Before Louisi-
ana Board of Pardons, Testimony of Vincent Venezia, Inmate, Angola Penitentiary (May
31, 1946) (copy on file with author) [*hereinafter* Pardons Board Testimony of Vincent
Venezia]; Transcript of Hearing Before Louisiana Board of Pardons, Testimony of Dr. S.D.
Yongue, Coroner, St. Martin Parish (May 31, 1946) (copy on file with author) [*hereinafter*
Pardons Board Testimony of Dr. S.D. Yongue]; Pardons Board Testimony of Gilbert
Ozenne, *supra* note 14; Affidavit of Louie M. Cyr (Mar. 19, 1947) (copy on file with author);
Affidavit of Ignace Doucet (Apr. 3, 1947) (copy on file with author); Affidavit of Sidney
Dupois (May 23, 1946), *reprinted in* Brief in Behalf of Petitioner, *supra* note 24, at 20–21;
Affidavit of Rev. Maurice L. Rousseve (May 25, 1946), *reprinted in* Brief in Behalf of
Petitioner, *supra* note 24, at 16–17; Affidavit of Harold Resweber (May 23, 1946), *reprinted
in* Brief in Behalf of Petitioner, *supra* note 24, at 18–19; Affidavit of Ignace Doucet (May
30, 1946), *reprinted in* Brief in Behalf of Petitioner, *supra* note 24, at 17–18; Affidavit of
Willie Olivier (May 24, 1946), *reprinted in* Brief in Behalf of Petitioner, *supra* note 24, at
15–16; Interview with Thomas Nelson, *supra* note 6; Interview with Winfield Ledet,
Faculty Member, Pearl River High School, Pearl River, La., in St. Martinville, La. (June 14,
2007); Photographs from the Mary Alice Fontenot Papers, University Archives and Acadia-
na Manuscripts Collection, University of Louisiana at Lafayette, Collection 97, Box 7,
Folder 15; KING, *supra* note 3, at 7, 9, 11–12, 19, 28, 220, 245; MILLER & BOWMAN, *supra* note
3, at 11; Deborah W. Denno, *Is Electrocution an Unconstitutional Method of Execution? The
Engineering of Death over the Century*, 35 WM. & MARY L. REV. 551, 608 (1994); *Defense
Attorney to Seek Commutation of Sentence on 'Double Jeopardy' Plea*, LA. WKLY. (New
Orleans, La.), Nov. 16, 1946, at 1; and Elliott Chaze, *'Plumb Mizzuble' Covers Willie
Francis' Idea of Electric Chair*, DAILY ADVERTISER (Lafayette, La.), July 1, 1946, at 1.

Willie was still housed in a New Iberia Parish jail cell with "bright pink" walls. On May 3 an inmate came to Willie's cell to shave his head to ensure maximum electrical conductivity for the 2,500 volts of electricity that would flow through the wires attached to Willie's head and leg. In Willie's account of this episode the tone was light; people were trying to joke to make him feel better, even the inmate-barber: " 'Well, Willie, I guess that's one hair-cut you won't have to pay for.' " Everyone laughed. On Willie's cell wall a journalist noticed a phrase Willie had written about a month earlier: "Of Course I Am Not a Killer." Yet no one at the time would ever comment on what the phrase possibly meant.

In shackles, Willie got into a black sedan that took him to the St. Martinville jail—driving first through the city and even past his house on Washington Street. En route, a deputy commented: " 'Don't worry, Willie—it won't hurt you very much. You won't even feel it!' " But at that point, pain was not Willie's concern. "I wasn't worried at all whether it would hurt me. I was more worried about the fact it was going to kill me." After pulling up to the courthouse and proceeding through the crowd of spectators—"both colored and white"—a sheriff and deputy took Willie to the St. Martin Parish jail. A two-story redbrick building located behind the courthouse, the jail would be the site of Willie's execution. It has since been demolished.

A.   The Executioners

Unlike most states at that time, Louisiana did not execute prisoners in the state penitentiary. Instead, the State delivered a portable, hardwood electric chair to the town where the crime had been committed. This chair, "Gruesome Gertie," was housed at the notoriously dangerous and deplorable Louisiana State Penitentiary in Angola, Louisiana.

Willie had two executioners: Ephie Foster, a captain at the Louisiana State Penitentiary, and Vincent Venezia, an inmate serving hard time there. Venezia was an electrician who worked as an assistant to U.J. Esnault, the prison's chief electrician. Venezia managed the generator while Foster threw the switch. Evidence shows that en route to St. Martinville with Louisiana's portable electric chair both men had spent the evening of May 2 drinking in bars in New Iberia and talking about Willie's execution.

The next day, Foster drove the oak chair into the city in a large truck. Photographs taken of the delivery evoke contradictory images. The first photo of the truck winding through the street looks so ordinary—as though it is transporting household furniture, such as a couch or living room table. But, the additional photos showing the unloading of Gruesome Gertie indicate that the truck's contents are anything but normal. Mayor Nelson, age ten at the time, told me that he and his friends were intensely curious about the chair and all that was going on, while never fully comprehending the consequences. "I can remember the day of the execution when they set up the chair and everything.... I remember playing hooky from school, a bunch of us, to go watch the execution.... But we couldn't, they ran us off.... We'd go back and they'd run us off. You see there was a wooden fence along the sidewalk, so you could look through the cracks.... [T]hey had the chair on the front porch" before moving it inside the jail. As Mayor Nelson explained, age ten in those days was a lot younger than it is today. He and his friends weren't "that knowledgeable" about the meaning behind the events. But, their naivety aside, the young children saw Willie's fate before he did.

Once Foster and Venezia unloaded Gruesome Gertie, they had to carry it to the second floor of the jail. They then ran the chair's wires out of the window so that they could connect to the gasoline-powered generator, which was located in the truck. According to one eye witness, during this task, Venezia handed a flask of alcohol to Foster from which both men drank.

B.   The Execution

When Willie arrived at the second floor of the jail, he entered the small L-shaped room where Gruesome Gertie had been set up. Shortly thereafter, Sheriff Resweber led him to a nearby cell, so that Willie could meet with Father Maurice Rousseve, the pastor of Willie's church. Father Rousseve attempted to console him and said he would "take care" of Willie's family; then Willie returned to the execution room. Everyone was ready. Willie's time had come.

"[S]oaking with perspiration," Willie was strapped to the chair. Someone in the room put a wet hood over Willie's head that covered his eyes but not his nose, so that he could breathe freely. Not being able to see frightened him all the more. But the next step was even more terrifying. Willie heard an unfamiliar voice—Foster's—state the last words he presumably would ever hear: "Good–Bye Willie." As Willie would later recount, "It was funny the way he said it—like he was telling me good-bye and I was going off on a trip." When the generator was finally turned on, the "sound was deafening" and could be heard for blocks. Willie described the details:

> I wanted to say good-bye, too, but I was so scared I couldn't talk. My hands were closed tightly. Then—I could almost hear it coming.
>
> The best way I can describe it is: Whamm! Zst!
>
> It felt like a hundred and a thousand needles and pins were pricking in me all over and my left leg felt like somebody was cutting it with a razor blade. I could feel my arms jumping at my

sides and I guess my whole body must have jumped straight out. I couldn't stop the jumping. If that was tickling it was sure a funny kind. I thought for a minute I was going to knock the chair over. Then I was all right. I thought I was dead.... Then they did it again! The same feeling all over. I heard a voice say, "Give me some more juice down there!" And in a little while somebody yelled, "I'm giving you all I got now!" I think I must have hollered for them to stop. They say I said, "Take it off! Take it off!" I know that was certainly what I wanted them to do—turn it off.

Amazingly, Willie was still alive after the first current subsided. Foster threw the switch again—asking Venezia to provide more current, juice that the generator did not have. With one final yell, Willie stuttered, " 'I am not dying.' " " 'Take it off! Take it off!' " [30] Quickly, Willie was unstrapped and walked away from the chair. As Willie would later explain, it took him a while to realize he was still alive; at first "it seemed like they were in an awful hurry to get me out of that chair so they could bury me."

Although Willie was silent during the medical examination immediately after the attempted execution, Dr. Yongue, the coroner, claimed he "found nothing wrong with" Willie apart from a fast pulse; there were no burn marks or burnt flesh. It appears, however, that Yongue never even asked Willie any questions. Sheriff Ozenne stated that Willie appeared "just a little nervous and shaky," but that Willie said he was " 'alright' " when Ozenne asked him how he felt. Foster, the executioner, did not even feign concern about Willie. In fact, he was livid, yelling out as Willie exited the room, " 'I missed you this time, but I'll get you next week if I have to use an iron bar!' " [30] Willie would later recount, "He [Foster] was plenty mad, I guess." But, of course, Willie was thrilled.

C. The Reaction

Willie's survival was greeted with ecstatic delight by his family.[31] The moment was interpreted by many, including Willie, as a blessing

---

[30] The works of Gilbert King and Miller and Bowman describe Foster as threatening Willie with a "rock," not an iron bar. KING, *supra* note 3, at 28; MILLER & BOWMAN, *supra* note 3, at 11. Presumably the references to a "rock" follow from the March 19, 1947, affidavit of Louie M. Cyr, where Cyr claims that George Etie stated that the "drunken executor cursed Willie Francis and told him that he would be back to finish electrocuting him, and if the electricity did not kill him, he would kill him with a rock." Affidavit of Louie M. Cyr, *supra* note 29.

[31] The discussion in this Section draws from FRANCIS AS TOLD TO MONTGOMERY, *supra* note 11; Pardons Board Testimony of Dr. S.D. Yongue, *supra* note 29; Pardons Board Testimony of E. Foster, *supra* note 29; Pardons Board Testimony of Vincent Venezia, *supra* note 29; Pardons Board Testimony of E.L. Resweber, *supra* note 14; Pardons Board Testimony of

from God, even inspiring a published song mimicking Willie's words to explain what had happened: "De Lord Fool'd Around Wid Dat Chair." According to witnesses, Willie's first comments when he rose out from the chair were, " 'The Lord was sho with me!' " Unfortunately, like everything else Willie experienced, such joy would be fleeting. Soon after the first failed attempt, Louisiana's Governor James (Jimmie) Davis decided that Willie would be executed again on May 9, 1946—six days later.

That week would turn into eight months and then, with the help of some extraordinary attorneys, into an entire year. Indeed, the failed event would mark the start of Willie's doomed fight to live. But it would be greatly downplaying the human side of this part of his story to view it only in terms of Willie's ultimate death by execution. The year would be filled with a national coalition of forces unlike that seen in any other case.

In many respects, Willie's story was a local one—specific to St. Martinville or to Louisiana—followed sporadically by the *Messenger*. On another level, however, the story was distinctly national—one that reporters and newspapers throughout the country covered because people everywhere were entranced by Willie's survival. As one paper noted, "Hundreds of letters from all parts of the country were received by Francis, the governor and Willie's lawyers, nearly all of them urging or hoping for clemency." Willie talked about the letters and support he got from people who were praying for him just days after the botched execution. "I felt just like a movie star, and didn't have any idea I had so many friends," Willie would comment. Over time, those "friends" included the likes of Fiorello LaGuardia, then mayor of New York City, and Herbert Lehmann, then governor of New York State, as well as the famed commentator Walter Winchell. Religion was often a strong theme

---

Gilbert Ozenne, *supra* note 14; Brief in Opposition to the Writ Granted, *supra* note 24, at 4; Affidavit of Sidney Dupois, *supra* note 29; Affidavit of Rev. Maurice L. Rousseve, *supra* note 29; Affidavit of Harold Resweber, *supra* note 29; Affidavit of Ignace Doucet (May 30, 1946), *supra* note 29; Affidavit of Willie Olivier, *supra* note 29; Affidavit of Luke LaViolette (May 24, 1946) (copy on file with author); Telegram from J.H. Davis, Governor, La., to E.L. Resweber, Sheriff, St. Martinville, La. (May 3, 1946) (copy on file with author); KING, *supra* note 3, at 34, 120; Hamm, *supra* note 17; Tom Gillen, Jr., *Around the Capitol*, WKLY. MESSENGER (St. Martinville, La.), Jan. 31, 1947, at 4; *My Time Has Come, Says Willie, Facing Death Again*, TIMES-PICAYUNE (New Orleans, La.), Jan. 14, 1947, at 6; Taylor, *supra* note 12; *Negro Lives to Tell Death Chair Story*, *supra* note 24; Chaze, *'Plumb Mizzuble' Covers Willie Francis' Idea of Electric Chair*, *supra* note 29; *Many Sought to Save Willie Francis*, LA. WKLY. (New Orleans, La.), May 18, 1946, at 9; *Court Rules Negro Must Go to Chair Again*, STATE (Columbia, S.C.), May 16, 1946, at 1; "Blackie," Editorial, *This & That*, WKLY. MESSENGER (St. Martinville, La.), May 10, 1946, at 1; *Comments on Fluke Execution Here*, WKLY. MESSENGER (St. Martinville, La.), May 10, 1946, at 2; and *Urge All Executions at State Pen*, Editorial, WKLY. MESSENGER (St. Martinville, La.), May 10, 1946, at 5.

in people's communications with Willie. "The people who wrote said they were sure the Lord had a hand in what happened.... "

Many of St. Martinville's residents greatly resented such outside interference with a criminal justice process they thought fair. The local community was particularly irritated by the intense national reaction to Willie's unfinished execution as it was expressed in newspapers in other states. Several *Messenger* articles on May 10, 1946, one week after Willie's execution attempt, focused on this matter. According to Marcel Bienvenu, the *Messenger*'s editor, "The large Northern papers played up the story so much that a flood of sympathetic letters have been reaching the Governor [of Louisiana] and other officials all asking for clemency of Francis." Another *Messenger* article derided *The Chicago Tribune* for assuming "an interest" in the case, calling it a "notorious South-hating sheet." As the article spewed, "You can generally count on the *Tribune* not to be up to any good." The *Messenger*'s take on the "metropolitan press" was also cynical and distrusting.

Yet one May 10 *Messenger* editorial, reprinted from the *Shreveport Times*, showed that the State's portable electric chair had long been a known problem within Louisiana; the writer suggested legislation enabling executions to be carried out in a "permanent execution building at the state penitentiary." "[T]he Louisiana Police Jury association ha[d] been urging the adoption of such a statute" for several years. The jurors knew that the portable electrocution method had "serious defects." "Certainly capital punishment, if it is to be inflicted, should be imposed inexorably, not haphazardly." Also problematic was the barbaric interest of "the throngs which wait to hear the roar of the machinery that signals the exacting of the death penalty." For "sensitive natures," such an experience can cause "real distress," and the "effect of the proceedings on young minds ... could hardly be called beneficial."

Of course, newspaper coverage also examined Willie's legal case. Whether or not any electrical current actually reached Willie would be a key matter of contention. Some sources stated that Willie had not received any current and appeared uninjured. According to one account, Willie had said that the chair only " 'kinda tickled a little.' " Yet reliance on such quotes from Willie was incredibly misleading. The "tickling" depiction was what Father Hannigan had told Willie to expect in an effort to make Willie feel less frightened and to be brave. After Willie survived the electrocution, Hannigan recalled that "Willie looked at me very seriously and said: 'Father, it tickled—but it hurt, too,' " a phrase Willie repeated in *The Chair*. Time and again, Willie attempted in his comments to juxtapose how people, especially Father Hannigan, told him the electrocution would feel and how it really did feel. "If that was tickling it was sure a funny kind," Willie lamented. In Willie's need-to-please world, the calculated opinions of others, who had never even sat in an electric chair, were a far better characterization of Willie's experiences than his own unique reality.

In *The Chair*, Willie left no question that the execution attempt caused acute pain, even though some of Willie's accounts to journalists were so colorfully put it could be hard to tell. As Willie said to one reporter, "you feel 'like you got a mouth full of cold peanut butter, and you see little blue and pink and green speckles, the kind that shines in a rooster's tail.' " Willie insisted that "when the switch was thrown he got some of the current." Indeed, witnesses to the execution detailed Willie's extreme reaction to the current, noting that Willie's "lips 'puffed out' and he rocked the chair." While predictably the electrician in charge disagreed, the matter was surely ambiguous enough to litigate. If only Willie had a good lawyer this time.

VI. MUCH TO DO IN LITTLE TIME

A. Willie's New Lawyer

On May 3, 1946, after Willie's flawed execution, Frederick Francis visited the law office of Jerome Broussard, a St. Martinville attorney, asking if Broussard would take Willie's case.[32] Frederick had performed odd jobs for Broussard in the past and he was determined not to have court-appointed counsel represent Willie again. Although Broussard was aware of Willie's situation, as a business lawyer he possessed neither the expertise nor the financial flexibility to accept a complex criminal case with few prospects for remuneration. Instead, Broussard referred Frederick to Bertrand de Blanc, an attorney who worked next door. Recently returned from World War II, de Blanc was refurbishing a law practice he had started before he left. De Blanc's family had a long and prominent presence in St. Martinville, and, like the rest of the city, de Blanc was familiar with Willie's botched electrocution attempt. Indeed, Sheriff Resweber had asked de Blanc to witness Willie's execution on May 3, but de Blanc refused. Referring to Willie, de Blanc told Resweber, "I like that guy."

Frederick Francis informed de Blanc that "he had no money but he would work to repay him." De Blanc responded "it was all right," he would still take Willie's case. Money was not the issue. De Blanc believed

---

[32] The discussion in this Section draws from the following sources: FRANCIS AS TOLD TO MONTGOMERY, *supra* note 11; Bertrand de Blanc, *Letter to the Editor*, WKLY. MESSENGER (St. Martinville, La.), May 17, 1946, at 6; Interview by Jeffrey H. Bowman with Bertrand de Blanc, *supra* note 14; KING, *supra* note 3, at 41–45; MILLER & BOWMAN, *supra* note 3, at 30; FRED W. FRIENDLY & MARTHA J.H. ELLIOTT, THE CONSTITUTION: THAT DELICATE BALANCE 166 (1984); LEMANN, *supra* note 19, at 90; *The Case of Condemned Negro is Story of Fighting Lawyer and His Aged Father Who Waits*, JEANERETTE ENTERPRISE (Jeanerette, La.), Jan. 16, 1947, at 1; and *Louisiana Stays Electrocution of Colored Boy*, MOBILE REG. (Mobile, Ala.), May 9, 1946, at 1.

that " '[i]t's not human' " to make a man " 'go to the chair twice.' "
" '[T]he state fell down on its job.' ... 'It made [Willie] suffer the
torture of facing death without completing it.' " Married, age 35, and the
father of three children, de Blanc would labor to save Willie from a
second execution for an entire year, his only remuneration some vegetables given to him by Frederick. One news article about de Blanc stated
that "[s]aving Willie has become a sort of obsession with him."

Yet de Blanc also felt he had some explaining to do to the St.
Martinville community. In a May 8, 1946, letter sent to the Editor of the
Messenger, de Blanc acknowledged the criticism he faced from town
members for representing Willie. He had "no apologies," however, for
accepting the case because, as an attorney, he had taken an oath to
defend people; whether "rich or poor, black or white" everyone is
"entitled to be heard." At the same time, de Blanc wanted the community to know how "shocked" he was upon hearing of the "brutal murder."
He "was one of Andrew's best friends." As neighbors, de Blanc "spent a
lot of time going to the drugstore just to talk to him," and de Blanc's
children "spent most of their time" at the drugstore too. Andrew "liked
them and they liked him." De Blanc further urged that the matter was
legal, not personal. While Willie should not be "set free," neither should
he die; the right course was that he be sentenced to life in prison. De
Blanc then provided an eloquent end to his letter that succinctly summarized what would fuel him through the next year: "[M]y few critics will
soon be dead and buried but the principles involved in this case of
freedom from fear of cruel and unusual punishment and that of due
process and double jeopardy will live as long as the American flag waves
on this continent."

B.   The Supreme Court of Louisiana

De Blanc realized he had only a few days left to block another
execution attempt.[33] Therefore, on May 7, 1946, he filed a petition for a
writ of habeas corpus in Louisiana state district court, arguing that
Willie's sentence had already been carried out and that a second electrocution attempt would deny him due process of law and constitute cruel
and unusual punishment.[34] De Blanc knew that it was unlikely that
Judge Simon, the judge considering the petition and the same judge who

---

[33] The discussion in this Section draws from State *ex rel.* Francis v. Resweber, 31 So.
2d 697 (La. 1947); Transcript of Record at 12, 17, 27, Louisiana *ex rel.* Francis v. Resweber,
329 U.S. 459 (1947) (No. 142); Brief in Behalf of Petitioner, *supra* note 24, at 3; Brief in
Opposition to the Writ Granted, *supra* note 24, at 4–5; Reprieve, State of Louisiana,
Executive Department (May 8, 1946) (copy on file with author) [*hereinafter* May 8, 1946
Reprieve]; KING, *supra* note 3, at 121; and *Lt-Governor Grants Negro Reprieve*, JEANERETTE
ENTERPRISE (Jeanerette, La.), May 9, 1946, at 1.

[34] A second petition for a writ of habeas corpus was filed in Louisiana state district
court the next day, May 8, 1946, by NAACP representatives A.P. Tureaud and Joseph R.

had presided over Willie's trial, would release Willie from jail; indeed, Simon denied the request the very same day. Two days later, on May 9, 1946, de Blanc appealed the decision by submitting a petition for writs of certiorari, prohibition, mandamus, and habeas corpus to the Supreme Court of Louisiana.[35] Realizing that the court would not have sufficient time to reach a decision before Willie's scheduled execution on May 9, 1946, the court's chief justice asked the acting governor to recall Willie's death warrant, which he agreed to do. Willie was granted a thirty-day reprieve, until June 7, 1946.

Willie and his family were elated, but the good feelings were short-lived. On May 15, 1946, the Louisiana Supreme Court refused to grant the writs de Blanc and two NAACP attorneys[36] had requested. The court concluded that, "[i]nasmuch as the proceedings had in the district court, up to and including the pronouncing of the sentence of death, were entirely regular," the Louisiana Supreme Court was not authorized "to set aside the sentence and release [Willie Francis] from the Sheriff's custody."[37] Indeed, the Louisiana Supreme Court also had "no authority to pardon [Francis] or to commute his sentence." Only the governor could pardon and commute, and this authority could "be exercised only upon the recommendation of the Board of Pardons" or any two of its three members.

With limited time remaining, de Blanc decided not to apply for a rehearing with the Louisiana Supreme Court and instead placed his hopes on the Pardons Board. Although the Board included Judge Simon,

---

Thornton. State *ex rel.* Francis v. Resweber, 31 So. 2d 697, 698 (La. 1947); Brief in Opposition to the Writ Granted, *supra* note 24, at 4; *see also Supreme Court Rejects Plea for Willie Francis*, LA. WKLY. (New Orleans, La.), May 18, 1946, at 1.

[35] De Blanc also submitted a supplemental petition on May 14, 1946. Transcript of Record, *supra* note 33, at 17. De Blanc took Willie's case directly to the Supreme Court of Louisiana because Louisiana's intermediate appeals court did not hear criminal cases at that time. *See* A Brief History of the Louisiana Appellate Court System, http://www.la-fcca.org/history.htm (last visited Aug. 20, 2008); *see generally* John T. Hood, Jr., *History of Courts of Appeal in Louisiana*, 21 LA. L. REV. 531 (1961).

[36] NAACP representatives A.P. Tureaud and Joseph R. Thornton submitted a separate petition for writs of certiorari, mandamus, and prohibition on May 8, 1946, a day before de Blanc submitted his petition. Brief in Opposition to the Writ Granted, *supra* note 24, at 4–5. Tureaud and Thornton's petition was given docket number 38219, and de Blanc's was given docket number 38221. Brief in Opposition to the Writ Granted, *supra* note 24, at 5. The Louisiana Supreme Court combined the petitions and considered both in its May 15, 1946, decision. *See* State *ex rel.* Francis v. Resweber, 31 So. 2d 697, 697 (La. 1947) (listing two docket numbers—38219 and 38221).

[37] The Louisiana Supreme Court's decision was published under the date of May 15, 1947, but in reality the decision was handed down on May 15, 1946. *See* Transcript of Record, *supra* note 33, at 27; State *ex rel.* Francis v. Resweber, Nos. 38219, 38221 (La. May 15, 1946).

de Blanc was banking on the knowledge that it would also include two
state officials who might be influenced by the rising public opinion in
support of Willie.

C.   The Hearing Before the Louisiana Board of Pardons

On May 31, 1946, Willie's case was heard by the Louisiana Pardons
Board, which consisted of Lieutenant Governor J. Emile Verret, Attorney General Fred S. LeBlanc, as well as Willie's trial judge, James
Simon.[38] Despite previous scuffles over the territorial handling of Willie's
case, de Blanc and the two attorneys associated with the New Orleans
NAACP who had filed writs with the Louisiana Supreme Court—A.P.
Tureaud and his associate, Joseph A. Thornton—agreed to work together
at the hearing.[39] The three men were opposed by District Attorney Pecot,
representing Sheriff Resweber. The transcript of the testimony would
end up being invaluable to all because it is one of the few sources of
documented information on Willie's case.

---

[38] The discussion of the hearing before the Pardons Board draws from the following
sources: Louisiana *ex rel.* Francis v. Resweber, 328 U.S. 833 (1946); Louisiana *ex rel.*
Francis v. Resweber, No. 1302 (U.S. June 10, 1946); Pardons Board Address of L.O. Pecot,
supra note 19; Transcript of Hearing Before Louisiana Board of Pardons, Testimony of U.J.
Esnault, Chief Electrician, Louisiana State Penitentiary, Angola, La. (May 31, 1946) (copy
on file with author); Transcript of Hearing Before Louisiana Board of Pardons, Testimony
of Dennis D. Bazer, Warden, Louisiana State Penitentiary, Angola, La. (May 31, 1946)
(copy on file with author); Pardons Board Testimony of E.L. Resweber, *supra* note 14;
Pardons Board Testimony of Gilbert Ozenne, *supra* note 14; Pardons Board Testimony of
E. Foster, *supra* note 29; Pardons Board Testimony of Vincent Venezia, *supra* note 29;
Pardons Board Testimony of Dr. S.D. Yongue, *supra* note 29; Brief in Behalf of Petitioner,
supra note 24, at 15–21; Brief in Opposition to the Writ Granted, *supra* note 24, at 53–101;
Petition for Executive Clemency (May 13, 1946) (copy on file with author); Reprieve, State
of Louisiana Executive Department (June 3, 1946) (copy on file with author); May 8, 1946
Reprieve, *supra* note 33; Letter from Bertrand de Blanc to Wilbert Rideau, Editor, *The
Angolite* (July 9, 1979); Letter from Charles Elmore Cropley, Clerk, U.S. Supreme Court, to
E.L. Resweber (June 11, 1946); KING, *supra* note 3, at 141–42; MILLER & BOWMAN, *supra* note
3, at 7, 42, 141; BARRETT PRETTYMAN, JR., DEATH AND THE SUPREME COURT 106, 108–11 (1961);
Arthur S. Miller & Jeffrey H. Bowman, *"Slow Dance on the Killing Ground": The Willie
Francis Case* Revisited, 32 DePAUL L. REV. 1, 14 n.81 (1983); Michael S. Bernick, *The
Unusual Odyssey of J. Skelly Wright*, 7 HASTINGS CONST. L.Q. 971, 974–75 (1980); *New
Prayer Book in Negro's Cell*, JOPLIN GLOBE (Joplin, Mo.), June 12, 1946, at 1; *High Court
Erred; Negro Gets Stay*, N.Y. TIMES, June 12, 1946, at 10; *No Clemency in Francis Case is
Board's Ruling*, DAILY ADVERTISER (Lafayette, La.), June 3, 1946, at 1; *Board Considers Fate
of Slayer*, TIMES-PICAYUNE (New Orleans, La.) June 1, 1946, at 4; and *Execution of Francis
Stayed 29 Days*, WKLY. MESSENGER (St. Martinville, La.), May 10, 1946, at 1.

[39] The State attached a portion of the Pardons Board hearing transcript to the brief it
submitted to the U.S. Supreme Court, Brief in Opposition to the Writ Granted, *supra* note
24, at 53–101; but there are inconsistencies between this version of the transcript and a
certified copy of the transcript found among de Blanc's papers. In de Blanc's copy both he
and Tureaud question witnesses while Thornton is silent. In the copy attached to the
State's brief, Tureaud and Thornton question witnesses while de Blanc is silent.

In his closing argument, District Attorney Pecot laid out the state's arguments against commuting Willie's sentence to life imprisonment:

[T]his case is a question as to whether or not this Board is going to follow the judgment of the jury of twelve men who listened most carefully to the evidence before bringing in their verdict, or whether or not because of an unfortunate happening due to no fault of anyone, but just a mechanical defect, the Board is going to say "for that reason we are going to extend this man an extra portion of mercy."

In order to show that the malfunction was accidental, two Angola prison employees testified: U.J. Esnault, the chief electrician, and Dennis D. Bazer, the warden. Warden Bazer had assigned Ephie Foster to Willie's execution. Both Esnault and Bazer asserted that they had never known the chair to fail before and that it operated properly after Willie's botched electrocution. Testimony designed to demonstrate Willie's guilt was provided by Sherriff Resweber and Sheriff Ozenne.

Willie's attorneys challenged the evidence of Willie's guilt. Tureaud had previously investigated the activities of Sheriff Ozenne and Gus "Killer" Walker—Willie's caretakers in the New Iberia Parish jail—who were known for their histories of coercion and violence; he questioned Resweber's account that Willie had offered full confessions without force. Indeed, the probing of witnesses before the Pardons Board accentuated the incompetence of Willie's trial attorneys.

In addition, the State produced witnesses to testify that Willie had not been harmed by the attempted electrocution because no (or only a minute amount of) electricity had entered his body. Both Ephie Foster and Vincent Venezia, Willie's executioners, agreed that electricity did not enter Willie. According to Foster, "There was a shortage—a little wire was loose and the current went back into the ground instead of going into the *nigger*," an account Venezia confirmed. Foster acknowledged, however, that Willie might have moved the approximately three-hundred-pound chair during the electrocution. The coroner, Dr. Yongue, testified that the chair moved two or three times right after Foster threw the switch but, upon examining Willie afterwards, he found that there was "no serious impairment and no burn marks."

Rather than focusing on Willie's trial, which de Blanc assumed would have little effect given societal attitudes and Judge Simon's presence, de Blanc emphasized Willie's torturous experience during the first attempted electrocution. Therefore, among de Blanc's first moves was to prove with affidavits from official witnesses that electricity did in fact reach Willie's body. Sidney Dupois, a barber, provided a typical description: "At that very moment [that the switch was turned on] Willie Francis' lips puffed out and he grunted and made the chair jump."

This approach meshed with de Blanc's additional argument that Willie should not face electrocution again because he had already "suffered the torture of death." To bolster his points, de Blanc listed historical examples of failed executions where the condemned individuals succeeded in having their sentences reduced as a result, thus avoiding the experience of another execution.[40]

De Blanc's arguments were as emotional as they were legal. Additional witnesses appeared before the Pardons Board, reflecting public sentiment against Willie's execution. De Blanc stressed that the State had never before given a death sentence to a fifteen-year-old. He raised examples of biblical stories and divine intervention as a way of making the point that God's law had interrupted Willie's execution, and that citizens should respect that law. And in an effort to bring back the theme of cruel and unusual punishment, de Blanc presented the Board with a photograph of Willie that Father Rousseve had taken at Willie's execution, just moments before Foster had pulled the switch. In de Blanc's view, it was " 'a picture that speaks a thousand words.' " " '[W]ere it not for a quirk of fate,' " Willie would be dead.

With Willie's picture before them, de Blanc's arguments stressed the future risks that Willie faced in another execution, and how religion, through "the hand of God," played into that risk. " 'What assurance,' " de Blanc asked, " 'does this boy have that he will go to his death in a humane manner, quickly and painlessly? Supposing that the chair doesn't work a second time? Suppose it doesn't work a third time? That could happen; it's happened once and it could happen again.' " De Blanc also emphasized how such risks could affect the country's acceptance of the death penalty generally. " '[U]nless this board sees fit to say that this boy will not suffer the torture of death again,' " " 'the whole system of capital punishment ... is in jeopardy because of the inhumane method in which it is being inflicted in this case.' " " 'People all over America have written to me expressing their sincere belief that it was the hand of God that stopped the electrocution,' " de Blanc noted, referring to the national outpouring on Willie's behalf. But " '[f]ate acts in strange ways. I, for one, would want no part in his re-execution. When I meet my God face to face, I would not want the stain of his blood on my hands.' "

De Blanc's arguments ended the session. If Willie's fate was in God's hands, it was also clearly in the hands of the Pardons Board. The approach also accentuated the contrasting ways that de Blanc and the

---

[40] Miller and Bowman cite directly to the transcript of de Blanc's statement before the Pardons Board. Miller & Bowman, *supra* note 38, at 14 n.81. However, that transcript no longer appears to be available. The author conducted an extensive search for it but was unable to uncover an extant copy.

two NAACP attorneys framed Willie's case. For de Blanc, the cruel and unusual nature of the punishment was foremost in his mind; for Tureaud and Thornton, the gross problems with the trial and those handling it were most significant.

The Pardons Board deliberated quickly. On June 3, 1946, without providing any opinion, the Board unanimously refused to commute Willie's sentence. Willie was scheduled to be electrocuted again in only four days, at noon on June 7, 1946. Now de Blanc would have to take Willie's case to the U.S. Supreme Court, a contingency for which he was prepared despite his surprise at the Board's decision.

A friend had suggested that de Blanc contact James Skelly Wright, a former assistant U.S. attorney for Louisiana who, while New Orleans-born, was then practicing law in Washington, D.C. Shortly after the Pardons Board's decision, de Blanc wired Wright, asking that he file a petition for a writ of certiorari. As a result, Louisiana's Governor Jimmie Davis issued a reprieve: "in the interests of justice [Davis did] not desire to order the execution of said Willie Francis until final action by the Supreme Court of the United States."

Any optimism about Willie's future would soon be dashed, however. On June 10, 1946, the Supreme Court handed down an order denying the writ. Willie told reporters, " 'I'm praying harder than ever. Got myself a new prayer book. All I can do is wait.' "

Incredibly, the next day a Supreme Court clerk announced that a mistake had been made: the writ of certiorari had been granted, not denied, and the Court would hear arguments. Such a stunning development was thought to be "virtually unparalleled" in the Supreme Court's history. While Willie was reported as being "stoic about [the] series of ups and downs," de Blanc was much more "voluble." In the eyes of Willie's supporters, it must have seemed as if divine intervention had, once again, intercepted Willie's life path.

VII. *LOUISIANA* EX REL. *FRANCIS v. RESWEBER*

The Supreme Court that would be hearing Willie's case was a tribunal in transition, situated between the "drama of the Roosevelt Court-packing plan [in 1937] and the nobility of the Warren Court's striking down racial segregation" in 1954.[41] Just six weeks before the

---

[41] The discussion of the Supreme Court that would hear Willie's case draws from, among other sources, MICHAL R. BELKNAP, THE VINSON COURT: JUSTICES, RULINGS, AND LEGACY 40 (Peter G. Benstrom ed., ABC–CLIO Supreme Court Handbook Series, 2004); MELVIN I. UROFSKY, DIVISION AND DISCORD: THE SUPREME COURT UNDER STONE AND VINSON, 1941–1953 (1997); WILLIAM F. SWINDLER, COURT AND CONSTITUTION IN THE TWENTIETH CENTURY: THE NEW LEGALITY 56–80, 137, 157–61 (1970); EUGENE C. GERHART, AMERICA'S ADVOCATE: ROBERT H. JACKSON 235–88 (1958); John P. Frank, *Fred Vinson and the Chief Justiceship*, 21 U. CHI. L.

Court granted certiorari in Willie's case, on April, 22, 1946, Chief Justice
Harlan Fiske Stone fell ill on the bench and died later that day of a
massive cerebral hemorrhage. Justice Stone left behind a feuding and
fractured body, marked by its 4–4 decisions, and many dissents and
"diverging concurrences." (Justice Robert Jackson was away at the time,
serving as the American prosecutor at the Nuremberg War Crimes
Trial.) The strains reflected both jurisprudential disagreements and
personal conflicts.

The opening for a Chief Justice heightened—and further revealed—
tensions among the Justices. Finally, President Harry Truman decided
to appoint as Chief Justice his close friend and Secretary of the Treasury, Frederick M. Vinson, in the hope that Vinson, "a skilled concilia-
tor," would be able to heal the divisiveness on the Court. As a result, in
line for Willie's argument were nine Justices, including the new Chief
Justice and Justice Jackson, who had returned from Nuremberg.

A. Skelly Wright's and Bertrand de Blanc's Arguments

Although all of the Justices hearing Willie's case had been appointed
by Democratic presidents—seven by President Franklin Delano
Roosevelt and two by President Harry Truman—the Court was not
liberal in the modern sense of that word.[42] Both Justice Hugo Black,
considered the leader of the liberal wing of the Court, and Justice Felix
Frankfurter, considered the leader of the conservative wing, agreed on
the importance of judicial restraint. In appointing Justices, Roosevelt's

---

REV. 212, 241 (1954); *Vinson Excelled in Federal Posts*, N.Y. TIMES, Sept. 9, 1953, at 26;
Jackson Attacks Black for Judging Ex–Partner's Case, N.Y. TIMES, June 11, 1946, at 1;
Lewis Wood, *Vinson Expected to Bring Supreme Court Harmony*, N.Y. TIMES, June 9, 1946,
at 10E; Felix Belair, Jr., *Vinson Named Chief Justice; Snyder to Head Treasury; Truman to
Let OWMR Lapse; Forrestal Stays*, N.Y. TIMES, June 7, 1946, at 1; and *Chief Justice Stone
of Supreme Court is Dead*, N.Y. TIMES, Apr. 23, 1946, at 1.

[42] The discussion that follows draws from the following sources: Louisiana *ex rel.*
Francis v. Resweber, 329 U.S. 459 (1947); State *ex rel.* Francis v. Resweber, 31 So. 2d 697
(La. 1947); *In re* Kemmler, 136 U.S. 436 (1890); Application for Writ of Certiorari at 3,
Louisiana *ex rel.* Francis v. Resweber, 329 U.S. 459 (1947) (No. 1302) (available at National
Archives, Box No. 4661); Brief in Behalf of Petitioner, *supra* note 24, at 15–21; Brief in
Opposition to the Writ Granted, *supra* note 24, at 53–101; Stanley F. Reed, Draft Opinion
in Louisiana *ex rel.* Francis v. Resweber 2–5 (Jan. 1947) (available at Library of Congress);
Letter from Charles Elmore Cropley, Clerk, U.S. Supreme Court, to Bertrand de Blanc
(Feb. 14, 1947) (available at National Archives, Box No. 4661); BELKNAP, *supra* note 41, at
26, 47; UROFSKY, *supra* note 41, at 7, 153, 213, 215–19, 223; FRIENDLY & ELLIOTT, *supra* note
32, at 169; SWINDLER, *supra* note 41, at 137; Denno, *Is Electrocution an Unconstitutional
Method of Execution?*, *supra* note 29, at 607; Jacob Balick, *Recent Cases*, 20 TEMPLE L.Q.
584 (1947); Norman L. Schatz, *Recent Decisions*, 31 MARQ. L. REV. 108 (1947); Elliott Chaze,
Francis Must Die in Electric Chair, JEANERETTE ENTERPRISE (Jeanerette, La.), Jan. 16, 1947,
at 1; Elliott Chaze, *"Death My Neighbor But Lord Closer," Says Willie, Facing Electric
Chair*, TIMES-PICAYUNE (New Orleans, La.), Jan. 15, 1947, at 4; *Killer to Face Chair 2d
Time; Gives Up Hope*, CHI. DAILY TRIB., Jan. 14, 1947, at 1; and Wood, *supra* note 41.

primary concern was that they uphold the New Deal legislation Congress passed under his leadership. In *Louisiana* ex rel. *Francis v. Resweber*,[43] this belief in restraint made the Court reluctant to overrule the decisions of the Louisiana legislature and the Louisiana Board of Pardons. For Wright and de Blanc, then, the legal battle would be uphill.

When petitioning the Supreme Court of Louisiana, de Blanc had argued that subjecting Willie to a second electrocution would violate both the Louisiana state constitution and the Constitution of the United States. Now, before the Supreme Court of the United States, Wright and de Blanc could not point to the provisions of the state constitution that echoed the Fifth Amendment prohibition on double jeopardy and the Eighth Amendment prohibition on cruel and unusual punishment because a state's highest court is the ultimate arbiter of that state's laws and constitution. Instead, the attorneys either needed to convince the Court of the most controversial argument made on Willie's behalf before the Supreme Court of Louisiana—that these safeguards in the federal constitution applied to Willie's case—or that some other aspect of due process would be violated by a second execution. Indeed, the Supreme Court had previously held, in many different kinds of circumstances, that the Bill of Rights, including these provisions, did not apply to the states; therefore, defendants prosecuted at the state level did not have the federal protections available today concerning violations of double jeopardy and tortuous punishments. Nevertheless, Wright and de Blanc were compelled to argue in the petition for certiorari that Willie had been denied the protection of the Due Process Clause of the Fourteenth Amendment because of violations of both the Fifth and Eighth Amendments—that Willie was "being placed in jeopardy of life and liberty a second time for the same offense and that to subject [him] a second time to final preparation for his execution, and execution itself would be cruel and inhuman punishment."

In the Supreme Court's first case dealing with the constitutionality of electrocution, In re *Kemmler*,[44] decided in 1890, the Court had refused to confront the petitioner's claim that New York's use of electricity to inflict death was cruel and unusual punishment under the Eighth Amendment. Instead, the Court had held that the Eighth Amendment did not apply to the states and therefore left unexamined the New York state legislature's conclusion that electrocution produced " 'instantaneous, and, therefore, painless death.' " Thereafter, a series of state courts relied on *Kemmler* to reject summarily challenges to the use of electrocution as an execution method. In 1915, the Supreme Court used New York's conclusion, citing *Kemmler*, to resolve an ex post facto provision

---

[43] 329 U.S. 459 (1947).

[44] 136 U.S. 436 (1890).

challenge to electrocution in *Malloy v. South Carolina*,[45] ruling that South Carolina's implementation of death through electrocution rather than hanging (the state's prior execution method) did not increase the punishment for murder but only changed its mode.

Unlike *Kemmler* and *Malloy*, the issue in *Resweber* was not whether electrocution was unconstitutional per se or more cruel than hanging, but whether the State of Louisiana constitutionally could execute Francis after the electric chair had malfunctioned during the first attempt. Indeed, by the time Willie's case came before the Court, decades had passed since *Kemmler* and *Malloy* were decided. Wright and de Blanc must have hoped that Justice Black would be open to their argument because Justice Black believed the Due Process Clause of the Fourteenth Amendment incorporated the entire Bill of Rights, making them applicable to the states. Three other Justices in the liberal wing of the Court typically voted with Justice Black: William O. Douglas, Wiley B. Rutledge, and Frank Murphy. If these four Justices and only one additional Justice could be convinced, Willie would not suffer a second electrocution attempt.

Wright and de Blanc faced further hurdles. Willie's official record before the Court had no specifics concerning Willie's attempted execution; the Court could review only the evidence presented to the Louisiana state courts, and such information was limited. Thus, the attorneys were forced to provide evidence in other ways, including describing the details of Willie's experiences in their briefs and attaching affidavits of witnesses to the execution. Fortuitously, additional details about Willie emanated from the partial record of the Louisiana Pardons Board hearings, which the State's attorneys attached to their brief; the State's evidence therefore included both testimony that Willie had not been harmed during the attempted electrocution and accounts of Willie's suffering. On November 18, 1946, Willie finally got his day in Court. Wright argued his case before the nine Justices who would now be the ones holding Willie's fate in their hands.[46]

The path of that fate, while never certain, would continue with startling twists and turns. On January 13, 1947, two months after oral arguments, Wright spoke with a Supreme Court clerk who informed him of the most extraordinary outcome: the Court had reversed the Louisiana Supreme Court's decision. Willie now had a chance. Thrilled, Wright headed over to the Supreme Court to read the Court's opinion to de Blanc over the phone. Yet in no time Wright's and de Blanc's expecta-

---

[45] 237 U.S. 180 (1915).

[46] De Blanc was unable to argue Willie's case because he was not admitted to the U.S. Supreme Court Bar. Letter from Charles Elmore Cropley, Clerk, U.S. Supreme Court, to Bertrand de Blanc, *supra* note 42.

tions for Willie were quashed. Once again, a Supreme Court clerk had been mistaken. The Court had actually *upheld* the Louisiana Supreme Court's decision, 5–4. That same day, the Supreme Court released *Resweber*.

B.   The Court's Decision

The *Resweber* Court's outcome defied prediction. In the plurality's view, Willie's execution presented "a unique situation" in which "[t]he executioner threw the switch but, presumably because of some mechanical difficulty, death did not result." However, the Court's conclusion that a second execution would be constitutional brought some surprises in the Justices' lineup. Justice Black, considered the leader of the liberal faction, voted to affirm the Louisiana Supreme Court's decision. In contrast, Justice Burton, whose "background gave him a 'generally conservative mindset,'" wrote the dissent. Justice Frankfurter concurred with the plurality's conclusion upholding the Louisiana Supreme Court's decision; but he wrote a separate opinion to accentuate his view that the Bill of Rights, and the Cruel and Unusual Punishments Clause in particular, do not apply to the states. Especially striking is the degree to which the plurality and Justice Frankfurter accepted the State's arguments that Willie's execution was properly conducted.

Today *Resweber* is primarily used as Eighth Amendment precedent; but, surprisingly, the plurality's decision was originally written as a Fourteenth Amendment due process analysis. When drafting the plurality opinion, Justice Reed began his legal analysis with the following sentence: "To determine whether or not the execution of the petitioner may fairly take place after the experience through which he passed, we examine the circumstances *in the light of the due process clause* of the Fourteenth Amendment." This sentence was followed by a footnote citing four cases—all of which hold that the Eighth Amendment and/or the Fifth Amendment do(es) *not* apply to the states. To persuade Justice Black to join the Court's opinion, however, Reed revised this draft sentence and added a phrase (italicized below) indicating that the Court would undertake its analysis in the same manner *as if* the Fifth and Eight Amendments were incorporated.

> To determine whether or not the execution of the petitioner may fairly take place after the experience through which he passed, we shall examine the circumstances *under the assumption, but without so deciding, that violation of the principles of the Fifth and Eighth Amendments, as to double jeopardy and cruel and unusual punishment, would be violative* of the due process clause of the Fourteenth Amendment.

That Justice Reed's change was made hastily, without development of a Fifth or Eighth Amendment standard, is evidenced by the fact that, despite the change from a Fourteenth Amendment due process standard to Fifth and Eighth Amendment standards, the text of the opinion and of the draft are almost identical. Even the draft's footnote citing four cases that hold that the Fifth and Eighth Amendments do not apply to the states was retained. In addition, when discussing the issue of double jeopardy the opinion still declares that "[a]s this is a prosecution under state law the *Palko* case is decisive." In *Palko v. Connecticut*,[47] the Court ruled that as a result of the Fourteenth Amendment "those 'fundamental principles of liberty and justice which lie at the base of all our civil and political institutions' " apply to the states, but *not* the Fifth Amendment. Because the *Resweber* plurality initially designed its cruel and unusual punishments guideline to apply to the Fourteenth Amendment under the belief that the Eighth Amendment would not be pertinent, *Resweber* never created a robust Eighth Amendment standard for future use.

While ultimately assuming the Eighth Amendment's incorporation, the plurality interpreted the Cruel and Unusual Punishments Clause as prohibiting only the "infliction of unnecessary pain" (or "the wanton infliction of pain") during the death sentence, not the suffering created by an "unforeseeable accident." This view held that even if Willie had actually experienced some electrical current during the first execution, "[t]he cruelty against which the Constitution protects a convicted man is cruelty inherent in the method of punishment, not the necessary suffering involved in any method employed to extinguish life humanely." The Justices thus accepted that State officials had "carried out their duties . . . in a careful and humane manner." "Accidents happen for which no man is to blame," the Court stressed. Using this accident analogy, the Court equated Willie's suffering to the "identical amount of mental anguish and physical pain" he would have experienced in any other accident, such as a fire in the cell block. No cruelty took place because there was "no purpose to inflict unnecessary pain nor [was] any unnecessary pain involved in the proposed execution." Ironically, a footnote in the opinion suggests that the Court's determination of the standard for cruel and unusual punishment under the Eighth Amendment is based on the *Kemmler* Court's understanding of the same clause in the New York constitution.

The plurality ended its brief opinion by dismissing another aspect of Willie's legal account—arguments that "the original trial itself was so unfair" and Willie's counsel so inadequate, that Willie's conviction should be reversed and a new trial granted. In the plurality's view, nothing in the original trial's record would "show any violation of [Willie's] constitutional rights."

---

[47] 302 U.S. 319 (1937).

The plurality's conclusions were fervently countered by the four dissenting Justices. Using language that echoed Justice Frankfurter's anti-incorporation standard for the Due Process Clause of the Fourteenth Amendment, the dissent found that "[t]aking human life by unnecessarily cruel means shocks the most fundamental instincts of civilized man." Indeed, the dissent recommended issuing a stay of execution and remanding the case to determine not only the nature of the punishment already inflicted on Willie but also that which could be imposed.

In the dissent's view, Willie's case more clearly violated constitutional due process than "many lesser punishments prohibited by the Eighth Amendment or its state counterparts." Relying on *Kemmler*, the dissent also stressed the Court's determination that " 'the application of electricity ... must result in instantaneous, and consequently in painless death.' " Therefore, the "all-important consideration is that the execution shall be so instantaneous and substantially painless that the punishment shall be reduced, as nearly as possible, to no more than that of death itself." In determining whether the procedure is unconstitutional, "instantaneous death" must also be measured against the administration of "death by installments," which is caused when electric shocks are applied after one or more intervening periods to a victim who is conscious.

The dissent particularly questioned the plurality's requirement of intentionality on the part of State officials. Such an onus was irrelevant: "The intent of the executioner cannot lessen the torture or excuse the result." The State's statutory duty was to ensure a proper execution with a single, continuous, current; yet the steps followed in Willie's execution "contrast[ed] with common knowledge of precautions generally taken elsewhere to insure against failure of electrocutions." In addition, the Louisiana legislature and courts had never "expressed approval of electrocution other than by one continuous application of a lethal current," the standard stipulated in Willie's death warrant. In other words, the plurality's assertion that "[l]aws cannot prevent accidents" evaded the issue of the State's responsibility to administer executions properly.

For Justice Frankfurter the issues took on a somewhat different form; he was the only member of the Court who based his decision on a belief that the Bill of Rights should not be incorporated. Citing history and precedent, Frankfurter stressed his opinion of the proper role for the Due Process Clause. The Clause "did not withdraw the freedom of a State to enforce its own notions of fairness in the administration of criminal justice unless ... 'in so doing it offends some principle of justice so rooted in the traditions and conscience of our people as to be ranked as fundamental.' " Unlike the dissent, however, Justice Frankfurter expressed his disbelief that Louisiana's "innocent misadventure" with Willie's execution would be found to "offend[] a principle of justice 'rooted in the traditions and conscience of our people.'" Rather, the "Court must abstain from interference with State action no matter how strong one's personal feeling of revulsion against a State's insistence on its pound of flesh." While Frankfurter conceded his shared "sentiments" with the dissenting Justice Burton, he also affirmed his convictions concerning the detrimental potential of the dissent's approach: "I would be enforcing my private view rather than that consensus of society's opinion which, for purposes of due process, is the standard enjoined by the Constitution." Such a stance did "not mean that a hypothetical situation, which assumes a series of abortive attempts at electrocution . . . would not raise different questions." But Willie's experience did not meet this standard. "Since I cannot say that [a second execution] would be 'repugnant to the conscience of mankind,' . . . I cannot say that the Constitution withholds it."

Resweber generated considerable legal commentary when it was released. Both the plurality and the dissent relied on *Kemmler*'s "torture or lingering death" standard for cruelty, thereby enabling that standard to be applied to the State of Louisiana. At the same time, the *Resweber* Court never reviewed evidence of any potential pain that an individual may suffer during electrocution. Even the dissent appeared to assume that, properly conducted, electrocution would be painless and instantaneous.

On January 13, 1947, the same day *Resweber* was released, Sheriff Ozenne informed Willie of the Court's decision. Willie had worried all along about the outcome, but he still was surprised and " 'sat down hard on his cot.'" By all accounts, however, Willie's response was composed. De Blanc reported that Willie was " 'a lot calmer than he was last May when he walked away from the chair. He's amazing.'" As before, a primary concern of Willie's was that he be "brave" and "die like the man [he] thought [he] was." He wanted to appear strong in the way that everyone around him was urging. Even during his final moments, Willie would abide by what others told him to do.

VIII.   NATIONWIDE SUPPORT FOR WILLIE

The *Resweber* Court's decision belied the extraordinary level of public support for Willie "from all over the country" following his May 3, 1946, botched electrocution.[48] In an era decades before cheap, rapid

---

[48] The majority of the letters referenced in this Section were part of a collection of materials provided by Allan Durand. Other letters were found on file at the St. Martin Parish Courthouse in St. Martinville, Louisiana. Copies of all of the letters referenced in this Section are on file with the author. The discussion in this Section also draws from the following sources: FRANCIS AS TOLD TO MONTGOMERY, *supra* note 11; RIVERDALE CHILDREN'S

technological communications, Willie's case would become a national and international phenomenon. That force would spur intense news coverage as well as scores of letters, most destined for Willie while others went straight to de Blanc, Sheriff Resweber, the Louisiana Pardons Board, and Governor Jimmie Davis. Through it all, Willie attained a near-celebrity status[49] that de Blanc utilized with letters of appeal published in newspapers across the country garnering donations to Willie's defense fund.

When not answering his mail, Willie spent most of his time behind bars reading and awaiting visitors. The full content of Willie's feelings and conversations will, of course, never be known, but the letters people wrote to him speak for themselves. The de Blanc family (as well as the St. Martinville Courthouse) retained a cache of some of the correspondence that people sent Willie and those involved with his case. Through these writings, a separate story can be told, a narrative not just touching on Willie's experiences but also an expression of how people perceived their post-war world—their thoughts, their hopes, their fears. Willie's case, then, helped mirror a slice of American culture.

A. The Bonds Across Races

Many of the letters to Willie conveyed a degree of sympathy and outrage that made clear the public did not want him to endure the physical and mental anguish of the electric chair a second time. Willie's youth and circumstances were particularly inspirational for a number of Willie's correspondents, even those younger than he. Orphans from the

---

ASSOCIATION, 120TH ANNIVERSARY, 1836–1956, at 2 (1956); Melinda Shelton, *Teen Twice Sent to Die in Electric Chair*, SUNDAY ADVOC. (Baton Rouge, La.), Sept. 8, 1985, at 1B; *"Be Careful How Ye Spend Thy Days," Warned Willie Francis*, SHREVEPORT SUN, May 24, 1947, at 3; *Willie Francis To Be Electrocuted Friday, May 9*, SHREVEPORT SUN, May 10, 1947, at 5; *Willie Francis Doomed to Die*, ILL. TIMES, May 8, 1947, at 1; *Willie Francis Faces Electric Chair Again*, COLO. STATESMAN, May 3, 1947, at 1; *The Case of Willie Francis*, OKLA. INDEPENDENT, Feb. 28, 1947, at 1; *Willie Francis Fights Second Walk to Chair*, CHI. DEFENDER, Jan. 25, 1947, at 2; *Rehearing Plea Before U.S. Supreme Court Slated for Youth Electric Chair Didn't Kill*, COLO. STATESMAN, Jan. 18, 1947, at 1; Chaze, *'Plumb Mizzuble' Covers Willie Francis' Idea of Electric Chair*, *supra* note 29; Taylor, *supra* note 12, at 20–22; *Negro Lives to Tell Death Chair Story*, *supra* note 24; Mary Barrow Collins, Letters From Item Readers, *What is Jeopardy?*, NEW ORLEANS ITEM, May 16, 1946, at 16; *Willie Hinges Fate on Faith*, DETROIT NEWS, May 16, 1946, at 9; and *Willie Francis, A Magic Name*, OKLA. INDEPENDENT, Mar. 21, 1946, at 1.

[49] As with any kind of celebrity, there were autograph seekers as one letter to Resweber revealed. *See* Letter from William E. Tolbert, Maugansville, Md., to Sheriff Leonard Resweber (May 8, 1946) (copy on file with author) ("I read about Willie Francis in the paper and I know this will be out of the ordinary but I will appreciate it more than you will ever know Sheriff Resweber if you could or rather if you will get Mr. Willie Francis to let me have one of his pictures and autograph it to me personally for my collection in my album in which I have quite a few famous people who have been kind enough to grant me my request.").

Riverdale Children's Association in New York, "the first institution in the United States dedicated to the care of Negro children," collectively sent Willie messages of good will. "We are very sorry to hear that you are in jail," wrote one child, while another, Willis Price, hoped "that God will spare you as he did before." Alfred Jarvis informed Willie that "we have been praying to ask God ... that you will not get the chair again." Carol Allen, a fourteen-year-old white girl from Pennsylvania, commended Willie on taking his death sentence better than anyone at any age, and wishing that he not endure electrocution a second time.

Mothers across the nation felt a maternal tie to Willie. Several wrote him and upon receiving a quick and personal reply, continued to write more often. "I can't hardly find words to write to express my sympathy with you," shared Margaret Dixon from Winston–Salem, North Carolina. "Willie it's amazing to think of the courage you have ... I just wanted you to know that along with me, my family, and the world at large is thinking of you.... " One Texas woman, who was a Christian "mother" to the boys and girls behind bars in her state, said she felt urged to include Willie among the "children" with whom she corresponded. Mrs. Nancy Lewis from Ohio, the mother of nine boys, four of them already dead and five who served in the army, wrote Willie to say that she felt toward him like she would one of her own. Mrs. Doris McClain from Houston, Texas, also corresponded with Willie, the depth of their relationship evidenced by Mrs. McClain's response to Willie's concerns about his girlfriend.

Ruth Kingcade, a thirty-five-year-old woman from Dayton, Kentucky, wrote to Willie at least four times throughout the month of May 1946, and Willie responded at least three times. Kingcade began one letter: "Honestly, I just had to answer your lovely letter right away," and, after telling Willie about her eighteen-year-old daughter, wrote "I don't have any more children so I'm going to borrow you (whether you like it or not! ha!)." In subsequent letters, something of a friendship appears to have emerged between the two; Kingcade conveys her thoughts about a variety of topics ranging from her health to the birth of her pet kittens. Willie, meanwhile, apparently told her about his family. Yet part of the tie between the two seemed based on Kingcade's knowledge that she too could die soon. Sick for fourteen years and bedridden for nine, the nearly deaf Kingcade informed Willie that she prayed for him but that she needed his prayers too. In awe of Willie's lack of fear, she claimed that she "could use a little of that courage.... So, trade me just a little prayer will you?" She also requested from Willie a picture as well as his mother's address. "Toodle doo for today. I will write again soon, just for a little chat. God Bless you dear Boy. Love, Ruth Kingcade."

Many writers mentioned to Willie that they felt a connection with him. Some expressed a paternalistic concern by calling him "son," while others referred to him as a brother and friend. Empathy and sympathy abounded for his mother and his family. Although many of the people who wrote to Willie did not know much about him, they still claimed a link. "I have read and reread your letter to [Governor] Davis and realy it seems as though i have know you and seem as if there was blood connections there somewhere," wrote Eleanor Smith of Houston, Texas. Another writer from Detroit, Michigan, made the following plea: "If for no other reason, then to [spare] the poor, innocent mother of this boy the tons of sorrows the Louisiana State authorities will heap ... upon her head ... if they take the life of her humble son Willie.... I beg, that you will not forsake this boy and his parents in their darkest hours ... in this great battle for young WILLIE'S LIFE."

One of Willie's most passionate and eloquent supporters was an English woman, Cicilie Taylor, who wrote a burning indictment of the American judiciary, blaming "white American prejudice" for "[t]his ghastly execution experience." Taylor's letter deplored the American attitude that blacks are "not supposed to be human," wondering if *Resweber* would have been decided differently if Willie's "judges had been born less fortunate" and "experienced [Willie's] unhappy plight." Perhaps through a shared background, the Justices could realize the "terrible life" blacks had to tolerate "because of a tradition that should never have existed in the first place." Taylor also reminded Willie of the black citizens who "fought died shed blood for Uncle Sam" and how the English "rated the Colored [American] soldiers higher in manners than the average white [soldier.]" Taylor ended her letter expressing her sympathies for Willie's parents and of course for him, emphasizing his age: "May the Lord continue to spare so young a life[,] a life that had only just begun."

B.   The Bonds of Religion and Risk

Predictably, a number of letters were religious in nature. Some contained quotes from various parts of the Bible, and one letter had enclosed a few religious tracts for Willie to read. Others referenced the 23rd Psalm, the story of Daniel in the lion's den, and the three Hebrew children. Mrs. Miller from Fort Worth, Texas, who addressed her letter to "Willie Francis (Negro who survived death chair)," asked Willie to "please let me know immediately" if he was without a Bible. Other religious letters were more foreboding. Mr. A.G. Louis–Luecke of Clifton, New Jersey, warned Willie that men who do not believe that they have been saved by Jesus will "go to hell," then demanded to know: "Do you, Mr. Francis, believe this?" In another letter, marked "urgent," an unidentified individual from Detroit, Michigan, wrote: "I guess by now you realize how short life is compared to eternity.... Where are you going to Heaven or to hell. You know Willie God has wonderfully blessed you by sparing your life for a few more days (which will seem like seconds). Are you saved Willie if you are you go to Heaven for *Eternity* if you aren't you know where you will go." Some writers simply wanted to let Willie know that someone was praying for him, that he was not alone.

At least two of the more religious letters were written in response to pictures of Willie clutching his prayer book. Other letters appeared to be responding to Willie's comment that, while he sat in the electric chair, he wondered what heaven and hell would be like. Arnold Drange, who introduced himself as "a veteran and a student at Augsburg College" in Minneapolis, Minnesota, wrote: "I have been deeply touched in reading the story of your being spared from death.... What touched me most, however, was that you said you wondered what hell is like." Drange then launched into a three-page letter providing his answer to that question. Mrs. R.S. Engel from Amsterdam, New York, wrote to Willie that she was "deeply concerned" upon reading that during the execution attempt, he was unsure as to whether he was going to heaven. "Evidently you have never thot of these things before," she wrote. "Will you go with me now to God's word and see what he has to say." Five pages of scripture and religious teachings followed.

The notion that God had spared Willie's life was a recurring theme. Many saw Willie's botched execution as a sign of divine intervention. "I ben reading the paper how God has delivered you from the electric chair and didn't allow the power of the electricity to harm you," wrote Sylvester Coleman from Winston–Salem, North Carolina, who identified his age as "around 20 years old." "The 'Good Master' saved you once as he will save you again," wrote Margaret Dixon, while Rosa Cole from Louisville, Kentucky, conjectured, "You are so young may be God wants to give you another chance."

Similarly, Willie's survival was viewed by many of his correspondents as something of a miracle. "Your miraculous escape from death several days ago has interested me greatly," began a letter from Laura Stephens of San Antonio, Texas, while Mrs. Ludwig Bergum of New London, Minnesota, declared her firm belief that "God has a purpose in sparing your life so miraculously." Evelyn Moyer from Wheeling, West Virginia, seemed to suggest that Willie would cheat death again when he returned to the electric chair, as long as he "believe[d] with all [his] heart." Dorothy Barbara Kingcade of Newark, New Jersey, echoed that sentiment: "If god don't want you to die in that electric chair you won't." A few letters, directed toward Willie's jailers, took on a more ominous tone, such as one addressed to Sheriff Ozenne from an unidentified individual in Chicago, Illinois: "I have heard when a person is saved from [the] chair it means he is not to go to his death.... If this boy is put to death again some thing will come of it.... " Estelle Hoffstadt of Los Angeles, California, went so far as to say "it is the

Lord's will that William Francis should be pardoned.... [I] would be afraid to try the death sentence again if I were those men."

If these statements encouraged Willie to hope that divine intervention might result in his sentence being commuted, his optimism was likely countered by letters from writers who were less certain of God's intentions. "A God who could save you from the electric chair is well able to save you from it again, *if it is His will*," wrote Mrs. William Sydow of Girard, Pennsylvania. "We must always pray 'Thy will be done.' Perhaps God wanted you to get better fitted for Heaven and then take you Home soon." "Received your letter and was glad to hear from you," began Lorena Hamm of Oak Park, Illinois. "We have talked about writing letters as you suggested; but we have prayed that the Lord should get His Will done. You see, He is Sovereign and He can put forth His hand to do that which is best." Rosa Cole of Louisville, Kentucky, approached the subject of Willie's possible death more delicately: "I believe that if you are given a chance you will try to make good.... If, however, it is your time to go pray hard that your soul may be saved if the body isn't."

Others felt God was not ready for Willie, at least not yet, for God had to prepare Willie's place in heaven. Heaven became the only future Willie and so many readers could look forward to in the midst of this not only cruel and unusual punishment, but cruel and unjust punishment. Willie should not be executed if for no other reason than the fact that Jesus had already died for the sins of others. Perhaps God had also prevented Willie's execution because Willie still had work to do here on this earth. Willie could improve prison morale, for example, or he could be a preacher; to condemn Willie is to "rob God."

Ministers, reverends, and priests from around the country tried to use their influence to spare Willie's life. As Father Flanagan of Boys Town, Nebraska, wrote the Louisiana Pardons Board, "Deeply interested in saving life of Willie Francis, would you, my dear Chairman, use your power of authority to commute the death sentence? May God direct you to do His Holy Will!" Yet, as letters and donations poured in, some simply wanted Willie to write them. They found comfort in corresponding with him as they faced their own fears of mortality. Ruth Kingcade in particular appeared at ease in communicating with Willie about her hopes for heaven and the role of risk in the future of their lives. "Funny things happen in this world and no one knows how anything will work out in advance, but the main thing for you to do and I know you are doing it, is to keep in your mind and heart that god is running the whole show, and everything happens for the best—even if we can't see it that way at the time."

C.   The Bonds of Punishment and Forgiveness

As the date of Willie's appeal to the Louisiana Pardons Board approached, he often asked his supporters to write letters to the Pardons Board on his behalf. It appears that most were happy to comply, although Mrs. W.H. Petersen of Downers Grove, Illinois, seemed to take some umbrage at his plea: "I received a letter signed by you yesterday, with the request that I write to your lawyer and to the Pardon Board, for a commutation of sentence. . . . I would have liked to receive a letter from you in answer to the one I sent you. Your soul's eternal salvation is of infinite more importance than to have your life spared." Notwithstanding her pique, however, Mrs. Petersen did send the letters that Willie requested.

Letters to the Pardons Board typically invoked Willie's suffering or God's will. "Put yourself in [Willie's] position and think how you would feel," implored Magnolia Milton of Los Angeles, California. "If God spared his life once from the chair why try to undo what God has done." Richard Hall of Haverhill, Massachusetts, asked the board to "consider the nerve wrecking strain of one time facing death," while Lillian Overy of Berkeley, Missouri, reminded them that "God knows best." George White of Harlem, Georgia, took a more cautious approach: "I would not like for it to be said at any time that I would condone crime, but under the existing circumstance I wish to make just this plea for Willie Francis, provided that you would feel that it is reasonable or justifiable, that you would commute his sentence to life imprisonment." Reverend L.H. Lewis, a Louisiana native serving in Madera, California, offered to accept responsibility for Willie: "Should you let him go free send him to me and I shall do all I can to help him to be a better boy and I shall make reports to you as often as you wish."

De Blanc also frequently received communications related to Willie. Forty-six students of criminology and penology at Temple University in Philadelphia wanted to help de Blanc by sending him a copy of their class textbook, calling his attention to pages "graphically describ[ing] the mental anguish experienced by one who is about to be executed" that they thought would be "of service to [him] in defending [his] client." They expressed concern for Willie and praised de Blanc for his efforts to save "that poor negro boy." One letter was unusual for its suggestion that Willie be "put to . . . sleep with some aneasthetic forever" rather than be electrocuted, to prevent his corneas from burning. This proposal, made by Mrs. J.R. Nichols of Timpson, Texas, stemmed from Willie's publicized willingness to donate his eyes to a blind man after his death.[50]

---

[50] It is evidence of de Blanc's dedication that, like Willie, he often responded personally to the letters he received. De Blanc wrote numerous notes thanking members of the public

Willie's culpability, or lack thereof, did not appear to have been a driving force among those who wrote in support of him. Some letter-writers professed a belief in his innocence, such as Sherman Green of New York City, who explained to Willie that "we are going to help you all we can because I feel like you are not guilty, of the crime that you are charge with." Many believed that Willie's sentence should be commuted to life in prison, and felt he had suffered enough. Others acknowledged the crime but nonetheless expressed support: "[S]o sorry that you did what you did but some times sin will make us do things that rong," wrote Mrs. White and Mrs. Wilson of Asheville, North Carolina. "[D]o hope that you can live," they continued. "Keep faith in God. Tell . . . your family we are deeply impressed." In a letter to Governor Jimmie Davis, an unidentified individual from Steubenville, Ohio, wrote: "Please do not electrocute the young man Negro. . . . He should not of kille either. Let this be a good lesson to him & all others." Hardy Hollingquest of Grambling, Louisiana, phrased a similar sentiment directly to Willie: "[I]f you get out of this let this be a lesson to you Willie. . . . We are praying to God for you to get a fair trial."

Other references to the crime were more oblique. Mrs. Wilbur Knight of Cokeburg, Pennsylvania, implored Willie to "call on Jesus to forgive you of any thing that you've done." Eleanor Smith of Houston, Texas, meanwhile, candidly informed Willie that she "w[ould] not say anything about [his] crime" in her letter. Indeed, many letters made no reference at all to the murder; it appears that Mrs. McAvena from Canada spoke for many of Willie's supporters when she expressed the belief that "[i]t matters not if you are guilty or not in the sight of God." Some wondered how any man of God could send a child to the electric chair in the first place, while others sent letters sharing their experiences or knowledge of the electric chair. Mrs. Mary Barrow Collins was perhaps most direct in her letter to the editor of the *New Orleans Item* challenging readers on the meaning of double jeopardy: "This letter is not prompted by pseudo-sentiment, although I do feel sorry for this poor, little, stuttering scrap of humanity, maybe more fit for a mental institu-

---

for their support of Willie, often including a sentence similar to this one, from a letter addressed to Reverend D.W. Perkins of Troy, Alabama: "[W]hen this case is finally over, I want you to feel that you have done as much as any one in helping [Willie's] noble cause." Letter from Bertrand de Blanc to Rev. D.W. Perkins, Troy, Ala. (Feb. 26, 1947) (copy on file with author). In another letter, de Blanc's fervor compelled him to pressure even Father Hannigan: "A tremendous flood of criticism will arise against the Catholic Church if Willie Francis goes to the chair again. . . . Do, please, come out of your obscurity; you do not have to say anything; just, do please, be present. Please remember that you live in this vicinity and you will be branded a coward and it will harm your spiritual work in the future. In other words, my dear Father Hannigan, you are 'on a spot.' " Letter from Bertrand de Blanc to Rev. Charles Hannigan, New Iberia, La. (May 24, 1946) (copy on file with author).

tion. But my deep and abiding love for the Constitution of the United States, which is the supreme law of the land, is my reason for writing."

Inspired by such Constitutional fervor, many letter-writers made tangible efforts to assist Willie. They offered to diagnose his speech impediment, sent him money, sponsored petitions, and, in several instances, volunteered legal advice, including evidence of other botched electrocutions. Through all these efforts, the same themes emerged, most particularly, the racial, legal, and moral/ethical issues of sending Willie back to the chair for the second time. These were matters that Willie's family most of all would have to face.

D.   The Bonds of Family and the Future

Willie's family visited him throughout his year-long stay in jail. Those members of his family in Texas and California sent letters updating him on various friends and relatives, while encouraging him to continue praying.[51] Willie's family would also get involved in addressing

---

[51] The collection of materials provided by Allan Durand contained eight letters from various members of Willie's family. *See* Letter from Beulah Francis, Los Angeles, Cal., to Willie Francis (May 14, 1946) (copy on file with author) ("You can image How glad I was to hear from you. It find me and my husband doing fine. I hope you are doing ok. . . . We are praying for you and every one in California is praying for you. Mrs. Fize said she is praying for you every night and morning. You must pray hard too."); Letter from Beulah Francis, Los Angeles, Cal., to Willie Francis (Jan. 13, 1947) (copy on file with author) ("Had a letter from Cecelia telling me all the children was sick with a cold. I hope they are better now. I can image she have a time with tham because they are so bad. We really been having some nice weather. It really do remind me of the spring. It be so Sunny. We are still praying and hoping every thing will turn out fine."); Letter from Mae Ella Francis, St. Martinville, La., to Willie Francis (May 7, 1946) (copy on file with author) ("every body is well. Mother feeling much better. Nonnely Lee was here but she come Friday Evening."); Letter from Doris Francis, Dallas, Tex., to Willie Francis (May 14, 1946) (copy on file with author) ("We arrived back home safely. All of the family is well in health but not in mind. You brother Joseph Nega says please don't will your eyes to nobody forget about that and pray. If there is anything that you want anything that we can do let us know. We have all the churches over here praying for you. And we are fasting and praying ourselves. And don't you for get to pray."); Letter from Scerita Francis, Port Arthur, Tex., to Willie Francis (May 6, 1946) (copy on file with author) ("Sammie is the badest little thing you could see & he so fat. Mrs. Branch have a time with him. Willie I want you to contain praying & pray as hard as you could. You know God will answer all prayer."); Letter from Emily Francis, Port Arthur, Tex., to Willie Francis (May 13, 1946) (copy on file with author) ("Every body over here are doing o.k. Sammie is bad as can be I cant do anything with Sammie. Willie I wont you to contained praying God will ans all pray is Is their a praying this is a time to pray."); Letter from Emily Francis, Port Arthur, Tex., to Willie Francis (May 14, 1946) (copy on file with author) ("I'm sending your dollar. I have just wrote you a letter. So their is two dollar Susie is sending you one two. She send her best regard. Well keep on praying. Do you want your bible I will send it to you."); Letter from Jane Gage, Beaumont, Tex., to Willie Francis (May 6, 1946) (copy on file with author) ("Bill just don't what to say that why I havnt writen befor now. So may God Bless You and keep you for us he save you once he is able to do it again You just rust in god I just cant write so pleas for give me Love Sis.").

perhaps the most unusual collection of letters Willie received, those sent from Mrs. Wilmer Cox of Dallas, Texas. Mrs. Cox asked Willie if he would donate his eyes to her brother if Willie was forced to face the electric chair a second time. At first, Willie obliged. Willie's eagerness to pass along his sight may have been connected to the friendship he formed as a child with an elderly blind neighbor in St. Martinville. But, just as likely, Willie's acquiescence was also part of his continual and lifelong effort to satisfy just about any request made of him.

Mrs. Cox's request was not solely self-interested, however; she was clearly concerned about Willie. She contacted at least one newspaper to relay the news of Willie's offer and her desire that Willie be saved. She also sent petitions on Willie's behalf and, in a letter to de Blanc, expressed her belief that Willie was innocent. By that time, de Blanc had drawn up Willie's will in which he left nothing to anyone except his eyes to Mrs. Cox.

In the end, the gift was not carried out. It is unclear which party was responsible for breaking the deal. One view is that Willie's mother forced him to forego his promise to Mrs. Cox. While Willie fretted over withdrawing his commitment, in the end, as an obedient son, he listened to his mother and wrote Mrs. Cox a letter of apology for changing his mind. Another possibility is that Mrs. Cox broke the agreement and wrote to de Blanc explaining that she thought the operation was too risky.

Apart from such highly publicized exchanges, Willie's fame also came from his frequent jailhouse interviews. Of all the topics discussed, Willie's plans for the future, a life without fear of the death penalty, were among the most compelling. After telling an interviewer that " 'maybe God will save me again,' " Willie said he would " 'be satisfied with life imprisonment.' " When asked what he would do if he were freed, Willie replied "that he would go to Los Angeles and work there— 'any kind of work.' " Willie's sister lived in Los Angeles. To another paper, Willie stated that he would " 'be happy to be a cook in the pen[itentiary]. I use to cook for my daddy pretty good and he says I got a knack with mustard greens and sidemeat.' " Willie added that he would also "like to be a priest, 'and maybe ride a ferris wheel and go swimming sometime.' " As de Blanc himself noted in an interview nearly forty years after Willie's death, " 'I think [Willie] would have made a good citizen if his sentence had been commuted to life. Back then he would have gotten out after about 10 years for good behavior.' "

Of course, none of Willie's aspirations would ever be realized. While the entire country was writing Willie about their hopes and dreams, Willie would soon learn that the only future he faced was his own demise.

IX. POST-*RESWEBER* DYNAMICS

A. The Media's Views

Resweber's outcome gripped the press and public nearly as much, it seems, as the initial botched electrocution.[52] Many were strongly critical of the Court. Of course, some news accounts and commentary supported the Court's opinion, stressing that the decision was fair and the controversy costly. Predictably, a front-page article with a photograph of Willie in the January 17, 1947, *Messenger* declared that "[i]n St. Martinville . . . the verdict of the Supreme Court is looked on as just and favorable." Commentary by the *Messenger*'s editor, Marcel Bienvenu, that same day, also leaves no ambiguity about the city's sentiments.

> Everyone in St. Martinville will be glad when this Willie Francis case is finally ended with his execution. Most of us just can't see why all those big newspapers up North are playing him up to be such a repentant little boy when he's fully grown and a confessed murderer and from his own confession and reports from his arrest in Texas he was not about to stop being a tough and dangerous character.

Indeed, a *Messenger* commentary the following week complained that "this negro arch-murderer has been, and is being given an overdose of notoriety by the press—including the local press." The writer noted that the *Messenger* would have exhibited "better taste, had the picture of the late Mr. Thomas been given prominence instead of that of this negro." Regardless, the *Messenger* continued its coverage.

As would be expected, one group harshly critical of *Resweber* was the NAACP. The focus now was on Louisiana's governor, Jimmie Davis, to intervene. A.P. Tureaud, legal counsel to the Louisiana Conference of the NAACP who had appeared with de Blanc at the Pardons Board hearing, once again became involved with Willie's case. He wired Governor Davis urging him to follow the precedent set by a previous Louisiana

---

[52] The discussion in this Section draws from, among other sources, KING, *supra* note 3, at 224–29; MILLER & BOWMAN, *supra* note 3, at 123–24; Bob Hamm, *Willie Becomes a Federal Case*, DAILY ADVERTISER (Lafayette, La.) Apr. 26, 1993, at B1; *Commutation of Sentence from Death to Life Term Sought by Atty. DeBlanc*, LA. WKLY. (New Orleans, La.), Feb. 15, 1947, at 1; Tom Gillen, Jr., *Around the Capitol*, WKLY. MESSENGER (St. Martinville, La.), Jan. 31, 1947, at 4; *New Plea Filed for Francis*, WKLY. MESSENGER (St. Martinville, La.), Jan. 31, 1947, at 1; P.L. Begnaud, *Breaux Bridge Chronicle*, WKLY. MESSENGER (St. Martinville, La.), Jan. 24, 1947, at 1; *Rehearing Plea Before U.S. Supreme Court Slated for Youth Electric Chair Didn't Kill*, *supra* note 48; *Counsel Seeks Rehearing, NAACP Urges Gov. Davis Commute Death Sentence*, LA. WKLY. (New Orleans, La.), Jan. 18, 1947, at 1; *Francis Must Die in Electric Chair*, WKLY MESSENGER (St. Martinville, La.), Jan. 17, 1947, at 1; "Blackie," Editorial, *This & That*, WKLY. MESSENGER (St. Martinville, La.), Jan. 17, 1947, at 1; James Marlow, *Francis Gets the Details of His Case*, RALEIGH TIMES (Raleigh, N.C.), Jan. 16, 1947, at 4; and Editorial, *Willie Francis Case*, TIMES-PICAYUNE (New Orleans, La.), Jan. 14, 1947, at 8.

governor who had commuted to life imprisonment the capital sentence of a prisoner whose execution date the sheriff forgot. However, "[u]nder Louisiana law [Davis could] not extend executive clemency unless the Board of Pardons and Reprieves so recommend[ed]." So Davis did nothing.

Additional barbs were directed at Justice Frankfurter's concurrence both in the form of public criticism as well as scores of heated letters sent to him personally. Commentary not only came from the syndicated news but also well known celebrities. Famed newspaper and radio commentator Walter Winchell and "most eastern columnists" demanded that Willie's sentence be commuted. Prominent columnist James Marlow's "Dear Willie"—a long open letter to Willie explaining the Court's decision—was particularly poignant. Marlow closed his letter by focusing on Frankfurter.

> Dear Willie—I thought you'd like to know how it was when nine men you never saw, sitting in a marble palace, talked about your future.
>
> . . . .
>
> [Justice Frankfurter] said the whole situation was very "disturbing."
>
> I bet you never dreamed in all your life that some day you'd be very "disturbing" to a Supreme Court justice.
>
> But in the end he agreed with the other four justices, that sending you back to the chair isn't cruel.

B.   Justice Felix Frankfurter's Response

In his concurrence Justice Frankfurter had suggested that the choice before the Court was whether mitigation of Willie's death sentence should be left to Louisiana's "executive clemency" or required by the Court.[53] Less than three weeks after *Resweber*—whether because of personal "revulsion against a State's insistence on its pound of flesh" or in response to public criticism—Justice Frankfurter took secret action to induce that "executive clemency." He wrote to his Harvard Law School

---

[53] The discussion that follows regarding Justice Frankfurter draws from Louisiana *ex rel.* Francis v. Resweber, 329 U.S. 459 (1947); Letter from Felix Frankfurter, Justice, U.S. Supreme Court, to Monte W. Lemann (Feb. 3, 1947) (copy on file with author); Letter from Monte W. Lemann to Hon. James D. Simon (Apr. 19, 1947) (available at Library of Congress, Manuscript Division, The Papers of Harold H. Burton, Box 69, Folder 3); Letter from Felix Frankfurter, Justice, U.S. Supreme Court, to the Justices of the U.S. Supreme Court (Apr. 23, 1947) (available at Library of Congress, Manuscript Division, The Papers of Harold H. Burton, Box 69, Folder 3); MILLER & BOWMAN, *supra* note 3, at 127; Melvin I. Urofsky, *The Court at War, and the War at the Court*, 1 J. SUP. CT. HIST. 1, 2 (1996); Miller & Bowman, *supra* note 38, at 37; *Must Go to Chair Again: Willie Francis Loses Plea to Louisiana Pardon Board*, N.Y. TIMES, Apr. 23, 1947, at 52; and *Vinson Excelled in Federal Posts, supra* note 41.

roommate, Monte E. Lemann, a member of the Louisiana bar, to explore options. Ironically, in his letter to Lemann, Frankfurter used the same kind of "risk of error" language he applied to the *Resweber* case itself, albeit in the opposite direction; he had different goals now. Frankfurter argued that clemency would be likely "if leading members of the bar pressed upon the authorities that *even to err on the side of humaneness* in the Francis situation can do no possible harm and might strengthen the forces of goodwill, compassion, and wisdom in society." Frankfurter also sent a "strictly confidential" copy of his letter to Justice Burton.

Two months later, Lemann responded by writing to Judge Simon, a former student of his at Tulane Law School, urging clemency for Willie based on Willie's prior botched electrocution. The next day, without revealing his own role, Frankfurter sent a copy of Lemann's letter (to Judge Simon) to each of his fellow Justices. Despite Frankfurter's enthusiastic praise of Lemann's letter, the attempt was unsuccessful. On April 22, 1947, the Pardons Board once again denied Willie's appeal. Neither Frankfurter nor, it seems, Burton ever conveyed to their colleagues on the bench that Frankfurter had asked Lemann to help Willie.

If Frankfurter's contemporaries had been aware of his attempt to save Willie, they might not have viewed his involvement in a political decision in the same manner it would be regarded today. Justices Douglas, Murphy, Jackson, and Frankfurter had all helped the Roosevelt administration "in many ways, from drafting speeches and legislation to suggesting" individuals to serve in "key roles," before and during the recently concluded World War. Chief Justice Vinson offered private, bedtime "advice and counsel on many problems" to President Truman. Nonetheless, authors Arthur Miller and Jeffrey Bowman ask the right question: "If Frankfurter's extrajudicial actions to try to save Willie's life were proper for a Supreme Court justice, why the secrecy?"

C. Wright's and De Blanc's Continuing Efforts

In the meantime, Wright and de Blanc pressed on.[54] On January 29, 1947 (a few days before Justice Frankfurter's letter to Lemann), they

---

[54] The discussion in this Section draws from Louisiana *ex rel.* Francis v. Resweber, 329 U.S. 459 (1947); Louisiana *ex rel.* Francis v. Resweber, 330 U.S. 853 (1947); Francis v. Resweber, 331 U.S. 786 (1947); State v. Francis, No. 2161 (16th Jud. Dist. Ct. La. May 5, 1947); Affidavit of Louie M. Cyr, *supra* note 29; Affidavit of Ignace Doucet (Apr. 3, 1947), *supra* note 29; Petition for Rehearing, Louisiana *ex rel.* Francis v. Resweber, 329 U.S. 459 (1947) (No. 142); Motion for a New Trial, State v. Francis, No. 2161 (16th Jud. Dist. Ct. La. Apr. 23, 1947); Motion in Arrest of Judgment, State v. Francis, No. 2161 (16th Jud. Dist. Ct. La. Apr. 23, 1947); Notice of Intention to Apply for Writs, State v. Francis, No. 2161 (16th Jud. Dist. Ct. La. May 5, 1947); Application for Certiorari, Mandamus and Prohibition, State v. Francis (La. May 5, 1947) (available at St. Martin Parish Courthouse, St. Martinville, La.); State v. Francis, No. 38,578 (La. May 6, 1947); State v. Francis, No. 38,580 (La. May 7, 1947); Death Warrant, Executive Department, State of Louisiana (Apr.

filed a petition for rehearing with the Supreme Court focusing on a 1946 amendment[55] to the Louisiana electrocution statute. That amendment now specified that the " 'operator of the electric chair ... shall be a competent electrician who shall not have been previously convicted of a felony.' " Neither the executioner, who "had no knowledge whatever of electricity," nor his assistant, who "was a convict from the state penitentiary," would have qualified under the amendment. As Wright and de Blanc asserted:

> A study of the change [in the electrocution statute] shows that the legislature of the State of Louisiana believed that the failure of the execution of Willie Francis resulted from the incompetence of the execution officials. In other words, the State of Louisiana has publicly confessed her error and has made provision to eliminate a repetition thereof.

Supreme Court rules mandated that a petition for rehearing not be granted unless a Justice who agreed with the judgment of the Court "desires it, and a majority of the court so determines."[56] Knowing this, Wright and de Blanc referred directly to Justice Frankfurter's concurrence in their petition. They argued that the plurality had erred by limiting the meaning "of due process under the Fourteenth Amendment to the Fifth and Eighth Amendments" instead of considering " '[p]rinciple[s] of justice rooted in the traditions and conscience of our people.' " In contrast, "[t]he concurring opinion of Mr. Justice Frankfurter recognizes the full and broad concept of due process in the Fourteenth Amendment, but does not and cannot apply those concepts to this case because the facts of this case are not before the Court." Without "a hearing on the facts and circumstances attending the abortive execution," which the Louisiana courts had denied to Willie, there was no way to know whether the case fell within Justice Frankfurter's " 'hypothetical situation.' " According to Frankfurter's concurrence, such a situation might violate due process because it "would ... raise different questions." Once again, however, Frankfurter declined the opportunity to

---

28, 1947) (copy on file with author); KING, *supra* note 3, at 241, 246; MILLER & BOWMAN, *supra* note 3, at 132, 135–38; Lewis Wood, *Youth Due to Go to Chair Again Today as High Court Denies Plea*, N.Y. TIMES, May 9, 1947, at 1; *Francis to be Electrocuted Today*, WKLY. MESSENGER (St. Martinville, La.), May 9, 1947, at 1; *Final Plea for Willie Francis*, N.Y. TIMES, May 8, 1947, at 52; John LeFlore, *Continue Fight to Save Francis*, CHI. DEFENDER, May 3, 1947, at 1; *Execution of Francis Set for May 9*, WKLY. MESSENGER (St. Martinville, La.), May 2, 1947, at 1; John LeFlore, *"Drunk" Charge in Francis Case*, CHI. DEFENDER, Apr. 26, 1947, at 1; *Executioner "Drunk" Pardon Board Told*, N.Y. TIMES, Apr. 19, 1947, at 8; *Willie Francis' Plea Set for April*, WKLY. MESSENGER, (St. Martinville, La.), Apr. 4, 1947, at 3; and *Francis Ruling Blamed on Last–Minute Switch*, WASH. DAILY NEWS, Jan. 14, 1947, at 2.

55 1946 La. Acts 425.

56 SUP. CT. R. 33 (amended Oct. 13, 1947).

vote to grant Willie relief. On February 10, 1947, the Court denied Wright's and de Blanc's petition.

Still, the attorneys refused to relent. De Blanc applied for yet another hearing before the Louisiana Pardons Board, which the Board granted. About three weeks before the hearing date, de Blanc received information that underscored the need for an investigation of the facts surrounding Willie's botched electrocution. Louie M. Cyr, a former New Iberia Parish city judge, paid a social visit to de Blanc. Upon learning that de Blanc was still working on Willie's case, Cyr lamented "that Willie had to suffer so much at the hands of the two drunken executioners." De Blanc was stunned. This was evidence he had never heard before. Cyr explained that the day after Willie's attempted electrocution, George Etie, a friend of Cyr's who had witnessed the execution, said that he and the executioners had been visiting bars in New Iberia only hours before the execution started. Etie blasted the inhumanity of the electrocution, stating that the two executioners "were so drunk that it was impossible for them to have known what they were doing." According to Etie, Willie also was in great pain, kicking and jumping so much he turned the 300–pound electric chair a quarter of the way around. Faced with the chair's failure, the executioner swore at Willie.

While Wright and de Blanc had contended that a full investigation of Willie's execution was necessary, such an investigation had never transpired. Unfortunately, too, Etie, for whatever reason, feared putting his account in an affidavit. Instead, Cyr stepped forward to provide an affidavit describing his conversation with Etie. Ignace Doucet, another witness to the flawed execution, also agreed to sign an affidavit stating that the two executioners had been "drinking during the whole last part of the morning."

With these two affidavits, de Blanc appeared before the Louisiana Pardons Board—once again asking that Willie's sentence be commuted to life imprisonment. But the move was to no avail. On April 22, 1947, the Pardons Board denied de Blanc's request, despite the many letters they had received supporting Willie's plea.

In desperation, de Blanc tried a different approach. The next day he filed a motion for a new trial in Louisiana district court based on the argument that crucial evidence existed that had not been presented during the first trial, specifically, Ida Van Brocklin's eye witness testimony about seeing a car with its lights on in front of Andrew Thomas's house. Because of the nature of her potential testimony, "the ends of justice would be served by the granting of a new trial." (De Blanc filed a motion for arrest of judgment at the same time.) Questioning Willie's guilt departed from de Blanc's prior strategy of focusing solely on the inhumanity of a second execution. At long last, de Blanc's thinking was coinciding with the original arguments offered by Tureaud and the NAACP. The change in strategy was more risky for de Blanc, both legally and politically. In essence, he would be claiming that the all-white jury wrongly convicted a young black for the murder of a white man, a position that could cause Louisiana whites to view Willie with far more hostility.

Before de Blanc had an opportunity to argue in favor of the motion, Willie received his next death warrant; he was to be executed on May 9, 1947. Four days before this new execution date, on May 5, 1947, de Blanc and District Attorney Pecot appeared before Judge Simon. Simon denied both motions based on Louisiana law which required that "every motion for a new trial or in arrest of judgment must be filed and disposed of before sentence." Willie's original trial attorneys had never raised the issues. In response, de Blanc served notice that he intended to apply to the Louisiana Supreme Court. In his Application for Certiorari, Mandamus and Prohibition, de Blanc argued that because the execution statute under which Willie was sentenced had been repealed (and replaced with a statute requiring that the electrocutioner be a "competent electrician, who shall not have previously been convicted of a Felony"), Willie's sentence was "without force and effect." Therefore Willie had yet to be sentenced and the motions for a new trial and arrest of judgment were timely. The Louisiana Supreme Court denied the application on May 6, 1947. The following day the court denied a different application for writs including habeas corpus.

One more move remained for Willie's attorneys. While de Blanc was making his two now-denied requests in Louisiana, Wright had been devising a last-chance petition for habeas corpus to be filed with the Supreme Court. De Blanc flew to Washington, D.C. for oral argument on May 8, 1947. Once again the two attorneys planned to change Justice Frankfurter's mind. According to Wright, it appeared as though Justice Burton's dissent may at one time have constituted the majority opinion and that one change in vote, possibly Justice Frankfurter's, moved it to the minority opinion. Justice Frankfurter, therefore, was key.

In his habeas petition, Wright argued that " 'the executioner and other persons connected with carrying out the execution were so drunk that it was impossible for them to know what they were doing.' " The State was negligent because there was " 'only a convict' " in charge and not a competent electrician. " 'The scene was a disgraceful and inhuman exhibition, that as soon as the switch controlling the current was taken off, the drunken executioner cursed Francis and told him he would be back to finish electrocuting him, and if the electricity did not kill him he would kill him with a rock.' " At the end, Wright expounded on the mental state of the executioners. According to Wright, the two men were propelled by " 'sadistic impulses and either willfully, deliberately or intentionally applied less than a minimal lethal current, for the purpose of torturing the petitioner.' " Therefore, Willie was "cruelly, inhumanely and excrutiatingly tortured." Ultimately, Wright made two requests of the Court: first, stay the execution and, second, either select a special commissioner to research the facts behind the first attempted electrocution or order the Louisiana courts to mandate an investigation. In addition, de Blanc presented a separate petition asking the Court to review the denial of the Louisiana Supreme Court "to grant such a writ."

The petitions arrived ten minutes before the beginning of oral arguments and a mere twenty-four hours before Willie's scheduled May 9 execution. As a result of the rush, Chief Justice Vinson called an immediate recess for the Justices to meet together and address, yet again, Willie's future. The conference lasted more than an hour, but at its conclusion Vinson announced that Willie's petition had been denied because the petitioners had not exhausted all their lower court remedies before seeking habeas in the Supreme Court. Vinson, however, added an important phrase: "In view of the grave nature of the new allegations, set forth in this petition, the denial is expressly without prejudice to application to proper tribunals."

Despite the denial, the Court's recognition of the "grave nature" of the claims and the fact that the denial was "expressly without prejudice" gave Wright and de Blanc hope. They felt that the Court would be more receptive to their plea if the federal district court in Louisiana decided the petition first. They also realized that Willie could be executed even before their petition could be reviewed. On the evening of May 8, 1947, de Blanc left Washington, D.C. to return to New Orleans, all the while drafting the petition he intended to file with the Louisiana Supreme Court the next morning, May 9, Willie's execution date.

X.   WILLIE IS FINALLY EXECUTED

By the time de Blanc returned to St. Martinville, Willie's execution was being readied.[57] Coverage in the *Messenger* was a reminder of the

---

[57] The following discussion of Willie's final execution draws from KING, *supra* note 3, at 269, 276–77, 280–81; MILLER & BOWMAN, *supra* note 3, at 139, 141; Ron Wikberg & Wilbert Rideau, *The Deathmen*, ANGOLITE, Jan./Feb. 1991, at 29, 41, 43; *Willie Francis Goes to Electric Chair*, COLO. STATESMAN, June 10, 1947, at 1; *Willie Francis Pays Penalty*, TAMPA BULL., May 17, 1947, at 1; *LA. Boy Makes Second Trip To 'Hot Seat'*, INDIANAPOLIS RECORDER, May 17, 1947, at 1; *'Nothing at All', Willie Francis' Last Words; Goes To Death Smiling; Reprieve Attempts Failed Three Times*, SHREVEPORT SUN, May 17, 1947, at 1; *Willie Francis Goes to Death Without Fear*, CHI. DEFENDER, May 17, 1947, at 1; *Walks to the Chair*, SHREVEPORT SUN, May 17, 1947, at 1; Elliott Chaze, *Willie Francis Wears Sunday Pants for Trip to Heaven as Chair Takes Life on Second Try*, WASH. POST, May 10, 1947, at 5; *Francis Dies in Chair on Second Try*, NEW ORLEANS STATES, May 9, 1947, at 1; *Expert Set to Throw Switch on Willie*, LOWELL SUN (Lowell, Mass.), May 9, 1947, at 1; Flannery Lewis, *Willie*

times and of race relations in St. Martinville. From January 3 to May 16, 1947, for example, there were articles concerning a state politician's support for white supremacy and discrimination in schools, as well as a run of racist jokes and commentary questioning blacks' desire for higher education. Willie's date with death was also the talk of the town.

On the eve of Willie's second scheduled execution, an interview with Frederick Francis revealed that Louise Francis would not be present for Willie's execution. According to Frederick, "she couldn't stand bein' in this town today." That same evening, Willie was practicing his walk to the electric chair—his "last mile"—focused on the next day's events. As Willie had stated over a year ago, he wanted to fulfill his promise to Father Hannigan and behave " 'like a man' " on his execution day. Indeed, Hannigan had been visiting Willie daily.

A.   Execution Morning

On the morning of May 9, 1947, Willie dressed in his Sunday best to prepare for his electrocution—a sharp contrast from the prior year when he had gone to his execution in his prison uniform. An Associated Press photo showed Willie outfitted in dark formal slacks and shoes and a white shirt. He had grown considerably taller and larger over the year.

Trusting that Willie would not give him any trouble, Sheriff Ozenne allowed him out of his cell that morning without chains. Thereafter, journalist Elliott Chaze documented Willie's next moves, from his leaving the New Iberia Parish jail, to his getting into the car going to St. Martinville, to his arriving at the St. Martinville jail, where he would be executed. This time, Willie's father, Frederick, stayed at the family home with several of Willie's siblings, so that Frederick would be prepared to receive Willie's body and make burial arrangements. Before de Blanc arrived, several members of Willie's family visited Willie in his cell. When they left his cell and entered the jailhouse yard to exit, a looming crowd had already gathered. Knowing they were Willie's relatives, one

---

Francis Faces Death in Resignation, NEW ORLEANS ITEM, May 9, 1947, at 1; *'I'm Gonna Die Like a Man,' Says Willie Francis, Due for Second Walk to Chair This Afternoon*, BEAUMONT ENTERPRISE, May 9, 1947, at 1; *Willie Hopes to Go Like Man at Second Death Try Today*, TIMES-PICAYUNE (New Orleans, La.), May 9, 1947, at 1; Elliott Chaze, *Willie Francis is to Face Electric Chair for Second Time at St. Martinville Today*, DAILY TIMES-NEWS (Burlington, N.C.), May 9, 1947, at 1; *Senator Overton Oppose* [sic] *Federal Aid to Schools*, WKLY. MESSENGER (St. Martinville, La.), Mar. 21, 1947, at 1; *Co-Operation Noted*, WKLY. MESSENGER (St. Martinville, La.), Feb. 21, 1947, at 4; WKLY. MESSENGER (St. Martinville, La.), Feb. 14, 1947, at 1; *Capitol Headlines*, WKLY. MESSENGER (St. Martinville, La.), Jan. 31, 1947, at 5; *Jimmy Morrison Announces for Governor*, WKLY. MESSENGER (St. Martinville, La.), Jan. 24, 1947, at 2; Tom Gillen, Jr., *Around the Capitol*, WKLY. MESSENGER (St. Martinville, La.), Jan. 24, 1947, at 5; and Tom Gillen, Jr., *Around the Capitol*, WKLY. MESSENGER (St. Martinville, La.), Jan. 3, 1947, at 4.

crowd member pressed into them hostilely: " 'They ought to do away with all the [niggers].' "

De Blanc arrived at the St. Martinville jail a little less than two hours before Willie's noontime execution. Immediately, he informed Willie of his plans to petition the Louisiana courts, and of his optimism that, this time, the results would be different. But Willie had given up hope and wanted no more legal attempts on his behalf. He could not put his parents, especially his ill mother, through more stress. Willie emphasized that he was ready to die. De Blanc struggled with Willie's decision but eventually relented. Sadly, he and Willie said their final goodbyes. Father Hannigan also visited Willie, letting him know that at noon sharp, the executioner would pull the switch and Willie would die immediately. Hannigan asked that, when Willie met with the Lord, Willie say good things about his family and his lawyer.

After Willie finished his last meal,[58] Father Rousseve arrived with another black priest to administer Willie's last rites. At this point, the generator had started and, at noon, the bells of Notre Dame church across the street marked the time. Unseen by Willie, a quiet, orderly crowd of nearly five hundred people gathered outside the jail, mostly expressing their disdain for him. Inside the jail, Elliott Chaze and Police Chief Claude Thomas, Andrew's brother, were among those present for the execution.

B.   The Time Has Come

Willie concluded his thirteen-step walk to the electric chair at 12:02 p.m. Having practiced this walk, Willie informed Father Hannigan that he did not need his help, instead indicating to the priest that he should go first.

This time, the State had selected a purported "expert," Grady Jarratt, to execute Willie, not the amateurs it had used before. Although Jarratt, a Texan, had been the operator of Louisiana's electric chair since 1941, when the State switched from hanging to electrocution, he was apparently not available for Willie's prior execution. Jarratt was known for his care and precision.

As soon as Willie sat in Gruesome Gertie, officials started strapping him in, while also cutting a slit in his left pant's leg in order to attach the electrode. When Willie looked up, Elliott Chaze mouthed him a

---

[58] Mrs. Paul Guilbeaux, the wife of Willie's jailor, prepared his last meal. Although Willie's favorite food was fried chicken, he requested fried fish and potatoes. The day of Willie's execution was a Friday, and, as a practicing Catholic, he was prohibited from eating meat. Chaze, *Willie Francis Wears Sunday Pants for Trip to Heaven as Chair Takes Life on Second Try, supra* note 57.

"hello." Willie also managed to ask Sidney Dupois about his son, and requested that Dupois " 'tell him to be a good boy....' "

When Jarrett asked Willie if there was anything he wanted to say, he replied, " 'nothing at all.' " At 12:05 p.m., Jarratt pulled the switch, and the chair surged with 2,700 volts of electrical current. According to one account, Willie was "motionless," and Jarratt applied another current as insurance. At 12:10 p.m. Jarratt announced that Willie was dead. It seemed that the chair worked this time, at least from the outside. It would never be known what happened to Willie on the inside.

Contrary to Frederick Francis's statements, Louise Francis stayed in St. Martinville for Willie's execution. One news account described her as "sobbing" amongst the crowd that had gathered outside the jail for Willie's execution. There is little information available about the rest of the family's immediate reaction.

Willie was able to have a funeral—from a fund donated by The Good Will Mutual Aid Association. Everyone attending walked with Willie's casket through the streets until the group reached the Union Baptist Cemetery. Although de Blanc did not attend the funeral, Willie Francis's saga would continue to affect both him and Wright for the rest of their lives.

C.   Wright and de Blanc in the Following Years

In their own way, both de Blanc and Wright achieved remarkable careers.[59] De Blanc became District Attorney for the parishes of Lafayette, Vermilion, and Acadia. In this capacity, he even became friendly with L.O. Pecot, the man who had prosecuted Willie; when Pecot died de Blanc was appointed to take over Pecot's district until an election could be held. However, de Blanc would always remember Willie. After working as a District Attorney for many years, he became an indigent defender. In 1986, four decades after taking Willie's case, de Blanc,

---

[59] The following discussion regarding the careers of de Blanc and Wright draws from the following sources: Bush v. New Orleans Parish School Bd., 187 F. Supp. 42, 46 n.2 (E.D. La. 1960); Interview by Jeffrey H. Bowman with Bertrand de Blanc, *supra* note 14; ERNEST J. GAINES, MOZART AND LEADBELLY: STORIES AND ESSAYS 58–59 (2005); WILLIE FRANCIS MUST DIE AGAIN (KUHT/Houston PBS 2006); Louis F. Oberdorfer, *In Memoriam: Judge J. Skelly Wright*, 57 GEO. WASH. L. REV. 1037, 1038–39 (1989); Bernick, *supra* note 38, at 989–91; Shelton, *supra* note 48; Marjorie Hunter, *Judge J. Skelly Wright, Segregation Foe, Dies at 77*, N.Y. TIMES, Apr. 8, 1988, at D10; Claude Sitton, *U.S. Court Orders New Orleans to Start Pupil Integration in Fall*, N.Y. TIMES, May 17, 1960, at 1; Barbara Ann Worthy, The Travail and Triumph of a Southern Black Civil Rights Lawyer: The Legal Career of Alexander Pierre Tureaud 1899–1972 (Jan. 30, 1984) (unpublished Ph.D. dissertation, Tulane University) (on file with author); and Senior Judge Louis F. Oberdorfer—U.S. District Court, Washington, D.C., http://www.dcd.uscourts.gov/oberdorfer-bio.html (last visited Nov. 3, 2008).

overcome by emotion while describing his experiences with Willie to novelist Ernest J. Gaines, put his head in his hands and wept.

Shortly after Willie's execution, Wright returned to his hometown of New Orleans as U.S. Attorney. In 1948 he became the youngest federal judge in the country when President Truman appointed him to a judgeship on the Federal District Court in New Orleans. With time, the careers of Wright and A.P. Tureaud would once again intersect. For many years, Tureaud had been bringing NAACP suits in the federal court in New Orleans to obtain equality for the black residents of Louisiana. One of these suits brought national attention to Judge Wright in 1960, when Wright created an integration plan for the New Orleans public schools after the school board refused to do so. However, because Wright was breaking racial barriers, within Louisiana he faced vilification and ostracism publicly and politically.

In 1962, President Kennedy nominated Wright for the D.C. Circuit Court, a promotion supported by southern senators because it would remove Wright from the controversial progress he was making in Louisiana. While on the D.C. Circuit Wright became good friends with Justice Hugo Black, whom he had always admired. In a memorial article following Wright's death, Judge Louis Oberdorfer, Justice Black's clerk for the 1946 term, referred to *Resweber* and Justice Frankfurter's concurrence in particular to pay Wright the highest compliment: "One reconstructing Judge Wright's faith may well find that Judge Wright tried to see to it that, unlike Justice Frankfurter, he never let such an unsupported assumption as the 'consensus of society's opinion' overcome his innate sense of justice." Of course, such a tribute to Wright revealed a longstanding acknowledgment that Justice Frankfurter's stance in *Resweber* was sorely misguided.

XI. EPILOGUE

The epilogue to Willie's story, like his life and death, is both personal and legal. In contrast to the accounts provided for Wright and de Blanc, little information exists about Willie's immediate family after his execution. Yet my 2007 visit to St. Martinville uncovered a host of relatives and townspeople who helped piece together glimpses of how Willie's case affected them. The impact has reverberated over the decades during which time this country and St. Martinville have changed— albeit not sufficiently to provide minority youths, like Willie, with adequate legal protection.

A. The Personal Story

With all of its deep South history and intrigue, present-day St. Martinville remains small and poor.[60] Numbering approximately 7,000 residents, it has nearly twice the population the city reported in the mid–1940s, with most of the increase having occurred during the 1950s. The racial makeup of the city is now the reverse of that of the 1940s, with nearly two-thirds of the population black and about one-third white.

Not surprisingly, the racial divisions are far less and different today. St. Martinville now spotlights its first black mayor, Thomas Nelson. And, in Sister Helen Prejean's renowned 1993 book, *Dead Man Walking*, the city is characterized as among the "friendliest, most hospitable places on earth"—a "place one would least expect" a murder to occur. Indeed, New Orleans residents who were evacuated to St. Martinville in 2005 because of Hurricane Katrina said that "the people there treated them like kings and queens" during their stay.

At the same time, a visitor would notice that modern-day St. Martinville is a scene of past Parisian glory, but present poverty, celebrated for its Acadian heritage and a few distinguishing features. One such feature, is the Evangeline Oak, made famous by Henry Wadsworth Longfellow's poem, *Evangeline*, and still growing beautifully alongside the Bayou Teche.[61] "Were it not for [Evangeline] and what America thinks of her, St. Martinville might be a forgotten spot on the map."

---

[60] The discussion that follows regarding present-day St. Martinville draws from the following sources: Interview with Keith Landry, *supra* note 12; Interview with Thomas Nelson, *supra* note 6; KING, *supra* note 3, at x, xiv; HELEN PREJEAN, DEAD MAN WALKING: AN EYEWITNESS ACCOUNT OF THE DEATH PENALTY IN THE UNITED STATES 4 (Vintage Books 1994) (1993); CAPUDER, *supra* note 6, at 152–53; HARNETT T. KANE, THE BAYOUS OF LOUISIANA 257 (1943); HENRY WADSWORTH LONGFELLOW, EVANGELINE: A TALE OF ACADIE (1847); LOUISIANA ALMANAC: 2006–2007 EDITION, *supra* note 8, at 245; U.S. DEP'T OF COMMERCE, BUREAU OF THE CENSUS, COUNTY AND CITY DATA BOOK: A STATISTICAL ABSTRACT SUPPLEMENT 210 (1953); U.S. DEP'T OF COMMERCE, BUREAU OF THE CENSUS, COUNTY DATA BOOK: A SUPPLEMENT TO THE STATISTICAL ABSTRACT OF THE UNITED STATES 186 (1947); U.S. Census Bureau, Population of St. Martinville, La., http://factfinder.census.gov/servlet/SAFFPopulation?_event=Search&_name=st.+martinville&_state=&_county=st.+martinville&_cityTown=st.+martinville&_zip=&_sse=on&_lang=en&pctxt=fph (last visited Aug. 9, 2008); U.S. Census Bureau, 2000 Fact Sheet for Louisiana, http://factfinder.census.gov/servlet/SAFFFacts?_event=&geo_id=04000US22&_geoContext=01000US@04000US22&_street=&_county=&_city Town=&_state=04000US22&_zip=&_lang=en&_sse=on&ActiveGeoDiv=&_useEV=&pctxt=fph&pgsl=040&_submenuId=factsheet_1&ds_name=ACS_2006_SAFF&_ci_nbr=null&qr_name=null&reg=&_keyword=&_industry= (last visited Aug. 9, 2008); and *Weekend Edition Saturday: New Orleans Braces for Gustav,* (NPR News radio broadcast Aug. 30, 2008), *available at* http://www.npr.org/templates/story/story.php?storyId=94140546.

[61] According to a plaque under the Evangeline Oak in St. Martinville, Longfellow is believed to have learned about the Acadians in St. Martinville and "the geography and local color of the Teche country" from a native of St. Martinville, Emile Edouard (Edward) Simon. Edward was a Louisiana district judge and the grandfather of the judge who presided over Willie's trial. Celia R. Cangelosi, *The Simons: Six Generations of Legal Service (If You Count the Family's Belgian Patriarch!)*, 54 LA. BAR J. 427, 427–28 (2007).

Indeed, like sixty years ago, the St. Martinville of today appears insular. During my 2007 stay, it was difficult to locate a detailed street map of any kind—even from the city's tourist office. Surely the residents would know the layout of such a small area, however, a visitor would not. The lack of a map was not just a metaphor for St. Martinville's isolation but also a pragmatic reality. As writer Gilbert King concluded from his own visits, "St. Martinville is a whole different world." Without question, Willie's case helped shape that world.

I also learned during my visit that Willie's house had been dismantled only a few months before I arrived. The destruction of the home was of no historic consequence to most St. Martinville residents and it revealed the dearth of knowledge regarding Willie. Only the older people I interviewed could answer questions about the Willie Francis saga; the younger residents either retained little or were totally unaware.[62] Willie's obscurity is regrettable not only because of the injustice of his case but also because of the historic racism that fueled it. These are stories worth remembering.

Pictures help recall a story.[63] Willie's grandnephew, Joseph Davis, Jr., provided me with the only known photograph of Willie's remaining siblings and associated family members. The picture was taken in St. Martinville in April 1971, following Frederick Francis's funeral. In the picture nine of Willie's sisters and brothers, as well as a niece and nephew, are standing next to the Francis family home. The nephew, Allen Francis, age 64, is the only person in the picture who is still living today. Now burdened with a serious heart condition and a long history of hospital stays, Allen told me that for one year in the 1960s, he was Frederick's caretaker in St. Martinville. Frederick, a diabetic amputee in his later years, had always insisted to Allen that Willie was innocent.

The matter of Willie's execution was also troubling to other family members, so much so that they had difficulty talking about it. Hilda Henry, Willie's niece and, until recently, the closest remaining relative,

---

[62] Gilbert King reported a similar lack of awareness among St. Martinville's residents of Willie's trial or execution. KING, *supra* note 3, at x.

[63] See *infra* page 94 for a reproduction of the family photograph described in this Section. The following discussion of Willie's family draws from the following sources: Letter from MaEsther Francis, Willie Francis's niece, Port Arthur, Tex., to Deborah W. Denno, Professor, Fordham Law School, New York, N.Y. (Aug. 22, 2008) (copy on file with author); E-mail from MaEsther Francis, Willie Francis's niece, to Deborah W. Denno, Professor, Fordham Law School, New York, N.Y. (Nov. 30, 2008) (copy on file with author); Telephone Interview with Hilda Henry, Willie Francis's niece, in Beaumont, Tex. (June 13, 2007); Telephone Interview with Allen Francis, Willie Francis's nephew, in Garland, Tex. (Sept. 28, Oct. 3, Nov. 26, 2008); Telephone Interview by Lisa–Sheri Torrence with MaEsther Francis, Willie Francis's niece, in Port Arthur, Tex. (Aug. 11, 2008); and Interview with Joseph Davis, Jr., Willie Francis's grandnephew, in St. Martinville, La. (June 14, 2007).

had initially agreed to meet with me for an interview in 2007 in her hometown of Beaumont, Texas; but she changed her mind at the last minute.[64] When I spoke with her on the phone about why she cancelled the visit, she explained that she was in her early seventies and had been ill for some time. She was only ten when Willie died. For Hilda, Willie's execution represented not simply the sorrow about his death but also a public humiliation and level of exposure that roused fear among the Francis family members left in St. Martinville.[65] Hilda started to cry after I had asked her only a few questions. I had to cut short the conversation; the weeping said it all.

MaEsther Francis, also a niece of Willie's, talked with me about Hilda's fear. Now in her late forties, MaEsther never knew Willie. But her father (Early Francis) told her about Willie's execution when she was a teenager. Yearning to learn more details, MaEsther conducted research about the execution during her college years. Like Joseph Davis, Jr., MaEsther found a blood association with Willie to be "a source of pride." Yet, when MaEsther tried to ask Hilda questions about Willie during a family reunion, Hilda became "extremely upset and began crying." "Through her sobbing" Hilda "said that [MaEsther] should not have brought up Willie Francis because [they] still had family members living in St. Martinville and the people who were actually responsible for Andrew Thomas's death and falsely accusing Willie were still alive and might try to hurt them if [the Francis family] started asking questions." Hilda ascribed to the belief held by others in town that Willie had been framed and used as a cover for Andrew's real murderers. As MaEsther recounted, Hilda's "tears were real, the trembling in her voice was real, and the fear in her eyes evident nearly fifty years later as long buried memories were brought to the surface." These were "[m]emories [Hilda] would have preferred to have left buried, memories that were taken to their graves by other family members, and memories that were never disclosed" to MaEsther.

Hilda died on September 11, 2008, but she did not take all of her memories to the grave. While Hilda informed me that she "couldn't go through" with our interview because Willie's execution was "too painful" to discuss, there was one statement she made to me firmly and with resolve: "Blame the white people of St. Martinville."

---

[64] Willie Francis was the brother of Hilda Henry's mother, Marie Francis Neal. Interview with Keith Landry, *supra* note 12.

[65] Years ago, after Willie was executed, a Hollywood production company taped discussions with Willie's siblings in an effort to devise plans for a major movie production about Willie's case. However, by the end of the taping, Emily Branch, the oldest sibling, decided she had no interest in a movie nor in the recordings, and the effort was abandoned. Keith Landry, Willie's grandnephew, has a copy of the taped discussions, but he has never revealed them publicly. Interview with Keith Landry, *supra* note 12.

Race, risk, and religion—all were pervasive themes that others in St. Martinville revealed to me in interviews along with their own personal stories.[66] Velma Johnson, a tour guide at the St. Martinville Cultural Heritage Center, was nine when Willie was executed. She reminded me that as a black resident of St. Martinville, if she and I had conversed decades ago, she would have had to avert her eyes while talking to me, a white. Velma has always believed that Willie was never executed but rather secretly released by those recognizing his innocence. James Akers informed me that the fear linked to Willie's death extended even to the lower class whites in the city who were distinguished from the white "St. Martinville elite." For example, Akers's own white, working class parents had squelched family discussion of Willie's case or execution, explaining that they must as long as those associated with Andrew Thomas's murder were still alive—a concern over potential reprisal that paralleled Hilda Henry's own account. Akers claimed that as a young boy of four or five years, he remembers the lights blinking from the generator on the day of Willie's execution. St. Martinville's Mayor Nelson told me that the majority of people in St. Martinville, even those in the white community, did not believe Willie committed the murder. Some thought that Willie was protecting his family with his silence out of concern that something might happen to them if he professed his innocence.

More than anyone in St. Martinville, Allan Durand, an attorney and Bertrand de Blanc's grandnephew, has tried to revive the accounts of Willie's ordeal. In 2006, Durand produced and directed an award-winning documentary about Willie, *Willie Francis Must Die Again*, promoting the film to generate public discussion. Yet he too acknowledged the kind of disquiet and denial particular community members felt about Willie's case. Durand especially appreciated the legal hurdles de Blanc had faced.

B.   The Legal Story

The legal system also documents memories and life narratives, either through the reporting of the facts of a case, the use of precedent, the overturning of a decision, or other vehicles. Today, of course, Willie's story would have had a different ending. Because of the Court's recent decision in *Roper v. Simmons*[67] to bar the death penalty for juveniles, Willie would never have been executed. Regardless, even if Willie had been age-eligible for the death penalty, his future would still be unclear. Mandatory death sentences, like the one under which Willie was sen-

---

[66] The remainder of this Section draws from the following sources: Interview with Velma Johnson, *supra* note 17; Interview with James Akers, *supra* note 6; Interview with Allan Durand, *supra* note 17; Interview with Thomas Nelson, *supra* note 6; WILLIE FRANCIS MUST DIE AGAIN, *supra* note 59.

[67] 543 U.S. 551 (2005).

tenced, are no longer constitutional.[68] Moreover, Willie would have been entitled to a reading of his *Miranda* rights. Present-day knowledge of the hazards of execution methods might have further prompted de Blanc to investigate the technical problems surrounding Willie's first attempted execution sooner rather than focusing on simply preventing Willie's subsequent execution.

There are numerous other ways to consider Willie's case from a "what if" perspective in light of the sea change in criminal law and procedure over the past decades. But that viewpoint is part of someone else's legal story, not Willie's. Willie was not afforded modern-day legal protections and he faced the death penalty, realities that are this Chapter's focus over and above musings of what might have been. Also unknown is precisely how Willie's experiences in the criminal justice system would be different today. Countless minority males still share many of Willie's challenges. Not nearly enough has been achieved to ensure them sufficient safeguards.

This country's continuing problems with botched execution methods exemplifies this point. While electrocution was once the dominant method, it is no longer used exclusively by any state; rather, lethal injection accounts for nearly all executions.[69] Initially, lethal injection was viewed as a more humane way of carrying out the death penalty; however, this new method also has proven to be a technical failure continually ripe for Eighth Amendment challenges.

1. From Electrocution to Lethal Injection

This country's turn to lethal injection reflects states' growing reliance on medicine as a response to philosophical, financial, and political pressures to eliminate the death penalty.[70] For example, New York

---

[68] Woodson v. North Carolina, 428 U.S. 280 (1976); Roberts v. Louisiana, 428 U.S. 325 (1976).

[69] On February 8, 2008, the Nebraska Supreme Court declared electrocution unconstitutional under the State's constitution. State v. Mata, 745 N.W.2d 229, 279–80 (Neb. 2008). At that time, Nebraska was the only state that used electrocution as its only method of execution. *Id.* at 257. So far, *Mata* has left a death penalty statute in place in Nebraska but no method to implement it.

[70] The following discussion of execution methods draws from Provenzano v. Moore, 744 So. 2d 413 (Fla. 1999) (Shaw, J., dissenting); Fierro v. Gomez, 77 F.3d 301 (9th Cir. 1996), *vacated and remanded*, 519 U.S. 918 (1996); Campbell v. Wood, 18 F.3d 662 (9th Cir. 1994); Gregg v. Georgia, 428 U.S. 153 (1976) (plurality opinion); Furman v. Georgia, 408 U.S. 238 (1972) (per curiam); *In re* Kemmler, 136 U.S. 436 (1890); STUART BANNER, THE DEATH PENALTY: AN AMERICAN HISTORY 169–70 (2002); RICHARD MORAN, EXECUTIONER'S CURRENT: THOMAS EDISON, GEORGE WESTINGHOUSE, AND THE INVENTION OF THE ELECTRIC CHAIR 15–16 (2002); IVAN SOLOTAROFF, THE LAST FACE YOU'LL EVER SEE: THE PRIVATE LIFE OF THE AMERICAN DEATH PENALTY 7 (2001); CRAIG BRANDON, THE ELECTRIC CHAIR: AN UNNATURAL AMERICAN HISTORY 32–38 (1999); PHILIP ENGLISH MACKEY, HANGING IN THE BALANCE: THE ANTI-CAPITAL PUNISHMENT

State's increasing opposition to capital punishment in the early 1800s led to the abolition of public hangings in 1835. By the late 1870s, graphic newspaper accounts of hangings—many of them botched—fed the public appetite for sensationalism and led the State's governor to ask the legislature in 1885 " 'whether the science of the present day' " could not find a less barbaric means to execute criminals. The legislature's appointed commission of three "well known citizens" ultimately selected the electric chair, following the commission's impressively detailed two-year study of every execution method used throughout history.[71]

New York's decision to enact electrocution spurred intense legal and scientific battles, momentarily resolved only when the Supreme Court decided that the Eighth Amendment did not apply to the states and that the State's statute was constitutional. In 1890, the murderer William Kemmler became the first person in the country to be electrocuted after the Court ruled against him. Kemmler's execution was a scene of confusion and horror, his slow death a spectacle of blood from ruptured capillaries and roasting flesh. This catastrophe did not dissuade states from adopting a method hailed as a scientific advancement. Electrocution was deemed superior to hanging or, at the very least, was far less visible.

The problems with electrocution increased with the passing decades, despite (or perhaps because of) enhanced scrutiny of the method's application. By the time Allen Lee Davis was executed in Florida in 1999, over a century after Kemmler, the tortuous issues surrounding the method appeared insurmountable: Davis suffered massive bleeding from

---

MOVEMENT IN NEW YORK STATE, 1776–1861, at 118 (1982); N.Y. COMM'N ON CAPITAL PUNISHMENT, REPORT OF THE COMMISSION TO INVESTIGATE AND REPORT THE MOST HUMANE AND PRACTICAL METHOD OF CARRYING INTO EFFECT THE SENTENCE OF DEATH IN CAPITAL CASES 3, 18–77, 95 (1888); Marian J. Borg & Michael L. Radelet, *On Botched Executions*, in CAPITAL PUNISHMENT: STRATEGIES FOR ABOLITION 143 (Peter Hodgkinson & William A. Schabas eds., 2004); Deborah W. Denno, *The Lethal Injection Quandary: How Medicine Has Dismantled the Death Penalty*, 76 FORDHAM L. REV. 49 (2007); Atul Gawande, *When Law and Ethics Collide—Why Physicians Participate in Executions*, 354 NEW ENG. J. MED. 1221, 1222 (2006); Deborah W. Denno, *When Legislatures Delegate Death: The Troubling Paradox Behind State Uses of Electrocution and Lethal Injection and What It Says About Us*, 63 OHIO ST. L.J. 63, 78–79 (2002); Christopher Q. Cutler, *Nothing Less Than the Dignity of Man: Evolving Standards, Botched Executions and Utah's Controversial Use of the Firing Squad*, 50 CLEV. ST. L. REV. 335, 413–14 & n.441 (2002); *Millions Flock to US Execution Site*, SCOTSMAN (Edinburgh, Scot.), Nov. 1, 1999, at 22; Deborah W. Denno, *Getting to Death: Are Executions Constitutional?*, 82 IOWA L. REV. 319, 364–70, 375 (1997); Denno, *Is Electrocution an Unconstitutional Method of Execution?*, *supra* note 29, at 604–07; and *Far Worse Than Hanging*, N.Y. TIMES, Aug. 7, 1890, at 1.

[71] The Commission consisted of its Chair, Elbridge T. Gerry, a New York City attorney, founder of the American Society for the Prevention of Cruelty to Animals, and founder and president of the American Society for the Prevention of Cruelty to Children; Dr. Alfred P. Southwick, a dentist from Buffalo who was a leading proponent of electrocution; and

the nose, deep burns on his face, head and leg, and partial asphyxiation from the mouth strap that belted him to the chair's headrest. Millions of people around the world viewed the results through the Florida Supreme Court's web site postings of Davis's post-execution color photographs—ultimately crashing the Florida court's computer system and intermittently disabling it for months. While the botched Davis execution did not halt electrocutions, it did prompt the Florida legislature to allow inmates to choose between electrocution and lethal injection.[72] By 2008, when the state of Nebraska found electrocution unconstitutional, the method was moving from a rarity to a relic.

Over time, other execution methods also showed obvious challenges. Like their predecessors, modern-day hangings risked being too long and cruel. Lethal gas, first enacted in 1921, has been judged to be the worst of all. In 1992, for example, Donald Harding's ten-minute execution and suffocating pain were so disturbing for witnesses that one reporter cried continuously, "two other reporters 'were rendered walking "vegetables" for days,'" the attorney general ended up vomiting, and the prison warden claimed he would resign if forced to conduct another lethal gas execution. While the firing squad has not been systematically evaluated, and may even be the most humane of all methods, it carries with it the baggage of its brutal imagery. This image has held despite the Court's 1878 conclusion in *Wilkerson v. Utah*[73] that the firing squad is not a cruel and unusual punishment under the Eighth Amendment.

In light of the troubling history of other execution methods, the quick popularity of lethal injection is understandable. When Oklahoma first adopted lethal injection in May 1977, one year after *Gregg v. Georgia*,[74] many states rapidly followed Oklahoma's lead. There was simply no other new and seemingly viable method on the capital punishment horizon. Besides, doctors had created the lethal injection formula incorporating chemicals applied in surgery. The procedure seemed to have the medical profession's stamp of approval.

With lethal injection, then, the law turned to medicine to rescue the death penalty. In due time, however, the humane veneer of lethal injection would start to crack as the method evidenced more and more flaws and inept application. Once again, as in past decades, execution problems would require the Supreme Court's response. But with such an underdeveloped Eighth Amendment caselaw pertaining to execution methods, the Supreme Court would have to turn to *Resweber* to rescue

---

Matthew Hale, a prominent constitutional attorney from Albany. BRANDON, *supra* note 70, at 14–15, 51–53.

[72] FLA. STAT. ANN. § 922.105 (West 2008).

[73] 99 U.S. 130 (1878).

[74] 428 U.S. 153 (1976) (plurality opinion). The *Gregg* decision ended a four-year moratorium on the death penalty prompted by *Furman v. Georgia*, 408 U.S. 238 (1972) (per curiam).

the meaning of "cruel and unusual punishments." Unfortunately, that rescue effort too has failed. As the next section discusses, *Resweber* has proven far too limited and inappropriate to take on the task expected by some members of the Court.

2.   From *Lousiana* ex rel. *Francis v. Resweber* to *Baze v. Rees*

Resweber's holding and history are controversial. Nonetheless, over the last sixty years of changing execution methods and incorporation status the decision has consistently served as precedent. Regrettably, some of this reliance has been erroneous or misleading. For example, of the 184 federal court opinions that have cited to one or more of the three opinions in *Resweber*,[75] twenty-two, or nearly twelve percent, cited the plurality opinion to support the proposition that the Eighth Amendment's prohibition on cruel and unusual punishments was incorporated into the Due Process Clause of the Fourteenth Amendment.[76] These courts cited *Resweber* even though, as a number of other opinions have noted, the *Resweber* plurality merely assumed, without deciding, that the Eighth Amendment was applicable to the states.[77] It would take the Court another fifteen years to hold explicitly (in a case not concerning an execution method) that the Eighth Amendment applied to the states through the Fourteenth Amendment's Due Process Clause.[78] While the federal courts have used *Resweber* in a variety of other ways,[79] not

---

[75] A search of LexisNexis yielded 184 federal court opinions citing *Resweber*. The opinions are listed and categorized in a memorandum on file with the author.

[76] *See, e.g.*, United States v. Georgia, 546 U.S. 151, 157 (2006). In *Robinson v. California*, 370 U.S. 660, 666–67 (1962), the Supreme Court concluded that the Eighth Amendment applies to the states. Ten opinions cited *Resweber* along with *Robinson* for the proposition that the Eighth Amendment is incorporated into the Due Process Clause of the Fourteenth Amendment. *See, e.g.*, Roper v. Simmons, 543 U.S. 551, 560 (2005).

[77] *See, e.g.*, Browning–Ferris Indus. v. Kelco Disposal, Inc., 492 U.S. 257, 284 (1989) (O'Connor, J., dissenting).

[78] *See* Robinson v. California, 370 U.S. 660, 666–67 (1962).

[79] The federal courts have used the principal opinion in *Resweber* in the following ways: (1) Forty-nine opinions cited *Resweber* for its conclusion that the Eighth Amendment proscribes the purposeful infliction of unnecessary pain and is directed towards cruelty inherent in the punishment, not unforeseeable accidents in its administration, *see, e.g.*, Taylor v. Crawford, 487 F.3d 1072, 1080 (8th Cir. 2007); (2) Twenty-six opinions cited *Resweber* because the decision implied that the death penalty (or electrocution specifically) was not per se unconstitutional, *see, e.g.*, Furman v. Georgia, 408 U.S. 238, 284–85 (1972) (per curiam) (Brennan, J., concurring); (3) Three opinions cited *Resweber* to support the proposition that an otherwise constitutional sentence can be rendered unconstitutional if it is not carried out properly, *see, e.g.*, Ingraham v. Wright, 430 U.S. 651, 670 n.38 (1977); (4) Three opinions cited *Resweber* to support the proposition that the need to apply more than one current of electricity does not violate the Eighth Amendment, *see, e.g.*, Williams v. Hopkins, 130 F.3d 333, 337–38 (8th Cir. 1997); (5) Twenty opinions cited *Resweber* for its

surprisingly, three opinions cited *Resweber*, along with other cases, to support the position that Eighth Amendment jurisprudence is not clear,[80] a perspective consistent with this Chapter's viewpoint.

One of the more recent and prominent examples of the variability of *Resweber*'s use appears in the various opinions in *Baze v. Rees*.[81] In *Baze*, the Supreme Court considered whether the lethal injection protocol promulgated by the State of Kentucky violated the Eighth Amendment's prohibition of cruel and unusual punishments. In order to effect capital punishment Kentucky uses a series of three drugs: sodium thiopental, a common anesthetic for surgery that is intended to cause unconsciousness; pancuronium bromide, a total muscle relaxant that stops breathing by paralyzing the diaphragm and lungs; and potassium chloride, a toxin that induces cardiac arrest and permanently stops the inmate's heartbeat. The concern is that the second drug can cause an inmate excruciating pain and suffering if administered without adequate anesthesia. The inmate, while paralyzed and unable to cry out, would slowly suffocate from the drug's effects. Injection of the third drug only increases the agony. In 2005, two prisoners, Ralph Baze and Thomas C. Bowling challenged the constitutionality of Kentucky's lethal injection protocol, contending that it created an " 'unnecessary risk' of pain." The Kentucky trial and appellate courts rejected their arguments, and the Supreme Court granted certiorari—a dramatic move given that over a century had passed since the Court had agreed to review the constitutionality of a state's execution method. In a splintered 7–2 plurality ruling, the *Baze* Court upheld Kentucky's lethal injection protocol,

---

discussion of double jeopardy, *see, e.g.*, Burks v. United States, 437 U.S. 1, 6 (1978); and (6) Four opinions cited *Resweber* for its discussion of equal protection, *see, e.g.*, Camacho v. Bowling, 562 F. Supp. 1012, 1026 (N.D. Ill. 1983). Moreover, ten opinions cited to Justice Frankfurter's concurrence in *Resweber* for his warning regarding judicial restraint and deference towards legislatures, *see, e.g.*, United States *ex rel.* Hetenyi v. Wilkins, 348 F.2d 844, 857–58 (2d Cir. 1965), and twenty-six opinions referred to one of the various Fourteenth Amendment Due Process Clause standards he sets forth, *see, e.g.*, Arroyo v. Schaefer, 548 F.2d 47, 50 & n.3 (2d Cir. 1977). The dissent in *Resweber* was cited in twelve opinions for its statement that "[t]aking human life by unnecessarily cruel means shocks the most fundamental instincts of civilized man." *See, e.g.*, Jackson v. Bishop, 404 F.2d 571, 576, 578 (8th Cir. 1968). The three opinions in *Resweber* have also been cited in support of a number of other less common propositions. *See, e.g.*, Robinson v. California, 370 U.S. 660, 675 (1962) (Douglas, J., concurring) ("The command of the Eighth Amendment, banning 'cruel and unusual punishments,' stems from the Bill of Rights of 1688.").

[80] *See* Trop v. Dulles, 356 U.S. 86, 99 & n.29 (1958); Jackson v. Bishop, 404 F.2d 571, 576, 579 (8th Cir. 1968); Fierro v. Gomez, 865 F. Supp. 1387, 1409 & n.24 (N.D. Cal. 1994).

[81] 128 S. Ct. 1520 (2008). The remainder of this Section draws on the following sources: Baze v. Rees, 128 S. Ct. 1520 (2008); Louisiana *ex rel.* Francis v. Resweber, 329 U.S. 459 (1947); *In re* Kemmler, 136 U.S. 436 (1890); Wilkerson v. Utah, 99 U.S. 130 (1879); and Deborah W. Denno, Introduction, *The Lethal Injection Debate: Law and Science*, 35 FORDHAM URB. L.J. 701, 702 (2008).

concluding that the risk of severe pain associated with the protocol was not substantial when compared to known and available alternatives. Three of the seven opinions filed in *Baze* (those of Chief Justice Roberts and Justices Thomas and Ginsburg) cited *Resweber*.

Baze is broad and complex. This Chapter's focus is limited to the Justices' use of *Resweber* in their Eighth Amendment analyses. Such an application of *Resweber*, however, seems to be aimed more at compensating for the dearth of such precedent in the execution methods context rather than at providing a coherent foundation for problem solving. As Justice Ginsburg's dissent states most clearly (and the other *Baze* opinions seem to take as given), "The Court has considered the constitutionality of a specific method of execution on only three prior occasions."

Those three occasions were *Wilkerson*, *Kemmler*, and *Resweber*, and all are paltry guides for tackling the jurisprudential hurdles in *Baze*. None of the cases involved a review of execution methods evidence under the Eighth Amendment. In *Wilkerson*, the Court concluded that the firing squad is not a cruel and unusual punishment under the Eighth Amendment. However, the Court never reviewed evidence on the cruelty of shooting because the issue was never raised by the plaintiff. The plaintiff's contention was that because the method of execution was not specified by the statute, the trial "court possessed no authority to prescribe the mode of execution." The Court disagreed.

In *Kemmler*, the Court held that the Eighth Amendment did not apply to the states and deferred to the New York legislature's conclusion that electrocution was not a cruel and unusual punishment under New York's Electrical Execution Act. For this reason, the Court never conducted an Eighth Amendment analysis of electrocution, and whatever legal standards the Court employed "were made *en passant*."

In *Resweber*, the issue was not whether the method of execution—electrocution—violated the Eighth Amendment, but whether the State of Louisiana could constitutionally execute the appellant after the electric chair had malfunctioned during the first attempt. Because the question of electrocution's constitutionality was not presented, there were no facts or legal arguments in the record on this issue; therefore, the *Resweber* Court's assumption that electrocution passed Eighth Amendment muster was unsupported. Moreover, the *Resweber* Court's failure to actually incorporate the Eighth Amendment meant that the plurality did not need to fully develop an Eighth Amendment standard. Although a majority of the *Resweber* Court found that a second execution would not violate the Due Process Clause of the Fourteenth Amendment, only four Justices agreed that it would not violate the Eighth Amendment.

Justice Frankfurter, the necessary fifth vote to uphold the Louisiana Supreme Court, did not consider the Eighth Amendment at all.

3.   The *Baze* Justices on *Resweber*

The three *Baze* opinions citing *Resweber* took a range of perspectives.[82] Most troublesome were Chief Justice Roberts's citations. His final reference to *Resweber*, a quotation from Justice Frankfurter's concurrence, bolsters Roberts's belief in judicial restraint: " 'One must be on guard against finding in personal disapproval a reflection of more or less prevailing condemnation.' " Yet Justice Roberts's other two *Resweber* references are not fully on point.

When articulating his Eighth Amendment standard, Roberts quotes from Frankfurter's concurrence referring to " 'a hypothetical situation' involving 'a series of abortive attempts at electrocution' [that] would present a different case." Although Roberts accurately notes that the concurrence is based on the Due Process Clause, it might not be clear to a modern reader of the opinion that Frankfurter did not consider the appropriate Eighth Amendment standard because he did not believe that the Eighth Amendment applied to the states. In other words, Roberts never explains why Frankfurter's Fourteenth Amendment due process standard is pertinent to an Eighth Amendment cruel and unusual punishments analysis. A good argument can be made that Frankfurter's standard is not applicable.

In addition, Justice Roberts refers to the plurality opinion in *Resweber* for the proposition that " 'an accident, with no suggestion of malevolence,' ... [does] not give rise to an *Eighth Amendment* violation." However, the internal quote from *Resweber* is not discussing the Eighth Amendment but rather whether a second execution would violate the Fifth Amendment prohibition on double jeopardy. The sentence following the quoted phrase from *Resweber* reads, "We find no *double jeopardy* here which can be said to amount to a denial of federal due process in the proposed execution." Once again, Justice Roberts misses the Eighth Amendment trail.

Justice Thomas, by contrast, depends less on precedent than on his conception of the "original understanding of the Cruel and Unusual Punishments Clause" when determining the appropriate Eighth Amendment standard. Thomas uses the *Resweber* plurality's suggested standard of a " 'purpose to inflict unnecessary pain' " to support his contention " 'that it was the original understanding and intent of the framers of the Eighth Amendment ... to proscribe as "cruel and unusual" *only* such modes of execution as compound the simple infliction of death with added cruelties or indignities.' " However, the *Resweber* Court never examined the mode of execution. The actual conclusion of the plurality was that the botched first execution attempt did not add to the cruelty of a second electrocution.

---

[82] The discussion in this section draws from Baze v. Rees, 128 S. Ct. 1520 (2008) and Louisiana *ex rel.* Francis v. Resweber, 329 U.S. 459 (1947).

Justice Thomas also stresses that the *Resweber* Court "was confronted in dramatic fashion with the reality that the electric chair involved risks of error or malfunction that could result in excruciating pain"; yet it still "concluded that the Constitution did not prohibit Louisiana from subjecting the petitioner to those very risks a second time in order to carry out his death sentence." Although Justice Thomas is correct, it might be more precise to think of the *Resweber* Court's conclusion as following a Fourteenth Amendment due process standard rather than an Eighth Amendment cruel and unusual punishment standard because the Court did not actually decide that the Eighth Amendment was applicable to the states. As previously noted, Justice Frankfurter, the necessary fifth vote to allow the second execution, determined that the Eighth Amendment is not incorporated; likewise, the plurality only considered the Eighth Amendment with respect to whether the botched first execution attempt would make a subsequent attempt unconstitutional, not whether the execution method itself was unconstitutional. Again, Justice Thomas fails to keep in mind the constitutional constraints and confusion the *Resweber* Court faced in a pre-incorporation legal world.

Justice Ginsburg fully comprehends these constraints. She points out that *Resweber* did not create a clear Eighth Amendment standard for determining the constitutionality of an execution method but rather used different guidelines. As Justice Ginsburg notes, "The plurality opinion in [*Resweber*] first stated: 'The traditional humanity of modern Anglo–American law forbids the infliction of unnecessary pain in the execution of the death sentence.' ... But the very next sentence varied the formulation; it referred to the '[p]rohibition against the wanton infliction of pain.'" Rather than turning to *Resweber* (or *Kemmler* or *Wilkerson*) as existing precedent, she believes the Court should develop an alternative guide.

Justice Ginsburg was also concerned with issues pertaining to risks of error—a common theme that *Resweber* addressed but never clearly or adequately resolved. Therefore, in Ginsburg's view, *Baze* should have been vacated and remanded with instructions to consider whether Kentucky's omission of safeguards used by other states "poses an untoward, readily avoidable risk of inflicting severe and unnecessary pain." She recommended a balancing approach in which the Court would weigh the degree of risk associated with an execution method, the magnitude of pain associated with that risk, and the availability of alternatives. Such an approach reasonably complies with the kinds of legal, medical, and technical problems that execution methods challenges have recently raised.

In sum, *Baze* exemplifies a modern decision that relies heavily on *Resweber*, in various ways, none of which (besides Justice Ginsburg's dissent) satisfies the doctrinal needs of a post-incorporation world accompanied by massive changes in criminal case law and standards. As Justice Ginsburg notes, in light of past precedent, the Eighth Amendment must comport with " 'evolving standards of decency that mark the progress of a maturing society.' " By sharp contrast, the "society" surrounding *Resweber*—and Willie Francis—did not represent progress either legally or socially. Thus, in *Baze*, there was needless regression to a point in sociolegal history not worth reviving. The Court now has opportunities to create a more advanced and just Eighth Amendment standard.

C. Willie's Final Words

On May 24, 1947, *The Shreveport Sun* published a letter Willie wrote just a day before he was executed; in it, Willie says goodbye and cautions the public about what can happen if a person commits a crime.[83] Yet, the warnings about law-breaking and punishment stopped with Willie; those in charge of the criminal justice system offered no comparable notice to *Shreveport Sun* readers that they could be convicted for a crime they may never have committed, particularly if they had grossly inadequate counsel. Nor were the readers ever informed that they could get death for a crime that might never even be prosecuted if they were someone else. In his letter, Willie told people not to engage in evil acts, but no one alerted them to their potential legal fate simply because of who they were, evil or not.

While such warnings about the inequities of the present criminal justice system perhaps blare somewhat louder today, many still ignore them. And there are few cautionary concerns about the inadequacies of long past precedent such as *Resweber*. One value of telling a defendant's story is to alert legal actors so they avoid repeating the past. Willie in particular seemed to have this goal in mind. "To every one, my best farewell wishes I send," said Willie in his *Shreveport Sun* letter.[84] And then Willie completed the rhyme with words that could move in so many different directions: "[A]nd may none reach my dreadful end."[85]

---

[83] *See "Be Careful How Ye Spend Thy Days," Warned Willie Francis*, *supra* note 48.

[84] *Id.*

[85] *Id.*

**WILLIE FRANCIS'S REMAINING SIBLINGS and
OTHER FAMILY MEMBERS (April 1971)**

Courtesy of Joseph E. Davis, Jr.,
grand-nephew of Willie Francis

2

Carol S. Steiker

Furman v. Georgia: Not an End, But a Beginning

In the early morning hours of August 11, 1967, William Henry Furman broke into the home of William and Lanell Micke in Savannah, Georgia. Hearing a sound, William Micke went to investigate, but Furman ran away, slamming the kitchen door behind himself. Furman stated at trial that he tripped over a cord on the porch while backing away and accidentally discharged his gun;[1] in contrast, a Detective testified that Furman had told him that after slamming the door, he turned around and fired one shot before fleeing.[2] Whether or not the gun went off accidentally, it was clear that the single bullet that was fired passed through the closed, wooden door to strike William Micke in the chest, killing him. At trial, the jury was instructed that it could find Furman guilty of murder on a "felony murder" theory even if the shooting was accidental.[3] As for the sentencing decision, the jury was instructed that it was to choose between life in prison and death by electrocution "as the jury sees fit" and that it was not required to give "any reason for its action in fixing the punishment at life or death."[4] After deliberating on the combined questions of guilt and punishment for about an hour and a half (after an entire trial that lasted less than a single day), the jury convicted William Furman of murder and sentenced him to death.

The facts of Furman-the-defendant's crime and punishment perfectly encapsulate the nature of the challenge raised by *Furman*-the-Su-

---

[1] *See* Brief for Respondent at 8, citing Appendix at 54–55, Furman v. Georgia, 408 U.S. 238 (1972) (No. 69–5003).

[2] *See id.* at 5, citing Appendix at 47.

[3] Brief for Petitioner at 7, citing Appendix at 62–63, Furman v. Georgia, 408 U.S. 238 (1972) (No. 69–5003).

[4] *Id.* at 8, citing Appendix at 64.

preme-Court-case.[5] As stated by Furman's petition for certiorari, the question presented by his case was "Whether Georgia's practice of allowing capital trial juries absolute discretion to impose the death penalty, uncontrolled by standards or directions of any kind, violates the Due Process Clause of the Fourteenth Amendment?"[6] The lack of any "standards or directions" allowed capital juries—in Georgia and elsewhere—to select defendants for death who did not represent the worst offenders. A thwarted burglar who shot—quite possibly accidentally— toward a closed door while fleeing is hard to rank among the worst of the worst, those whose crimes call for society's ultimate penalty. The two other defendants whose cases were decided by the Supreme Court along with Furman's had not even taken a life: they were each convicted of rape, Lucious Jackson in Georgia, and Elmer Branch in Texas.[7] Yet, without any guidance from judges about how to make their decisions, capital sentencing juries could and did end up selecting for death a group of defendants whose death-worthy characteristics seemed random at best, and invidious at worst. (Furman, Jackson, and Branch were all black; their victims were all white.)

While the facts and the legal claim of *Furman* had a harmonious fit, the larger "meaning" or legacy of the case, when viewed through the lens of the following 35–plus years of legal developments and scholarly consideration, appears profoundly contradictory. Both in terms of what the *Furman* decision *did* (as a matter of practical consequences in the world) and in terms of what it *said* (as a matter of doctrine), little is as it might seem on the surface. As a matter of practical consequences, *Furman* abolished (temporarily) the death penalty in America and spared (permanently) hundreds of death row prisoners. But in the longer term, the political and legal backlash engendered by *Furman* led to a period of strong resurgence of capital punishment in law and practice in the United States. As a matter of legal doctrine, *Furman* has been depicted both by the Court and scholars as primarily a rejection of standardless capital sentencing discretion. But *Furman*'s more robust doctrinal legacies have been the vigorous protection of individualized capital sentencing and the categorical exemption of certain kinds of offenders from capital punishment—doctrines less procedurally focused than the regulation of sentencing discretion and even in tension with such regulation. In short, *Furman* has been a study in contradictions, leaving a complex legacy different from what was widely predicted at the

---

[5] Furman v. Georgia, 408 U.S. 238 (1972).

[6] Petition for Writ of Certiorari to the Supreme Court of Georgia, Furman v. Georgia (No. 69–5003). After McGautha v. California, 402 U.S. 183 (1971), was decided rejecting a Due Process challenge to standardless discretion, *Furman*'s claim was recast as an Eighth Amendment challenge to the imposition of "cruel and unusual punishment."

[7] *See* Jackson v. Georgia, 408 U.S. 238 (1972); Branch v. Texas, 408 U.S. 238 (1972).

time of its decision, and different as well from what many courts and scholars have portrayed over the years since 1972. This chapter will explore those contradictions and conclude—perhaps foolhardily—with another prediction of sorts. After exploring how *Furman* not only failed to end the death penalty, but rather began a period of great flourishing of the practice of capital punishment, I will suggest, perhaps quixotically, that *Furman* nonetheless may *also* have left a legacy—both doctrinal and institutional—that might usher in the beginning of the end of the death penalty in America.

I. What *Furman* Did

A. The Triumphant Story

Although the three cases decided together in *Furman* involved capital statutes from only two states, the momentous 5–4 decision declaring those statutes unconstitutional under the Eighth Amendment's ban on "cruel and unusual punishment" was widely understood to invalidate capital punishment throughout the United States. Fred Graham's article reporting the decision in the *New York Times* stated, under a front-page banner headline, that "the effect of the decision appeared to be to rule out executions under any capital punishment laws now in effect in this country."[8] Although no one had been executed in the United States in the previous five years (largely as a result of pre-*Furman* litigation strategy), there were approximately 600 inmates on death row at the time of the decision whose lives were spared, along with Furman, Jackson, and Branch.[9]

The decision was momentous not only because of its sweeping, nationwide effect, but also because it was the culmination of a long legal battle that had been waged for the better part of a decade. *Furman* was the antithesis of, say, *Gideon v. Wainwright*,[10] in which a *pro se* litigant

---

[8] Fred P. Graham, "Supreme Court, 5–4, Bars Death Penalty As It Is Imposed Under Present Statutes," N.Y. Times, June 30, 1972, at A1.

[9] It is interesting how difficult it is to get the precise number of those on death row at the time of the *Furman* decision. One of the Justices refers to "almost 600" condemned prisoners, 408 U.S. at 316 (Marshall, J., concurring), while another refers to "some 600" on death row in state and federal prisons. 408 U.S. at 417 (Powell, J., dissenting). The New York Times sub-heading on the day after the decision reads: "Court Spares 600." Writing one year later, Michael Meltsner, a member of Furman's litigation team in the Supreme Court, calls the number at 633, without citing a source. Michael Meltsner, *Cruel and Unusual: The Supreme Court and Capital Punishment* 293 (1973). More recently, legal journalist Joan Cheever describes her efforts to ascertain precisely the number of those spared in 1972 and reports that her research into parole records, newspaper accounts, law journal articles, books, and conversations with corrections officials led her to a final accounting of 589. Joan M. Cheever, *Back From the Dead* 274 n.2 (2006).

[10] 372 U.S. 335 (1963) (announcing a constitutional right to counsel for indigent defendants in all non-petty criminal cases).

with a hand-written petition happened to provide the catalyst for a path-breaking Supreme Court decision.[11] Rather, *Furman v. Georgia* was the carefully planned result of the legal strategy of a group of civil rights lawyers at the NAACP Legal Defense Fund (LDF), who worked in close association with lawyers from the ACLU. This coordinated cadre of lawyers made a strategic decision in the mid–1960's that the time was ripe to challenge the constitutionality of capital punishment wholesale—first on racial justice grounds, but as the strategy unfolded, also on other aspects of unfairness in its administration.[12] The lawyers' attention was captured by a 1963 dissent from denial of certiorari by Justice Arthur Goldberg during his first Term on the Court, who called upon the Court to take up the issue of the constitutionality of the death penalty for the crime of rape, suggesting that the Court should consider whether death was a disproportionate or unnecessarily cruel punishment in such cases, out of line with "evolving standards of decency that mark the progress of [our] maturing society."[13]

At the present moment, it is perhaps difficult to recapture the sense in which capital punishment could be viewed as primarily an issue of racial justice. Current critics of capital punishment tend to focus more on the problems of wrongful conviction of the innocent, inadequate counsel or procedures, and unacceptable cost, or on absolute moral or religious objections to the practice, than on the problem of racial discrimination (though this criticism has by no means disappeared). Two features of the 1960's, however, made capital punishment an obvious target for an organization like the NAACP LDF, which focused on issues of racial justice. First, capital punishment was still widely authorized, at least in the South, as a punishment for rape, and it was used almost exclusively as a punishment for the rape of a white woman by a black

---

[11] *See* Anthony Lewis, *Gideon's Trumpet* (1964) (describing Clarence Earl Gideon's legal odyssey).

[12] The best and most comprehensive account of LDF's strategy leading up to the *Furman* decision is Michael Meltsner's book, *see* Meltsner, *supra* note 9. Meltsner was a key player on the core LDF team from the beginning and wrote his account of the litigation leading up to *Furman* within a year of the decision. Other book-length treatments of the case include Leonard A. Stevens, *Death Penalty: The Case of Life vs. Death in the United States* (1978) and Burton H. Wolfe, *Pileup on Death Row* (1973).

[13] Rudolph v. Alabama, 375 U.S. 889, 890 (1963) (Goldberg, J., dissenting from denial of certiorari) (quoting Trop v. Dulles, 356 U.S. 86, 101 (1958)). Goldberg's law clerk on the *Rudolph* case was Alan Dershowitz, who worked on the detailed memorandum that Goldberg circulated to his brethren on the Court, urging them to grant review in six pending capital cases in order to decide in a comprehensive fashion whether and under what circumstances the death penalty was constitutional. Goldberg's dissent from denial of certiorari represented only a "shard" of this larger memorandum. *See* Meltsner, *supra* note 9, at 31.

man.[14] Second, the Warren Court's "criminal procedure revolution" of the 1960's—which brought the exclusionary rule to state courts, imposed *Miranda* warnings on police interrogations, and required counsel for most criminal defendants and juries for most criminal trials—was widely understood to be a response to the treatment of indigent and minority defendants in criminal cases, especially in the South, where the criminal justice process at times still justly earned the derisive description of "legal lynching." In this context, Justice Goldberg's suggestion that the Court should take up the issue of capital punishment, especially for the imposition of the crime of rape, was a clarion call to LDF.

The LDF lawyers' strategy was multi-faceted. In keeping with their civil rights orientation, they began collecting data on the impact of race in capital rape prosecutions with an eye toward raising a direct racial challenge. But the lawyers also targeted several other aspects of the way that capital punishment was commonly administered that seemed to raise serious fairness or Due Process concerns. First, when capital juries were selected, it was common to exclude not only jurors who flat out refused to consider the possibility of sentencing the defendant to death for religious or moral reasons, but also all jurors who expressed any conscientious scruples whatsoever about capital punishment. This weeding-out process, known as "death qualification," resulted in juries that were thought to be both more likely to convict the defendant of a crime and biased in favor of the use of capital punishment. Second, as in William Furman's own case, it was common for capital trials to be unitary affairs, where jurors were asked to decide on the defendant's guilt and punishment in a single proceeding. If a defendant sought to offer his own testimony or other evidence solely in order to seek mercy as to his punishment, he had to essentially admit his guilt and open the door to the admission of character evidence and prior convictions that would otherwise be inadmissible against him. Third, capital statutes were commonly exceedingly broad, authorizing death sentences not only for murder, but also for rape, kidnapping, armed robbery, and burglary, among other things. As Justice Goldberg's dissent from denial had suggested, perhaps capital punishment was simply excessive for most crimes other than murder. Finally, even if death was not constitutionally excessive punishment for any particular subset of offenses, capital jurors were typically given no direction about how to exercise their sentencing discretion among so broad a class of eligible defendants; instead, they

---

[14] Between 1930 and 1972, 89% of all of those executed for rape in the United States were black men convicted of raping white women. Marvin E. Wolfgang, "Racial Discrimination in the Death Sentence for Rape," in *Executions in America* 109, 113 (William J. Bowers, ed., 1974). In Georgia alone during that period, the percentage was even higher (58 out of 61). Marvin E. Wolfgang & Marc Riedel, *Rape, Race, and the Death Penalty in Georgia*, 45 Am. J. Orthopsychiatry 658, 663 (1975).

were instructed, as Furman's jury was, that the choice was to be according to their conscience or "as the jury sees fit." The combination of wide eligibility for capital punishment and standardless discretion in capital sentencing generated concerns about arbitrariness and discrimination in sentencing outcomes.

Having identified the key constitutional issues, LDF adopted a "moratorium" strategy, essentially seeking to raise all possible issues in all capital cases nationwide, so as to bring the already declining number of executions down to zero. Obviously, the small cadre of lawyers working at LDF in New York could not possibly handle every case, even with the assistance of the more far-flung ACLU, which at the time had 48 state affiliates. Consequently, the lawyers coordinating the moratorium strategy developed some leveraging techniques that allowed them to mount a nationwide attack on executions. First, they created "Last Aid Kits," which included drafts of "petitions for habeas corpus, applications for stays of execution, and legal briefs that put forth every significant constitutional argument against the death penalty."[15] These kits were disseminated to capital defense lawyers around the country so that "even an attorney totally unfamiliar with the Fund's legal strategy found himself able, upon minimum inspection, to present a court with substantial legal reasons for postponing an execution."[16] Second, LDF worked with ACLU lawyers in Florida and California, two of the biggest death penalty states, to bring federal class action litigation raising constitutional issues on behalf of all death row inmates in the state—a procedural move that when successful (Florida), earned a state-wide stay of executions when the class was certified and that even when unsuccessful (California), engendered further time-consuming litigation.[17] Third, LDF lawyers either directed or played a substantial role in the litigation of the constitutional issues in a series of important capital cases leading up to *Furman*.

The Supreme Court granted review in four cases raising key constitutional challenges to capital punishment in the four years leading up to *Furman*. In the first one decided by the Court, opponents of the death penalty won a startling and significant victory: in *Witherspoon v. Illinois*,[18] the Court accepted one of the main procedural challenges to capital punishment, ruling that a capital defendant's sentence could not stand when all jurors with any conscientious scruples against the death

---

[15] Meltsner, *supra* note 9, at 112.

[16] *Id.*

[17] *See id.* at 129–41.

[18] 391 U.S. 510 (1968).

penalty were disqualified from the sentencing jury.[19] This decision was greeted as a ruling of enormous consequence by death penalty supporters and opponents alike. Death penalty supporters worried that death sentences would become much harder to achieve, now that at least some opponents of capital punishment would sit on sentencing juries. Indeed, Justice Black in dissent suggested that the Court's ruling might "mak[e] it impossible for States to get juries that will enforce the death penalty."[20] Death penalty foes saw *Witherspoon* as a sign that the Court might open to even broader constitutional assaults on capital punishment. However, in two capital cases decided on the heels of *Witherspoon*— *Boykin v. Alabama*[21] and *Maxwell v. Bishop*[22]—the Court ducked the opportunity to address other major challenges to capital punishment (that it was disproportionate punishment under the Eighth Amendment for the crime of robbery in *Boykin*, and that racial disparities, unitary proceedings, and standardless discretion violated Equal Protection and Due Process under the Fourteenth Amendment in *Maxwell*), by ruling in favor of the capital defendants on other grounds. Finally, in *McGautha v. California*,[23] the Court directly addressed and rejected Due Process challenges to unitary guilt/punishment proceedings and to standardless discretion in capital sentencing. This apparently decisive 6–3 loss on two of its central constitutional challenges was a crushing blow to LDF, but hope was not dead for long. Less than two months later, apparently determined to put to rest the continuing questions swirling around the constitutionality of capital punishment, the Court granted certiorari in *Furman* and its companion cases to consider the petitioners' Eighth Amendment (as opposed to Due Process) challenges to their death sentences.

   Initially, the grant of certiorari included not only Furman, Jackson, and Branch's cases, but also a challenge by one Earnest Aikens from California, a three-time rapist and murderer. But shortly after the four *Furman* cases had been briefed and argued, the California Supreme Court rendered Aikens' pending federal constitutional challenge moot by

---

[19] The *Witherspoon* Court confined its ruling to the impact of overly broad "death qualification" on the impartiality of the sentencing jury, concluding that the data was "too tentative and fragmentary," *id.* at 517, to make the case that death-qualified trial juries were biased in favor of conviction. Eventually, the Court rejected the claim that "death qualification" of juries at the guilt phase violates the constitution, even accepting that the practice may render trial juries more conviction prone. *See* Lockhart v. McCree, 476 U.S. 162 (1986).

[20] *Witherspoon*, 391 U.S. at 533 (Black, J., dissenting).

[21] 395 U.S. 238 (1969).

[22] 398 U.S. 262 (1970).

[23] 402 U.S. 183 (1971).

abolishing capital punishment by a 6–1 vote under California's constitutional provision banning "cruel *or* unusual punishment" (in contrast to the federal constitution's Eighth Amendment ban on "cruel *and* unusual punishment").[24] The lawyer who won the California case was the same lawyer who had just argued *Furman*—Tony Amsterdam, the "authentic genius"[25] at the center of LDF's 9–year strategy to abolish capital punishment through constitutional litigation. The California's Court's decision cleared the way for *Furman* in more ways than one: it provided the example of a respected court squarely rejecting capital punishment on constitutional grounds; it cleared more than 100 defendants from death row, reducing the volume of inmates who would be affected by the Supreme Court's ruling; and it got rid of the most heinous of the cases on which the Supreme Court had granted review (a brutal rape/murder). To many, the California Supreme Court's momentous and widely reported decision was an omen that the end of the American death penalty was approaching.

Thus, when *Furman* was decided only a few months later, one can understand the jubilation, relief, and sense that history was being made that swept through LDF and the wider abolitionist community. Michael Meltsner describes the high emotion in LDF's offices the June morning the decision was announced by the Court—the tears, laughter, and embraces led one LDF lawyer to shout into a phone, "This place looks like we just landed a man on the moon."[26] Many believed that the Court's decision would mark the permanent end of the practice of capital punishment in the United States, a practice that its critics believed rightly belonged in the dustbin of history. The sense that *Furman* marked a final end point was articulated not only by abolitionist activists like LDF Director–Counsel Jack Greenberg (who issued a statement proclaiming "There will no longer be any more capital punishment in the United States"[27]), but also by sympathetic news media (such as the *Washington Post*, which editorialized "We trust that the death chambers will now be dismantled"[28]). Some of the *Furman* opinions (at least of the Justices in the majority) also reflected a sense of closure: Justice Marshall hailed the Court's decision as "a major milestone in the long road up from barbarism,"[29] while Justice White observed that capital punish-

---

[24] *See* People v. Anderson, 6 Cal.3d 628, 493 P.2d 880, 100 Cal. Rptr. 152 (1972).

[25] Edith M. Lederer, "Lawyer Who Won Death Penalty Case Rated 'Authentic Genius,'" Sheboygan Press, Feb. 19, 1972 at 12.

[26] Meltsner, *supra* note 9, at 290.

[27] *Id.* at 291.

[28] "Dismantling the Death Chambers," Washington Post, June 30, 1972, at A18.

[29] 408 U.S. at 371 (Marshall, J., concurring) (citation omitted).

ment had declined in use so substantially in the years leading up to the Court's decision that it "has for all practical purposes run its course."[30] Shortly after the Court issued its decision in *Furman*, Justice Douglas sent a handwritten note to Justice Brennan stating, "I hope 'total abolition' is what we accomplished."[31]

B.   The Counter–Story: Not an End, But a Beginning

Of course, looking back, it is clear that capital punishment in America had not remotely "run its course" or succumbed to "total abolition" in 1972. The "major milestone" of the Court's invalidation of the death penalty turned out to be, in words of an editorial written less than a year later, "one of the briefest vanishing acts, after one of the longest buildups, in jurisprudential history."[32] Signs of its transience were apparent from the moment *Furman* was decided. The same *New York Times* front page that trumpeted the news of the decision in a banner headline also contained an above-the-fold story entitled "Nixon Backs Death Penalty," which was soon followed by other news reports of wide support for the president's plan to ask Congress to reinstate the death penalty for a variety of federal crimes, including treason, hijacking, the bombing of public buildings, and the killing of law enforcement officers.[33] Dozens of state officials, including Governor Ronald Reagan of California (later President) and Georgia State Representative Sam Nunn, Jr. (later U.S. Senator), immediately decried the ruling and urged reinstatement of the death penalty. Outrage at the Court's decision was especially fierce in the South. Lt. Governor Lester Maddox of Georgia called the decision "a license for anarchy, rape, and murder," while Lt. Governor (at the time Acting Governor) Jere Beasley of Alabama declared that the Justices in the majority had "lost contact with the real world."[34]

Moreover, states across the country immediately swung into action to try to find ways to bring the death penalty back to life. The voters in California lost little time in amending their state constitution to override the California Supreme Court's decision; "Prop. 17" passed by a 2–1 margin in November of 1972.[35] But most of the action in the states was

---

[30] *Id.* at 313 (White, J., concurring).

[31] Note provided by Professor Michael Klarman from his on-going research on the *Furman* decision in the Justices' private papers; copy on file with author.

[32] "Revival of the Death Penalty," Austin American–Statesman, Mar. 24, 1973, at 4.

[33] *See, e.g.*, Franz Scholz, "Nixon's Stand on Death Penalty Reflects U.S. Opinion," Lowell Sun, Mar. 18, 1973, at 1.

[34] Morton Mintz, "Joy on Death Row; Praise, Scorn on Hill," Wash. Post, June 30, 1972, at A13.

[35] *See* John Eagan, "Voters' Death Penalty Mandate Ignored," Star–News, Dec. 14, 1972, at 17 (describing "Prop. 17," which declared that capital punishment was not

legislative. The day after *Furman* was decided, the chairs of the Georgia
Senate and House judiciary committees scheduled joint hearings to draft
new death penalty legislation.[36] During the state legislative sessions of
1973, the vast majority of states saw the introduction of bills to reinstate
capital punishment—including even states like Michigan, which had
abolished the death penalty more than a century earlier.[37] By 1976, 35
states had passed legislation reinstating capital punishment with new
statutory schemes designed to address the constitutional defects described in *Furman*. As Hugo Bedau's chapter on *Gregg v. Georgia*[38] and
its accompanying cases describes,[39] *Furman*'s temporary abolition was
replaced by only four years later by *Gregg*'s regimen of reinstatement
with continuing constitutional oversight, a regimen that governs to this
day.

Not only did *Furman* fail to enact more than an extremely ephemeral abolition of capital punishment, it inaugurated an era of enormous
resurgence in the use of capital punishment. Many acute observers in
the months and years immediately following *Furman* understood that
the Court's rejection of capital punishment would not likely prevail in
the long term. Just days after the decision, a New York Times "Week in
Review" article bore the headline, "Banned, But for How Long?"[40] One
month after the decision, criminal law professor Yale Kamisar wrote an
editorial opining that "the death penalty is badly battered, and almost
dead—but not so dead that the next Nixon appointee cannot breathe
some life back into it."[41] Less than a year later, another editorial writer
mused: "[W]ill the nation ever have an intelligible and rational policy
concerning the death penalty? Amazingly, the answer . . . may be in the
affirmative."[42] He went on to note that newly drafted reform proposals
"anticipate favorable action by the court."[43] But while the constitutional

---

precluded by the provision of the California constitution banning "cruel or unusual
punishment").

[36] B. Keith Crew, *Furman v. Georgia*, in Melvin I. Urofsky, ed., *The Public Debate Over
Controversial Supreme Court Decisions* 291, 295 (2005).

[37] *See* Meltsner, *supra* note 9, at 308.

[38] 428 U.S. 153 (1976).

[39] *See* Hugo Adam Bedau, "*Gregg v. Georgia* and Allied Cases: Protecting the Death
Penalty from Abolition."

[40] Lesley Oelsner, "Banned—But for How Long? Capital Punishment" N.Y. Times,
July 2, 1972, at E1.

[41] Yale Kamisar, "The Death Penalty: It's Not Dead Yet," L.A. Times, July 30, 1972.

[42] James Halley, *Confusing Policies on Death Penalty*, San Mateo Times, Mar. 19, 1973,
at 12.

[43] *Id.*

reinstatement of capital punishment in 1976 did not come as a surprise, few would have predicted in the early 1970's that by the end of the 1990's death row would number in the thousands rather than hundreds, and executions would reach almost 100 a year—the highest in nearly 50 years.[44]

Moreover, the early 1970's also inaugurated an era of sharp divergence between the United States and the rest of the Western industrialized world. In the post-World War II era leading up to *Furman*, the use of the death penalty in the United States did not seem strikingly different from its deployment in the rest of the West. Executions in the U.S. and most of its peer nations declined in the decades after the war, taking the biggest dive (along with public support for the practice) during the turbulent 1960's. In England, for example, the death penalty was provisionally abolished in 1965, and the abolition was made permanent in 1969. But as of 1972, still only a minority of European countries had completely abolished capital punishment. In the next few decades, as the practice of capital punishment in the United States revived and then soared, Europe led the industrialized West toward complete abolition of the practice. Countries like Canada, Spain, and France abolished the death penalty for murder in the late 1970's and early 1980's, while countries like the Netherlands, Denmark, and Sweden that had already abolished capital punishment for murder in the 19th or early 20th century abolished it for all crimes. Eventually, partly by conditioning membership in the European Union on abolition of capital punishment, Europe achieved virtually universal abolition of the death penalty for all crimes.

One might say that the appearance of *Furman* as the fulcrum or turning point of American capital practices is simply fortuitous, that *Furman* merely coincidentally marked the timing of a shift that would have occurred anyway rather than played a causal role in that shift. However, there are several good reasons to think that the Court's intervention in *Furman* did more than mark a misunderstanding of where the nation was heading in terms of capital punishment. Rather, the *Furman* decision itself and the continuing constitutional regulation of capital punishment that it engendered may well have helped to shore up the beleaguered practice of capital punishment—a conclusion that represents an ironic and cautionary twist to the familiar, triumphant story of a "landmark victory" in the Supreme Court.

What are the reasons for attributing to *Furman* this causal role? First, we should not underestimate the role of backlash against the

---

[44] Information on executions in the United States in the modern era is available at http://deathpenaltyinfo.org. Information on yearly execution totals from before 1976 (back to 1930) is available in Bureau of Justice Statistics, "Capital Punishment 1978," p. 16, Table 1, in Hugo Adam Bedau, ed., *The Death Penalty in America: Current Controversies* 11 (1997).

Court's intervention as a spark that ignited the flame of renewed passion for capital punishment. Perhaps the strongest evidence of backlash lies in two 1972 Gallup polls asking the same general question about support for capital punishment for murder—one taken a few months before the *Furman* decision and one taken a few months afterwards. The gap between those who favored the death penalty in this fairly abstract sense and those who opposed it (in both polls, more favored the practice than opposed it) changed from a difference of 8 percentage points to a difference of 25 percentage points.[45] In a matter of months! What had happened during those months? The only plausible explanation is that the Court's decision in *Furman* generated strong political backlash. To be sure, the opponents of the Court's decision had powerful material to work with. Defendants on death row who escaped execution in 1972 included scary cult killer Charles Manson, mass murderer of student nurses Richard Speck, and Sirhan Sirhan, who declared in open court that he had assassinated presidential hopeful Bobby Kennedy "with 20 years malice aforethought."[46] Combine these high profile cases with rising homicide rates, increased shootings of police officers, and a rash of airline hijackings (more than 300 worldwide between 1968–72), and it seems obvious in retrospect that *Furman* touched a nerve in an especially fearful time. Even committed abolitionists were taken aback at the intensity of the reaction to *Furman*. A spokesman for the ACLU's Washington legislative office ruefully observed early in 1973, "The move to reinstate the death penalty is bigger and faster than we had expected."[47]

Moreover, the backlash was strongest and most vitriolic in the South. Of those who spoke out against the Court's decision, none were more vehement than ardent segregationists like Senator James Eastland of Mississippi, Senator Herman Talmadge of Georgia, and Lt. Governor (and former Governor) Lester Maddox of Georgia. The ferocity of Southern outrage in response to *Furman* was likely fueled by the fact that the case and the entire issue of capital punishment had been championed by LDF, the same organization that had brought desegregation to an unwilling South through constitutional litigation. Both Eastland and Talmadge seemed to allude to the link between the Court's holdings on capital punishment and desegregation in their criticisms of *Furman*.

---

[45] *See* Robert M. Bohm, "American Death Penalty Opinion 1936–1986: A Critical Examination of the Gallup Polls," in Robert M. Bohm, ed., *The Death Penalty in America: Current Research* 113, 116 (1991) (finding 50% "for" to 42% "against" pre-*Furman*, and 57% to 32% post-*Furman*).

[46] Douglas Robinson, *Sirhan Plea to Die Is Denied by Court*, N.Y. Times, Mar. 1, 1969, at 1.

[47] David Mutch, *States Battle High Court for Death Penalty Revival*, Chronicle–Telegram, Jan. 26, 1973 at 3.

Talmadge declared, "Five of the nine members of the Supreme Court have once again amended by usurpation the Constitution. We have had too much of that already."[48] Eastland similarly accused the Court of "again legislating and destroying our system of government."[49] Even the origins of the cases themselves—two from Georgia and one from Texas— reinforced the perception that the Court's ruling was specifically targeted at the South (due to the fortuity of the *Aikens* case becoming moot after the decision of the California Supreme Court). Not coincidentally, it was only *after* the Court's intervention that a clearly discernible "death belt" emerged in the South (a play on the more commonly used "Bible belt"). In the earlier part of the 20th century, a number of big states outside of the South—notably California, New York, Pennsylvania, and Ohio—were major death penalty states conducting a substantial portion of the nation's executions. After *Furman*, when executions resumed again, they became much more highly concentrated in the South. The racial origins of the *Furman* litigation and the virulent Southern backlash that it inspired no doubt played a role in this development.

Second, *Furman* helped to enshrine the death penalty as a potent symbol in the politics of crime. By 1972, the politicization of crime policy (and of the constitutional regulation of crime policy by the Court) was nothing new. Richard Nixon ran his 1968 campaign for President on an aggressive "law and order" platform with the Warren Court's criminal procedure revolution, most notably the *Miranda* decision, squarely in his sights. What is not as obvious now as it was in 1972 is the breakdown of the *Furman* Court along the lines of presidential appointment. During his first Term in office, Richard Nixon was able to appoint four new Justices to the Court. The *Furman* decision was the first major criminal case with all four new appointees voting, and the 5–4 decision aligned the five non-Nixon appointees in the majority against the four dissenting Nixon appointees. Indeed, the sub-heading of the lead article announcing the *Furman* opinion in the *New York Times* read: "4 Justices Named by Nixon All Dissent in Historic Decision." The rising homicide and violent crime rates of the 1970's and 1980's assured the continuing success of "law and order" politics, but *Furman* helped to transform the death penalty into a powerful symbol within those politics.

It stands to reason that, *Furman* or no *Furman*, the death penalty would remain a highly charged issue in local and state elections, because local and state elected officials play such substantial roles in crime policy, death penalty prosecutions, and the exercise of the clemency power in capital cases. *Furman*'s enduring legacy, however, is its role in catapulting the issue into national presidential politics, despite the

---

[48] Crew, *supra* note 36, at 293 (citing the *Atlanta Journal*, June 29, 1972).

[49] Mintz, *supra* note 34.

insignificance of the contribution of the federal government to the national practice of capital punishment, which is overwhelmingly a state affair. Nixon, of course, played the issue for all it was worth, taking to the airwaves to defend his re-introduction of a federal death penalty and lambasting "soft-headed judges."[50] The role of capital punishment loomed largest the following decade in the 1988 presidential race between George H.W. Bush and Michael Dukakis. Many remember as a turning point in the race Dukakis' emotionless rejection of capital punishment in response to a question—during a televised debate—about how he would react if his wife, Kitty, were raped and murdered. Indeed, a 1988 presidential election exit poll revealed that more voters identified the death penalty as an issue that was "very important" to them in the presidential election than identified social security, health care, education, or the candidates' political party.[51] Capital punishment continued to be significant in the next presidential campaign, when then-Governor Bill Clinton, avoiding Dukakis' disastrous example, flew back to Arkansas from the campaign trail in 1992 to oversee the execution of a severely mentally disabled murderer.[52] George W. Bush called upon his experience as the Governor of Texas, the nation's death penalty powerhouse, in making the death penalty issue work for him against his Democratic rivals in the 2000 and 2004 elections, especially against John Kerry, who modified his anti-capital punishment stance in response to the 9/11 attacks.[53] Most recently, in the 2008 presidential race, candidates from both major parties lost no time in repudiating the Supreme Court's invalidation of the death penalty for offenders who rape but do not kill child victims.[54] Liberal law professor and strong Barack Obama supporter Laurence Tribe leapt to the defense of Obama's position in an Op–Ed in the *Wall Street Journal*.[55] Clearly, the death penalty's star has not yet waned in the realm of the symbolic politics of crime.

Finally, *Furman* has played a role in reinforcing capital punishment by injecting the Supreme Court and the constitution into the ongoing

---

[50] Meltsner, *supra* note 9, at 309.

[51] *See* Phoebe C. Ellsworth & Samuel R. Gross, *Hardening of the Attitudes: Americans' Views on the Death Penalty*, J. Soc. Issues, Summer 1994 at 19, 23 (citing ABC News exit poll of 23,000 voters in the 1988 presidential election in which George H.W. Bush overwhelmingly defeated Michael Dukakis).

[52] *See* Marshall Frady, *Death in Arkansas*, New Yorker, Feb. 22, 1993, at 105.

[53] *See* David M. Halbfinger, *Kerry's Shifts: Nuanced Ideas or Flip–Flops?*, N.Y. Times, Mar. 6, 2004.

[54] *See* Linda Greenhouse, *Supreme Court Rejects Death Penalty for Child Rape*, N.Y. Times, June 26, 2008.

[55] Laurence H. Tribe, *The Supreme Court Is Wrong on the Death Penalty*, Wall St. J., July 31, 2008, at A13.

regulation of capital punishment. Having failed to abolish capital punishment, *Furman* instead has been invoked, by legislatures and the Court alike, as establishing a blueprint for constitutional amelioration of problems in its administration. As I have explained elsewhere at much greater length (with my co-author and one of the editors of this volume, Jordan Steiker),[56] the Court's ongoing constitutional regulation of capital punishment has helped to legitimate the practice of capital punishment in the eyes of both participants and observers. The role of the Court as overseer of the administration of the death penalty, combined with the absence of meaningful regulation of the capital process, has led actors within the criminal justice system, as well as the public at large, to overestimate the extent to which capital verdicts are the product of a fair and rational process. As for institutional actors within the criminal justice system, we observed that the "aura of science and shared responsibility created by the Court's doctrine comforts actors within the system who have the discretion to bring capital charges, impose the death penalty, or commute a capital sentence."[57] As for the public at large, we worried that members of the public might presume "that the highly visible continuing involvement of the Supreme Court in regulating capital punishment insures—perhaps *over*-insures—against arbitrary or unjust executions."[58] We concluded "with gloomy irony" that "the Supreme Court's Eighth Amendment jurisprudence [inaugurated by *Furman*], originally promoted by self-consciously abolitionists litigators and advanced by reformist members of the Court, not only has failed to meet its purported goal of rationalizing the imposition of the death penalty, but also may have helped to stabilize and entrench the practice of capital punishment in the United States."[59]

II. What *Furman* Said

The Court's decision in *Furman* was not merely an event whose impact (on politics, public opinion, etc.) can be assessed and debated; it was also a source of legal doctrine whose meaning can be parsed. Here, too, contradiction—indeed, multiplicity—abounds. The task of assigning doctrinal meaning to the decision is complicated by the fact that there was no majority or even plurality opinion for the Court. Rather, each of the five Justices in the majority wrote his own opinion, and none of them joined any of the others' opinions. (Each of the four dissenters wrote his own opinion as well, though they also joined in each other's opinions to a

---

[56] Carol S. Steiker & Jordan M. Steiker, *Sober Second Thoughts: Reflections on Two Decades of Constitutional Regulation of Capital Punishment*, 109 Harv. L. Rev. 355 (1995).

[57] *Id.* at 360.

[58] *Id.*

[59] *Id.*

great extent.) Thus, the only part of the decision that constituted the "law" of the majority was a brief, *per curiam* opinion that stated simply, "The Court holds that the imposition and carrying out of the death penalty in these cases constitute cruel and unusual punishment in violation of the Eighth and Fourteenth Amendments."[60] In addition to being fractured, the *Furman* decision was very long—at 50,000 words and 232 pages, it was the longest decision in the Court's history.[61] Finally, the grounds on which the Justices in the majority based their decisions to invalidate the three death sentences before them varied profoundly. Let us consider the opinions (much more briefly than they appeared in U.S. Reports!) in turn.

A.   The Furman *Opinions*

Only two of the Justices in the majority—Brennan and Marshall—were prepared to hold capital punishment unconstitutional in all cases. In later years, Brennan and Marshall would frequently join each other's opinions in death penalty cases, continuing to insist that the imposition of the death penalty always violated the Eighth Amendment. But in *Furman* itself, each authored a solo opinion. The opinions of Brennan and Marshall together account for nearly half of the entire *Furman* decision, including dissents, and there is a substantial degree of overlap between them, in both style and substance. Justice Brennan's opinion began with a detailed consideration of the "cruel and unusual punishments" clause during the drafting of the Bill of Rights and its treatment in the Court's prior precedents outside of the death penalty context. From this survey, Brennan concluded that the foundation of the clause lay in the protection of "human dignity."[62] Acknowledging that it may be difficult to determine when a punishment fails to accord with a concept as amorphous as human dignity, Brennan adduced four principles that would enable courts to make such determinations: 1) the degree to which a punishment is severe or degrading; 2) the probability that a punishment is inflicted arbitrarily; 3) the rejection of a punishment by contemporary society; and 4) the extent to which a punishment fails to serve penal purposes more effectively than a less severe punishment. In an extended discussion, Brennan found that capital punishment is inconsistent with all four principles, in that it is "unusually" severe and

---

[60] 408 U.S. at 239–40.

[61] At least, this is what Woodward and Armstrong report in their blockbuster account of the Supreme Court, though they, oddly, count 243 pages, whereas I find only 232 in U.S. reports. *See* Bob Woodward & Scott Armstrong, *The Brethren: Inside the Supreme Court* 220 (1979). *Furman*'s asserted record was as short-lived as its abolition of capital punishment: it was broken in 1976 by the Court's campaign finance decision in Buckley v. Valeo, 424 U.S. 1 (1976), which, at 294 pages, exceeds *Furman*'s verbosity by 62 pages.

[62] *Id.* at 270 (Brennan, J. concurring).

degrading, there is a "strong" probability that it is inflicted arbitrarily, its rejection by contemporary society is "virtually total," and there is "no reason" to believe that it serves "any" penal purpose more effectively than the less severe punishment of imprisonment.[63]

Justice Marshall's concurrence, like Brennan's, sought to generate from the history of the "cruel and unusual punishments" clause a set of foundational principles. Like Brennan, Marshall offered four general factors to consider in determining whether a punishment is "cruel and unusual," factors that overlapped substantially with Brennan's four principles of human dignity: 1) the degree of physical pain and suffering inflicted; 2) the extent to which the punishment is new, or "previously unknown;"[64] 3) whether the punishment is excessive and serves no valid legislative purpose; and 4) whether "popular sentiment abhors it."[65] In assessing whether death is an excessive or unnecessary penalty, Marshall broke new ground, emphatically rejecting "retribution," which he equated with "retaliation" and "vengeance," as an "intolerable aspiration[] for a government in a free society."[66] Reasoning that capital punishment had not been proven to be a more effect deterrent than imprisonment, that capital punishment was not necessary to prevent recidivism, and that no other important state goals would be substantially advanced by maintaining the death penalty, Marshall concluded that capital punishment constituted "excessive" punishment under the Eighth Amendment.[67] In addition to being excessive, Marshall concluded that it was also "morally unacceptable to the people of the United States at this time in their history."[68] This argument, of course, ran into some difficulty, given the prevalence of capital statutes and public opinion polls showing substantial support for capital punishment. Marshall—in what might be viewed as a show of either breathtaking optimism or insufferable condescension—concluded that a substantial proportion of American citizens would find capital punishment to be "barbarously cruel" if only they were exposed "to all information presently available"[69] about its application and consequences.

Justice Douglas, the most senior member of the majority whose concurrence thus appears first, based his vote to vacate the defendants'

---

[63] *Id.* at 305.

[64] *Id.* at 331 (Marshall, J., concurring).

[65] *Id.* at 332.

[66] *Id.* at 343.

[67] *Id.* at 359.

[68] *Id.* at 360.

[69] *Id.* at 362.

death sentences not on the grounds of human dignity or the moral unacceptability of the death penalty, but rather on the grounds of inequality and discrimination in the administration of the penalty. He sought to forge a link between the Eighth Amendment's ban on "cruel and unusual punishments" and the Fourteenth Amendment's guarantee of "equal protection of the laws." Douglas asserted, "There is increasing recognition of the fact that the basic theme of equal protection is implicit in 'cruel and unusual' punishments."[70] Interestingly, the source cited by Douglas for this "increasing recognition" is a law review article co-authored by none other than former Justice Arthur Goldberg and his law clerk of the 1963 Term of Court, Alan Dershowitz—the architects of Goldberg's dissent from denial of certiorari in the *Rudolph* case that galvanized the LDF lawyers to take up capital punishment.[71] Douglas went on to survey available data that suggested that capital punishment was disproportionately imposed and carried out on offenders who were poor, young, ignorant, mentally impaired, or black. He then observed that Furman, Jackson, and Branch were all young, black men with white victims and that evidence suggested that Furman and Branch were either mentally deficient or mentally ill or both, though Douglas acknowledged that the evidence was insufficient to prove that the defendants were singled out on the basis of their race. Nonetheless, Douglas argued that history had demonstrated that uncontrolled discretion in punishment was linked to vengeance against unpopular individuals and groups, and he contended that limitations on "cruel and unusual punishments" were created to respond to this evil. Because the administration of the American death penalty was—in Douglas' colorful phrase—"pregnant with discrimination,"[72] he concluded that it was incompatible with the Eighth Amendment. Douglas specifically withheld judgment on the question whether a mandatory (as opposed to discretionary) death penalty would comport with the Eighth Amendment.

Justices Stewart and White were the two Justices in the majority whose votes changed in the single year separating *McGautha* and *Furman*. In the Court's 1971 decision in *McGautha*, both Stewart and White had voted with the 6–3 majority *rejecting* a challenge to standardless capital sentencing discretion on Due Process grounds. In *Furman*, they both apparently changed their minds, accepting exactly the same challenge under the "cruel and unusual punishments" clause of the Eighth Amendment. Both Justices were careful to say in *Furman* that they were

---

[70] *Id.* at 249 & n.12 (Douglas, J., concurring).

[71] *See* Arthur J. Goldberg & Alan M. Dershowitz, *Declaring the Death Penalty Unconstitutional*, 83 Harv. L. Rev. 1773 (1970). Brennan also cited Goldberg & Dershowitz in his opinion. See 408 U.S. at 268, 275 n.17 (Brennan, J., concurring).

[72] 408 U.S. at 27 (Douglas, J., concurring).

not ruling on the constitutionality of capital punishment in all circumstances; rather, it was the discretionary way in which the penalty was
currently administered that rendered it unconstitutional. Stewart emphasized how "wantonly and freakishly"[73] the uniquely severe punishment of death appeared to be imposed, describing the petitioners as
being among "a capriciously selected random handful"[74] out of a wide
group of offenders eligible for capital punishment. Under these circumstances, Stewart concluded—in the most memorable and widely quoted
line of the *Furman* decisions—that the death penalty as administered in
the cases before the Court was "cruel and unusual in the same way that
being struck by lightning is cruel and unusual."[75]

So Justice White articulated similar concerns, but grounded them in
what he took to be a deficit of "legislative will."[76] In the absence of a
mandatory death penalty, White reasoned, the unwillingness of juries to
impose capital punishment could not be said to frustrate legislative will.
And once a certain level of infrequency of the imposition of the death
penalty is reached, capital punishment is simply no longer able to serve
as "a credible deterrent or measurably to contribute to any other end of
punishment in the criminal justice system."[77] Without a legislative
mandate, and with negligible returns as a matter of penal policy, the
death penalty amounted to "the pointless and needless extinction of life
with only marginal contributions to any discernible social or public
purposes."[78]

So, 136 pages and five opinions later, it became clear that only two
Justices—Brennan and Marshall—would hold that capital punishment
was *per se* unconstitutionally "cruel and unusual," no matter how
carefully it was administered. The other three Justices in the majority
focused their objections on the way that capital punishment was presently administered, and all three specifically reserved the question whether
a "mandatory" death penalty could survive constitutional scrutiny. In
case anyone missed this possible "fix" to the *Furman* problem, Chief
Justice Burger in dissent invited state legislatures and Congress to make
the "significant statutory changes" that would be necessary to satisfy
the Court's majority.[79] But he warned of the problems that a mandatory

---

[73] *Id.* at 310.

[74] *Id.* at 309–10.

[75] *Id.* at 309.

[76] *Id.* at 311 (White, J., concurring).

[77] *Id.* at 311 (White, J., concurring).

[78] *Id.* at 312.

[79] *Id.* at 400 (Burger, C.J., dissenting).

death penalty would create, lamenting darkly, "If this is the only alternative that the legislatures can safely pursue under today's ruling, I would have preferred that the Court opt for total abolition."[80]

Quite apart from these concerns about the advisability and constitutionality of a mandatory death penalty, the prime focus of the dissenters' ire was the Court's usurpation of the proper role of the legislature. As the Chief Justice urged, "[I]t is essential to our role as a court that we not seize upon the enigmatic character of the guarantee [against cruel and unusual punishment] as an invitation to enact our personal predilections into law."[81] In the view of the dissenters, the determination of whether capital punishment serves valid penological ends, or serves such ends any more effectively than less severe punishment, is a determination reserved for legislatures, not courts. As for concerns about unfairness in the administration of the penalty, the dissenters maintained that the Eighth Amendment's ban was a substantive rather than a procedural one: "The Amendment is not concerned with the process by which a State determines that a particular punishment is to be imposed in a particular case."[82] And as for the petitioners' specific objections to standardless capital sentencing discretion, the dissenters noted that this challenge had been argued and resolved the previous year in *McGautha*, which deserved respect under the doctrine of *stare decisis*.[83] Justice Powell's and Justice Rehnquist's dissents emphasized similar themes, especially the need for "judicial self-restraint,"[84] and each of their opinions was joined by all four dissenters, as was Burger's.

Justice Blackmun's dissent, written for himself alone, also maintained that the decision was a legislative rather than a judicial one, but it took on a more personal cast and anguished tone. Blackmun described the "excruciating agony of the spirit" that he suffered in facing the clash between his personal beliefs about capital punishment and his views about the limits of his role as a judge. Wrote Blackmun, "I yield to no one in the depth my distaste, antipathy, and, indeed, abhorrence, for the death penalty.... For me, it violates childhood's training and life's experiences...."[85] Yet, he concluded, "Although personally I may rejoice at the Court's result, I find it difficult to accept or to justify as a matter of history, of law, or of constitutional pronouncement. I fear the Court

---

[80] *Id.* at 401.

[81] *Id.* at 376.

[82] *Id.* at 397.

[83] *Id.* at 408.

[84] *Id.* at 431, 433 (Powell, J., dissenting); *id.* at 470 (Rehnquist, J., dissenting).

[85] *Id.* at 405 (Blackmun, J., dissenting).

has overstepped.''[86] In light of his agony of spirit, it is perhaps not surprising that Blackmun, alone among the *Furman* dissenters,[87] officially repudiated the view that he espoused in 1972. More than two decades later (and shortly before the end of his career on the Court), Blackmun joined the ranks of Brennan and Marshall by proclaiming that "the death penalty experiment has failed"[88] and announcing that he would no longer vote to sustain executions: "I no longer shall tinker with the machinery of death."[89]

B.   *What* Furman *Meant, Take One: Confusion*

Early on, there was remarkable agreement about what *Furman* meant: nobody knew, and nobody thought anyone else knew, either. Chief Justice Burger's charge that the Court's decision left capital punishment "in an uncertain limbo"[90] was widely repeated in the press. Michael Meltsner, writing in 1973, warned that predicting how the Supreme Court would respond "in 1975 or 1977" to mandatory capital sentencing laws that were already being enacted "is as risky as forecasting the weather for those years."[91] Another observer in the same year editorialized, "Although capital punishment has been hotly debated in America since the founding of the Republic, its legal status is now more confused and uncertain than ever before. No one can foresee what the outcome is going to be."[92] Widespread uncertainty about what *Furman* meant prompted *Congressional Digest* to devote its entire January 1973 issue to the topic, explaining: "Confusion resulting from the Supreme Court's ruling has resulted in a variety of responses among the States to different—and frequently conflicting—interpretations of how the decision affects their capital punishment laws."[93] This confusion, combined with the steady drumbeat to reinstate capital punishment in Congress and the vast majority of states, virtually ensured that the Supreme Court would have to revisit the issue—and soon.

---

[86] *Id.* at 414.

[87] Justice Powell, too, eventually came to repudiate the death penalty—but only after his retirement from the Court, in an interview for his official biography. *See* David Von Drehle, "Retired Justice Changes Stand on Death Penalty: Powell Is Said to Favor Ending Executions," Wash. Post, June 10, 1994 (based on interview with John C. Jeffries, Jr., Powell's official biographer).

[88] Callins v. Collins, 510 U.S. 1141, 1145 (1994).

[89] *Id.* at 1130.

[90] 408 U.S. at 403 (Burger, C.J., dissenting).

[91] Meltsner, *supra* note 9, at 310.

[92] Clayton Fritchey, *Confusion in Capital Punishment*, Fresno Bee Republican, Dec. 8, 1973, at A9.

[93] Crew, *supra* note 36, at 293 (quoting *Congressional Digest*, January 1973).

C. What Furman *Meant, Take Two: The Rejection of Standardless Capital Sentencing Discretion*

In 1976, the Court decided *Gregg v. Georgia* and its four accompanying cases,[94] addressing the constitutionality of five of the 35 new death penalty schemes passed since *Furman*. While the Court struck down mandatory capital statutes[95] as incompatible with the Eighth Amendment on the ground that individualized sentencing is a constitutional essential in capital cases, the Court nonetheless firmly rejected the Brennan/Marshall view that the Eighth Amendment precluded all use of the death penalty. Rather, the Court upheld non-mandatory capital sentencing schemes that offered "guided discretion" through consideration of aggravating and mitigating factors or specific questions, combined with other procedural checks on unfettered sentencing discretion.[96] The vote upholding the new "guided discretion" death penalty schemes was 7–2, reflecting both Justice Douglas' replacement on the Court by Justice Stevens, and Justices Stewart and White's joining of the majority for reinstatement of capital punishment. In this set of decisions, which is the subject of another chapter of this volume,[97] the plurality gave pride of place to Stewart and White's opinions in *Furman*. In *Gregg*, the plurality began its analysis in the central analytical section ("We now consider whether Georgia may impose the death penalty on the petitioner in this case"[98]) by quoting extensively from the Stewart and White opinions. The *Gregg* plurality justified this focus by noting that other Justices in the *Furman* majority agreed with Stewart and White's constitutional concerns and by quoting Chief Justice Burger's *Furman* dissent to the effect that Stewart and White had expressed "the decisive grievance" in the case.[99] In this way, Stewart and White's particular procedural concerns about standardless discretion became enshrined as "what *Furman* meant." Stewart's quotable "struck by lightning" line helped, too, to frame that idea as the focus of the case. My own framing of the issue posed by *Furman* in the introduction to this essay reflects this standard account of what *Furman* was "about."

---

[94] Gregg v. Georgia, 428 U.S. 153 (1976); Proffitt v. Florida, 428 U.S. 242 (1976); Jurek v. Texas, 428 U.S. 262 (1976); Woodson v. North Carolina, 428 U.S. 280 (1976); and Roberts v. Louisiana, 428 U.S. 325 (1976).

[95] Two of the five statutes reviewed—those from North Carolina and Louisiana—involved mandatory capital statutes.

[96] The statutes from Georgia, Florida, and Texas all were upheld as providing sufficient "guided discretion" to capital sentencers.

[97] *See* Hugo Adam Bedau, "*Gregg v. Georgia* and Allied Cases: Protecting the Death Penalty from Abolition."

[98] *Gregg*, 428 U.S. at 187 (opinion of Stewart, Powell, and Stevens, JJ.).

[99] *Id.* at 188 n.36 (quoting *Furman*, 408 U.S. at 398–99 (Burger, C.J., dissenting)).

The standard account of *Furman* has sources of support beyond the *Gregg* plurality's framing of the case. First, there is the framing of the issue by the litigants themselves. The "Question Presented" by LDF in *Furman's* petition for certiorari to the Court challenged the constitutionality of the "absolute discretion" of capital trial juries to impose death "uncontrolled by standards or directions of any kind."[100] Moreover, during oral argument in the case, Tony Amsterdam focused on the disjunction between the "hundreds and hundreds and hundreds"[101] of people eligible for the death penalty and the "very, very few"[102] people who actually received it. In addition, the *Furman* majority consisted of the three Justices who had dissented in *McGautha* the previous year, plus Stewart and White, who changed their views about the constitutionality of standardless capital sentencing discretion between *McGautha* and *Furman*. In light of this remarkable about-face, it seems reasonable to consider their views the "decisive" ones in the case.[103] Finally, later cases built on the "standardless discretion" concern of *Furman* and *Gregg*, striking down aggravating factors that failed to provide adequate guidance to sentencing juries. For example, only a few years after the Court upheld Georgia's new "guided discretion" statute in *Gregg*, the Court struck down one of Georgia's statutory aggravating factors because it failed to provide sufficient guidance to sentencing juries.[104] Aggravator (b)(7) asked the jury to determine whether the offense was "outrageously or wantonly vile, horrible or inhuman in that it involved torture, depravity of mind, or an aggravated battery to the victim." The Court concluded that this aggravator was too "broad and vague" to give

---

[100] Petition for Writ of Certiorari to the Supreme Court of Georgia, Furman v. Georgia (No. 69–5003).

[101] Transcript of Oral Argument, Furman v. Georgia (No. 69–5003), Jan. 17, 1972, at 859.

[102] *Id.* at 862.

[103] It remains mysterious exactly why Stewart and White changed their votes between *McGautha* and *Furman*. Blackmun speculates that the Court was influenced by the intervening action of the California Supreme Court, striking down capital punishment by a lopsided 6–1 vote based on a state provision similar to the federal Eighth Amendment. *See Furman*, 408 U.S. at 411 (Blackmun, J., dissenting) ("The Court, in my view, is somewhat propelled toward its result by the interim decision of the California Supreme Court, with one justice dissenting."). Or it may be that Amsterdam's impressive advocacy in *Furman* won the day (LDF had filed as *amicus* rather than served as counsel of record in *McGautha*). According to Woodward and Armstrong, Justice White "told his clerks that Amsterdam's oral argument had been possibly the best he had ever heard." Woodward & Armstrong, *supra* note 61, at 209. Once White changed his vote, Stewart did not want to be the single vote in favor of capital punishment that would send the hundreds waiting on death row to the execution chamber. *See id.* ("If [the Court's vote] came out 5 to 4, Stewart decided, he would have to vote to strike the laws.").

[104] *See* Godfrey v. Georgia, 446 U.S. 420 (1980).

adequate guidance to the sentencing jury.[105] Thus, a superficial reading of *Furman*, *Gregg*, and some of the early post-*Gregg* cases offers support for what has become the "standard account" of *Furman*'s essential mandate—a rejection of standardless capital sentencing discretion.

D. What Furman *Meant, Take Three: The Importance of Individualized Capital Sentencing and Proportionality*

Despite the reasonableness of the standard account of *Furman* in the years immediately following *Gregg* and the apotheosis of "guided discretion," the account lost its explanatory power as the Court elaborated its Eighth Amendment capital jurisprudence over the next two decades. Looking back from the vantage point of the 21st century, the major innovations wrought by the inauguration of constitutional regulation of capital punishment in *Furman* and *Gregg* have less to do with the guiding of discretion and owe less to the views of Stewart and White than the standard account allows. The two most profound changes to the practice of capital punishment that have ensued under the Eighth Amendment have been 1) the absolute protection of individualized capital sentencing, and 2) the more recent proliferation of categorical exemptions of groups of offenders and offenses from execution under an analysis focused on the disproportionality or excessiveness of the death penalty in certain circumstances. These developments are either in conflict with the goal of limiting discretion or only tangentially related to it. Moreover, the intellectual and doctrinal origins of these developments lie in the *Furman* opinions of Justices Brennan and Marshall, despite the Court's rejection of their abolitionist stance.

First, consider the Court's mandate regarding individualized sentencing. In striking down mandatory capital sentencing in 1976, a plurality of the Court recognized a right of capital defendants to be treated "as uniquely individual human beings" rather than "as members of a faceless, undifferentiated mass."[106] The Court went on to give this right expansive protection, eventually striking down aspects of the other two capital statutes that it had provisionally upheld in 1976. Florida's statute, upheld in *Proffitt*, was invalidated as applied in *Hitchcock v. Dugger*[107] on the ground that consideration of mitigating circumstances was limited only to those enumerated in the statute. Texas's statute, upheld in *Jurek*, was invalidated as applied in *Penry v. Lynaugh*[108] on the ground that the specific statutory questions posed to the sentencing jury

---

[105] *Id.* at 423.

[106] Woodson v. North Carolina, 428 U.S. 280, 304 (1976) (opinion of Stewart, Powell, and Stevens, JJ.).

[107] 481 U.S. 393 (1987).

[108] 492 U.S. 302 (1989).

(whether the defendant had killed deliberately and whether the defendant would pose a danger in the future) did not allow it to consider the full range of the petitioner's mitigating evidence. Moreover, even though Oklahoma's statute, unlike those of Florida and Texas, permitted consideration of all relevant mitigating evidence, the Court overturned a capital sentence imposed under it when the trial judge refused to treat as relevant the defendant's evidence of his mental and emotional problems and troubled family history.[109]

These cases and their many progeny dwarf, both in number and in impact, the cases that deal with guiding discretion. While the Court's guided discretion cases, like *Godfrey*, invalidated "broad and vague" aggravating factors that rendered defendants eligible for the death penalty, the Court never restricted the number of aggravating factors that statutes could contain or the proportion of convicted murderers who could be rendered eligible for capital punishment. As a result, aggravating factors have proliferated,[110] and the number of defendants eligible for the death penalty under these new statutes has not changed dramatically from pre-*Furman* days.[111] In contrast, the requirement of individualized sentencing has had a much greater impact on sentencing practices, giving rise to a cottage industry of "mitigation specialists"[112] and engendering a line of cases holding capital defense lawyers constitutionally "ineffective" for failing to pursue and present evidence in mitigation during capital sentencing proceedings.[113]

The Court's cases on individualized sentencing not only outweigh the Court's cases on guided discretion, but the former also stand in significant tension with the latter. To require that capital sentencers be open to any and all reasons *not* to impose a sentence seems indistinguishable from allowing sentencers *to* impose death sentences for any

[109] Eddings v. Oklahoma, 455 U.S. 104 (1982).

[110] *See* Jonathan Simon & Chris Spaulding, "Tokens of Our Esteem: Aggravating Factors in the Era of Deregulated Death Penalties," in Austin Sarat, ed., *The Killing State: Capital Punishment in Law, Politics and Culture* (1999).

[111] *See, e.g.,* David C. Baldus, George Woodworth & Charles A. Pulaski, Jr., *Equal Justice and the Death Penalty: A Legal and Empirical Analysis* 102 (1990) (concluding that over 90% of persons sentenced to death before *Furman* would also be eligible for capital punishment under the post-*Furman* statute).

[112] *See* Carol S. Steiker, "Darrow's Defense of Leopold and Loeb: The Seminal Sentencing of the Century," in Michael E. Tigar & Angela J. Davis, eds., *Trial Stories* 117, 142 ("Not only is there a professional *term* for the process of deep investigation into a defendant's background, there is a specialized professional *role* in capital trials for a person who conducts a social history and develops mitigating evidence—the 'mitigation specialist.'").

[113] *See* Williams v. Taylor, 529 U.S. 362 (2000); Wiggins v. Smith, 539 U.S. 510 (2003), and Rompilla v. Beard, 545 U.S. 374 (2005).

and all reasons. As LDF observed in its amicus brief in *McGautha*, " 'Kill him if you want' and 'Kill him, but you may spare him if you want' mean the same thing in any man's language."[114] As Justice Scalia even more pungently observed, "To acknowledge that 'there is perhaps an inherent tension' [between the Court's twin requirements of individualized sentencing and guided discretion] is rather like saying that there was perhaps an inherent tension between the Allies and the Axis powers during World War II. . . . They cannot be reconciled."[115]

Justice Scalia traces the requirement of guided discretion back to *Furman* and locates the origins of the requirement of individualized sentencing four years later in *Woodson*, one of the two 1976 cases in which the Supreme Court invalidated *mandatory* capital statutes. This chronology, while it helps to frame the binary opposition that Scalia decries, is inaccurate. In fact, *Woodson*'s rejection of mandatory sentencing finds its roots in the conception of "human dignity" fleshed out at length in Justice Brennan's opinion in *Furman*. As Justice Brennan described the meaning of human dignity, "The State, even as it punishes must treat its members with respect for their intrinsic worth as human beings."[116] To be sure, Justice Brennan had a more categorical view of the implications of this general principle, but *Woodson*'s requirement that the sentencing process treat defendants as "uniquely individual human beings" strongly echoes Brennan's conception of human dignity. In light of the power of *Furman*'s legacy in terms of individualized sentencing, one scholar has dismissed the idea that *Furman*'s central requirement was the promotion of consistency in sentencing as a "mythical mandate."[117] One needn't go so far as to consign the standard view to the realm of myth in order to re-calibrate the relative significance of the competing strands of doctrine that have evolved from *Furman*.

The second of the two most significant developments to flow from *Furman* has been the Court's categorical rejection of capital punishment for certain offenses and groups of offenders. Only one year after reinstating capital punishment in *Gregg*, the Court directly addressed the issue raised by Justice Goldberg in 1963 and struck down the death penalty as constitutionally excessive punishment for the crime of rape, at least when the victim was an adult woman. In this decision, *Coker v. Geor-*

---

114 Brief Amici Curiae of the NAACP Legal Defense and Educ. Fund, Inc. and the National Office for the Rights of the Indigent at 69, McGautha v. California, 402 U.S. 183 (1971) (No. 71–203).

115 Walton v. Arizona, 497 U.S. 639, 664 (1990) (Scalia, J., concurring) (citation omitted).

116 *Furman*, 408 U.S. at 270 (Brennan, J., concurring).

117 *See* Scott W. Howe, Furman's *Mythical Mandate*, 40 U. Mich. J. L. Ref. 435 (2007).

gia,[118] the Court engendered a line of analysis that it has used with increasing vigor in recent years to limit the ambit of the death penalty. The *Coker* Court did not focus upon—or even mention—the racially discriminatory application of the death penalty for rape; rather, it addressed the excessiveness of the punishment of death to the crime of rape in general, finding that the use of the death penalty in such circumstances made no measurable contribution to the goals of capital punishment and that the death penalty was grossly disproportionate to the underlying crime. In making the proportionality determination, the Court looked to "objective evidence" [119]of society's evolving views in the decisions of legislatures and sentencing juries. Noting that Georgia was the only state that still authorized the death penalty for the rape of an adult woman, the Court discerned a societal consensus that death was a disproportionate punishment for such crimes. Moreover, this consensus was confirmed by the Court's "own judgment"[120] that death was an excessive punishment for someone who had not deliberately taken a life.

This "excessiveness" analysis, like the Court's requirement of individualized sentencing, has its roots in the *Furman* opinions—but these roots are far deeper and more developed in the opinions of Justices Brennan and Marshall than in those of Justices Stewart and White. Three of Justice Brennan's four "principles" of human dignity are discernible in the methodology of the *Coker* Court—concern with the "severity" of punishment, with its "rejection by contemporary society," and with the degree to which it serves "penal purposes." Justice Marshall emphasized similar concerns; indeed he focused a large part of his dissent on capital punishment's "excessiveness" in general, focusing on its failure to serve valid legislative purposes. Moreover, Justice Marshall added to this excessiveness analysis a consideration of evolving societal consensus, concluding that "popular sentiment abhors" the death penalty. To be sure, Justice White also inquired whether capital punishment could be said to measurably advance penal purposes, but his inquiry was a procedural rather than a substantive one, focusing on the rarity of application of the death penalty. Only Brennan and Marshall looked to penal purposes and social consensus as benchmarks for the constitutionality of capital punishment as a *substantive* rather than procedural matter.

The *Coker* Court's proportionality limit on the use of a capital punishment has proven to be an increasingly strong constraining force on the use of the death penalty. In the first dozen years after *Coker*, the proportionality principle appeared to be a fairly weak constraint. Initial-

---

[118] 433 U.S. 584 (1977).

[119] *Id.* at 593.

[120] *Id.* at 597.

ly, the Court used its *Coker* analysis to strike down capital punishment for felony murderers who did not themselves kill, attempt to kill or intend to kill, in a case involving a getaway car driver who was not even present when his co-defendants entered a home during a robbery and ended up killing the occupants.[121] This precedent, however, did not last long. Just a few years later, the Court modified its holding to allow capital punishment for "non-triggermen" in felony murders, as long as the defendant played a substantial role in the underlying felony and evinced a mental state of reckless indifference toward human life.[122] Moreover, in 1989, the Court rejected two significant challenges to the proportionality of the death penalty across the United States—the execution of juvenile offenders and of offenders with mental retardation.[123] In neither of these cases did the Court discern an objective societal consensus against the practice or resort to its "own judgment" to preclude the use of capital punishment for such offenders.

These 1989 decisions appeared to signal the demise of the Court's capital proportionality principle. Then, in a controversial series of opinions in 2002, 2005, and 2008, the Court breathed new life into its proportionality constraint, invalidating capital punishment for offenders with mental retardation,[124] for juvenile offenders under the age of 18,[125] and for offenders convicted of raping, but not killing, children (and by extension, offenders charged with ordinary crimes short of homicide).[126] This movement was made possible by Justice Kennedy's consistent support for more restrictive constitutional regulation of capital punishment; indeed, Kennedy authored the majority opinion in two of the three recent proportionality cases, both of which were 5–4 votes. In these recent cases, the mechanisms by which the Court's proportionality test became more demanding were both a widening of the sources of evidence of objective societal "consensus" and the Court's greater willingness to rely upon its "own judgment" to bolster less-than-overwhelming demon-

---

[121] *See* Enmund v. Florida, 458 U.S. 782 (1982).

[122] *See* Tison v. Arizona, 481 U.S. 137 (1987).

[123] *See* Stanford v. Kentucky, 492 U.S. 361 (1989); Penry v. Lynaugh, 492 U.S. 302 (1989). Two years prior to *Stanford*, in Thompson v. Oklahoma, 487 U.S. 815 (1988), a majority of the Court invalidated a 15–year-old offender's death sentence, but stopped short of finding a consensus against the practice of executing 15–year-old juveniles (only four Justices discerned such a consensus). Justice O'Connor added her fifth vote to set aside the sentence on the ground that there was enough evidence of a societal rejection of the practice of executing such youthful offenders that statutes, like Oklahoma's, that *failed to state a minimum age* for execution were unconstitutional because they failed to reflect that the question had been given serious consideration and passed upon by the legislature.

[124] *See* Atkins v. Virginia, 536 U.S. 304 (2002).

[125] *See* Roper v. Simmons, 543 U.S. 551 (2005).

[126] *See* Kennedy v. Louisiana, 128 S.Ct. 2641 (2008).

strations of emerging consensus. As for sources of evidence, the Court in
Coker had suggested that objective evidence of consensus lay solely in
legislative judgments and jury verdicts. In exempting offenders with
mental retardation from the death penalty in 2002, however, the Court
expanded the range of relevant evidence of societal consensus by referring, in a tentative footnote, to the views of expert organizations (for
example, professional organizations of psychological experts), religious
leaders, and the world community, as well as public opinion polling data.
Three years later, in exempting juvenile offenders from the death penalty, the Court moved its reference to the views of the world community
from a footnote to the text and offered a ringing defense of the relevance
of the views and practices of peer democracies. As for its own judgment,
all three recent opinions contained extended discussions of how the goals
of retribution and deterrence were not served (or were actually undermined) by the execution of offenders with mental retardation, juvenile
offenders, or offenders convicted of the rape of children.

These three recent decisions constitute a significant expansion on
the Court's early proportionality cases and amount to a much more
substantial limit on the practice of capital punishment than the fairly
minimal constraints imposed in the name of "guided discretion." While
the narrowing of the ambit of capital punishment through the exclusion
of certain offenders and offenses is not in *conflict* with the goal of
guiding discretion (as individualized sentencing is thought to be, by
Justice Scalia among others), neither is categorical narrowing the *same*
as guiding discretion. Like the requirement of individualized sentencing,
the requirement of proportionality flows from an entirely different set of
constitutional presuppositions than the requirement that discretion be
guided, and it entails an entirely different constitutional methodology.
These presuppositions and methodology are more rooted in the approaches of Brennan and Marshall's *Furman* opinions than those of
Stewart and White, and they are more likely to eventually yield the
result—wholesale constitutional abolition—that Brennan and Marshall
sought in 1972.

III. Furman's Future Legacy?

Having just canvassed three contradictory "takes" on the question
of what *Furman* "meant," it may seem foolhardy to offer any predictions, however hazy or qualified, about the future. After all, the constitutional regulation of capital punishment has been full of internal contradictions from its inception, with more twists and turns in its relative
brief life as constitutional law than many far more hoary doctrines.
Nonetheless, LDF's victory in *Furman* has left two legacies that together
may eventually achieve what the LDF litigators had initially and perhaps
naively hoped to achieve—the permanent, nationwide abolition of the
practice of capital punishment in America.

The first legacy is the one briefly canvassed in the preceding section—the Court's recent embrace of a constitutional methodology that calls upon a wide range of materials to chart the country's "evolving standards of decency" in a way that might allow relatively modest movement toward abolition to count as an emerging consensus for the purposes of the Eighth Amendment. After all, the Court found evidence of a societal consensus against executing mentally retarded and juvenile offenders even though only 18 out of 50 states had banned the specific practice in each instance. The Court counted the pre-existing 12 abolitionist states along with the other 18 to reach a majority (30–20) sufficient for a consensus, taking into account the speed and consistency of change in the 18 states that specifically changed their practices. To this concrete evidence of legislative change, the Court added evidence of relatively few jury verdicts imposing death sentences on mentally retarded or juvenile offenders and the more expansive evidence of expert, religious, and world views, as well as public opinion polling.

It is possible—though by no means guaranteed—that the kind of movement that the Court discerned in the context of mentally retarded and juvenile offenders could be mimicked in the context of the use of capital punishment writ large. This past year, New Jersey became the first state to legislatively abolish capital punishment in the "modern era" of the death penalty since 1976. Further legislative votes for abolition (in addition to votes for restriction, moratorium or reform), along with declining numbers of executions nationwide,[127] combined with growing consensus among experts, religious leaders, and the world community against the death penalty, could make a plausible case for constitutional abolition, especially given the reservations that some members of the current Court have recently expressed about the practice of capital punishment.[128] I explore at greater length, with co-author Jordan Steiker, the doctrinal path toward abolition that has been opened by the Court's recent proportionality cases in a chapter entitled "The Beginning of the End?" in a collection of essays on *The Road to Abolition*.[129] Our primary observation is that we are in "a moment of

---

[127] Both execution rates and sentencing rates have been falling consistently in recent years. *See* "Facts" at http://www.deathpenaltyinfo.org.

[128] *See* Baze v. Rees, 128 S.Ct. 1520, 1546–1552 (2008) (Stevens, J., concurring) (canvassing problems with the justification and administration of capital punishment that lead him to conclude that it is *per se* unconstitutional, while accepting that *stare decisis* requires him to continue to uphold it); Kansas v. Marsh, 548 U.S. 163, 207–211 (2006) (Souter, J., dissenting) (describing concerns about erroneous capital convictions); Ring v. Arizona, 536 U.S. 584, 614–619 (2002) (Breyer, J., concurring) (canvassing problems with the justification and administration of capital punishment).

[129] *See* Carol S. Steiker & Jordan M. Steiker, "The Beginning of the End?" in Austin Sarat & Charles Ogletree, eds., *The Road to Abolition* (forthcoming, 2009) (draft manuscript on file with author).

possibility for constitutional change in the status of the capital punishment"—a moment that "bears some resemblance to the period preceding *Furman*." We conclude that "some combination of various forms of movement toward abolition might be held to constitute a new consensus against the practice, even while a majority of states still officially authorizes it."[130] While we remain deeply ambivalent about "these new, albeit faint, prospects for judicial nationwide abolition"[131] in light of the experience of backlash and legitimation that attended *Furman* itself, we nonetheless credit *Furman* with creating the foundations for the new doctrinal path toward constitutional abolition that we discern. Of course, plausible doctrinal foundations are a far cry from a predictable result. But the foundations identified above both reflect the growing skepticism of a current majority of the Court about the legitimacy of state death penalty practices and offer that majority a means by which it can continue to express that skepticism through constitutional adjudication.

Furman left a second legacy as well—one that lies outside of U.S. Reports even as it influences the content of what is reported. Quite apart from the competing strands of doctrine that flow from the rich source of the *Furman* opinions are the doctrine "spinners"—the lawyers who have continued in the path of the LDF & ACLU litigators, raising various constitutional challenges to the administration of capital punishment (including new versions of some of the same claims that LDF had identified and pursued during its original moratorium strategy). At the time of *Furman*, there was no capital defense bar to speak of. The defense of death cases was considered the work of local defense attorneys, and there simply was no national law of the death penalty to bring these lawyers together in a shared mission. The Supreme Court's constitutionalization of capital punishment under the Eighth Amendment, inaugurated by *Furman*, changed the very nature of capital defense work and created a national network of capital defense lawyers, of which LDF is now merely a small player. State and federal public defender organizations specializing in capital cases have proliferated, as have non-profit organizations across the country, like the Texas Defender Service, the Southern Center for Human Rights in Atlanta, and the Equal Justice Initiative in Alabama. In addition to government-funded specialized defenders and NGOs, numerous law schools operate capital defense "clinics" in which law students provide legal services to capital defendants under the supervision of experienced lawyers.

Like *Furman*'s doctrinal legacy, *Furman*'s institutional legacy—the creation of a sprawling, specialized capital defense bar—is a double-edged sword. Undoubtedly, the development of a national capital defense bar has helped to raise the general quality of capital defense services in

---

[130] *Id.*

[131] *Id.*

individual cases and has ensured that *Furman*'s constitutional legacy will continue to be fleshed out through litigation. If a successful constitutional challenge to capital punishment ever inaugurates nationwide abolition in the United States, it will be through the work of this new generation of specialized capital defense lawyers. What has been lost in the proliferation of the capital defense bar, however, is the central planning capacity of a small group of legal strategists. In the years leading up to *Furman*, the constitutional attack on capital punishment was tightly coordinated from the center by a coalition of LDF and ACLU lawyers. Today, the litigation of *Furman*'s constitutional legacy is fractured, even hydra-headed—emanating from a wide array of institutional actors who might or might not be in touch with one another, and who might or might not share similar incentives and strategic views.

The task of coordinating the multiplying strands of constitutional litigation in capital punishment has largely fallen, by default, to none other than Tony Amsterdam—the architect of LDF's legal strategy who argued and won *Furman*. Amsterdam's career reflects the rise and fall and recasting of the meaning of his most famous case. Hailed as an "authentic genius" for his stunning victories in the California abolition case[132] and *Furman*, Amsterdam argued the abolitionist cause again in the 1976 cases but was unable to preserve *Furman*'s holding in the light of the massive backlash in favor of restoring capital punishment. In the decades since the constitutional reinstatement of capital punishment, Amsterdam, who moved to the faculty of N.Y.U.'s law school in 1981, has taken a less visible but still central role in the constitutional litigation of capital punishment issues. A mentor to capital defense lawyers nationwide, Amsterdam offers breathtakingly detailed edits at all hours of the day and night in response to briefs sent to him by lawyers on pressing deadlines from states across the country, in addition to running a clinic at N.Y.U. that hosts moot courts for lawyers arguing capital cases.

Furman is thus Amersterdam's legacy as much as Amsterdam and the new breed of specialized capital defense lawyers are *Furman*'s legacy. Consequently, in predicting where *Furman* will eventually bring us, it is fair to turn to Amsterdam himself. A recent interview reports that while Amsterdam remains fairly pessimistic about the chances for abolition of the death penalty, he does concede some recent movement in criminal justice policy. "It's true that history has moved in a pendulum, and we may be moving a little toward humanity, toward egalitarianism. But we've gone so far in the other direction that it will take a long, long time to get back."[133] In the meantime, Amsterdam acknowledges that he is

---

[132] *See* People v. Anderson, 6 Cal.3d 628, 493 P.2d 880, 100 Cal. Rptr. 152 (1972), discussed *supra* in Part I.

[133] Jeffrey Toobin, *Talk of the Town, The Bench: Comeback*, The New Yorker, Mar. 26, 2007, at 35.

consulting on forty capital cases at any given time[134]—*Furman*'s architect still hard at work on *Furman*'s legacy.

IV. Furman the Man: A Final Contradiction

Having charted the path of *Furman*'s lawyer, it is only fair to consider the path of Furman the person, saved from the death chamber in 1972. Fairness aside, William Henry Furman's personal odyssey works well as a metaphor for the profound contradictions engendered by *Furman*-as-law. Legal journalist Joan Cheever sought to find as many as possible of the hundreds spared by the *Furman* decision in 1972 in order to explore how so many for whom society had abandoned hope managed to find rehabilitation and redemption.[135] After a long and frustrating search, Cheever eventually located Furman, who had been released from prison in 1984. She describes watching a football game on T.V. and sharing a meal of fried shrimp with a physically debilitated and mentally slow gentleman, who speaks to her with great politeness and tears up when discussing his past. It is these difficult memories, in Cheever's view, that kept Furman out of trouble in the more than 21 years since his release from prison.[136]

Yet in 2006, the same year that Cheever's book was published, William Furman pleaded guilty to the very same kind of charge that had landed him on death row decades earlier—burglary. Furman admitted to burglarizing a home in Macon, Georgia, occupied by a mother and her 10–year-old daughter, and he was sentenced to 20 years in prison. Perhaps most disturbingly, news accounts of the case reported that when Furman was arrested in the home, police found a pair of panties belonging to the 10–year-old girl in his pocket.[137]

What does William Furman's story mean? Does Furman's life, especially his two decades of apparently peaceful and law-abiding existence, represent a story of redemption that calls into question Georgia's willingness to electrocute him in 1972? Or does his recent recidivism undermine that story with a darker and less hopeful denouement? The contradictions in Furman's personal story parallel the multiplicity and fragmentation of meaning in the legal story—the end of which has yet to be written.

---

[134] *Id.*

[135] *See* Cheever, *supra* note 9.

[136] *Id.* at 244 ("It isn't religion that has kept William Henry Furman out of trouble since his release from prison more than 21 years ago. It is the memories. Ones too painful to share.").

[137] Tim Sturrock, *Subject of Historic Death Penalty Case Pleads Guilty*, Macon Telegraph, Oct. 5, 2006, at B1.

*

3

Hugo Adam Bedau

Gregg v. Georgia and Allied Cases: Protecting the Death Penalty from Abolition

I. Introduction

The year 1976 was a banner one for the jurisprudence of capital punishment in the United States. On July 2 the Supreme Court announced its decisions in a quintet of cases that made history and that were in subsequent decades to prove unparalleled in their influence. Leading the way was *Gregg v. Georgia*[1], in which a seven-justice majority of the Court—in the aftermath of *Furman v. Georgia*[2] (decided four years earlier, in 1972)—paved the way for subsequent decisions and legislation in support of the lawfulness of capital punishment. The tale told by this set of 1976 decisions is nothing less than the story of how the death penalty was re-animated by the Supreme Court after its decision in *Furman* and given new life for years to come.

For several reasons, the Supreme Court's ruling in *Gregg* and its four companion cases was of paramount importance for all of the nation's future death penalty jurisprudence. By far the most important ruling of the Court in these cases was its pronouncement on the constitutional status of the death penalty. The Justices voted, seven to two, that this punishment (redesigned and re-enacted in Georgia, Florida, Texas and nearly three dozen other states after the abolitionist ruling in *Furman* four years earlier) "does not invariably violate the Constitution."[3]

Second, the Court—again by a vote of seven to two—upheld three different models of death penalty statutes intended to guide jurors' exercise of discretion in death penalty sentencing in compliance with *Furman*. Its decisions in this trio of cases—*Gregg, Proffitt v. Florida*,[4] and *Jurek v. Texas*[5]—effectively endorsed the recently enacted capital sentencing statutes of sixteen states,[6] and cleared the way for others (e.g., Oregon) to enact similar statutes in the near future.[7]

---

[1] *Gregg v. Georgia,* 428 U.S. 153 (1976), hereinafter *Gregg.*

[2] *Furman v. Georgia*, 408 U.S. 238 (1972), hereinafter *Furman.*

[3] *Gregg*, at 169.

[4] *Proffitt v. Florida*, 428 U.S. 242 (1976), hereinafter *Proftitt.*

[5] *Jurek v. Texas,* 428 U.S. 262 (1976), hereinafter *Jurek.*

[6] The post-*Furman* statutes in Arkansas, Arizona, California, Colorado, Connecticut, Illinois, Maryland, Montana, Nebraska, Ohio, Pennsylvania, Utah, and Virginia shared the relevant features of the Georgia, Florida, and Texas statutes upheld in the 1976 cases. See: *Ariz. Rev. Stat. Ann.* §§ 13–452 to 13–454 (Supp. 1973); *Ark. Stat. Ann.* § 41–4706 (Supp. 1975); *Cal. Penal Code* §§ 190.1, 209, 219 (Supp. 1976); *Colo. Laws* 1974, c. 52, § 4; *Conn. Gen. Stat. Rev.* §§ 53a–25, 53a–35(b), 53a–46a, 53a–54b (1975); *Fla. Stat. Ann.* §§ 782.04, 921.141 (Supp. 1975–1976); *Ga. Code Ann.* §§ 26–3102, 27–2528, 27–2534.1, 27–2537 (Supp. 1975); *Md. Ann. Code*, art. 27, § 413 (Supp. 1975); *Mont. Rev. Codes Ann.* § 94–5–105 (Spec. Crim. Code Supp. 1976); *Neb. Rev. Stat.* §§ 28–401, 29–2521 to 29–2523 (1975); *Ohio Rev. Code Ann.* §§ 2929.02–2929.04 (1975); *Pa. Laws* 1974, Act. No. 46; Tex. Penal Code Ann. § 19.03(a) (1974); *Utah Code Ann.* §§ 76–3–206, 76–3–207, 76–5–202 (Supp. 1975); *Va. Code Ann.* §§ 18.2–10, 18.2–31 (1976).

[7] See Lee Epstein and Joseph F. Koblyka, *The Supreme Court and Legal Change* 86–7, Table 4–1 (1992), and Mark Vilaboy, "Comment & Legislative Review: Playing the

Third, the Court ruled (this time by a vote of five to four) against the constitutional permissibility of the mandatory death penalty statutes that had been enacted in North Carolina, Louisiana, and seventeen other states,[8] citing—in *Woodson v. North Carolina*—their "incompatibility . . . with contemporary values . . ."[9] as well as their "failure to allow the particularized consideration of relevant aspects of the character and record of each convicted defendant before the imposition upon him of a sentence of death"[10] as required by *Furman*.

Fourth, the appellate litigation provided an opportunity for the Justices in the minority in *Furman* to revive a prominent role for deterrence and retribution, conspicuous in the amicus brief in *Gregg* by the Solicitor General.[11]

II. The National Death Penalty Culture and the Road to *Gregg*

Georgia was the political and legal setting for the crime, trial, and sentence of Troy Gregg.[12] How appropriate that one of the leading post–*Furman* death penalty jurisdictions should be the Peach State, for Georgia is not just one among the many states that restored capital punishment. Together with Texas and Florida, Georgia can claim premier status among today's three dozen death penalty states:[13]

- The modern system of capital punishment in the United States is shaped above all by the Supreme Court in three Georgia cases: *Furman* (1972), *Gregg* (1976), and *McCleskey* (1987).[14]

Apprendi Card: Revisiting Judicial Fact–Finding in Arizona's Death Penalty Scheme," 33 *Ariz. St. L. J.* 363, 368 (2001).

[8] The other states that had embraced such mandatory schemes in hopes of satisfying *Furman*'s commands were Alabama, Delaware, Idaho, Indiana, Kentucky, Mississippi, Missouri, Nevada, New Hampshire, New Mexico, New York, Oklahoma, Rhode Island, South Carolina, Tennessee, Washington, and Wyoming. See: *Ala. H.B.* 212, §§ 2–4, 6–7 (1975); *Del. Code Ann.* tit. 11, § 4209 (Supp. 1975); *Idaho Code* § 18–4004 (Supp. 1975); *Ill. Ann. Stat.* c. 38, §§ 9–1, 1005–5–3, 1005–8–1A (Supp. 1976–1977); *Ind. Stat. Ann.* § 35–13–4–1 (1975); *Ky. Rev. Stat. Ann.* § 507.020 (1975); *La. Rev. Stat. Ann.* § 14:30 (Supp. 1976); *Miss. Code Ann.* §§ 97–3–19, 97–3–21, 97–25–55, 99–17–20 (Supp. 1975); Mo. Ann. Stat. § 559.009, 559.005 (Supp. 1976); Nev. Rev. Stat. § 200.030 (1973); N.H. Rev. Stat. Ann. § 630:1 (1974); N.M. Stat. Ann. § 40A–29–2 (Supp. 1975); *N.Y. Penal Law* § 60.06 (1975); *N.C. Gen. Stat.* § 14–17 (Supp. 1975); *Okla. Stat. Ann.* tit. 21, § 701.1–701.3 (Supp. 1975–1976); *R.I. Gen. Laws Ann.* § 11–23–2 (Supp. 1975); *S.C. Code Ann.* § 16–52 (Supp. 1975); *Tenn. Code Ann.* §§ 39–2402, 39–2406 (1975); *Wash. Rev. Code* §§ 9A.32.045, 9A.–32.046 (Supp. 1975); *Wyo. Stat. Ann.* § 6–54 (Supp. 1975).

[9] *Woodson v. North Carolina*, 428 U.S. 280 (1976), 194 hereinafter *Woodson*.

[10] *Woodson*, 303.

[11] Robert H. Bork, "Brief for the United States as Amicus Curiae, Oct. Term 1975."

[12] Sources for details regarding Gregg's life, crime, and disposition can be found in Christopher Davis, *Waiting for It* (1980) and in various newspaper columns.

[13] Department of Justice, Bureau of Criminal Justice Statistics, *Capital Punishment* (1973–) and NAACP Legal Defense and Educational Fund, *Death Row U.S.A.* (1975–).

[14] *McCleskey v. Kemp*, 481 U.S. 279 (1987), hereinafter *McCleskey*.

- When *Furman* was decided in 1972, Georgia had more crimes punishable by death than any other American jurisdiction.

- Since *Furman* (as of 2005) the Georgia legislature has made more crimes punishable by death than any other state legislature.

- Since 1930, more black Americans have been executed in Georgia than in any other jurisdiction.

- In total executions since 1930, Georgia ranked second (behind Texas).

- In the period 1930–1972 (in other words, the four decades immediately pre–*Furman*) Georgia had more persons under death sentence than any other jurisdiction did.

- All but three of the 61 persons executed for rape in Georgia between 1930 and 1972 were black Americans whose victims were white.

- In the aftermath of *Furman,* Florida was the first state to re-enact the death penalty, followed closely by Georgia and Texas.

- Georgia was the first state to sentence someone to death under a post–*Furman* statute.[15]

During the years after *Furman*, the death penalty enjoyed considerable public support across the nation. Only five months after the decision, in November 1972, Gallup recorded the highest poll number it had ever tallied in favor of the death penalty, finding that 57% of the country supported it. That figure represented an increase of 7% from Gallup's most recent poll in March 1972—before the Supreme Court handed down its decision in *Furman*.[16] By the time the Court heard *Gregg* and its companion cases, 65% of the country supported the death penalty.[17] Furthermore, the capital punishment laws passed after *Furman* did not merely reinstate capital punishment; they apparently reinvigorated it. Prior to *Furman*, support for the death penalty was at a historic low and the number of persons sentenced to death had been

---

[15] "Death Penalty Laws Enacted in 13 States, Issue Pending in 16 Others; Gubernatorial Action Awaited in Arizona and Tennessee," *L.A. Times,* May 13, 1973, at K4. (Jesse Le Conley, a black man convicted of raping a white woman, was sentenced to death under Georgia's new statute in April of 1973).

[16] Michael Kuhn, Note, "House Bill 200: The Legislative Attempt to Reinstate Capital Punishment in Texas," 11 *Hous. L. Rev.* 410, 416 (1973–1974) (citing *The Gallup Opinion Index,* Dec. 1972, at 28–29).

[17] Tom Goldstein, "Issue and Debate: Capital Punishment: Confusion Reigns as Law is In Limbo," *N.Y. Times,* Dec. 10, 1976, at 35 (citing Gallup polling).

steadily declining. In 1974, however, 149 people received death sentences, more than any year since 1942, and in 1975, 298 people were sentenced to death, "more than any year for which data exist[ed]."[18] Abolition was essentially confined to the handful of long-standing pre–*Furman* abolitionist jurisdictions,[19] and even in those jurisdictions popular support for abolition was weak. Writing in 1994, social psychologist Phoebe C. Ellsworth and law professor Samuel R. Gross endorsed the view that "the best known fact about American attitudes toward capital punishment is that support for the death penalty is at a near record high . . . [roughly 70% of the public]."[20]

In the face of this unpopularity, what was the national strategy designed by the NAACP Legal and Educational Fund (LDF) to undermine the constitutional status of the death penalty? It has been related with clarity and precision by law professor Michael Meltsner in his book, *Cruel and Unusual: The Supreme Court and Capital Punishment* (1973). The strategy was to postpone as long as possible any attempt to argue that the death penalty was per se unconstitutional, in violation of the eighth and fourteenth amendments. The likelihood of winning such an argument in the late 1960s or early 1970s was disturbingly small. In any case, aggressive argument on that point would be deferred until there were no other arguments to be made. Thus the LDF piled up cases, one after another, devoted to testing procedural objections that might have a chance of winning a five to four decision. But as bad luck would have it, the Fund found itself required to develop just such an argument in *Gregg*, a bare two years after the decision in *Furman*.

Not helping was the unsurprising fact that, no sooner was *Furman* decided in the summer of 1972 than state legislatures from the Atlantic to the Pacific fell all over themselves in a head-long rush to restore the lawfulness of execution.[21] In fact, the day after the Supreme Court announced its decision in *Furman*, five legislatures immediately declared their intention to draft new death penalty statutes.[22] Within a year, several states had formed exploratory commissions to consider how to restore capital punishment, and three dozen bills to do so had been

[18] Stuart Banner, *The Death Penalty* 270 (2002).

[19] Hugo Adam Bedau, ed., *The Death Penalty in America: An Anthology* 12 (1964).

[20] Phoebe C. Ellsworth and Samuel R. Gross, "Hardening of the Attitudes: Americans' Views on the Death Penalty," 50 *J. of Social Issues* (1994).

[21] Restoration of the death penalty in Florida has received the most careful study. See Charles W. Ehrhardt et al., "I. The Future of Capital Punishment in Florida: Analysis and Recommendations," 64 *J. Crim. L. and Crimin.* 2 (1973), and Charles W. Ehrhardt and L. Harold Levinson, "II. Florida's Legislative Response to *Furman*: An Exercise in Futility." 64 *J. Crim. L.* and Crimin.10 (1973).

[22] Jonathan Simon, *Governing Through Crime* 117 (2007).

introduced in as many legislatures. On the second anniversary of *Furman*, twenty-eight states had new death penalty laws.[23] By 1976 that number had grown to thirty-five.[24]

The country's new zeal for the death penalty dismayed and baffled abolitionists. Law professor Charles L. Black, Jr., attributed "the post–*Furman* legislative frenzy . . . [to] 'the operation of causes which those of us who oppose capital punishment can only guess at.' "[25] Moreover, the LDF did not anticipate such a backlash. One attorney who worked on *Furman* later commented that he and his colleagues were "surprised" that states chose to return so "quickly and enthusiastically" to capital punishment.[26] In retrospect, it appears that the LDF and its allies failed fully to appreciate the country's changing mood regarding criminal justice issues.

Furman provoked many angry responses from death penalty supporters.[27] For example, on the day of the decision, Georgia Lt. Governor (and former Governor) Lester Maddox called it a " 'license for anarchy, rape, and murder,' "[28] acting Alabama Governor Jere Beasley said that the five Justices in the majority had " 'lost contact with the real world,' "[29] and Attorney General Robert List of Nevada "denounced the decisions as 'an insult to Nevada', to its laws and to its people."[30] At the

---

[23] Frank E. Zimring and Gordon Hawkins, *Capital Punishment and the American Agenda* 38–39 (1989), quoting Hugo Adam Bedau, *The Courts, the Constitution, and Capital Punishment* 93 (1977).

[24] Zimring and Hawkins, *supra* note 23, at 41. The following states passed new capital punishment laws after *Furman* but before *Gregg*: "Florida (1972), New Mexico (1973), Rhode Island (1973), Arizona (1973), Arkansas (1973), Georgia (1973), Idaho (1973), Indiana (1973), Louisiana (1973), Nevada (1973), Nebraska (1973), Texas (1973), Virginia (1973), Washington (1973), Wyoming (1973), California (1974), Delaware (1974), Illinois (1974), Mississippi (1974), Montana (1974), New Hampshire (1974), North Carolina (1974), Ohio (1974), Pennsylvania (1974), South Carolina (1974), Tennessee (1974), Colorado (1975), Kentucky (1975), Maryland (1975), Missouri (1975)." Epstein and Koblyka, *supra* note 7, at 86–87 tbl. 4–1 (1992).

[25] Zimring and Hawkins, *supra* note 23, at 41, quoting Charles L. Black, Jr., *Capital Punishment: The Inevitability of Caprice and Mistake* 12–13 (1974).

[26] Epstein and Koblyka, *supra* note 7, at 90.

[27] Others, of course, praised the decision. For example, Senator Ted Kennedy (D–MA), hailed *Furman* as " 'one of the great judicial milestones in American history.' The Court, he said, 'has ruled for life, and it has thereby given new life to our democracy and to the quality of American justice.' Morton Mintz, 'Joy on Death Row; Praise, Scorn on Hill,' " *Wash. Post*, June 30, 1972, at A13.

[28] *Id.*

[29] *Id.*

[30] *Id.*

national level, Senator James O. Eastland of Mississippi, powerful chairman of the Senate Judiciary Committee, accused the Court of "again legislating and destroying our system of government."[31] On the night of the *Furman decision,* President Nixon stated that he believed the death penalty was "needed,"[32] and held a press conference the next day during which he argued that the Court's holding "must not be taken ... to rule out capital punishment."[33] Some media outlets also spoke against the decision. The New York *Daily News,* for example, "urged State legislators to readopt the death penalty with all of its 'old time' severity in order to see 'what the Supreme Court does about that.' "[34]

Perhaps in a different political and social climate the highly charged rhetoric invoked by *Furman* opponents would have faded away. In the early 1970s, however, "anti-crime politics were beginning to reshape the political identities of American policy-makers."[35] The intensity with which state legislators pursued new death penalty statutes and their success in doing so reflected "the growth of crime, spreading anger and fear, and [the] increase of punitive attitudes" among the public.[36] That same public transformation contributed to the open (but measured) support from President Nixon, and his attorney general John Mitchell, for legislative efforts to restore capital punishment.[37] While the federal government had stayed completely out of *Furman* (suggesting "some uncertainty within the Nixon administration in 1971 as to the possible political costs of taking a position"[38]) by 1975, "supporting capital punishment entailed no political cost at all."[39]

---

[31] *Id.*

[32] Robert Young, "Nixon Hopes Federal Death Rulings Stand," *Chi. Trib.,* June 29, 1972, at Backpage.

[33] Epstein and Koblyka, *supra* note 7, at 84.

[34] Michael Meltsner, *Cruel and Unusual: The Supreme Court and Capital Punishment* 291 (1973).

[35] Bryan A. Stevenson, "Two Views on the Impact of Ring v. Arizona on Capital Sentencing: The Ultimate Authority on the Ultimate Punishment: The Requisite Role of the Jury in Capital Sentencing," 54 *Ala. L. Rev.* 1091, 1091 n4 (2003).

[36] J. Gorecki, *Capital Punishment: Criminal Law and Social Evolution* 112–13 (1983). The exact cause of the large number of new death statutes is not a settled question. For example, Zimring and Hawkins believe explaining the new statutes by reference to changing attitudes towards crime is "one guess that seems clearly mistaken." Zimring and Hawkins, *supra* note 23, at 49 n58. Instead, they view the response as frustration with the Court's decision manifesting itself in overly aggressive legislative behavior and "psychological reactance." *Id.* at 41–42.

[37] See Hugo Adam Bedau, "The Nixon Administration and the Deterrent Effect of the Death Penalty," 34 *U. Pittsburgh L. Rev.* 557 (1973).

[38] Banner, *supra* note 18, at 270–71.

[39] *Id.,* at 271.

Consequently, the strong feelings provoked by *Furman* carried over into the legislative process, where tensions also ran high and support was strong for restoring capital punishment. Death penalty supporters and abolitionists alike made impassioned pleas for their cause on the floor of legislatures across the country, including the United States Senate and House of Representatives. Generally speaking, opponents characterized the death penalty as excessively cruel, unconstitutional, and motivated by revenge rather than justice.[40] Proponents, on the other hand, focused on capital punishment's supposed deterrent effects and emphatic retribution.[41]

In Texas, for example, a minority of anti-death legislators lambasted the practice as " 'barbaric,' 'unconstitutional' and 'inconsistent with contemporary standards of decency and morality.' "[42] Moreover, they introduced amendments meant to sabotage the statute. One representative, inspired by biblical scripture, suggested executions be performed with " 'instruments of iron, wood, or stone.' "[43] Still another proposed that the legislature be forced to vote on each death sentence and witness the execution which would occur on the House floor, reasoning that "there would never be a majority with the 'moral conviction' to watch a convict 'fry on the floor of the [H]ouse.' "[44]

In Georgia, however, legislative supporters of capital punishment were equally animated. One representative—responding to critics who claimed capital punishment did not deter crime—proposed conducting executions in the courthouse squares of the counties in which the crime was committed.[45] Another brought the legislative session to a halt by pointing a .22 caliber pistol at the House Minority Leader.[46] He did so to

---

[40] For further discussion of the legislative response, see Zimring and Hawkins, *supra* note 23, at 42–45.

[41] Tom Goldstein, "Issue and Debate: Capital Punishment: Confusion Reigns as Law is In Limbo," *N.Y. Times*, Dec. 10, 1976, at 35 (noting that "[t]he chief justification given by proponents of the death penalty is that society is entitled to satisfy its moral outrage at offensive conduct").

[42] David Crump, "Capital Murder: The Issues in Texas," 14 *Hous. L. Rev.* 531, 533 n8 (1977), quoting *Hous. Chron.*, Jan. 28, 1973, § 1, at 19.

[43] *Id.*, quoting *Hous. Chron.*, May 14, 1973, § 5, at 8. The reference is to Numbers 35:15–31.

[44] *Id.*, quoting *Hous. Chron.*, Jan. 31, 1973, § 1, at 12.

[45] "Wild Georgia Session: Gun Waved in Debate on Death Penalty Bill," *L.A. Times*, Jan. 18, 1973, at A9.

[46] *Id.*

make a point: "had he fired and killed [the Minority Leader] he could not be sentenced to death because none of the aggravating factors provided under the bill would be present."[47]

The high levels of emotion, coupled with confusions about how to design a constitutionally acceptable statute, lent itself in many instances to a rushed and *ad hoc* process. Because all nine justices in *Furman* wrote separate and sometimes conflicting opinions, legal commentators were unsure how, if at all, to remedy the constitutional infirmities identified in the case.[48] Thus, legislatures were left to make their best guess concerning what mechanisms would ensure that their new laws passed constitutional muster.[49] Many states looked to the American Law Institute's Model Penal Code for guidance,[50] but as that provision had been drafted a decade before *Furman*, it offered no sure solution (particularly since the drafters had originally voted 18–2 to abolish the death penalty before concluding they should nevertheless address the issue).[51]

Despite the mounting opposition, LDF and other attorneys worked in concert to involve themselves in as many appeals as possible springing from the states' new post–*Furman* laws. A large number of these appeals came from North Carolina, Georgia, and Florida, as these three states accounted for 65 percent of the death sentences imposed between *Furman* and *Gregg*.[52] By October 1974, more than 150 people had been sentenced to death under the new statutes, and the LDF was representing twenty-nine of them—at least nine of whom had petitions pending before the Supreme Court.[53] In one of those cases, that of Jesse Fowler of North Carolina, the Court granted review.

North Carolina, Louisiana, and seventeen other states had enacted mandatory death penalty statutes, perhaps reading Chief Justice Burger's *Furman* dissent to suggest that any degree of sentencing discretion would produce intolerably arbitrary sentencing verdicts and thus violate

---

[47] *Id.*

[48] See, e.g., David A. Johnston, Staff Research Report No. 107 of the Ohio Legis. Service Comm'n: "Capital Punishment: Legislative Implications of the U.S. Supreme Court Decision in *Furman v. Georgia*" 1 (1972).

[49] "The issue has caused some heated debate and some confusion over how capital punishment statutes should be worded." *L.A. Times*, see *supra* n15.

[50] Zimring and Hawkins, *supra* note 23, at 41; ALI, *Model Penal Code* (Proposed Official Draft 1962) Sec. 210.6.

[51] ALI, *Model Penal Code*, Sec. 210.6, comment 1, at 111 (1980).

[52] Epstein and Koblyka, *supra* note 7, at 95.

[53] *Id.*, at 50.

the Eighth Amendment.[54] The LDF lawyers, by contrast, felt that these inflexible schemes were least likely to survive review in the Supreme Court, and from their point of view *Fowler v. North Carolina*[55] represented perhaps their best chance to win a narrow 5–4 ruling. Oral argument was set for April 21, 1975, and the LDF's hopes were high.[56]

But two things frustrated the LDF's plan. First, Solicitor General Robert Bork weighed in on behalf of the federal government and redirected the Court's focus to the constitutionality of the death penalty as such, in all states. Bork also forced the LDF, and the Court, to confront emerging social science research that purported to support the deterrent value of capital punishment. Suddenly, the LDF lawyers were on shakier ground, as they had no choice but to reassert the abolitionist arguments that had failed to garner a majority only three years earlier in *Furman*.[57]

Second, Justice Douglas suffered a stroke. Although he attended oral argument in *Fowler*, he was too ill to participate in the conference. The Court deadlocked 4–4, and upon the news of Justice Douglas' resignation a decision in *Fowler* was postponed until the next Term. This development did not bode well for the remaining *Furman* dissenters, the LDF, or the more than 450 convicts who had accumulated on death rows across the country under the new post–*Furman* statutes.[58]

In the meantime, petitions for certiorari were piling up at the Court (thirty-seven by September 1975 and more than fifty by December 1976), and it was becoming clear that the Court had to address the emerging controversy more broadly than *Fowler* would allow.[59] And so, less than a month after Justice Douglas's replacement, John Paul Stevens, was confirmed to the Court, certiorari was granted to consider five capital cases encompassing the full range of post–*Furman* legislation—mandatory systems from North Carolina and Louisiana, and various guided-discretion statutes from Georgia, Florida, and Texas.

Three of the cases (those from Texas, North Carolina, and Louisiana) had been filed by the LDF, and one each was filed by Florida and Georgia public defenders.[60] At this point, however, all the defense attorneys knew that in contrast to their experience four years earlier in *Furman*, there was only a slim chance that they could prevail. The case

---

[54] *Furman*, at 401; Burger, C.J., dissenting.

[55] *Fowler v. North Carolina*, 428 U.S. 904 (1976), hereinafter *Fowler*.

[56] Epstein and Koblyka, *supra* note 7, at 97–99.

[57] Banner, *supra* note 18, at 270–72; Epstein and Koblyka, *supra* note 7, at 97–99.

[58] *Id.*

[59] *Id.*

[60] Banner, *supra* note 18, at 270–72; Epstein and Koblyka, *supra* note 7, at 100–03.

from Georgia, in which the Court would consider whether Furman's challenge to capital punishment had been overcome, involved Troy Leon Gregg, convicted of killing two men in a robbery-murder.

III. The Offender

Troy Leon Gregg,[61] age 21 at the time of his crime, was a typical product of a dysfunctional rural family. "Dysfunctional" hardly does justice to the awful facts. Growing up in a small rural community in western North Carolina, he witnessed at an early age his step-father assaulting his mother—a commonplace event when his step-father arrived home drunk, as he often did. His great grandfather had murdered his wife. Worse than that, as a teenager in 1960 Gregg witnessed mass murder in his own family. The killer was Gregg's drunken step-father, Wayne Franks, who on entering the house shot and killed the boy's much-loved grandmother. He then turned the gun on his own mother-in-law. His three nephews and nieces were next. Except for young Troy, the whole family had been murdered in a fusillade of bullets. The insane shooting spree came to an end when Franks shot himself; the next day he became the sixth victim to die. A neighbor was prompted to observe, "This family had a history in which violent death played a part." Another said laconically "There's a lot of death in that family."

At trial, Gregg took the stand in his own defense. (For reasons not entirely clear, his attorney G. Hughel Harrison did not call any witnesses.) Gregg did not claim in his testimony that his wretched adolescence or the horrible crimes he had witnessed years earlier were causal factors (and thus to some degree a mitigating excuse) for the murders and robberies he committed and for which he faced a possible death sentence. As for a serious criminal record as a juvenile or adult, he had none. He was not a hard drinker. He had recently bought a .25 caliber pistol—for self-defense, he said. Indeed, Gregg was so slight and thin that his friends and family since childhood had called him "Shadow."[62]

IV. The Offense

The crimes for which Gregg was convicted and sentenced to death were nothing remarkable, as murders and robberies go—except for the fact that the crime involved multiple (two, to be exact) murders. He was charged with the armed robbery and murder of Fred Simmons and Bob "Tex" Moore on November 21, 1973. Simmons and Moore, both of whom were drunk at the time, had given a lift to Gregg and another fellow, Fred Allen, while they were hitchhiking in Florida. Their car had broken down, but they continued on their way in another vehicle, a 1960

---

[61] The factual information in Sections III, IV, and V is based on the account in Davis, *supra* note 12.

[62] *Id.*, at 49.

Pontiac, that Simmons purchased with some of the fistful of cash he was carrying. While still in Florida they picked up yet another hitchhiker, Dennis Weaver, and proceeded north to Atlanta. Weaver was dropped off about 11 p.m. Shortly after that, the four men turned into a rest stop. The next morning the bodies of Simmons and Moore were discovered in a nearby ditch.

Two days later, after reading about the killings in an Atlanta newspaper, Weaver contacted the Gwinnett County (Georgia) police and told them about the journey by car and the shooting of the two hitchhikers. The next day Gregg and Allen, while driving north in Simmons's car, were arrested in Asheville, North Carolina. A search of the car and riders produced a .25 caliber pistol. Later it was established that this was the weapon with which Simmons had been killed. After receiving a *Miranda* warning of his rights, Gregg signed a statement in which he admitted shooting and then robbing Simmons and Moore. He claimed, however, that he acted in self-defense.

On the following day, Gregg and Allen were taken to the scene of the crime, and Allen told the police a somewhat different version of the crimes: When Simmons and Moore left the car to relieve themselves in a ditch, Gregg told Allen he intended to rob the two. Taking out his pistol, he fired three shots at close range, and the two victims fell dead into the ditch. After the robbery and murder, Gregg and Allen drove off. Medical examination of the two victims established that Moore died from bullet wounds in the face and head, and that both victims had severe bruises consistent with falling (or being dragged) into a ditch. A police detective affirmed that the substance of Allen's testimony was an accurate account of the crimes.

Gregg testified in his own behalf and advanced a different story of the crime. In claiming that he had shot Simmons and Moore in self-defense, he alleged that they had attacked him and Allen, one with a steel pipe and the other with a knife. The prosecutor, Gwinnett County District Attorney Bryant Huff, argued otherwise. Gregg and his companion, he said, murdered the car driver and his friend as they were taking a leak by the side of the road. Gregg then robbed them, took their car, and drove off—only to be arrested on his way home for Thanksgiving. The jury agreed with the prosecution.

That was not quite the end of Gregg's story. After seven years on death row, Gregg and three other convicts—dressed like prison guards—escaped from prison. The next night, following a barroom fight in Asheville, North Carolina, Gregg was killed by one or more of his companions. His body was thrown into a nearby lake.

Born in 1953, Gregg was 27 when he died on July 29, 1980—but his death was not carried out, as he was afraid it would be, in the electric

chair. His undistinguished life ended in an undistinguished death. Little
did he know that his case would make constitutional law.[63]

V. The Trial

Gregg's trial lawyer, Harrison, died in 2007; Harrison's son Sam
said of his father, "He was a lawyer's lawyer. He lived it. He breathed
it." He took his role seriously. He provided Gregg with suitable clothes
to wear during the trial and ran up more than a thousand dollars in
expenses for which he was not reimbursed. Harrison thought Gregg's
claim that he killed in self-defense was probably true; despite the love
affair with violence in so many of his family, Gregg was passive and by
all accounts would prefer to flee rather than stand and fight.

Presiding at the trial was Judge Reid Merritt. He submitted the
charges to the jury on both felony-murder and non-felony-murder theories. He also permitted the defense to submit the case to the jury on the
issue of self-defense. He did not (as the defense had hoped) instruct the
jury on the issue of manslaughter. Merritt submitted the robbery charge
to the jury on both an armed-robbery theory and on the lesser included
offense of robbery by intimidation.

The jury of nine men and three women began its deliberations on
the morning of Thursday, February 7, 1974; the jurors required less
than an hour to find Gregg guilty of two counts of armed robbery and
two counts of murder (one of each for Simmons and for Moore).[64] The
court moved immediately to the penalty phase. Neither the prosecution
nor Gregg presented any evidence, either in aggravation or mitigation,
regarding the appropriate punishment. Instead, the attorneys simply
proceeded to closing argument. Demanding a death sentence, prosecutor
Huff quoted the Bible and read ringing phrases from an 1873 opinion of
the Georgia Supreme Court: "[T]he false humanity that starts and
shudders when the axe of justice is ready to strike is a dangerous
element for the peace of society."[65] For his part, Harrison asked the

---

[63] Nor, ironically, was either of the other two condemned men—whose death sentences
the Supreme Court upheld in the seminal 1976 cases—ever executed. Jerry Lane Jurek, the
petitioner in *Jurek v.Texas*, won relief from his conviction in federal court several years
later on the ground that his confession had been coerced. See *Jurek v. Estelle*, 623 F.2d 929
(5th Cir. 1980) (*en banc*). Facing retrial, Jurek entered a guilty plea in return for the
State's abandoning its efforts to seek a death sentence. See James Kimberley, "Case That
Revived Death Penalty Ended Ironically," *Hous. Chron.*, Feb. 3, 2001. Charles William
Proffitt, the petitioner in *Proffitt v. Florida*, was saved from the electric chair by the
Florida Supreme Court, which eventually—after more than a decade of appeals in state and
federal courts—concluded that Proffitt's death sentence was excessive after all, and
reduced it to life imprisonment. *Proffitt v. State*, 510 So.2d 896 (Fla. 1987).

[64] "Death Asked by Jury in Gwinnett," *Atl. Jour.-Const.*, Feb. 8, 1974.

[65] Davis, *supra* note 12, at 119. Exhorting jurors with this hoary and hot-tempered
quotation from *Eberhart v. State*, 47 Ga. 598 (1873), was a favorite tactic of Georgia

jurors for mercy and cautioned them against making an irrevocable error in case they had been mistaken in convicting Gregg.[66] After three hours of deliberation, foreman Cecil Shealy announced the jury's verdict: a death sentence on each count.[67]

Judge Merritt formally pronounced sentence the following day. After setting Gregg's execution for April Fool's Day 1974, the judge intoned, "And may God have mercy upon your soul."[68] Harrison asked that the phrase be deleted from the record, saying that he saw no place for such language in a judgment condemning a man to death.[69] The court granted Harrison's request.[70]

VI.   The Sentence

Gregg was convicted and sentenced to death in February 1974; the date of execution was set for early April. The smart money said Gregg had nothing to worry about. Although during the winter of 1973–74 several hundred prisoners across the nation were on death row, including thirty-four in Georgia, no prisoner had been executed in Georgia's electric chair since 1964, eight years before the *Furman* ruling in 1972. Despite the extensive role of race in the administration of Georgia's death penalty jurisprudence, race played no role in *Gregg*. The victims, the offenders, and the court officers—all were white males. Only the demography of the trial jury reflected the fact that in 1976 women as well as men, and African Americans as well as whites, were declared competent to serve on a capital jury in Georgia.

The statute under which Gregg was sentenced, like others across the nation, was a direct reaction to *Furman*. One day after the decision in

---

prosecutors in death penalty trials under the post–*Furman* statute, but reviewing courts consistently found its use in closing argument "improper," "clearly improper," "highly improper," and "undeniably wrong." *Romine v. Head*, 253 F.3d 1349, 1367–68 (11th Cir. 2001) (noting that the court had forbidden use of "the now-infamous *Eberhart* quotation . . . on at least seven occasions").

[66] *Id.*, at 120.

[67] *Id.*, at 121. Shealy later remarked, "There wasn't a whole lot of disagreement [during the penalty phase deliberations]. Only one person in particular said they felt awfully *burdened* by the death penalty." *Id.*, at 125. According to Shealy, the holdout juror's reluctance arose from "sort of putting herself in a position where individual responsibility was being sought;" "some discussion by [the other jurors] got through [to her] that it wasn't a matter of the individual but of the law." *Id.* Shealy described his own feelings, by saying, "I'm not responsible. The state says that if certain parameters are met, then the death penalty is appropriate and no other penalty is. . . ." *Id.*, at 125–26.

[68] *Id.*

[69] "Troy Gregg Sentenced to Death," *Atl. Jour.-Const.*, Feb. 9, 1974. See also Davis, *supra* note 12, at 121–22.

[70] *Id.*

Furman was announced, the chairmen of the Georgia House and Senate Judiciary committees called for a joint hearing to draft a new death penalty law, declaring, "We certainly want to conform to the Supreme Court ruling and have the legislation ready to do so...."[71] One pro-death penalty representative, James "Sloppy" Floyd, called it "one of the saddest days in American history."[72]

Ignoring warnings that their action could be overturned by the Supreme Court, state legislators passed a bill based loosely on the death penalty provisions of the Model Penal Code, and Governor Jimmy Carter signed it into law in March, 1973.[73] The new statute introduced several novel features that would prove of enormous influence in all other American death penalty cases, as friends of the death penalty searched for statutory schemes that would be consistent with the holding in *Furman*.

The essential ingredients of the new Georgia death penalty scheme were five in number. First, the prosecution was required to make known to the defense prior to the trial of any and all aggravating circumstances it intended to cite in its effort to pave the way for a death sentence. This introduced what amounts to discovery—long a familiar feature in non-capital and civil cases—into death penalty practice, thereby evening the playing surface and bringing more transparency into the sentencing phase of the trial. (The seeming failure of the Georgia attorney general's office to comply with this requirement played a significant role in the notorious Georgia death penalty case of the Dawson Five in 1975–76.[74])

Second, the scheme imposed a mandatory appeal of the conviction and the sentence to the state supreme court. This innovation was designed to end the hit-or-miss quality of post-conviction review (or failure to review) that was so typical of death penalty practice around the nation prior to *Furman*. Reviewing the trial jury 's death sentence on appeal would no longer rest on the uncertain initiative of defense counsel. (Mandatory review on appeal in capital cases had been recently pioneered in California and adopted in a few other states.)

---

[71] Milo Dakin and Bob Hurt, "State Lawmakers to Keep Death Penalty," *Atl. Jour.-Const.*, June 30, 1972, at 1–A.

[72] *Id.*

[73] Milo Dakin, "Carter Signs Death Penalty Bill," *Atl. Jour.-Const.*, Mar. 29, 1973, at 18–A; Tom Linthioum, "Senate Approves the Death Penalty," *Atl. Jour.-Const.*, Feb. 23, 1973, at 1–A; "Wild Georgia Session: Gun Waived in Debate on Death Penalty Bill," *L.A. Times,* Jan. 18, 1973, at A9.

[74] Hugo Adam Bedau, "Witness to a Persecution: The Death Penalty and the Dawson Five," 8 *Black L. J.* 7 (1983).

Third, in its review, the Georgia Supreme Court had to decide whether a death sentence in the case at hand was warranted or whether it would be arbitrary, disproportionate, or in some other way not consistent with the decisions made in other Georgia death penalty cases.

Fourth, the Georgia Supreme Court had to give "special expedited direct" review of the defendant's conviction and sentence on appeal. The intention here was to speed up the appellate review of death penalty cases so that they would not be forced to linger along with the rest of the criminal cases in the queue waiting for appellate review.

Finally—and by far the most important element—the trial was to be divided into two parts or stages. (The Supreme Court had recently declared that such separation was not constitutionally required in *McGautha v. California*.[75]) Stage one was designed so that the trial court could determine whether the defendant was guilty as charged beyond a reasonable doubt. If he was so judged, the second stage of the trial then took place; its purpose was to determine whether it was permissible for the defendant to be sentenced to death rather than to prison for life. In this so-called bifurcated or two-stage trial, the prosecution was required to establish to the satisfaction of the sentencing judge or jury that at least one of ten statutory "aggravating circumstances" was present in the crime. The finding of one or more such circumstances was a necessary (but not a sufficient) condition of imposing a death sentence. (Georgia's ten statutory aggravating circumstances are listed in Appendix A.)

As for mitigating circumstances, none was mentioned in the Georgia statute—the idea explicitly surfaced in the state court's opinion but was given no precision or definition. (Mitigating circumstances were identified, however, in the new Florida death penalty statute and ratified in *Proffitt*; see Appendix B.) It looked as though neither the legislative drafters nor the supreme court of Georgia thought that there would be many (or perhaps even any?) efforts to undo a death sentence by relying, wholly or mainly, on an effective plea of mitigating circumstances.

The role assigned to mitigating circumstances was narrow at best. For one thing, no mitigating circumstances used in a given case were allowed to cancel or nullify any aggravating circumstances (if there were any) in the same case. No matter how many mitigating circumstances might be invoked by the defense and endorsed by the jury, they could not outweigh a solitary aggravating circumstance. It simply remained for the sentencer (judge or jury) to impose a death sentence (if one was to be imposed). The crucial issue was always and only this: Does the sentencer find any aggravating circumstances? As for the mitigating circumstances, no law required defense counsel to introduce any for the sentencer's

---

[75] *McGautha v. California*, 402 U. S. 183 (1971).

evaluation. The record in capital cases would soon show that defense counsel in the sentencing phase of a capital case all too frequently wandered all over the map in the failure to make effective use of potentially available mitigating circumstances.[76]

There is a somewhat unsettling feature of this two-stage trial scheme. Suppose that the defendant in the first stage enters a plea of not guilty. Assume he is nonetheless found guilty. The defendant's best hope now is to try to take advantage of one or more of the available mitigating circumstances. But to do that the defendant in effect must repudiate his earlier plea of not guilty. Now he must concede, explicitly or implicitly, that he was guilty all along. Only in this way can he hope to persuade the trial court that despite being found guilty of the crime he is undeserving of death—thanks to being saved by one or more of those mitigating factors. An exception to this practice could occur only in those infrequent capital cases where the defense believed that there was a "lingering doubt" regarding the defendant's guilt.

How did the new Georgia scheme apply in Gregg's case? Neither the prosecution nor the defense submitted any evidence in support of a lesser sentence than death. Mitigation thus played no role (though it might have[77]) in deciding Gregg's sentence. Aggravating circumstances, however, were crucial. Here is how Judge Merritt instructed the jury on the three aggravating circumstances that the prosecution intended to use to support its effort to secure a death sentence for Gregg:

> "One—That the offense of murder was committed while the offender was engaged in the commission of two other capital felonies, to wit, the armed robbery of [Simmons and Moore].

> "Two—That the offender committed the offense of murder for the purpose of receiving money and the automobile described in the indictment.

> "Three—The offense of murder was outrageously and wantonly vile, horrible and inhuman, in that [it] involved the depravity of [the] mind of the defendant."[78]

A look at Appendix A will confirm that these three are Georgia's statutory aggravating circumstances (b), (d), and (g).

VII. The State Appeal

The state appeal was held in the Tattnall County Courthouse in Reidsville, described by one observer as "a dirt farmer's town (and a prison town), unaffected, utilitarian, and quiet." Probably the most

---

[76] See, e.g. *Watkins v. Murray*, 493 U.S. 907 (1989); Marshall, J., dissenting.

[77] *Gregg*, at 194.

[78] *Id.*, at 161.

memorable event in the town's recent history was the filming of *The Longest Yard*, starring Burt Reynolds and using prisoners and prison staff.

The appeal, now made mandatory under the new Georgia death penalty statutes, was argued in July of 1974; it was decided in October of that year. Again defending Gregg was his court-appointed trial attorney, Harrison. Arguing for the state was G. Thomas Davis, a Senior Assistant Attorney General for Georgia. The Georgia Supreme Court upheld the trial court's verdict and sentence on the two counts of murder but vacated the death sentences in the robberies on the ground that a death penalty for robbery was (in the language of the eighth amendment) "unusual" in its severity and therefore unconstitutional. This may have been the first post–*Furman* state death penalty statute declared by a state supreme court to be unconstitutional because it violated the eighth amendment prohibition of "unusual" punishments.[79]

Dissent on the bench from the majority judgment was confined to one vote. The ruling had little or no explicit effect upon death penalty deliberations in other cases or jurisdictions. However, it did foreshadow the possibility that the death penalty would henceforth be confined to homicide-related cases—as proved to be true in *Coker v. Georgia* (death penalty for rape [1977] [80]) and *Eberheart v. Georgia* (death penalty for kidnapping [1977] [81]). As of 2008, the Supreme Court had yet to sustain the constitutionality of any non-homicidal death penalty statute. Seldom noticed is the fact that the Texas death penalty statute approved by the Supreme Court in *Jurek* was formulated by reference to the crime of "murder" (variously defined).[82] This had the result that nine of the ten pre–*Furman* capital crimes under Texas law were invalidated.[83]

The most important provision in the state supreme court's ruling was its endorsement of the statutory standards defining a permissible death sentence, with emphasis on the requirement that the sentence not be "excessive or disproportionate" to the penalties for homicide imposed in similar cases, or "imposed under the influence of passion, prejudice,

---

[79] For a partial list of other post–*Furman* cases where state supreme courts have invalidated the constitutionality of the state's capital statutes, see Hugo Adam Bedau, "The Death Penalty and State Constitutional Rights in the United States of America," United Nations, *Crime Prevention and Criminal Justice Newsletter* 16 (Nov.1986).

[80] *Coker v. Georgia*, 433 U.S. 584 (1977).

[81] *Eberheart v. Georgia*, 433 U.S. 917 (1977).

[82] For the text of the Texas statute, see *Jurek*, 269; White, J., concurring.

[83] For pre–*Furman* capital statutes in Texas, see Hugo Adam Bedau, ed., *The Death Penalty in America: Current Controversies* 9 (1997).

or any other arbitrary factor.''[84] Exactly how the supreme court of Georgia established that the standards in question had been satisfied— or even how those standards were to be interpreted—was not explained. Nor was it clear how the eighteen Georgia death penalty cases cited in support really did support the interpretation given to them. So-called proportionality review would have a difficult time getting integrated into the new Georgia sentencing scheme. Would it be unfair to suggest that these crucial aspects of the court's appellate decisions were left to guesswork by the parties concerned? (Eight years later, in *Pulley v. Harris* [1984], a California case, the Supreme Court effectively brought this experiment to an end: proportionality review of death sentences was ruled not required by the federal constitution.[85])

The Georgia court's decision did have the arguable merit of moving any further developments in the case into the federal courts. There the Supreme Court granted Gregg's petition for review.

VIII. The Case at The Supreme Court

Gregg and its four companion cases from Florida, Texas, North Carolina and Louisiana were tied together by the LDF's main brief in the Texas case (*Jurek*), an amicus brief filed by the LDF for *Gregg* in the Florida case (*Proffitt*), and references to the LDF's brief previously filed in *Fowler*[86]—now being held pending resolution of the new North Carolina case, *Woodson*. The LDF's main argument compared the current state of capital punishment to the circumstances found unconstitutional by the Court four years earlier in *Furman*. Evolving standards of decency, the LDF argued, led to the conclusion that the death penalty violated the eighth amendment; and the states' asserted desire to impose death sentences, the argument went, was belied by the manifold outlets that permitted the punishment not to be imposed.

The Ford administration had no intention of permitting, much less encouraging, an abolitionist outcome in these important cases. Accordingly, it again called on Solicitor General Bork, who filed a 134–page amicus brief on behalf of the Georgia statute and any future parallel federal statute. Bork's brief outlined a lack of support in constitutional history for abolishing capital punishment, argued the illegitimacy of moral decisions made by judges and academics rather than by state legislatures and their constituents, and defended the social purposes of retribution and deterrence.

Oral argument in all five cases was set for a two-day period at the end of March 1976. Appearing for the petitioners in *Jurek*, *Woodson*, and

---

[84] *Gregg v. The State*, 210 S.E.2d 659 (Ga.1974).

[85] *Pulley v. Harris*, 465 U.S. 37 (1984).

[86] For further discussion of *Fowler*, see Bedau, *supra* note 23, at 103–09.

Roberts v. Louisiana,[87] was Anthony G. Amsterdam, the LDF's abolition-ist litigator nonpariel,[88] already famous for his arguments in *Furman* and its predecessors. G. Hughel Harrison argued *Gregg*, and another appointed counsel argued *Proffitt*. State prosecuting attorneys also ar-gued in all five cases, but the Justices focused on Amsterdam and Bork.

By all accounts, argument went poorly for Amsterdam and the LDF, despite the willingness of Justices Stewart, Powell, and Stevens to rely on a doctrine emerging from *Furman*—that "death is different."[89] Bork strenuously argued that this doctrine had no support in the Constitu-tion; he spent the second half of his argument defending the States' legitimate legislative prerogatives and endorsing the societal ends served by capital punishment, all the while stirring animosity toward Amster-dam. "The Court," Bork insisted, "must look to the legislature, not the more enlightened professor for the morals of society." Bork's approach was so well received that at the end of his half hour at the podium, Justice Powell gave him an additional five minutes by way of a softball question: "Would you care to comment, elaborate, or state your views with respect to the deterrent effect, if any, of the death sentence?"[90]

In sharp contrast, Powell and Chief Justice Burger pummeled Am-sterdam with questions, including one exchange in which Burger stated, "Since there is always an initial discretion on the part of the prosecutor, and . . . at the far end of a power of clemency by an executive, then no statutes can meet [your] standards." In response, Amsterdam admitted he would "[e]ventually take the position" articulated by Burger, but that it was "not a position that needs to be taken in this case[.]" As one scholar has commented, Amsterdam's "dilemma was irresolvable. Either the states could draft constitutional statutes or they could not. There was no way to have both at once."[91]

The LDF's response to the claims for capital punishment's retribu-tive value also proved to be a weak spot for Amsterdam, as evidenced by the following exchange:

> *Court*: If one wanted to argue retribution, one could say that the victims, whom you never mention, have already lost.

---

[87] *Roberts v. Louisiana*, 428 U.S. 325 (1976), hereinafter *Roberts*.

[88] See Meltsner, *supra* note 34.

[89] *Gregg*, at 188; Edward Lazarus, *Closed Chambers: The Rise, Fall, and Future of the Modern Supreme Court* 117(1999).

[90] Epstein and Koblyka, *supra* note 7, at 108–09; Bob Woodward and Scott Armstrong, *The Brethren: Inside the Supreme Court* 434 (1979); *Rupert V. Barry*, Note, "Furman to Gregg: The Judicial and Legislative History," 22 *How. L. J. 53*, 106–07 (1979).

[91] Banner, *supra* note 18, at 273–74.

Amsterdam: What did you say?

Court: I say if one wanted to argue retribution, one could say that the victims, whom you never mention, have already lost.

Amsterdam: If one wanted to argue that the system of killing [the defendants] was retributive, yes, but there is no rational retributive justification for killing people who killed . . .

Court: I guess you missed my point. [I] mentioned [the] victims of the four defendants.

Amsterdam: Yes. Victims are unquestionably—

Court:—Dead.[92]

Still, Amsterdam made unmistakable the overall position of the petitioners and the LDF. "What we have now in 1976," he argued, "is not change in the arbitrary and capricious nature of the death sentencing statutes of four years ago, only the technical illusion of such a change."

IX.   The Texas and Florida Schemes

Let us shift our attention from Georgia and imagine that *Gregg's* case had arisen in Florida or in Texas. What differences, if any, might this have made to the outcome and to the steps taken to reach it?

Both Florida and Texas had moved quickly to re-enact capital punishment laws in the wake of *Furman*. Florida was first, ignoring the recommendations of its Committee to Study Capital Punishment (appointed by the Governor immediately after *Furman* to study the feasibility of reinstating the death penalty), which had recommended that capital punishment was likely unconstitutional and should not be restored until further study could be undertaken.[93] Not to imply that Florida was oblivious to constitutional concerns; on the contrary, legislators' debates centered on how to comply with *Furman*.[94] At the Governor's request, the legislature held an emergency session where legislators quarreled past midnight "nearly to a stalemate over the type of sentencing reform."[95] What they finally produced, signed into law December 9, 1972,[96] was a bill similar to the capital sentencing provisions of the Model Penal Code—a classic model "guided-discretion" statute.

---

[92] As recounted in Epstein and Koblyka, *supra* note 7, at 109.

[93] Epstein and Koblyka, *supra* note 7, at 85–86. After the Florida bill's passage, members of the Committee condemned the new law as "seriously defective," and called it "an expedient response to election-time politics rather than a sound response to constitutional and penological needs of the state." *Id.*

[94] Martin Dyckman, "New Death Penalty Enacted by Florida," *Wash. Post,* Dec. 2, 1972, at A3.

[95] *Id.*

[96] "Florida Becomes First to Reinstate the Death Penalty," *N.Y. Times,* Dec. 9, 1972, at 32.

In Texas, the process of re-enacting capital punishment was undertaken with less careful consideration. After debate over *Furman*'s requirements, and several different proposals including a mandatory system, the legislature ultimately passed with little floor discussion a statute that had been hastily drafted in committee. Former U.S Representative Craig Washington, a member of the Texas House during the 1973 session, described the process: "Nobody sat down and thought through these things to come up with a rational way [to address the problems identified in *Furman*]. They made up something that sounded like it would give the jury some guidance.... You have to remember these questions were ... thought up on the spur of the moment in conference committee."[97] The new Texas statute mandated a death sentence upon "yes" answers to prescribed special verdict questions, and—despite its quasi-mandatory aspects—it was treated as a "guided discretion" statute by the Court.

Had Gregg been tried in Florida, three factors of note would have been different. First, the Florida statute provided the trial court with an explicit list of mitigating circumstances for guidance in deciding on the sentence.[98] Second, no proportionality review was required. Third, and by far the most important factor, is that the statute empowered the trial judge to override the jury's sentence, turning the jury's sentence into no more than a recommendation.[99] (Only a few states in addition to Florida adopted the jury-override provision.[100]) Subsequent years would prove two things. First, the jury-override would reintroduce the very arbitrariness in sentencing that *Furman* was supposed to remedy. Second, the override provision would result in more rather than fewer death sentences—the very opposite of the intention with which the Florida legislature introduced the practice in the first place.[101] As a side issue, *Proffitt* shared with *Gregg* the invalidation of his death sentence (1982) by the federal courts; years later (1996), he was transferred to prison in Connecticut so he could serve out the rest of his life sentence near his family.[102]

---

[97] Tex. Defender Serv., "Deadly Speculation: Misleading Texas Capital Juries with False Predictions of Future Dangerousness" 2–3 (2004); see http://texasdefender.org/DEADLYSP.pdf (quoting Kathy Walt, "Debate Over Death Penalty Is Renewed; Predicting Future Threats Raises Question of Flaws," *Hous. Chron.,* July 9, 2000, at B1).

[98] *Proffitt*, 249; Stewart, J., plurality opinion.

[99] The Supreme Court upheld a challenge to the Florida judicial override. *Spaziano v. Florida*, 468 U.S. 447 (1984).

[100] Florida, Alabama, Delaware, and Indiana were the other jury-override jurisdictions. See Michael Mello, "The Jurisdiction to do Justice: Florida's Jury Override and the State Constitution," 18 *Florida State U. L. Rev.* 923 (1991).

[101] Katheryn K. Russell, "The Constitutionality of Jury Override in Alabama Death Penalty Cases," 46 *Ala. L. Rev.* 5 (1994).

[102] *The [Florida] Stuart News*, July 4, 1996, A1.

In the case of Texas, the differences in sentencing practice under the new statute are more dramatic. The first difference would have been that the apparatus of an explicit list of aggravating (and mitigating) circumstances would play no role in deciding between death and life imprisonment. Put aside also any proportionality review. Disregard the demand for discovery governing the employment of aggravating circumstances by the prosecution. Introduce the sole criterion that required the jury to predict whether the defendant would be a danger to others. Only if the court affirmed that he would be could they sentence him to death. This criterion, so it was averred, would narrow the class of murders eligible for a death sentence so that, in the words of Justice Stewart, "this system serves to assure that sentences of death will not be 'wantonly' or 'freakishly' imposed" in violation of the Constitution.[103] As later years were to prove, a closer look at the Texas system would lead one to doubt whether that system really could accomplish what Stewart claimed for it. Not many states reintroduced the death penalty by means of a scheme like the one enacted in the Lone Star State.[104] Apparently there were more statutory ways than one to skin a constitutional cat.

The new Texas scheme deserves a closer look. As noted above, if the trial judge or jury was to impose a death sentence, it had to answer three questions in the affirmative: "(1) [Was] the conduct of the defendant that caused the death of the deceased committed deliberately and with the reasonable expectation that the death of the deceased or another would result; (2) [Is] there a probability that the defendant would commit criminal acts of violence that would constitute a continuing threat to society; and (3) if raised by the evidence, [was] the conduct of the defendant in killing the deceased ... unreasonable in response to the provocation, if any, by the deceased."[105]

The contrast between this set of three criteria in Texas and the five-fold scheme created in Georgia could hardly be greater. Or more perplexing. The most pointed critique of the Texas statute, given in a lecture a few months after the decision in *Gregg*, was offered by Charles L. Black, Jr. One cannot do better than follow the critique he offered in his short (two dozen pages) essay on the subject.[106]

Black considered each of the three Texas questions in turn. They constitute an odd trio. The first condition is presumably guaranteed to

---

[103] *Gregg*, at 207; Stewart J., plurality opinion.

[104] According to James W. Marquart and Jonathan R. Sorenson, in 1989 there were only eight states whose capital statutes contained a "future dangerousness" provision. See Bedau, *supra* note 83, at 162.

[105] *Jurek*, 269; Stewart, J., plurality opinion.

[106] Black, *supra* note 25, at 111–34 (1981 2d).

be satisfied in *every* capital case. *Every* capital jury or judge must answer the first question in the affirmative; how else could the defendant have been properly convicted of murder in the first place? This makes the first of the three criteria redundant. The same is true with respect to the third question; if the jury were to answer in the negative, that would impeach its prior guilty verdict. As for the second question, Black correctly noted that "it is, at the very least, almost always going to be the only [question] on which the jury actually decides anything it has not already decided. It is the life-or-death question."[107] It is troubling on moral as well as on empirical grounds. Black asked rhetorically, "What is wanting is . . . one single example in the whole range of civilized law outside of this one statute, that explicitly . . . makes a person's cruel death [by execution] depend on a prediction of that person's *future* conduct."[108]

From the empirical point of view, gathering and interpreting the evidence of a defendant's future dangerousness is no small matter. Social science evidence prior to *Gregg* gave ample warning that such predictions were of little or no value.[109] Perhaps the best evidence of their unreliability in the post–*Gregg* environment is found in the research conducted in Texas by social scientists James W. Marquart and Jonathan R. Sorenson on the relative lack of recidivism among death row prisoners who (for one reason or another) were not executed. In their cautious words, "capital murderers on parole do not represent a disproportionate threat to the larger society."[110] As a final word they added this cool assessment: "over-prediction of secondary violence is indicated."[111] So much for the improvements in Texas's death penalty jurisprudence thanks to the provisions ratified by the Court in *Jurek*. Unfortunately, this research was unavailable to Gregg's legal team until several years after *Gregg* had been decided.

As with Gregg's and Proffitt's stories, Jerry Lane Jurek's did not end with his sentence of death. In 1980 the federal courts overturned his conviction, thus nullifying his sentence to death by lethal injection. Two years later at retrial, he reached a plea bargain in which he confessed to

---

[107] *Id.*, at 115.

[108] *Id.*, at 124.

[109] John Monahan, "The Prediction of Violent Criminal Behavior: A Methodological Critique and Prospectus," in Alfred Blumstein et al., eds., *Deterrence and Incapacitation: Estimating the Effects of Sanctions on Crime Rates* (1978).

[110] James W. Marquart and Jonathan R. Sorensen, "A National Study of the *Furman*-Commuted Inmates: Assessing the Threat to Society from Capital Offenders," in Bedau, *supra* note 83, at 172.

[111] *Id.*, at 174.

murder and in exchange the prosecution agreed to sentence him to life in prison.[112]

X.   A Divided Court Speaks

As in *Furman*, so in *Gregg*. The Supreme Court split in several ways when it came to explaining the rationale for its ruling. These divisions, however, did not significantly weaken the holding; the seven to two judicial lineup in *Gregg* was much stronger than the five to four vote in *Furman*, which lacked even a plurality (much less a majority) opinion.

The plurality opinion for the *Gregg* Court, authored by Justice Potter Stewart and joined by Justices Lewis F. Powell, Jr., and John Paul Stevens, was controlling. Stewart, along with Justice Byron R. White, had provided one of the two swing votes in the five-justice holding in *Furman;* both now reversed course. White concurred in the judgment but also offered his own conservative opinion. He was joined by Chief Justice Warren E. Burger and Justice William H. Rehnquist. The seventh vote to uphold the Georgia statute was cast by Justice Harry A. Blackmun, who contented himself (as he had in his *Furman* opinion) with a single short sentence expressing his concurrence only in the judgment. Shrewd Court watchers would later see in Blackmun's relative silence the seed that eventually blossomed into his full-scale opposition to the death penalty years later in *Callins v. Collins* (1994).[113]

The dissenting opinions by Justices William J. Brennan, Jr., and Thurgood Marshall did little more than provide a very brief version of their lengthy opinions in *Furman*, although there was one major novelty in Justice Marshall's opinion. He chose to unravel the econometric argument for the deterrent effect of executions advanced by Justice Stewart and Solicitor General Bork. Brennan and Marshall once again favored complete abolition, as was to be expected given their opinions in *Furman*. They were undone, however, by the silence of Justice Blackmun and the shift of Justice Stewart and Justice White into the retentionist column. The abolitionists had failed to carry the day for complete abolition on eighth amendment grounds, and there was little left for them to say to smooth the way for some future constitutional argument.

XI.   Constitutional Norms and the Stewart Plurality Opinion.

What was the argument that persuaded the Court that the new Georgia, Texas, and Florida death penalty statutes were not in violation of the eighth and fourteenth amendments' prohibition of "cruel and unusual punishment"? Why was the death penalty per se not in violation of the Constitution? These were the crucial questions left unanswered

[112] *Hous. Chron.*, Feb. 4, 2001, A28.

[113] *Callins v. Collins*, 510 U.S. 1141 (1994); Blackmun, J., dissenting.

(indeed, left unasked) by *Furman*. Justice Stewart's plurality opinion
provides the answers. They resulted from identifying both the purposes
of punishment and the normative principles on which the *Furman*
majority relied. How did these purposes and principles fare in Stewart's
plurality opinion for the Court in the *Gregg*?

The principles in question were five in number. They can be stated
in categorical form as follows:

- An arbitrary death penalty is unconstitutional.

- A discriminatory death penalty is unconstitutional.

- A death penalty that flouts evolving standards of decency is
  unconstitutional.

- A death penalty that flouts substantive due process is unconstitutional.

- A death penalty that flouts the dignity of man is unconstitutional.

Substantive Due Process. As far as the Stewart plurality was concerned, the least influential normative principle of the five was the
principle of substantive due process. As a principle of constitutional law,
it permits a court to nullify a statute that invades some fundamental
value—such as liberty, privacy, or autonomy—when there is available a
less invasive law that can provide the same degree of protection. In the
present context the inference is obvious. If you believe that long-term
imprisonment can protect society as well as the death penalty does,
which is what Justices Brennan and Marshall believed, then the extra
severity of a death penalty has lost its rationale for you. Powerful though
this principle is, it has been highly controversial for more than a
century,[114] because it licenses the courts to intervene as super-legisla-
tures, endorsing laws that suit the court's pleasure—or so its critics
allege—under the guise of interpreting the Constitution. As Justice
Stewart put it in *Gregg*, "We may not require the legislature to select
the least severe penalty possible so long as the penalty selected is not
cruelly inhumane or disproportionate to the crime involved."[115] It is not
surprising that most of the Justices would refuse to avail themselves of
this norm.

The Dignity of Man. Respecting the dignity of man is the most
abstract as well as the vaguest of the five principles. It entered into
constitutional interpretation only a half century ago with the decision in

---

[114] Kermit L. Hall, ed., *The Oxford Companion to the Supreme Court of the United
States* 237–38 (1992).

[115] *Gregg*, at 182–83; Justice Stewart quotes Justice Powell in *Furman* at 451: "[W]e
cannot invalidate a category of penalties because we deem less severe penalties adequate to
serve the ends of penology."

Trop v. Dulles (1958).[116] Since then this principle has figured in all the Supreme Court's rulings that have interpreted the eighth amendment favoring abolition, and it is reflected in nine of the ten *Furman* opinions (the holdout, it will be recalled, was Justice Blackmun). However, it plays a very insignificant role in Justice Stewart's plurality opinion in *Gregg*. He writes there that "The Court also must ask whether [the punishment] comports with the basic concept of human dignity at the core of the Amendment."[117] But he does not go on to explain how the death penalty accomplishes this prodigious task.

Is it possible to invoke the principle of human dignity to better effect by arguing that the death penalty, no matter how it is administered, is and will remain an affront to human dignity? Consider in this light the five methods of administering executions that have been adopted at one time or another by American legislatures during the twentieth century. What could be a greater affront to human dignity than killing offenders in the electric chair, or in the gas chamber, or by hanging, or by a firing squad, or by the latecomer, lethal injection? In these sordid practices the dignity of man has been conspicuous by its absence, as even a superficial acquaintance with these methods of execution proves.[118]

Evolving Standards of Decency. The idea that there are objective standards of decency, that they evolve over time, and that they have played a dominant role in determining constitutionally permissible punitive practices figures prominently in the abolition arguments of Justices Brennan and Marshall in both *Furman* and *Gregg*. Thanks to this principle one could acknowledge that although the text of the Constitution mentions the death penalty several times without disapproval, this tolerance does not protect the constitutional status of that penalty for all time. Indeed, the importance of this principle can hardly be denied. It figured in death penalty jurisprudence from the very beginning of the modern constitutional abolition campaign, launched in a 1961 law review article by California lawyer Gerald Gottlieb[119], and relied upon two years later in the case of *Rudolph v. Alabama*.[120] What was true about the doubtful moral acceptability of the death penalty in the early 1960s[121] is

---

[116] *Trop v. Dulles*, 356 U.S. 86 (1958).

[117] *Gregg*, at 182. See also Hugo Adam Bedau, "The Eighth Amendment, Human Dignity, and the Death Penalty," in Michael J. Meyer and William A. Parent, eds., *The Constitution of Rights: Human Dignity and American Values* 145 (1992).

[118] Deborah Denno, "Lethally Humane? The Evolution of Execution Methods in the United States," in James R. Acker et al., eds., *America's Experiment with Capital Punishment* 2d, 693 (2003).

[119] Gerald H. Gottlieb, "Testing the Death Penalty," 34 *South. Cal. L. Rev.* 268 (1961).

[120] *Rudolf v. Alabama*, 375 U.S. 889 (1963); Goldberg, J., dissenting.

[121] See, e.g., Bedau, *supra* note 19; James Avery Joyce, *Capital Punishment: A World View* (1961).

even truer half a century later.[122] There are evolving standards of decency and they show up in the degree of tolerance being afforded to the death penalty over the past half century in much of the world.

The Stewart plurality in *Gregg* was quite ready to challenge the claim that evolving standards of decency condemned the death penalty insofar as those standards were manifest in various forms of public opposition to executions. Justice Stewart cited three independent kinds of evidence to that effect (the dissenters apparently were unable to cite anything to the contrary). First, most state legislatures promptly re-enacted death penalty statutes in the aftermath of *Furman*. True. Second, in the one state where a post-*Furman* death penalty referendum had been held (California), the state constitution was promptly amended to permit enactment of a death penalty statute. Also true. Finally, capital trial juries in the four years since *Furman* had no difficulty in meting out dozens of death sentences. Alas, all too true. As for the modest fraction of capital cases that actually ended with a death sentence and execution—more than 250 death sentences had been handed down within two years after the decision in *Furman*, and more than 400 by the time *Gregg* was decided—Stewart argued that "the reluctance of juries in many cases to impose the sentence may well reflect the humane feeling that this most irrevocable of sanctions should be reserved for a small number of extreme cases."[123] (Stewart cited no evidence in support of this conjecture, and in recent years the evidence against it is quite powerful.)

Today, forty years after *Gregg* was decided, there are several kinds of evidence—especially two—to which the death penalty in America is vulnerable as never before. One is the tidal wave of literature subjecting the death penalty to every kind of attack: moral, political, legal, histori-cal, sociological, criminological, and economic.[124] The other is the steady attack it has come under from international organizations (chiefly Am-nesty International), international conferences, and international human rights law.[125] The kinds of evidence that the Stewart plurality in *Gregg* cited in 1976 against the claim that evolving standards of decency

---

[122] See, e.g., J. Michael Martinez et al., eds., *Leviathan's Choice: Capital Punishment in the Twenty-First Century* (2002); Austin Sarat, *When the State Kills: Capital Punishment and the American Condition* (2001).

[123] *Gregg*, at 184.

[124] See Hugo Adam Bedau, "Death Penalty Research Today and Tomorrow," in Charles S. Lanier, William J. Bowers, and James R. Acker, eds., *An Agenda for the Next Generation of Capital Punishment Research* (2008).

[125] See, e.g., Roger Hood and Carolyn Hoyle, *The Death Penalty: A Worldwide Perspec-tive.* 4th ed. (2008); William A. Schabas, ed., *The International Sourcebook on Capital Punishment* (1977); and Council of Europe, *The Death Penalty—Beyond Abolition* (2004).

condemned the death penalty could easily be reformulated in light of today's knowledge and would serve to undermine the complacent support the post–*Furman* death penalty system received in the recent past. Probably the single most dramatic evidence of this sort is in the mass commutation of death row prisoners by Governor George Ryan in Illinois in 2003,[126] unimaginable in 1976.

Arbitrariness and Discrimination. How should we define arbitrariness and discrimination in a system of punishment? Here is one way: A punishment is *arbitrary* when there are no coherent or rational reasons for inflicting it instead of some more or less severe alternative, as when a prosecutor seeks the death penalty for a defendant chosen at random. A punishment is *discriminatory*, however, when it is based on irrelevant factors, such as race, class, or gender. (The two concepts ought to be defined independently, because a punishment can be arbitrary without being discriminatory, and it can be discriminatory without being arbitrary.) Death penalty statutes as administered prior to *Furman* suffered from both kinds of flaws.

These norms dominated the thinking of all five Justices in the *Furman* majority. They agreed that the death penalty as administered in 1972 was both arbitrary and discriminatory and therefore unconstitutional. The post–*Furman* statutes crafted by legislatures, such as those we have examined in Georgia, Florida, and Texas, were aimed at remedying these faults. (We have seen how, and how differently, these three state legislatures discharged that task.) These administrative defects could, in principle, be remedied—or so it seemed reasonable for friends of capital punishment to believe at the time. As for abolition arguments of this sort, they permitted the Justices to adopt a cautious and piecemeal approach to the larger issue of abolition, if indeed they were ever to approach that issue at all. Research in subsequent years, however, would prove beyond a reasonable doubt that it was far more difficult—indeed, perhaps impossible—to draft and comply with death penalty statutes that were neither arbitrary nor discriminatory. In particular, race and class would continue to exert their malign influence, distorting the process and the outcome.[127]

The *Gregg* majority did not dispute the relevance of the anti-discrimination and anti-arbitrariness principles. These two norms were too deeply embedded in constitutional law to be dismissed so crudely. Accordingly, the Stewart plurality undertook to dispute, and vigorously,

---

[126] George Ryan, "I Must Act," in Hugo Adam Bedau and Paul G. Cassell, eds., *Debating the Death Penalty*, 218–34 (2004).

[127] See, e.g., Bryan Stevenson, "Close to Death: Reflections on Race and Capital Punishment in America," in Bedau and Cassell, *supra* note 126, at 76–116; Stephen B. Bright, "Counsel for the Poor," in Bedau, *supra* note 83, at 275–309.

the evidence that the new statutes in fact violated these principles. Unlike the dissenters, the Stewart plurality did not believe that the new laws introduced remedies that were purely "cosmetic"[128] and thus failed to improve on the procedures held to be unconstitutional in *Furman*.

The Purposes of Punishment. Stewart then turned from empirical judgments that he believed nullified the abolitionist attack on the death penalty to more abstract considerations. First, he argued that the death penalty (like most punishments) serves two "principled social purposes: retribution and deterrence...."[129] (In a footnote he mentioned another purpose: "incapacitation of dangerous criminals."[130]) In support of the first principle Stewart added: "Indeed, the decision that capital punishment may be the appropriate sanction in extreme cases is an expression of the community's belief that certain crimes are themselves so grievous an affront to humanity that the only adequate response may be the penalty of death."[131] In another footnote Stewart quoted an English authority, Lord Justice Denning, Master of the Rolls, who observed that "Punishment is the way in which society expresses its denunciation of wrong doing: ..."[132] (We might add denunciation of wrong doing as a fourth principle animating the purposes of punishment.) Stewart did not pause to note that of course punishment is not the only and arguably not even the main way society expresses its disapproval of wrong doing; this makes appealing to denunciation an ambiguous support for the Stewart plurality's argument. How we are to regard retribution for homicide as best obtained by the death penalty when only a small fraction of criminal homicides result in a death sentence and only a smaller fraction of those result in an execution apparently did not trouble Justice Stewart; he expressed no worries on this score. We are left having to conclude that either retribution does not count for much where murder is concerned or it is adequately satisfied without recourse to the death penalty—or that a little retribution goes a long way.

Does deterrence fare any better? Stewart disposed of this consideration with a quotation from Professor Black, a deterrence skeptic if ever there was one. Black's view can be summarized in two of his sentences: "Statistical attempts to evaluate the worth of the death penalty as a deterrent to crimes by potential offenders have occasioned a great deal of debate. The results simply have been inconclusive."[133] There is, of

---

128 *Gregg*, at 198.

129 *Id.*, at 183.

130 *Id.*, at n28.

131 *Id.*, at 184.

132 *Id.*, at n30.

133 Black, *supra* note 25, at 25–26; quoted in Stewart, J., plurality opinion, 184.

course, much more to be said on this dispute (much of it took place in the mid–1970s around the time *Gregg* was decided). A fuller account of the deterrence controversy is to be found in the Justices' opinions in *Gregg* and in the amicus brief filed by the Department of Justice over the signature of the Solicitor General and contested by Justice Marshall in his dissenting opinion in *Gregg*. So much, then, for how the death penalty—according to the Stewart plurality—serves the purposes of punishment.

Here is how Justice Stewart summed up his defense of the constitutional status of the death penalty: "[W]hen a life has been taken deliberately by the offender we cannot say that the punishment is invariably disproportionate to the crime. It is an extreme sanction, suitable to the most extreme of crimes. We hold that the death penalty is not a form of punishment that may never be imposed, regardless of the circumstances of the offense, regardless of the character of the offender, and regardless of the procedure followed in reaching the decision to impose it."[134]

XII.   The White Plurality Opinion

Although the Stewart plurality wrote for the Court, the plurality argument of Justice White—written for himself, Chief Justice Burger, and Justice Rehnquist—needs to be examined for the contribution it made to the strength of the overall retentionist argument. The White plurality focused on assessing the adequacy of the Georgia death penalty statute in satisfying the requirements of *Furman*. The twin constraints of federalism and deference to the legislature, exceeding in this regard the concern of the Stewart plurality, governed their opinion.

White then turned to the central issue of excessive discretion; he did so by addressing the extent to which the jury, the state supreme court, and the state legislature in death penalty jurisdictions had made marked improvements in these three areas of their capital jurisprudence. "The Georgia Legislature has plainly made an effort to guide the jury in the exercise of its discretion while at the same time permitting the jury to dispense mercy on the basis of factors too intangible to write into a statute, . . ."[135] That is not all: "[T]he Georgia Legislature has made an effort to identify those aggravating factors which it considers necessary and relevant to the question whether a defendant convicted of capital murder should be sentenced to death." This was true. The Georgia legislature had, apparently in good faith, tried to identify these factors. White continued his review of the novel features of the Georgia death penalty scheme as enacted by the state legislature, which prompted him

---

[134] *Gregg*, at 187.

[135] *Gregg*, at 222; White, J., concurring.

to add: "There is ... reason to expect that Georgia's current system would escape the infirmities which invalidated its previous system under *Furman*."[136] Reason, indeed, there might be; it is an empirical question deserving to be treated as such. One might think that in some future case Justice White would have returned to this issue and rendered a judgment on whether our "reason to expect" such results had turned out to be well or ill founded. Evidence in his subsequent death penalty opinions is lacking, as he has remained silent on this issue.

As for the alleged unreliability (according to the dissenters) with which the supreme court of Georgia was carrying out its new duties of proportionality review on expedited appeal, Justice White was unpersuaded. "Petitioner has wholly failed to establish, and has not even attempted to establish, that the Georgia Supreme Court failed properly to perform its task in this case or that it is incapable of performing its task adequately in all cases; and this Court should not assume that it did not do so."[137] What went unmentioned was the fact that Gregg's attorneys had been able to gather only two years worth of empirical data (1972 to 1974) on this and the other empirical issues on which their argument rested; not surprisingly, this was insufficient to persuade, much less prove their claims.

White finally turned to review the use and abuse of discretion by the Georgia prosecutors: "[T]hat prosecutors behave in a standardless fashion in deciding which cases to try as capital felonies is unsupported by any facts."[138] He concluded the essence of his position thus: "I decline to interfere with the manner in which Georgia has chosen to enforce such laws [including the criminal laws against murder] on what is simply an assertion of lack of faith in the ability of the system of justice to operate in a fundamentally fair manner."[139] In the light of the past thirty years it is touching to see Justice White's confidence in the system, especially as it affects prosecutorial decision-making, and the wealth of research that incontrovertibly shows how unfair the current system really is.

Professor Black did not assess the evidence as Justice White did. He closed his essay with a review of the unregulated discretion left untouched by the rulings in *Gregg*, *Jurek*, and *Proffitt*. "[T]oo much arbitrary discretion" remains in the system, he argued.[140] "This discretion exists as to the prosecutor, who decides, without constraints what to charge," and especially to "whether the accused person is to be allowed

---

[136] *Id.*

[137] *Id.*, at 224.

[138] *Id.*, at 225.

[139] *Id.*, at 226.

[140] Black, *supra* 25, at 125–26.

to plead guilty to a lesser charge." The discretion further extends to "the jury's virtually uncontrollable power to find 'not guilty' or 'guilty' of a lesser offense—..." And, he added, "It exists, in the decision on insanity—... It exists in the administration of clemency." And what did this add up to? "The net effect of all this is that, quite aside from the step formally devoted to a sentencing decision, the actual selection of persons for death is made by a series of choices not governed by any articulated standards."[141] So much for Justice White's confidence in the post–*Furman* constraints on sentencing discretion in capital cases. The best counter-assessment on the breadth of discretion allowed by these cases is to be found in the Solicitor General's amicus brief and the twenty pages of analysis he offered there.

XIII.   The Mandatory Death Penalty

The cases of *Woodson* and *Roberts*, from North Carolina and Louisiana respectively, presented statutes for review that, upon conviction, mandated sentences of death. The Court's reasoning in these cases showed its reliance on the reasoning in *Gregg*. Taking up the hint in Chief Justice Burger's dissent in *Furman* that a mandatory death penalty might satisfy the constraints imposed by *Furman*,[142] nineteen state legislatures by 1976 had rejected the complex features of capital sentencing endorsed by the Georgia, Florida, and Texas legislatures in favor of the historically prior practice of mandatory death sentences for some or all capital crimes.

North Carolina settled on a mandatory penalty not adopted via the legislative process, but as a result of a state supreme court decision in 1973 finding that any discretion in capital sentencing would violate *Furman*.[143] In April 1974, North Carolina's General Assembly ratified changes in the law to "[c]onform the punishment ... to the current case law: mandatory death penalty for first-degree murder."[144] Louisiana, through its legislature, enacted a mandatory death penalty for reasons identical to those of the North Carolina court: "removing the discriminatory application of the death penalty, which the United States Supreme Court held last year is imposed almost always only on the poor, the black and those with inadequate legal defense."[145]

---

[141] *Id.*

[142] *Furman*, at 401; Burger, C.J., dissenting.

[143] *State v. Waddell*, 282 N.C. 431, 445 (N.C. 1973).

[144] Dexter Watts, *Capital Punishment Legislation, Memorandum of Institute of Government* 1 (1974).

[145] James H. Gillis, "House Concurs on Share Bill," *New Orleans Times–Picayune*, June 13, 1973.

LDF attorneys were involved in considerable litigation over North Carolina's mandatory statute, because of the large number of people being sentenced under it. Their strategy focused on the claim that the mandatory system did not eliminate discretion but merely hid it, and that the resulting discrimination was apparent from the makeup of the new death row population.[146] By 1976 LDF's efforts had brought North Carolina's—first via *Fowler,* and ultimately via *Woodson*—and Louisiana's schemes under the Supreme Court's scrutiny.

In analyzing the mandatory laws, the three justices in the Stewart plurality were content to receive guidance from history on the point. "The consistent course shared by the state legislatures and by Congress since the middle of the past century demonstrates that the aversion of jurors to mandatory death penalty statutes is shared by society at large."[147] Why this unpopularity?

After a review of the nation's history with mandatory death penalties, the Stewart plurality identified three kinds of deficiency in the new North Carolina law. First, "the practice of sentencing to death all persons of a particular offense has been rejected as unduly harsh and unworkably rigid." The second deficiency was the "failure to provide a constitutionally tolerable response" to *Furman*'s rejection of unbridled jury discretion in the imposition of capital sentencing. The third "constitutional shortcoming" in the new death penalty scheme was its "failure to allow the particularized consideration of relevant aspects of the character and record of each convicted defendant before the imposition upon him of a sentence of death."[148] Here, too, Justice Brennan and Justice Marshall concurred in the judgment of the majority, as was to be expected, given their belief (expressed at length in *Furman*) that all death penalties were unconstitutional.

The Chief Justice, Justice White, and Justice Rehnquist were of a contrary persuasion. Their reasoning, however, consisted of little more than a reliance on their views as expressed in *Proffitt,* since the issues in *Woodson* and *Proffitt*—though not identical—were very similar. The real argument in dissent was provided by Justice Rehnquist, writing for himself. He began with a very different history of the American experience in the use and disuse of mandatory death sentencing from the version proposed by the Stewart plurality. As for the three "deficiencies" in capital sentencing that Justice Stewart identified, Justice Rehnquist rejected them all; there were no such deficiencies, in his opinion.

---

[146] Epstein and Koblyka, *supra* note 7, at 96.

[147] *Gregg,* at 295.

[148] *Gregg,* at 293, 302, 303.

XIV.   The Constitutional Argument of Solicitor General Bork

The Solicitor General's comprehensive defense of the death penalty unfolded as follows: First, the origins of the eighth amendment show that a legislature may enact death penalty statutes without violating the Constitution. Bork enlisted five different considerations in support of this conclusion: (1) The language of the Constitution shows that the framers intended to allow capital punishment; (2) for most of our history no one doubted that the Constitution permitted death penalties; (3) the experience in England with its counterpart to our eighth amendment supported this view; (4) the origin of the prohibition of "cruel and unusual punishment" reflected this derivation; (5) finally, the role this constitutional provision has played in the last century of judicial interpretation shows its relevance to the acceptability of various forms of punishment but without empowering the Court to be a "super-legislature."

Bork then asserted several propositions of current relevance and diverse character. First, the duty of the Court is to uphold penalties (such as any of the post–*Furman* death penalty statutes) that have full-scale legislative validity and also enjoy popular respect. A raft of considerations supported this view: (1) The death penalty serves legitimate public purposes; (2) it deters crime; (3) it reinforces "important social values"; (4) it is a legitimate expression of moral outrage; (5) it is not excessive in pursuit of these values; (6) the death penalty effectively incapacitates dangerous offenders. These are the essential empirical and normative propositions undergirding the constitutionality of death penalties—according to Bork.

Other considerations also need to be kept in mind, he insisted. As to public opinion, capital punishment is currently accepted by the public. Where, as here, there is a difference of opinion over the adequacy of a regulated practice, it is proper to defer to the wishes of the legislature. Finally, the main empirical claims on which the Stewart plurality in *Furman* had relied for support no longer apply—if they ever did.

To complete his argument, Bork advanced several further propositions. We need to consider only those concerning discretion. Bork argued that discretion is central to the effective operation of our current system of criminal justice. Furthermore, it does not result in a "freakish" imposition of death sentences. Finally, discretion in charging, plea bargaining, jury nullification, lesser included offenses, jury sentencing, and clemency—all involve essential reliance on discretion; taken together they prevent the imposition of a death sentence from being invalid.

Let us take a closer look at a few of these two dozen claims. In the three decades since the decision rendered in *Gregg*, each of the Solicitor General's allegations has been challenged and found wanting. Literally a

whole bookcase of materials on these claims is now available for consul-
tation for anyone who wishes to decide what to believe and on whom to
rely in regard to each claim. (This is not the place to undertake such a
comprehensive review.)

Of the several issues the Solicitor General addressed in his amicus
brief, one of the most important was the perennial issue, one may safely
say, of deterrence. Bork's position could not have been put more bluntly:
"Capital punishment deters crime."[149] In the 1970s he was quoted right
and left in discussion of this judgment. No one seems to have noticed
that one might well concede that the death penalty does sometimes deter
crime—and then argue that this is not the issue. Rather, the issue is
whether any evidence exists that death deters *better* than the alternative
of life imprisonment and enough better to make it worthwhile to have
such a system with all its unsavory and unavoidable costs. It is the issue
of *marginal* deterrence that is badly in need of empirical support. Bork's
brief showed he had no interest in that matter. The evidence on which
he did rely—the econometric number-crunching initially marshaled by
economist Isaac Ehrlich in his pioneering research of 1975,[150] according
to which each execution deterred "approximately eight murders"—also
failed to make this distinction. For all we know, even today, each
execution might deter eight murders; but it is equally possible, for all we
know, that each life imprisonment would deter eight murders—or three,
or twelve. But there were many other grounds, technical and otherwise,
on which to suspend judgment of a deterrent effect. Perhaps it is
sufficient here to quote the words of Professor Lawrence R. Klein, at the
time (1978) president of the American Economic Association, and his
associates: "[I]t seems unthinkable to us to base decisions on the use of
the death penalty on Ehrlich's findings, as the Solicitor General of the
United States has urged. They simply are not sufficiently powerful,
robust, or tested at this stage to warrant their use in such an important
case."[151]

That was the state of things deterrent and the death penalty in the
late 1970s. How does the issue look today? The most recent comprehensive assessment of deterrence and the death penalty was published in
1997, a decade ago, by sociologists William C. Bailey and Ruth D.
Peterson. Their conclusion? "The available evidence remains 'clear and
abundant' that, as practiced in the United States, capital punishment is

---

[149] Bork, *supra* note 11, at 34.

[150] Isaac Ehrlich, "The Deterrent Effect of Capital Punishment: A Question of Life and
Death," 65 *American Economic Review* 397–417 (1975).

[151] Lawrence R. Klein et al., "The Deterrent Effect of Capital Punishment: An
Assessment of the Estimates," in Alfred Blumstein et al., *Deterrence and Incapacitation:
Estimating the Effects of Criminal Sanctions on Crime Rates,* 336 (1978).

not more effective than imprisonment in deterring murder."[152] More recent econometric research conducted by economists at Emory University, attempting to breathe new life into the application of Ehrlich's methods and thereby achieve comparable (even superior) results to his, have not altered the Bailey–Peterson reading of the deterrence evidence: There is none to the effect that executions are a marginally superior deterrent over life imprisonment for the crime of murder.[153]

Another claim deserving at least passing notice here is the Solicitor General's observation that the death penalty "is not imposed on the basis of race."[154] That might have been a reasonable judgment prior to the late 1990s, when law professor David Baldus and his associates published their research[155] in connection with the litigation in *McCleskey*. It has not been a reasonable judgment in the decade since then.

Finally, there is the complete omission of any reassurance on the issue of wrongful convictions in capital cases or from the Solicitor General on the risk of executing the innocent. (Those issues did not become of paramount interest in the debate over the death penalty, as they are now, until 1987.[156])

XV.   The Argument of the Dissenters

As noted earlier, the Supreme Court did not achieve unanimity in advancing the arguments of the Stewart and White coalitions. These arguments left two of the justices—Brennan and Marshall—unpersuaded (and the ninth—Justice Blackmun—all but speechless in bare-bones concurrence). So much were Brennan and Marshall unpersuaded that, as noted earlier, neither justice ever spelled out his dissent in any future capital case (excepting only their dissents more than a decade later in *McCleskey*).

Justice Brennan did add a few new thoughts. Pointing out that he "will not again canvas the reasons that led him to [favor complete abolition]," he did repeat himself when he "emphasized only that foremost among the 'moral concepts' recognized in our cases and inherent in the Clause is the primary moral principle that the State even as it

---

[152] William C. Bailey and Ruth D. Peterson, "Murder, Capital Punishment, and Deterrence: A Review of the Literature," in Bedau, *supra* note 83, at 135.

[153] See Jeffrey Fagan, "Death and Deterrence Redux: Science, Law and Causal Reasoning on Capital Punishment," 4 *Ohio State J. Crim. L.*, 255 (2006).

[154] Bork, *supra* note 11, at 65.

[155] See David C. Baldus et al., *Equal Justice and the Death Penalty: A Legal and Empirical* Analysis (1990).

[156] The origin of the modern interest in wrongful convictions in capital cases can be dated from Hugo Adam Bedau and Michael L. Radelet, "Miscarriages of Justice in Potentially Capital cases," 40 *Stanford L. Rev.* 22 (1987).

punishes, must treat its citizens in a manner consistent with their intrinsic worth as human beings—a punishment must not be so severe as to be degrading to human dignity."[157] Perhaps his most effective criticism occurred when he pointed out that "three of my Brethren hold today that mandatory infliction of the death penalty constitutes the penalty cruel and unusual punishment. I perceive no principled basis for this limitation."[158] He used the opportunity to quote his *Furman* opinion yet again: "The fatal constitutional infirmity in the punishment of death is that it treats 'members of the human race as nonhumans, as objects to be toyed with and discarded' "[159] And more in the same rhetorical vein, which reached a fever pitch in his quotation from the French novelist and philosopher Albert Camus: "Justice of this kind is obviously no less shocking than the crime itself, and the new 'official' murder far from offering redress for the offense committed against society adds instead a second defilement to the first."[160]

Justice Marshall also dissented; in his opinion, however, he devoted himself to a completely new line of argument. "My sole purposes here are to consider the suggestion that my conclusion in *Furman* has been undercut by developments since then, and briefly to evaluate the basis for my Brethrens' holding that the extinction of life is a permissible form of punishment under the Cruel and Unusual Punishments Clause." Marshall reminded his readers that he rested public disapproval of the death penalty on the views of "an *informed* citizenry,"[161] and he implied that the American public was hardly informed on the subject of the death penalty. In the years after *Furman*, the view that an informed citizenry would oppose capital punishment came to be known as the Marshall Hypothesis.[162] To date, however, it has received very little support from empirically minded social scientists.

Justice Marshall then turned to evaluate the research on deterrence conducted by Professor Ehrlich. His few paragraphs offered his readers a clear and concise critique of Ehrlich's views. Marshall reached the same conclusion that was reached by independent scholars of many persuasions before him: "The Ehrlich study, in short, is of little, if any,

---

[157] *Gregg*, at 229–30; Stewart, J., dissenting.

[158] *Gregg*, at 230; Brennan, J., dissenting.

[159] *Id.*

[160] *Id.*, at 231, quoting Albert Camus, *Reflections on the Guillotine* 5–6 (1960).

[161] *Gregg* at 232; Marshall, J., dissenting; italics in original.

[162] "[T]he American people are largely unaware of the information critical to a judgement of the morality of the death penalty … and … the opinions of an informed public would differ significantly from those of a public unaware of the consequences and effects of the death penalty." *Gregg* at 232.

assistance in assessing the deterrent impact of the death penalty."[163] If public opinion was unreliable and the evidence for deterrence wholly inadequate (what a pity the Solicitor General chose to rest so much weight on it), little evidence was left on which to support the death penalty—except for retribution.

XVI. Conclusion

Candid observation more than thirty years after the rulings in *Gregg* and its allied cases leads unerringly to the conclusion that the attempt to bring efficiency and fairness into death penalty sentencing by means of the statutory measures enacted into law by legislatures and the rulings of state and federal appellate courts in the aftermath of *Gregg* has turned out to be more than a disappointment; it has become a colossal and embarrassing failure.

Or so the friends of abolition will insist. The Supreme Court's attempt to regulate the American system of capital punishment reached its peak with *Gregg, Jurek, Woodson, Roberts,* and *Proffitt.* Three decades later, following a series of rulings by an increasingly conservative Supreme Court, we find capital punishment jurisprudence in disarray. There is no obvious path to follow in further efforts to repair the tattered fabric of the law created by the Court's own rulings over these years.

Friends of the death penalty take a very different stance. They will be glad that the holdings in *Gregg* confirmed their belief in the constitutionality of the death penalty per se. They are less happy with the rulings made by the Court in the three leading cases that attempted to regulate the use of the death penalty. The rulings in *Woodson* and *Roberts* must have been another disappointment. Some will say the decisions in this series of cases was the best that could be achieved given the on-again, off-again discontent with capital punishment evidenced by the Court and manifest in the various coalitions of the nine Justices. Three decades of rulings—beginning with *Coker v. Georgia, Eberheart v. Georgia,* and *Lockett v. Ohio*[164]—followed by two dozen important subsequent cases, have all but dismantled the death penalty. What we have as a result of these rulings is a form of creeping abolition: piecemeal abolition by the courts, but not by the legislatures,[165] and half-hearted abolition by judges whose efforts to narrow the death penalty constantly

---

[163] *Id.,* at 236; Marshall, J., dissenting.

[164] Lockett v. Ohio, 438 U.S. 586 (1978).

[165] In December 2007, however, New Jersey became the first jurisdiction in America post-*Furman* to abolish capital punishment, when Gov. Jon S. Corzine "signed into law a measure repealing New Jersey's death penalty, ..." Jeremy W. Peters, "Death Penalty Repealed in New Jersey," *N.Y. Times,* Dec. 17, 2007. See also http://cbsnews.com/stories. 2007/12/17/national.

verge on outright failure. The ruling in *Gregg* stands at the head of this troubling list.

* * *

Appendix A

According to Georgia statute 27–2534.1 (b) (Supp. 1975), the ten statutory aggravating circumstances are:

(a) The offense of murder, rape, armed robbery or kidnapping was committed by a person with a prior record of conviction for capital felony, or the offense of murder was committed by a person who has a substantial history of serious assaultive criminal convictions.

(b) The offense of murder, rape, armed robbery, or kidnapping was committed while the offender was engaged in the commission of another capital felony, or aggravated battery, or the offense of murder was committed while the offender was engaged in the commission of burglary or arson in the first degree.

(c) The offender by his act if murder, armed robbery, or kidnapping knowingly created a great risk of death to more than one person in a public place by means of a weapon or device which would normally be hazardous to the lives of more than one person.

(d) The offender committed the offense of murder for himself or another, for the purpose of receiving money or any other thing of monetary value.

(e) The murder of a judicial officer, former judicial officer, district attorney or solicitor or former district attorney during or because of the exercise of his official duty.

(f) The offender caused or directed another to commit murder or committed murder as an agent or employee of another person.

(g) The offense of murder, rape, armed robbery, or kidnapping was outrageously or wantonly vile, horrible or inhuman in that it involved torture, depravity of mind, or an aggravated battery to the victim.

(h) The offense of murder was committed against any peace officer, corrections employee or fireman while engaged in the performance of his official duties.

(i) The offense of murder was committed by a person in, or who has escaped from, the lawful custody of a police officer or place of lawful confinement.

(j) The murder was committed for the purpose of avoiding, interfering with, or preventing a lawful arrest or custody in a place of lawful confinement, of himself or another.

Appendix B

According to Florida statute 921.141 (6) (Supp. 1976–1977), the eight mitigating circumstances are:

(a) The defendant has no significant history of prior criminal activity.

(b) The capital felony was committed while the defendant was under the influence of extreme mental or emotional disturbance.

(c) The victim was a participant in the defendant's conduct or consented to the act.

(d) The defendant was an accomplice in the capital felony committed by another person and his participation was relatively minor.

(e) The defendant acted under extreme duress or under the substantial domination of another person.

(f) The capacity of the defendant to appreciate the criminality of his conduct or to conform his conduct to the requirements of law was substantially impaired.

* * *

*

4

Sheri Lynn Johnson

Coker v. Georgia: Of Rape, Race, and Burying the Past

"... I come to bury Caesar, not to praise him.
The evil that men do lives after them.
The good is oft interred with the bones."[1]

I. Introduction

Coker v. Georgia, decided on March 28, 1977, less than a year after the blow of *Gregg v. Georgia,*[2] had to be encouraging to the anti-death penalty community of lawyers and activists. *Coker* reversed the death sentences of Ehrlich Coker, as well as those of two other Georgia defendants, John Eberheart and John Hooks, and it struck down the death penalty for the crime of rape, beginning a line of cases that required "proportionality" of the death penalty to the conduct of the defendant. While, at least from the perspective of the anti-death penalty advocacy community—one that I share—these two consequences were indubitably good, subsequent case law suggests that this good may be largely "interred with the bones." Moreover, *Coker* was surprisingly silent on the matter of race, despite the egregious record of the imposition of the death penalty on black men for the rape of white women, and this silence is an evil wrought by the members of the *Coker* Court that plainly "lives after them."

In this chapter, I will tell three stories. First is the story of the man, Ehrlich Coker, or at least the bits of his story that can be pieced together, including the story of his crimes and capital trial. Second is the story of rape and the death penalty; this part of the chapter summarizes

---

[1] William Shakespeare, Julius Caesar, Act III, scene II (the opening lines of Marc Antony's speech, which, as it turns out, *is* designed to praise Caesar, as well as bury him, a matter to which I will return in the conclusion).

[2] 428 U.S. 153 (1976) (upholding Georgia's death penalty for murder against due process and cruel and unusual punishment challenges).

the Supreme Court's decision in *Coker*, and the role of that decision in the proportionality line of cases. Last is the backstory, the shameful story of race that the Court elected to avoid in its opinion in *Coker*, the avoidance of which has cast a very long shadow.

II. Ehrlich Coker's Story

A. Coker's background

Judging from the reactions of colleagues, the most surprising fact about Ehlich Coker is that he is white; all but one person I asked had assumed he was black. He was born on August 31, 1949, in Atlanta Georgia to Jasper Coker, a house painter, and Mary Coker, a housewife. Almost nothing is known about his childhood, in part because Coker has never granted an interview. From the trial transcript, it can be gleaned that when he was eleven or twelve years of age, he was knocked out when hit by a baseball bat.[3] His grandmother, who was taking care of him at the time, did not bring him to a doctor.[4] It was only to this grandmother that Coker felt an emotional attachment. The rest of his family was hostile, and engaged in a lot of drinking, fighting, and cursing. Coker himself fought often as a child, both because he was combative, and because he was very sensitive.[5] The presentence report provides a little additional information: Coker was not a large man; at the age of 25, when he was arrested for the rape of Elnita Carter, he was 5' 7" tall, and weighed only 145 pounds. At the age of 15, he was arrested for breaking and entering, and placed on probation; at 16, he was found ungovernable and beyond the control of his parents, and continued on probation; and at 16 and a half, he was found delinquent for running away, and once more continued on probation.[6]

At that point, Coker had finished the tenth grade. He dropped out and immediately joined the military. After infantry training at Fort Benning, he served for three years in Korea as a corporal in an artillery unit, and was honorably discharged. In Korea, he drank heavily enough to suffer from blackouts.[7]

In the half dozen years between his release from the army and his arrest for the rape of Elnita Carver, Ehrlich Coker got married to Brenda Williams Coker, and had a son, also named Ehrlich.[8] He worked

---

[3] Appendix, *Coker v. Georgia* 12 (trial testimony of Ehrlich Coker).

[4] Id. at 17–18.

[5] Id. at 37 (trial testimony of Dr. Clarence Johnson).

[6] Appendix, *Coker v. Georgia*, pp. 257, 259 (presentence report).

[7] Id. at 13–14; 20–22 (trial testimony of Ehrlich Coker). There is no indication of what he did while in Korea, but given the timing, it would not have involved combat.

[8] Id. at 13–14.

for a carwash company in Forest Park Georgia, and then an oil company in Augusta.

B.   Coker's prior criminal history

Despite the jobs and family, all was not well. Shortly after his discharge, in 1969, Coker was accused of felony child molestation in Atlanta, though no disposition of the case is recorded. From the outside, things were quiet until 1972, when Coker's criminal charges began to snowball. In September of 1972 Coker and a co-defendant, Glenn Stacey, were charged with the July rape and kidnapping of sixteen year old, Susan Jones, crimes which occurred on the premises of Coker's employer. Jones had been kidnapped from a phone both, raped multiple times, beaten, and then dragged naked through the brush and left in the woods. Because Coker and his co-defendant forced Jones across a county line and raped her in the second county as well, two months later he was also charged and convicted of rape and aggravated assault in that county. In the spring of 1973, Coker entered guilty pleas to the indictments in both counties, receiving a life sentence for each rape, a twenty year sentence for kidnapping, and an eight year sentence for aggravated assault.

As a result of investigators' conversations with Coker concerning the crimes against Jones, Coker was soon charged with—and, also in the spring of 1973, pleaded guilty to—the unsolved rape and murder of Sue Wick on December 5, 1971, a murder that had occurred in yet a third county. For his rape and murder of Wick, Coker received sentences of 20 years and life imprisonment, respectively.

Coker was imprisoned at Ware Correctional Institution, with three life sentences, and presumably *for* life, when an awful fortuity permitted his final crime. During an Alcoholics Anonymous Meeting on the evening of September 24, 1974, six inmates mounted an escape attempt. According to the warden, Coker was not among them. He was, however, present, and he refused orders to join the guards. With two other inmates, one of whom had been involved in plotting the escape, Coker escaped through a fire hatch, a crime for which he was subsequently sentenced to five years, though by that time, the sentence itself hardly mattered, given his three life sentences, and capital sentence for the rape of Elnita Carter.

C.   The Rape of Elnita Carter[9]

About three hours after Coker escaped from prison, he arrived at the home of sixteen year-old Elnita Carver, her sixteen year-old husband Allen, and their three-week old baby. Coker, who by now had separated from his escape-mates, but was still in his prison clothes, entered the

---

[9] The facts in this section are not in dispute, and come from the petition for certiorari and briefs filed.

unlocked kitchen door, surprising Elnita and Allen. Coker held a "board" over his head, and told the Carvers not to try anything "and nobody will get hurt." He then ordered the Carvers to go into the bedroom and Elnita Carver to tie her husband's feet together with a blouse. Despite Coker's small stature, and lack of a weapon, the Carters complied, perhaps a reflection of their young age. Apparently not satisfied, Coker tied Allen to a shower rod in the bathroom. He then changed into a pair of Allen's pants, and asked for cigarettes, a gun, and something to drink. Elnita gave Coker some iced tea in the kitchen, and while there, he picked up a steak knife; he then took Allen's wallet, and the keys to family car. After Coker pushed the Carvers' sleeping baby into the bathroom, Allen complained that his hands were growing numb. Although Coker replied that it was "better than being dead," he nonetheless untied Allen, retied him to the bathroom sink, and put a pillow under his head, warning Allen not to try anything funny because he (Coker) did not want to hurt him.

Coker then told Elnita, who was in her nightgown, to get dressed in order to show him how to start the family car. When she asked whether she could go into the bathroom to change clothes, Coker said no, and when she took off her nightgown, Coker came up behind her and started "feeling" her. After she cried and repeatedly told him to quit, Coker promised he would not hurt her, gagged Allen, and closed the bathroom door. Coker insisted Elnita tell Allen he was not hurting her, then showed her the knife, and had sexual intercourse with her. Without causing her additional injury, Coker got dressed, allowed Elnita to dress, and asked her if she could give him directions to Atlanta. When she could not, Coker announced that he was taking her with him. He promised Allen that he would not hurt Elnita, provided he was not stopped by the police before he got Waresboro, but that if Allen were to get lose and call the police, Allen's "wife [was] going to be dead."

Despite these instructions, Allen got loose and called the police, setting in motion a widespread search for Coker and Elnita. When an unmarked police car passed the two a few miles beyond Waresboro, Coker suspected the police, and expected a roadblock ahead. He turned onto a dirt road, but it was a dead end, so he stopped, telling Elnita they would wait there until the roadblock was gone. He unbuttoned Elnita's blouse, but when she complained of mosquitos (!), he desisted. He also described for her a plan to get another car. Ten minutes later, when police cars appeared, he opined that "I reckon they are going to get me now," and that "I won't never get away." When told to get out of the car, he did, and according to the Sheriff, though he had "ample opportunity" to harm Elnita with the knife stored behind the car visor, he did not attempt to do so.

D. Coker's Capital Trial

Coker was charged with rape and kidnaping as well as several lesser offenses. He was represented by E. Kontz Bennett, Jr., of the public defenders office. Were Coker tried today, a competent attorney would have performed a family social history investigation,[10] and in particular, given Coker's sex offenses and the alcoholic home in which he grew up, investigated the possibility that Coker himself was the victim of sexual abuse as a child. That said, considering that Coker's trial occurred only between the Supreme Court's decisions in Furman and Gregg, when there was little experience with the new statutory scheme, Coker's attorney did a surprising number of things right, some of which mattered in the ultimate resolution of his case, and others which might have mattered.[11] Most importantly, less than a month after the grand jury indicted Coker, Bennett entered a plea of not guilty, along with a motion to quash the indictment on the ground that imposition of the death penalty for rape constituted cruel and unusual punishment in violation of the Eighth and Fourteenth Amendments to the United States Constitution. Several days later, he filed an amended motion to quash, one claiming that the death penalty for rape also violated the Equal Protection and Due Process clauses of the Fourteenth Amendment to the federal constitution, as well as parallel state constitutional provisions, and raising parallel complaints concerning the imposition of the death penalty for the crime of kidnaping.

After meeting with his client, and becoming convinced that Coker was not a typical defendant,[12] but "definitely disturbed," and "unable to give me substantial facts in the case," Bennett entered a special plea of not guilty by reason of insanity to the five counts of the indictment, and then filed a Petition for Examination, requesting the appointment of a psychiatrist to determine whether Coker was criminally responsible, and whether he was competent to stand trial. He then requested the impaneling of a separate jury to determine Coker's competence.

At this hearing, Coker himself testified, describing the blow to his head as child, his heavy drinking, his blackout spells and memory lapses, and his experiences of hearing voices. Bennett testified that Coker was

---

[10] See *Williams (Terry) v. Taylor*, 529 U.S. 362 (2000); *Wiggins v. Smith*, 539 U.S. 510 (2003).

[11] For example, he moved to sever the escape count from the indictment; he objected to the Court's refusal to allow Coker to be present during voir dire; and he objected to improper summation comments, including one quite similar to remarks later condemned by the Supreme Court as diminishing the jurors sense of responsibility for their own decision.

[12] Appendix, *Coker v. Georgia* 25–27 (insanity hearing testimony of E. Kontz Bennett, Jr.).

unable to assist in his own defense, citing Coker's lack of concern over the charges he faced, inability to relate key facts, and his frequent—but apparently sincere—alterations in his account of the crime. Dr. Johnson, who examined Coker for 50 minutes and examined his psychiatric record, found that Coker exhibited symptoms of a temporal lobe seizure disorder, likely caused by the childhood blow to the head, a disorder that might prevent him from fully cooperating with counsel, and when aggravated by alcohol, might account for his aggressive behavior. He could not, however, reach a definite conclusion on either criminal responsibility or competence in the absence of psychological testing and an EEG. The state responded with the testimony of three police officers, the warden of the prison, and a medical technician at the prison, each of whom stated that Coker appeared mentally competent. The special jury found Coker competent.

One day later, Coker's trial began. At the guilt phase, Dr. Johnson was the only witness, who again testified that his evaluation was inconclusive, though temporal lobe disorder was a possibility, and that further testing was necessary. The following day, the jury rejected the insanity defense, finding Coker guilty of all charges. And the next day, now a scant month and a day after Coker was indicted, his capital sentencing proceeding began.

At his sentencing proceeding, prison guards, the Carvers, the neighbor from whose house Allen Carver called the police, and the officers who pursued and arrested Coker provided undisputed descriptions of his escape and rape of Elnita Carver. The jury also heard accounts of Coker's rape of Susan Jones and rape/murder of Sue Wick by the Georgia Bureau of Investigation officer assigned to those cases. Defense counsel presented no witnesses, and the jury's verdict on the rape count was death by electrocution, and for the armed robbery, a recommendation of mercy.

E. Appeal and Certiorari

The speed of these early cases is breathtaking. Bennett, assisted by Dennis Strickland, appealed Coker's conviction to the Georgia Supreme Court.[13] Six months after Coker's sentencing, that court affirmed Coker's convictions.[14] Coker's brief asserted 79 errors, each of which the Georgia Supreme Court dismissed with the briefest discussion. With respect to Coker's constitutional challenge to the imposition of the death penalty for the crime of rape, the majority said only that "This statute has been

---

[13] *Coker v. State*, 216 S.E.2d 782, 786 (Ga. 1975).

[14] *Id.* Justice Gunter dissented without filing an opinion.

repeatedly upheld by a majority of this court," cited four cases, and announced that it "affirm[s] those rulings here."[15]

F.   The Aftermath of *Coker* for Ehrlich Coker

After the United States Supreme Court decision was released, Coker was brought in for resentencing. E. Kontz Bennett and Dennis Strickland, local counsel in the Georgia Supreme Court, appeared with Coker for his resentencing to life imprisonment. Strickland[16] remembers the proceeding as brief and uneventful. He has no recollection of Coker himself, whom he had not met before, other than that he was quiet.[17] Coker, now almost sixty years old, is incarcerated at Phillips State Prison. In his online photo, he looks prison-worn. It seems the years since the Supreme Court case have been quiet. In a letter, he describes himself as deeply grateful to David Kendall, his advocate in the Supreme Court, and as trusting his advice above that of anyone else.[18] For him, at least, the case ended very well, or at least as well as it could, given how it began.

III.   The Rape and Proportionality Story of *Coker v. Georgia*

A.   The Proportionality Prologue to *Coker*

The Eighth Amendment forbids "cruel and unusual punishment," and the earliest cases interpreted the prohibition to apply only to "punishments of torture . . . and all others in the line of unnecessary cruelty,"[19] and clearly held that the death penalty was not unnecessarily cruel.[20] However, in 1910, in *Weems v. United States*,[21] the Supreme Court held that punishment not proportional to the severity of a crime is also cruel and unusual, opening the possibility that some applications of the death penalty might be disproportionate.

The first suggestion that the Court might be receptive to a proportionality argument against the imposition of the death penalty came in a capital rape case. In 1963, newly appointed Justice Goldberg was joined by Justices Douglas and Brennan in a dissent from the denial of certiorari in *Rudolph v. Alabama*.[22] *Rudolph* involved the capital convic-

---

[15] Id. at 788.

[16] Coker's trial counsel, and Strickland's co-counsel on the appeal, E. Kontz Bennett no longer practices law, and did not return phone calls.

[17] Telephone conversation with Dennis Strickland, October 5, 2007.

[18] Letter on file with the author.

[19] *Wilkerson v. Utah*, 99 U.S. 130, 136 (1878); *In re Kemmler*, 136 U. S. 436, 447 (1890).

[20] *Id.*

[21] 217 U.S. 349 (1910).

[22] 375 U.S. 889 (1963) (Goldberg, J., dissenting).

tion of a black man for the rape of a white woman, and the dissent (without noting the racial identity of the defendant or victim) protested that the Court should at least consider whether "[i]n light of the trend both in this country and throughout the world against punishing rape by death, ... the imposition of the death penalty by those States which retain it for rape violate[s] 'evolving standards of decency that mark the progress of our maturing society,' or standards of decency more or less universally accepted[.]"[23]

But before the Supreme Court would address the question of the proportionality of the death penalty for rape (or for any crime other than murder), it was faced with an assault on the death penalty as *per se* cruel and unusual. The story of that assault, and its apparent—albeit transient—success, is told in the chapter on *Furman v. Georgia*.[24] But for my purposes here, it is worth noting only two things. First, of the three cases joined for consideration in *Furman*, only *Furman* itself was a murder case; the other two were rape cases, one from Georgia and one from Texas.[25] And second, despite 114 pages, and nine separate opinions, *Furman* contains no hint that the legitimacy of capital punishment might hinge on its proportionality to the crime.

One might have thought that it was all or nothing, but most state legislatures did not read *Furman* that way. As the chapter on *Gregg* details, 35 states refused to think that *Furman* spelled the end of capital punishment, and made their best guess at the kind of statute that might survive the assorted objections to capital punishment raised in the Justices' opinions in *Furman*. Prior to *Furman*, sixteen states statutes provided capital punishment as a possible penalty for the rape of an adult woman,[26] but only three states—Georgia, North Carolina, and Louisiana—made rape a capital felony after *Furman*. Because the revised statutes of North Carolina and Louisiana made the death penalty for rape mandatory, they were invalidated by *Woodson v. North Carolina*[27] and *Roberts v. Louisiana*.[28] When Louisiana and North Carolina responded to Woodson and Roberts by revising their capital punishment statutes, both states reenacted the death penalty for murder, but not for rape. This left Georgia alone in its authorization of the death penalty for

---

[23] *Id.*

[24] 408 U.S. 238 (1972).

[25] *Furman* at 240, n. 1 (Douglas, J., concurring).

[26] *Coker* at 593. Those states were: Alabama Arkansas, Florida, Georgia, Kentucky, Louisiana, Maryland, Mississippi, Missouri, Nevada, North Carolina, Oklahoma, South Carolina, Tennessee, Texas and Virginia. *Id.* at n. 6.

[27] 428 U.S. 280 (1976).

[28] 428 U.S. 325 (1976).

rape, though three more states—Florida, Mississippi, and Tennessee—authorized the death penalty for the rape of a child by an adult.

Once certiorari was granted, Georgia's isolation became even more apparent. No amicus filed a brief in support of the Georgia law. Moreover, the amicus brief submitted in support of the petitioner was signed not only by the ACLU and the Center for Constitutional Rights but also by four women's advocacy groups, including the NOW Legal Defense and Education Fund.[29] These signatories hint that the brief is not reflexively anti-death penalty, and indeed, it is not. The brief was co-authored by now-Justice Ginsburg, who was at the time Director of the Women's Rights Project of the ACLU. Rather than urging abolition of the death penalty, "amici, interested in the effective enforcement of laws against rape, urge that the death penalty for rape be invalidated because it stems from archaic notions which demean women and gross racial injustice and does not serve the goal of convicting and subjecting to criminal sanctions those who are in fact guilty of rape."[30] The brief both traces the historical origins of the death penalty for rape as a property crime, and documents the history of its racially disparate application. Ultimately, it argues that the goal of equitable enforcement of rape laws would be better served by a law that neither imposed extreme penalties on the defendant nor granted him special evidentiary protections.

B.   The Decision and Dissents in *Coker*

Neither the origin of rape laws in a vision of women as property nor their subsequent use as an instrument of racist oppression is acknowledged (or disputed, for that matter) in the *Coker* opinions. *Coker* lacks a majority opinion. Justice White announced the judgement of the Court, striking down Coker's sentence, and filed an opinion joined by Justices Stewart, Blackmun, and Stevens. Justices Marshall and Brennan concurred in the judgment, Justice Powell concurred in the judgment, but dissented in part, while Justices Burger and Rehnquist dissented.

1.   Justice White's plurality opinion

Justice White's opinion is relatively brief. After explicitly eschewing reconsideration of *Gregg*, the opinion points to *Gregg's* acceptance of the *Weems* holding that the Eighth Amendment bars not only "barbaric" punishments, but also "excessive" ones.[31] Excessiveness, said White,

---

[29] 1976 WL 181482 (Appellate Brief) (U.S. December 03, 1976), Brief Amici Curiae of the American Civil Liberties Union, the Center for Constitutional Rights, the National Organization for Women Legal Defense and Education Fund, the Women's Law Project, the Center for Women Policy Studies, the Women's Legal Defense Fund, and Equal Rights Advocates, Inc. (No. 75–5444.)

[30] *Id.* at 7.

[31] *Coker* at 592 (White, J.).

occurs when either the penalty 1) "makes no contribution to acceptable goals of punishment," or 2) "is grossly out of proportion to the severity of the crime." Both of these determinations should be informed by "public attitudes, ... precedent, legislative attitudes, and the response of juries in their sentencing decisions...."

At least purporting to seek such guidance, White first reviewed the number of states that authorized the death penalty for rape of an adult woman in 1925 (18 plus the federal government), in 1971 (prior to *Furman*—16), and, most tellingly, Georgia's total isolation at the time of oral argument.[32] He concluded that the view of state legislatures therefore "weighs very heavily on the side of rejecting capital punishment as a suitable penalty for the rape of an adult woman."[33]

White next turned to the behavior of juries. Rather curiously, White did not consider the history of the imposition or rape by juries, but looked only at the number of cases in which the death penalty had been imposed in Georgia since *Furman*. Of the 63 rape cases reviewed by the Georgia Supreme Court since *Furman*, only six had resulted in the imposition of a death sentence, a number White had to concede was "not ... negligible." White noted the state's contention that this merely showed that juries properly reserved death sentences for the most aggravated of cases, but did not respond to it except to say that"in the vast majority of cases," juries did not impose the death sentence.[34]

White then turned to the Court's own judgment of the disproportionality of the death penalty as punishment for the rape of an adult woman, which, he said, the "legislative rejection of capital punishment for rape strongly confirms."[35] In making his own assessment, White first noted the reprehensibility of rape as a crime, "both in a moral sense and in its almost total contempt for the personal integrity and autonomy of the female victim and for the latter's privilege in choosing those with whom intimate relations are to be established." He noted its violence, and the frequency with which rape is accompanied by physical injury and psychological damage. Then, however, he distinguished it from homicide, both in terms of moral depravity and the injury inflicted, and concluded that the death penalty with its unique severity and irrevocability, "is an excessive penalty for the rapist, who as such, does not take human life."[36] In the course of this discussion, the opinion includes a line subsequently criticized for its insensitivity: "Life is over for the victim of

---

[32] *Id.* at 595–96.

[33] *Id.* at 596.

[34] *Id.* at 596–97.

[35] *Id.* at 597.

[36] *Id.* at 598.

the murderer; for the rape victim, life may not be nearly so happy as it was, but it is not over and normally is not beyond repair."[37]

Interestingly, throughout the analysis of the Court's own view of the seriousness of the crime, the crime is referred to as "rape," rather than "rape of an adult woman," and the rest of the opinion drops the qualifying phrase. This suggests that the Court itself thought that rape—whether of a child or an adult—is not permissibly punished by death because, whatever the age of the victim, "the rapist, ... as such, does not take human life."

The plurality opinion then dismissed as irrelevant the fact that the death penalty for rape was only available if the jury or judge found the existence of an aggravating circumstance, since that provision did not alter the fact "that the instant crime being punished is a rape not involving the taking of life." It ended by noting the further disproportion created by the fact that under Georgia law, deliberate killing, absent proof of aggravating circumstances, is not punishable by death, and rejects "the notion ... that the rapist, with or without aggravating circumstances, should be punished more heavily than the deliberate killer...." This disproportion, of course, was not really fairly attributable to the Georgia legislature; it was the product of the legislature's attempt to respond to the Court's own *Furman* constraints.

2. The concurrences

Justices Marshall and Brennan did not comment on capital punishment and rape at all. Brennan's one line opinion simply stated his concurrence in the judgment of the Court, and his adherence to the views he expressed in *Gregg*.[38] Justice Marshall's did the same, except that he noted he had "set forth at some length" his views on capital punishment in *Furman*.[39] Justice Powell concurred in the judgment, and "in the plurality's reasoning that *ordinarily* death is a disproportionate punishment for the crime of raping an adult woman,"[40] but dissented because he was not persuaded by the plurality's "bright line between murder and all rapes regardless of the degree of brutality of the rape or the effect on the victim."[41] In Powell's view, there were some rapes in which the majority's comparisons to homicide may be wrong, either with respect to the moral heinousness of the offense or to the harm created, or both. He thought that whether the death penalty was disproportion-

---

[37] *Id.*

[38] *Coker* at 600 (Brennan, J., concurring).

[39] *Id.* (Marshall, J., concurring).

[40] *Id.* at 601 (Powell, J. concurring and dissenting).

[41] *Id.* at 603.

ate for rapes involving excessive brutality or severe injury should be the subject of a more discriminating inquiry than the "plurality undertakes," and would not "prejudge the issue."[42]

3. Justice Burger's Dissent

Burger, joined by Rehnquist, filed by far the longest opinion, and it made several interesting arguments that were really not addressed by the plurality opinion. The overarching importance of federalism, and its implication that states should be left to experiment unless the constitution speaks directly to prohibit such experimentation is a familiar refrain.[43] But Burger had several quite specific complaints as well. First, he objected that the Court looked at the question too broadly; rather than ask abstractly whether the rape of an adult woman can be punished by death, he thought the case required only the determination of whether Georgia could punish Coker for the particular rape he committed, considering all the facts and circumstances revealed by the record: Whether "the Eighth Amendment's ban against cruel and unusual punishment prohibit[s] the State of Georgia from executing a person who has, within the space of three years, raped three separate women, killing one and attempting to kill another, who is serving three prison terms exceeding his probable lifetime and has not hesitated to escape confinement at the first available opportunity?"[44] Because Coker was a "chronic rapist whose continuing danger to the community [was] abundantly clear,"[45] Burger would have held that the sentence imposed was within the power reserved to the state.

Burger attacked both the plurality's calculation of the consensus of the states and its analysis of the seriousness of rape as compared to homicide. He deemed the majority's focus on the immediate past "truly disingenuous," given that the diminished number of states whose statutes made rape a capital felony may well be attributable to the "great uncertainty arising from our less than lucid holdings on the Eighth Amendment."[46] He also took the majority to task for referring to rape victims who are "unharmed," given the extreme psychological consequences for rape victims,[47] and chastised Powell for his characterization of Coker's crime as not "excessively brutal," given the "profound suffer-

---

[42] *Id.* at 604.

[43] *See e.g., id.* at 610–611; 618–19; 622 (Burger, J., dissenting).

[44] *Id.* at 607.

[45] *Id.*

[46] *Id.* at 614.

[47] *Id.* at 611–12.

ing the crime imposes upon the victims and their loved ones,"[48] and the impossibility of estimating the harm done to Coker's 16–year–old victim when he raped her in the presence of her husband three weeks after she had given birth.[49]

Burger argued that the constitutional test cannot be "life for life, eye for eye, tooth for tooth," because "States must be permitted to engage in a more sophisticated weighing of values in dealing with criminal activity which consistently poses danger of death or grave bodily harm,"[50] noting that legislatures routinely make the penalty for a criminal act (such as stealing) more severe than the act it punishes in order to deter wrongdoing.[51] He also expressed concern that the Court's ruling in *Coker*, to the extent it is based upon this life for life principle, casts doubt on the constitutional validity of statutes imposing the death penalty for other non-homicidal offenses such as kidnaping, treason and airplane hijacking.[52]

While Burger did not explicitly refer to the contentions of the amici that the imposition of the death penalty for rape will actually impair enforcement of rape laws, he did respond to them by noting that a range of enforcement consequences may be predicted from making rape a capital crime, but that it is impossible to know which ones will actually ensue.[53] This, he thought, was among the reasons that Georgia's legislative program "must be given time to take effect so that data may be evaluated for comparison with the experience of States which have not enacted death penalty statutes."[54]

C. "The Good is Oft Interred with the Bones"

Part III will complain about the harm that *Coker* did by ignoring the extraordinary racial disparities in the imposition of the death penalty for rape. I assess this harm from the perspective of a scholar and practitioner committed to the abolition of the death penalty. But before castigating the Court for the road not taken, the benefits the proportionality approach the Court instead employed should be considered. What "good" (from the perspective of an abolitionist) might fairly be attributed to *Coker*?

---

[48] *Id.* at 612.

[49] *Id.* at 609 n. 2.

[50] *Id.* at 620.

[51] *Id.* at 619.

[52] *Id.* at 621.

[53] *Id.* at 617–18.

[54] *Id.* at 618.

1. The death penalty for rape

One might start with the reversal of Ehrlich Coker's death sentence, and those of the four other men on Georgia's death row at that time.[55] Then, one might speculate about the number of sentences likely to have been imposed had *Coker* been decided the other way; Georgia was averaging a little more than one death sentence a year for rape. Furthermore, if the Georgia capital rape statute had been upheld, might not other states have broadened their statutes as well? The problem with attributing these positive consequences to *Coker* is that it compares upholding the Georgia statute with striking it down. But, as I shall argue in Part IV, the real alternative was to strike down the death penalty for rape as racially discriminatory, and considering that alternative, the lives of Ehrlich Coker and other potentially capital rape defendants would have been spared either way. Thus, thinking about the good done by the approach taken in Coker requires evaluating *Coker's* progeny

2. *Coker's* Felony Murder Progeny

Reading only *Coker's* firstborn, *Enmund v. Florida*,[56] one might be ready to congratulate (or at least exonerate) the *Coker* plurality's choice of proportionality as the tool for striking down the death penalty for rape. Earl Enmund was sentenced to death as an accomplice to murder merely because he was "the person in the car by the side of the road at the time of the killings, waiting to help the robbers escape."[57] *Enmund* holds that imposition of the death penalty for an accomplice to felony murder who "does not himself kill, attempt to kill, or intend that a killing take place or that lethal force will be employed"[58] violates the Eighth Amendment because the punishment is disproportionate to his culpability. Justice White's opinion follows his methodology in *Coker*, and makes several explicit comparisons to *Coker*. Comparing the eight jurisdictions that permitted capital punishment for felony murder-without-more to the one jurisdiction that permitted it for rape, the Court observed that the legislative judgment was not "as compelling as [those] considered in *Coker*, [but] nevertheless weighs on the side of rejecting capital punishment for the crime at issue."[59] On the other hand, it pointed out that the evidence of jury consensus was stronger for felony murder than rape, concluding that "the evidence is overwhelming that American juries have repudiated the death penalty for crimes such as

---

[55] *Coker* at 596–97 (plurality opinion) (noting that six sentences had been imposed, and that the Georgia Supreme Court had reversed one).

[56] 458 U.S. 782 (1982).

[57] *Id.* at 788.

[58] *Id.* 797.

[59] *Id.* at 793.

petitioners."[60] With respect to the Court's own judgment of proportionality, White's opinion quotes *Coker's* comparison of rape to murder, then concludes, "As was said of the crime of rape in *Coker*, we have the abiding conviction that the death penalty, which is 'unique in its severity and irrevocability,' is an excessive penalty for the robber, who as such, does not take life."[61]

Unfortunately, any enthusiasm for *Enmund* must be tempered by its less than righteous siblings, *Cabana v. Bullock*,[62] and *Tison v. Arizona*.[63] *Cabana* is a distinct cutback; it holds that the requirements of *Enmund* need not be submitted to a jury, but can be determined after-the-fact of the jury verdict by a court.[64] Some might try to dismiss *Cabana* as the Court's attempt to clean up a case tried before *Enmund*— just a short-term procedural compromise with past practices. But regardless of one's view of *Cabana*, it is clear that *Tison* is a huge cutback on the promise of *Enmund*.

In *Tison*, Justice O'Connor, who dissented in *Enmund*, wrote the majority opinion, She quickly abandoned its narrow "kill, attempt to kill, or intend that a killing take place or that lethal force will be employed" test, adding the alternative of "major participation in the felony committed, combined with reckless indifference to human life."[65] After *Tison*, it is hard to see much value in *Enmund*; if all *Enmund* assures is that no death sentences may be imposed for minor participation in the underlying felony, then proportionality does very little more than juries do on their own. As *Enmund* points out, there were very few nontriggerman felony murder death sentences anyway. So it is hard to make the case that any significant good still flows from *Coker* to felony murder capital defendants.

3.   *Coker* redux: *Kennedy v. Louisiana* and Child Rape

As noted in the section describing the plurality opinion, *Coker* is ambiguous as to whether the Eighth Amendment prohibits punishment of the rape of a child by death. That ambiguity was not resolved for more than twenty years, but in *Kennedy v. Louisiana*[66] the Court finally held that punishing child rape with death is also disproportionate. There are no big surprises in *Kennedy*.

---

[60] *Id.* at 794.

[61] *Id.* at 797.

[62] 474 U.S. 376 (1986).

[63] 481 U.S. 137 (1987).

[64] *Cabana, supra.*

[65] *Tison* at 158.

[66] *Kennedy v. Louisiana*, 554 U.S. ___ (2008).

At the time *Coker* was decided, two states, Mississippi and Florida, authorized imposition of the death penalty for the rape of a child. The Mississippi Supreme Court subsequently upheld its statute,[67] concluding that *Coker* was limited to the rape of an adult woman, but the Florida Supreme Court, reasoning that *Coker* extended to offenses that did not involve the taking of a life, overturned its statute.[68] In 1989, the Mississippi court struck down its statute on state grounds, leaving no states that capitally punished child rape.[69] Then in 1995, Louisiana passed legislation authorizing the death penalty for "aggravated rape . . . if the victim was under the age of twelve years . . . ",[70] and in 1996, in two consolidated pretrial cases, the Louisiana Supreme Court upheld the statute against a proportionality challenge.[71] Following this decision, five other states—Georgia, Montana, Oklahoma, South Carolina and Texas— enacted capital child rape statutes.[72]

By 2007, when the Supreme Court granted certiorari in *Kennedy v. Louisiana*,[73] two men—Patrick Kennedy and Richard Davis—had been sentenced to death for child rape, both in the state of Louisiana. Amicus briefs in support of Louisiana were filed by three of the five other states with capital child rape statutes—Texas, Oklahoma and South Carolina— and interestingly, were also filed by Missouri, Idaho, Mississippi, and Alabama urging the Court to permit those states to make their own judgments about the wisdom of such statutes.[74] Several amicus briefs were filed in support of the petitioner, including one from the ACLU and NAACP focused on the long history of racial disparity in the imposition

---

[67] *Upshaw v. State*, 350 So.2d 1358 (Miss. 1977).

[68] *Buford v. State*, 403 So.2d 943 (Fla. 1981).

[69] *Leatherwood v. State*, 548 So.2d 389 (Miss. 1989).

[70] La. Rev. Stat. Ann. § 14–42 (1) (West 1998 Supp.).

[71] *State v. Wilson and Bethley*, 685 So.2d 1063 (La. 1996). Certiorari was sought by Bethley, and denied in *Bethley v. Louisiana, cert. denied*, 520 U.S. 1259 (1997), where Justice Stevens, joined by Justices Breyer and Ginsburg, issued a "statement regarding the denial of certiorari," which pointed out that the denial was not a ruling on the merits, and that there was arguably a jurisdictional bar to Supreme Court review because of the pretrial posture of the case. Id. (Stevens, J.).

[72] *Kennedy v. Louisiana*, 554 U.S. __ (2008). All but Georgia, however, made the crime death-eligible only for offenders with a previous rape conviction. *Id.*

[73] *Kennedy v. Louisiana*, 554 U.S. __ (2008).

[74] Brief of Amici Curiae Missouri Governor Matt Blunt and Members of the Missouri General Assembly in Support of Respondent in Kennedy v. Louisiana, 2008 WL 742922; Brief of Texas, Alabama, Colorado, Idaho, Mississippi, Missouri, Oklahoma, South Carolina, and Washington as Amici Curiae Supporting Respondent in Kennedy v. Louisiana, 2008 WL 782550.

of the death penalty for rape,[75] and one from a number of child advocacy organizations,[76] urging the Supreme Court to strike down the Louisiana statute because "[b]y permitting the execution of perpetrators of child sexual abuse, the statute will likely have exactly the wrong effect: rather than protecting children, this statute will increase the number of victimized children, encourage offenders to kill their victims, and interfere with victims' healing process."[77]

As in *Coker*, both majority and dissent eschew any discussion of race. Oral argument suggested the possibility that *Kennedy* would be decided on the very narrow ground that the Louisiana statute (unlike the statutes of the five other states that authorized the death penalty for the rape of a child) did not require the presence of an aggravating factor to make the rape of a child death eligible.[78] But it was not. Instead, it holds that the Eighth Amendment bars imposition of the death penalty for the rape of a child where the rape did not result, and was not intended to result, in the victim's death.

Justice Kennedy wrote the opinion for the five-four majority. Consulting several sources of contemporary norms, he found a national consensus against capital punishment for child rape and other non-homicide crimes. First, he relied upon the fact that of the thirty seven jurisdictions that impose capital punishment, only six authorize it for child rape.[79] In so doing, he rejected Louisiana's argument that the apparent consensus was in part the product of the Court's own opinion in *Coker*, which was understood by state legislatures as forbidding the death penalty for rape,[80] declaring that *Coker* was unambiguously limited in scope to the rape of an adult woman. He also rejected the state's argument that it had demonstrated a consistent trend toward capital child rape statutes, deeming the five new statutes insufficient in number to constitute a trend, and dismissed the pending legislation in five

---

[75] Brief Amicus Curiae of the American Civil Liberties Union, The ACLU of Louisiana, and the NAACP Legal Defense and Educational Fund, Inc., In Support of Petitioner in Kennedy v. Louisiana, 2008 WL 503591.

[76] Brief of the National Association of Social Workers; The National Association of Social Workers, Louisiana Chapter; The National Alliance to End Sexual Violence; The Louisiana Foundation Against Sexual Assault; The Texas Association Against Sexual Assault; The New Jersey Coalition Against Sexual Assault; and The Minnesota Coalition Against Sexual Assault as Amici Curiae in Support of Petitioner in Kennedy v. Louisiana. 2008 WL 494945.

[77] *Id.* at 1.

[78] *See* http://www.supremecourtus.gov/oral_arguments/argument_transcripts/07–343.pdf at 32 et. seq.

[79] *Kennedy v. Louisiana*, 554 U.S. ___ (2008).

[80] *Kennedy v. Louisiana*, 554 U.S. ___ (2008).

additional states as unreliable. The opinion then noted execution data as further evidence of social consensus against the death penalty for child rape and pointed out that no one had been executed for rape of a child or adult since 1964, or for any other non-homicide offense since 1963.

Turning to the Court's own judgment on the proportionality question, the *Kennedy* opinion took pains to be more sensitive than *Coker* to the possibility of permanent and devastating harm from rape, but nonetheless determined that in terms of both moral depravity and severity of harm inflicted, child rape did not compare to murder.[81] Before concluding, Justice Kennedy nodded to both the arguments of the child advocacy amici and those of the defense bar amici. He observed that capital rape statutes may harm child victims in three ways: first by causing the child victim to feel moral responsibility for the perpetrator's death; second by deterring any prosecution at all in some cases, particularly in intra-familial rapes; and third by removing any incentive for the child rapist to spare the life of the child. He also noted the greater risk of wrongful execution presented by child rape cases. These factors, taken together, he said, supported the conclusion that the Court's decision was consistent with principals of retribution and deterrence. Interestingly, Justice Kennedy did not note the gross racial disparities in prior capital rape prosecutions as an additional reason for the Court's own proportionality judgment, despite the fact that the briefs addressed them, and despite the fact that the petitioner Kennedy himself, unlike Coker, was black.

Justice Alito, joined by Justices Scalia, Thomas and Chief Justice Roberts, dissented. He disputed the majority's conclusion about the existence of a societal consensus against the death penalty for child rape, arguing that state legislatures have "operated under the ominous shadow of the *Coker* dicta, and therefore have not been free to express their own understanding of our society's standards of decency."[82] He also challenged the Court's own evaluation of the proportionality of capital punishment for child rape, using examples to demonstrate that the moral depravity of some child rapists is arguably greater than that of some intentional murderers.[83]

Assuming, as I do, that the result in *Kennedy* is desirable, it is hard to praise the *Coker* route to that result. The alternative approach to capital rape available to the Court at the time of *Coker*—as unconstitutional because it was racially discriminatory—would not have left the child rape question open. Leaving it open has allowed for political

---

[81] *Kennedy v. Louisiana*, 554 U.S. ___ (2008).

[82] *Kennedy v. Louisiana*, 554 U.S. ___ (2008) (Alito, J., dissenting).

[83] *Kennedy v. Louisiana*, 554 U.S. ___ (2008).

backlash just because of the emotional volatility of the child rape issue; both candidates for President in 2008 declared their opposition to the decision when it was announced. Moreover, Justice Kennedy's opinion makes it clear that he intends no broadening of the proportionality-to-the-offense doctrine that might compensate for the political backlash. The opinion explicitly limits the reasoning of *Kennedy* (and by implication, *Coker)* to "crimes against individuals."[84] "[C]rimes defining and punishing treason, espionage, terrorism, and drug kingpin activity, which are offenses against the State," apparently are still fair game.

4. *Atkins* and *Simmons* as Offspring.

Thus, if the good of *Coker* is weighed solely by the proportionality-to-the-offense line of cases, there isn't much on the positive side of the scale. But perhaps that measure is too narrow. Shouldn't we count the proportionality-to-the-offender line of cases as *Coker*'s progeny as well? More specifically, *Atkins v. Virginia*[85] provided a categorical exemption from the death penalty for persons with mental retardation, and *Roper v. Simmons*[86] did the same for juvenile offenders. Only the most curmudgeonly (or uncompromising) of abolitionists could avoid praising *Atkins* and *Simmons*; hundreds will be saved by these decisions.[87] So I am happy to praise *Atkins*, and happy to praise *Simmons*, but dubious that *Coker* should get much of the credit. True, both *Atkins* and *Simmons* cite *Coker*. Though *Atkins* does so primarily for the largely undisputed principle that the Court's own judgment must be brought to bear on proportionality questions,[88] *Simmons* cites *Coker* as support for the principle that the views of the international community are relevant to the assessment of whether a punishment is cruel and unusual,[89] a principle that certainly has the potential for broader application to the death penalty as a whole. That's nice, but the difficulty isn't so much with what *Coker* is cited for in *Atkins* and *Simmons*, but the fact that *Coker* was also cited in *Thompson v. Oklahoma*,[90] which in 1988 upheld the death penalty for juveniles, and in *Penry v. Lynaugh*,[91] which in 1989 had upheld its application to persons with mental retardation. Neither of

---

[84] *Kennedy v. Louisiana*, 554 U.S. ___ (2008).

[85] 536 U.S. 304 (2002).

[86] 543 U.S. 551 (2005).

[87] Numbers aside, most people would find a strong appeal to eliminating the rank barbarism of executing our young and our helpless.

[88] *Atkins* at 313.

[89] *Roper* at 575–75.

[90] 487 U.S. 815, 823 (1988).

[91] 492 U.S. 302, 331 (1989).

those decisions cared a fig for international opinion, so it's hard to imagine that *Coker* itself demanded that concern. In my view, *Coker* doesn't deserve much more credit for *Atkins* and *Simmons* than it deserves blame for *Thompson* and *Penry*.

Coker is the first Supreme Court decision to reject a punishment as disproportionate to a crime. And as such, it *was* one step on the way to other categorical bans, bans that saved the lives of defendants who would not have been directly aided by a race discrimination resolution of the question of capital rape. By establishing a two-part methodology for evaluating disproportionality, *Coker* gave the Court precedent to cite that made *Atkins* and *Simmons* look less like judicial activism. But given the quite different uses that were made of *Coker* in *Thompson* and *Penry*, I don't think *Coker* compelled, or even caused adoption of the categorical bans on executing juveniles and persons with mental retardation.

IV. The Race Story Whited Out by *Coker*.

Though Ehrlich Coker's own story has a happier ending than most capital punishment stories, and the rape and capital punishment story (a.k.a. the proportionality story) has a moderately positive ending in *Kennedy*, those outcomes must be balanced against the road not taken. Prior to *Coker*, it was impossible to think about rape and capital punishment without thinking about race; it was also impossible to think about race and capital punishment without thinking about rape. But by choosing to grant certiorari in one of the very few white defendant capital rape cases, and by ignoring the bleak history of race, rape and capital punishment when considering that case, the Supreme Court whited out the ugliest corner of capital punishment. These choices, by design or default, made possible the moral debacle of *McCleskey v. Kemp*.[92]

A.   The Bleak Pre-*Coker* History of Race, Rape and Capital Punishment.

The story of race, rape and capital punishment is easily summarized: In this country, race—of victim and offender—has virtually always been the driving force behind capital punishment for rape, and race has often heavily influenced the imposition of the death penalty for other crimes. This story has never been a secret, though the details are uglier than the summary suggests.

---

[92] 481 U.S. 279 (1987) (holding that general statistical evidence that Georgia's capital punishment scheme operated in a racially discriminatory manner did not establish either an Eighth Amendment Cruel and Unusual Punishment Clause violation or a Fourteenth Amendment Equal Protection Clause violation).

In colonial times, many states made eligibility for capital punishment depend both upon the offense committed and the race and/or status of the offender.[93] By the time of the Civil War, none of the northern states provided for capital punishment for any crime other than murder, and in many the institution itself was questioned, but "[m]uch of the debate that took place in the North simply did not occur in the South because of the perceived need to discipline a captive workforce."[94] Nonetheless, in the first half of the 19th century, all of the Southern states had abolished the death penalty for certain previously death-eligible crimes committed *by whites*.[95] Moreover, the change in practices—for whites—was even more progressive than the change in theoretical eligibility: "Between 1800 and 1860 the southern states are known to have executed only seven white burglars ... six white horse thieves ... four white robbers" and *no* white rapists.[96]

On the other hand, in Texas, African Americans, whether slave or free (unlike whites) were subject to capital punishment for insurrection, arson, attempted murder of a white victim, rape or attempted rape of a white victim, robbery or attempted robbery of a white person, and assault with a deadly weapon upon a white person.[97] In Virginia, free African Americans (but not whites) could get the death penalty for rape, attempted rape, kidnapping a woman, and aggravated assault—all provided the victim was white; slaves in Virginia were eligible for death for commission of a mind-boggling sixty-six crimes.[98] In Mississippi, that number was thirty-eight,[99] and though most Southern states did not have such a staggering number of capital felonies for slaves, all had statutes that differentiated between crimes that were capital if committed by a slave, but not if committed by a white man.[100] In all slaveholding

---

[93] A. Leon Higginbotham, Jr. IN THE MATTER OF COLOR: RACE AND THE AMERICAN LEGAL PROCESS 181–82, 256–57, 262–63 (1978).

[94] Stuart Banner, THE DEATH PENALTY: AN AMERICAN HISTORY 112 (Harvard University Press 2002).

[95] *Id.* at 139.

[96] *Id.*

[97] *Id.* at 141. Free African Americans were death eligible for the kidnapping of a white woman. *Id.*

[98] *Id.*

[99] *Id.*

[100] *Id.*; Kenneth M. Stampp, THE PECULIAR INSTITUTION: SLAVERY IN THE ANTEBELLUM SOUTH 210–11 (1956); George M. Stroud, A SKETCH OF THE LAWS OF SLAVERY IN THE SEVERAL STATES OF THE UNITED STATES OF AMERICA 75–87 (2d ed. Philadelphia: Henry Longstreth 1856).

states, the rape of a white woman by a black man was a capital crime.[101] In Georgia, the disparity in penalty was particularly notable; rape of a white woman by a white man was punishable by imprisonment of twenty years or less, and attempted rape, by not more than five years, but rape or attempted rape of a white woman by an African American was punishable by death.[102] Equally importantly, a slave could not be raped by her owner, and the rape of a slave by another white man was not punished as rape, but as a trespass against the owner's property.[103] Indeed, in antebellum Louisiana, rape of a black woman, whether slave or free, was no crime at all.[104]

Nor were these differences merely theoretical. This "black-white divergence in southern criminal codes was reflected in actual practice;"[105] in the antebellum South, African Americans were hung in numbers far out of proportion to their representation in the population, and for many more crimes than were whites.[106]

After the Civil War, the Black Codes in some states served to punish African Americans by death for crimes that incurred lesser punishments for white offenders,[107] while in others, such as Georgia, the same discrimination was accomplished by facially neutral statutes that accomplished discrimination by making the death penalty available at the discretion of the jury.[108]

The Fourteenth Amendment did away with the formal sources of discrimination, as it was intended to,[109] but left untouched the disparate applications made possible by discretion. From 1930, when national statistics began to be kept, to 1972, when the Supreme Court struck down unguided discretion statutes, about half of the defendants executed

---

[101] John Hope Franklin & Alfred A. Moss, Jr., FROM SLAVERY TO FREEDOM 115 (1988).

[102] Ga. Penal Code of 1816, No. 508 § 1, Lamar, Compilation of the Laws of Georgia, 571, 804 (1821).

[103] Franklin & Moss at 114.

[104] Judith Kelleher Schafer, SLAVERY, THE CIVIL WAR, AND THE SUPREME COURT OF LOUISIANA 85–87 (1994).

[105] Banner at 141.

[106] Id.

[107] See e.g., Randall Kennedy, RACE, CRIME AND THE LAW 84–85 (1997); Theodore Brantner Wilson, THE BLACK CODES OF THE SOUTH 97, 105–06 (1965).

[108] Id. at 101, 104–05, 113–14.

[109] When Senator Howard introduced the Fourteenth Amendment in the Senate, he described it as "prohibit[ing] the hanging of a black man for a crime for which the white man is not to be hanged." Cong. Globe, 39th Cong. 1st Sess. 2766 (May 23, 1866).

for murder in the United States were African American, which is clearly disparate whether considered in comparison to their proportion in the population or to their proportionate share of murderers. But that disparity pales when compared to the racial disparity in executions for rape: Of the 455 men executed for rape, 405, or 89 percent, were African American men,[110] virtually all of whom were accused of raping white women.[111] Indeed, it appears that no white man has ever been executed for raping a black victim.[112]

These stark raw numbers reflect disparities that persisted even when possible confounding factors were investigated. When the Legal Defense Fund of the NAACP commissioned a comprehensive study by Professor Marvin Wolfgang of capital rape prosecutions between 1945 and 1965, Wolfgang considered over two dozen possibly aggravating nonracial factors, and concluded that none of those variables accounted for racial disparities; controlling for those factors, African American defendants whose victims were white were sentenced to death approximately 18 times more frequently than any other racial combination of defendant and victim.[113]

Evidence of racial bias in the imposition of the death penalty for rape is not (and was not, at the time of *Coker*) limited to statistics, but was corroborated by a variety of other sources, both formal and informal. Most dramatically, everyone knew that the horrible history of lynching in this country was closely tied to hysteria over the purported threat of interracial rape, as "the most common public reason for lynching was that White women needed to be protected from Black rapists and attempted rapists."[114] The Supreme Court was also aware of the flimsiness of the evidence that sufficed to convict black capital rape defendants, having reviewed several notorious cases in which the guilt of the defendants was at best dubious, most notably *Powell v. Alabama*,[115] and *Hamilton v. Alabama*.[116] Finally, the amicus brief submitted by the

[110] U.S. Dep't of Justice, Bureau of Prisons, National Prisoner Statistics, Bulletin No. 45, *Capital Punishment* 1930–1968, 7 (1969). Unofficial statistics from the longer period of 1864 to 1972, are similar, Amsterdam at 38.

[111] Jack Greenberg, CRUSADERS IN THE COURTS 440 (Harper Collins 1994).

[112] Michael L. Radelet, Executions of Whites for Crimes Against Blacks: Exceptions to the Rule? 30 SOC. Q. 529, 537–41 (1989).

[113] Marvin E. Wolgang & Marc Riedel, *Race, Judicial Discretion, and the Death Penalty*, 407 ANNALS AM. ACAD. POL. & SOC. SCI. 126–33.

[114] Jeffrey J. Pokorak, *Rape as a Badge of Slavery: The Legal History of, and Remedies for, Prosecutorial Race-of-Victim Charging Disparities*, 7 NEW. L.J. 1, 23–24 (2007).

[115] 287 U.S. 45 (1932).

[116] 368 U.S. 52 (1961).

ACLU and LDF in *Coker* pointed out language in earlier Georgia state court opinions that approved racially discriminatory standards of proof in rape cases.[117]

Thus, it was not surprising that three of the five concurring opinions in *Furman* acknowledged the obvious connection between race, rape and capital punishment.[118] One might read *Coker*, however, and never realize that race, rape, and capital punishment were so closely entwined.

B. *Coker* Looks Away

One might begin by asking just how it happened that when nearly ninety percent of the men sentenced to death for the crime of rape were black,[119] the Supreme Court chose to review the case of a white defendant. My review of the available papers of Justices Marshall and Blackmun revealed no evidence that Coker's race was the reason his petition for certiorari was granted. The circumstances, however, more than suggest that this was not the operation of chance.

Six years earlier, when faced in *Maxwell v. Bishop* with a statistical challenge by a black death-sentenced rape defendant, the Court had granted certiorari—but limited consideration to the non-racial issues.[120] I interpret *Maxwell* as evidence that the Court did not want to face the question of racial disparities. I admit that a more generous a generous (or optimistic) observer might, *at the time Maxwell was decided*, have defended the Court's sidestepping of the racial disparity question on two grounds: First, that Maxwell's case was a less than perfect vehicle for the statistical challenge;[121] and second, that because the Court did reverse Maxwell's sentence on other grounds, it therefore did not permit

---

[117] *See e.g., McCullough v. State*, 73 S.E. 546, 547 (1912) (allowing a jury to infer intent to commit rape when the evidence showed only an assault by a black man on a white woman due to "racial differences and established customs"); *Dorsey v. State*, 34 S.E. 135, 136, 137 (1899) (race may rebut any presumption that the defendant intended to obtain consent and would abandon purpose of sexual intercourse if he failed to obtain it).

[118] It is noteworthy that even Solicitor General Bork's amicus brief in *Gregg v. Georgia* carefully confines its argument that race is not a factor in the imposition of capital punishment to capital punishment for the crime of murder. Brief for the United States as Amicus Curiae in *Gregg v. Georgia* at 65–68.

[119] *See Furman v. Georgia*, 408 U.S. 238, 364 (Marshall, J., concurring noting that of the 455 men executed for rape after the Justice Department began compiling statistics, 405 were Black).

[120] 393 U.S. 997 (1968) (granting certiorari limited to questions two and three).

[121] 398 F.2d 138, 156 (8th Cir. 1968), *rev. on other grounds*, 398 U.S. 262 (1970) (noting that the statistical study had not included the county in which Maxwell had been convicted).

Maxwell's execution to occur without examining the question or racial bias.[122]

But after *Coker*, no such defense is plausible. Two other Georgia capital rape defendants, John Eberheart, and John Hooks, were before the Supreme Court on petition for a writ of certiorari at the same time as was Ehrlich Coker. In fact, the petitions in those cases were filed before Coker's. Both Eberheart and Brooks—co-defendants—were Black. Rather than reviewing either of their cases, the Court chose *Coker*.[123]

Is there any non-racial reason that Court might have preferred to grant certiorari in Coker's case than in Eberheart or Hook's cases? There is none that is apparent on the face of the records. One could imagine circumstances in which the Court might want to take a case with a very sympathetic defendant, or circumstances in which it might want to take a case with a very unsympathetic defendant, but both Coker and Eberheart/Hooks present quite aggravated rape cases, albeit aggravated in different ways.[124] Likewise, one could imagine a preference for one state (or one statute) over another, but all three cases arose in Georgia. Hooks pled guilty and was sentenced by a judge, which procedurally distinguishes him from Coker, but Eberheart was convicted and sentenced by a jury. The only significant difference between Coker and Eberheart is the race of the defendant. Finally, we know that the race of Eberheart and Hooks would have been apparent to the Court on the most cursory review of the record because the state court opinion recounts that the defendants called the victim "honkey bitch," and "white bitch."[125]

It's worth noticing that choosing either Eberheart or Hooks would not have precluded the Court from looking at the proportionality to the offense issue; it could have done that as well in a black defendant case as in a white defendant case. Moreover, the choice to look away really was twice: both at the cert. grant and at the consideration of the merits stages. This is because both the brief for Coker as petitioner, and the amicus brief from the ACLU made extensive arguments based upon racial disparity. Indeed, even if the Court had chosen the proportionality route to the exclusion of a race discrimination route to the unconstitutionality of capital rape statutes, one might have expected consideration of the penalty's extraordinary history of discrimination and animus; that history would seem relevant to the Court's own judgment of proportion-

---

[122] 398 U.S. 262 (1970).

[123] It reversed and remanded both cases for reconsideration in light of *Coker*.

[124] Although the rape with which Coker was charged did not involve physical injury to the victim, Coker had a history of rape and homicide, and had committed the capital rape while escaped from prison. The rapes committed by Eberheart and Hooks were especially ugly, and involved significant lasting injury to the victim. *Eberheart* at 14.

[125] *Id.*

ality, even if not relevant to the evaluation of consensus. But not a footnote, not a word.

C. "The Evil That Men Do Lives After Them": *McCleskey* and Beyond

In Chapter 6, Professor Baldus tells the story of *McCleskey v. Kemp*.[126] Obviously I won't retell it here, but only highlight how *Coker* facilitated the Court's refusal "to assume that what is unexplained is invidious."[127]

In *McCleskey*, the Supreme Court finally faced directly the influence of race upon the imposition of the death penalty. McCleskey argued both that racial discrimination in the imposition of the death penalty in Georgia violated the Equal Protection Clause of the Fourteenth Amendment, and that the influence of race rendered Georgia's capital sentencing scheme arbitrary and capricious in violation of the Cruel and Unusual Punishment Clause of the Eight Amendment. The evidence supporting these two claims was identical, and for both claims, the most important evidence proffered was the Baldus study. That study examined over 2,000 Georgia murder cases that had occurred during the 1970s. Baldus extensively analyzed his data, examining the effects of 230 variables. He found that, controlling for the relevant variables to avoid spurious correlations,[128] Georgia murder defendants were 4.3 times more likely to be condemned to death if their victims were white than if their victims were black, and that black murder defendants were 1.1 times more likely to receive death sentences than were white defendants. Thus, unlike the racial disparity statistics cited by the petitioner and amici in *Coker*, and before *Coker*, in *Maxwell*, the big racial disparity in *McCleskey* was between white and black *victim* homicides, rather than white and black *defendant* homicides. This was not the result of the new sentencing schemes approved in *Gregg*, but the direct result of *Coker*, for, as Stuart Banner observed, "rape had always been the crime for which the race of the defendant made the biggest difference, so *Coker* instantly wiped away more discrimination that any reform of murder sentencing could have."[129]

As Banner also observed, before *Coker*, racial disparities had yielded clear moral positions: Racial bias was causing too many black defendants

---

[126] 481 U.S. 279 (1987).

[127] *McCleskey v. Kemp* at 313.

[128] One of his models incorporated all 230 variables, and one considered the effects of the thirty-nine most powerful non-racial variables (as well as race if the defendant and race of the victim), and it is the latter model that the majority in *McCleskey* addresses.

[129] Stuart Banner, THE DEATH PENALTY: AN AMERICAN HISTORY 289 (Harvard University Press 2002).

to be sentenced to death.[130] But because most murders are intraracial, the Baldus statistics could be read to mean that *too few* black defendants were being sentenced to death, a reading which hardly creates a unanimous outcry for reform. Of course, another interpretation of those statistics is possible: White victim's lives were being *over*valued. This interpretation would suggest too many executions, some of white defendants and some of black defendants. Or the data might have hinted at a more complex race story, one that would have incorporated the modest race of defendant effects Baldus found: White lives were overvalued, especially when taken by black defendants. And this in turn might have suggested the operation of race in capital sentencing was not uniform, but may have varied with the case, depending on the race of the jurors, the nature of the mitigation presented, the racial identities of the lawyers, and a myriad of other factors. And in fact, empirical evidence since developed suggests just this kind of variability.

But whatever the possible interpretation of stronger race of victim disparities than race of defendant disparities, according to his biographer, Justice Powell found the absence of strong race of defendant effects critical. In his view, the Baldus study showed that the guided discretion approved in *Gregg* had in fact increased the rationality of capital sentencing, producing more death sentences in the more highly aggravated cases. The race of victim disparities didn't bother him because, in his view, if race discrimination had been infecting Georgia's capital sentencing, Baldus would have found "a bias based on the *defendant's* race."[131]

Although Powell came to regret his vote in *McCleskey*,[132] it is not clear whether his view of the significance of this evidence changed.[133] In any event, his opinion for the Court shows no signs of ambivalence. His characterization of the empirical evidence presented by McCleskey was almost a yawn: "At most, the Baldus study demonstrates a discrepancy that appears to correlate with race."[134] Because "[a]pparent disparities in

---

[130] *Id.*; Stephen Carter, *When Victims Happen to Be Black*, 97 YALE L.J. 420, 433 (arguing that the wrong done to McCleskey "pales" compared to the "massive discrimination against black victims.").

[131] John C. Jeffries, JUSTICE LEWIS F. POWELL, JR.: A BIOGRAPHY 439 (New York: Scribners 1994).

[132] *Id.* at 451–52. (When asked after his retirement whether he would change his vote in any case, Powell answered, "Yes," McCleskey v. Kemp).

[133] Q: Do you mean you would now accept the argument from statistics?

A: "No, I would vote the other way in any capital case."

Id.

[134] *McCleskey* at 312.

sentencing are an inevitable part of our criminal justice system," and because "the discretion [involved] is fundamental to our criminal process," Justice Powell "decline[d] to assume that what is unexplained is invidious."[135] The Baldus study, he complacently concluded, "does not demonstrate a constitutionally significant risk of racial bias"[136] in the determination of whom the state will execute.

Many others have written about the many things wrong with Powell's analysis,[137] but I only want to point out its flagrant ahistoricity. If Baldus' data had shown a statistically significant correlation between left-handed victims and imposition of the death penalty, it might have been defensible to declare that what is unexplained is not necessarily invidious. But that's because most jurors are right-handed (and therefore less likely to discriminate against others like themselves); because juries generally wouldn't know whether a victim was right-handed (the lack of salience making discrimination difficult); and—most importantly—because we have no history of animus or discrimination against the right-handed (making discrimination against them inexplicable, or at least surprising enough to make us search for other explanations). But most jurors are white; and the race of the victim would be apparent to juries; and—most importantly—the whole of American history reflects widespread animus and discrimination toward African Americans.[138]

Yet Powell relegates the historical evidence McCleskey proffered to a footnote consisting of one short paragraph. In that footnote, Powell made the doctrinal concession that "the historical background of the decision is an evidentiary source for proof of intentional discrimination." He described McCleskey's historical evidence as "focuse[d] on Georgia laws in force during and just after the Civil War,"[139] a characterization which permitted him to dismiss the probative value of that evidence:

---

[135] *Id.* at 313.

[136] *Id.*

[137] *See e.g.*, Samuel R. Gross & Robert Mauro, DEATH AND DISCRIMINATION: RACIAL DISPARITIES IN CAPITAL SENTENCING 159–211 (1989); Randall Kennedy, McCleskey v. Kemp: *Race, Capital Punishment, and the Supreme Court*, 101 HARV. L. REV. 1388 (1988); Hugo Bedau, *Someday McCleskey Will Be Death Penalty's Dred Scott*, LA Times, May 1, 1987, § 2 at 5, col. 1. As will not surprise the reader by this point, I have done so myself. Sheri Lynn Johnson, Unconscious Racism and the Criminal Law, 73 CORNELL L. REV. 1016 (1988).

[138] *See McCleskey* at 329 (Brennan, J. dissenting) ("Evaluation of McCleskey's evidence cannot rest solely on the numbers themselves. We must also ask whether the conclusion suggested by those numbers is consonant with our understanding of history and human experience.")

[139] *McCleskey* at 298 n. 20.

But unless historical evidence is reasonably contemporaneous with the challenged decision, it has little probative value.[citations omitted]. Although the history of racial discrimination in this country is undeniable, we cannot accept official actions taken long ago as evidence of current intent.[140]

At the least, this footnote is mistaken and misleading. McCleskey's historical evidence *encompassed* racially discriminatory statutes from the antebellum and Reconstruction periods, but it was not *limited* to those periods. Indeed, what figured most prominently in the more modern evidence were the racial patterns in capital rape prosecutions. There is no chance that this evidence escaped Powell's attention, for Justice Brennan's dissent referred to it—and to *Coker*:

> Five years later, the Court struck down the imposition of the death penalty in Georgia for the crime of rape. *Coker v. Georgia*, 433 U.S. 584 (1977). Although the Court did not explicitly mention race, the decision had to have been informed by the specific observations on rape by both the Chief Justice and JUSTICE POWELL in *Furman*. Furthermore, evidence submitted to the Court indicated that black men who committed rape, particularly of white women, were considerably more likely to be sentenced to death than white rapists. For instance, by 1977, Georgia had executed 62 men for rape since the Federal Government began compiling statistics in 1930. Of these men, 58 were black and 4 were white. See Brief for Petitioner in Coker v. Georgia, O.T. 1976, No. 75–5444, p. 56; see also Wolfgang & Riedel, Rape, Race, and the Death Penalty in Georgia, 45 Am. J. Orthopsychiatry 658 (1975).[141]

Ignoring facts asserted by a party is easy, and ignoring inferences made by a colleague in dissent is not much harder; in contrast, it would have been very difficult to ignore the Court's own precedent had the Court held that the death penalty for rape violated the prohibition against race discrimination. And it is hard to imagine that the Court could have avoided that holding if it had taken the other fork when deciding between petitioners Coker and Eberheart. Would *any* Justice have called the racial patterns in the imposition of the death penalty for rape "unexplained," or denied that those patterns reflected "invidious" racial animus? I think the starkness of the statistical pattern, the intuitively accessible nature of race of defendant discrimination, the well-established fact of white fear, anger, violence and stereotyping associated with black sexuality in general, and interracial sexual liaisons in particular, would have made it impossible to avoid the answer of racial

---

[140] *Id.*

[141] *Id.* at 332 (Brennan, J., dissenting); *see also id.* at 359 (Blackmun, J., dissenting) (referring to Justice Brennan's recitation of the historical evidence).

discrimination, had the Court been willing to entertain the question with respect to capital rape prosecutions. Moreover, the race and capital rape statistics (as well as the race-specific antebellum statutes) support the inference of discrimination in murder cases in another way: The capital rape statistics, like the capital murder statistics, reflect both race of defendant and race of victim effects. Viewed through the lens of the capital rape data, it is neither surprising nor coincidental that Baldus found large race of victim effects in the capital murder cases; certainly no one would argue that the fact that capital rape executions were limited to white victim cases was anything but intentional, or anything but invidious. Had the Court first considered the race of victim effects in capital rape cases, it would not likely have characterized those same effects "unexplained" in capital murder prosecutions.

And then? Then it would have been a short step to a different outcome in *McCleskey*. If the Court had to add racial discrimination *in the same state* in the administration of the death penalty for rape, to the dramatic racial disparities based on race of victim in capital homicide case and then add modest race of defendant disparities in those cases (inexplicably ignored by the majority),[142] how could the sum be less than racial discrimination in capital sentencing?[143] I don't claim to know whether the corrected calculation would have meant the end of all capital punishment, or merely the narrowing of capital punishment statute to the most highly aggravated cases, where Baldus's data showed that racial disparities did not exist.[144] Either way, for capital defendants, it would have been better than *Coker*. And apart from capital defendants, the truth would have been better for us all.

CONCLUSION

When Marc Antony says (as Shakespeare has it) "I come to bury Caesar, not to praise him," he doesn't mean it, as becomes obvious when he reviews Caesar's life for the crowd. But after reviewing the life of the

---

[142] McCleskey's argument included both disparities, and emphasized their interaction, though it relied most heavily on race of victim disparities, which were much stronger. Brief for Petitioner, McCleskey v. Kemp, 481 U.S. 279 (1987) at 13–16, 33–41, 80–87.

[143] Moreover, the Court had already recognized the phenomenon of unconscious racial bias in *Turner v. Murray,* 476 U.S. 28 (1986), which would have aided in explaining why race of victim effects might be more prominent than race of defendant effects. *See* Johnson, *supra*, note 111.

[144] "One of the lessons of the Baldus study is that there exist certain categories of extremely serious crimes for which prosecutors consistently seek, and juries consistently impose, the death penalty without regard to the race of the victim or the race of the offender. If Georgia were to narrow the class of death-eligible defendants to those categories, the danger of arbitrary and discriminatory imposition of the death penalty would be significantly decreased, if not eradicated. Justice Stephens urged this possibility." *McCleskey* at 367 (Stephens, J., dissenting).

Coker decision, I find relatively little to praise, and much to condemn, or at least to mourn. Hearing from Ehrlich Coker made me pause, and reading Jack Greenburg's assessment—that *Coker* was "like a touchdown following a 90 yard march"[145]—made me pause again. For quite different reasons, they each should know. But in the end, I think the peculiar virtues of deciding the death penalty for rape through *Coker's* proportionality approach have been largely interred, while the evil of separating race from the three-strand braid of race, rape, and capital punishment lives on and on.

Ehrlich Coker—and John Eberheart and John Hooks, and all the potential capital rape defendants—would have been just as well served by an examination of capital rape prosecutions that was true to their history as an instrument of racial discrimination, oppression, and animus. Facing that history would have made it much harder for the Court to blithely declare in *McCleskey* that "unexplained" racial patterns were not necessarily "invidious." As it did happen, *McCleskey* has shut down virtually all statistical-based challenges to administration of the death penalty, including those focused on a particular decisionmaker,[146] and those attempting to demonstrate race of defendant disparities.[147] That shut-down tells a lie about our country, and allows people to die for that lie. I lay part of the blame at the feet of *Coker*.

---

[145] Jack Greenberg, CRUSADERS IN THE COURTS 454 (Harper Collins 1994).

[146] See John H. Blume, Theodore Eisenberg & Sheri Lynn Johnson, *Post–McCleskey Racial Discrimination Claims in Capital Cases,* 83 CORNELL L. REV. 1771 (1998).

[147] Anthony G. Amsterdam, *Opening Remarks: Race and the Death Penalty Before and After McCleskey v. Kemp,* 39 COL. H.R. L.REV. 34, 45 (2007).

*

5

John H. Blume*

Gilmore v. Utah: The Persistent Problem of "Volunteers"

"Let's do it."

Gary Gilmore

I. Introduction

On January 17, 1977, after a ten year hiatus, the United States re-entered the execution business. Just a few months earlier, the Supreme Court had taken the first step when it held that the death penalty was not in all respects cruel and unusual punishment prohibited by the Eighth Amendment and placed its stamp of approval on several of the new, and supposedly improved, death penalty statutes.[1] Most knowledgeable observers believed it would be years before the first execution took place. They were wrong. They did not anticipate that one of the newly condemned inmates would volunteer for execution. But Gary Gilmore, a Utah death row inmate, did just that. At 8:06 in the morning, five sharpshooters chosen by the Warden took aim at a target pinned on Gary Gilmore's shirt by a physician to indicate where Gilmore's heart was located and, on command, fired. Gilmore was quickly pronounced dead, taken to a hospital, where his eyes were harvested and donated, his

---

* Professor of Law, Cornell Law School and Director, Cornell Death Penalty Project.

[1] In 1972, in *Furman v. Georgia*, 408 U.S. 238 (1972), the Court determined that the death penalty, as then administered in this country, violated the Eighth Amendment's prohibition against cruel and unusual punishment. Many states, including Utah, scurried to enact new capital punishment statutes which would satisfy the Supreme Court's rather vague mandate. In 1976, the High Court approved some of the new law, the "guided discretion" statutes, *see Gregg v. Georgia*, 428 U.S. 153 (1976); *Profitt v. Florida*, 428 U.S. 242 (1976); *Jurek v. Texas*, 428 U.S. 262 (1976), but found that mandatory capital punishment schemes violated the Eighth Amendment. *Woodson v. North Carolina*, 428 U.S. 280 (1976); *Roberts v. Louisiana*, 428 U.S. 325 (1976).

body cremated, and his ashes subsequently distributed according to his wishes.

By any standard, Gilmore was executed with breathtaking speed. The crimes leading to his convictions, death sentence and executions took place on July 19th and 20th of 1976. Gilmore was arrested on July 21st, the trial commenced on October 5th and culminated in a death sentence on October 7th. Several weeks later, Gilmore requested that all appeals be waived and several days after that he wrote a letter to the Utah Supreme Court requesting that any and all appeals be declared null and void. After a few brief stays of execution—and several suicide attempts—Gilmore was executed, without any appellate review of his convictions and sentence on January 17th, 1977, just a few days shy of the six month anniversary of the offense.

Gilmore was the first, but certainly not the last, person executed in the modern era of capital punishment who waived his appeals and chose death. Since Gilmore's death by firing squad, another 129 death sentenced inmates, out of the 1104 inmates who have been executed, have waived their appeals and volunteered for execution.[2] Gilmore's case, and that of every other death row volunteer since his case was decided, also raised the following question: how should a death sentenced inmate who wishes to waive his appeals be viewed? As a client making a legal decision to accept the outcome of a prior proceeding, or as a person seeking the aid of the state in committing suicide? In this chapter, I will discuss the events giving rise to Gilmore's execution, the Supreme Court's decision in his case, and its impact on the subsequent legal struggle against capital punishment in the United States, especially as it pertains to the persistent problem of volunteers.

II. Gilmore's Story

The Early Years

Gary Mark Gilmore was born on December 4, 1940 in Texas. Gilmore's father, Frank, was a conman and wanderer with a long criminal record.[3] He was also an abusive alcoholic given to fits of rage. His mother, Bessie, a lapsed Mormon, was emotionally distant. She would not allow any of her children to touch her, and she believed that she and her family were cursed by ghosts.[4] After years of traversing

---

[2] http://www.deathpenaltyinfo.org/article.php?scid=8 & did=146 (last checked June 9, 2008).

[3] M. Gilmore, Shot in the Heart, p. 91; Famous American Crimes and Trials, p. 176.

[4] For example, Bessie's sister, Alta, was killed in an accident when Bessie was a teenager. Bessie believed her sister was killed by the demon of a dead man she had conjured up during a seance with a Ouija board that had occurred a few days earlier. Mikal

Texas, often under assumed names to avoid the law, the family settled down in Portland, Oregon in the late 1940's, and Frank stopped drinking and started a legitimate business.[5] Steady, gainful employment and sobriety, however, did not cure Frank's violent temperament. It appeared to make him more violent towards Bessie and the children.[6] While all the Gilmore boys would be whipped,[7] often for no reason, Gary felt the wrath of his father more than his other brothers due to his father's suspicion, apparently incorrect, that he was not the child's father and also because Gary would fight back, which made Frank more angry and violent.[8] Frank, Sr. beat the boys with razor straps, belts and his fists, often for nothing or for trivial offenses such as being five minutes late for dinner.[9]

Gilmore, despite his high I.Q.,[10] never did particularly well in school. He was involved in numerous fights and he was frequently disciplined for disrespectful conduct towards his teachers and altercations with other students. He finally quit school for good when he was 14, after which his daily existence consisted of drinking, using heroin, speed and other drugs, stealing and fighting.[11] He became known for his bravado and death-defying acts. One of his favorites stunts was to walk out to the middle of a train trestle, wait for the train to reach the start of the bridge, and then run to the opposite side, jumping to safety at the last possible moment.[12] Many who knew him thought, even then, that Gilmore had a death wish.

Prior Incarcerations

Not surprisingly, Gilmore was arrested numerous times as a teenager. Initially, his father hired lawyers and investigators and Gilmore was able to avoid any lengthy juvenile incarcerations the first several times

---

Gilmore, SHOT IN THE HEART, p. 39. Later in life, Bessie became convinced that this same evil spirit possessed Gary. *Id.* at 115.

[5] *Id.* at 79; *see also* FAMOUS AMERICAN CRIMES AND TRIAL, p. 176.

[6] M. Gilmore, SHOT IN THE HEART, p. 108. Mikal Gilmore described the fights between the parents as "nightmarish and brutal."

[7] Gilmore had three brothers. Two were older, Frank Jr. And Gaylen, one, Mikal, was younger.

[8] Mikal Gilmore, SHOT IN THE HEART, p. 87.

[9] *Id.* at 124.

[10] N. Mailer, THE EXECUTIONER'S SONG, p. 379; *see also* Interview with Gary Gilmore, *Playboy Magazine* (April 1977), p. 76.

[11] *Id.* at 74.

[12] *Id.* at 135.

he was caught.[13] However, he eventually stole one car too many and was sentenced to a juvenile term at MacLaren's Reform School for Boys.[14] Gilmore, who detested authority, quickly became a "leader" at MacLaren and he spent a good deal of his year at the institution in maximum security.[15] He was released but soon wound up in the Oregon State Correctional Institution after engaging in additional car thefts. During one of his incarcerations, his father died, and Gilmore was not allowed to attend the funeral. When the prison authorities broke the news to him, Gilmore destroyed most of the contents of his cell, acted out against staff, and attempted suicide.[16]

Gilmore was released, reoffended, and in 1964 he was sentenced to a term of fifteen years imprisonment for assault and robbery. Due to his bad institutional behavior, he was placed on an anti-psychotic medication, Prolixin.[17] Gilmore hated the drug, claiming it made him a "zombie." His mother eventually convinced the prison to take him off the medication. During this incarceration, his brother Gaylen died. This time he was allowed to attend the funeral.[18] But, his behavior did not improve, and he continued to spend long stretches of his sentence in solitary confinement. By some measures, he spent his time in solitary confinement productively; he worked on his drawing, wrote poetry, and read classical literature. Because of his artistic talent, he was recommended for an early release to attend art school. But freedom was again short lived. Less than a month after his release, Gilmore was arrested for armed robbery and he was again confined in the Oregon State Prison system.[19] His continued bad behavior and suicide attempts convinced the prison that Gilmore should be placed back on Prolixin.[20] Gilmore detested the idea of being involuntarily medicated, and he convinced the prison to instead transfer him to the federal maximum security prison in Marion, Illinois.[21] While incarcerated in Marion, he began writing his

---

[13] FAMOUS AMERICAN TRIALS, pp. 177–78.

[14] Id. at 178.

[15] M. Gilmore, SHOT IN THE HEART, pp. 154–155. According to Gilmore's brother, Mikal, Gilmore "had a penchant for hard time punishment" that "became a pattern . . . for the rest of his prison career." Id. Gilmore himself estimated that he spent almost four years in isolation. Interview with Gary Gilmore, Playboy Magazine, p. 86.

[16] FAMOUS AMERICAN TRIALS, p. 178.

[17] Mailer, p. 398. He was also given electric shock treatments against his will. Interview with Gary Gilmore, Playboy Magazine, p. 176.

[18] FAMOUS AMERICAN TRIALS, p. 179.

[19] Id.

[20] M. Gilmore, SHOT IN THE HEART, p. 313.

[21] Id.

maternal cousin Brenda, who lived in Provo, Utah. Brenda eventually was instrumental in convincing the parole board to release Gilmore to her custody. Prior to his release, she arranged for him to work for his uncle, Vern Damico, in Damico's shoe repair business. On April 9, 1976, Gilmore was released and traveled to Utah to begin a new life.[22]

The Last Gasp of Freedom

Gilmore was thirty-five years old when he went to Utah. He had been incarcerated for almost half of his life. Because he was so "institutionalized," Gilmore had great difficulty adjusting to life on the outside in general and life in conservative, Mormon Utah in particular. For example, his uncle repeatedly had to rebuke him for making sexually suggestive comments to and about the shoe repair shop's female customers.[23] He also began drinking steadily and taking Fiorinal, a headache medication.

Not long after arriving in Provo, he met a young woman named Nicole Barrett. Just nineteen, Nicole had been married and divorced three times and had two children.[24] Gilmore fell hopelessly in love with Nicole and the relationship was, by all accounts, very intense. Gilmore believed (literally) that he and Nicole were "twin souls," who had "known and loved each other for thousands of years."[25] He soon left Brenda's house and moved in with Nicole and her children. Alcohol and drugs were a staple of the relationship, and Gilmore began to drink even more as his use of Fiorinal escalated. The drug exacerbated his mood swings and another common side effect, sexual dysfunction, contributed to building tension in his relationship with Nicole.[26] The stress led to more binges, and because he needed money to support his drug and alcohol use, Gilmore began stealing. After two months, Gilmore's unpredictable and increasingly violent mood swings and the sometimes physical abuse of Nicole and her children, convinced Nicole she had to leave Gilmore. Gilmore tried to talk her into coming back, but she had had enough. His entreaties continued and Nicole decided to hide from him.[27]

The Crimes

After the breakup with Nicole, Gilmore became even more unstable. By his own account, he could not sleep or eat.[28] Persistent financial

---

[22] Famous American Trials, p. 179.

[23] Famous American Trials, p. 179.

[24] M. Gilmore, Shot in the Heart, p. 324.

[25] Interview with Gary Gilmore, *Playboy* Magazine, p. 77.

[26] *Id.*

[27] *Id.*

[28] Interview with Gary Gilmore, *Playboy* Magazine, p. 78.

problems, including making the payments on a truck he loved but could not afford and increased alcohol and drug abuse, led to even more pronounced mood swings and angry outbursts. Gilmore began thinking about killing Nicole.[29] But she was hiding from him, and his attempts to locate her for the most part proved unsuccessful.[30]

On July 19, 1976, Gilmore went to Nicole's mother's house. Nicole was not there, and no one would tell him where she was staying Gilmore cajoled Nicole's sister April, a drug addict with her own psychiatric problems, into going with him to see the movie "One Flew Over the Cuckoo's Nest." Later that evening, Gilmore parked the truck, told April he needed to make a phone call and walked into a Sinclair Gas Station in Orem, Utah. Twenty-four-year-old Max Jensen, a law student, was working that evening. Gilmore pulled out a gun, told Jensen to empty his pockets and to give him the coin changer Jensen wore around his waist.[31] Jensen was completely compliant. Gilmore told Jensen to kneel on the bathroom floor, and then shot him twice in the head. Gilmore purportedly said "This one's for me" before firing the first shot, and "This one's for Nicole," before firing the second shot.[32] Gilmore walked out without taking a large sum of money sitting on the service station desk. He later said he was distracted by Jensen's blood, which had splattered on his pants. Gilmore and April spent the night at a local Holiday Inn, where she rebuffed his sexual advances.[33]

The next afternoon, while mechanics were working on Gilmore's truck, Gilmore went to see if he could find his uncle Vern. After failing to find Vern at home, Gilmore walked into the nearby Center City Hotel in Provo and shot and killed the manager, Ben Bushnell.[34] A witness saw Gilmore leaving the hotel with a cash box in one hand and a gun in the other. Gilmore decided he needed to dispose of the gun; while holding it by the barrel and attempting to shove it into a bush, the gun discharged and blew a hole in Gilmore's left hand.[35] Bleeding and in pain, Gilmore

---

[29] *Id.* at 79.

[30] The day before the first murder, he did briefly encounter Nicole when she came to the house they had been living in to get some of her belongings. She did not know he was there. When he attempted to stop her from leaving, she pulled out a pistol and pointed it at him. *Id.* at 178.

[31] M. Gilmore, Shot in the Heart, p. 324.

[32] *Id.*

[33] *Id.*

[34] Playboy Magazine Interview with Gary Gilmore, p. 80. Ironically, Gilmore had lived with his mother and brothers in this hotel years earlier for a short period of time when his father was incarcerated. M. Gilmore, Shot in the Heart, p. 95.

[35] M. Gilmore, Shot in the Heart, p. 325.

ran into the gas station bathroom where his truck was being repaired. An employee saw the trail of blood, and then heard on a police scanner that there had been an assault and robbery at a nearby hotel. After Gilmore left the station, the employee took down the truck's license number, called the police and gave them the tag number, a description of the driver and the direction he was headed. After trying unsuccessfully to get a friend to take him to the airport, Gilmore called his cousin Brenda. She called the police.[36] Not long thereafter, Gilmore was arrested in front of Nicole's mother's house. Nicole witnessed Gilmore's arrest.[37]

The Trial

Believing the evidence was stronger in the Bushnell case, the prosecution elected to first try Gilmore for that murder. Given Gilmore's criminal record and poor disciplinary history during his prior incarcerations, the prosecution also announced that it would ask the jury to sentence Gilmore to death.[38] Gilmore's three day trial, the first capital trial since *Furman* in Utah, began on October 5, 1976, less than three months after the crimes. Gilmore was represented by two public defenders, Craig Snyder and Mike Esplin; neither had any capital trial experience. The prosecution's case against Gilmore was solid. It was built primarily on ballistics evidence tying the gun Gilmore placed in the bush to cartridges found at the scene; the testimony of an eyewitness who placed Gilmore near the motel where Bushnell was murdered with a cashbox in one hand and a gun in the other; the testimony of the gas station employee who saw the trail of blood into the bathroom and took down Gilmore's tag number as he left the service station; and a statement Gilmore made to his cousin Brenda when, after his arrest, she asked him what to tell his mother and he replied, "Tell her it's true."[39] Defense counsel's cross-examination of the state's witnesses was perfunctory and the evidence came in largely unchallenged.[40]

After the prosecution rested, Gilmore's trial counsel indicated they did not intend to call any witnesses. Gilmore became irate, convinced his

---

[36] Interview with Gary Gilmore, *Playboy* Magazine, p. 80.

[37] FAMOUS AMERICAN TRIALS, p. 182.

[38] By several accounts, the lead prosecutor, Noall Wooten, was not a strong supporter of capital punishment but did not believe that, given Gilmore's history, he could be rehabilitated. Mailer, p. 413–14. It is also reported that Wooten believed that even if the jury sentenced Gilmore to death, there was little likelihood that Gilmore would actually be executed. Crime Library, www.crimelibrary.ccm/notorious_murders/mass/gilmore/trial_5. html.

[39] FAMOUS AMERICAN TRIALS, p. 182.

[40] Barbara Babcock, *Gary Gilmore's Lawyers*, 32 Stan. L. Rev. 865, 867 (1980).

lawyers were trying to railroad him.[41] Apparently, he was under the impression that his lawyers intended to contest the charges (or at least his mental state). Faced with the prospect of certain conviction and a return to prison for, in all likelihood, the rest of his life, Gilmore encouraged his lawyers to do something. They attempted to mollify him by pointing out some weakness in the state's circumstantial case. But Gilmore was no fool, and he knew that if no defense was presented, his conviction was guaranteed. The next day, he asked the trial judge to reopen the testimony and allow him to testify. Gilmore wanted to present an insanity defense. His attorneys informed the court that Gilmore had been evaluated by four different psychiatrists, and the experts all agreed that Gilmore knew the difference between right and wrong at the time he killed Bushnell and thus was not legally insane under Utah law.[42] Gilmore soon withdrew his request.

In his summation, defense attorney Esplin argued that the gun could have discharged accidently, just as it had accidently gone off when Gilmore tried to get rid of it, and asked the jury to convict Gilmore of second degree murder. The jury thought otherwise, and after only an hour and twenty minutes of deliberation, it returned with a verdict finding Gilmore guilty of first degree murder.[43]

After a lunch break, the sentencing phase of the trial began. Things went quickly but not well for Gilmore. The prosecution called a police officer who testified as to his belief that Gilmore also killed Jensen, and another officer was called who recounted his telephone conversations with correctional staff in Oregon about Gilmore's bad behavior during his various incarcerations.[44] Gilmore testified on his own behalf, and by all accounts, did much more harm than good. He appeared angry, belligerent, and completely devoid of any remorse,[45] remarking at one

---

[41] FAMOUS AMERICAN TRIALS, p. 183.

[42] Gilmore's counsel also did not present any type of diminished capacity defense based on Gilmore's alcohol and drug abuse, the stress of the breakup with Nicole, and the resulting lack of sleep. Babcock, Stan. L. Rev. at 867. To be fair to Snyder and Esplin, Gilmore made their job difficult. He refused to allow them to call Nicole as a witness and he reportedly stared menacingly at the jury. M. Gilmore, SHOT IN THE HEART, at 325. He also refused to allow them to invoke the sequestration rule because he wanted Nicole to be able to sit in the courtroom. Given that she was a potential witness for both the prosecution and the defense, sequestration would have prevented her from observing the proceedings. Mailer, THE EXECUTIONER'S SONG, p. 414. However, there is also no evidence that counsel made any real effort to explain to Gilmore the consequences of his choices and to convince him to change his mind. Babcock, 32 Stan. L. Rev. at 869.

[43] Mailer, THE EXECUTIONER'S SONG, p. 433.

[44] Mailer, THE EXECUTIONER'S SONG, pp. 434–35.

[45] When asked why he killed Bushnell, Gilmore responded, "Well I felt like there was no way what happened could have been avoided." *Id.* at 439.

point, "I am finally glad to see that the jury is looking at me." One observer noted that the jury appeared "stunned" by his testimony.[46] The defense did not call several mental health experts who had evaluated Gilmore while he was incarcerated in Oregon and who believed that Gilmore had been permanently damaged by the prior forcible administration of anti-psychotic medications.[47] Instead, they called a local psychiatrist who examined Gilmore after the two Utah murders and who testified that Gilmore was a sociopath.[48] After summations, the jury retired to decide whether Gilmore should live or die. It did not dally long with the decision. By late afternoon, the jury returned with a death verdict. Under Utah law, Gilmore had to choose whether he wanted to die by hanging or firing squad.[49] Gilmore responded: "I think I'd prefer to be shot."[50] Knowing the decision would be appealed, the trial judge set Gilmore's execution for November 15, 1976.

Gilmore's decision to die, the "waiver" of his appeals and the legal battle over his execution.

It is unclear exactly when Gilmore decided to waive his appeals, but within two weeks of the sentence being imposed, his letters to Nicole indicated his "inclination" was to let the sentence be carried out.[51] But, in addition to his own death, he wanted Nicole to commit suicide.[52] During a meeting with his trial counsel, Gilmore informed them that he wanted to be executed in order to atone for a crime he committed in a prior life in eighteenth century England.[53] He became angry when they insisted on pursuing the appeal. At a court hearing on November 1, Gilmore informed the judge of his decision in his characteristically brusque manner: "You sentenced me to die. Unless it's a joke or

---

[46] *Id.* at 441.

[47] Babcock, 32 Stan. L. Rev. at 869; *see also,* Mailer, The Executioner's Song, p. 400.

[48] Mailer, The Executioner's Song, pp. 437–38.

[49] Utah retained the firing squad even after hanging became the primary method of execution due to its commitment to the Mormon doctrine of blood atonement. Some Mormons believe that some sins, including murder, are so serious that they place the sinner beyond the saving power of Christ's crucifixion. Gilmore, Shot in the Heart at 351. Thus, in order to be forgiven, the sinner's blood has to be spilled. Joseph Smith, Documentary History of the Church, 5:296 ("I am opposed to hanging, even if a man kill another, I will shoot him or cut off his head, spill his blood on the ground and let the smoke ascend thereof up to God.").

[50] Mailer, The Executioner's Song, p. 438.

[51] *Id.* at 473.

[52] *Id.*

[53] *Id.* at 490.

something I want to go ahead and do it."[54] The judge informed Gilmore he could still change his mind and appeal, but told Gilmore that unless he decided to do so, the sentence would be carried out as ordered.[55]

Gilmore's trial counsel, despite being dismissed by the trial court, filed a notice of appeal on November 3rd.[56] Other death row inmates in Utah also attempted to intervene, arguing that Utah's post-*Furman* death penalty statute was unconstitutional.[57] The Utah Supreme Court stayed the execution on December 5th, indicating they would entertain the merits of the appeal.[58] Gilmore then retained Dennis Boaz, a former prosecutor from California, who agreed to help Gilmore in his quest to die. Gilmore wrote a letter to the Court asking "Don't the People of Utah have the courage of their convictions. Let's do it and to hell with all the bullshit."[59] After the Attorney General's office filed a motion for reconsideration and Boaz moved to dismiss the appeal and to vacate the stay, the Court agreed to reconsider its decision to stay the execution and Boaz and Gilmore were permitted to appear before them to argue for Gilmore's right to be executed.[60]

The mood was set from the beginning when the Chief Justice announced, "We want this to be very brief, because we have a regular calender at 9:00 a.m."[61] The entire "waiver" of Gilmore's right to appeal consisted of the following questions and answers:

Boaz: Gary Gilmore, do you realize you have an absolute right to appeal the conviction and sentence rendered in this case?

Gilmore: Yes Sir.

Boaz: Did you previously indicate to your attorneys of record that you did not wish an appeal taken in this case.

Gilmore: I told them during the trial and perhaps before that, that if I were found guilty and sentenced to death that I would prefer to

---

[54] *Id.* at 492.

[55] *Id.*

[56] Earl F. Dorius, *Personal Reflections of my Involvement and the Involvement of the Attorney General's Office Staff with the Cary Gilmore Case: Between November 1, 1976 and January 17, 1977,* (on file at Brigham Young University School of Law, p. 2).

[57] *Id.* at 4.

[58] *Id.* at 5.

[59] *Id.* at 7–8.

[60] *Id.* at 9–10.

[61] Petition for Rehearing filed in U.S. Supreme Court, p. 5, *Bessie Gilmore v. Utah* (on file with author).

accept without any delay.... But I fired them and they understood that.

Boaz: Gary Gilmore, are you in fact at this moment ready to accept execution?

Gilmore: Not at this moment but I am ready to accept it next Monday morning at 8:00 a.m. That is when it was set and that is when I am ready to accept it.[62]

Gilmore's dismissed trial counsel, Mr. Snyder, argued that the appeal should be heard because Gilmore was under "tremendous emotional stress and strain" and that what he was attempting to do was "tantamount to suicide." Thus, counsel argued, the court should review and consider "the substantial matters which are raised both by the trial conviction and subsequent proceeding."[63] At a minimum, Gilmore's trial counsel argued, there needed to be a formal hearing to determine Gilmore's competency to waive his appeals and whether there had been a knowing and intelligent waiver of the right to appeal.[64] One member of the Court asked counsel, "Why won't you accept in good grace his firing you, like he is willing to accept in good grace the sentence of the court." When asked if he had any final words, Gilmore stated, "I believe I was given a fair trial and I think the sentence is proper and I am willing to accept it like a man. I don't wish to appeal.... I desire to be executed on schedule, and I just wish to accept that with the grace and dignity of a man and I hope you will allow me to do that."[65] Later that day, by a vote of 4 to 1, the Utah Supreme Court vacated the stay of execution.[66] By most accounts, Gilmore was very happy.

The day after the state court's decision, the outgoing Governor asked the Board of Pardons to review Gilmore's case prior to the execution.[67] Because the Board would not meet until November 17th, Gilmore's date with death was postponed. Angered by the delay, Gilmore and Nicole entered into what proved to be an unsuccessful suicide pact the evening the execution was originally scheduled. Both took an overdose of barbiturates, but neither died.[68]

---

[62] Mailer, THE EXECUTIONER'S SONG at 533.

[63] Id.

[64] Dorius, *supra* p. 11.

[65] Id.

[66] Id.

[67] Mailer, THE EXECUTIONER'S SONG, p. 548.

[68] Id. at 590.

Gilmore had his date with the Board of Pardons. He was represented by new counsel. Boaz had been fired, apparently for talking too much to the press, and Gilmore's new attorneys were two Utah lawyers, Robert Moody and Ronald Stanger. As he had in prior proceedings, Gilmore taunted the Board: "I seek nothing from you, don't desire anything from you, haven't earned anything, and I don't deserve anything either."[69] At one point he stated, "Let's do it you cowards."[70] He also urged the ACLU and various ministers who argued for clemency to "butt out."[71] On November 30th, the Board voted 3–2 not to commute the sentence. The sentence was to be carried out on December 6th.

But it was not over. Boaz' former local counsel, Tom Jones, attempted to lodge an appeal in the Utah Supreme Court arguing that Gilmore's mental condition had deteriorated and questioning Gilmore's capacity to make an informed decision.[72] Anthony G. Amsterdam, a professor at Stanford University who had argued many of the leading cases challenging the death penalty in the Supreme Court of the United States, also filed a motion for stay of execution in the Utah Supreme Court, the United States Supreme Court, and the federal district court on behalf of Gilmore's mother Bessie as "next friend."[73] Amsterdam's submissions challenged Gilmore's competency relying upon Gilmore's prior "history of emotional disturbance," his two recent suicide attempts, a hunger strike and Jones' affidavit filed in the Utah Supreme Court which expressed Jones' opinion that Gilmore was not competent. Given that the only competency hearing had been conducted prior to Gilmore's trial, Amsterdam argued that a formal competency hearing and determination was needed before Gilmore could waive his appeals. Amsterdam also attacked the validity of Gilmore's alleged waiver of his right to appeal on the bases that Gilmore was represented during the waiver proceeding in the Utah Supreme Court by a conflicted lawyer—Boaz—who stood to gain financially if Gilmore was executed,[74] and the lack of an adequate

---

[69] *Id.* pp. 674–75.

[70] Dorius, p. 21.

[71] *Id.*

[72] *Id.* p. 23.

[73] Dorius, p. 28. Gilmore's former trial counsel, Craig Snyder contacted Amsterdam about the case. Amsterdam then talked to Gilmore's brother, Mikal, and mother, Bessie, discussed the potential problems with Gilmore's purported waiver and competency and obtained their permission to proceed with Ms. Gilmore as the "next friend." Mailer, THE EXECUTIONER'S SONG, pp. 701–03.

[74] Boaz' deal with Gilmore called for him to get the media rights to Gilmore's case in exchange for assisting Gilmore in his effort to be executed. Gilmore subsequently sold the publication rights and motion picture rights to Lawrence Schiller for a little more than fifty thousand dollars. M. Gilmore, SHOT IN THE HEART, p. 331. Schiller conducted the interviews

judicial inquiry to determine whether Gilmore's waiver was knowing and intelligent, and since there was no trial transcript, none of the attorneys who had been involved in the case could possibly advise Gilmore as to what he might be waiving since they had no idea what potential avenues of attack there might be.[75] Amsterdam also challenged the yet untested Utah death penalty statute, arguing that because it did not provide for automatic appellate review, a key feature in the Georgia, Florida and Texas regimes recently upheld by the Supreme Court, it was unconstitutional.[76]

On December 3rd, the United States Supreme Court stayed the execution.[77] But that victory was short lived. After the Attorney General's office responded, the Supreme Court vacated the stay on December 13th. Given its brevity, I will set it out the Court's order in its entirety:

> On October 7, 1976, Gary Mark Gilmore was convicted of murder and sentenced to death by a judgment entered after jury trial in a Utah Court. On December 3, 1976, this Court granted an application for a stay of execution of the judgment and sentence, pending the filing here by the State of Utah of a response to the application together with transcripts of various specific hearing in the Utah courts and Board of Pardons, and until "further action of the Court of the application for stay."
>
> The State of Utah has now filed its response and has substantially complied with the Court's requests for transcripts of specified hearings. After carefully examining the materials submitted by the State of Utah, the Court is convinced that Gary Mark Gilmore made a knowing and intelligent waiver of any and all federal rights he might have asserted after the Utah trial court's sentence was imposed, and specifically, that the State's determinations of his competence knowingly and intelligently to waive any and all such rights were firmly grounded.
>
> Accordingly, the stay of execution granted on December 3, 1976 is hereby terminated.

Chief Justice Burger, joined by Justice Powell, concurred. The Chief Justice stated that the case was "unique in the annals of the Court."[78] It was unique, he said, because Gilmore had requested no relief himself,

---

with Gilmore which were the basis of the interview in Playboy magazine, he also wrote the screenplay for the movie adaption of Mailer's book, THE EXECUTIONER'S SONG.

[75] Petition for rehearing at 10.

[76] *Id.* at 23–25.

[77] Doirus, p. 31.

[78] 429 U.S. at 1013, n. 1.

Gilmore stated that he had "received a fair trial," Gilmore did not claim to be innocent of the crime and "his only complaint ... has been with respect to the delay on the part of the State in carrying out the death sentence."[79] As to the "merits," the Chief Justice stated that Gilmore's mother could only possibly have standing to seek relief if Gilmore was "incompetent to waive his right or appeal under state law and was at the present time incompetent to assert rights or to challenge Bessie Gilmore's standing to assert rights in his behalf as 'next friend.' "[80] However, the Chief Justice stated he had examined "with care the pertinent portions of the transcripts and reports of state proceedings and the response of Gary Mark Gilmore ... and [he was] in complete agreement with the conclusion ... that Gary Mark Gilmore knowingly and intelligently, with full knowledge of his right to seek an appeal in the Utah Supreme Court has waived that right."[81] He also agreed with the State's "determination of [Gilmore's] competence to waive his rights knowingly and intelligently were firmly grounded."[82]

Justice Stevens, joined by Justice Rehnquist, also concurred on the basis that, given the state court's finding of competence and given that Gilmore's access to the courts was "entirely unimpeded," a third party had no standing.[83] "Without a proper litigant before it, this Court is without power to stay the execution."[84]

Justices White, Brennan, Marshall and Blackmun dissented. Justice White, joined by Brennan and Marshall noted that "substantial questions" existed about the constitutionality of the Utah death penalty statute, none of which were resolved by the state courts due to Gilmore's "purported waiver."[85] Unlike the majority, however, he did not believe that the "consent of a convicted defendant" privileged the state to "impose a sentence otherwise forbidden by the Eighth Amendment."[86] Thus he did not believe there was any "jurisdictional barrier" to the Court's consideration of the questions raised in Bessie Gilmore's submissions and he would have continued the stay pending the filing of a timely petition for certiorari and then vacate the state court's judgment and

---

[79] Id.

[80] Id. at 1014.

[81] Id. at 1014–15.

[82] Id.

[83] Id. at 1017.

[84] Id.

[85] Id. at 1017–18.

[86] Id.

remand the case for reconsideration "in light of the death penalty decisions announce by this Court last term."[87]

Justice Marshall's dissent focused on Gilmore's waiver. First, he noted that less than five months had passed since the commission of the crime, which—in his view—was "hardly sufficient time for mature consideration of the question [of waiver]."[88] He also pointed out that Gilmore had acted erratically since the sentence was imposed; he had attempted suicide and had filed one state habeas petition, which he subsequently withdrew.[89] Marshall also focused on the lack of any adversarial testing of the state experts who indicated Gilmore was competent. Finally, he excoriated the Utah Supreme Court for treating as irrelevant to the issue of waiver trial counsel's assertion that Gilmore was possibly incompetent and for failing to transcribe the state supreme court proceeding upon which the state court's waiver finding was based. "These inexplicable actions by a court charged with life or death responsibility underscore the failure of the State to determine adequately the validity of Gilmore's purported waiver and the propriety of imposing capital punishment."[90]

Finally, Justice Blackmun dissented because, in his view, the questions of Bessie Gilmore's standing and the underlying constitutional issue were not "insubstantial."[91] Thus, he believed the proper course was "plenary, not summary, consideration."

On December 17th, the Court denied Gilmore's petition for rehearing.

Gilmore's final days

But this was not the final judicial word; the courts were not quite done with Gilmore's case. Gilmore's execution was scheduled for January 17th, 1977.[92] One suit was soon filed by other death row inmates in Utah, and the ACLU filed another suit on behalf of Utah taxpayers, seeking to stay the execution on the basis that the statute was unconstitutional because it did not provide for mandatory appellate review.[93] At 1:00 a.m. on the day of the execution, a federal district court judge

---

[87] *Id.* at 1018–19.

[88] *Id.* at 1019.

[89] *Id.*

[90] *Id.* at 1020.

[91] *Id.*

[92] M. Gilmore, Shot in the Heart, p. 331.

[93] Dorius, p. 59.

granted a temporary restraining order in the ACLU's taxpayer suit.[94] The Attorney General's office appealed, and the attorneys were ordered to be in Denver for a hearing as soon as possible. Pleadings were filed via teletype, the attorneys took a state plane to Denver and the hearing commenced at 6:50 a.m.[95] The execution was scheduled for 7:49 a.m. because the trial judge had ordered the execution to occur before sunrise on the 17th, and there was some concern that the execution might not be legal if it was carried out after daybreak.[96] At 7:32 a.m., the panel announced its decision unanimously vacating the stay.[97] While the Attorney General's office attempted to contact the prison to tell them to carry out the execution before sunrise, the ACLU attorneys were attempting to contact the United States Supreme Court. The Supreme Court denied the stay at 8:03 a.m.[98]

The execution

While the last minute appeals were being heard, Gilmore was eating his last meal consisting of a hamburger, a few hard boiled eggs, and several shots of whiskey.[99] Once the news came in that the Tenth Circuit had vacated the stay, Gilmore was taken to an unused cannery on the prison grounds where the execution was to take place. Several observers remarked afterwards that the cannery was very crowded; there were numerous police officers and law enforcement personnel who had been given permission to watch the first execution.[100] Due to fear of ricochet, a dirty old mattress and sandbags were placed behind the chair where Gilmore would sit. Gilmore was tied to the chair, and a white paper target was placed over his heart.[101] The five executioners stood behind a black curtain that had holes cut in it for the rifle barrels.[102] Gilmore's witnesses were allowed to come forward and they exchanged their

---

[94] *Id.* p. 53.

[95] *Id.* at 57.

[96] *Id.* While the argument was taking place, the prosecuting attorney who tried the case, Noall Wooton, contacted the trial judge at the Attorney General's request and asked if he would amend the execution order to read "anytime during the day of January 12, 1977," instead of "at sunrise." The judge agreed to amend the order. *Id.* at 60.

[97] *Id.* at 62.

[98] *Id.* at 66.

[99] Mailer, THE EXECUTIONER'S SONG, p. 973.

[100] *Id.* at 980.

[101] *Id.* at. 985.

[102] Interview with Gary Gilmore, *Playboy* Magazine, p. 186. Obviously this information did not come from Gilmore. Schiller was allowed to witness the execution and this statement comes from his account of the execution.

"parting words."[103] Gilmore was asked if he had any last words, and he responded, "Let's do it."[104] After a priest finished administering the last rites, Gilmore uttered his last words: "There will always be a father."[105] A black hood was placed over Gilmore's head.[106] On command, they fired.[107] Larry Schiller, the only journalist allowed to witness the execution reported that after the shots rang out, Gilmore's arm rose slowly and then fell limp.[108] Gilmore was pronounced dead, and his body was taken to a hospital where his corneas were harvested and used in several transplants.[109] Gilmore was cremated and his ashes distributed according to his wishes.[110]

The moratorium on executions in the United States was officially over.

The Volunteer Phenomena

A. The Law of Volunteering

Despite Chief Justice Burger's statement to the contrary in *Gilmore*, Gilmore's desire to die was not "unique in the annals of the Court." In fact, the Court first faced the issue ten years prior to *Gregg* in *Rees v. Payton*.[111] Rees, a Virginia death row inmate, directed his attorney to withdraw a petition for certiorari filed on his behalf, but counsel refused to do so, ostensibly due to doubts about his client's competency. After reports from several mental health professionals were filed, the Supreme Court remanded the case to the district court for a hearing to determine whether Rees should be permitted to waive his appeals and let the death sentence be carried out,[112] directing the district court to determine Rees'

---

[103] *Id.*

[104] Famous American Trials, p. 185.

[105] M. Gilmore, Shot in the Heart, p. 351.

[106] Gilmore did not want to wear the hood, but the Warden believed the executioners would be unnerved by having to look at Gilmore's face when they fired. Mailer, The Executioner's Song, p. 852.

[107] According to the protocol, the gun of one of the five executioner's would be loaded with a blank so no individual marksman would be sure that he had fired a fatal shot. Gilmore's uncle, who received Gilmore's clothing after his death, reported, however, that there were five bullet holes in Gilmore's shirt. M. Gilmore, Shot in the Heart, p. 390.

[108] *Id.* at 350.

[109] Mailer, The Executioner's Song, p. 973. In fact, the doctor who removed Gilmore's eyes, came to the prison to facilitate the removal. *Id.*

[110] *Id.* at. 1021–22.

[111] *Rees v. Peyton*, 384 U.S. 312 (1966).

[112] *Id.* at 313. Since the Supreme Court is not a fact-finding court, the remand was necessary "in aid of the proper exercise of [the Supreme Court's] certiorari jurisdiction." *Id.*

"mental competence," or whether "he has [the] capacity to appreciate his position and make a rational choice with respect to continuing or abandoning further litigation or on the other hand whether he is suffering from a mental disease, disorder, or defect which may substantially affect his capacity in the premises."[113]

Even a quick parsing of *Rees* foreshadows difficulties in application, largely because the two alternatives posed by *Rees* are not mutually exclusive. A defendant could both have the capacity to "make a rational choice" and also be suffering from a mental illness which "substantially affect[s]" his capacity to make a decision. As the Eighth Circuit has noted, there is an "overlap" in these two categories.[114] This logical difficulty may explain the Court's odd reticence in *Gilmore*, where neither the majority nor the dissents even referred to *Rees*. Instead, the majority said only that the Court was "convinced that Gary Mark Gilmore made a knowing and intelligent waiver of any and all federal rights he might have asserted after the Utah trial court's sentence was imposed, and specifically, that the State's determination of his competence knowingly and intelligently to waive any and all such rights."[115]

Post-*Gilmore*, the Court further muddied the waters in *Whitmore v. Arkansas*,[116] by *both* referring to *Gilmore* and its waiver standard of whether "the defendant has given a knowing, intelligent, and voluntary waiver of his right to proceed....",[117] *and* also citing *Rees* in the course of stating that "there was no meaningful evidence that [the defendant] was suffering from a mental disease, disorder, or defect that substantially affected his capacity to make an intelligent decision."[118] Eventually, however, in *Demosthenes v. Baal*,[119] the Court embraced only that aspect of *Whitmore* that focused on whether the defendant was competent to

---

[113] *Id*. at 314.

[114] *See Smith v. Armontrout*, 812 F.2d 1050, 1056 (8th Cir. 1987) (noting an "overlap" in the categories of cases established in *Rees*).

[115] *Gilmore, supra* n. 4, 429 U.S. at 1013.

[116] 495 U.S. 149 (1990).

[117] *Id*. at 165. The proper interpretation of *Whitmore* was further complicated by its unusual procedural posture. The actual question before the Court involved the circumstances under which a third party could intervene to challenge a death sentenced's inmates death sentence. The Court held that "next friend" standing could not be obtained "where an evidentiary hearing has established that the defendant has given a knowing, intelligent, and voluntary waiver of his right to proceed." *Id*. Whether that standard is only applicable to next friend intervention, or whether it also governs the withdrawal of an appeal is not clear.

[118] *Id*. at 166.

[119] *Demosthenes v. Baal*, 495 U.S. 731 (1990).

give a " 'knowing, intelligent, and voluntary waiver of his right to proceed.' "[120]

Finally, in *Godinez v. Moran*[121] the Court attempted to rationalize its wandering precedents. According to the Court, the phrase "rational choice" in *Rees* was equivalent to "rational understanding"[122] as used in *Dusky v. United States*.[123] *Dusky*, which addressed the question of when a defendant is competent *to stand trial*, established a two-pronged test for competency. According to *Dusky*, a defendant is competent to stand trial if: 1) he has a rational and factual understanding of the charges; and, 2) he has the ability to assist counsel.[124] Because the ability to assist counsel is not typically at issue in waiver of appeals, there is only one prong to competency: a defendant is competent to waive his appeals and permit the state to carry out the death sentence if he has a rational and factual understanding of the consequences of his decision.[125] If he does, then he can waive his appeals—assuming of course that the waiver is knowing, intelligent and voluntary. Thus it was not until almost fifteen years after *Gregg* was decided that the standard for assessing waiver of a death row inmate's appeals became relatively speaking, settled.[126]

B. *Another look at Gilmore's Case*

Aside from ignoring *Rees*, the Court's decision in *Gilmore* rested on shaky factual ground. The only competency hearing ever conducted in Gilmore's case took place prior to his two-day trial. After Gilmore expressed a desire to die, no court ever convened a hearing to hear evidence from mental health professionals who evaluated Gilmore's

---

[120] *Id.* at 734 (quoting *Whitmore*).

[121] *Godinez v. Moran*, 509 U.S. 389 (1993).

[122] *Id.* at 398, n. 9.

[123] *Dusky v. United States*, 362 U.S. 402 (1960).

[124] *Id.* at 402.

[125] In the post-conviction setting, as opposed to the direct appeal of a conviction or sentence, an inmate can present new evidence challenging his conviction and/or death sentence. Thus, in that procedural posture, some courts have indicated that the ability to assist counsel is a relevant consideration. *See, e.g., Council v. Catoe*, 597 S.E.2d 782 (S.C. 2004).

[126] While I do not intend to critique the Court's legal standard for permitting waiver in this piece, it is important to note that there is arguably a significant broader societal interest in having a mandatory appeals process in capital cases. Wholly apart from the client's desire to die, there is a systemic interest in making sure that the "undeserving"—both legally and factually—are not executed. A myopic focus on the knowing and intelligent nature of the waiver would allow someone who is actually innocent or categorically ineligible for the death penalty, i.e., a juvenile or a person with mental retardation, to waive their appeals and submit to execution. John H. Blume, *Killing the Willing: "Volunteers," Suicide and Competency*, 103 Mich. L. J. 939, 969 (2005).

competency at the time he was permitted to waive his appeals. Given his erratic behavior, his multiple suicide attempts, and the statements submitted to the courts from two different lawyers questioning his competency, it is difficult—if not impossible—to see what the determination that Gilmore was competent was based upon. Presumably, the Court relied on Gilmore's statements, but that hardly seems sufficient. Gilmore said very little when he was brought before the Utah Supreme Court and even a seriously mentally ill person could have stumbled through the cursory and frequently leading questioning.

The Court's determination that Gilmore's waiver of his right to appeal was "knowing and intelligent" is even more deficient. In prior (and subsequent) decisions, the Court had stated that there was a presumption against the waiver of constitutional rights.[127] And the Court had also said that it was reversible error to allow a defendant to waive constitutional rights when there had been no inquiry or hearing into the defendant's competence.[128] In addition to the failure to conduct a competency hearing, however, Gilmore's purported waiver had other significant problems. The Court based its waiver determination on the Utah Supreme Court proceedings. But, as noted above, the hearing was rushed, and Gilmore was asked only a few perfunctory questions establishing that he knew he had a right to appeal and he had instructed his lawyers not to file an appeal. The Utah Supreme Court never questioned Gilmore at all; the few questions asked were put to Gilmore by Dennis Boaz, a lawyer who stood to gain financially if the execution went forward. This was hardly the searching judicial inquiry one would expect before a literally life or death decision of this magnitude was permitted.[129] There was no evidence before the Court indicating that any attorney had explained to Gilmore that the new Utah death penalty statute's constitutional status was still in doubt and no attorney ever reviewed the record of the trial to determine whether there were viable issues that could have been raised in an appeal. Nor did any member of the Court explain this to Gilmore.[130] In sum, the Court's conclusion that

---

[127] *Johnson v. Zerbst,* 304 U.S. 458, 468 (1938).

[128] *Westbrook v. Arizona,* 384 U.S. 150 (1966).

[129] Even Boaz' limited questioning was cut short by the Chief Justice. When Boaz attempted to ask another question, the Chief Justice interrupted, saying: "No we don't want to get into a full blown trial in this case and this gentleman has made a statement and I don't think under the circumstances that he should be subjected to any intense cross-examination."

[130] In addition to possible constitutional defects in the Utah capital sentencing scheme, there were a number of potentially meritorious trial-specific issues that could have been raised on Gilmore's behalf, especially as to the validity of the death sentence. For example, the evidence of Gilmore's prior poor prison behavior offered by the prosecution at the sentencing phase of Gilmore's trial was rank hearsay. A Utah police officer was permitted

the waiver was knowing and intelligent can not be squared with an objective review of the record.

C. Gilmore as a Paradigmatic Volunteer

Gilmore was the first, but certainly not the last volunteer in the "modern era." Since his execution, more than a hundred other death sentenced inmates have waived their appeals and submitted to execution.[131] Approximately 12% of all persons executed have been volunteers.[132] In some states, especially those with small death rows which do not actively sentence persons to death, all or the overwhelming majority of the executions which have taken place involved volunteers.[133] Gilmore was also a harbinger of volunteers to come. Gilmore was white, he had a history of substance abuse, mental illness and had a number of prior suicide attempts. The overwhelming majority of subsequent volunteers fit the same basic profile: 87.4% of all volunteers are white and the same percentage (87.74%) had mental health and substance abuse problems.[134] Many had also previously attempted suicide.[135]

The volunteer profile overlaps substantially with the profiles of those who commit suicide in the "free world." Suicide in the United States is an overwhelmingly white, male phenomena. As a general matter, men are four times more likely to commit suicide than women.[136] In 1997, for example, 72% of all suicides were committed by white males.[137] In 1998, 73% of all suicides involved white males;[138] and in 1999, the percentage was again 72%.[139] White men commit suicide at a higher rate than every other group except Native American men; and white

---

to testify about Gilmore's bad conduct in the Oregon prison system based upon a conversation he had with an Oregon prison official.

[131] Blume, *Killing the Willing,* 103 Mich. L. J. at 940.

[132] 130 of 1104 individuals executed have been volunteers. *See also Id.* at 959.

[133] For example, the only individuals executed in Connecticut, Idaho, New Mexico, Oregon South Dakota in the modern era of capital punishment were both volunteers. Four of six executions in Utah have involved volunteers., as have three of the four executions which have taken place in the state of Washington and one of the two executions in Kentucky.

[134] *Id.* at 962.

[135] *Id.*

[136] *Supra,* n. 87.

[137] *In Harm's Way: Suicide in America at* http://www.nimh.nih.gov/publicat/harmaway. cfm (last viewed March 5, 2004).

[138] (www.psycom.net/depression.central.suicidefacts.html).

[139] *Suicide Facts,* Supra, n. 87.

men commit suicide at twice the rate of black or Latino men.[140] Further-more, according to the Nation Institute of Mental Health, over ninety percent of suicide victims suffer from a diagnosable mental disorder, most commonly a depressive disorder or a substance abuse disorder.[141] There is also a high prevalence of bi-polar disorder,[142] post-traumatic stress disorder and other personality disorders.[143] Substance abuse is found in 25 to 55 percent of suicides, although two-thirds of suicide victims who were substance abusers also suffered from a major depres-sive episode.[144] One-third of suicides by suicide victims suffering from substance abuse were precipitated by loss or anticipation of loss of a close personal relationship.[145]

These commonalities between volunteers and those who commit suicide are relevant to the ongoing debate regarding how to characterize volunteers: are they best seen as clients making a legal decision to accept the outcome of a prior proceeding, or as persons seeking the aid of the state in committing suicide? I will not enter that debate in this chapter except to say that the Court's focus on competency and the knowing, voluntary and intelligent nature of the waiver of appeals ignores the often critical issue of motivation. Why does the death sentence inmate want to waive his appeals? Is the motivation acceptance of responsibility, or is it suicide.[146] We do not allow citizens in the "free world" to commit suicide, even if they are terminally ill. Why should death sentenced inmates be allowed to waive their appeals if the motivation is suicide?[147]

In Gilmore's case, there is evidence suggesting that acceptance of responsibility and suicide were both in play. His statements to the Utah Supreme Court, and a number of other statements suggest the motivat-ing factor was an acceptance of punishment. For example, he told the Utah Supreme Court: "I believe I was given a fair trial and I think the sentence is proper and I am willing to accept it like a man. I don't wish to appeal.... I desire to be executed on schedule, and I just wish to

---

[140] *Id.* (The overall national suicide rate is 10.7 suicides for every 100,000 people).

[141] JOUKO LONNQUIVIST, *Psychiatric Aspects of Suicidal Behavior: Depression*, THE INTER-NATIONAL HANDBOOK OF SUICIDE AND ATTEMPTED SUICIDE 107 (Keith Hawton & Kees van Heeringen eds., 2000).

[142] Kent R. *Jamison, Suicide and Bipolar Disorder*, J. CLINICAL PSYCHIATRY, 2000; 61.

[143] MATTHEW K. NOCK & PETER M. MARZUK, *Suicide & Violence*, THE INTERNATIONAL HANDBOOK OF SUICIDE AND ATTEMPTED SUICIDE, *supra* n. 94, at 438–39.

[144] George E. Murphy, *Psychiatric Aspects of Suicidal Behavior: Substance Abuse*, in THE INTERNATIONAL HANDBOOK OF SUICIDE AND ATTEMPTED SUICIDE, *supra* n. 94, at 135.

[145] *Id.* at 140.

[146] For a detailed view of my views on the subject *see Killing the Willing, supra.*

[147] *Id.*

accept that with the grace and dignity of a man and I hope you will allow me to do that.''[148] But, there is also evidence that not only his decision to waive his appeals, but the crime itself were motivated by suicide. Gilmore had been incarcerated more than half of his life, and he told his family and Nicole that he could not bear the thought of spending the rest of his life in prison.[149] While that may be rational, it is suicidal. Furthermore, his history of suicide attempts, both before and after he was sentenced to death, suggest that his primary concern was to end his life, and death by firing squad was a means to that end.[150] More speculative is whether the murders themselves were also part of his plan to end his life. But, his decision to be paroled to Utah, a state that still executed by firing squad, the timing of the crimes—they occurred on the heels of his break up with Nicole—and the brazen manner in which he committed the murders, making little or no effort to avoid being identified and captured, suggests that the crimes as well may have been a means to an end, death.[151] If so, he would not be the first or last death row inmate who killed to achieve their own demise.

Final Reflections: The Frenzy to Kill, Gilmore as a Cultural Icon, and the Significance of the Court's Decision.

The most striking thing about Gilmore's case is the speed with which the trial, the "appeals" and the execution took place. Gilmore was executed less than six months after the crimes occurred. There was a frenetic feel to the entire case. This is especially striking given that the Supreme Court had only recently placed its stamp of approval on a few of the supposedly new and improved death penalty statutes, while finding several others to be constitutionally inadequate. Utah's post-*Furman* capital sentencing scheme was untested.

The frenzy to kill Gilmore is best evidenced by the events that occurred in the final hours of his life. The execution was stayed by the federal district court at 1:00 a.m. the day of the execution. Pleadings were hurriedly prepared and sent by teletype to the federal court of

---

[148] Dorius, p. 11.

[149] Gilmore told his brother Mikal:

They'd never let me be free and I've spent too much time in jail. I don't have anything left to me. I killed two men. I don't want to spend the rest of my life in jail. If some fucker gets me set free, then I'm going to get a gun and kill a few of those damn lawyers that keep interfering. Then I'll say to you, "See what your meddling accomplished? Are you proud?"

M. Gilmore, SHOT IN THE HEART, p. 339.

[150] Gilmore told his brother Mikal that he would commit suicide if the sentence was commuted. *Id.* at 343.

[151] By one account, Gilmore told another inmate before his release that "I am going to go get me a couple of Mormons." M. Gilmore, SHOT IN THE HEART, p. 314.

appeals. A hearing was set in Denver for early the same morning, and the lawyers for both side boarded a plane to attend the argument which took place before dawn. While the argument was taking place, Wooten, the trial prosecutor, rushed to find the trial judge. He obtained an amended execution order allowing Gilmore to be executed in the event the sun should rise before the court of appeals ruled. But the court did rule, and the lawyers for the state ran from the courtroom to call the prison and exhorted them to shoot Gilmore before sunrise and before the Supreme Court had the opportunity to further delay the proceedings.[152] Gilmore's lawyers simultaneously rushed to file a stay application in the United States Court, but Court personnel at the court of appeals would not allow them to use the phones.[153] And, the execution took place before the final word was received from the Court that a stay of execution had been denied.[154]

There are several possible, and not mutually exclusive explanations for the frenzy to kill. At certain points in the history of the death penalty, in fact when it appears most fragile, there is a dogged determination by its supporters to press on. The recent executions in Texas and other states following the Supreme Court's rejection of the challenge to lethal injection in *Baze v. Rees* and California's execution of Stanley "Tookie" Williams had a similar frenzied "feel." Or maybe it was because Gilmore was such an attractive candidate to be the first person executed. He was white, thus issues of racial bias which had been the center of many legal attacks on capital punishment were not at issue. There was no lingering doubt about his guilt, the evidence was clear. He was intelligent, and there did not seem to be any compelling evidence of any major psychiatric illness. Gilmore demonstrated no remorse. He also had a long criminal record and a history of poor behavior in prison, thus it was unlikely he could be rehabilitated. He also taunted the system for its lack of will and courage in going forward with the death sentence. He was, in many respects, the perfect person to usher in the new era of executions.[155] Supporters of capital punishment desperately wanted to

---

[152] The Attorney General representing the state in the appeals, when asked by prison officials if they should wait to see if the Supreme Court acted, gave the following instructions: "No. Just go ahead and see if you can get it in. Well, we're going to be close. We might be able to get it in under the sunrise requirement." Dorius, p. 66.

[153] Dorius, p. 64.

[154] When the clerk of the Supreme Court, Michael Rodak, called the Attorney General's office to tell them the stay had been denied, they were informed that the execution had already taken place. In a tremendous understatement, the state's lawyer responded, "that would have been just a horrible thing" if the Court had stayed the execution. Dorius, p. 67.

[155] *See also* Robert W. Jolly, Jr. & Edward Sagarin, *The First Eight After Furman: Who was Executed with the Return of the Death Penalty*, 30 Crime & Delinquency 610 (1984).

end the ten year moratorium because they realized, as did opponents of the death penalty, that the longer the United States went without executions, there was a greater likelihood citizens and lawmakers would conclude it was unnecessary. Gilmore's decision to die could not have come at a more opportune time for those who wanted an "active" death penalty.

Gary Gilmore is probably the most famous death row inmate in American History. He achieved "icon" status not because of his crimes— many death row inmates have committed far worse crimes, and not because of the doctrinal significance of his case, the Court's decision is in many respects not a legal landmark. Rather, Gilmore is an icon because, and only because, he was the first to die. By volunteering for execution, Gilmore became the subject of a Pulitzer prize winning book by one of the greatest American writers,[156] a famous punk rock song,[157] a Hollywood movie starring one of the leading actors of this generation,[158] an interview in one of the most widely read magazines in the world,[159] and even a skit on "Saturday Night Live."[160] He was on the cover of almost all the leading periodicals, and he received thousands of letters from people from all over the world.[161] All because he allowed—no because he dared—the state of Utah to shoot him and end his life.

Had Gilmore pursued his appeals, it is almost certain that no one reading (or writing) this chapter would have heard of him. It is possible he would have eventually been executed, but the execution would not have been carried out for another ten years or so thus making him just another faceless individual whose life was taken by the American capital punishment system.[162] Texas, for example, whose capital sentencing

---

[156] Norman Mailer won the Pulitzer Prize in 1980 for his book, THE EXECUTIONER'S SONG, which was published in 1979.

[157] The English punk rock bad, The Adverts, released "Gary Gilmore's Eyes," in 1977. The song, told from the perspective of one of the recipients of Gilmore's corneas, made it into the Billboard top 10.

[158] In the movie version of Mailer's Book, The Executioner's Song, Oscar winner Tommy Lee Jones played Gilmore.

[159] As noted above, Schiller's interview with Gilmore was published after his death in *Playboy* magazine.

[160] On December 11, 1976, Saturday Night Live featured a skit called "Let's Kill Gary Gilmore for Christmas," featuring host Candice Bergen and performers Gilda Radner, Dan Aykrod, Jane Curtin, John Belushi, Laraine Newman and Garrett Morris. In the skit, songs about Gilmore's execution were performed to the tunes of various Christmas Carols. (http://snltranscripts.jt.org/76/76jgilmore.phtml).

[161] Diane Ratcliff, *The Gary Gilmore Letters: A Study of People who Wrote a Condemned Killer*, (Dissertation manuscript) (on file with author).

[162] Utah did not conduct another execution until August 28, 1987, when Dale Pierre Selby, who was sentenced to death before Gilmore,was executed by lethal injection. (http://www.deathpenaltyinfo.org/article.php?scid=8&did=466).

scheme was approved by the Supreme Court in 1976 did not carry out its first execution until 1982. It is also very possible that his convictions or sentence would have been reversed on appeal and he may well have avoided execution as have most of the other death sentenced inmates who were successful on appeal. He might currently be serving a life sentence in Utah, have died in prison or even been released on parole. We will never know, of course, because he chose death.

As noted previously, one could argue that doctrinally his case is not that significant. In some respects that is true, but in another important way it is not. Because the Supreme Court so quickly, and cavalierly, decided that Gilmore could "waive" his appeals, without regard to his primary motivation—suicide—the legality of his underlying conviction and death sentence, or even the shoddy nature of the purported waiver hearing and competency determination, the Court set an incredibly low bar for subsequent volunteers to hurdle. That explains, in turn, why such a high percentage of those executed in the "modern era" of capital punishment have been volunteers.[163] It did not have to be that way, but once the Court allowed Gilmore to die, the path was set.

---

[163] As noted above, in some states all, or nearly all, of those executed have been volunteers. A number of these jurisdictions have a low commitment to actually executing those sentenced to death. In these states, the execution of volunteers conveys the impression that the death penalty enjoys more contemporary support in this country than it in fact does. Furthermore, without these volunteer executions, the "Southern" character of the current death penalty regime would be even more pronounced.

6

David C. Baldus, George Woodworth, John Charles Boger, and Charles A. Pulaski

McCleskey v. Kemp (1987): Denial, Avoidance, and the Legitimization of Racial Discrimination in the Administration of the Death Penalty*

* An earlier version of this paper was presented as part of a symposium entitled "Capital Punishment Stories" at the University of Texas School of Law, November 2–3, 2007. John Blume, William Buss, Randall Bezanson, Gary Goodpaster, Catherine Grosso, Lyell Henry, David McCord, Jordan Steiker, Teresa Wagner, Adrien Wing, and the participants at the symposium provided helpful comments and advice as did the members of the University of Iowa College of Law Workshop, May 16, 2008. Peter D'Angelo, Jonathan Gallagher, Jonathan Hendricks, and David Franker contributed valuable research assistance and Lisa Jo Schomberg expertly prepared the table and figures. We are particularly grateful for the contribution of Robert Stroup, Warren McCleskey's Atlanta co-counsel. We acknowledge with gratitude the support of the University of Iowa Law School Foundation.

TABLE OF CONTENTS

Part I.   Introduction

McCleskey v. Kemp (1987) was a death penalty case arising in Fulton
County, Georgia.[1] The defendant, Warren McCleskey, was an African
American charged with murdering an off-duty white police officer, Frank
Schlatt, during an armed robbery of the Dixie Furniture Company in
Atlanta. He was convicted and sentenced to death in 1978 by a jury with

---

[1] 481 U.S. 279 (1987).

one African American member.[2] His attorneys contended before the lower courts and, eventually before the Supreme Court of the United States, that McCleskey's death sentence violated both the cruel and unusual punishment clause of the Eighth Amendment and the Equal Protection Clause of the Fourteenth Amendment.[3]

The principal basis for this claim was a statewide statistical study of 128 death sentences imposed in more than 2,000 murder and voluntary manslaughter cases from Georgia between 1973 and 1979. The study documented statistically significant statewide race-of-victim disparities in capital charging and sentencing outcomes after adjustment for a large array of non-racial offender characteristics that bear on offender culpability and deathworthiness. Throughout this Chapter we refer to this research as the "Baldus study." Its core findings indicated that, after adjustment for differing levels of criminal culpability, the odds that a defendant would receive a death sentence were, on average, 4.3 times higher in white-victim cases than they were in black-victim cases, a result that could occur by chance less than 1 in 1000 times in a race neutral system.[4] The study also showed that the victim's race had the

---

[2] McCleskey had grown up in the Atlanta area under the care of relatives who ran an illegal "juke joint." At the time of the furniture store robbery, he had two prior convictions for armed robbery. Four men indisputably conspired to plan and carry out the furniture store robbery, including McCleskey and Ben Wright, an eventual co-defendant. During the robbery, as furniture store employees were being detained in the back of the store, off-duty Police Officer Schlatt arrived on the scene answering a silent alarm. He entered the front of the store and proceeded toward the middle. Someone, whom Fulton County officials later charged was Warren McCleskey, fired two shots at Officer Schlatt. One ricocheted off a cigarette lighter in his chest pocket. Another entered his head, killing him.

McCleskey initially confessed to the police that he had taken part in the robbery but denied any participation in the murder. At trial, he repudiated his confession and argued that he had not been present during the robbery. The State's murder case was built on three prongs. First, the bullet from the ricochet was recovered and it proved to match a .38 Rossi pistol used during the robbery. Although Ben Wright's girlfriend, when initially questioned, informed police officers that Wright had been carrying a .38 Rossi during the armed robbery, she changed her testimony at trial to put the murder weapon in Warren McCleskey's hands. Second, in his testimony during McCleskey's trial, Ben Wright denied any part in the murder and asserted that McCleskey had shot Officer Schlatt. The third and perhaps most important prong of the State's case came from Offie Evans, a jailhouse informant who testified that, while he and Warren McCleskey were incarcerated in adjoining cells in Fulton County, McCleskey had acknowledged committing the homicide and bragged that he would have shot a dozen officers if necessary to get out of the store. *See infra* part VI for the post-McCleskey implications of Evans' testimony.

[3] John C. Boger, a co-author of this chapter, was McCleskey's lead counsel throughout his 10 years of federal habeas corpus litigation. The other three co-authors of this chapter, David C. Baldus, George Woodworth and Charles A. Pulaski Jr., were the architects of the empirical study on which McCleskey's claims of racial discrimination were based. Baldus and Woodworth were the principal witnesses on his behalf in McCleskey's first federal habeas corpus proceeding.

[4] The estimated race-of-victim disparity was statistically significant at the .0003 level. *See infra* p. 251 Table 2, Line 9, Column C. *See also* David C. Baldus, George Woodworth,

most pronounced influence on death sentences imposed among cases that fell into a midrange of criminal culpability—being neither excessively aggravated nor only minimally so. Significantly, McCleskey's case fell within that midrange.[5] In addition, the statistics from Fulton County, where McCleskey was prosecuted, reflected comparable white-victim disparities.[6]

The legal foundation of the Georgia study was the proposition, distilled from earlier Supreme Court decisions, that a statistical demonstration of *systemic* purposeful racial discrimination in the imposition of death sentences would justify some form of sentencing relief under the Equal Protection Clause of the Fourteenth Amendment or the cruel and unusual punishments provision of the Eighth Amendment.[7] Further-

---

and Charles A. Pulaski, Jr., EQUAL JUSTICE AND THE DEATH PENALTY: A LEGAL AND EMPIRICAL ANALYSIS 319–320, tbl. 52 (1990). The only statewide statistically significant black-defendant disparities were concentrated among the most aggravated 472 cases in the universe which were represented by 285 cases in the sample. Among these cases in a well controlled multivariate statistical analysis, black defendants faced odds of receiving a death sentence that were 2.4 times higher than the odds faced by similarly situated white defendants. *Id.* at 328–29. Georgia's rural judicial circuits were the principal source of these black-defendant disparities. *Id.*, at 362–64.

[5] *See* Figure 1 *infra,* p. 253 and *infra* note 59 for a discussion of this midrange finding and the "liberation hypothesis" which it implicates.

[6] Indeed, our study indicated that between 1973 and 1979, there were 32 prosecutions in death-eligible cases from Fulton County that were comparable to McCleskey's case in terms of offender culpability. Among those cases, defendants in white-victim cases were 3.6 times (47% vs. 13%) more likely to be sentenced to death than defendants in black-victim cases without regard to the race of the defendant. Baldus et al. *supra* note 4 at 334–40, tbls. 59–63.

[7] *See infra* Part II for a discussion of the relevant law. Throughout this chapter, our references to "purposeful" discrimination do not refer to conscious racially motivated decisions, although they may occur in some situations. Consistent with the literature and much law, we define purposeful discrimination in this context as the differential treatment of similarly situated defendants that cannot be explained by race-neutral case characteristics, which is the product of stereotypes and other racially biased preconceptions which unconsciously influence decision making. Sheri Lynn Johnson, *Unconscious Racism and the Criminal Law,* 73 CORNELL L. REV. 1016 (1988); Samuel R. Sommers and Phoebe C. Ellsworth, *White Juror Bias: An Investigation of Racial Prejudice Against Black Defendants in the American Courtroom,* 7 PSYCHOLOGY, PUBLIC POLICY, AND LAW 201 (2001); Samuel R. Sommers and Phoebe C. Ellsworth, Race in the courtroom: Perceptions of guilt and dispositional attributions, 26 PERSONALITY AND SOCIAL PSYCHOLOGY BULLETIN 1367 (2000).

Justice Scalia in a memorandum prepared for the Court in *McCleskey* refers to the "unconscious operation of irrational sympathies and antipathies, including racial" on prosecutorial and jury decision making. *Infra* note 119 and accompanying text. Justice White, *infra* note 40 and accompanying text describes well the impact of stereotypes and unconscious fears on decision making in black-defendant/white victim cases. As he indicates, racial bias takes two forms: first it can *inflate aggravation*—by erroneously and improperly *increasing* the risk that a fact-finder will find that a defendant was *more culpable* than was factually the case, and second prejudice can *deflate mitigation*—by

more, it was clear that, despite the reforms that Georgia adopted after *Furman v. Georgia,* the Georgia system created an opportunity for racial discrimination to occur. Although Georgia's post-*Furman* sentencing statute imposed a variety of substantive and procedural requirements upon the trial judge and jury, it imposed no limitations or restrictions whatsoever on prosecutors' exercise of discretion. In addition, the data indicate that the principal source of these disparities were prosecutorial charging decisions.[8]

Nevertheless in Warren McCleskey's case, the United States Supreme Court ruled 5–4 that, even accepting the study's methodological validity, its statistical evidence of racial discrimination had no bearing on the validity or invalidity of McCleskey's death sentence. Rather, Justice Powell's majority opinion ruled that evidence of systemic racial discrimination was irrelevant under both the Equal Protection Clause of the Fourteenth Amendment and the cruel and unusual punishments provision of the Eighth Amendment.

A main theme of this Chapter is that *McCleskey v. Kemp* represents a closely divided (5–4) resolution of tension among several lines of authority that developed in the Supreme Court's jurisprudence in the last half of the twentieth century. The first line of authority, based on the concept of a *prima facie* case of discrimination, developed in the late 1960s. Embedded in these rulings was the Court's growing appreciation of the fact-finding capacity of social science and statistical methodology to promote the interests of justice under the Equal Protection Clause of the Fourteenth Amendment and federal civil rights statutes.

A second line of authority, supportive of the first, evolved from *Furman v. Georgia* (1972), a 5–4 decision that invalidated Georgia's traditional capital punishment law. In *Furman,* a plurality of the Court ruled that the death sentencing outcomes of the Georgia system, combined with a complete absence of standards to guide jury discretion,

---

erroneously and improperly *decreasing* the weight that a fact finder places on the mitigation that is factually present in the case. The first form of bias is consistent with stereotypical perceptions of minorities, such as the violence prone and moral inferiority stereotypes mentioned by Justice White. The second form of bias (deflating mitigation) is also consistent with stereotypical perceptions of minorities, whereby the race of the defendant and victim may affect the empathy of fact-finders toward each. Caucasian charging authorities and jurors may be more likely to identify with white defendants than with black defendants and to identify more strongly with white victims than with black victims, thereby producing a more punitive response in the white-victim cases. In the grand jury and jury venire selection and the employment discrimination cases discussed in Part II A & B *infra,* the focus is not on "conscious" discrimination but on whether racial bias was a factor or substantial factor in the adverse treatment of minorities classwide or in individual cases. A similar test is applied to *Batson* allegations of racial discrimination in the selection of jurors, *infra* note 102.

[8] Baldus et al., supra note 4 at 326–27 (statewide) and 338–39 (Fulton County).

produced an unacceptable level of arbitrariness under the Eighth Amendment. *Furman* embodied the Court's conclusion, based upon the facts and outcomes of hundreds of capital murder cases that the Court had observed over many years, that there was no meaningful way to distinguish the cases in which defendants were sentenced to death from those in which defendants received lesser sentences.[9]

However, during the 1970s, a divergent line of authority under the Equal Protection Clause of the Fourteenth Amendment emerged that did not bode well for the use of evidence of system-wide deficiencies as a basis for resolving claims of racial discrimination in individual cases. The chief decision in this respect was *Washington v. Davis* (1976)[10] in which the Court rejected claims of racial discrimination against government actors in the absence of "smoking gun" evidence of purposeful discrimination. *Davis* very much foreshadowed the Court's subsequent decision in *McCleskey*, and, like *McCleskey*, seemingly reflected a historical concern that ground-breaking decisions to protect black citizens against racial discrimination might unduly antagonize the white population.[11]

Another relevant line of authority was the 1976 *Gregg/Proffitt/Jurek* trio of cases[12] that sustained the constitutionality of the Georgia, Florida, and Texas statutes after they had been rewritten to satisfy the arbitrariness concerns expressed by the Court in *Furman*. These new statutes adopted procedural rules, as opposed to outcome-oriented obligations, such as the enumeration of aggravating circumstances as a necessary predicate for the imposition of a death sentence. The NAACP Legal Defense and Educational Fund (LDF) challenged these statutes for their failure to impose meaningful limitations on the exercise of discretion in the application of Georgia's death sentencing process, particularly by

---

[9] Justice White explained the basis for his judgment in *Furman*. *Furman*, 408 U.S. 238, 312 (1972) ("Nor can I 'prove' my conclusion [concerning the infrequency and arbitrariness of the death sentencing outcomes] from these data. But, like my Brethren, I must arrive at judgment; and I can do no more than state a conclusion based on 10 years of almost daily exposure to the facts and circumstances of hundreds and hundreds of federal and state [death eligible cases].").

[10] 426 U.S. 229 (1976).

[11] We have drawn here on the insightful analyses of the Supreme Court's Equal Protection jurisprudence by Derrick Bell, RACE RACISM AND AMERICAN LAW 421 (5th ed. 2004) ("Despite the outcry which the *McCleskey* outcome triggered, the Court's decision is neither surprising nor a departure from the Supreme Court's race jurisprudence") and Donald E. Lively and Stephen Plass, *Equal Protection: The Jurisprudence of Denial and Evasion*, 40 AM. U. L. REV. 1307, 1334 (1991) (The Court countenances a "[m]otive-based inquiry [that] facilitates the jurisprudence of denial and evasion by detaching the process of review from the persistent realities and consequences of racism.").

[12] *Gregg v. Georgia*, 428 U.S. 153 (1976); *Proffitt v. Florida*, 428 U.S. 242 (1976); and *Jurek v. Texas*, 428 U.S. 262 (1976).

prosecutors. The Court's 1976 decisions sustained the constitutionality of these new statutes on the ground that, on their face, they were capable of preventing constitutionally arbitrary death sentences. These decisions could also be read to suggest that how these facially valid statutes were actually applied in individual cases was not a cause for constitutional concern.

There was also a belief in the early 1980s that the post-*Furman* system that the Court developed after 1976 for regulating the states' administration of capital punishment was unduly antagonizing support-ers of capital punishment (and their elected representatives) who consti-tuted a substantial majority of the population.[13] In fact, a series of decisions enforcing the procedural requirements endorsed by the 1976 trilogy led to considerable resentment and complaints that the standards set by *Gregg, Proffitt,* and *Jurek* were, as a practical matter, unattaina-ble. There is evidence that this rising tide of resentment was of consider-able concern to the Justices even before they decided *McCleskey.*[14]

There were three other features of McCleskey's case that likely drew his claims into question. First, McCleskey principally alleged race-of-victim discrimination against defendants whose victims were white rath-er than race-of-defendant discrimination directed against black defen-dants.[15] Second, we believe that some of the Justices may have chosen to

---

[13] After 1976, the Court overturned a long series of death sentences, which created some concern that the Court's requirements for the constitutional imposition of death sentences were unattainable. The roll back began in 1983 with the Court sustaining death sentences in *Zant* v. *Stephens,* 462 U.S. 862 (1983), *Pulley v. Harris,* 465 U.S. 37 (1984), and *Darden v. Wainwright,* 477 U.S. 168 (1986).

[14] *Pulley v. Harris,* 465 U.S. 37 (1984) supports this interpretation. It rejected a claim that the Constitution requires states to conduct an outcome based proportionality review of each death sentence imposed along the lines envisioned by Georgia's proportionality review requirement, which the Court applauded in *Gregg v. Georgia.*

[15] Justice Powell stated such a viewpoint to his biographer after his retirement from the Court. *Supra* note 103 and accompanying text. For a discussion of the moral and legal foundations of the Constitutional prohibition against purposeful discrimination based on the race of either the defendant or the victim, see David C. Baldus and George Woodworth, *Race Discrimination and the Legitimacy of Capital Punishment: Reflections on the Interac-tion of Fact and Perception,* 53 DE PAUL L. REV. 1411, 1444, 1450–53 (2004). (From a legal perspective, both forms of discrimination are a "race-based distortion of the system that offends not only the Constitution but also basic principles of comparative justice." In terms of morality there are distinctions: "The victims of race of defendant discrimination are easy to identify-black defendants. The adverse effects of race-of-victim discrimination are more subtle. Within the black community, there are two levels of victimization. First are the black victims (and their families) whose losses are undervalued. . . . Second, race-of-victim discrimination results in unfair treatment of the black community because it undermines for it, the goals of retribution and deterrence that justify the use of capital punishment. . . . The third class of victims, who are predominately white, are the defendants whose victims are white who would have received a life rather than a death sentence if their victim had

back away from the use of complicated, empirically based methodology like that employed in *McCleskey* because of concerns about the ability of judges to understand the social science, together with a concern about over-burdening the federal judiciary in case after case with an obligation to settle conflicting arguments about "regression theory," "sampling error," and similar issues. From that perspective, *McCleskey* decided that judges and traditional methods of jurisprudence, not social scientists and statistical methodology, should decide what the law should be in capital cases.[16] Third, Justice Powell's opinion reflects resistance to the imposition of stringent limitations on the freedom of juries to make sentencing decisions, which may be viewed by some Justices as a virtue to be celebrated rather than as a potentially dangerous source of arbitrariness and discrimination. In the end, these considerations appear to have prevailed over concerns about racial justice in the administration of capital punishment.

Part II of this Chapter describes in more detail the relevant legal theories of racial discrimination and the evidentiary frameworks used to support them and how they had been applied in post-*Furman* capital cases prior to *McCleskey*. Part III reviews the empirical evidence offered by McCleskey, and Parts IV and V consider the rulings of the lower federal courts and the United States Supreme Court. Part VI describes the aftermath of the decision.

Part II. Legal Background: Legal Theories of Purposeful Discrimination and the Evidentiary Frameworks Used to Support Them[17]

In the late 1970s and early 1980s, two provisions of the United States Constitution appeared to be candidates to support claims of racial

---

been black ... [Race-of-defendant discrimination implicates the] traditional goal of antidiscrimination law—the protection of minorities from adverse treatment because of their race. In contrast, race-of-victim discrimination does not harm a minority defendant because of his or her race. The core of the black defendants' claims of race-of-defendant discrimination is that they are being punished for a factor over which they have no control—their race. For defendants claiming race-of-victim discrimination, their heightened risk of a death sentence is the product of a characteristic of the victims *they* selected.... The beneficiaries of race-of-defendant discrimination are nonblack, generally white, offenders.... In contrast, the beneficiaries of race-of-victim discrimination are most commonly black defendants whose victims are black. Indeed, those defendants represent the largest pool of death-eligible offenders.").

[16] *See Bell, supra* note 11 at 421. ("At the doctrinal level, the decision is consistent with the Court's distrust of statistical evidence and its insistence on direct evidence of purposeful discrimination. *McCleskey* makes clear the Courts' unwillingness to accept less than direct proof of discrimination which renders it incapable of recognizing, let alone remedying, the more subtle forms of racism that characterize contemporary institutions.").

[17] *See generally* Robert H. Stroup, *The Political, Legal, and Social Context of the* McCleskey *Habeas Litigation*, 39 COLUM. HUM. RTS. L. REV. 74 (2007) (McCleskey's Atlanta

discrimination in capital charging and sentencing decisions. First, was the Equal Protection Clause of the Fourteenth Amendment. Second was the cruel and unusual punishments provision of the Eighth Amendment. What was not at all clear, however, was the precise factual basis of such claims and the "evidentiary frameworks" that federal courts might apply in their assessment of statistical evidence offered to support them.

A. The Original *"Prima Facie Case"* Evidentiary Framework

The *prima facie* case evidentiary framework had its roots in the famous 19th century case *Yick Wo v. Hopkins* (1886),[18] which involved discrimination against Chinese nationals by the San Francisco Board of Supervisors in its allocation of authority to operate a laundry in a wooden building. The applications of all 200 Chinese applicants were denied such permission, whereas the request of only one of 110 white applicants was denied. There was no evidence in the record of discrimination directed individually against Yick Wo, who challenged a criminal conviction based on his operating a laundry in a wooden building without a permit. Solely on the basis of evidence of *systemic* purposeful discrimination, the Supreme Court held that Yick Wo's prosecution was barred by the Equal Protection Clause of the Fourteenth Amendment.

A comparable *prima facie* case approach has been applied since the 1960s in cases in which black criminal defendants challenge their convictions on the basis of statistical evidence of systemic purposeful discrimination in the selection of either the grand jury that indicted them or the venire from which their juries were selected. For example, blacks might constitute 40% of the citizens of the county but the grand jury that indicted the defendant, or the venire members from which his jury was selected, may have had no or very few black members. This disparity would strongly suggest systemic purposeful discrimination against black citizens by the county's jury commissioners. The state could rebut this inference with evidence that the black citizens were excluded from the grand jury or the venire, not on the basis of race, but because they were not qualified for grand or petit jury service. However, in the absence of such a rebuttal by the state, the defendant won and was granted a new trial. In these cases, the defendant was required to establish neither that his jury discriminated against him nor that any individual citizen was excluded from jury service because of his or her race.[19] In short, the

---

co-counsel during his 10 years of federal habeas corpus litigation explaining his perception of the law in the early to mid–1980s).

[18] 118 U.S. 356 (1886). It is worth noting that the protected class in this case was distinctly not African Americans.

[19] *Castaneda v. Partida*, 430 U.S. 482 (1977) (concerning the appointment of grand jurors). With this evidentiary framework, the defendant can establish a *prima facie* case of discrimination with evidence of "unadjusted" disparities that do not control for the

evidence of classwide systemic purposeful discrimination against black citizens tainted the system to such a degree that its decisions could not stand.

By the 1980s it was clear that an Equal Protection claim of the type eventually alleged by McCleskey would require more than the proof of systemic discrimination of the type that succeeded in the grand jury and jury venire cases. However, the *prima facie* approach of those cases was quite relevant to a potential Eighth Amendment claim. Such a claim would require very little extension of *Furman*'s logic to hold that a system characterized by systemic purposeful racial discrimination was arbitrary under the Eighth Amendment. Also, the logic of *Furman*, would entitle such a claimant to complete relief from his death sentence if the court found that the statute under which he was prosecuted was unconstitutional because of its arbitrary application.[20]

B.   The Title VII Evidentiary Framework

Since the late 1970s, Title VII, a federal statute that prohibits employment discrimination, has provided a potentially applicable evidentiary framework for the presentation of Equal Protection claims in the death penalty context. Specifically, the Title VII approach used evidence of systemic discrimination to evaluate claims of purposeful discrimination against *individual* employees. In this context, the complaining employee could establish a *prima facie* case of discrimination against him or her with statistical evidence of systemic discrimination in hiring, promotion, or salary decisions, as the case may be. As in the jury selection cases, this evidence could be rebutted by the employer. However, if the employer failed to rebut the evidence, the plaintiff did not win, like defendants did in the grand jury and venire member selection cases. Rather, under the leading Title VII case on the issue, the plaintiff's

---

qualifications for jury service of the protected and unprotected citizens on the master juror rolls. The state carries the burden of explaining the racial disparities on the basis of non-racial factors bearing on juror qualifications or losing the case. *Whitus v. Georgia,* 385 U.S. 545, 552 (1967) is to the same effect with respect to discrimination in the selection of both grand-juries and petit-jury venires. Blacks constituted 27.1% of the tax digest from which venires were drawn but only 9.1% of the grand jurors and 7.8% of the petit jury venire members.

[20] This was the theory applied by the New Jersey Supreme Court in 1992 when it rejected *McCleskey* as a matter of New Jersey constitutional law. *State v. Marshall,* 613 A.2d 1059 (N. J. 1992) (holding that compelling evidence of systemic racial discrimination comparable to the evidence before the Supreme Court in *McCleskey* would justify the New Jersey court's modification or abolition of the state's system of capital punishment). Also, by the logic of the grand jury and venire-member selection cases, a successful claimant would be entitled to relief from his death sentence with the state retaining the option of capitally charging him again in a system that was administered in a race-neutral manner.

unrebutted evidence of systemic discrimination shifted to the employer a *burden of persuasion* concerning the employer's adverse decision against the plaintiff. To avoid liability to such a plaintiff, the employer had to establish by a preponderance that the employee was adversely affected by the employer's decision, not because of his or her protected status but because of the employee's lack of qualifications.[21]

The application of this Title VII evidentiary framework to a claimant like McCleskey would, upon proof of systemic purposeful discrimination, shift to the state a burden of proving that the charging and sentencing decisions in his case were not based on his race, or the race of his victim, but instead were based on the comparative death worthiness of his case defined in terms of race-neutral factors.[22]

---

[21] *International Brotherhood of Teamsters v. United States*, 431 U.S. 324, 336 (1977) is the leading authority. *See also Bazemore v. Friday*, 478 U.S. 385 (1986). *See generally* Barbara T. Lindemann et al. 1 EMPLOYMENT DISCRIMINATION LAW 104 (2007) ("During the remedial stage, each class member who has suffered the adverse employment action as to which discrimination has been proven is entitled to a rebuttable presumption that he or she has been the victim of the pattern or practice of unlawful discrimination. The employer carries the burden of persuasion to overcome this rebuttable presumption.") Under this approach, the employer will also prevail if it can demonstrate that there was no pattern and practice of purposeful discrimination in which event the burden of proof would not shift to the employer. *Id.* at 106–07. For recent applications, *see Munoz v. Orr*, 200 F.3d 291, 298–301 (5th Cir. 2000) and *Obrey v. Johnson*, 400 F.3d 691, 694–95 (9th Cir. 2005). It is also worth noting that the *Teamsters* Title VII evidentiary framework commonly relies on multiple regression models to document systematic purposeful discrimination. *Bazemore v. Friday*, 478 U.S. 385 (1986) (racial disparities in the salaries of black and white employees). This authority provided legal support for our use in *McCleskey* of multiple regression analysis as the basis for documenting systemic racial discrimination. The more fundamental reason for our use of logistic regression analysis is that it is the approach generally accepted by statisticians and the federal courts for the analysis of such decisions.

[22] In fact, this is the evidentiary framework that Justice Blackmun applied in his dissenting opinion in *McCleskey* to support his conclusion that McCleskey satisfied the *Washington v. Davis* 426 U.S. 229 (1976) standard: McCleskey had proven by a preponderance of the evidence that "racial factors entered into the decision-making process that yielded McCleskey's death sentence." *Infra* note 143 and accompanying text. It is also the evidentiary framework that Justice Brennan used to support his conclusion that McCleskey established by a preponderance of the evidence that a constitutionally unacceptable "risk" of racial discrimination existed under the Eighth Amendment. *Infra* note 140 and accompanying text.

In the absence of statistical evidence of systemic purposeful discrimination, under both the Equal Protection Clause and Title VII, the evidentiary frameworks are quite different. *Batson v. Kentucky*, 476 U.S. 79 (1986) (Equal Protection Clause) and *McDonnell Douglas Corp. v. Green*, 411 U.S. 792 (1973) (Title VII). *Bell, supra* note 11 at 767–71. What is common to both the Equal Protection and Title VII approaches in these contexts is that the burden of proof with respect to the purposeful discrimination against the individual (venire member or employee) always remains on the claimant alleging the purposeful discrimination.

C.   The *Washington v. Davis* "Smoking Gun" Evidentiary Framework

Washington v. Davis (1976)[23] involved an Equal Protection challenge to the District of Columbia's use of written exams to qualify applicants for admission to a police academy. This requirement had an adverse-impact on black applicants. The first holding of *Washington* was that under the Equal Protection Clause, proof of an adverse impact on a protected group did not shift to the government a burden of persuasion to provide a justification for its adoption of the facially neutral rule that produced the adverse impact.[24] The second holding of the case was that proof of *purposeful* discrimination on the part of the government actor, whose decision was at issue, was required to sustain an Equal Protection claim. The third holding was that evidence of the adverse impact of a single governmental decision would not sustain a finding of purposeful discrimination on the part of the decision maker. Thus, *Washington* holds that claimants in such cases must rely on direct "smoking gun" evidence of purposeful racial discrimination on the part of the government decision-maker involved. This holding is methodologically sound because evidence of the adverse impact of an actor's single decision rarely provides compelling evidence of purposeful discrimination on the part of that official. That situation stands in sharp contrast to those presented in the grand jury, venire member selection, and Title VII cases in which the statistical evidence underlying the evidence of racial disparities is the product of many, often hundreds, of decisions. Statistical evidence in this context provides a compelling basis for assessing whether race or gender is a significant influence in the decisions at issue. Indeed, in the absence of such statistical evidence, it is impossible to evaluate claims of racial discrimination in any meaningful way.[25]

---

[23] 426 U.S. 229 (1976).

[24] Through this holding, the court rejected under the Equal Protection Clause the approach it had applied in Title VII cases according to which employers had the burden of justifying their application of facially neutral rules when such applications had an adverse impact on protected groups of employees and job applicants. Griggs v. Duke Power Co., 401 U.S. 424 (1971).

[25] In re Proportionality Review Project (II), 757 A.2d 168, 171–72 (N.J. 2000) ("The study of system-wide discrimination requires the use of statistical techniques in complex socio-political settings. The process is far more complicated than counting the number of defendants by race and the number of death penalties meted out, although it certainly includes such elementary comparative analyses. A myriad of discretionary decisions are made at every level in the system, and sorting out their relationship to the race of either defendants or victims is complex and difficult. . . . We make these choices because we know of no other means by which the relationship, if any, between race and the death penalty system in New Jersey may be reviewed. The importance of understanding whether racial discrimination infects our system of capital punishment requires that we make this effort.") (Poritz, C.J.).

Except for *McCleskey,* none of the cases since the 1970s in which relief has been denied on the basis of *Washington v. Davis* involved evidence of systemic purposeful discrimination among similarly situated individuals. On the contrary, all of those cases involved a *single* governmental decision that produced an adverse impact on a protected group. Examples include claims that a town's zoning decision adversely affected blacks seeking low-income housing in the community,[26] and a state legislature's decision to give preferential treatment to military veterans, which disproportionately benefited men.[27]

D. Which Evidentiary Standard?

The Supreme Court's willingness to decide Equal Protection and Title VII cases by applying the *prima facie* case approach or the *Washington v. Davis* smoking gun evidentiary framework may be explained by two factors.[28] First, the Court appears to believe that federal courts should defer to high-level elected officials, especially legislators. As a result, they enjoy the benefit of the *Washington v. Davis* standard. In contrast, the *prima facie* case model is applied to low-level government officials (jury commissioners in grand jury and venire-selection Equal Protection cases) and private individuals (employers in Title VII cases) whose discretion in the eyes of the Court is entitled to far less deference and a far weaker presumption of regularity. The second consideration noted above is that statistical evidence provides a weak basis for inferring discriminatory intent in a single decision case, to which the *Washington v. Davis* approach is routinely applied, while it provides a very strong basis for the evaluation of claims of purposeful discrimination in cases in which the *prima facie* case evidentiary framework is applied to patterns of repeated behavior.

At a doctrinal level, therefore, the *McCleskey* Equal Protection issue boiled down to which evidentiary framework best fit the case. McCleskey argued that the *prima facie* case approach was more appropriate because his claim was based on evidence of systemic purposeful discrimination affecting nearly two thousand similarly situated defendants, including McCleskey. He could also have argued that the decision makers (prosecutors and jurors) in his case were low-level government officials whose discretionary decisions were not entitled to great deference. In its response, the State of Georgia argued that because the decisions of both

---

[26] *Village of Arlington Heights v. Metropolitan Hous. Dev. Corp.*, 429 U.S. 252 (1977).

[27] *Personal Adm. of Massachusetts v. Feeney*, 442 U.S. 256 (1979).

[28] We draw here on an insightful analysis of Sheila R. Foster, *Causation in Antidiscrimination Law: Beyond Intent Versus Impact*, 41 Hous. L. Rev. 1469, 1541 (2005) (*McCleskey* marked a shift not only in capital punishment jurisprudence, but also in "the Court's recent jurisprudence . . . in the evidentiary frameworks that . . . [it had] set up to detect discrimination.").

prosecutors and jurors were entitled to great deference, the *Washington v. Davis* approach best fit the case, thereby taking McCleskey's statistical evidence off the table.[29]

For the Eighth Amendment claims, the issue was whether the Court would consider the evidence of systemic racial discrimination relevant to the issue of arbitrariness under *Furman* or ignore that evidence because the procedural protections in the Georgia statute foreclosed all concerns about the actual operation of the system.

E.   Claims of Racial Discrimination in post-*Furman* Death Penalty Cases

Our expectations in the early 1980s about the Supreme Court's likely reaction to race based claims, such as McCleskey's, and its reaction to the statistical evidence supporting such claims were influenced by *Furman* and lower court post-*Furman* cases in which racial claims had been raised.

Racial discrimination was an important consideration in *Furman v. Georgia* (1972),[30] even though the question certified by the Court was whether the application of the death penalty in Furman's case constituted "cruel and unusual punishment" within the meaning of the Eighth Amendment. The claimants raised the race issue[31] but the Justices were not persuaded. Nevertheless, a number of Justices intimated that proof of purposeful racial discrimination in the administration of the death penalty could implicate the Equal Protection Clause or could create a sufficient risk of "arbitrariness and caprice" to violate the Eighth Amendment's cruel and unusual punishments provision. Against this background, Justice Powell's dissenting opinion in *Furman* was especially interesting:

> Although not presented by any of the petitioners today, a different argument, premised on the Equal Protection Clause, might well be made. If a Negro defendant, for instance, could demonstrate that members of his race were being singled out for more severe

---

[29] The legislature would have been implicated in *McCleskey* if he had challenged the motives of the Georgia legislature in adopting its death penalty statute or in keeping it on the books with knowledge of its adverse impact. But McCleskey made no such claims.

[30] 408 U.S. 238 (1972).

[31] Brief of Petitioner at 11–13, *Furman v. Georgia*, 408 U.S. 238 (1972) (No. 71–5003). The Petitioner's briefs addressed the race issue as one important evidentiary indication of "arbitrariness" due to the rare and uneven use of the death penalty, and its apparent imposition based upon such factors as race, especially in rape cases (two of the three defendants before the court in *Furman* had been sentenced to death for rape). The *amicus* brief of the National Association for the Advancement of Colored People ("NAACP") also dwelt at length on the race issue, although it presented no data on disparities adjusted for offender culpability.

punishment than others charged with the same offense, a constitutional violation might be established.[32]

As executions under post-*Furman* death sentences became imminent in the late 1970s, LDF commenced a campaign of race-based challenges to the administration of the death penalty in the South. All of its claims were denied, but two Fifth Circuit Court of Appeals decisions, which based their rulings in part on what the court perceived to be methodological shortcomings in the studies on which the claimants relied, left the impression that with improved methodology, some courts might give such claims serious attention.[33] The methodological concerns stated in these Fifth Circuit cases guided us in the development of the Baldus study.[34]

However, two Supreme Court cases decided after our research had been presented in federal district court (but was not yet in the Supreme Court) raised red flags, particularly in retrospect. Both cases indicated that the Court was aware of *McCleskey* long before it agreed to hear the case and that several members were unreceptive to McCleskey's claims. In the first case, *Stephens v. Kemp* (1983),[35] four dissenting members of the Court addressed the evidence in the pilot study that underlay the final Charging and Sentencing Study that we ultimately presented in *McCleskey*. As we explain in more detail below,[36] the pilot study had been presented in a number of Georgia capital habeas corpus cases in which counsel was seeking a full blown hearing in which we could present our final results. On the basis of the pilot study alone, the Eleventh Circuit Court of Appeals stayed the execution of Alpha Otis Stephen's death

---

[32] *Furman*, 408 U.S. at 449.

[33] *See, e.g., Spinkellink v. Wainwright*, 578 F.2d 582, 613–14 (5th Cir. 1978) (the analysis had only one control for offender culpability, it failed to model the procedural stages involved in the flow of cases through the system, and if a state has enacted a "properly drawn statute in imposing the death penalty, then the arbitrariness and capriciousness and therefore the racial discrimination condemned in *Furman* have been conclusively removed"); *Smith v. Balkcom* 671 F.2d 858, 859–60 (5th Cir. Unit B 1982) (rejecting a racial claim on grounds similar to those relied on in *Spinkelink*).

[34] In addition, dictum in *Zant v. Stephens*, 462 U.S. 862 (1983), decided six weeks before the evidentiary hearing in *McCleskey,* suggested that the court may be receptive to claims based on reliable evidence of systemic discrimination in the administration of a state death penalty system. Justice Stevens' opinion held that a jury's application of an admittedly defective statutory aggravating circumstance was not problematic because it was not equivalent to attaching "the 'aggravating' label to factors that are constitutionally impermissible or totally irrelevant to the sentencing process, such as for example the race, religion, or political affiliation of the defendant." *Id.* at 885. This language implied that systemic purposeful race-of-defendant or race-of-victim discrimination was impermissible.

[35] *Stephens v. Kemp*, 464 U.S. 1027 (1983).

[36] *Infra* note 48 and accompanying text.

sentence on the ground that the Baldus study may eventually provide a basis for relief in his case. On the state's appeal, the Supreme Court affirmed the stay, a decision that drew a strong four member[37] dissenting opinion stating with force that the pilot study was irrelevant and weak. This was Justice Powell's critique:

> The Baldus study, relied upon by Stephens, has not been presented to us. It was made in 1980 and apparently has been available at least since 1982. Although characterized by the judges of the Court of Appeals who dissented from the denial of hearing *en banc,* as a "particularized statistical study" claimed to show "intentional race discrimination," no one has suggested that the study focused on this case. A "particularized" showing would require-as I understand it that there was *intentional* race discrimination in indicting, trying, and convicting Stephens, and presumably in the state appellate and state collateral review that several times followed the trial. If the Baldus study is similar to the several studies filed with us in *Sullivan v. Wainwright,* 464 U.S. 109, 104 S.Ct. 450, 77 L.Ed.2d ___ (1983), the statistics in studies of this kind, many of which date as far back as 1948, are merely general statistical surveys that are hardly *particularized* with respect to any alleged "intentional" racial discrimination. Surely, no contention can be made that the entire Georgia judicial system, at all levels, operates to discriminate in all cases. Arguments to this effect may have been directed to the type of statutes addressed in *Furman v. Georgia,* 408 U.S. 238, 92 S. Ct. 2726, 33 L.Ed.2d 346 (1972). As our subsequent cases make clear, such arguments cannot be taken seriously under statutes approved in *Gregg.*[38]

The second case, *Turner v. Murray* (1986), decided three months before the Court agreed to hear *McCleskey,* raised an additional red flag.[39] *Turner* was a black-defendant/white-victim capital case from Virginia in which the Court ruled 7–2 that "the trial judge committed reversible error at *voir dire* by refusing petitioner's request to question prospective jurors on racial prejudice." Justice White's opinion for the Court presented an insightful analysis of the "unique opportunity for racial prejudice to operate [in a case] but remain undetected."[40] He

---

[37] The four members were Chief Justice Burger and Justices Powell, Rehnquist, and O'Connor.

[38] *Stephens v. Kemp,* 462 U.S. at 1030.

[39] *Turner v. Murray,* 476 U.S. 28 (1986). The case was decided while McCleskey's petition for a writ of certiorari requesting Supreme Court review was pending in the Court.

[40] *Id.* at 35. ("On the facts of this case, a juror who believes that blacks are violence prone or morally inferior might well be influenced by that belief in deciding whether petitioner's crime involved the aggravating factors specified under Virginia law. Such a

further explained that the Court found "the risk that racial prejudice may have infected petitioner's capital sentencing unacceptable *in light of the ease with which the risk could have been minimized*" (emphasis added). The clear implication of this test was that cases calling for remedies of the type requested by McCleskey, of which he was well aware at the time, were quite a different matter.[41]

In sum, prior to *McCleskey*, the Supreme Court had in other contexts approved statistical methods of the type employed by the Baldus study. The Court had also approved evidentiary frameworks that could have supported McCleskey's contention that the Georgia statute was arbitrarily applied, that there was a great risk that his death sentence was a product of racial discrimination, or that it was in fact the product of such discrimination. However, what the Court had not approved since *Furman*, was a legal claim based on an outcome-oriented analysis of charging and sentencing outcomes or one that had challenged the capital punishment status quo to a degree approaching *Furman v. Georgia* (1972).

Part III.   The Empirical Studies and Getting a Case to Federal Court

A.   Research Design and Data Collection

The principal "Charging and Sentencing Study" of Georgia's death penalty system used in *McCleskey* evolved over four years. In 1979 Professors Baldus, Woodworth, and Pulaski had undertaken what we called the "Procedural Reform Study" with 594 Georgia murder cases solely for academic research purposes, with no expectation that the results would be used in litigation.[42] In the course of the study, which became a pilot study for the larger Charging and Sentencing Study, Baldus developed a common interest in Georgia's death sentencing system with Jack Boger, who then led LDF's capital punishment project

---

juror might also be less favorably inclined toward petitioner's evidence of mental distur-bance as a mitigating circumstance. More subtle, less consciously held racial attitudes could also influence a juror's decision in this case. Fear of blacks, which could easily be stirred up by the violent facts of petitioner's crime, might incline a juror to favor the death penalty.")

[41] It is worth noting that Justice White, the author of the Court's *Turner* opinion, had voted three years earlier to stay the execution of the defendant in *Stephens v. Kemp*, the case discussed *supra* note 35 and accompanying text.

[42] For details on the first study see Baldus et al. *supra* note 4 and accompanying text at 42–44. Our research design built upon the pioneering work of Professors Marvin E. Wolfgang, a sociologist, and Anthony G. Amsterdam, a lawyer. Marvin E. Wolfgang, *Blacks and the Law*, 407 Annals of the American Academy of Political and Social Science 119, 126–29 (1973) (a study of death sentencing outcomes in 1265 capital rape case convictions in the South, 1945–1964). The results were eventually presented in *Maxwell v. Bishop*, 398 F.2d 138 (8th Cir. 1968) a federal habeas corpus proceeding challenging on racial grounds an Arkansas death sentence imposed in a black-defendant/white-victim rape case. *Infra* note 141.

and handled many capital cases in Georgia as co-counsel with local counsel. In 1980, on the basis of the evolving pilot study, Boger, Professor Anthony Amsterdam, a LDF consultant, and Jack Greenberg, the Director of the LDF at the time, invited Baldus, Woodworth, and Pulaski to conduct a study in a then undetermined jurisdiction with the support of a $250,000 grant to LDF from the Edna McConnell Clark Foundation, which they agreed to do.[43]

From mid–1980 through the spring of 1981, with substantial input from counsel, Baldus, Woodworth, and Pulaski focused on the research design for the new study. The first goal was to include all potentially death-eligible cases, which we defined as cases that resulted in a murder or voluntary manslaughter conviction. Accordingly, our universe included 2,484 defendants who were convicted of murder or voluntary manslaughter from 1973 through 1979.[44] The second goal was to collect sufficient procedural data on each case to track it longitudinally from the homicide charge to final disposition through the successive points of decision in the process. This information would enable us to identify the sources of any racial disparities documented among all death-eligible cases. The third goal was to develop a data collection instrument and database that would include not only information on the statutory aggravating and mitigating factors under Georgia law, but also all other non-racial case characteristics relating to offender culpability that might explain or reduce the statistical significance of any race effects initially documented in the system. We also sought information on the race, ethnicity, and socioeconomic status of each defendant and victim.[45]

Our goal was to develop a research design that would produce a manageable sample of approximately 1000 cases.[46] During the summer of

---

[43] One term of this agreement was that Baldus, Woodworth, and Pulaski would control the conduct of the study and the publication of their findings. During the fall of 1980, LDF counsel, Baldus, and Pulaski considered the pros and cons of Texas, Mississippi, Florida, and Georgia as possible locations for the study. Georgia emerged as the first choice because Baldus and Woodworth had recently obtained access to individual case files of the Georgia Board of Pardons and Paroles, a body established by the Georgia Constitution to ensure the delivery of justice in the state's criminal justice system. This access was crucial because the Board's staff investigates and prepares a post-conviction contemporaneous record of the facts of each case within its jurisdiction. Moreover, these files are centrally maintained in the Board's Atlanta office. In contrast, in the other states we considered, data collection would have required coders to review case records in county court houses across the state.

[44] For more detail see Baldus, et al., *supra* note 4 at 44–45.

[45] Race and ethnicity are the legally-suspect variables. The socioeconomic-status (SES) of defendants and victims, are morally but not legally suspect. However, they are important to include in such a study because they may be correlated with and explain away race-of-defendant and race-of-victim disparities in the system.

[46] The final sample was 1083 cases that included 128 death sentences.

1981 five law students coded the 1000 plus cases that constituted the database for the Charging and Sentencing Study on which McCleskey's case was principally based.[47]

B.   Data Entry, Preliminary Findings, and Getting a Hearing

The process of entering 1000 + sets of data in a single machine-readable database commenced in September of 1981 and consumed the fall.

Since 1978, LDF attorneys had been working with local counsel in Georgia to include generalized allegations of racial discrimination in the administration of Georgia's death penalty—that might be supported by the results of future research.[48] In early 1982, the challenge was to persuade a federal judge to order a hearing in which we could present our Georgia evidence in full. This required offering to a court (in which the appropriate pleadings had been filed) whatever preliminary findings were available at the time of filing to preview the shape that the evidence would likely take in a subsequent hearing. In this regard, the finding of the Georgia pilot study documented strong white-victim disparities in charging and sentencing outcomes. With these findings in hand, Jack Boger and local counsel began their search for a court that would order a hearing.

As a matter of professional principle, LDF lawyers did not reserve their racial discrimination claims for use in the most factually favorable cases or those pending before sympathetic judges. Instead, they alleged racial discrimination claims in the pleadings of every client they represented, leaving to chance and the response of federal and state judges the identification of the case in which the evidence supporting those claims would be presented.

As chance would have it, Warren McCleskey, a client of Jack Boger and co-counsel Atlanta attorney Robert Stroup, completed his first federal habeas proceedings shortly after the 1982 data from the pilot study became available. On McCleskey's behalf, Boger and Stroup filed the pilot study findings with United States District Judge J. Owen Forrester in the Northern District of Georgia and asked him to reopen

---

[47] During the spring of 1981, we conducted a nationwide solicitation of law schools and recruited a data collection team of five law students. Working under the supervision of Edward Gates, who had coded cases for this project during the fall of 1980, these students hand entered data for each of the 1000 + cases on printed data collection documents (one per case). The data collection instrument used for this purpose is at App. E, pp. 512–48, Baldus et al., *supra* note 4. They completed the coding process by working full-time for nearly three months during the summer of 1981.

[48] By June of 1982, when preliminary findings from the pilot study became available LDF lawyers had filed some form of pleading alleging racial discrimination and requesting a full hearing on the issue in over 30 Georgia death sentenced cases.

McCleskey's habeas corpus case (which he had denied within the last 30 days) and hear the new evidence.[49]

In October of 1982, he agreed.[50] Judge Forrester stated to Jack Boger that he had an interest in the statistical issues because of his background in science and engineering. He added further that every year he liked to allocate two weeks of his calendar to issues of concern to "the poor and down trodden" and that for 1983, Boger and Stroup could have that time on behalf of Warren McCleskey. And so it came to pass that the Georgia sentencing study was presented in a relatively unsympathetic case, in which the defendant had been convicted of murdering a white police officer who had responded to an armed robbery in progress, and was allegedly shot by McCleskey, a black defendant with two prior armed robbery convictions. It was heard by a former Drug Enforcement Agency strike force prosecutor, appointed to the federal bench by President Ronald Reagan. While fair and open-minded, Judge Forrester was not likely to have a receptive ear to a claim of racial discrimination, especially on behalf of a convicted murderer of an Atlanta police officer.[51]

C. The August 1983 Hearing

In January 1983, Judge Forrester scheduled a hearing date for the first two weeks of August, which lasted eight trial days, nearly all of which were devoted to the statistical issues.[52] Jack Boger and co-counsel Tim Ford of Seattle devoted several days to documenting the data collection process and the basics of the methodology for the two studies. More than once, Judge Forrester asked: "Mr. Boger, when are we going to get to the pudding?"

With respect to our findings, Table 1 presents the evidence proffered to the court of "unadjusted" systemic disparities in death sentencing rates among all defendants that took no account of differing levels of

---

[49] McCleskey exhausted state remedies for his federal habeas racial claims by virtue of his having pled his Eighth and Fourteenth Amendment race-based claims in his January 5, 1981 state habeas petition, which was dismissed by the state courts without a hearing.

[50] Judge Forrester agreed to reopen the case and hear the race claims under Federal Rule 60 (b) (2) on the basis of "newly discovered evidence which by due diligence could not have been discovered in time to move for a new trial under Rule 59(b)."

[51] Ideally the claim would have been presented in a case that involved a youthful black defendant, a white store clerk victim, substantial mitigating circumstances and was prosecuted in a rural community in which prosecutors had a strong reputation for hostility to African Americans.

[52] The witnesses for McCleskey were Edward Gates, who oversaw the data collection process in Georgia, Professors Baldus and Woodworth, Dr. Richard Berk, a sociologist rebuttal witness, and officials with the Georgia Board of Pardons and Paroles. The state's witnesses were Dr. Joseph Katz, Assistant Professor, Department at Quantitative Methods, Georgia State University, and Dr. Roger Burford, Professor of Quantitative Business Analysis, Louisiana State University.

defendant culpability.[53] The results in Row I Column B reveal no statewide race-of-defendant effects. In fact, the unadjusted death sentencing rate for white defendants is higher (7%) than the rate for black defendants (4%).[54] Row II Column B of the table, however, reveals a large white-victim disparity, with a death sentencing rate of 11% for the white-victim cases vs. a rate of 1.33% for the black-victim cases.[55] Even more striking is the magnitude of the death sentencing rate among the black-defendant/white-victim cases shown in Part III compared to the rates for the cases with other defendant/victim racial combinations.[56]

TABLE 1

UNADJUSTED RACE-OF-VICTIM AND RACE-OF-DEFENDANT DISPARITIES
IN DEATH-SENTENCING RATES AMONG ALL MURDER AND
VOLUNTARY MANSLAUGHTER CASES.

(Georgia Charging and Sentencing Study:1973–79)[1]

A.	B.
	Rates and Disparities

I.   Race-of-defendant disparity
     a.   Black-defendant cases   (BD)
     b.   White-defendant cases   (WD)
             Difference   (BD–WD)
             Ratio   (BD/WD)
	
	4% (68/1676)
	7% (60/808)
	-3 pts.
	.57

II.   Race-of-victim disparity
     a.   White-victim cases   (WV)
     b.   Black-victim cases   (BV)
             Difference   (WV–BV)
             Ratio   (WV/BV)
	
	11% (108/981)
	1.33% (20/1503)
	9.7 pts.
	8.5

---

[53] Baldus et al., *supra* note 4 at 315, tbl. 50. Disparities in these outcomes reflect the combined impact of prosecutorial charging and jury sentencing decisions. The death sentencing rate among all cases with indictments for murder was 4% (68/1676) for the black-defendant cases and 7% (60/808) for the white-defendant cases.

[54] This is a product of the white-victim disparities in the system, which elevate the death sentencing rate for killers of whites who are predominately white.

[55] Baldus et al., *supra* note 4 at 315, tbl. 50.

[56] The death sentencing rate for the black-defendant/white-victim cases was 21% (50/233), while the rates for the other three defendant/victim racial combinations ranged from 1.2% (18/1443) for the black-defendant/black-victim cases to 8% (58/748) for the white-defendant/white-victim cases. Among white-victim cases, the death sentencing rate for the black-defendant cases was 21% compared to 8% for the white-defendant cases. *Id.*

	Rates and Disparities
III. Defendant/victim racial composition	
a. Black-defendant/white-victim (B/W)	21% (50/233)
b. White-defendant/white-victim (W/W)	8% (58/748)
c. Black-defendant/black-victim (B/B)	1.2% (18/1443)
d. White-defendant/black-victim (W/B)	3% (2/60)
All Cases	5% (128/2484)

1. The disparities reported in Table 1 are estimated for the universe of all cases that resulted in a murder or voluntary manslaughter conviction. When the analysis is limited to death-eligible cases, the race-of-victim disparity is 12 percentage points. (14% for white-victim cases versus 2% for black-victim cases), while the race-of-defendant disparity is–3 points (7% for black defendants versus 10% for white-defendants). The rates by defendant/victim racial combination in the death-eligible cases are B/W 23%, W/W 11%, B/B 2%, and W/B 4%. Baldus et al., *supra* note 4 at 315, tbl. 50, note 1. *See* Baldus et al., *supra* note 4, at 72, note 38, on the use of all cases and those deemed death-eligible by our measures as a basis for estimating racial disparities.

The core model on which we relied to document adjusted statewide racial-disparities among all death-eligible cases contained 39 non-racial variables, deemed important because of their practical effect, statistical significance, or conceptual importance. Table 2 presents the results from that model limited to the 19 non-racial variables from the core model that were statistically significant beyond the .10 level.[57] It documents a strong statistically significant race-of-victim disparity, which supports an inference of systemic purposeful racial discrimination.

TABLE 2

THE IMPACT OF RACE AND 19 STATISTICALLY SIGNIFICANT AGGRAVATING AND MITIGATING FACTORS IN THE CORE 39 NON-RACIAL VARIABLE McCLESKEY MODEL OF DEATH SENTENCING OUTCOMES AMONG MURDER AND VOLUNTARY MANSLAUGHTER CASES: 1973–79[1]

(Georgia Charging and Sentencing Study: 1973–79)

A.   B.   C.

Variable Label and Name	Odds Multiplier	Logistic Adjusted Regression Coefficient with Level of Statistical Significance in Parenthesis
1. Defendant not triggerman (NOKILL)	.08	-2.5 (.0001)
2. History of Drug or Alcohol Abuse (DRGHIS)	.36	-1.02 (.0023)
3. Defendant was black (BLACKD)	1.1	.10 (.76)

[57] The two race variables in Table 2 are items 3 and 9. The names of the variables in the database are in capital letters.

Variable Label and Name	Odds Multiplier	Logistic Adjusted Regression Coefficient with Level of Statistical Significance in Parenthesis
4. Multiple shots (MULTSH)	1.8	.61 (.0633)
5. Defendant prime mover in planning Homicide contemporaneous offense (DLEADER)	2.3	.83 (.0751)
6. Victim was a stranger (STRANGER)	2.4	.88 (.0054)
7. Co-perpetrator received a lesser sentence (CPLESSEN)	2.6	.96 (.0048)
8. Multiple stabbing (MULTSTAB)	3.6	1.29 (.0021)
9. One or more white victims (WHVICRC)	4.3	1.45 (.0003)
10. Prior record of murder, armed robbery, rape, kidnapping with bodily injury (LDFBI)	4.9	1.6 (.0004)
11. Defendant killed two or more people (TWOVIC)	5.1	1.63 (.0012)
12. Armed robbery involved (ARMROB)	6.1	1.8 (.0001)
13. Kidnapping involved (KIDNAP)	6.1	1.8 (.0001)
14. Defendant prisoner or escapee (LDFB9)	6.7	1.9 (.0019)
15. Murder for hire (LDFB6)	6.8	1.92(.0088)
16. Mental torture (MENTORT)	7.2	1.98(.0035)
17. Victim was 12 or younger (VICCHILD)	8.2	2.1(.0011)
18. Victim tortured physically (TORTURE)	11.1	2.4 (.0024)
19. Defendant motive to collect insurance (INSMOT)	14.9	2.7 (.0003)
20. Rape involved (RAPE)	14.9	2.7 (.0001)
21. Motive to avenge role by judicial officer, D.A., lawyer (AVENGE)	40.1	3.69 (.0160)
n = 1066		

1. Baldus et al., *supra* note 4 at 319–20, tbl. 52, presents the model with 39 non-racial variables, while this Table 2 is limited to the 19 non-racial variables that were statistically significant at the .10 level or beyond. *Supra* note 58 explains that the Table 2 model shown here was McCleskey's exhibit.

Specifically, Column A identifies the variables in the analysis and Column B lists the odds multiplier (also known as an adjusted odds ratio) for each variable. The statistics for the black-defendant and white-victim variables are in Column B, Rows 3 and 9 of Table 2.[58] The most salient finding, shown in Row 9, Column B, is that, statewide, defendants in white-victim cases, faced odds of receiving a death sentence that were, on average, 4.3 times higher than the odds faced by similarly situated defendants in black-victim cases.

---

[58] An odds multiplier indicates the degree on average that an offender's odds are enhanced or diminished by the presence of a given case characteristic listed in Column A, holding constant all of the other variables in the analysis. For example, Row 11, Column B reports a 5.1 odds multiplier for multiple victims in the case. This means that, on average, a defendant's odds of receiving a death sentence are 5.1 times higher in multiple victim cases controlling for all of the other variables in the analysis. Column C lists the adjusted logistic regression coefficient with the level of statistical significance in parentheses. Row 3, Column B reports for the black defendant variable an adjusted 1.1 odds multiplier that is not statistically significant. This means that statewide among all cases there was no black-defendant effect in the analysis. However, Row 9, Column B reports a highly significant 4.3 odds multiplier for white-victim cases, which means that, on average, statewide, the odds of receiving a death sentence were 4.3 times higher in white-victim cases than they were in black-victim cases. When the analysis included all 39 non-racial variables, the white-victim odds multiplier is 4.3 and the black-defendant odds multiplier is .94. Baldus et al., *supra* note 4, at 319–20, tbl. 52. The 19 non-racial variable version in Table 2 was McCleskey's exhibit. The data in Column B indicate that the average impact of a white victim in the case (Row 9) is comparable to the impact of multiple stabbings (Row 8) or a defendant's prior record for a serious offense (Row 10). These findings were replicated across more than a dozen analyses involving different combinations of non-racial variables. *See* Baldus et al., *supra* note 4, at apps. J and L. Justice Blackmun discusses this aspect of the evidence in *McCleskey*, 481 U.S. at 351–56.

FIGURE 1

RACE-OF-VICTIM DISPARITIES IN BLACK-DEFENDANT CASES, AFTER ADJUSTMENT
FOR DEFENDANT CULPABILITY IN A MULTIPLE REGRESSION ANALYSIS:
GEORGIA CHARGING AND SENTENCING STUDY, 1973–1979*

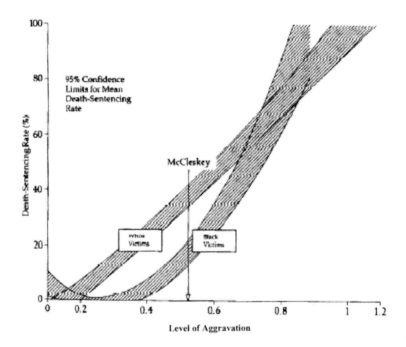

The evidence also documented adjusted white-victim disparities in
the 20–percentage point range among cases that fell in the "midrange"
of cases in terms of offender culpability.[59] Figure 1 illustrates this effect
among the black-defendant cases.[60]

---

* The curves represent 95% confidence limits on the average death-sentencing rate at
increasing levels of aggravation (redrawn from computer output). Baldus et al., *supra* note
4 at 321, fig. 32.

[59] The culpability scale underlying Figure 1 is the logistic regression model referred to
supra note 57 and accompanying text with 39 non-racial variables. The midrange effect is
known as the "liberation hypothesis," developed by Harry Kalven and Hans Ziesel,
AMERICAN JURY (1964). It postulates that among the most and least aggravated cases,
decision makers are in the grip of fact, while, among the close cases in the midrange,
decision makers are "liberated" from the grip of fact, and inappropriate factors, such as
race, are more likely to have an impact on their decisions.

[60] Table 1 referred to above documents a 20–percentage point unadjusted white-victim
effect among all of the black-defendant cases, i.e., a death sentencing rate of 21% when the
victim is white (III. a.) and a 1.2% rate when the victim is black (III. c.). Figure 1 plots on
the vertical Y axis the predicted probability of a death sentence for white-victim and black-

Part IV.   The Lower Court Rulings

A.   The District Court Ruling

Throughout the August 1983 hearing, Judge Forrester treated all participants in the hearing with respect. The same cannot be said about his February 1, 1994 decision, which almost contemptuously dismissed the scientific validity of our Georgia research.[61] His unsparing approach was nonetheless prescient in terms of foreshadowing how the Supreme Court would ultimately address the case.[62]

He reasoned that statistics do not generally show the intentional discrimination required under the *Washington v. Davis* evidentiary standard and that McCleskey's evidence also failed to meet the requirements for a *prima facie* case.[63] He further stated that even if it was assumed that the study had made out a *prima facie* case of discrimination, the state had effectively rebutted it by showing that the study did not employ good statistical methods and that factors other than race explained the results.[64]

Although Judge Forrester rejected McCleskey's racial claims, he vacated his murder conviction because the state had failed to disclose to the defendant or to the trial jury that it had promised and given favorable treatment to a prisoner (Offie Evans) in exchange for his

victim cases after adjustment for their "Level of Aggravation" indicated along the X axis. The width of each set of plots indicates a 95% confidence interval around the death sentence probability estimated at each point on the level of aggravation scale. The open space between those plots indicates the location on the aggravation scale where the race-of-victim effects are strongest. At the low and high end of the level of aggravation scale, the predicted likelihood of a death sentence is essentially the same for white and black-victim cases. However in the midrange of cases from about .3 to .6 on the aggravation scale, there are strong white-victim disparities. The figure places McCleskey in the midrange of cases at a point where the adjusted white-victim disparity is approximately 20–percentage points (40% for the white-victim cases, 20% for the black-victim cases). Among the white-defendant cases, the number of white-defendant/black-victim cases (n=19) with only 2 death sentences is too small to support analysis. *See* Baldus et al., *supra* note 4 at 322 tbl. 53, col. H.

[61] *McCleskey v. Zant*, 580 F.Supp. 338 (N.D. Ga. 1984). *See* Baldus et al., *supra* note 4 at App. B, pp. 450–53 for a more detailed methodological critique of Judge Forrester's opinion.

[62] His opinion suggests he had paid careful attention to Justice Powell's dissenting opinion (December 1983) in *Spencer v. Zant*, *supra* note 38 and accompanying text, which had belittled the results of our Georgia pilot study.

[63] *McCleskey*, 580 F.Supp. at 361–62. (Overall, Judge Forrester believed that statistical methods were incapable of proving discrimination, and, as a consequence, our Georgia study failed "to contribute anything of value" to McCleskey's cause.).

[64] The court appears to have accepted Dr. Katz's thesis that the white-victim cases were more aggravated while black-victim cases were shown to have more mitigating factors in general. However, the court failed to mention that Dr. Katz presented no multivariate statistical analyses in which the race-of-victim effects in the system were explained away by race-neutral variables bearing on the criminal culpability of the offenders in the study.

damaging testimony against McCleskey in violation of *Giglio v. United States*.[65]

B.   The Eleventh Circuit Court of Appeals

Appeals in federal habeas cases are normally heard by a three-judge panel. Because of the perceived importance of this case, the United States Court of Appeals for the Eleventh Circuit heard the case directly en banc, which meant that all 12 members of the court heard the argument.[66]

Because of concerns about the interest of the appellate judges in the methodological and statistical issues presented by the case, counsel for McCleskey focused on those issues in their brief and stressed the constitutional issues during the oral argument. At oral argument, June 12, 1984, the court appeared to accept the approach as none of the methodological and statistical issues were raised by counsel or the court during the argument.

At the outset, the Eleventh Circuit's majority opinion written by Judge Roney reversed Judge Forrester's order of a new trial on McCleskey's *Giglio* theory.[67] With respect to McCleskey's racial claims, he made two points that are relevant to the Supreme Court's eventual decision. First he "assum[ed] the validity of the [Georgia] research [but held that] it would not support a decision that the Georgia law was being unconstitutionally applied, much less would it compel such a finding . . . ."[68] In addition, he faulted the racial claim for its failure to present a "particularized" showing of race discrimination in McCleskey's case.[69] He then

---

[65] 405 U.S. 150 (1972); *McCleskey v. Zant*, 580 F.Supp. 338, 384 (1984). ("Because disclosure of the promise of favorable treatment and correction of the other falsehoods in Evans' testimony could reasonably have affected the jury's verdict on the charge of malice murder, petitioner's conviction and sentence on that charge are unconstitutional. The writ of habeas corpus must therefore issue.") Offie Evans importantly appears in McCleskey's second federal habeas corpus petition *infra* note 148 and accompanying text.

[66] In retrospect, some members of the court regretted having heard the case initially *en banc*. Their view after the court's en banc decision was that a decision by a three-judge panel would have prepared the court for a subsequent *en banc* argument and given them better control of both the legal and statistical issues. Interview, November 2, 2007 with Professor John Blume, a judicial clerk on the Eleventh Circuit at the time of the *en banc* argument.

[67] *Id.* at 883. Had the district court's judgment in favor of McCleskey been a not guilty jury verdict on a charge of murder, it would have been final and could not have been appealed by the State. However, in state and federal post-conviction judicial proceedings, a judicial decision supporting a defendant's claim for a new trial based on a violation of state or federal law is always subject to appeal by the State and reversal by an appellate court.

[68] *Id.*

[69] *Id.* at 893. On this point, the opinion relies on the dissenting opinion referred to above in *Stephens v. Kemp, supra*, note 38. With respect to discrimination in McCleskey's

proceeded to trivialize the racial harm documented by McCleskey's evidence of systemic race-of-victim discrimination and concluded that, in fact, the evidence revealed an "essentially rational system."[70]

The three dissenting opinions[71] accepted the validity of the Baldus study and disagreed with the court's holding that McCleskey had to establish purposeful discrimination in his case. They also argued that systemic Eighth Amendment claims were sufficient and that they did not require proof of "intent to discriminate in order to show that the death penalty is being applied arbitrarily and capriciously."[72] They argued that the evidence supported his Eighth Amendment and Equal Protection systemic claims as did the history of racial discrimination in Georgia's criminal justice system.

Part V.   The Supreme Court

A.   Getting There

The process of obtaining Supreme Court review of an adverse lower-court decision, especially in a death-sentence case, is fraught with uncertainty. Few petitions for a writ of certiorari filed with the Court are granted in capital cases. Moreover, unknown to McCleskey's counsel, the 5–4 division between the Justices which eventually emerged in the 1987 *McCleskey* opinion, had occurred long before the Court considered

---

case, he states: "The Baldus study statistical evidence does not purport to show that McCleskey was sentenced to death because of either his race or the race of his victim." *Id.* at 895.

[70] On the first "harm" point, he characterized a 6–percentage point white-victim regression coefficient as a "6% bottom line" disparity, which was not "sufficient to overcome the presumption that the statute is operating in a constitutional manner." For two reasons, he also rejected the 20–percentage point white-victim disparity among the midrange cases in terms of offender culpability as inadequate. First, he believed that the concept of the midrange of cases was not adequately defined. In addition, he believed that the analysis was not a proper basis for a "systemwide challenge" because it does not embrace all of the cases in the system. *Id.* at 888. Judge Roney also stated his belief that the evidence "revealed an essentially rational system" because the "high aggravation" cases were more likely to result in the death sentence than low aggravation cases. *Id.* at 896.

[71] Judge Johnson, *Id.* at 907–18; Judge Hachett, *Id.* at 918–19; and Judge Clark, *Id.* at 920–27.

[72] *Id.* at 908 (Johnson, J.). The proof required is that race "enters into" charging and sentencing decisions. Judge Johnson further argued that ... "[A] pattern of death sentences skewed by race alone will support a claim of arbitrary and capricious sentencing in violation of the Eighth Amendment." *Id.* at 910.

McCleskey's petition for a writ of certiorari.[73] The conservatives[74] preferred to leave the issue to the lower courts, an approach that was likely to perpetuate the unanimous rejection of race based claims since the late 1970s.[75]

Why then was the case taken by the Court?[76] The threshold answer is that review will be granted under the Court's rules if four justices vote to hear it, and the four liberal justices wanted to hear *McCleskey*, even though they knew they would lose. But what would be accomplished by a decision that would likely foreclose consideration of the issue for decades, as in fact has happened? According to Edward Lazarus, the votes of Justices Brennan and Marshall were "automatic" and Justices Blackmun and Stevens believed that in the face of the trend of LDF's racial claims in the federal courts "the Court had no choice but to confront" the issue ". . . whether the other Justices wanted to or not."[77]

B. The Oral Argument

In the oral argument, the Court allowed McCleskey's counsel Boger to begin and argue without interruption for an unusually long time, five or six minutes, before posing its first question.[78] Justice White's first

---

[73] Edward Lazarus, CLOSED CHAMBERS 190–191, 205 (1998). Lazarus was a law clerk for Justice Harry Blackmun during the term that *McCleskey* was considered by the Supreme Court. We found his book a particularly valuable source of information on the Supreme Court's handling of *McCleskey*. The book has been criticized for its use of confidential sources and its accuracy. Alex Kozinski, *Conduct Unbecoming,* 108 YALE L. J. 835 (1999). We have relied on the information in Lazarus' book that appears on the basis of what we know from other sources to be factually accurate.

[74] Counsel for McCleskey believed they had a chance of reaching Justices White or Powell with these arguments. However, author Edward Lazarus reports that both of these Justices sought to keep the case out of the Court, and Justice White eventually became a vociferous opponent of the racial claims. *Id.* at 204–06.

[75] Federal district courts routinely denied requests for a hearing on racial claims, and such denials were routinely affirmed on appeal.

[76] *McCleskey v. Kemp*, 479 U.S. 806 (1986).

[77] The long delay in the Court's grant of the writ was the result of a "hold" placed on the case by virtue of the pendency of another case, *Lockhart v. McCree*. Lazarus, *supra* note 73 at 187–888. This is a common Supreme Court practice to promote efficiency in the Court's management of its docket. A favorable outcome for the petitioner in that case would have required a new trial for McCleskey and many other death row prisoners.

[78] As noted above, participants outside the Court did not realize that the case had been decided before the Court granted cert. We were also unaware that while the case was pending in the Supreme Court, Justice White had assumed a leadership role in opposing McCleskey's claim. In addition, it appears that before the oral argument, without the knowledge of the four eventual dissenting Justices, he sent his four conservative colleagues a detailed memo urging a "unified vote to reject McCleskey's claims," and organized the assault on Jack Boger's October 15, 1986 oral argument. Lazarus, *supra* note 73 at 202. All of Boger's questions came from the five members of the majority. The Oyez Project, *McCleskey v. Kemp–Oral Argument* (October, 15, 1986).

attack was on the reliability of a data collection process conducted by "law students" rather than "law graduates." He also suggested a conflict of interest by the authors of the Baldus study *vis a vis* the Legal Defense Fund.[79]

Chief Justice Rehnquist and Justice O'Connor asked about the constitutional proof requirements. Boger agreed that to establish an Equal Protection claim, he had to establish purposeful discrimination on the part of McCleskey's prosecutor or jury: "We've had to show it inferentially of course."[80] With regard to remedy, Boger's main theme was that Georgia's current system had failed, and, as in *Furman,* its "current statute need [sic] be struck."[81]

When asked by Justices Powell and Scalia whether, given McCleskey's crime, the death sentence in his case could easily be explained by non-racial factors, Boger replied that "Mr. McCleskey was undoubtedly sentenced to death, in part, because he committed a homicide and an armed robbery. But he was also sentenced to death, in part, we believe, because he was black."[82]

Mary Beth Westmoreland's argument on behalf of the State of Georgia had two main themes. First, the methodology used in the Baldus study was incapable of establishing racial discrimination because each case is "unique on its own individual facts." Her second theme was that McCleskey had identified no cases similar to his "in which the death penalty had not been imposed." "[O]ur . . . bottom line . . . is you cannot come up with two similar cases to compare because each case is unique on its own individual facts."[83]

Justice Scalia's questioning of Westmoreland took an unexpected turn when he asked her why the issue of proof in McCleskey's case is "different from Title VII [cases]."[84] When she resisted with her "unique" case argument he responded: "But certainly on the theoretical point of whether statistical evidence can properly be used, assuming it's reliable as . . . *prima facie* evidence of discrimination in a particular case, there's no basis for distinguishing this from the Title VII situation, is there?" She eventually agreed with qualifications.[85] Scalia's position in

---

[79] Boger explained that Baldus received no compensation for his time. *Id.* at 5.

[80] *Id.*

[81] *Id.* at 6. He later stated that it would be "a matter for the Georgia legislature to come up with some solutions remedially, but there are a number of solutions that are available to it."

[82] *Id.* at 10.

[83] *Id.* at 14.

[84] *Id.* at 17.

[85] *Id.* at 18.

the oral argument on the core evidentiary framework issue in the case, raises a question for us about how he was able to sign on to Justice Powell's opinion which explicitly rejects Scalia's position on this issue.[86]

C. The Decision and Majority Opinion

Because of his strong opposition to McCleskey's claims, Justice White apparently sought to author the Court's majority opinion. However, Chief Justice Rehnquist assigned the opinion to Justice Powell.[87]

As noted above, our analysis of Justice Powell's *McCleskey* opinion and the circumstances leading up to the decision convinces us that the Court's decision was principally based on the majority's belief that a recognition of McCleskey's claims could have put numerous state capital punishment systems at risk of invalidation.[88] An honest and forthright opinion would have justified the Court's decision on those grounds. *Swain v. Alabama* (1965)[89] is a relatively recent example of such an opinion on a closely related issue. *Swain* addressed the well known practice of prosecutorial discrimination against black venire members in the use of peremptory challenges, which resulted in many black defendants being tried by all white juries, often in capital cases. The Court justified its avoidance and denial of the racial issue through the creation of an unattainable burden of proof as follows:

---

[86] We recognize that questions of a Justice in an oral argument do not count as a committed position. However, the assumption of Scalia's question in the oral argument was completely consistent with his statement in a January memo to the court, while the case was pending, that he saw no problems of proof in McCleskey's case. ("I cannot honestly say that all I need is more proof.") Scalia's memo to the Court stated that he intended to file a concurring opinion but he never did. *Infra* note 101. The key provisions of Scalia's memorandum are also reported in David C. Baldus, George Woodworth & Charles A. Pulaski Jr., *Reflections on the "Inevitability" of Racial Discrimination in Capital Sentencing and the "Impossibility" of its Prevention, Detection, and Correction,* 51 Wash. & Lee L. Rev. 359, 371, n. 46 (1994).

[87] Lazarus, *supra* note 73 at 205. According to Lazarus, the other members of the five Justice majority to whom Powell's opinion was circulated suggested only marginal changes to his draft opinion. Three of the four dissenting Justices wrote separate opinions. Justice Brennan believed that he was writing for "the next generation." He and his clerks took two and one-half months to finish his opinion, which infuriated the Chief Justice who insisted on a one-month turn around. *Id.* at 210. Justice Blackmun finished his opinion in six weeks and Justice Stevens wrote only a brief but important dissent. Justice Marshall, the Court's only African–American Justice and the first Director Counsel of the NAACP Legal Defense and Educational Fund, perhaps cared more about this issue than anyone on the court. Yet he chose not to write separately but concurred in the three dissents.

[88] We mention *supra* note 15 and accompanying text additional concerns that may have influenced some members of the Court to join the majority.

[89] 380 U.S. 202 (1965) (a black-defendant/white-victim rape case with a death sentence imposed by an all white jury).

"To subject the prosecutor's challenge in any particular case to the demands and traditional standards of the Equal Protection Clause would entail a radical change in the nature and operation of the challenge. The prosecutor's judgment underlying each challenge would be subject to scrutiny for reasonableness and sincerity. And a great many uses of the challenge would be banned."

The tradeoff between the Court's tolerance of the possibility of potentially racially motivated peremptory strikes and the protection of prosecutorial prerogatives could not have been clearer.[90]

In 1987, this level of candor about the practical consequences of a McCleskey victory, may, in the Court's view, have run against existing standards of appropriate federal judicial conduct and could have undercut the perceived legitimacy of the Court's decision. It is our opinion that instead of candor, Justice Powell's *McCleskey* opinion presents an analysis designed to hide the realities of the Georgia death penalty system.

To be sure, there is language in Justice Powell's opinion suggesting what we believe were the Court's actual concerns. The opinion expresses a fear that recognition of McCleskey's claims would amount to a de facto overruling of *Gregg v. Georgia* (1976), which upheld the constitutionality of the Georgia system.[91] The opinion further stated that the law does not impose "totally unrealistic conditions"[92] on the use of the death penalty and that "McCleskey challenges decisions at the heart of the State's criminal justice system ..." which requires "discretionary judgments" ... that are "essential to the criminal justice process ..." Consequently "we would demand exceptionally clear proof before we would infer that the discretion has been abused."[93]

However, in lieu of what we would consider to be a reasoned defense of the Court's policy judgment, Justice Powell's opinion advances five arguments that, in our opinion, do not persuade.

---

[90] *Baze v. Rees*, 128 S.Ct. 1520, 1532 (2008) is a more recent example of a forthright opinion rejecting a challenge to the capital punishment status quo. In his opinion for the Court, Chief Justice Roberts rejected an Eighth Amendment challenge to lethal injection as a mode of execution. ("Permitting an Eighth Amendment violation to be established on such a showing would threaten to transform courts into boards of inquiry charged with determining 'best practices' for executions, with each ruling supplanted by another round of litigation touting a new and improved methodology. Such an approach finds no support in our cases, would embroil the courts in ongoing scientific controversies beyond their expertise, and would substantially intrude on the role of state legislatures in implementing their execution procedures-a role that by all accounts the States have fulfilled with an earnest desire to provide for a progressively more humane manner of death.").

[91] *McCleskey*, 481 U.S. at 313, n. 37.

[92] *Id*. (quoting *Gregg v. Georgia*, 428 U.S. 153, 199, n. 50).

[93] *Id*. at 297.

1. Unattainable Burdens of Proof

As noted above in more detail,[94] the key "legal" issue in the case was whether the Court would apply a *"prima facie* case" evidentiary framework or the unattainable *Washington v. Davis* (1976) evidentiary framework. Had Justice Powell considered the *prima facie* approach applicable, the Court could have remanded the case to the court of appeals to determine the validity of the Georgia research and to make the required findings of fact.[95]

Instead, Justice Powell ruled that evidence of systemic racial discrimination was irrelevant and essentially inadmissible because "the nature of the capital sentencing decision, and the relationship of the statistics to that decision, are fundamentally different from the corresponding elements in the venire-selection or Title VII cases." [96]

This determination resulted in two holdings that completely ignored McCleskey's statistical evidence of systemic discrimination. The first holding dismissed McCleskey's Fourteenth Amendment claim as follows:

> ... to prevail under the Equal Protection Clause, McCleskey must prove that the decisionmakers in *his* case acted with discriminatory purpose. He offers no evidence specific to his own case that would support an inference that racial considerations played a part in his sentence. Instead, he relies solely on the Baldus study.[97]

The second holding took a similar tack with respect to McCleskey's Eighth Amendment claim:

> In light of the safeguards designed to minimize racial bias in the process, the fundamental value of jury trial in our criminal justice system, and the benefits that discretion provides to criminal defendants, we hold that the Baldus study does not demonstrate a

---

[94] *Supra* note 28 and accompanying text.

[95] Another alternative would have been for Justice Powell to apply the *prima facie* approach himself by showing that McCleskey's evidence didn't meet the standards and in so doing challenge the inferences of purposeful discrimination and risk of arbitrariness drawn by the dissenting Justices. However, that approach would have left the federal courts open to future claims based on more compelling evidence of arbitrariness and racial discrimination than McCleskey had presented. There is also evidence that the Court considered but rejected a suggestion that the Court appoint a special master to apply the *prima facie* case approach to the evidence. This suggestion "presupposed that the conservative Justices were still open to convincing. But the evidence was increasingly to the contrary." Lazarus, *supra* note 73 at 202. *See* Marc Price Wolf, *Proving Race Discrimination in Criminal Cases Using Statistical Evidence*, 4 HASTINGS RACE & POVERTY L.J. 395 (2007) (explores the idea of a special master).

[96] *McCleskey*, 481 U.S. at 294.

[97] *Id*. at 292–93.

constitutionally significant risk of racial bias affecting the Georgia capital sentencing process.[98]

Because almost all decisions within the criminal justice system are discretionary, *McCleskey* in effect places all of them beyond the reach of the courts in the absence of direct "smoking gun" evidence from a prosecutor or jurors in the case.[99]

We believe that Justice Powell's distinctions between the decision-making processes in capital cases and those in other contexts were strained and unpersuasive.[100] They confirmed the validity of Powell's

---

[98] *Id.* at 313.

[99] It is worth noting, however, that the Supreme Court did not accept the Eleventh Circuit's holding that a violation of the Eighth Amendment required proof of purposeful racial discrimination. It also rejected Georgia's claim that a capital defendant had no standing to raise a racial claim based on the race of the victim. The Court held that McCleskey's standing existed because proof of racially based disparate treatment in government decision-making gives anyone adversely affected by such decisions the standing to raise a racial claim. *Id.* at 292, n. 8. Justice Powell properly relegated this holding to a footnote since the Court totally nullified its meaning with its subsequent holdings barring all statistically based claims of racial discrimination from the federal courts.

[100] Justice Powell's first distinction focused not on "the number of entities [decision makers] involved in a particular decision" but on the "number of entities whose decisions necessarily are reflected in a statistical display such as the Baldus study." *Id.* at 295. It is "incomparably more difficult to deduce a consistent policy by studying the decisions of these many unique entities." Thus, an inference of a "prosecutorial 'policy,' is of doubtful relevance." The opinion also focuses on the "uniqueness" of each jury as a point of distinction but does not explain how that would threaten the validity of inferences based on an analysis of jury decisions. As for Fulton County, he stated that the "weight to be given the results gleaned from this small sample is limited." These are uninformed social science claims supported by no expert opinion or reference to the relevant literature. *Id.* at 295. When relevant social scientific literature exists, Justice Powell's opinion cited it in detail, for example on the question of the impact of a defendant's appearance on his risk of conviction. *Id.* at 319. Also, Justice Blackmun documents that there are large numbers of actors involved in jury and employment cases. *Id.* at 362. It is true that the number of actors whose decisions are aggregated in a single analysis reduces the likelihood that any individual factor will emerge as significant because multiple actors may place differing weights on the same factors, thereby cancelling out an overall effect. However, the emergence of a single factor as important in a series of aggregated analyses, such as the race of the victim or any other factor, as important in a series of aggregated analyses gives one confidence that the effect is real. With respect to a local unit such as Fulton County, to which Powell referred, the key issue is the consistency of those results with the overall results. Moreover, a concern about Fulton County's sample size is questionable since it included 581 cases, and amounted to 23% (581/2484) of the universe. See Baldus et al., *supra* note 4 at 315, tbl. 50 (Part III for the 2484 case universe) and at 337, tbl. 61 (for the 581 Fulton County cases in the statewide universe).

Justice Powell's second point of distinction is the number of variables potentially involved in the analysis and their objective verifiability. In the jury and employment context, he perceives many fewer "uniform ... objectively verifiable" variables than exist in the capital sentencing context in which he also believes there is "no common standard[s]

later statement to his biographer that his "understanding of statistical analysis ... range[d] from limited to zero."[101]

The style and rhetoric of the *McCleskey* opinion is part of a long tradition of Supreme Court decisions imposing unattainable burdens of proof in order to deny and avoid claims of racial discrimination under the Equal Protection Clause. Our review of the Court's jurisprudence since the 1970s, in Part II above, documents the extent to which *Washington v. Davis* (1976) has reduced the number of successful claims to zero in cases involving only a single decision by a governmental actor.[102]

2. Denial and Trivialization of Documented Race Based Harms

Following the example of the Eleventh Circuit Court of Appeals, Justice Powell's opinion denies and trivializes the racial harms documented by McCleskey's evidence. At no point did Justice Powell's opinion criticize let alone condemn race-of-victim discrimination. Indeed, he stated later to his biographer that "[d]ifferential treatment based on the race of [the] victims was hard to understand as racial bias against defendants."[103]

---

by which to evaluate all defendants who have or have not received the death penalty." *Id.* at 295. Although there is some force to the "subjectivity" issue, his "common standard" argument appears to be inconsistent with his statement later in the opinion that "the Baldus Study in fact confirms that the Georgia system results in a reasonable level of proportionality among the class of murders eligible for the death penalty." *Id.* at 313, n. 36; *see also id.* at 290 (quoting the Eleventh Circuit to the same effect). For a more detailed methodological critique of the Supreme Court's methodological ruling, *see* Baldus et al., *supra* note 4 at 370–93.

[101] John C. Jeffries, Jr., JUSTICE LEWIS F. POWELL, JR. 439 (1994). Justice Powell's methodological analysis was inconsistent with the views of the amicus brief filed in the case by a group of eminent social scientists who endorsed the validity of methodology and findings of the Georgia research on which McCleskey relied even as they disclaimed any views on the death penalty. Brief Amici Curiae for Franklin M. Fisher, *et al.* cited in *McCleskey Reply Brief*, 1986 WL 727363 at 13. Recall that in the oral argument, *supra* note 84 and accompanying text, Justice Scalia stated his belief that the Title VII *prima facie* case clearly applied to *McCleskey* if the data were valid. So even though Justice Scalia appears to have accepted McCleskey's factual claim, according to Lazarus's sources, he "was willing to tolerate that bias and even thought that the other Justices, in candor should admit they were too." Lazarus, *supra* note 73 at 211. Lazarus speculated on Scalia's failure to write a separate concurrence: "Most likely, he decided that Powell's opinion all but foreclosed another statistical challenge—and that was good enough." *Id.* at 211.

[102] The only exceptions involve challenges against the discriminatory use of preemptory strikes by prosecutors in voir dire under *Batson v. Kentucky*, 476 U.S. 79 (1986), and few such claims are successful. Kenneth J. Melilli, Batson *In Practice: What We Have Learned About Batson and Peremptory Challenges,* 71 NOTRE DAME L. REV. 447, 462–3 (1996).

[103] Jeffries, *supra* note 101 at 439.

Not only did he see no race problem, his opinion went on to state that "[t]he Baldus study in fact confirms that the Georgia system results in a reasonable level of proportionality among the class of murderers eligible for the death penalty ... the system sorts out cases where the sentence of death is highly likely and highly unlikely, leaving a midrange of case where the imposition of the death penalty in any particular case is less predictable."[104] Justice Powell never explained, however, how he could simultaneously rely upon certain findings (showing the role of aggravating factors) but reject others (showing a comparable role of the race of the victim) from the same study.

When Justice Powell did address McCleskey's evidence of Georgia racial disparities, he reported that it merely *"purports* to show" racial disparities[105] (emphasis added). He later presented the following widely quoted claims which we believe have no support in either the data or the testimony of the state's experts:

1. "At most, the Baldus study indicates a discrepancy that appears to correlate with race. ... The discrepancy indicated by the Baldus study is a 'far cry from the major systemic defects identified in *Furman,*'"[106] and

2. "Where the discretion that is fundamental to our criminal process is involved, we decline to assume that what is unexplained is invidious."[107]

Because these two claims have a "scientific" ring to them, i.e., "correlate," and "unexplained," they may suggest to lay readers that they properly identify limitations of McCleskey's evidence of systemic race effects in the Georgia system. In fact neither of these two claims was presented by the state, nor by its experts, and neither is correct. The first claim incorrectly suggests that the evidence "appear[s]" to have documented race disparities in the system but did not do so in fact. Such a conclusion is completely at odds with the evidence, which established strong statistically-significant racial disparities that were not expressly denied by Justice Powell and were expressly recognized by both the dissenting Supreme Court Justices and the Eleventh Circuit. As Randall

---

[104] *McCleskey*, 481 U.S. at 313, n. 36. He later stated to his biographer that he thought the overall picture revealed by the Georgia evidence was "decidedly positive," since "[t]he pattern suggests precisely the kind of careful balancing of individual factors that the Court required in *Gregg*." Jeffries, *supra* note 101 at 439.

[105] *McCleskey*, 481 U.S. at 286.

[106] *Id*. at 312–313. The "far cry" assertion was lifted verbatim from *Pulley v. Harris*, 465 U.S. 37, 54 (1984). ("Any capital sentencing scheme may occasionally produce aberrational outcomes. Such inconsistencies are a far cry from the major systemic defects identified in *Furman*.")

[107] *Id*. at 313.

Kennedy has observed, the statement is comparable to stating that "at most studies on lung cancer indicate a discrepancy that appears to correlate with smoking."[108]

Justice Powell's claim that McCleskey's evidence was a far cry from "the major systemic defects identified in *Furman*" is remarkable since the *Furman* record contained no empirical evidence about the operation of any death penalty system.[109] In effect, Justice Powell applauded the anecdotal foundations of the *Furman* decision while disparaging the empirically documented racial disparities in the *McCleskey* record.

We also believe Justice Powell's additional argument that McCleskey's evidence assumed that what is "unexplained is invidious" is mistaken. There is no reference in the record to anything "unexplained," and McCleskey's counsel never asked the court to assume anything.[110]

Justice Powell addressed the statistical evidence that was actually in the record in a series of footnotes that first describe the methodological problems that led the district court to dismiss the study as fatally "flawed."[111] However, the opinion pointedly declines to rule on the validity of those findings and "assume[s] the study is valid statistically without reviewing the factual findings of the District Court," a move that left a cloud over the court's "validity" assumption.[112]

---

[108] Randall Kennedy, *McCleskey v. Kemp*: Race, Capital Punishment and the Supreme Court, 101 HARV. L. REV. 1388, 1415 (1988).

[109] As Justice White well noted, *supra* note 9, the factual judgments of the justices in *Furman* were based entirely on their own unquantified clinical assessments, developed from their decades long reading of capital and non-capital homicide appeals.

[110] At a statistical level, it is true of course that every multiple regression model has unexplained variance which normally is of no consequence to the substantive analysis. In *McCleskey*, the unexplained variance in the models existed *after* the substantive analysis had documented very strong race-of-victim disparities in the charging and sentencing outcomes. The analysis made no substantive assumptions about and offered no explanations for the unexplained variance and certainly did not attribute it to the influence of racial discrimination in the system.

[111] *McCleskey*, 481 U.S. at 288, n. 6. Justice Powell's opinion clearly supports author Edward Lazarus's statement that Powell's "basic opinion strategy was to avoid dealing with the substance of the Baldus study altogether. In this regard, he closely tracked the reasoning of the Eleventh Circuit, first claiming to 'assume the validity' of Baldus's study (though not without attacking it), then trying to show why the statistics were insufficient to support McCleskey's claims." Lazarus, *supra* note 73 at 205–06.

[112] The meaning of the Court's validity assumption was also drawn into question by its strong caveat that the assumption: "does not include the assumption that the study shows that racial considerations actually enter into any sentencing decisions in Georgia. Even a sophisticated multiple-regression analysis such as the Baldus study can only demonstrate a *risk* that the factor of race entered into some capital sentencing decisions and a necessarily lesser risk that race entered into any particular sentencing decision." *Id.* at 291, n. 7.

With respect to the risk that race was a factor in McCleskey's case, the opinion assumes that "absent far stronger proof," the outcome in his case is explained by the presence of two statutory aggravating circumstances.[113] The opinion ignored the fact that variables for these two aggravating circumstances were already included in numerous analyses that documented systemic race-of-victim effects. The opinion also ignored evidence of systemic race effects among 32 Fulton County cases that were similar to McCleskey's case, which supported an inference of discrimination.[114]

Justice Powell's denial and trivialization of racial harms was consistent with early Supreme Court cases in which the Court denied relief to African–American claimants.

A well known 19th century example is *Plessy v. Ferguson*, in which the Supreme Court held that state laws requiring racial segregation in public accommodations, such as passenger trains, did not violate the Equal Protection Clause of the Fourteenth Amendment so long as the separate facilities available to each race were equal.[115] The Court's rationale trivialized the harm to blacks by characterizing it as an "ordinary civil injury," as contrasted to a "political" injury, which would ostensibly implicate the Constitution.[116] The opinion also places on blacks responsibility for the stigma they suffered from racial segregation:

> We consider the underlying fallacy of the plaintiff's argument to consist in the assumption that the enforced separation of the two races stamps the colored race with a badge of inferiority. If this be so, it is not by reason of anything found in the act, but solely because the colored race chooses to put that construction upon it.[117]

---

[113] *Id.* at 296.

[114] Baldus et al., *supra* note 4 at 332–40, tbl. 59 at 335.

[115] 163 U.S. 537 (1896).

[116] In evaluating 19th century cases, it is important to recognize that in the late 19th century many jurists and legislators saw important distinctions between "civil" rights—which attached to the right to own property, contract, sue and testify in court, and be protected from physical violence—and social rights, which embraced such things as access to public accommodations (today viewed as civil rights). At that time, there was strong consensus about the importance of protecting civil rights but much less support for protecting the social rights of blacks, including, for example, the right to attend a privately owned theatre. Pamela Brandwein, *A Judicial Abandonment of Blacks? Rethinking the "State Action" Cases of the Waite Court*, 41 L. AND SOCY. REV. 343, 354–56 (2007). Justice Powell's distinction between race-of-defendant and race-of-victim discrimination noted above may reflect a similar distinction in his mind to the effect that race-of-defendant discrimination implicates important moral and constitutional interests that race-of-victim discrimination does not.

[117] *Plessy v. Ferguson*, 163 U.S. 537, 551 (1896).

3.   Assertions of the Inevitability and Ineradicabilty of the Alleged
Harms to Minorities

Justice Powell sought to minimize further the importance of the
documented race disparities in the Georgia system by reference to their
inevitability and ineradicability. By his words: "Apparent disparities in
sentencing are an inevitable part of our criminal justice system"[118] he
appeared to be assuming that the level of racial discrimination documented in our Georgia research is "inevitable" in all American death
penalty systems. His "inevitability" theme drew particular salience from
the memorandum noted above written by Justice Scalia to the other
members of the Court while they were reviewing Justice Powell's draft
opinion. In his memo, Justice Scalia stated: "Since it is my view that the
unconscious operation of irrational sympathies and antipathies, including racial, upon jury decisions and (hence) prosecutorial decisions is real,
acknowledged in the decisions of this Court and ineradicable, I cannot
honestly say that all I need is more proof."[119] In short, Justice Scalia
candidly embraced the theme of inevitability stated in Justice Powell's
opinion. And Scalia's "ineradicability" theory is clearly reflected in
Justice Powell's claim that short of the abolition of the Georgia statute
and overruling *Gregg v. Georgia*, any judicial remedy would be "uncon-
vincing," ineffective, and unworkable.[120]

Earlier Supreme Court opinions have also used inevitability and
ineradicability arguments to minimize the significance of racial discrimination legitimated by the Court. *Plessy v. Ferguson* developed such an
argument when it reasoned that "in the nature of things," the Fourteenth Amendment could not have intended to enforce "social as distinguished from political, equality, or a commingling of the two races upon
terms unsatisfactory to either."[121] The core of the *Plessy* rationale
emphasized the inevitability of the social gap between the races and the
incapacity of the law to change that reality.[122]

---

[118] *McCleskey*, 481 U.S. at 312. The opinion further explains that every system " 'has
its weaknesses and potential for misuse' " (quoting *Singer v. United States*, 380 U.S. 24
(1965)), and that there are " 'no perfect procedures' " (quoting *Zant v. Stephens*, 462 U.S.
862, 884 (1983)).

[119] Lazarus *supra* note 73 at 211.

[120] *McCleskey*, 481 U.S. at 319, n. 45. Thomas Ross, *The Rhetoric of Poverty: Their
Immorality, Our Helplessness,* 78 GEORGETOWN L. J. 1499, 1509 (1991) describes a similar
judicial approach to poverty in the United States. ("The central theme ... is helplessness.... First, poverty is said to be an inescapable societal tragedy that [judges] are
helpless to remedy" because the issue is "beyond the perimeters of their power and
jurisdiction." If the problem is not inevitable the legislature "is the body empowered to
solve it.").

[121] 163 U.S. 537, 544 (1896).

[122] Similarly in *Giles v. Harris*, 189 U.S. 475, 483, 488 (1903) *infra* note 126 and
accompanying text, Justice Holmes invoked judicial inability to protect Alabama voters

4. Assertions that the Federal Courts Are the Wrong Forum in Which to Seek Relief

Another move by Justice Powell to minimize the significance of the Court's denial of relief was to suggest that the federal courts were the wrong forum in which to obtain the type of relief the petitioner sought, stating that "McCleskey's arguments are best presented to the legislative bodies." Elected representatives, he wrote, are better " 'constituted to respond to the will and consequently the moral values of the people' "[123] and better able to "evaluate the results of statistical studies."[124] However, given the predictably meager results of a 20–year post-*McCleskey* legislative campaign,[125] it is hard to see how Justice Powell could have reasonably believed there was another forum in which meaningful relief might realistically be found.

There is also 19th century precedent for the "wrong forum" argument as a justification for the denial of racial claims, which says, in short, while we cannot help you, we can point you in a direction where you may find some relief. *Giles v. Harris*[126] dismissed with regret on jurisdictional grounds an action brought on behalf of 5,000 black residents of Montgomery, Alabama whose right to vote had been denied (in the words of Justice Holmes), by a "wholesale fraud" approved by the "white population" of the State through an amendment to the Alabama constitution.[127] Justice Holmes perceived a great injustice but painfully explained: "[R]elief from a great political wrong, if done, as alleged, by the people of the state and the state itself, must be given by them or by the legislative and political department of the government of the United States."[128]

5. The "Slippery slope:" Accepting McCleskey's Claim Will Upset the Status Quo in Other Areas of the Law

Justice Powell's final argument was to assure the reader that the denial of McCleskey's claims was in the best interest of law and the administration of the entire criminal justice system. Adoption of McCles-

---

from voting fraud: "The ... court has no constitutional power to control [the actions of the state] by any direct means. And if we leave the state out of consideration, the court has little practical power to deal with the people of the state in a body." *Id.* at 488.

[123] *McCleskey*, 481 U.S. at 319 (quoting from *Furman v. Georgia*, 408 U.S. 238, 383 (1972)).

[124] *Id.* (quoting from *Gregg v. Georgia*, 428 U.S. 153, 186 (1976)).

[125] *See infra* note 153 and accompanying text.

[126] 189 U.S. 475 (1903).

[127] *Id.* at 482–83.

[128] *Giles*, 189 U.S. at 488.

key's Eighth Amendment claim, he said, could disrupt the entire criminal justice system with discrimination claims:

> ... if we accepted McCleskey's claim that racial bias has impermissibly tainted the capital sentencing decision, we could soon be faced with similar claims as to other types of penalty. Moreover, the claim that his sentence rests on the irrelevant factor of race easily could be extended to apply to claims based on unexplained discrepancies that correlate to membership in other minority groups, and even to gender. Similarly, since McCleskey's claim relates to the race of his victim, other claims could apply with equally logical force to statistical disparities that correlate with the race or sex of other actors in the criminal justice system, such as defense attorneys or judges. Also, there is no logical reason that such a claim need be limited to racial or sexual bias. If arbitrary and capricious punishment is the touchstone under the Eighth Amendment, such a claim could—at least in theory—be based upon any arbitrary variable, such as the defendant's facial characteristics, or the physical attractiveness of the defendant or the victim, that some statistical study indicates may be influential in jury decision making. As these examples illustrate, there is no limiting principle to the type of challenge brought by McCleskey.

In his dissenting opinion, Justice Brennan characterized this statement as a fear of "too much justice."[129] More importantly, his dissenting opinion states three limiting principles that undercut the force of this "imaginary horrible." First, claims could be limited to capital cases under a "death is different" rationale.[130] Second, actionable claims could further be limited to allegations of racial discrimination, which command heightened scrutiny under the Constitution.[131] Third, relief could be limited to cases with compelling proof of discrimination.[132] Justice Powell cites mock jury studies that document disparities in criminal convictions and sentences based on characteristics beyond race and gender, such as the attractiveness of crime victims and criminal defendants, but they clearly fall short of the kind of compelling evidence of discrimination that would be required to support a legal claim. Moreover, to our knowledge, no one has ever based a claim of arbitrariness and discrimination on case characteristics beyond race and gender.

There is contemporaneous precedent for the use of the slippery slope argument as a justification for denying a race-based equal-protection

---

[129] *McCleskey*, 481 U.S. at 339.

[130] *Id*. at 339–40.

[131] *Id*. at 340–41.

[132] *Id*. at 341–42.

claim. As noted above, *Washington v. Davis* (1976) rejected the dispa-
rate-impact theory in equal protection claims against facially neutral
government regulations. Such a rule, said the Court, "would be far-
reaching and would raise serious questions about, and perhaps invalidate, a whole range of tax, welfare, public service, regulatory, and
licensing statutes that may be more burdensome to the poor and to the
average black than to the more affluent white."[133] We consider these
concerns equally unpersuasive.

D.   The Dissenting Opinions

The three dissenting opinions, which rest on two different theories
of liability, provide a good overview of how the law might have evolved if
Justice Powell had voted differently.[134]

1.   Justice Brennan

Justice Brennan's dissenting opinion concentrated on McCleskey's
Eighth Amendment claim. His point of departure was that McCleskey's
"challenge to the Georgia system is not speculative or theoretical; it is
empirical."[135] He believed that "[c]lose analysis of the Baldus study ...
in light of both statistical principles and human experience, reveals that
the risk that race influenced McCleskey's sentence is intolerable by any
imaginable standard."[136] In this regard, he relied on evidence of both
unadjusted disparities which did not control for offender culpability, and
adjusted disparities that did.[137] Brennan concluded that the "statistical
evidence ... relentlessly documents the risk that McCleskey's sentence
was influenced by racial considerations."[138] His study of the history of
Georgia's use of the death penalty convinced him that "McCleskey's
claim is not a fanciful product of mere statistical artifice."[139] He further
concluded that the risk of discrimination in his case is "precisely the

---

[133] *Washington v. Davis*, 426 U.S. 229, 248 (1976).

[134] In 1991, after his retirement from the bench, Justice Powell identified *McCleskey* as
one of two cases in which he regretted his vote. However, when asked if he accepted
McCleskey's statistical argument, he demurred and said merely that he regretted that he
did not, like Justices Brennan and Marshall, vote to abolish capital punishment under all
circumstances. Jeffries, *supra* note 101 at 451–52. Why, to make this point, he selected
McCleskey out of all of the other death sentenced cases he voted to affirm is unknown.

[135] *McCleskey*, 481 U.S. at 338.

[136] *Id*. at 325.

[137] *Id*. at 325–28.

[138] *Id*. at 328. The "relentlessly documents" standard was later adopted by the New
Jersey Supreme Court as the standard it would use to evaluate its system for evidence of
systemic racial discrimination. Proportionality Review II, 757 A.2d 168, 176 (N.J. 2000).

[139] *Id*. at 329.

type of risk of irrationality in sentencing that we have consistently condemned in our Eighth Amendment jurisprudence."[140]

He believed that McCleskey's evidence should lead to the same outcome as a facially discriminatory statute—invalidation of the statute and reversal of all death sentences imposed under it, regardless of the race of the victim or defendant just as in *Furman v. Georgia.*

2. Justice Blackmun

Justice Blackmun's dissenting opinion focused on McCleskey's Equal Protection claim. Perhaps this choice was motivated in part by his role 20 years earlier in *Maxwell v. Bishop* (1968).[141] As a judge on the Eighth Circuit Court of Appeals, he rejected Maxwell's statistical claim of racial discrimination in the application of the death penalty under Arkansas' rape statute that was based on an empirical study by sociologist Marvin Wolfgang.

Justice Blackmun's bottom line in *McCleskey* was that the historical record, the process of decision making in the Fulton County prosecutor's office, the evidence of systemic discrimination statewide and in Fulton County, and the failure of the state to explain the racial disparities in Fulton County or to establish that "legitimate racially neutral criteria and procedures yielded this racially skewed result" supported an "inference that racial factors entered into the decision-making process that yielded McCleskey's death sentence." This finding, he concluded, established "a constitutionally intolerable level of racially based discrimination leading to the imposition of his death sentence."[142]

To reach this decision Justice Blackmun applied a hybrid model of proof, based on *Castaneda v. Partida* and *Batson v. Kentucky*, that most clearly resembles the evidentiary framework used in class action employment-discrimination cases described in Part II.[143]

Blackmun added that he did not believe the "acceptance of McCleskey's claim would eliminate capital punishment in Georgia." He agreed with Justice Stevens that the narrowing of death-eligible cases to those most aggravated cases in which the risk of racial discrimination is low

---

[140] *Id.* at 321.

[141] *Maxwell v. Bishop,* 398 F.2d 138 (8th Cir. 1968). *See supra* note 42. In *McCleskey,* 481 U.S. at 354, n. 7, Justice Blackmun compares and contrasts the two studies as part of his explanation of why he had confidence in the Baldus study.

[142] *McCleskey,* 481 U.S. at 345 & 359.

[143] *Id.* at 360–61. See also *supra* note 19 and accompanying text (*Castaneda*) and note 22 (*Batson*). In a 2005 Ninth Circuit Court of Appeals case, *Belmontes v. Brown,* 414 F.3d 1094 (9th Cir. 2005), a federal district court applied this model and ruled that a prior murder in a defendant's case explained on non-racial grounds why the state sought a death sentence against a black defendant.

"is not too high a price to pay for a death penalty system that does not discriminate on the basis of race."[144] He also recommended the adoption of explicit guidelines for assistant district attorneys to promote consistency.[145]

3. Justice Stevens

Justice Stevens agreed with Justice Brennan that the evidence established an unconstitutional risk of race discrimination in McCleskey's case. "This sort of disparity is constitutionally intolerable. It flagrantly violates the Court's prior 'insistence that capital punishment be imposed fairly, and with reasonable consistency, or not at all.'"[146] However, like Justice Blackmun, he believed that death eligibility could be narrowed to a point that race effects could be eliminated or sufficiently reduced and thereby meet the requirements of the Eighth Amendment:

> The Court's decision appears to be based on a fear that the acceptance of McCleskey's claim would sound the death knell for capital punishment in Georgia. If society were indeed forced to choose between a racially discriminatory death penalty (one that provides heightened protection against murder "for whites only") and no death penalty at all, the choice mandated by the Constitution would be plain. ... But the Court's fear is unfounded. One of the lessons of the Baldus study is that there exist certain categories of extremely serious crimes for which prosecutors consistently seek, and juries consistently impose the death penalty without regard to the race of the victim or the race of the offender. If Georgia were to narrow the class of death-eligible defendants to those categories, the danger of arbitrary and discriminatory imposition of the death penalty would be significantly decreased, if not eradicated. As Justice Brennan has demonstrated in his dissenting opinion, such a restructuring of the sentencing scheme is surely not too high a price to pay.[147]

---

[144] *McCleskey*, 481 U.S. at 365.

[145] *Id*. It is assumed in Justice Blackmun's opinion that until a state like Georgia narrows its death-eligible defendants to the worst of the worst, death sentenced defendants can continue to raise *prima facie* claims like McCleskey's. Blackmun's guidelines recommendation resonated with the New Jersey Supreme Court, which made similar suggestions to its state prosecutors before the New Jersey legislature abolished capital punishment in 2007.

[146] *McCleskey*, 481 U.S. at 366–67 (quoting *Eddings v. Oklahoma*, 455 U.S. 104, 112 (1982)).

[147] *Id*. at 367. *See generally,* James S. Liebman, *Slow Dancing with Death: The Supreme Court and Capital Punishment, 1963–2006*, 107 COLUM.L.REV. 1, 86 & n. 434 (2007). ("[B]y requiring super aggravation ... the Court could have reduced the costs of the death penalty without ending its use") and James S. Liebman and Lawrence C.

Part VI.   Aftermath

Justice Powell's *McCleskey* decision did not end the matter in the federal courts. There was, in fact, *McCleskey* II, a 1991 6–3 Supreme Court decision that denied McCleskey's claim for relief in his second, "successor," federal habeas-corpus petition.[148] The petition was based on the 1987 discovery by McCleskey's counsel of Offie Evans's status as a government agent when in McCleskey's guilt trial Evans testified that McCleskey had admitted to him from an adjoining jail cell that he was the triggerman in the furniture store robbery/murder. McCleskey had long believed that Evans had been planted in the cell next to him because Evans falsely told him that he was a relative of one of the co-perpetrators in the robber/murder.

Evans' status as a government agent was important because proof of such status would provide the ground for a new trial under *Massiah v. United States*.[149] With that in mind, counsel raised a *Massiah* claim in McCleskey's first state habeas-corpus petition. However, the claim was dismissed by the state courts because it was denied by the state and McCleskey's counsel had no evidence with which to refute the denial. When counsel filed McCleskey's first federal habeas corpus claim following the dismissal of all of his state habeas claims, they did not plead the *Massiah* claim again because they had no evidence on the issue beyond what had been presented without success in the state post-conviction proceeding.

However, within months of the first McCleskey decision, McCleskey's counsel fortuitously obtained from the Atlanta police department a 21–page statement signed by Evans which reported his jail house conversations with McCleskey, and for the first time, provided compelling evidence that he had been planted in the cell next to McCleskey. On the basis of this newly discovered evidence, counsel filed a second federal habeas-corpus petition, and Judge Forrester, after a hearing in which the jailer confirmed McCleskey's original suspicions, ordered a new trial.

However, McCleskey never saw a second trial because the Supreme Court ruled that the filing of his second habeas-petition constituted an "abuse of the writ" because he had not filed the *Massiah* claim in his first federal habeas-petition and could not show good "cause" for his

---

Marshall, *Less is Better: Justice Stevens and the Narrowed Death Penalty*, 74 FORDHAM L.REV. 1607, 1621–23, 1632–38, 1673–75 (2006). ("A critical message of Justice Stevens' death penalty jurisprudence is that narrowing death eligibility is an important incremental step that remains open to the states and the Court. Those committed to enhancing the fairness and accuracy of the capital justice system should take this lesson to heart.")

[148] *McCleskey v. Zant*, 499 U.S. 467 (1991).

[149] 377 U.S. 201 (1964) (Evans' failure to reveal his status as a government agent would have violated McCleskey's Sixth Amendment right to counsel).

failure to do so. *McCleskey* II held that what McCleskey knew when he filed his first state-habeas petition put him "on notice to pursue the *Messiah* claim in his first federal habeas petition," even though he knew it would likely fail in federal court for the same reasons it had failed in the state habeas-proceeding.[150] The court further ruled that the reason given for his failure to raise the claim in the first habeas proceeding did not satisfy the standard for "cause" that must be satisfied to overcome the presumption that his second habeas petition constituted an "abuse of the writ."

McCleskey next sought clemency from the Georgia Board of Pardons and Paroles. When that petition failed, he returned to the state and federal courts to challenge the clemency denial.[151] A flurry of appeals to state and federal courts continued after the time scheduled for his execution, 7:00 pm September 24, 1991, which resulted in one stay of execution after he had been strapped into the electric chair. Following two 6–3 Supreme Court refusals to stay the execution, at approximately 10:00 pm and 3:00 am the next day, after the Justices had been polled by telephone, McCleskey was pronounced dead at 3:13 am September 25, 1991.[152]

Because *McCleskey* I, specifically relegated the issue of racial discrimination in the administration of capital punishment to the "legislative bodies," several legislatures took it up. In the late 1980s and early 1990s, Congress considered a Racial Justice Act that would have overruled *McCleskey* and given federal courts the power to hear claims of racial discrimination arising in state and federal courts. However, since *McCleskey*, only one state legislature, Kentucky, has responded—with a limited measure that relates only to prosecutorial decision making.[153]

Post–*McCleskey* claims for relief have also been presented to state and federal courts, but efforts in both these forums have failed largely because of *McCleskey*'s uncompromising rhetoric.[154] However, one state

---

[150] *McCleskey v. Zant*, 499 U.S. at 498. ("Omission of the claim will not be excused merely because evidence discovered later might also have supported or strengthened the claim.")

[151] The theory was that the Board ignored "statements from two jurors that information improperly withheld at trial tainted their sentence, and that they no longer supported an execution." Peter Applebome, *Georgia Inmate is Executed After "Chaotic" Legal Move*, THE NEW YORK TIMES, September 26, 1991.

[152] *Id.*

[153] *See* Olatunde C. A. Johnson, *Legislating Racial Fairness in Criminal Justice*, 39 COL. HUM. RTS. L. REV. 233 (2007).

[154] See generally, John H. Blume, Theodore Eisenberg, Sheri Lynn Johnson, *Post–McCleskey Racial Discrimination Claims in Capital Cases*, 83 CORNELL L. REV. 1771, 1803–07 (1998) (describing efforts to carve out a county-wide selective prosecution exception to

court, the New Jersey Supreme Court, took the issue seriously. Acting under the authority of the New Jersey Constitution, it created a system of comparative proportionality review designed to limit death sentencing to the most aggravated cases, which appears to have reduced the impact of race in the system before the New Jersey legislature abolished capital punishment in 2007.[155] The New Jersey court also considered empirically based claims of race discrimination in the system but denied relief in all of them because the level of proof of systemic racial discrimination did not rise to the level documented in *McCleskey*. The remaining state supreme courts that have heard such claims have dodged the issue, applied *McCleskey*, or imposed unattainable burdens of proof under state law. Thus, for the foreseeable future, *McCleskey* has effectively legitimated racial discrimination in the administration of the death penalty by placing it beyond the reach of the courts. And as noted earlier, the logic of the opinion does the same thing for the entire criminal justice system.

The *McCleskey* story is part of a larger tale well told elsewhere of the irony that efforts to cleanse the death penalty of arbitrariness and discrimination have "contribute[d] substantially to the stabilization and perpetuation of capital punishment as a social practice,"[156] with arbitrariness and discrimination still in place and beyond the reach of the law.

McCleskey); Anthony G. Amsterdam, "Opening Remarks": to *Symposium on Pursuing Racial Fairness in Criminal Justice: Twenty Years After McCleskey v. Kemp*, 39 COLUM. HUM. RTS. L. REV. 34 (2007) (recommending a supplementation of statewide proportionality studies with county level studies focusing on qualitative evidence of discriminatory attitudes on the part of prosecutors and law enforcement officials); Sheri Lynn Johnson, *Litigating For Racial Fairness After* McCleskey v. Kemp, 39 COLUM. HUM. RTS. L. REV. 178 (2007) (discussing three lessons learned from litigation efforts since *McCleskey*–think small, if you can't change how people decide, change who decides, and think small again.) For other post-*McCleskey* strategies, see Mirian S. Gohara, *Commentary, Sounding The Echoes of Racial Injustice Beyond The Death Chamber: Proposed Strategies for Moving Past* McCleskey, 39 COLUM. HUM. RTS. L. REV. 124 (2007) and Angela J. Davis, *Racial Fairness in the Criminal Justice System: The Role of the Prosecutor*, 39 COLUM. HUM. RTS. L. REV. 202 (2007); David McCord, *Lightning Still Strikes*, 71 BROOK. L. REV. 797 (2005).

[155] *See* David C. Baldus, George Woodworth, and Catherine M. Grosso, *Race and Proportionality Since McCleskey v. Kemp (1987): Different Actors with Mixed Strategies of Denial and Avoidance*, 39 COL. HUM. RTS. L. REV. 143 (2007) and Alex Lesman, *State Responses to the Specter of Racial Discrimination in Capital Proceedings: The Kentucky Racial Justice Act and the New Jersey Supreme Court's Proportionality Review Project*, 13 J.L. & POL'Y 359 (2005).

[156] Carol S. Steiker and Jordan M. Steiker, *Sober Second Thoughts: Reflections on Two Decades of Constitutional Regulation of Capital Punishment*, 109 HARV. L. REV. 355, 438 (1995).

*

7

Jordan M. Steiker*

Penry v. Lynaugh: The Hazards of Predicting the Future

I. Introduction

Over the past thirty years since executions resumed in this country, Texas has carried out over 36% of the executions nationwide.[1] This figure is surprising in itself, given that 36 states currently authorize capital punishment and Texas has accounted for less than 18% of the nation's death-sentenced inmates.[2] Even more surprising is that Texas has managed to lead the country in executions despite the fact that the death penalty statute it had in place for the first half of this period had the most serious constitutional difficulties of any of the state capital statutes conditionally approved by the U.S. Supreme Court in 1976.

The story of Johnny Paul Penry, whose case brought into focus the inadequacy of the former Texas statute, helps explain how Texas achieved the dubious distinction of executing the most inmates under the worst procedures. But the story of Penry provides a broader perspective on the recent American experience with capital punishment. The story stretches from the beginning of the modern era of capital punishment in the United States to the present. It offers an extraordinary window into the workings of a variety of institutional actors over that period, including the abolitionist lawyers who sought to invalidate the Texas statute in 1976, the small-town prosecutors who relentlessly

* I would like to thank Scot Powe, Larry Sager, and John Wright for their helpful comments and Meghan Shapiro for her tireless research.

[1] See Death Penalty Information Center, Executions by State and Region Since 1976, at www.deathpenaltyinfo.org/article.php?scid=8&did=186.

[2] See Death Penalty Information Center, Death Sentences in the United States From 1977 to 2006, at www.deathpenaltyinfo.org/article.php?scid=9&did=847.

pursued Penry's execution, and the various courts that struggled to make sense of the Supreme Court's ephemeral Eighth Amendment jurisprudence. The story illustrates the difficulty of translating lofty constitutional principles into concrete protections, especially in the face of determined resistance, and the unpredictable and often surprising consequences of constitutional litigation in the capital context.

Penry's story begins with extraordinary brutality, both in his crime and in his childhood, which led to his first case before the U.S. Supreme Court, *Penry v. Lynaugh* (*"Penry I"*)[3], in 1989. It continues with his retrial, new death sentence, and extensive appeals in state and federal court that culminated in an execution date in 2000. It is followed by a last minute reprieve and yet another case in the U.S. Supreme Court, *Penry v. Johnson* (*Penry II*)[4], in which his death sentence was again reversed based on essentially the same error that required reversal of his first sentence. Penry's success in his second Supreme Court case—twelve years after his first reversal—set in motion a reconsideration of the many state and federal decisions that had withered the protections afforded by the first *Penry* decision. Over the next several years, from 2001 to the present, the U.S. Supreme Court, despite its dwindling docket, heard an astonishing number of Texas death cases addressing the adequacy of the former Texas statute—a statute that had been repealed in 1991. In each of the five cases, the Court ruled that the Texas statute unconstitutionally precluded juror consideration of the defendant's mitigating evidence. The Court's decisions revealed that the old Texas statute was inadequate for the vast majority of defendants who had been sentenced to death under its terms. But by 2008, only a handful of the defendants sentenced under the old Texas scheme remained on death row. The scores of other inmates who had been condemned under that statute had already been executed, and thus the Court's recent decisions constitute a belated acknowledgement that a significant number of those executed in Texas over the past twenty-five years were unfairly and unconstitutionally condemned. In this respect, the *Penry* story is a story of the failure of the American death penalty in the modern era, with a troubling level of error—not just among those death-*sentenced* but among those actually *executed*—in the execution capital of the country. Penry's two victories in the U.S. Supreme Court regarding the defects in the Texas sentencing scheme are thus overshadowed by the fact that so many other inmates with *"Penry"* error were executed notwithstanding those decisions.

Penry's victories are overshadowed in another sense as well. In addition to his claim that the Texas statute did not allow jurors to

---

[3] 492 U.S. 302 (1989).

[4] 532 U.S. 782 (2001).

consider his extensive mitigating evidence, Penry also argued that he should be exempt from the death penalty entirely because of his mental retardation. At the time of his trial, no state had exempted persons with mental retardation from the death penalty, and it is fair to say that the states had simply not considered the issue as they enacted new death penalty statutes in the wake of *Furman v. Georgia*.[5] But as Penry's case worked its way through his appeals, the country's attention was captured by the execution in 1986 of Jerome Bowden, an inmate with mental retardation in Georgia. Two years later, the spectacle caused Georgia to become the first state to ban the execution of persons with mental retardation, though other states did not act quickly to join Georgia's ban. When Penry's case arrived at the Supreme Court in 1988, there was little legislative support for his claim that the execution of persons with mental retardation violated prevailing standards of decency. Although professional opinion and polling data revealed significant opposition to the practice, the Court's methodology—which emphasized state legislation as a window to current values—seemed inhospitable to Penry's claim. For that reason, Penry's own brief and oral argument focused almost entirely on his claim about the inadequacy of the Texas statute.

Penry's case, though, received extraordinary world-wide attention on the mental retardation issue because it highlighted the distance between the Texas death penalty and national and international norms. *Penry* became a barometer of just how far our criminal justice practices diverged from other Western democracies, as Texas sought to defend not only the right to execute offenders, but to execute offenders who fell within the bottom two-to-three percent of adult intellectual functioning. When Penry lost on this claim (by a narrow 5–4 margin), *Penry* symbolized the deregulation of the American death penalty. The popular press barely noted that Penry's death sentence had in fact been overturned because of defects in the Texas sentencing procedure and instead emphasized that the American death penalty, which seemed on the route to abolition just two decades earlier, now seemed both entrenched and invulnerable to significant legal challenge.

The irony of Penry's case is that the issue on which he "won" did not significantly impede Texas' implementation of the death penalty because the victory was undermined by subsequent retrenchment by the state and federal courts. Notwithstanding its defective statute, Texas emerged as the leading executing state and as the symbol of the ascendant American death penalty. But the issue on which he lost—and which was much more salient both politically and culturally—ultimately contributed to an unprecedented flurry of legislative attention to a death

---

[5] 408 U.S. 238 (1972).

penalty practice since the death penalty resumed in 1976. In the wake of *Penry I*, sixteen more states banned the execution of persons with mental retardation, and the Supreme Court revisited the proportionality claim just thirteen years later in *Atkins v. Virginia*.[6] In that opinion, the Court not only found the execution of persons with mental retardation to constitute excessive punishment, but also adopted a new proportionality methodology which is far more hospitable to judicial regulation of the death penalty. *Atkins* paved the way for the Court's revisiting and reversal of its decision upholding the execution of juveniles,[7] and the Court has planted the seeds for further constitutional regulation, perhaps even abolition, of capital punishment.

The strange course of *Penry* reveals that Supreme Court decisions are often the beginning rather than the end of a conversation. Defeats can become victories if they galvanize public attention and concern, and victories can become defeats if they engender resistance and the Court is unable or unwilling to police its mandate. As suggested above, Penry's story reflects both of these possibilities: the defeat of his proportionality claim was later reversed, while his first victory was rendered a virtual nullity for almost two decades as the state and federal courts refused to find the statute inadequate for any inmates other than Penry himself. But the story of victories becoming defeats was repeated in the course of Penry's own litigation. The victory in *Atkins*—with its constitutional prohibition against executing persons with mental retardation—has been undermined for many defendants because states have adopted difficult procedural barriers to the enforcement of that right.[8] At Penry's third punishment-phase trial, conducted in 2002, the jury was asked whether Penry had mental retardation only after it had heard all of the gruesome details of his offense and understood that a finding of mental retardation precluded the imposition of the death penalty. The jury found that Penry did not have mental retardation, and sentenced him to death. In yet another irony, Penry's sentence was invalidated not because the Texas Court of Criminal Appeals found him ineligible for the punishment, but because it concluded that the jury instructions did not adequately ensure that Penry's jury could consider as mitigating his mental impairment short of mental retardation. Penry thus won on yet another version of a *"Penry"* claim. Penry's three victories on *Penry* claims mean that he accounts for about one-fifth of all such reversals over the past eighteen

---

6 536 U.S. 304, 314–15 (2002) (discussing state legislative reform post-*Penry*).

7 Roper v. Simmons, 543 U.S. 551 (2005).

8 *See, e.g.,* Carol S. Steiker & Jordan M. Steiker, Atkins v. Virginia: *Lessons from Substance and Procedure in the Constitutional Regulation of Capital Punishment*, 57 DePaul L. Rev. 501 (2008).

years. Penry has since entered into a plea agreement to avoid a fourth punishment trial, and will likely spend the rest of his days in prison.

II. The Crime and the Trial

At about 10 a.m. on October 25, 1979, Cindy Gail Peters received a phone call from her close friend Pamela Moseley Carpenter.[9] Carpenter, twenty-two, lived in Livingston, a small town in East Texas. Livingston is something of a recreational town, because of its 93,000 acre Lake Livingston, but in most respects it is similar to many other close-knit, lightly-populated towns in East Texas. Carpenter told Peters, "This is Pam. I've been stabbed and raped. Mother's at the church. Help me and hurry." Carpenter, who had moved to Livingston from Houston in part to escape the dangers of a big city, had been sewing children's Halloween costumes when she was attacked that morning. She died at the hospital at about noon.

Before she died, Carpenter was able to give a description of her assailant—a young, short, thin white male—and when the description was sent over the police radio, Billy Ray Nelson, a deputy sheriff, thought of Penry. Penry had recently been released on parole from a neighboring Texas penitentiary in Huntsville after serving time for rape. Within hours of the offense, Nelson located Penry, who denied any knowledge of the rape or assault. Penry went with Nelson to the police station, where the police noticed blood on his shirt. Penry was then taken to the crime scene, though he was not formally placed under arrest. While several officers examined the crime scene, Penry sat in the back of the police car. When Nelson came back to the car, Penry confessed to the crime. The officers took Penry into Carpenter's house to "re-enact" the crime. By 2:45 that day, Penry appeared before a magistrate and was charged with capital murder.

By 6:45 that night, Penry, who could neither read nor write, had signed a typed, four-page, single-spaced confession. The confession began with legal boilerplate, using words strikingly beyond Penry's vocabulary ("I do hereby freely and voluntarily, without being induced by any compulsion, threats, promises or persuasion, make the following statement."). Penry then recounted his prior history of sexual assaults ("It was about three years ago when I first tried to rape someone."). During his third attempted rape, in which he assaulted a woman in his car, the car got "stuck." Penry then turned himself in to two "guys who came by" because "I could tell [the victim] was scared and was going to tell the police so I beat her to it and told the police myself." That offense resulted in a five year sentence. After he was released on parole two

---

[9] These facts, and the descriptions of Penry's retrials, come primarily from the trial transcripts of the proceedings.

years into his sentence, Penry again looked for potential victims. He first encountered Carpenter when he helped deliver appliances to her home. As he thought about her more, he chose to revisit her on a pretext. He came to Carpenter's home on the morning of October 25, asking if the stove he had helped fix was working. He then forced his way into her home and grabbed her while holding a knife. Carpenter struggled and knocked the knife out of Penry's hand. He slapped her several times and she fought back with a pair of scissors. He slapped her, raped her, and plunged the scissors she had used against him into her chest. Just before doing so, Penry told Carpenter he was going to kill her, that he "hated to," but "thought she would squeal" on him.

The confession recounts that Penry's father, in addition to the police, had read Penry his rights two or three times and explained them to him. According to the confession, after reading Penry his rights, his father asked Penry whether he had committed the crime, and left angrily after Penry answered affirmatively. Toward the end of his confession, Penry states that "I cannot read or write but this statement was read to me and it is the truth to the best of my knowledge. I can understand things, I just cannot read or write." At the very end of the typed statement, there is one additional, hand-written line: "I think I need some punishment for this and help."

The immediate reaction to Carpenter's killing was outrage over Penry's parole. The public attention was increased by the fact that Carpenter's brother—Mark Moseley—was a national celebrity, a professional football player who would go on to become the only place-kicker ever to win the NFL's most valuable player award. In response to press inquiries right after the crime, Joe Price, the attorney in the Polk County District Attorney's office who went on to prosecute Penry three times, acknowledged Penry's criminal history of three prior assaults. When asked how Penry could be released so soon after those offenses, Price explained: "Why was he on the streets? Well, we go to the extreme to protect a defendant's rights. Sometimes you protect them so much, something like this case happens."[10] Price also responded to the immediate "rumors" that Penry had mental retardation, stating that although he wasn't a doctor, he could say that he had talked to Penry and that Penry had no trouble communicating.

About two weeks after the crime, Penry was arraigned. His court-appointed lawyer, John Wright, was a thirty-year old civil lawyer without much criminal experience and no capital experience whatsoever. In response to the trial judge's first question—"how do you plead?"—Penry stated, "Guilty. No—I plead not guilty." Penry was later asked whether

---

[10] Polk County Enterprise, "Woman stabbed, no bond for suspect," Oct. 28, 1979, p. A1.

he had ever been confined to a mental institution, but Penry indicated that he didn't understand the question. The trial judge expressed an interest in expediting the trial date, but in light of Penry's prior institutionalizations, he ordered a competency evaluation in anticipation of a competency proceeding. Under Texas law, a jury, not a judge, was to determine whether Penry had a sufficient understanding of the proceedings to stand trial for capital murder.

The subsequent competency trial gave ample evidence of Penry's limited intelligence. Direct examination revealed that Penry did not know the day of the week or the current year. When asked whether he knew the days of the week, he stated that he knew "a few." He could not name all of the months of the year, and did not know how many hours are in a day. He could not count to eleven or add three to nine. He could not spell "bird" or "fun" or recite the alphabet. He indicated that, at the age of 23, he believed in Santa Claus. When asked about the twelve people behind the bench—the separate jury empanelled solely for the issue of his competency—he stated that they were the "grand jury." When asked if he knew what they were there for, he stated he didn't know, but when asked what they wanted to do, he said "kill me."

The rest of the competency hearing involved a typical battle of experts. On the defense side, Dr. Jerome Brown, a clinical psychologist who had examined Penry, testified that Penry had organic brain damage. Through Brown, the defense introduced detailed medical records and psychological evaluations of Penry, dating from his prior psychiatric hospitalizations as well as his placement at the Mexia State School, a school for persons with mental retardation. Penry's intelligence tests had produced full scale IQ scores of 50, 51, 56, and 63. Penry had also been diagnosed as psychotic, based on his fear of victimization, which Brown attributed in part to his history of being victimized. Brown also testified that Penry's records revealed very low functioning, with an inability to function independently in the community or in gainful employment. During cross-examination, Price introduced via Brown records documenting Penry's aggressive, anti-social behavior during his various institutionalizations. Penry apparently had assaulted other patients. Price pressed Brown about Penry's capacity to understand and assist his attorneys in his defense, and Brown emphasized Penry's inability to discuss events rationally and consistently. According to Brown, Penry shared a trait common among those with very low intelligence—an eagerness to please and a desire to appear to understand even when confused; in this respect, Brown insisted that Penry's simple "yes" answers to questions about whether he understood the purpose of the trial and the roles of the defense and prosecution lawyers should not be accepted at face value. Brown asserted that Penry's deficits caused him to have the intellectual knowledge and abilities of a 6½ year-old child; Brown measured his social maturity as that of a 9– or 10–year-old.

The state's experts, two psychiatrists, downplayed Penry's mental impairments, refusing to acknowledge that Penry's IQ scores placed him near the very bottom the population. One of the state's experts. Dr. Felix Peebles, Jr., sought to explain away Penry's inability to measure time on the ground that "it does not make a whole lot of difference whether or not it is June or July or morning or afternoon" for a person who doesn't have a job. Peebles also committed a cardinal sin in a competency hearing—he revealed to the jury, during direct examination by the prosecutor, that Penry's crime was a rape-murder and that Penry had confessed his involvement to Peebles. Under Texas law, the jury charged with the competency issue is not to hear evidence of the offense itself because of its obvious potential prejudicial impact. The trial judge sustained the defense objection to the testimony but denied a motion for a mistrial. The jury found Penry competent to stand trial.

The issue of Penry's mental capacity would pervade the rest of the proceedings. Penry sought to exclude his confession in part based on his inability to waive his right to an attorney. Penry also raised the insanity defense, claiming his impairments prevented him from understanding the wrongfulness of his behavior or conforming his conduct to the law. Penry's trial occurred just before Texas, like many jurisdictions, eliminated the volitional prong of the insanity test (inability to conform conduct) in response to John Hinckley's acquittal by reason of insanity after his attempted assassination of President Reagan. But the tests for establishing involuntariness and insanity were extremely demanding, and Penry's confession was admitted and his insanity defense rejected by the jury.

As in most capital murder trials in Texas during the early 1980s, the defense devoted virtually all of its efforts to the guilt-innocence phase of the trial. Indeed, the trial court had limited the defense investigation budget to a total of $300. The defense presented much the same expert testimony that it had put before the competency jury—evidence that Penry had not finished the first grade, that he had been hospitalized for psychiatric problems, and that he had been institutionalized in a state school for persons with mental retardation. His mother, sister, and aunt also testified to his limitations, including testimony regarding his aunt's year-long struggle to teach Penry how to print his name. During the course of this family testimony, evidence emerged that Penry had been severely disciplined as a child, including beatings over his head with a belt at the hands of his mother. Penry had also routinely been locked in his room for lengthy periods of time without access to a toilet. The apparent goal of this testimony was not to emphasize Penry's mistreatment but to illustrate his inability to learn and adjust his behavior.

After the jury rejected Penry's insanity defense, the case moved to
the punishment phase, with the state emphasizing Penry's previous
assaults and criminal record. The state also used the same experts that
had affirmed Penry's competence and sanity to testify to Penry's likely
dangerousness. Texas' death penalty—virtually unique among the statutes passed in the wake of *Furman*—required the state to prove a
defendant's dangerousness as a prerequisite to obtaining a death sentence. Unlike the vast majority of the post-*Furman* statutes that had
been endorsed by the Court, the Texas statute did not explicitly ask
jurors whether the defendant should live or die, or whether aggravating
circumstances outweighed mitigating circumstances. Instead, the Texas
statute required a verdict form that contained only three possible questions: whether the defendant acted deliberately, whether the defendant
constituted a future danger to society, and whether, if the victim had
provoked the defendant, the defendant had acted unreasonably.[11]

The defense's punishment-phase case was extraordinarily brief, oc-
cupying less than fifteen pages of the trial transcript. Penry's uncle was
called as a rebuttal witness to undermine the state's case concerning an
unadjudicated sexual assault, stating that Penry hadn't been out of his
sight at the time of the alleged offense. The defense also offered the
testimony of Frank Aragon, a prison security officer who preached on
weekends as a Baptist minister. He indicated that he regarded Penry as
not beyond redemption, though he added his view that no one was
beyond redemption. The state's sole question on cross-examination was
whether Penry's victim, Pam Carpenter, was beyond redemption, to
which Aragon replied, "no, sir."

The punishment-phase closing arguments revealed the underlying
constitutional problem regarding the Texas statute. From the state's
perspective, the jury's task was quite simple and straightforward: if the
evidence established affirmative answers to the three special issues, the
jury's task was done. There was no question that invited broader
reflection on whether Penry deserved to die. So the first prosecutor
quickly ran through the special issues, arguing that Penry's confession
reflected his deliberate choice to kill his victim, that Penry's history of
assaults as well as the state's psychiatric testimony showed a "very
strong probability" of Penry's future dangerousness, and that Penry's

---

[11] Former Tex. Code Crim. Proc. Ann., Art. 37.071(b) (Vernon 1981 and Supp. 1989)
provided the following three "special issues": "(1) Whether the conduct of the defendant
that caused the death of the deceased was committed deliberately and with the reasonable
expectation that the death of the deceased or another would result; (2) whether there is a
probability that the defendant would commit criminal acts of violence that would constitute a continuing threat to society; and (3) if raised by the evidence, whether the conduct of
the defendant in killing the deceased was unreasonable in response to the provocation, if
any, by the deceased."

decision to kill was not provoked by Carpenter but instead rooted in his desire not to get caught.

The defense, on the other hand, had very little it could say about these issues, because the best reason for withholding a death sentence—Penry's substantial and well-documented mental impairment—had nothing to do with the inquiries of the special issues. If anything, Penry's inability to learn from his mistakes—which was central to Penry's claim of insanity—virtually proved the state's case on future dangerousness. As a result, the defense closing arguments appeared to be non-sequiters—interesting observations unconnected to what the jury would actually decide. Wright, the lead defense attorney, spoke about the unequal application of the death penalty, and suggested in a self-deprecating way that Penry shouldn't be punished for Wright's poor representation ("I am very concerned with my own inadequacy in handling this case."). He also claimed that the death penalty wasn't a deterrent, especially given that it was administered privately, behind prison doors. Wright lamely sought to claim that Penry had not acted "deliberately," within the meaning of the first special issue, because only hardened criminals, like John Wayne Gacy, who killed many victims over many years, truly satisfied that standard. He argued that Penry's "mental condition and mental state," as well as his "environment," supported a life sentence, but he did not and could not explain how any of those facts justified a "no" answer to the special issues. He concluded by asking the jurors what Jesus Christ would do if seated in their chairs.

Wright's co-counsel likewise emphasized Penry's "mental affliction," telling the jurors that, notwithstanding their rejection of Penry's insanity defense, they all must have recognized "that there is something definitely wrong, basically, with this boy." But, like Wright, he was unable to make a dent against the state's case regarding the special issues and concluded with this final appeal: "I don't think [death] would be a proper verdict in this case, but that is with your conscience."

The state seized on the amorphous appeals of Penry's lawyers that had reminded the jury about Penry's deficits but could not find any persuasive way of connecting them to the special issues. In the last argument to the jury, the state emphasized that the jury should focus only on the instructions they were given and not venture beyond the inquiries of the special issues:

> You've all taken an oath to follow the law and you know what the law is. . . . You've all said you want to follow the law, and I trust that you will. I didn't hear [the defense attorneys] say anything to you about what your responsibilities are. In answering these question based on the evidence and following the law, and that's all that I asked you to do, is to go out and look at the evidence. . . . [The

defense] didn't pick out these issues and point out to you where the State had failed to meet this burden. [The defense] didn't point out the weaknesses in the State's case, because, ladies and gentlemen, I submit to you we've met our burden. So, what we have here is about forty-five minutes of emotional argument, and that's what exactly it all boils down to, pleading to your emotions.... But, ladies and gentlemen, your job as jurors and your duty as jurors is not to act on your emotions, but to act on the law as the Judge has given it to you, and on the evidence that you have heard in this courtroom, then answer those questions accordingly.

The state thus exploited the narrowness of the special issues by reminding the jurors of their obligation not to try to achieve broader justice in the case. The jury soon returned a verdict of death.

In this respect, the state's closing argument amplified the central difficulty with the Texas statute. By its restrictive focus, the statute discouraged extensive defense efforts devoted to the punishment phase of the case, because many of the traditional categories of "mitigating" evidence, such as evidence of a difficult background, the influence of intoxication or drugs at the time of the offense, psychiatric illness, and low intelligence, are simply unrelated to the inquiries of the special issues. Most Texas juries received only the two instructions on deliberateness and dangerousness, and the clumsily formulated deliberateness question did not offer a promising vehicle for considering a defendant's reduced culpability; by the punishment phase, virtually all defendants in Texas capital cases already had been found guilty of an "intentional" murder, and the purportedly different mens rea of a "deliberate" versus "intentional" attitude toward death was elusive at best. Worse still, in many cases, such as Penry's, the very evidence that in most jurisdictions was treated as mitigating (such as an abusive background or mental retardation) would have only *aggravating* significance in Texas, as enhancing the defendant's prospects for dangerousness.

Thus, Texas's restrictive death penalty statute exacerbated one of the central defects in capital litigation both then and now: inadequate punishment-phase investigation and presentation. At the time of Penry's trial, less than four years after the Court approved several of the post-*Furman* statutes in 1976, few lawyers in capital cases undertook the sort of punishment-phase investigation that has become, over the past fifteen years, part of the prevailing standard of practice. Most trial lawyers were accustomed to winning or losing their criminal trials at the guilt-innocence phase, either by obtaining non-guilty-verdicts or a conviction on a lesser offense. The idea of directing trial energies primarily to the issue of sentence had simply not permeated the defense-bar culture. Nor had many trial lawyers thought to engage defense-team "mitigation specialists," specifically charged with the task of developing a social history of the client via school and job records, interviews with family and friends, and psychological and psychiatric evaluations. The standard of practice in Texas, like most jurisdictions in the South, was particularly low given the extraordinarily inadequate compensation for trial attorneys and the absence of any state-wide system for training or assisting lawyers in capital cases. Capital trial lawyers were thus already disinclined to devote substantial efforts to costly and time-consuming punishment-phase investigation and presentation. Texas trial lawyers, moreover, knew that they would have no straight-forward way of appealing to a jury's sense of "justice" apart from their ability to demonstrate that their individual clients were extraordinarily aberrational either in failing to anticipate death or in not constituting a danger notwithstanding their commission of a capital offense.

Like many, but certainly not all Texas capital attorneys, Penry's lawyer recognized and challenged the inadequacy of the Texas statute to authorize a "discretionary grant of mercy based upon the existence of mitigating circumstances." He also requested an instruction that the jury could not impose death without concluding that the aggravating circumstances in Penry's case outweighed any mitigating circumstances. These challenges, though, had one enormous doctrinal impediment—the Supreme Court's decision in *Jurek v. Texas*,[12] which had upheld the Texas statute against constitutional challenge.

III. The Legacy of *Jurek*

The Texas statute was one of the five statutes addressed by the Court in the wake of *Furman*'s invalidation of all then-existing capital statutes in 1972.[13] *Furman* had notoriously given little guidance about how to save the American death penalty. The five Justices who supported the judgment had agreed that the challenged death penalty statutes—and by extension virtually all of the then-prevailing capital statutes—had produced intolerable arbitrariness in violation of the Eighth Amendment.[14] A common theme of the opinions was the failure of states to guide jury discretion in capital cases. An enormous number of offenders were ostensibly death-eligible under the existing state schemes, but very few inmates were sentenced to death; perhaps more importantly, the states gave little reason to believe that the few sentenced to death were among the worst offenders justifying the imposition of death in

---

[12] 428 U.S. 262 (1976).

[13] The other four statutes before the Court came from Florida, Georgia, Louisiana, and North Carolina.

[14] For a fuller discussion of the various opinions and themes in *Furman*, see Carol S. Steiker & Jordan M. Steiker, *Sober Second Thoughts: Reflections on Two Decades of Constitutional Regulation of Capital Punishment*, 109 Harv. L. Rev. 355 (1995).

their cases. This perception was heightened by the fact that two of the three offenders before the Court in the *Furman* litigation had been sentenced to death for non-homicidal rape.

But there were other themes in the concurring *Furman* opinions as well, including concerns about invidious race and class discrimination, the inconsistency of the death penalty with prevailing American values and conceptions of human dignity, and the inability of the death penalty to serve any significant social purposes given the sheer infrequency of its imposition. The failure of any of the five Justices in the majority to join any of the other concurring opinions made it difficult to speculate about the "core" *Furman* defect or, more importantly, how, or if, it could be solved.

The states had seemed to divide into two camps: those that would attempt to remove sentencing discretion entirely and those that would seek to control discretion by reserving the death penalty for the most aggravated cases. Many states, including Louisiana and North Carolina, adopted the former approach and enacted "mandatory" death penalty statutes that required imposition of a capital sentence upon conviction of particular crimes (usually first-degree murder). Most of the "guided discretion" statutes, such as Georgia's and Florida's, required sentencers to find the existence of at least one aggravating factor and to then consider mitigating factors in the course of deciding the ultimate sentence.

Texas' statute was an odd combination that did not fall neatly into either camp. On the one hand, Texas created a new crime, "capital murder," which narrowed the class of death-eligible murders at the guilt-innocence phase; the factors that transformed murder into capital murder at the guilt-innocence phase (e.g., murder in the course of a dangerous felony, murder of a peace officer, murder for remuneration) were very similar to the aggravating factors that triggered death eligibility at the punishment phase in Georgia, Florida, and other "guided discretion" states. On the other hand, the punishment phase in Texas bore little resemblance to the guided discretion statutes because there appeared to be little sentencer discretion: instead of asking jurors to decide whether aggravating factors outweighed mitigating factors or whether mitigating circumstances justified a sentence less than death, Texas jurors would decide only whether the defendant's conduct was committed "deliberately" and whether the defendant remained dangerous.

Notwithstanding the states' embrace of significant statutory changes, including changes that appeared to limit or remove sentencing discretion, the litigation strategy following *Furman*, designed and implemented by the NAACP Legal Defense Fund, was to continue to press on the issue of *excessive* discretion and resulting arbitrariness. For example, the petitioner's brief in *Gregg* claimed that the newly-enumerated aggravating factors in the Georgia statute were "amorphous, intangible, [and] elusive."[15] More significantly, the brief condemned the jury's ability to *withhold* the death penalty on virtual any grounds: "The statute does not specify or define 'mitigating circumstances,' and the sentencer is therefore free in any case to consider *anything* a mitigating factor which inspires mercy."[16] Likewise, in *Roberts*, attacking Louisiana's *mandatory* death penalty statute, the LDF emphasized that too much discretion remained within the system—most notably in prosecutorial charging and the power of jurors to convict on lesser-included offenses. Accordingly, the LDF insisted that the "ostensibly" mandatory scheme still permitted similar offenders to receive different treatment. Put in its most provocative formulation, the LDF insisted that "numerous interconnected procedures and practices in the administration of Louisiana's 1973 death penalty laws assure that capital punishment will remain 'a ghastly, brainless lottery.' "[17] Similarly, despite the narrow focus of the new special issues, the LDF brief in the Texas case claimed that jurors would nonetheless answer the issues in order to achieve their desired outcome: "In light of the nature of the inquiries, [the jury's] answers can hardly be thought to reflect anything more or less than its sentiments on 'the question whether this defendant was fit to live.' "[18]

The strategy of attacking all of the new statutes in the same way—insisting that they failed to solve the problem of arbitrariness wrought by unguided discretion—left open the possibility that *Furman*'s victory would be complete. If the Court agreed that impermissible discretion still permeated the actual administration of the death penalty, the death penalty would be effectively abolished. The strategy had several advantages. It took the dominant theme in *Furman*—inconsistent and discriminatory application of the death penalty—and made a plausible case that such discrimination could not be ameliorated by tinkering with statutory language. In this respect, the strategy found support in *McGautha v. California*,[19] where Justice Harlan had eloquently challenged the claim that states could meaningfully guide sentencer discretion (although he found no obligation for states to do so under the Due Process Clause). The strategy also avoided the charge of "bait-and-switch"—in which death penalty opponents first attacked statutes for allowing too much

---

[15] 1976 WL 178715, at *35.

[16] *Id.* at *34.

[17] 1976 WL 181300, at *30.

[18] 1976 WL 194471, at *58.

[19] 402 U.S. 183 (1971).

discretion and then attacked statutes for placing excessive *limits* on discretion. Perhaps the abolitionists' best hope was to defend a general constitutional principle prohibiting excessive discretion rather than to insist upon an unachievable web of rules designed to defeat the death penalty. The "excessive discretion" strategy also put all of the petitioners from the different states on the same page, so that the death-row inmates in North Carolina and Louisiana (the mandatory statutes) and the death-row inmates in Georgia and Florida inmates (the guided discretion schemes) would not end up defending each other's statutes as they sought to highlight the defects in their own schemes. Finally, the excessive discretion strategy fit well within a broader claim that the death penalty was no longer consistent with prevailing society values, and that its retention was possible only because there were numerous discretionary outlets to prevent its imposition.

But the strategy had significant drawbacks as well. The charge of excessive discretion was easier to lodge in the pre-*Furman* world because states had undertaken virtually no efforts to structure death penalty decisionmaking. This lack of effort was especially striking given the longstanding and ignored recommendation of the American Law Institute to structure death-penalty decisionmaking (embodied in the Model Penal Code, promulgated more than a decade before *Furman*).[20] But the claim of unbridled discretion was harder to defend after 35 states revamped their statutes in the wake of *Furman* and articulated new theories of capital murder. The petitioners in the 1976 cases were undoubtedly correct that some discretion unavoidably remained—in charging decisions, clemency, and elsewhere—but there was clearly a significant distance between the absolute discretion in the pre-*Furman* regime and the discretion embodied in the guided-discretion and mandatory schemes adopted post-*Furman*. Given that *Furman* was a 5–4 decision, it seemed unlikely that the Court's condemnation of unbridled discretion would be construed so broadly as to condemn any discretion at all, especially in light of the political support for the death penalty reflected in the states' adoption of their new statutory schemes.

Moreover, as Carol Steiker illuminates in her chapter on *Furman*, the seeds of a contra doctrine *requiring* discretion can also be found in *Furman* itself,[21] both in Justice Brennan's concurring opinion emphasizing an Eighth Amendment concern for human dignity and in Chief Justice Burger's dissenting opinion lamenting the prospect of mandatory capital sentencing schemes. The vesting of discretion in prosecutors, juries, and governors inevitably creates opportunities for arbitrary decisionmaking; but removing such discretion—by forbidding decisionmak-

---

[20] Model Penal Code § 210.6 (Proposed Official Draft, Adopted May 24, 1962).

[21] Carol Steiker, *Furman v. Georgia,* in this volume.

ers from considering mitigating facts—creates its own arbitrariness. Just
as decisionmakers vested with discretion can decide to treat similarly-
situated defendants differently, decisionmakers deprived of discretion
are *prevented* from treating differently-situated defendants differently,
and it is not obvious that the latter form of arbitrariness is any more
tolerable than the former.

Perhaps the most problematic aspect of the "excessive discretion"
strategy was the flipside of one of its virtues—the fact that it put all
death-sentenced inmates in the same boat. By insisting that the guided-
discretion and mandatory statutes were infected by the same error, their
lawyers maximized the possibility that none of the statutes would be
sustained. This strategy also appeared to reduce the conflict among the
inmates because they were all pressing the same claim. But this approach also increased the prospects for the *worst* possible outcome—that
all of the statutes, including the mandatory schemes, would be upheld.

In highlighting the residual discretion that remained in all of the
new capital schemes, the LDF downplayed the most obvious defect of the
mandatory schemes—that they precluded sentencer consideration of
mitigating evidence. Jurors had long been permitted to exercise "mercy"
and to return non-death sentences based on any sort of mitigating
evidence. Indeed, one of the defining characteristics of the American
death penalty had been the steady, near-universal shift from mandatory
to discretionary statutes beginning in the mid–19th century.[22] The re-
introduction of mandatory statutes was contrary to this longstanding
trend, and it had the obvious disadvantage of removing from jurors'
consideration factors long regarded as relevant to the life-or-death decision (including evidence of mental illness, youth, and non-triggerman
status). Although it was undoubtedly true that such discretion allowed
jurors to withhold the death penalty for impermissible reasons (such as
the race or status of the defendant or victim), such discretion seemed
essential to protecting undeserving defendants from the death penalty.

By emphasizing the amount of discretion that remained instead of
the amount of discretion that had been removed in the hope that the
new statutes would be invalidated *en masse*, the LDF failed to make the
case that mandatory capital schemes denied defendants their right to
have mitigating evidence considered at sentencing. A narrow ruling
invalidating the mandatory statutes was less likely given the LDF's
insistence that discretionary outlets for mercy remained even in the
purportedly mandatory jurisdictions. Indeed, part of the LDF strategy
was to convince the Court that such outlets confirmed that the death
penalty did not enjoy the level of popular support inferable from the
widespread adoption of new capital statutes; according to the LDF, the

---

[22] Hugo Bedau, *The Death Penalty in America* 3rd ed. 9–12 (1982).

death penalty continued to be tolerated because in every jurisdiction, including the mandatory ones, there was no genuine requirement that the death penalty be imposed.

Ultimately, the Court decisively upheld Florida and Georgia's guided discretion statutes,[23] with only Justices Brennan and Marshall dissenting. Indeed, even these Justices did not embrace the "excessive discretion" argument, and instead rested their conclusions on the incompatibility of the death penalty with human dignity and the absence of any penological justification for the punishment. At the same time, the Court narrowly invalidated North Carolina and Louisiana's mandatory statutes.[24] The plurality opinion which supplied the rationale for the result concluded that the mandatory scheme was inconsistent with "evolving standards of decency" and constituted an intolerable response to the *Furman* problem of unbridled discretion. Although some of the plurality's arguments were traceable to points made in the LDF briefs (insisting that the purportedly mandatory provisions could be avoided through juror nullification), the major thrust of the plurality opinion was formulated by the Justices and not the advocates: that individualized sentencing is an indispensable part of capital sentencing, and that the Constitution forbids treating capital defendants as "members of a faceless, undifferentiated mass to be subjected to the blind infliction of the penalty of death."[25]

Given that the Court struck down the mandatory statutes, albeit narrowly, it is tempting to say that the litigation strategy caused no harm. But the unified defense focus on the problem of excessive discretion (and the related claim that the death penalty remained inconsistent with prevailing standards of decency) might well have led the Court to uphold the Texas statute in *Jurek*.

At the time the Court addressed the constitutionality of the Texas statute, no one argued to the Court that the statute impermissibly constrained consideration of mitigating evidence. In fact, as indicated above, the LDF argument was precisely the opposite: that despite the limited inquiries of the special issues, jurors were likely to answer them to achieve the verdict that they believed was appropriate. Had the advocacy in *Jurek* not been part of a collective strategy, though, the Texas statute might have been challenged along the lines that ultimately prevailed in *Woodson*—that the Texas statute denied capital defendants consideration of their mitigating circumstances. Ironically, the only

---

[23] Proffitt v. Florida, 428 U.S. 242 (1976); Gregg v. Georgia, 428 U.S. 153 (1976).

[24] Woodson v. North Carolina, 428 U.S. 280 (1976); Roberts v. Louisiana, 428 U.S. 325 (1976).

[25] *Woodson*, 428 U.S., at 304 (opinion of Justices Stewart, Powell, and Stevens).

voices insisting that the Texas statute was much more similar to the mandatory statutes that the Court invalidated than to the guided-discretion statutes that the Court upheld are found in Justice Rehnquist's and Justice White's *dissenting* opinions in *Woodson* and *Roberts*. According to Justice Rehnquist, who would have upheld North Carolina's mandatory scheme, the "Texas system much more closely approximates the mandatory North Carolina system which is struck down today."[26] Likewise, Justice White, defending the Louisiana statute, maintained that the "two additional questions" under the Texas scheme did not change the mandatory character of the Texas scheme and thus concluded that "the Texas law is not constitutionally distinguishable from the Louisiana system."[27]

The timing of *Jurek*—the fact that the Texas statute was jointly considered with the guided-discretion and mandatory statutes—exacerbated the conflicts among inmates from the various states. Had the Texas statute arrived at the Court *after* it had invalidated the mandatory schemes, the LDF could have made the same sorts of arguments advanced by Justices Rehnquist and White—that the Texas scheme was essentially mandatory as well (because the deliberateness and dangerousness inquiries did not facilitate meaningful consideration of many, perhaps most, kinds of mitigating evidence). But the joint consideration of Texas with the other statutes led to the unified strategy of attacking excessive discretion, and that strategic decision ultimately left the Court to its own devices in classifying Texas as a guided-discretion rather than mandatory scheme.

In addition, because *Jurek* was one of the five "foundational" decisions post-*Furman*, it enjoyed a special status that ultimately prevented both the Supreme Court and the state and lower federal courts from acknowledging the defects in the Texas scheme. Soon after the 1976 decisions, the Court amplified its holdings in *Woodson* and *Roberts* and began to recognize a robust right to individualized sentencing. In *Lockett v. Ohio*[28] and *Eddings v. Oklahoma*,[29] the Court reversed death sentences where sentencers were able and willing to consider some but not all mitigating factors calling for a sentence less than death. But the Supreme Court did not question the general soundness of the Texas scheme in a post-*Lockett* case involving a *Witherspoon*[30] issue (death-

---

[26] 428 U.S. at 315.

[27] 428 U.S. at 359.

[28] 438 U.S. 586 (1978).

[29] 455 U.S. 104 (1982).

[30] Witherspoon v. Illinois, 391 U.S. 510 (1968).

qualification of jurors),[31] and for more than a decade following *Jurek*, Texas capital defendants were virtually alone nationwide in being subject to the death penalty without having a sentencer determine that they deserved to die. Although the Court's decision to view Texas as a guided-discretion state appeared tentative and provisional in *Jurek*—the Court emphasized that the Texas courts had not clearly spoken to the reach of the special issues—that subtlety was lost as inmates accumulated on Texas' death row.[32]

Thus, a significant part of the story of *Penry* is a cautionary tale about cause lawyering. The post-*Furman* collective strategy might well have contributed to the Court's endorsement of the flawed Texas statute in *Jurek*. Of course, the post-*Furman* situation was a genuine quagmire and it is not obvious that the collective strategy should have been rejected in favor of statute-specific challenges. Even from the perspective of Jurek himself, it is unclear whether the best course was to pursue a narrow challenge to the Texas statute (with the prospect of a retrial and resentencing if he prevailed) or a broad challenge that might have precluded the use of the death penalty altogether. A slightly broader perspective would have included all Texas inmates under a sentence of death prior to *Jurek* (whose interests were likely similar to Jurek's), and an even broader perspective would have included prospective death penalty candidates within Texas (presumably within this class, defendants with strong mitigation would have had different interests than those without such evidence). The broadest approach, of course, would also have considered the interests of inmates and potential defendants in other jurisdictions. As noted above, one problem in pursuing a purely "Texas" approach is that there was a substantial downside to having all death-sentenced inmates advance their own narrow interests, because such an approach would have inevitably led to highlighting the constitutional virtues of statutory provisions different from the ones within their jurisdiction (in the hope of persuading the Court that other statutes satisfied some constitutional minimum lacking at home). In this respect, the post-*Furman* world entailed some form of the familiar "prisoners' dilemma," in which cooperation offered some genuine benefits (and perhaps justified the LDF's global strategy). But unlike the classic formulation, this prisoners' dilemma not only maximized the odds of the preferred outcome (constitutional abolition), it also maximized the odds of the least desirable outcome (deregulation in the event that the "excessive discretion" argument failed).

---

[31] Adams v. Texas, 448 U.S. 38 (1980).

[32] For a detailed account of how Texas emerged as the execution leader in the modern era, see Carol S. Steiker & Jordan M. Steiker, *A Tale of Two Nations: Implementation of the Death Penalty in "Executing" versus "Symbolic" States in the United States*, 84 Tex. L. Rev. 1869 (2006).

What would have happened had Jurek's lawyers rejected the global strategy and successfully sought to invalidate the Texas statute as impermissibly mandatory? On the one hand, such a victory would have been both narrow and short-lived. Had the Court invalidated the Texas statute on such grounds, it would not have ended the death penalty in Texas; it would have likely accelerated by at least a decade Texas' legislative revision of its statute and the addition of a question inviting jurors to grant leniency based on mitigating circumstances. On the other hand, perhaps some of the inmates sentenced prior to *Jurek* (including Jurek himself) would have been spared at resentencing if their juries were given a meaningful vehicle for considering mitigation. The State's success rate at capital trials between *Furman* and *Jurek* was fairly high, possibly the result of its mandatory character. This fact gave ammunition to the State as it rebutted the LDF claim that the nebulous special issues would permit the "erratic escape" of capital murderers by Texas juries inclined toward leniency: only three of fifty-eight juries during this period had declined to answer the "deliberateness" question affirmatively, although fifteen juries had returned "no" findings to dangerousness.[33]

It is also possible that some number of the score of inmates sentenced to death in the fifteen year interval between *Jurek* and the 1991 amended capital statute would have received life sentences under the leniency provision.[34] Although it is unlikely that a different result in *Jurek* would have radically altered the administration of the death penalty in Texas, it certainly would have slowed Texas' move to executions and likely reduced the number of those ultimately executed. A collateral benefit to *Jurek*'s invalidation of the Texas statute might have been an earlier recognition in Texas of the importance of developing and presenting mitigating evidence. Texas was not alone in its appallingly poor level of trial defense in capital cases throughout the 1980s, but some of the blame for inadequate punishment-phase advocacy during that period is fairly attributable to the narrow focus of the Texas scheme; unlike defendants in other states, Texas inmates who presented mitigating evidence at the punishment phase faced the genuine prospect that such evidence (such as abusive or deprived background, mental illness, or mental retardation) would have had exclusively aggravating relevance to the special issues.

---

[33] 1976 WL 181479, at *28.

[34] The amended Texas statute added the following catch-all mitigation question: Tex. Code Crim. Proc. Ann., Art. 37.071(e)(1) ("whether, taking into consideration all of the evidence, including the circumstances of the offense, the defendant's character and background, and the personal moral culpability of the defendant there is a sufficient mitigating circumstance or circumstances to warrant that a sentence of life imprisonment without parole rather than a death sentence be imposed.").

In any case, *Jurek*'s unraveling did not begin until 1988, when the Court addressed whether its decisions in *Woodson*, *Lockett*, and *Eddings* required relief for a defendant who claimed that his evidence of "residual doubt" and good behavior in prison was not given constitutionally adequate consideration via the Texas special issues.[35] The Court rejected his claim, but Justice O'Connor's concurring opinion recognized that the Texas scheme would be inadequate in cases where a defendant's mitigating evidence had significance beyond the inquiries of the special issues.[36] That decision paved the way for the Court to hear Penry's claim.

IV. *Penry v. Lynaugh*: Two Decisions, Two Legacies

Penry I is truly two decisions, both authored by Justice O'Connor. The first, joined by the Court's liberals (Justices Brennan, Marshall, Blackmun, and Stevens), found that the Texas special issue scheme unconstitutionally precluded consideration of Penry's mitigating evidence of his mental retardation and history of abuse. The second, joined by the Court's conservatives (Chief Justice Rehnquist and Justices White, Scalia, and Kennedy), rejected Penry's claim that the Eighth Amendment altogether prohibits the execution of persons with mental retardation.

A. Revisiting the Special Issue Scheme

The portion of Justice O'Connor's decision regarding the inadequacy of the Texas scheme described *Jurek* as upholding the special issues only against facial attack, leaving open the claim that "in a particular case, the jury was unable to fully consider the mitigating evidence introduced by a defendant in answering the special issues."[37] But in describing the problem in Penry's case, Justice O'Connor's opinion cast great doubt on the general viability of the Texas scheme. The central problem with the special issues was that they did not give a vehicle for the jury to consider Penry's reduced culpability. The "deliberateness" question, though it ostensibly required the State to prove that Penry acted more than "intentionally," did not give the jury the opportunity to decide that Penry was undeserving of death in light of his mental retardation and abusive background; that is, the jury could have believed that Penry acted "deliberately" but also that he did not deserve to die, and the deliberateness question gave no means of expressing this view. The dangerousness question likewise did not provide a means of giving effect to Penry's reduced culpability and in fact treated his mitigation as *aggravating* because jurors could well have concluded that he was *more*

---

[35] Franklin v. Lynaugh, 487 U.S. 164 (1988).

[36] *Id.*, at 185 (O'Connor, J., concurring in the judgment).

[37] 492 U.S., at 321.

dangerous as a result of his abused background and cognitive impairments. Justice O'Connor also emphasized that the inadequacy of the special issues was evident in defense counsel's general appeal at closing argument to spare Penry (rather than focused argument under the special issues) and compounded by prosecutorial efforts to reinforce their limited scope (reminding jurors that they had "taken an oath to follow the law" and that the defense "didn't pick out these issues and point out to you where the State had failed to meet [its] burden").

The State's chief argument in defense of the Texas scheme was that Texas had sought to redress *Furman*'s concerns about unbridled discretion. The special issues, in the State's view, allowed for the consideration of mitigating circumstances but channeled that consideration through focused questions rather than allowing jurors to react with unfocused emotion. In this respect, the State highlighted the considerable tension between *Furman*'s condemnation of arbitrariness in sentencing (traceable to unguided discretion) and *Woodson*'s insistence that sentencer discretion to consider the circumstances of the offense and offender is constitutionally mandated. The war in *Penry* was essentially to decide whether the constitutional requirement of "guidance" or "discretion" was preeminent.

By the time of the decision, the Court had already scaled back its commitment to non-arbitrariness. The Court had recently rejected the claim in *McCleskey v. Kemp*[38] that the demonstrable influence of race—particularly the race of victims—in Georgia's capital scheme violated the Eighth Amendment. In so doing, the Court emphasized *Woodson*'s constitutional commitment to individualized sentencing and the unavoidable arbitrariness that it entailed. The Court also had been inhospitable to a variety of claims challenging the failure of states to suitably channel sentence discretion on the aggravating side (in their definition of aggravating factors and in structuring the ultimate life-or-death decision).[39]

In fact, the seventeen years of litigation post-*Furman* had brought the Court to a surprising doctrinal point: on the one hand, the Court had demanded little of the post-*Furman* schemes in terms of "guiding" or "structuring" the death penalty decision; and, on the other hand, the Court had *constitutionalized* preservation of the very discretion that had inspired the *Furman* challenge.[40] *Woodson, Lockett,* and *Eddings* had turned *Furman* on its head. Instead of demanding that states confine

---

[38] 481 U.S. 279 (1987).

[39] See, e.g., Zant v. Stephens, 462 U.S. 862 (1983); Lowenfield v. Phelps, 484 U.S. 231 (1988).

[40] For a discussion of this tension, see Carol S. Steiker and Jordan M. Steiker, *Let God Sort Them Out? Redefining the Individualization Requirement in Capital Sentencing*, 102 Yale L. J. 835 (1992).

discretion to assure consistent outcomes in capital cases, the Court insisted that States preserve and codify sentencer discretion to withhold the death penalty on the basis of mitigating facts. As Justice O'Connor explained in *Penry*, once states narrow the class of death-eligible defendants through the use of aggravating factors, the Constitution *requires* States to ensure that sentencers can react to mitigating facts related to their personal moral culpability. Rejecting the State's claim that this was unfaithful to *Furman*, Justice O'Connor insisted that "[r]ather than creating the risk of an unguided emotional response, full consideration of evidence that mitigates against the death penalty is essential if the jury is to give a 'reasoned *moral* response to the defendant's background, character, and crime.' "[41]

As a practical matter, Justice O'Connor's endorsement of a broad right to individualized sentencing—which included a defendant's right to "full" consideration of mitigating facts related to personal moral culpability—posed little threat to the imposition of the death penalty outside of Texas. In the wake of the Court's rejection of the mandatory schemes, virtually all states permitted wide consideration of mitigating factors and allowed sentencers broad discretion to determine whether a defendant deserved to die. Only Oregon had adopted a special issue scheme similar to the one in Texas, and Oregon had few death sentences (a death-row under twenty-five) and few executions in the modern era.[42]

But the fact that *Penry I* would have limited doctrinal significance outside of Texas did not mean that *Penry I* was unimportant to the American death penalty. *Penry* threatened to derail the death penalty in Texas, and because Texas had already emerged as the leader in executions in the post-*Furman* era (accounting for over 25% of the executions between 1977–1988 (29/104)),[43] a broad application of *Penry I* to Texas death-sentenced inmates threatened to reduce significantly the overall number of executions nationwide. One critical part of the *Penry* story, however, is its stingy application.

B. The Narrowing of *Penry*

A significant number of Texas inmates sentenced under the post-*Furman* statute had offered evidence of abused or deprived backgrounds, limited intelligence, learning difficulties, drug addiction, and psychiatric

---

[41] 492 U.S., at 328 (quoting *Franklin*, 487 U.S., at 184 (O'Connor, J., concurring)) (internal quotation marks omitted).

[42] See Death Penalty Information Center, Death Sentences in the United States from 1977 to 2006, at www.deathpenaltyinfo.org/article.php?Scid=9&did=847; Death Penalty Information Center, Executions in the United States, 1976–Present, at www.deathpenalty info.org/article.php?scid=8&did=1110.

[43] See Death Penalty Information Center, Searchable Database of Executions, at www. deathpenaltyinfo.org/executions.php.

problems. These inmates, like Penry, had been sentenced to death without an opportunity for the jury to consider whether they deserved to be spared in light of their impaired circumstances (and despite their dangerousness). Had *Penry I* been applied on its own terms, scores of inmates would have been entitled to relief and Texas would not have become the dominant death penalty state throughout the 1990s.

The resistance to *Penry I*, though, began almost immediately. Whereas the Oregon Supreme Court invalidated the death sentences of all inmates condemned under their special issue scheme,[44] the Texas Court of Criminal Appeals insisted that *Penry I* should be read narrowly, particularly in light of the Court's endorsement of the Texas scheme in *Jurek*. Although over three hundred inmates had been sentenced to death in Texas by juries who had never been asked whether they should live or die, the state and lower federal courts insisted that *Penry* error occurred only in a narrow subset of cases in which the defendant presented mitigating evidence virtually identical in quality and quantity to Penry's.

Four years after *Penry I*, during which the Texas courts had reversed fewer than five sentences on *Penry* grounds, the Supreme Court returned to the Texas statute and gave some support to the narrow reading of *Penry I*. Two Justices in the *Penry* majority (Justices Brennan and Marshall) had since retired, and there was reason to believe that the precarious 5–4 *Penry I* holding was in jeopardy. The two cases before the Court, *Graham v. Collins*[45] and *Johnson v. Texas*,[46] presented the narrow question whether a defendant's evidence of youth could be given constitutionally adequate consideration via the special issues. The defendants had argued that such evidence, like Penry's evidence of mental retardation and abuse, reduced their culpability, yet their juries were precluded from withholding the death penalty based on their reduced blameworthiness.

Retreating from Justice O'Connor's insistence that sentencers be empowered to give "full effect" to a defendant's mitigating evidence, the Court upheld the death sentences in both cases. Justice Kennedy, a *Penry I* dissenter who was now writing for the Court, argued that evidence of youth could be given significant consideration via the future dangerousness question, because jurors could well conclude that a defendant's immaturity and impulsivity would subside with age. Thus, the evidence of youth could be used to answer "no" to dangerousness, even

---

[44] See William R. Long, *A Time to Kill? Reflections on the Oregon Death Penalty*, Or. St. B. Bull., Apr. 2002 (available at www.osbar.org/publications/bulletin/02aps/kill.htm).

[45] 506 U.S. 461 (1993).

[46] 509 U.S. 350 (1993).

if jurors were not empowered to decide whether the defendants deserved to die. More importantly, Justice Kennedy argued that *Penry I* did not overrule *Jurek*, and that states must be permitted to "structure" consideration of mitigating evidence. Even as Justice Kennedy made this point, though, its significance was only backward looking and only relevant to Texas; by the time *Graham* and *Johnson* were decided, Texas had already amended its statute to permit broad consideration of mitigating evidence to avoid the problems identified in *Penry I*.

The State's victories in *Graham* and *Johnson* led to even greater restrictions on *Penry I* in the state and lower federal courts. The Texas Court of Criminal Appeals, in tandem with the Fifth Circuit Court of Appeals, insisted that virtually all evidence, including evidence of childhood trauma, drug addiction, sexual abuse, low intelligence, psychiatric illness, and post-traumatic stress disorder, could be adequately addressed via the dangerousness issue despite the fact that such evidence plainly supported rather than undermined a jury's finding of dangerousness.[47] In addition, the Texas and lower federal courts crafted new and unprecedented screening tests for "constitutional relevance" that required a defendant's mitigation to establish a "uniquely severe condition" with a "nexus" to the crime in order to reach the *Penry* inquiry (concerning the addressability of such evidence within the special issues). In fact, more than ten years after *Penry I*, in a 2003 opinion surveying its *Penry* case law, the Fifth Circuit Court of Appeals could point to only one case in which it had granted relief to that point.[48] Meanwhile, executions in Texas skyrocketed, with Texas executing 132 inmates in the four year interval between 1997 and 2000 (more than any state has executed over the past forty years).[49] Most of these inmates had been sentenced to death under the old Texas statute, and many were deserving of relief under a straightforward reading of *Penry I*.

C. Penry's Retrial

After Penry's death sentence was overturned in 1989, Terry Brown, the Polk County District Attorney, pledged to seek another death sentence against Penry. Although a retrial was estimated to cost as much as $500,000, more than Polk County's entire annual budget, Brown indicated "if I have to bankrupt this county, we're going to bow up and see that

---

[47] See Carol S. Steiker and Jordan M. Steiker, *A Tale of Two Nations: Implementation of the Death Penalty in "Executing" v. "Symbolic" States in the United States*, 84 Tex. L. Rev. 1869, 1892–95 (2006).

[48] Robertson v. Cockrell, 325 F.3d 243, 253 (5th Cir. 2003) (citing Blue v. Cockrell, 298 F.3d 318 (5th Cir. 2002), as case in which it granted relief under *Penry*).

[49] See Death Penalty Information Center, Searchable Database of Executions, at www.deathpenaltyinfo.org/executions.php.

justice is served.''[50] Over defense objections, the trial was held in Walker County, a short ride from Polk County. Walker County was ideal for the prosecution. It shares much of the same media market as Polk County, so most of the community was aware of Penry's previous trial, confession, conviction, and death sentence. Moreover, Walker County is home to several prisons within the Texas Department of Corrections, including the Ellis Unit, which housed death row at the time, and the Walls Unit, which performed—and still performs—executions. Indeed, the Texas Department of Corrections employs almost one-third of the workers in the county, and by the time of his retrial, Penry was arguably TDC's most famous prisoner. Although some of the major papers in Texas had reacted negatively to *Penry I*'s refusal to exempt persons with mental retardation from the death penalty, the Huntsville Item, centered in Walker County, reacted to the decision with an editorial (by its news editor): "Mitigating circumstances—a bunch of junk."[51]

The retrial covered some of the same ground as the first trial. In addition to the original trial lawyer John Wright, Penry was now represented by Robert Smith, a partner from the New York offices of Paul, Weiss, who offered his assistance pro bono (Smith, and several other lawyers from Paul, Weiss, would participate in Penry's defense for many years). The involvement of Smith and Paul, Weiss, as well as broader changes in capital trial practice, was reflected in the considerably expanded efforts to seek mercy for Penry. Whereas the evidence of Penry's intellectual deficits previously had been introduced to establish Penry's inability to stand trial and insanity at the time of the offense, at the second trial the defense introduced a more extensive mitigating case at punishment, including efforts from both professional and lay witnesses to establish Penry's mental retardation. Reports from Penry's childhood described him as "very brain damaged," and psychological testing at age nine indicated that Penry had "fairly severe retardation with a total IQ of just above 50."

In addition, the defense offered much more extensive evidence of Penry's abused background. Penry's siblings and aunts testified to the extraordinary abuse Penry suffered at the hands of his mother (who had died in the interval between trials). According to these witnesses, Penry's mother had beat him every day with belt buckles, brooms, and sticks, had forced him to drink his own urine and excrement, had burned him in scalding water and attempted to drown him, had threatened to cut off his genitals, and had locked him alone is his room for long periods

---

[50] Steve Brewer, "Penry likely to face retrial, officials say," The Huntsville Item, Jul. 1, 1989, p. 3A.

[51] Jean Ann Ruth, "Mitigating circumstances—a bunch of junk," Huntviles Item, Oct. 11, 1989.

of time without food or access to a bathroom. The State meanwhile sought to portray Penry as both dangerous and manipulative. Through the testimony of TDC officers, the state presented evidence of Penry's bad behavior in prison and purported "malingering" to support his claim of mental retardation. One officer stated that he had seen Penry reading and writing on a regular basis until his mental retardation claim came before the Supreme Court, after which Penry began to act more impaired.

The most striking legal aspect of the retrial concerned the trial court's response to the prior reversal. When *Penry I* was issued in late June, 1989, the Texas legislature had just adjourned. As a non-professional body, the Texas legislature meets for only 140 days every other year. Although the legislature can also meet in "special session," it did not amend its capital statute to comply with *Penry I* until it met again in regular session in 1991; the revised special issue scheme, made effective for offenses committed after September 1, 1991, removed the first and third special issues (on deliberateness and provocation) and added a new, catch-all question asking whether any mitigating circumstances call for a sentence less than death.

The looming problem was what to do during the interval between *Penry I* and the effective date of the new statute. The problem was exacerbated by the fact that all parties understood Texas law to forbid altering the special issues on the verdict form submitted to the jury. Accordingly, Penry's jurors at his retrial were to answer exactly the same three questions that the Supreme Court had declared constitutionally inadequate to facilitate consideration of his mitigating evidence.

Most trial courts during this period—including Penry's—sought to remedy the *Penry* problem via some form of a "nullification" instruction. Such an instruction directed jurors to consider all mitigating evidence and, if they found such evidence justified a sentence less than death, to answer the special issues to achieve a life sentence. This approach presented several obvious problems. First, and foremost, the nullification instruction essentially required jurors to lie in order to give effect to mitigating evidence. If, for example, a juror believed that the State had proved deliberateness and dangerousness, but also believed that the defendant should be spared based on mitigating factors, the juror would have to answer one of the special issues dishonestly in order to achieve a life sentence. Second, the verdict form—the sole document the jury had to complete—made no mention of mitigating evidence. There were obvious reasons to fear that the lengthy and cumbersome instructions about *how* to answer the questions would be lost when the jury actually focused on the special issues it was required to answer.

The nullification instruction given in Penry's case was actually less clear than others in communicating the power of the jury to nullify its answers to the special issues. Instead, it confusingly suggested that the jury *should* consider Penry's mitigating circumstances "at the time you answer the special issue[s]." The last sentence of the nullification instruction captures the awkwardness of this purported remedy: "If you determine, when giving effect to the mitigating evidence, if any, that a life sentence, as reflected by a negative finding to the issue under consideration, rather than a death sentence, is an appropriate response to the personal culpability of the defendant, a negative finding should be given to one of the special issues."

Penry's lawyers argued at trial that this instruction did not solve the *Penry I* problem and that Penry could not be subject to the death penalty because the legislative fix was prospective only. During the punishment phase argument, the defense emphasized Penry's intellectual deficits and, to a much greater extent, his history of abuse. The defense gamely tried to explain the jurors' right to answer the special issues falsely if they believed Penry deserved a life sentence: "Let me try to simplify [the instruction]. If, when you thought about mental retardation and the child abuse, you think that this guy deserves a life sentence, and not a death sentence, decide life in prison is punishment enough, then, you got to answer one of those questions no.... Not the easiest instruction to follow, and the law does funny things sometimes, but, it is what it says, and I have taken all of this time with you to make sure that you understand what it says."

The prosecution, on the other hand, argued that the evidence of abuse and impairment was overstated. More fundamentally, the prosecution maintained that such evidence was not truly mitigating, because the defense had failed to demonstrate a connection between being abused or having mental retardation and committing violent crimes. As to abuse, the prosecution stated: "There is no connection between child abuse and criminal acts. No connection." As to mental retardation, the prosecution declared: "We got mental retardation, and how is that a mitigating factor? How does that reduce his blame?" The prosecution also tried to exploit local distrust of Penry's New York lawyers: "A Defendant has got plenty of rights and they ought to be enforced and they have been. He has an attorney representing him throughout this trial, and that is well and good.... But, now we are down to society's part of the trial. And, society, has a direct say in this, and when I say society, I am not talking about some fancy group of folks somewhere or another ... I am talking about the people in Walker County, in Polk County, people out there on the streets...."

As in the first trial, the prosecution also sought to focus the jury's attention on the narrow inquiries of the special issues and to deflect a broader assessment of Penry's moral culpability. After describing Penry's specific actions and decisions leading up to the stabbing of Pamela Carpenter, the prosecution commented: "If that is not deliberate folks, there ain't a cow in Texas." Likewise, the prosecutor stated that "when you start talking about Special Issue Number Two [dangerousness], there is a limited amount of evidence that you can even use on that issue."

Penry was again sentenced to death. The involvement of Paul, Weiss was evident in Penry's direct appeal brief, which raised 132 points of error in a massive 375 page filing. The first eleven of the 132 claims presented variations of the same *Penry I* claim that had resulted in the reversal of his first death sentence, emphasizing the failure of the special issues in combination with the nullification instruction to ensure adequate consideration of his mitigating evidence. The brief effectively ridiculed the notion that the *Penry I* problem could be solved by instructing jurors to think about mitigation as they answered questions that the Supreme Court had already concluded were inadequate to facilitate such consideration: "It would be equally logical to tell someone: 'When you deliberate on whether the sky is blue, consider the music lesson you had last Thursday.'"

As Penry's "new" *Penry* claim worked its way through the state and federal courts, there was little reason for optimism. While Penry's case was pending on direct appeal, the Supreme Court retreated from its broad *Penry I* holding in *Graham* and *Johnson*, and the Texas and lower federal courts were aggressively diluting *Penry I*'s protections. In addition, as early as 1992 the Texas Court of Criminal Appeals had upheld the use of a nullification charge in another capital case (dozens of death-sentenced inmates had received a similar type of instruction), insisting that the supplemental instruction "was adequate to avoid the constitutional infirmity condemned by *Penry*."[52] The Texas Court of Criminal Appeals affirmed Penry's conviction on direct appeal in 1995, denied state habeas relief in 1998, and the Fifth Circuit Court of Appeals held that the new *Penry* claim did not even warrant a full appeal in 2000.[53] Penry's execution date was set for November 16, 2000. Few observers expected the Supreme Court to revisit the long-amended Texas capital scheme. Even fewer believed that Penry would receive a commutation from then-Governor George Bush, notwithstanding appeals from numerous groups, including the European Union, which had stated in a letter to Bush that the execution of an inmate "[w]ith a mental age of 6 and an IQ of 54" would "degrade the dignity and worth of the person." On the

---

[52] Fuller v. State, 829 S.W.2d 191 (Tex. Crim. App. 1992).

[53] Penry v. Johnson, 215 F.3d 504 (5th Cir. 2000).

eve of Penry's execution, the Supreme Court granted a stay and subsequently agreed to hear his case.

D. *Penry* Revived

In its review of Penry's second death sentence (*Penry II*), the Supreme Court unsurprisingly found the nullification instruction inadequate to cure the *Penry I* problem.[54] The Court was skeptical that the jury would have found much direction from the "confusing instruction," and the special issues—to which their verdict was tied—still made no mention of mitigating evidence. Moreover, even if the instruction, understood in the context of trial, clearly directed jurors to falsify their answers if they believed Penry should be spared, the Court was unwilling to endorse "nullification" as an acceptable means of ensuring individualized sentencing. Requiring jurors to answer the special issues *dishonestly* in order to give effect to Penry's evidence "made the jury charge as a whole internally contradictory, and placed law-abiding jurors in an impossible situation."[55]

Had the Court simply made these points, *Penry II* would have been an extremely modest decision, applicable only to those persons sentenced in the interval between *Penry I* and the effective date of the amended statute. Even within this small group, arguably only those inmates who had evidence precisely likely Penry's would have been entitled to relief, given the restrictive reading of *Penry I* prevailing in the Texas and lower federal courts; in all other cases, the use of the nullification instruction would have been unproblematic because the special issues would have been deemed adequate for the consideration of the inmate's mitigating evidence.

But changes on the Court (particularly the replacement of Justice White by Justice Ginsburg), had restored a working majority for the original *Penry I* decision. Justice O'Connor wrote the majority opinion, and she seemed committed to emphasizing the broad scope of her original *Penry I* opinion. Justice O'Connor and her colleagues were undoubtedly aware of the abandonment of *Penry I* in the Texas and lower federal courts over the past decade, as literally dozens of petitions for certiorari had complained of *Penry I*'s under-enforcement (and capital cases, particularly those with "real" execution dates, receive special attention from the Court).

In describing the scope of *Penry I*, Justice O'Connor insisted that constitutional error occurs whenever a sentencer is precluded from giving "*full* consideration and *full* effect to mitigating circumstances."[56]

---

[54] 532 U.S. 782 (2001).

[55] *Id.*, at 799.

[56] *Id.*, at 797.

She pointedly borrowed this language—italics and all—from her *dissenting* opinion in *Johnson*, which had lamented the Court's refusal to find *Penry* error whenever a defendant's mitigating evidence had significance beyond the special issues. Notably, Justice Kennedy, who had authored *Johnson*, joined Justice O'Connor's opinion, notwithstanding the invocation of language from her *Johnson* dissent.

Despite this clear shot across the bow, it was business as usual in the Texas courts and the Fifth Circuit Court of Appeals. Before *Penry II* was issued, the Texas Court of Criminal Appeals had denied *Penry I* relief to Robert Tennard, a defendant who had offered evidence of his 67 I.Q. during the punishment phase of his capital trial under the pre–1991 statute. Such evidence obviously presented the same problem as Penry's because Tennard's low intelligence reduced his culpability and yet supported an affirmative answer to dangerousness. Indeed, the prosecution had even discouraged jurors from paying attention to Tennard's low I.Q., insisting "the reasons why he became a danger are not really relevant." The CCA nonetheless found no *Penry I* error because Tennard had failed to prove full-blown mental retardation and had not offered independent evidence that he was unable to learn from his mistakes.[57]

Despite the intervening decision in *Penry II*, with its emphasis on the need for "*full* consideration" of mitigating evidence, the Fifth Circuit Court of Appeals held that the merit of Tennard's *Penry* claim was not debatable among reasonable jurists and hence denied a full appeal on his claim. The Fifth Circuit applied its test of constitutional relevance, concluding that Tennard's evidence of his 67 I.Q. was not mitigating because it did not amount to "a uniquely severe condition" and Tennard had not shown that his crime was "attributable" to his low I.Q.[58]

The Supreme Court reversed, in an opinion sharply critical of the decision below.[59] Justice O'Connor, again writing for the majority (the same six Justices who formed the *Penry II* majority), insisted that Tennard's evidence of his low I.Q. bore the same relation to the special issues as Penry's evidence of mental retardation and childhood abuse, and the state and lower federal courts were wrong to impose threshold tests of constitutional relevance to conclude otherwise. According to Justice O'Connor, the "Fifth Circuit's test [for constitutional relevance] ha[d] no foundation in the decisions of this Court."[60] Indeed, because the case arose on federal habeas, Tennard had to establish that the state court decision was not only wrong, but unreasonably wrong, and the

---

[57] Ex parte Tennard, 960 S.W.2d 57 (Tex. Crim. App. 1997).

[58] Tennard v. Cockrell, 284 F.3d 591 (5th Cir. 2002).

[59] Tennard v. Dretke, 542 U.S. 274 (2004).

[60] *Id.*, at 284.

Court's opinion strongly suggested that Tennard had met that standard (technically, the Court reversed only the Fifth Circuit's refusal to grant a full appeal of Tennard's claim).

While *Tennard* was pending, the CCA denied relief to LaRoyce Smith, who had likewise presented evidence of low intelligence under the pre–1991 statute.[61] His jury, like Penry's, had also received a nullification instruction. The CCA held that Smith's evidence was not constitutionally relevant, following the "severity" and "nexus" tests employed by the Fifth Circuit. The CCA also insisted that the nullification instruction in any case cured the *Penry* problem because it communicated clearly—more clearly than the instruction condemned in *Penry II*—the obligation of the jurors to falsify their answers if they believed Smith deserved a life sentence. On top of this hair-splitting, two members of the CCA, concurring in the result, openly ridiculed the Court's *Penry II* decision: "[H]aving decided that no federal constitutional error occurred in this case, we may disagree with the United States Supreme Court that Texas jurors are incapable of remembering, understanding and giving effect to the straightforward and manageable 'nullification' instruction such as the one in this case."[62] This quotation was followed by a "But see" citation to the Court's opinion in *Penry II*.

The Supreme Court summarily reversed in a per curiam opinion, *Smith v. Texas*,[63] with only Justices Scalia and Thomas dissenting. As in *Penry II*, the Court quoted Justice O'Connor's dissenting language from *Johnson* emphasizing a defendant's right to "*full* consideration" of his mitigating evidence. Indeed, the Court appeared to emphasize the breadth of the *Penry* problem by concluding that the inquiries of "deliberateness and dangerousness [ ] had little, if anything, to do with the mitigation evidence petitioner presented,"[64] which included evidence of learning disabilities, low intelligence, a difficult family background, and his youth. The Court also rejected the CCA's effort to salvage the use of nullification instructions, insisting that "*Penry II* identified a broad and intractable problem—a problem that the state court ignored here— inherent in any requirement that the jury nullify special issues contained within a verdict form."[65]

Despite these three decisions reversing and sharply criticizing denials of relief under *Penry I* and *Penry II*, the Texas and lower federal courts continued to read *Penry* narrowly. On remand in *Smith*, the CCA

---

[61] Ex parte Smith, 132 S.W.3d 407 (Tex. Crim. App. 2004).

[62] 132 S.W.3d, at 427 (Hervey, J., concurring).

[63] 543 U.S. 37 (2004).

[64] *Id.*, at 48.

[65] *Id.*, at 46.

remarkably found the *Penry* error to be harmless on the ground that the nullification instruction was so well explained to the jurors that they likely gave effect to Smith's mitigating evidence.[66] Moreover, two CCA judges again insisted "we are not bound by the view expressed in *Penry II* that Texas jurors are incapable of remembering, understanding and giving effect to the straightforward and manageable 'nullification' instruction such as the one in this case."[67] The Fifth Circuit, meanwhile found no *Penry* error in two cases involving evidence of mental illness and a defendant's deprived and abusive background.[68]

In 2007, almost twenty years after *Penry*, with only a small and dwindling number of inmates death-sentenced under the old special issue scheme remaining on death row, the Court agreed to hear these cases and reversed in all three, with Justice Kennedy supplying the decisive fifth vote.[69] Justice O'Connor, who had since retired, no longer carried the *Penry* banner, but the Court nonetheless embraced the broadest articulation of her *Penry* doctrine. According to the Court, the *Penry* line of cases stands for the proposition that sentencers must be allowed to respond to *all* evidence that reduces a defendant's moral culpability for his offense. Because the special issues often fail to permit meaningful consideration of such evidence, they are inadequate for a wide range of mitigating factors, including evidence of deprivation, abuse, psychiatric impairment, and low intelligence.

Thus, Penry's return to the Supreme Court after his second death sentence set in motion the revitalization of the *Penry* doctrine. The most recent trio of decisions appears to acknowledge that the former Texas statute was much closer in its operation to the mandatory statutes that the Court invalidated than the guided discretion statutes that it upheld. Indeed, this belated recognition is significant, because it suggests that a large proportion of the inmates executed in America's most active executing state were condemned unconstitutionally—without a genuine assessment of whether they deserved to die.

The Court's extraordinary attention to the deficiencies of the repealed Texas statute (five merits decisions between 2004–2007) is somewhat peculiar given the small number of surviving inmates affected by its decisions (probably no more than two dozen) and the issue's lack of any continuing doctrinal significance (all states presently permit essen-

---

[66] Ex parte Smith, 185 S.W.3d 455 (Tex. Crim. App. 2006).

[67] *Id.*, at 474 (Hervey, J., concurring).

[68] Cole v. Dretke, 418 F.3d 494 (5th Cir. 2005); Brewer v. Dretke, 442 F.3d 273 (5th Cir. 2006).

[69] Smith v. Texas, 550 U.S. 297 (2007); Abdul–Kabir v. Quarterman, 550 U.S. 233 (2007); Brewer v. Quarterman, 550 U.S. 286 (2007).

tially unbridled consideration of mitigating circumstances). Perhaps the Court was drawn to the cases by the defiant tone of the lower court opinions, particularly in the Texas Court of Criminal Appeals. Texas has become an outlier not only in the number of executions it has carried out, but also in its willingness to ratify outrageous conduct, ranging from sleeping lawyers,[70] brazenly discriminatory use of peremptory strikes,[71] prosecutorial failure to disclose exculpatory evidence,[72] and state-sponsored testimony regarding the "dangerousness" of Hispanics.[73] Or perhaps these decisions are part of a broader dynamic on the current Court to reign in perceived departures from its moderate regulation of the American death penalty, reflected in its seemingly constant reversals of decisions from the Ninth Circuit, on the one hand, and the Fourth and Fifth Circuits on the other (the former for excessive indulgence in its treatment of constitutional claims and the latter for their excessive restrictiveness). Whatever its cause, the Court's new-found willingness to enforce *Penry* is as important for its documentation of the flawed Texas death penalty in the modern era as it is for its relatively modest practical consequences—the removal of a small number of inmates from death row who managed, mostly through fortuity, to avoid execution in the most active death penalty state for at least seventeen years.

E. *Penry*'s Other Legacy: Proportionality Limits on Executing Persons with Mental Retardation

After Penry's second death sentence was reversed in June, 2001, he was sent back for retrial, this time in Montgomery County, just north of Houston and south of Huntsville. By the time the trial was to start in April, 2002, twenty-three years after the commission of the offense, the Supreme Court had already agreed to revisit *Penry*'s refusal to exempt persons with mental retardation from the death penalty in *Atkins v. Virginia*.[74] Although it was unusual for the Court to revisit one of its decisions after such a short interval (thirteen years), much had changed regarding the American death penalty generally and the status of executing persons with mental retardation in particular.

When *Penry I* was argued, only two states, Georgia and Maryland, had passed statutes prohibiting the execution of persons with mental retardation. Justice O'Connor, writing for a majority, insisted that the "clearest and most reliable objective evidence of contemporary values" is

---

[70] Ex parte Burdine, 901 S.W.2d 456 (Tex. Crim. App. 1995).

[71] Miller–El v. Dretke, 545 U.S. 231 (2005); Miller–El v. Cockrell, 537 U.S. 322 (2003).

[72] See, e.g., Ex parte Adams, 768 S.W.2d 281 (Tex. Crim. App. 1989).

[73] See Saldano v. Roach, 363 F.3d 545 (5th Cir. 2004).

[74] 533 U.S. 976 (2001).

state legislation,[75] and the absence of much legislative activity strongly weighed against Penry's claim. Writing just for herself, Justice O'Connor went on to consider whether the execution of persons with mental retardation made any "measurable contribution to acceptable goals of punishment." Penry had argued that the diminished culpability associated with mental retardation invariably rendered such offenders undeserving of the death penalty, especially in light of the commitment to reserve the death penalty for the "worst of the worst." In Justice O'Connor's view, though, the "diverse capacities and life experiences" of persons with mental retardation made it difficult to conclude that *all* members of that class could "never act with the level of culpability associated with the death penalty." Penry had sought to piggy-back on the claim that death penalty was disproportionate as applied to juveniles, which was before the Court at the same time and had greater "objective" support in the form of state legislation (15 states barred the execution of persons under the age of 17 at the time of the crime and 12 barred the execution of 17 year-olds). One of Penry's experts at trial had testified that Penry had a "mental age" of 6½, and in Penry's view, there was a clear societal rejection of executing persons with such limited capacity. Justice O'Connor, though, found significant flaws in the "mental age" concept, including the fact that after ages 15 or 16, "the mean scores on most intelligence tests cease to increase significantly with age."[76] As a result, the "mental age" of the average adult is about 16 years and 8 months; importing a ban on executing juveniles to persons whose "mental age" is below 18 would thus have the effect of prohibiting most executions altogether, and the imprecision of the "mental age" concept made the choice of a lower threshold appear arbitrary. In any case, in *Stanford v. Kentucky,*[77] a decision issued the same day as *Penry,* the Court upheld by the same five-to-four margin the death penalty as applied to 16 and 17 year-old offenders.

The Court's rejection of the claim in *Penry I* focused legislative attention on the propriety of executing persons with mental retardation. For opponents of the practice, the strategy was to bring mental health professionals, rather than abolitionist activists, to the legislative chambers to make the case for the exemption. By the time *Atkins* reached the Court, sixteen additional states outlawed the practice; in addition, no statutes explicitly *authorized* the practice, and few states or politicians seemed adamant in their support. The fact that many of the prohibiting states were active death penalty states (including Georgia, Arkansas, Florida, and Missouri), together with the paucity of such executions

---

[75] 492 U.S., at 331.

[76] *Id.*, at 339.

[77] 492 U.S. 361 (1989).

(five) nationwide since *Penry*, strengthened the claim that the practice was inconsistent with prevailing community values.

In Texas, unlike in most other states, the debate about exempting persons with mental retardation was less about *Penry* the case and more about John Paul Penry the inmate. Proposed bills to exempt persons with mental retardation were presented every legislative session after *Penry I*, but opposition to those bills invariably highlighted the gruesome facts of Penry's crimes. Ellen May, niece of victim Pamela Moseley Carpenter, attended hearings on the legislation and testified about the significance of her family's loss. State prosecutors opposed an exemption, and some of their opposition was likely traceable in part to their unwillingness to disturb Penry's own death sentence. While *Penry II* was pending in the Supreme Court—and it seemed possible that he would be spared the death penalty in any event—the Texas legislature passed the mental retardation exemption. Joe Price, the Inspector Javert of Penry's story, apparently was so incensed by the willingness of the Texas District and County Attorneys Association—the prosecutors' lobby—to support the legislation (even though it was designed to have prosecution-friendly procedures implementing the ban) that he sought (unsuccessfully) to have its executive director replaced. In any case, Governor Perry vetoed the legislation.[78] In a perplexing twist, Governor Perry declared in his Veto Proclamation that "[w]e do not execute mentally retarded murderers today."[79] This statement seemed particularly odd given that Texas led the country in executing persons with mental retardation during the modern era. But it also seemed to confirm the lack of genuine political support for the challenged practice.

Although state legislative reform quickly followed *Penry I* on the exemption front, the decade following the decision saw the increasing entrenchment of the death penalty as a national practice. Executions climbed from about twenty per year (nationwide) in the late 1980s to about eighty per year in the late 1990s.[80] Notwithstanding the increase in executions, the national death-row population increased significantly as death-sentencing rates climbed as well (the per capita rate for death sentences reached its modern-era high in the mid–1990s).[81] At the same time, the Court seemed disinclined to impose significant constitutional constraints on the imposition of the death penalty, and the prospects for future judicial regulation appeared to decline with the departures of

---

[78] See *Atkins*, 536 U.S., at 315 n.16.

[79] *Id.*, quoting Veto Proclamation for H.B. No. 236.

[80] See Death Penalty Information Center, Death Penalty Fact Sheet, p. 1, at www.deathpenaltyinfo.org/factsheet.pdf.

[81] See Death Penalty Information Center, Rate of Death Sentencing By Year (per population), at www.deathpenaltyinfo.org/article.php?did=840&scid=64.

Justices Brennan, Marshall, and Blackmun, the Court's three most reliable opponents of capital punishment.

But by turn of the millennium, the mood of the country palpably shifted with the discovery of numerous wrongfully-convicted inmates on Illinois' death row.[82] The magnitude of error (thirteen death-sentenced inmates) seemed significant in its own right, but was even more troublesome given that Illinois had executed only twelve inmates in the modern era. Governor Ryan, a Republican who had long supported the death penalty, insisted on an exhaustive audit of Illinois' capital punishment system. As the details of the wrongful convictions emerged, they painted a portrait of widespread dysfunction, including police misconduct, inadequate representation, and excessive prosecutorial zeal. Ryan issued a moratorium on executions and ultimately commuted the sentences of all 167 death-row inmates. In addition, the emergence of new DNA technology during the 1990s led to the exoneration of numerous capital and non-capital inmates nationwide. Although the public was likely aware in the abstract about the potential fallibility of the criminal justice system, the experience in Illinois and the DNA revolution attached scores of faces and stories to the underlying problems. As a result, legislative and popular attention shifted to reform rather than expansion of the American death penalty. Within a few years, the number of death sentences nationwide fell precipitously, dropping about 65% from the 1995 modern high (326) to the 2006 modern low (115),[83] a decline only partially explained by declining homicide rates. Executions slowed as well, from the modern era high of 98 nationwide in 1999 to less than 60 per year in each of the last four years (2003–07).[84]

This shift in mood perhaps contributed to the Court's willingness to revisit *Penry* on the exemption question. The grant in *Atkins* posed a substantial practical dilemma as Penry's third trial was about to begin: should the trial court abate the proceeding until the Court ruled in *Atkins*? And, if the Court were to ban executing persons with mental retardation, how should the trial court implement that ruling? Would the jury, a separate jury, or the judge make a finding as to whether Penry had mental retardation? Who bore the burden of proof on the issue and under what standard (proof by a preponderance of the evidence, clear and convincing evidence, or beyond a reasonable doubt)?

---

[82] Carol S. Steiker and Jordan M. Steiker, *The Seduction of Innocence: The Attraction and Limitations of the Focus on Innocence in Capital Punishment Law and Advocacy*, 95 J. Crim. L. & Crim. 587 (2005).

[83] See Death Penalty Information Center, Death Sentences by Year: 1977–2007, at www.deathpenaltyinfo.org/article.php?scid=9&did=873.

[84] See Death Penalty Information Center, Executions by Year, at www.deathpenalty info.org/article.php?scid=8&did=146.

Two years before, as Penry's execution date approached (before the Supreme Court stay), the District Attorney had aggressively opposed clemency for Penry, insisting that Penry did not have mental retardation. In the State's view, although Penry might have satisfied the prong requiring significantly sub-average intellectual functioning (reflected in I.Q. scores below 70), Penry had not established "deficits or impairments in adaptive functioning." Indeed, the State maintained that Penry's criminal misbehavior—his "ability to plan his prior crimes, think ahead, and think on his feet" illustrated adaptive qualities, and as the third trial was approaching, the State was prepared to defend its assertion that Penry did not have mental retardation.

Over defense objections, the trial court chose to proceed with the trial, and much of the evidence and argument tracked the second trial. The parties again wrangled over the admissibility of Penry's confessions and Penry's competence to stand trial. The competency trial, tried to a separate jury, took over a week, and was in many respects a rehearsal of the punishment phase. Both sides presented extensive expert and lay testimony about Penry's intellectual capacity, which was obviously relevant to the question of competency (whether he could "consult with his lawyer with a reasonable degree of rational understanding" and whether he had "a rational as well as factual understanding of the proceeding against him"). The defense emphasized Penry's early diagnosis of mental retardation, his placement at the Mexia State School for the Mentally Retarded, and the numerous tests over the years (administered by officials at Texas institutions) confirming his low I.Q. The defense also put on the testimony of lawyers who had served as Penry's attorneys who spoke to Penry's inability to understand the proceedings and to assist in his defense. The State, on the other hand, emphasized the low standard for competency to stand trial, remarking that "[c]riminals, as a general rule, aren't bright." It also emphasized testimony of prison personnel about Penry's adaptive behavior in prison, including writing and sending letters, making requests, and talking about his upcoming trial. The State made clear that the consequences of an incompetency finding would be to preclude serious punishment: "Do not let them raise the bar so high that people that go out and commit serious crimes here in the State of Texas cannot be held accountable for their actions." In less than an hour, the jury returned a verdict that Penry was competent to stand trial.

During the punishment phase, the Supreme Court issued *Atkins*. The defense insisted on a mistrial, asserting that the evidence before the trial court indisputably established Penry's mental retardation; the defense also made procedural objections, contending that the case could not proceed because only a jury could make the finding of mental retardation, and the jury currently empanelled had not been subject to voir dire on the exemption issue. The State, on the other hand, argued that if the jury sentenced Penry to death, the question whether Penry had mental retardation could be sorted out in postconviction litigation.

Governor Perry's veto of the exemption bill put the trial judge in a difficult position. The legislature had not established a mechanism for enforcing a ban on executing persons with mental retardation, and any procedures the trial court adopted were subject to challenge (including the burden issue, whether the determination belonged to judge or jury, whether a separate jury had to be empanelled, and whether the jury deciding the mental retardation question could be informed of the facts of the offense). Both sides cautioned the trial court about trying to improvise in response to *Atkins*.

The trial judge made her own finding that Penry did not have mental retardation. She also put the mental retardation question to the jury, structuring their deliberations so that they would decide between life and death and whether Penry had mental retardation at the same time. Because the verdict form could not be altered without the approval of the legislature, the trial judge could not directly ask whether Penry had mental retardation; remarkably, in light of the last reversal in Penry's own case, the trial judge gave a new "nullification" instruction. If the jurors believed Penry had mental retardation, they were to answer the mitigation question (whether there was sufficient mitigation to justify a sentence less than death) affirmatively; if not, they were to consider any *other* mitigation supporting a sentence less than death and decide the mitigation (life versus death) question on its own terms.

Penry's third jury again sentenced him to death, implicitly rejecting his claim of mental retardation. But given the trial court's ad hoc response to *Atkins*, Penry's sentence was precarious. Although the prosecution had repeatedly claimed that Penry's mental impairments were exaggerated and that he did not have mental retardation, there were strong reasons to believe that his sentence was vulnerable to appellate reversal. If Penry's claim of mental retardation could be rejected, it is hard to imagine any others being sustained. Penry had been placed in a school for the mentally retarded at a young age. Penry apparently wasn't even a particularly strong student at that school. Numerous I.Q. tests administered from childhood through adulthood uniformly produced scores in the 50s and low 60s. The only real argument on the other side was that Penry's actions during his crimes revealed "adaptive" behavior—as though committing violent crimes and getting immediately apprehended reflected skills beyond the capacity of persons with mental retardation.

Perhaps recognizing the vulnerability of Penry's third death sentence, the trial judge, Elizabeth Coker, refused to appoint Penry's longtime lawyers, John Wright and Julia Tarver (of Paul, Weiss) to work on Penry's direct appeal. Though the continuation of trial counsel on direct appeal is routine in Texas, Judge Coker insisted that Penry waive any claim to ineffectiveness of assistance of counsel on appeal in order to retain Wright and Tarver as his counsel. Penry had clearly expressed his desire for their continued representation; indeed, Wright had visited Penry in prison about once a month for the twenty two years while Penry languished on death row. But when Penry refused to waive this potential claim, new counsel was substituted to represent Penry. The irregularity of Judge Coker's decision to remove Wright and Paul, Weiss from the case was reflected in the decision of the New York Times to publish a story about the conflict.[85]

That Judge Coker's decision might have been motivated by a desire to undermine Penry's prospects on appeal (and to insulate her rulings from review) is evident in the campaign literature she distributed when she stood for reelection following Penry's trial: "Criminals fear walking into Judge Coker's courtroom because they know her reputation for handing down tough sentences. When the John Paul Penry capital murder trial came before her court in 2002, Judge Coker cleared the way for the jury to issue a death sentence."

The Texas Court of Criminal Appeals apparently thought that Judge Coker cleared too much, reversing Penry's third death sentence in 2005 based on her ad hoc instructions on mental retardation and mitigation.[86] The CCA concluded that jurors might have understood the instruction to preclude them from considering evidence of mental impairment *short* of mental retardation as they decided the mitigation question, because they were told to consider any *"other"* mitigating evidence in the event they rejected the retardation claim.

There is some irony in the CCA's careful parsing of these instructions given its virtual non-enforcement of *Penry* for over fifteen years. In case after case, the CCA upheld death sentences unsupported by a jury determination that the defendant deserved to die (indeed, given the jury's rejection of Penry's mental retardation claim, Penry himself would have been ineligible for *"Penry"* relief under the CCA's old approach, which required proof of a "severe" condition comparable to retardation). And yet, in Penry's case, where the jury was directly asked whether mitigating circumstances called for leniency, the CCA found that the inclusion of the word "other" fatally undermined his sentence. Perhaps the CCA's decision reflected a new-found commitment to a broad individualization principle, inspired in part by the Supreme Court's recent

---

[85] Adam Liptak, "Longtime Death Case Lawyer Appeals Ouster," New York Times, Mar. 24, 2003, p. A13.

[86] Penry v. State, 178 S.W.3d 782 (Tex. Crim. App. 2005).

reversals, but it is equally likely that the CCA anticipated enormous difficulties in Penry's case relating to his *Atkins* claim. Both the procedural mechanism by which Penry's claim of mental retardation was rejected at trial as well as the substantive case for withholding the *Atkins* exemption had serious problems, and the CCA probably did not want Penry to be the test case for administering *Atkins* in Texas.

When Penry's case returned for yet another sentencing, similar concerns likely prompted the District Attorney to allow Penry to plead to a life sentence. In the interim, Joe Price, who had led the State's efforts to punish Penry with death, had died in a car accident while returning from the rodeo. The prospect of relitigating Penry's competence, mental retardation, and death-worthiness seemed daunting, especially given the continuing failure of the Texas Legislature to pass a statute implementing *Atkins*. One of the key features—and certainly the oddest feature—of the plea bargain was for Penry to acknowledge that he does not have mental retardation. It is hard to imagine a provision with less legal significance than a concession obtained under such circumstances. John Wright, quoted in a news story ("John Paul Penry admits lying about retardation; gets off death row"[87]), made just this point: "My opinion is that he's retarded now and was retarded then. . . . When they say we'll give you a life sentence if you say you're not retarded, he took the deal."[88]

V. Conclusion

Penry is truly at the center of the modern American death penalty storm. The defects in the Texas statute that culminated in *Penry* are directly traceable to the Court's intervention in *Furman*. Texas, like many States, had read *Furman* to condemn discretionary grants of mercy based on mitigating evidence. When the Court stepped back from the brink of judicial abolition in 1976, and forged a path of continuing constitutional regulation, it misclassified the Texas statute as facilitating sentencer discretion, perhaps because of the ill-fated LDF abolitionist strategy. That misclassification in turn allowed hundreds of Texas inmates to be sentenced to death without a determination that they deserved to die.

The almost immediate retreat from *Penry* by the Texas and lower federal courts allowed Texas to become the national leader in executions and symbolized the extraordinary resistance, in certain jurisdictions, to the Court's moderate course of constitutional regulation. By the time Penry returned to the Court after his second trial, and the Court revived

---

[87] Jason Whitely, "John Paul Penry admits lying about retardation; gets off death row," 11 News, Livingston, TX, Feb. 15, 2008 (available at www.khou.com/topstories/khou 080215_rm_penrycase_c645b1e9.hrml).

[88] *Id.*

the *Penry* doctrine in *Penry II*, most of the inmates that had been unconstitutionally condemned had already been executed. In light of Texas' abandonment of the challenged statute in 1991 and the paucity of surviving inmates who had been sentenced under the old scheme, the Court's continued interest in the *Penry* issue (reflected in five merits opinion reversing decisions of the Texas and lower federal courts over a four year period) is striking. Overall, such interest more likely reflects the Court's concerns about lower court disobedience than its desire to craft new substantive law. In this respect, *Penry* is a story of both resistance and enforcement, and the saga illustrates the vulnerability of Court decisions absent determined supervision.

The other half of *Penry* likewise illustrates the interaction between decisions of the Court and other actors in our constitutional system. *Penry*'s refusal to craft an exemption for persons with mental retardation is one of the few constitutional decisions in which the denial of the claimed right mobilized states to grant greater protection for individual liberty. *Penry* set in motion an unparalleled moment of state death penalty reform, and the new statutes prohibiting the execution of persons with mental retardation led the Court to revisit its decision within only thirteen years.

The Court's resulting decision in *Atkins* not only indirectly led to Penry's relief from his own death sentence, it also inaugurated a new, more robust, era of federal constitutional regulation of the death penalty.[89] Whereas the Court's proportionality analysis in *Penry* and *Stanford* had suggested strongly that majority legislative practices were virtually immune from constitutional attack, *Atkins* invalidated the death penalty for persons with mental retardation even though a majority of death penalty states permitted it. More importantly, *Atkins* found support for its conclusion of a national consensus in non-legislative indicia of prevailing opinion, citing expert opinion (amicus briefs filed by the American Psychological Association and the American Association for Mental Retardation), religious opinion (an amicus brief filed on behalf of diverse religious communities), world opinion (an amicus brief filed by the European Union), as well as public opinion polls.

The reference to these gauges of "evolving standards of decency" appeared only in a footnote, but their potential import in broadening the Court's role in enforcing the Eighth Amendment was clear at the time of the decision. Justice Scalia, for example, complained about the Court's methodology to the point of bestowing a new award: "[T]he Prize for the

---

[89] Carol S. Steiker and Jordan M. Steiker, *Abolition in Our Time?* 1 Ohio St. J. Crim. L. 323 (2003); Steiker & Steiker, The Beginning of the End? in Sarat & Ogletree, The Road to Abolition (forthcoming) (describing the increased prospects for judicial abolition of capital punishment).

Court's Most Feeble Effort to fabricate 'national consensus' must go to its appeal (deservedly relegated to a footnote) to the views of assorted professional and religious organizations, members of the so-called 'world community,' and respondents to opinion polls.''[90] When the Court revisited *Stanford* three years later in *Roper v. Simmons*,[91] invalidating the death penalty as applied to juveniles, it expanded upon the *Atkins* footnote, and affirmed the importance of exercising its own "independent judgment" on proportionality,[92] rather than merely deferring to prevailing statutory schemes. The Court relied heavily on expert opinion regarding the mental and emotional development of juveniles. The Court also found "confirmation" for its judgment in the fact that the United States was alone among nations in the world giving official sanction to such executions. The off-hand reference to world opinion in *Atkins* became a separate full section of the opinion in *Simmons*—equal in length to its discussion of state legislative and sentencing practices. The Court also explicitly defended its canvassing of international opinion and practice on the ground that "the express affirmation of certain fundamental rights by other nations and peoples" underscores the "centrality" of those rights within our own culture.[93]

Like *Atkins*, *Simmons* invalidated a death-penalty practice notwithstanding its authorization by a majority of death penalty states. It focused less on what states declared legislatively and more on what states actually did. More generally, *Simmons'* amplification of *Atkins* provides a blueprint for the judicial abolition of capital punishment in the United States. It privileges non-legislative criteria that overwhelmingly point against the continued use of the death penalty. The increasing rarity of death sentences and executions supports the claim that the statutes on the books do not reflect genuine public support for the punishment (especially in light of the broad net of death-eligibility cases in the post-*Furman* statutes). Elite, social, and professional opinion— from religious groups, the ABA, criminologists, and others—generally rejects the notion that the death penalty serves any important penological purposes beyond those secured by the alternative of lengthy incarceration. World opinion increasingly condemns the death penalty as contrary to basic human rights.

The part of *Penry*, then, that most observers regarded as nearly fatal to the prospects for continued constitutional regulation of the death penalty, set in motion events that have now produced a remarkable

---

[90] 536 U.S., at 347–48 (Scalia, J., dissenting).

[91] 543 U.S. 551 (2005).

[92] *Id.* at 563.

[93] *Id.* at 578.

recalibration of the Court's Eighth Amendment methodology. The death penalty appears more vulnerable now to judicial regulation—or perhaps abolition—than at any other time since *Furman*. Indeed, Justice Stevens, who cast a critical vote sustaining the new death penalty statutes in 1976, recently expressed his view "that the imposition of the death penalty represents the pointless and needless extinction of life with only marginal contributions to any discernible social or public purpose" and is therefore "patently excessive and cruel and unusual punishment violative of the Eighth Amendment."[94] In another recent opinion, four Justices (Souter, Ginsburg, Breyer, and Stevens) announced that the discovery of pervasive error in capital cases (in Illinois and elsewhere) amounts to "a new body of fact [that] must be accounted for in deciding what, in practical terms, the Eighth Amendment guarantees should tolerate."[95] Although these Justices insisted that "it is far too soon for any generalizations about the soundness of capital sentencing across the country,"[96] this very disclaimer highlighted the possibility of revisiting the constitutionality of the death penalty at some future time.

This past term, in *Kennedy v. Louisiana*,[97] the Court added yet another proportionality constraint by invalidating the death penalty for child rape. Despite new legislative efforts to punish child rape with death, the Court crafted a broad rule prohibiting imposition of the death penalty for any non-homicidal ordinary crimes (distinguishing use of the death penalty to punish treason, espionage and other crimes against the "State"). The Court again placed great weight on its own "independent judgment" and discounted the legislative trend in light of the infrequency of the practice. More importantly, the Court highlighted the deep tensions in current capital punishment law—indeed, the very same problem of balancing guidance and discretion that gave rise to *Penry*—and expressed its reluctance to permit expansion of the death penalty in light of its already apparently flaws: "[T]he resulting imprecision and the tension between evaluating the individual circumstances and consistency of treatment have been tolerated where the victim dies. It should not be introduced into our justice system, though, where death has not occurred."[98] Nothing in *Kennedy* suggests that abolition is around the corner (though it continues the trend of drawing attention to prevailing defects in the administration and legal regulation of the death penalty), but the Court's refusal to sustain the new child rape statutes is enor-

---

[94] Baze v. Rees, 128 S.Ct. 1520, 1551 (2008) (Stevens, J., concurring in judgment).

[95] Kansas v. Marsh, 548 U.S. 163, 207 (2006) (Souter, J., dissenting).

[96] *Id.*, at 210.

[97] 128 S.Ct. 2641 (2008).

[98] *Id.*, at 2661.

mously significant. A contrary decision would have effectively removed the incipient radical potential of the Court's emerging proportionality doctrine, and a door unclosed is a door still open.

It is hard to gauge whether the emerging popular and judicial reservations about capital punishment will culminate in the judicial abolition of the death penalty. Indeed, *Penry*'s greatest lesson is that judicial decisions often chart a course quite different from what its authors or audiences expect, and the Court's words frequently begin rather than end a constitutional conversation.

*

8

Austin Sarat

The Story of *Payne v. Tennessee*: Victims Triumphant*

In April of 1991 the United States Supreme Court heard the appeal of Pervis Payne who, four years earlier, had been convicted of assault and murder and sentenced to death by a Tennessee jury. The victims of these crimes were a young mother, Charisse Christopher, and her two children. Among the evidence presented by the State during the sentencing phase of his trial was testimony by Charisse's mother, Mrs. Zvalanek, who at that time was legal guardian of Charisse's son Nicholas who had survived the attack. When the prosecutor, Thomas Henderson, asked her about the impact of the crime on her grandson she replied:

> He cries for his mom. He doesn't seem to understand why she doesn't come home. And he cries for Lacie. He comes to me many times during the week and asks me 'Grandmama, do you miss my Lacie?' And I tell him yes. He says, 'I'm worried about my Lacie.'[1]

During his closing argument Henderson told the jury

> There is nothing you can do to ease the pain of any of the families in this case . . . there is obviously nothing you can do for Charisse and Lacey Jo. But there is something that you can do for Nicholas. Somewhere down the road Nicholas is going to grow up, hopefully. He's going to want to know what happened. And he is going to know

* I want to thank Tovah Ackerman and Charlie Quigg for their invaluable research assistance and Jordan Steiker for his helpful comments on a previous version of this essay. I am grateful for financial support from the Axel Schupf Fund for Intellectual Life at Amherst College and Amherst's Dean of the Faculty, Greg Call, and from the University of Alabama Law School Foundation and Dean Kenneth Randall.

[1] Payne v. Tennessee, 501 U.S. 808, 814–815 (1991).

what happened to his baby sister and his mother. He is going to want to know what type of justice was done. He is going to want to know what happened. Your verdict, you will provide the answer.

Payne's case gave the Supreme Court the occasion to revisit the question of whether statements of the kind made by Nicholas's grandmother and the prosecutor, so called victims' impact evidence, should have been admitted or whether they violated his 8th and 14th Amendment rights. Just four years earlier, in *Booth v. Maryland* the Court had barred the use of such evidence in capital cases.[2] But, by 1991 with the composition of the Court altered by the retirements of Justices Brennan and Powell (both of whom were in the *Booth* majority), only three members of that majority remained on the Court—Justices Blackmun, Marshall, and Stevens. The replacements for Brennan and Powell— Justices Souter and Kennedy—shifted the balance, with the result that what the *Booth* Court held to be unconstitutional, the *Payne* Court found to have no significant constitutional defects.

For twenty years after its decision in *Furman v. Georgia*,[3] striking down the death penalty, for the next twenty years, the Supreme Court purported to construct an elaborate system of "super due process" through which capital defendants could be assured an extra-measure of protection from arbitrariness, caprice, or emotionalism.[4] In the sentencing phase of capital trials, attention was to be directed exclusively to the task of ascertaining the precise, personal culpability of the defendant. Did this particular murderer, given the full circumstances of his or her life, deserve to die at the hands of the state? Here the most exacting calculus of retribution was carried out.

Payne marked an important moment in the Court's late twentieth century retreat from its previous quest for super due process and a sharp escalation in what the *New York Times* labeled the Court's "Death Agenda."[5] It meant that constitutional scrupulousness would no longer

---

[2] *Booth v. Maryland*, 482 U.S. 496 (1987).

[3] 408 U.S. 238 (1972).

[4] Margaret Radin, "Cruel Punishment and Respect for Persons: Super Due Process for Death," 53 *Southern California Law Review* (1980), 1143. For a discussion of the abandonment of super due process in death penalty cases see Franklin Zimring, "Inheriting the Wind: The Supreme Court and Capital Punishment in the 1990s," *Florida State University Law Review* 20 (1992), 7.

[5] See "The Court Sets a Death Agenda," *New York Times* (April 27, 1991), 24. Indeed so hostile have the courts become to extended litigation in capital cases that even new evidence of actual innocence was found to be inadequate as the basis for challenging a death sentence. See *Herrera v. Collins*, 504 U.S. 971 (1992). In response to *Herrera*, Justice Blackmun charged the Court with coming "perilously close to murder." For the current Supreme Court "finality is more important than hearing every meritorious legal claim;

be a barrier to hearing the voice of the victim. Moreover, *Payne* brought to light a central fact of contemporary legality, namely its inability to rid itself of vengeance.

Vengeance is at once the "threatening evil" which provides the *raison d'etre* of law, and an unwelcome guest which is nonetheless indispensable to legal justice itself. Moreover, vengeance is the ultimate measure of loyalty to those who cannot avenge themselves. It is the supreme test of social bonds, of blood ties called to let blood. Played out as an address to a jury, victim impact evidence in capital cases subjects the claims of blood to judgment in accordance with rules whose substance is not fully encompassed by the imperatives of loyalty or kinship.

The story of *Payne v. Tennessee* is a story of the Supreme Court's dramatic reversal of precedent and change of the direction of its death penalty jurisprudence. It was also a significant milestone in an ongoing political struggle, the struggle of victims for inclusion and recognition in America's criminal justice process. This struggle took place across the entire nation, in city halls, state legislatures, and the Congress, as well as the courts. The Court's *Payne's* decision was a crucial marker of the success of the victims' rights movement.

The Crime

The crimes for which Payne was convicted took place in Millington, Tennessee, a suburb of Memphis. Established in 1878 by a plantation owner, George Millington, who offered to donate land for a town and to help build a railroad station on the newly established Chesapeake and Ohio Railroad line, the town was formally incorporated in 1903. Its current population of around 10,000 is almost 70% white and 22% African American, roughly what it was twenty years ago when Charisse Christopher was murdered. Described on its web site as "dotted with peach orchards, cotton fields, a myriad of lakes and crisscrossed by bridle paths through the scenic wooded countryside ...", the town boasts that it has "some of the finest schools in the nation," is "home of the world's largest inland Navy Base," and is "a community with just the right balance of yesterday and today."[6]

---

there simply comes a point when legal proceedings must end and punishment must be imposed." See Evan Caminker and Erwin Chemrinsky, "The Lawless Execution of Robert Alton Harris," *Yale Law Journal* 102 (1992), 226. "[T]he Court's desire to expedite the process of death ... has now accrued a life of its own." at 253. Also Joseph Hoffman, "Is Innocence Sufficient? An Essay on the United States Supreme Court's Continuing Problems with Federal Habeas Corpus and the Death Penalty," *Indiana Law Review* 68 (1993), 817.

6 http://www.ci.millington.tn.us/millhistory.html.

A headline in the June 28, 1987 edition of the Memphis *Commercial Appeal* announced "Man Held in Slayings of Mom and Tot."[7] The newspaper told of the murder of Charisse and Lacey in their apartment and reminded its readers that these were the "first homicides in the North Shelby County city ... in three years."[8] As Millington Police Captain W. J. Orman put it, "Things like this aren't supposed to happen in small towns."[9]

The next day the newspaper reported that a man had been arrested in connection with the killings and identified him as "Pervis Tyronne Payne, 20, a painter and carpenter from Drummonds, Tenn ..."[10] The paper said that he had been charged with "two counts of second-degree murder (charges that were changed to 1st degree murder two days later) and one count of assault to commit murder."[11] Payne, the newspaper told its readers, was the son of a minister, had two sisters, played football in high school and "was a drummer in the band for several years."[12] At the time of his arrest he had no criminal record. One of the members of his father's church, The Church of God in Christ, described Payne as a "moral young fellow, nice sense of humor, kind. His personality is just such that you couldn't help but love him if you knew him."[13]

In all of the litigation associated with Payne's case, courts seemed to go out of their way to provide unusually detailed descriptions of his crimes. The most extensive of these is found in the 1990 decision of the Supreme Court of Tennessee on Payne's direct appeal from his conviction and death sentence. I quote it at length because it gives a flavor of how the courts understood the context of Payne's constitutional claims.

> Defendant was found guilty of the first degree murder of Charisse Christopher and her daughter, Lacie, and guilty of assault with intent to commit murder in the first degree of her son, Nicholas. He was given the death penalty for each of the murders and thirty (30) years for the assault with intent to commit murder offense.

> Charisse Christopher was 28 years old, divorced, and lived in the Hiwassee Apartments, in Millington, Tennessee, with her two children, three and one-half year old Nicholas and two and one-half year old Lacie. The building in which she lived contained four units, two

---

[7] *The Commercial Appeal* (June 28, 1987), A1.

[8] *Id.*

[9] *Id.*, A4.

[10] *The Commercial Appeal* (June 29, 1987), B1.

[11] *Id.*

[12] *Id.*, B2.

[13] *Tri-State Commercial Appeal eDition*, (June 30, 1987), B1–B2.

downstairs and two upstairs. The resident manager, Nancy Wilson, lived in the downstairs unit immediately below the Christophers. Defendant's girlfriend, Bobbie Thomas, lived in the other upstairs unit. The inside entrance doors of the Christopher and Thomas apartments were separated by a narrow hallway. Each of the upstairs apartments had back doors in the kitchen that led to an open porch overlooking the back yard. In the center of the porch was a metal stairway leading to the ground. There was also an inside stairway leading to the ground floor hallway and front entrance to the four-unit building.

Bobbie Thomas had spent the week visiting her mother in Arkansas but was expected to return on Saturday, 27 June 1987, and she and Defendant had planned to spend the weekend together. Prior to 3:00 p.m. on that date, Defendant had visited the Thomas apartment several times and found no one at home. On one visit he left his overnight bag, containing clothing, etc., for his weekend stay, in the hallway, near the entrance to the Thomas apartment. With the bag were three cans of Colt 45 malt liquor.

Nancy Wilson was resting in her apartment when she first heard screaming, yelling, and running in the Christopher apartment above her. She heard a door banging open and shut and Charisse screaming, "get out, get out." She said it wasn't as though she was telling the intruder to get out, it was like "children, get out." The commotion began about 3:10 p.m., subsided momentarily, then began again and became "terribly loud, horribly loud." She went to the back door of her apartment, went outside and started to go to the Christopher apartment to investigate, but decided against that, and returned to her apartment and immediately called the police. She testified that she told the police she had heard blood curdling screams from the upstairs apartment and that she could not handle the situation. The dispatcher testified he received her disturbance call at 3:23 p.m. and immediately dispatched a squad car to the Hiwassee Apartments. Mrs. Wilson went to her bathroom after calling the police. The shouting, screaming and running upstairs had stopped, but she heard footsteps go into the upstairs bath, the faucet turned on and the sound of someone washing up. Then she heard someone walk across the floor to the door of the Christopher apartment, slam the door shut and run down the steps, just as the police arrived.

Officer C. E. Owen, of the Millington Police Department, was the first officer to arrive at the Hiwassee Apartments. He was alone in a squad car when the disturbance call was assigned to Officers Beck and Brawell. Owen was only two minutes away from the Hiwassee Apartments so he decided to back them up. He parked and walked toward the front entrance. As he did so, he saw through a large picture window that a black man was standing on the second floor landing of the stairwell. Owen saw him bend over and pick up an object and come down the stairs and go out the front door of the building. He was carrying the overnight bag and a pair of tennis shoes. Owen testified that he was wearing a white shirt and dark colored pants and had "blood all over him. It looked like he was sweating blood." Owen assumed that a domestic fight had taken place and that the blood was that of the person he was confronting. Owen asked, "[H]ow are you doing?" Defendant responded, "I'm the complainant." Owen then asked, "What's going on up there?" At that point Defendant struck Owen with the overnight bag, dropped his tennis shoes and started running west on Biloxi Street. Owen pursued him but Defendant outdistanced him and disappeared into another apartment complex.

Owen called for help on his walkie-talkie and Officer Boyd responded. By that time Owen had decided Defendant was not hurt and the blood was not his own—he was running too fast. Owen told Boyd that "there's something wrong at that apartment." They returned to 4516 Biloxi. Nancy Wilson had a master key and let them in the locked Christopher apartment. As soon as the door was opened they saw blood on the walls, floor—everywhere. The three bodies were on the floor of the kitchen. Boyd discovered that the boy was still breathing and called for an ambulance and reported their findings to the chief of police and the detective division. A Medic Ambulance arrived, quickly confirmed that Charisse and Lacie were dead, and departed with Nicholas. He was taken to Le Bonheur Children's Hospital in Memphis and was on the operating table there from 6:00 p.m. until 1:00 a.m., Sunday, 28 June. In addition to multiple lacerations, several stab wounds had gone completely through his body from front to back. One of those was in the middle of his abdomen. The surgeon, Dr. Sherman Hixson, testified that he had to repair and stop bleeding of the spleen, liver, large intestine, small intestine and the vena cava. During the surgery he was given 1700 cc's of blood by transfusion. Dr. Hixson estimated that his normal total blood volume should have been between 1200 and 1300 cc's. He was in intensive care for a period and had two other operations before he left the hospital, but he survived.

Charisse sustained forty-two (42) knife wounds and forty-two (42) defensive wounds on her arms and hands. The medical examiner testified that the forty-two (42) knife wounds represented forty-one (41) thrusts of the knife, "because there was one perforated wound to her left side that went through her—went through her side. In and out wounds produce two." He said no wound penetrated a very large vessel and the cause of death was bleeding from all of the wounds; there were thirteen (13) wounds "that were very serious and may have by themselves caused death. I can't be sure, but certainly the combination of all the wounds caused death." He testified that death probably occurred within, "maybe 30 minutes, that sort of time period," but that she would have been unconscious within a few minutes after the stabbing had finished.

The medical examiner testified that the cause of death of Lacie Christopher was multiple stab wounds to the chest, abdomen, back and head, a total of nine. One of the wounds cut the aorta and would have been rapidly fatal.

Defendant was located and arrested at a townhouse where a former girlfriend, Sharon Nathaniel, lived with her sisters. Defendant had attempted to hide in the Nathaniel attic. When arrested he was wearing nothing but dark pants, no shirt, no shoes. As he descended the stairs from the attic he said to the officers, "Man, I ain't killed no woman." Officer Beck said that at the time of his arrest he had "a wild look about him. His pupils were contracted. He was foaming at the mouth, saliva. He appeared to be very nervous. He was breathing real rapid." A search of his pockets revealed a "pony pack" with white residue in it. A toxicologist testified that the white residue tested positive for cocaine. They also found on his person a B & D syringe wrapper and an orange cap from a hypodermic syringe. There was blood on his pants and on his body and he had three or four scratches across his chest. He was wearing a gold Helbrose wristwatch that had bloodstains on it. The weekend bag that he struck Officer Owen with was found in a dumpster in the area. It contained the bloody white shirt he was wearing when Owen saw him at the Hiwassee Apartments, a blue shirt and other shirts.

It was stipulated that Charisse and Lacie had Type O blood and that Nicholas and Defendant had Type A. A forensic serologist testified that Type O blood was found on Defendant's white shirt, blue shirt, tennis shoes and on the bag. Type A blood was found on the black pants Defendant was wearing when seen by Owen and when arrested. Defendant's baseball cap had a size adjustment strap in the back with a U-type opening to accommodate adjustments. That baseball cap was on Lacie's forearm—her hand and forearm sticking through the opening between the adjustment strap and the cap material. Three Colt 45 beer cans were found on a small table in the living room, two unopened, one opened but not empty, bearing Defendant's fingerprints, and a fourth empty beer can was on the landing outside the apartment door. Defendant was shown to have purchased Colt 45 beer earlier in the day. Defendant's fingerprints were also found on the telephone and counter in the kitchen.

Charisse's body was found on the kitchen floor on her back, her legs fully extended. The right side of her upper body was against the wall, and the outside of her right leg was almost against the back door that opened onto the back porch.

During his trial, Payne took the stand to explain how his fingerprints could have been all over the apartment and why he was splattered with the victim's blood. The Supreme Court of Tennessee summarized his testimony as follows:

His defense was that he did not harm any of the Christophers; that he saw a black man descend the inside stairs, race by him and disappear out the front door of the building, as he returned to pick up his bag and beer before proceeding to his friend Sharon Nathaniel's to await the arrival of Bobby Thomas. He said that as the unidentified intruder bounded down the stairs, attired in a white tropical shirt that was longer than his shorts, he dropped change and miscellaneous papers on the stairs which Defendant picked up and put in his pocket as he continued up the stairs to the second floor landing to retrieve his bag and beer. When he reached the landing he heard a baby crying and a faint call for help and saw the door was ajar. He said curiosity motivated him to enter the Christopher apartment and after saying he was "coming in" and "eased the door on back," he described what he saw and his first actions as follows: "I saw the worst thing I ever saw in my life and like my breath just had—had tooken—just took out of me. You know, I didn't know what to do. And I put my hand over my mouth and walked up closer to it. And she was looking at me. She had the knife in her throat with her hand on the knife like she had been trying to get it out and her mouth was just moving but words had faded away. And I didn't know what to do. I was about ready to get sick, about ready to vomit. And so I ran closer—I saw a phone on the wall and I lift and got the phone on the wall. I said don't worry. I said don't worry. I'm going to get help. Don't worry. Don't worry. And I got ready to grab it—the phone but I didn't know no number to call. I didn't know nothing. I didn't know nothing about no number or—I just start trying to twist numbers. I didn't know nothing. And she was watching my movement in the kitchen, like she—I had saw her. It had been almost a year off and on in the back yard because her kids had played with Bobbie's kids. And I have seen her before. She looked at me like I know you, you know. And I didn't know what to do. I couldn't leave her. I couldn't leave her because she needed—she needed help. I was raised up to help and I had to help her."

He described how he pulled the knife out of her neck, almost vomited, then kneeled down by the baby girl, had the feeling she was already dead; said the little boy was on his knees crying, he told him not to cry he was going to get help. His explanation of the blood on his shirt, pants, tennis shoes, body, etc., was that when he pulled the knife out of her neck, "she reached up and grab me and hold me, like she was wanting me to help her …", that in walking and kneeling on the bloody floor and touching the two babies he got blood all over his clothes. He said he went to the kitchen sink, probably twice, to get water to drink when he thought he was going to vomit, but he denied that he went into the bathroom at any time or used the bathroom lavatory to wash up, as Nancy Wilson testified she heard someone do after the violence subsided.

He was then suddenly motivated to leave and seek help and he described his exit from the apartment as follows: "And I left. My motivation was going and banging on some doors, just to knock on some doors and tell someone need help, somebody call somebody, call the ambulance, call somebody. And when I—as soon as I left out the door I saw a police car, and some other feeling just went all over me and just panicked, just like, oh, look at this. I'm coming out of here with blood on me and everything. It going to look like I done this crime."

The shoulder strap on the left shoulder of the blue shirt he was wearing while in the victim's apartment was torn, a fact he did not seem to realize and could not remember when it happened. He said he ran because the officer did not seem to believe him. He claimed that he had the Colt 45 beer with him as he ran; that the open can with beer in it spilled into the sack, as he ran from Owen, the bottom of the sack broke, the beer and tennis shoes were scattered along his route. He said that what witnesses had described as scratches were stretch marks from lifting weights.

Neither the jury nor the courts that reviewed his conviction and sentence believed his account. As one court put it, "The appellant's own testimony was damning."[14] Even the lawyer who represented him at trial acknowledged that the state had a "powerful circumstantial case" and conceded that Payne's testimony "really was the nightmare."[15] As he told me,

I don't know if you've ever read the transcript—alright, you always do a lot of soul-searching about whether your client's going to take the witness stand, whether he wants to or doesn't want to. Now, he absolutely wanted to. And there really was no other way to get his version of the facts across to the jury anyway, so there wasn't a whole lot of choice in it. And, he took the witness stand. And he

---

[14] *Payne v. State*, 1998 WL 12670.

[15] Interview with Jim Garts, January 24, 2007.

probably made one of the worse witnesses that I've ever seen. One thing is, Pervis is fairly low on the IQ scale. Did not use common sense and good judgment in spite of whatever efforts I made to prepare him. And, surely into the cross-examination, he got at odds with Tom Henderson who is a very abrasive cross examiner. And, the two of them kind of got in to a donny brook you know, Pervis did not respond the way I would have wanted him to, to that environment. And then wound up getting kind of excited and when Tom asked him a question about certain blood that was you know on a particular part of his anatomy whether it was his shoes, or the back of his arm or something—because he had a lot of blood on him—he said, "well, then how did you get that blood on you?"—you know, inconsistent with whatever he had said. And Pervis said, "It must have been when she hit the wall," which was totally inconsistent with him bending over her and her grabbing him trying to get help and maybe being pulled up a little bit. And I think he tried to correct it a bit by saying, "hit the floor" or whatever, but I mean when he said that, I remember, I've tried hundreds of cases and I've been doing this for 32 years now. But I've never seen any statement in a trial one phrase have more impact. It was just one of those pregnant, whatever, remarks, because the court reporter quit typing. She just stopped. The jury was dead silent. Tom used it as a theatrical moment, stopped for a second, and then started yelling, "Hit the wall, hit the wall?" at Pervis and Pervis tried to straighten it out a bit. But I don't know that it really made much difference because I think the jury probably didn't have a real doubt at least most of them didn't at that point anyway.[16]

The gruesome facts of the kind of crime Payne was convicted of committing played into a powerful 1980s narrative of an escalating crime wave, of dangerous cities, and of a criminal justice system whose lenient treatment of predatory criminals endangered innocent citizens everywhere.[17] It also focused attention of the courts who heard Payne's case on, what Markus Dubber calls, "the 'icon of the victims' rights movement.'"[18] As he observes, "To trigger the desired sympathetic response at the desired intensity, the victim must be the victim of a serious crime.... This leads the victims' rights movement to put homicide front and center."[19] That Payne was accused of murdering a woman and a

---

[16] *Id.*

[17] For a more complete description of this narrative see Stuart Scheingold, *The Politics of Law and Order: Street Crime and Public Policy*, New York: Longman, 1984.

[18] Markus Dubber, *Victims in the War on Crime: The Use and Abuse of Victims' Rights*, New York: New York University Press, 2002, 179.

[19] *Id.*

child deepened the resonance of his case for those who wanted to put preventing the victimization of the "innocent" at the center of the criminal justice system.

Victims' Rights

By the time Payne's case reached the Supreme Court, the victims' rights movement had established itself as an important force in the American criminal justice system and had taken on a distinctively conservative, tough-on-crime, cast. In the United States and elsewhere that movement mobilized a tide of resentment against a system of justice which traditionally tried to substitute public processes for private action and, in so doing, to justify the criminal sanction as a response to injuries to public order rather than to harms done to particular individuals.[20] The tendency of criminal justice systems in western democracies has been to displace the victim, to shut the door on those with the greatest interest in seeing justice done. In response, victims demanded that their voices be heard throughout the criminal process.

At its inception, the movement brought together progressives and conservatives, women's groups seeking to advance the cause of victims of sexual assault, families victimized by drunk drivers, child abduction, and other crimes.[21] It contested the fairness of legal procedures that are distant and unresponsive to crime victims' grief and rage.[22] By trans-

---

[20] "Hard on the heels of the civil rights movement, the women's liberation movement, and the movement to expand the rights of criminal suspects, the victims' rights movement burst on the scene in the early 1970s and quickly became a potent political force. Part backlash against what it considered the pro-defendant romanticism of the 1960s, the victims' rights movement was also a spiritual heir to the '60s ethos. With its suspicion of bureaucratic government and its concern for the disempowered, the victims' rights movement spoke for the 'forgotten' men and women of the criminal justice system." See Stephen Schulhofer, "The Trouble with Trials: The Trouble with Us," 105 *Yale Law Journal* (1995), 825. Also David Roland, "Progress in the Victim Reform Movement: No Longer the 'Forgotten Victim,'" 17 *Pepperdine Law Review* (1989), 35, and Stuart Scheingold, Toska Olson, and Jana Pershing, "Sexual Violence, Victim Advocacy, and Republican Criminology: Washington State's Community Protection Act," 28 *Law & Society Review* (1994), 736.

[21] Donahoe argues that the victims' rights movement is less like movements for civil rights or women's suffrage than it is "a continuing shift in conventional wisdom in reaction to the landmark decisions of the Warren Court that extended constitutional rights to defendants, suspects, and prisoners." See Joel F. Donahoe, "The Changing Role of Victim Impact Evidence in Capital Cases," 2 *Western Criminology Review* (1999). Found at http://wcr.sonoma.edu/V2n1/donahoe.html.

[22] Wendy Kaminer, *It's All the Rage: Crime and Culture*. Reading, MA.: Addison–Wesley, 1995. "To a victim," Kaminer writes, "the notion that crimes are committed against society, making the community the injured party, can seem both bizarre and insulting: it can make them feel invisible, unavenged, and unprotected." 75. See also Angela Harris, "The Jurisprudence of Victimhood," 1991 *Supreme Court Review* (1991),

forming courts into sites for the rituals of grieving, that movement tries to make private experiences part of public discourse.

In its earliest stages the victims' rights movement seemed "humanitarian and 'liberal.' "[23] Jonathan Simon persuasively argues that in its initial incarnation the crime victim was "once framed by the civil rights subject. Jim Crow segregation came to be seen as a kind of crime against African Americans.... Feminists made the link between crime victims and the civil rights subject even stronger when they presented the raped woman as the idealized subject of second wave feminism."[24] At its origins, in the 1960s, the movement advanced a social welfarist case on behalf of victim compensation programs, the first of which was established in California in 1965, "a good three years before President Nixon launched the war on crime in earnest and seventeen years before the punitive incarnation of victims rights first made national headlines with the passage of California's Proposition 8, the first 'Victim's Bill of Rights.' "[25] By the end of the 1960s five other compensation programs were established in New York, Hawaii, Massachusetts, Maryland, and the Virgin Islands.[26] And, even today, long after the call for victims' rights has become a staple of the conservative political agenda, some contend that victims' rights are "not antithetical to liberalism and to a liberal vision of criminal law in particular...."[27]

Throughout its history, politicians have garnered considerable mileage from encouraging and manipulating victim politics. They marginalize the pragmatic interest of victims in more effective crime prevention and fan their anger and desire for punishment. Thus criminal victimization has been linked to political mobilization by a host of Republican politicians starting with Richard Nixon's 1968 "law and order" campaign.[28] By the early 1990s the movement had become so powerful that one

---

77, and Susan Bandes, "Empathy, Narrative, and Victim Impact Statements," 63 *University of Chicago Law Review* (1996), 361.

[23] Henderson, "The Wrongs of Victim's Rights," 944.

[24] Simon, *Governing Through Crime*: How the War on Crime Transformed American Democracy and Created a Culture of Fear, New York: Oxford University Press (2007), 108.

[25] See Dubber, *Victims in the War on Crime*, 170.

[26] Currently all 50 states plus the federal government have such programs. The Office for Victims of Crime was established in the United States Department of Justice by the 1984 Victims of Crime Act to oversee diverse programs that benefit victims of crime. See http://www.ojp.usdoj.gov/ovc/help/links.htm.

[27] Dubber, 154.

[28] Jonathan Simon, *Governing Through Crime: How the War on Crime Transformed American Democracy and Created a Culture of Fear*. New York: Oxford University Press, 2007, 109.

commentator argued that it had succeeded in "creating a new era in American criminal law and procedure."[29] Today, "constitutions, statutes, and court opinions proclaim the victim's right to have a voice in all aspects of American criminal law."[30]

The success of the victim's rights movement in securing recognition of victims and in reorienting the criminal justice system has been remarkable and its victories legion.[31] Let me note several of those achievements, some of which have been mainly symbolic and ceremonial, some quite tangible.[32] In 1975, The District Attorney of Philadelphia, Pennsylvania organized the first "Victims' Rights Week," and that same year saw the formation of the National Organization for Victim Assistance. One year later a probation officer in Fresno County, California created the first victim impact statement, an inventory of injuries and loses presented to a judge prior to sentencing. In 1980 Wisconsin passed the first Crime Victims' Bill of Rights.

The election of Ronald Reagan as President put an important and vocal ally of the victims' rights movement in the White House. In 1981 he became the first President to proclaim "Crime Victims' Rights Week," and a year later he appointed a Task Force on Victims of Crime which ultimately proposed that a victim rights amendment by added to the United States Constitution.[33] That same year Congress "passed the first federal victims' rights statute, the Victim and Witness Protection Act,"[34] and in 1983, then Chief Justice Burger stated that "in the administration of justice, courts may not ignore the concerns of victims."[35]

1984 saw the passage by Congress of the Victims of Crime Act which established a National Crime Victims Fund and by the late 1980s state constitutional amendments granting rights to victims had been intro-

---

[29] Lynne Henderson, "The Wrongs of Victim's Rights," 37 *Stanford Law Review* (1985), 938. As Dubber observes, "Two phenomena have shaped American criminal law for the past thirty years: the war on crime and the victims' rights movement." See Dubber, *Victims in the War on Crime*, 1 and Robert Mosteller, "Victim Impact Evidence: Hard to Find the Real Rules," 88 *Cornell Law Review* (2003), 550.

[30] Dubber, *Victims in the War on Crime*, 173.

[31] See "Crime Victims Seeking a Greater Legal Voice," *New York Times* (March 6, 1985, B2).

[32] A more complete chronology can be found at www.ojp.usdoj.gov/ovc/ncvrw/2004.

[33] The text of that amendment stated; ". . . the victim, in every criminal prosecution, shall have the right to be present and to be heard at all critical stages of judicial proceedings."

[34] Dubber, *Victims in the War on Crime*, 175.

[35] See *Morris v. Slappy*, 461 U.S. 1, 15 (1983).

duced in nine states. By 1989, 30 states had created a right of "allocution" for victims[36] and Alabama state law accorded victims of crime the right to sit at the prosecution table during criminal trials.[37]

In 1991, the year the Supreme Court's *Payne* decision, the first effort to place victims' rights in the Constitution got underway in Congress.[38] To date, despite the support of Presidents Clinton and Bush the victims' rights amendment has not yet been added to the US Constitution. Nonetheless, 33 states have added victims' rights amendments to their constitutions.[39] So successful has the victims' rights movement been that Simon contends, "Crime victims are in a real sense the representative subjects of our time. . . . The vulnerabilities and needs of victims define the appropriate conditions for government intervention."[40]

Victim Impact Evidence in Capital Cases: The Constitutional Context

In the last four decades one of the most visible defeats for the victims' rights movement was the Supreme Court's 1987 decision in *Booth*.[41] As a result, almost as soon as the decision was announced leaders of that movement targeted it for reversal.[42]

Booth was the case of two men, John Booth and William Reid, who in 1983 entered the West Baltimore home of Irvin and Rose Bronstein, Booth's neighbors, with the intent to steal money. Finding the Bronsteins at home, Booth and Reid bound, gagged, and stabbed them several times in the chest with a kitchen knife. The killers were subsequently

---

[36] "Victim and Sentence: Resetting Justice's Scales," *New York Times* (September 29, 1989), B5.

[37] "Crime Victims Getting a Day, and a Say, in Court," *New York Times* (April 1, 1988), B7.

[38] Six years later Congress enacted the Victims Rights Clarification Act to ensure the rights of victims to attend trials and present victim impact evidence in both capital and non-capital federal cases.

[39] See Mosteller, "Victim Impact Evidence: Hard to Find the Real Rules," 552.

[40] Simon, *Governing Through Crime*, 75–76.

[41] As the *New York Times* noted "The decision was denounced by groups advocating the rights of crime victims in the criminal process, which have become increasingly active in recent years. It delighted and surprised some opponents of the death penalty who had not been optimistic about the outcome." "Justices, 5–4, Deal Blow to Backers of Victim Rights," *New York Times* (June 16, 1987), A1.

[42] As leader of the victims' rights movement put it on the day the *Booth* decision was announced, " 'This is exactly the type of decision that would be reversed if Ronald Reagan had one more vote on the Supreme Court.' " "Justices, 5–4, Deal Blow to Backers of Victim Rights," *New York Times* (June 16, 1987), A28.

arrested and convicted on two counts of first-degree murder, two counts of robbery and one count of conspiracy to commit robbery.

As in the Payne case, during the sentencing phase of the trial, jurors were presented with victim impact statements, this time in the form of a third person account of interviews with the Bronsteins's son, daughter, son-in-law, and granddaughter.[43] While the victim impact statement in this case contained an elaborate description of the reaction of each of those people to the death of the Bronsteins, it concentrated on the daughter and the son. The jury was told that:

> "The victims' daughter ... states that she doesn't sleep through a single night and thinks a part of her died too when her parents were killed. She reports that she doesn't find much joy in anything and her powers of concentration aren't good. She feels as if her brain is on overload.... The victims' daughter states that wherever she goes she sees and hears her parents."[44]

This statement, presented as the clinical narrative of a state official, nonetheless conveys the pain, grief, and torment of the daughter left behind. It describes her as a kind of corpse yet suggests that she is haunted by uncontrollable memories. It is as if her parents are not entirely dead; they live on in visions and voices known only to her. Such haunting visions and voices create empathetic bonds between speaker and listener by evoking an artificial and incomplete portrait of a formerly blissful family life, ruined by villainous acts.

Similarly eerie suggestions concerning visions of the dead are found in the statement of the Bronsteins's son.

> The victims' son states that he can only think of his parents in the context of how he found them that day, and he can feel their fear and horror. It was 4:00 p.m. when he discovered their bodies and this stands out in his mind. He is always aware of when 4:00 p.m. comes each day, even when he is not near a clock.... He is unable to drive on the streets that pass near his parents' home.... He is constantly reminded of his parents. He sees his father coming out of

---

[43] To some extent the full force of the victim impact statement is blunted when it is reported in a third person account. To take but one contrasting example, the trial, more than a decade ago, of Colin Ferguson for murdering commuters on the Long Island Railroad provides a more compelling version of the genre of the victim impact statement. " 'I know I have an impossible request, Your Honor. But given five minutes alone with Colin Ferguson, this coward would know the meaning of suffering.... (To Ferguson): Look at these eyes. You can't look at 'em, right? You can't. You remember these eyes. You're nothing but a piece of garbage. You're a (expletive) animal. Five minutes. That's all I need with you. Five minutes,' " said Robert Giugliano, who was one of Ferguson's victims. Quoted in Jeffrey Rosen, "Victims and the Interest of Justice," *The San Diego Union–Tribune* (March 31, 1995), Opinion, B–5.

[44] See *Booth*, 512.

synagogues, sees his parents' car, and feels very sad whenever he sees old people.

Murdered parents discovered in a grizzly scene live on as ghosts. For this victim, memory is the true source of pain. He lives in a present in which the past refuses to die. The call of the victim is to rectify the past, to placate memory by silencing the ghosts whose constant call is for vengeance.

The voice of the victim is an urgent call both to remember and to obliterate memory, to attend to the past and to forge a different recollection. One hope is that a new memory of a vengeful punishment, can eradicate the memory of the crime.[45]

This desire to replace an unendurable past with a new image of the suffering of the criminal is also apparent in the victim impact statement of the Bronstein children. Thus the son contended that

> 'his parents were not killed, but were butchered like animals. He doesn't think anyone should be able to do something like that and get away with it. He is very angry . . . He states that he is frightened by his own reaction of what he would do if someone hurt him or a family member.'

And the daughter noted that

> 'her parents were stabbed repeatedly with viciousness and she could never forgive anyone for killing them that way. She can't believe that anyone could do that to someone. The victims' daughter states that animals wouldn't do this. They didn't have to kill because there was no one to stop them from looting . . . The murders show the viciousness of the killers' anger. She doesn't feel that the people who did this could ever be rehabilitated and she doesn't want them to be able to do this again or put another family through this.'[46]

---

[45] As Aladjem notes, "Vengeance expresses 'a wish to change the world and right the past, to be seen and counted in a private and ultimately a public conversion of memory, to reassign guilt and to end that unending memory of horror that is, says Aeschylus, "a relentless anguish gnawing at the heart." ' " See Terry Aladjem, "Vengeance & Democratic Justice: American Culture and the Limits of Punishment," unpublished manuscript, 1992, 26.

[46] "Probably the most controversial type of information a victim could provide . . . is the victim's opinion of the defendant and what sentence the defendant should receive. . . . Victim opinion is probably the type of victim information that proponents of victim participation at sentencing most want to be allowed in sentencing proceedings. Asking for a victim's opinion best recognizes his dignity and his role in the prosecution and punishment of the defendant. However, the victim's opinion may be the most inflammatory and prejudicial evidence the victim could provide." See Phillip Talbert, "The Relevance of Victim Impact Statements to the Criminal Sentencing Decision," 36 *U.C.L.A. Law Review* (1988), 210.

In both these statements we can see how a dynamic of responsibility and monstrosity works in victim impact evidence. "They didn't have to kill ..." suggests beings capable of calculating, of knowing what has to be done, and of making decisions about how to act. The killers are, at the same time, presented as inferior to "animals." In addition, while the daughter's words contain an element of generality, her statement, as well as that of her brother, is cast in a kind of personal, emotional tone. Finally, the son's self-described anxiety about his own reaction suggests just the kind of uncontrollable response to injury which public justice hopes to displace if not fully satisfy. That anxiety contains a kind of threat, or a reminder of the possibility of a more dangerous violence lurking just below the surface of civil society.

The legal question presented in *Booth* was whether victim impact evidence rendered the death sentences of Booth and Reid unconstitutional under the Eighth Amendment's ban on "cruel and unusual punishment." The Court, with Justice Powell writing for the majority, held that it did. In his judgment, because the victim impact statement in Booth's case presented the jury with emotionally compelling testimony, it created a substantial risk of prejudice. The very power of the victim's voice represents its greatest danger. The victim impact statement, despite its obvious rhetorical force, was "irrelevant" to the capital sentencing decision because, as Powell observed, it did not and could not contribute to an assessment of the "blameworthiness" of the defendants.[47]

For any defendant to be blameworthy, Powell contended, he would have to have known about and contemplated the damaging impact on the victims' family that the murder of the Bronsteins would have. A legal wrong is different from a harm, and while Powell had no doubt about the harm done to the family, he insisted that the mere fact of harm was irrelevant in a capital case. There the focus should be on whether the wrong committed was sufficiently egregious as to warrant the death penalty. To allow the jury to hear the Bronsteins' victim impact statement would focus their attention on factors of which the defendants were "unaware" and would "divert the jury's concern from the defendant's background and record, and the circumstances of the crime."[48]

Moreover, the use of victim impact statements, in Powell's view, turned capital sentencing into a test of the rhetorical proficiency of surviving relatives.[49] Rather than skill at arms, verbal acumen would

---

[47] *Booth*, 504.

[48] *Id.*, 505.

[49] Powell limited his holding to capital cases. He noted that "our disapproval of victim impact statements at the sentencing phase of a capital case does not mean, however, that

become a tool for exacting revenge. The opportunity to present victim impact evidence placed the family in the position of seeking a champion, of enlisting the jury to do what the law forbids the family from doing directly. "Articulate" and "persuasive" family members would be able to secure a result unavailable to those who were less well able to express their "grief."[50]

Finally, Powell rejected victim impact statements because they introduce passion and emotion, and threaten to overwhelm the "reasoned decision making we require in capital cases."[51] The voice of the victim breaches the delicate boundary between passion and reason, serving to "inflame the jury and divert it from deciding the case on the relevant evidence.... As we have noted, any decision to impose the death sentence must 'be, and appear to be, based on reason rather than caprice or emotion.' "[52] Here the construction and policing of a boundary between retribution and revenge is fully on display.

However, Powell's was not the only voice in *Booth*, nor the only one who responded to the call to hear the voice of the victim. Justices White and Scalia both produced dissenting opinions which would provide the basis for *Payne's* reversal of this case just four years later.

White asserted that the proper focus of sentencing in capital cases was not only the "internal disposition" of the murderer, but "the full extent of the harm he caused."[53] He said that it was not "unfair to confront a defendant with an account of the loss his ... act has caused the victim's family...."[54] In this view, punishment could and should be based on a calculus of harms and injuries as well as of wrongs. Punishment might properly be enhanced, White said, "on the basis of harm caused, irrespective of the offender's specific intention to cause such harm."[55]

White saw victim impact statements in capital cases as essential in counteracting the "mitigating evidence which the defendant is entitled

---

this type of information will never be relevant ... in a non-capital criminal trial.... We note ... that our decision today is guided by the fact that death is a 'punishment different from all other sanctions ... and that therefore the considerations that inform the sentencing decisions may be different from those that might be relevant to other liability or punishment determinations.' " *Id.*, 507, 509, notes 10 and 12.

[50] *Id.*, 507.

[51] *Id.*, 509.

[52] *Id.*, 508.

[53] *Id.*, 516.

[54] *Id.*, 518.

[55] *Id.*, 516.

to put in."[56] Victim impact evidence reminds the sentencer, he noted, that the "victim is an individual whose death represents a unique loss to ... his family."[57] But who would need to receive such a reminder and hear such an assertion? Insisting that punishment should be aimed at responding to the family's loss, White seems to want to privatize public processes.

Scalia too suggested that harm is separate from moral guilt and that it provides an equally valid reason for imposing the death penalty.[58] As he put it, harm and moral guilt are "distinct justifications that operate independently of each other."[59] In addition, Scalia, acknowledging the power of the victims' rights movement, insisted that the Court should acknowledge "an outpouring of popular concern for what has come to be known as 'victims' rights' ...."[60] The victim impact statement lays before the jury "the full reality of human suffering the defendant has produced ..." which Scalia contended is "one of the reasons society deems his act worthy of the prescribed penalty."[61] Scalia's references to an "outpouring of popular concern" and what society "deems" necessary in the way of punishment indicates that legal values are too far removed from social values. His reaction to this problem was to insure that punishment would be, and would appear to be, responsive to suffering and that law itself would heed the "outpouring of popular concern" as well as what society "deems" appropriate.[62]

Two years after *Booth*, the Court reaffirmed its central holding in *South Carolina v. Gathers*.[63] In that case, the defendant, Gathers, was tried and convicted of murder and first-degree criminal sexual conduct. He and three other youths had encountered a self-proclaimed preacher in a wooded section of a park at night and had beaten him on the head with a bottle. The defendant perforated the man's rectum with an

---

[56] *Id.*, 517.

[57] *Id.*, 517.

[58] *Id.*, 520.

[59] *Id.* See also Steven Gey, "Justice Scalia's Death Penalty," 20 *Florida State University Law Review* (1992), 121.

[60] *Booth*, 520.

[61] *Id.*

[62] Scalia's efforts, first to distinguish between the defendant's moral guilt and the victim's harm, and, second, to emphasize the assertion of a generalized public sense of justice through the criminal justice process, are both deeply inconsistent with the retributivist tradition. In *Booth*, "Justice Scalia implies that the potential for injustice regarding a particular capital defendant is outweighed by society's need to use capital trials to purge its collective anger and moral outrage at violent crime." Gey, "Justice Scalia's ...," 69.

[63] 490 U.S. 805 (1989).

umbrella and stabbed him with a knife. The youths, looking for something to steal, rummaged through the victim's belongings, which consisted mainly of some bibles and various other religious tracts and articles, and scattered them on the ground. Those items were later introduced into evidence without objection at the guilt phase of the trial, but no reference was made at that time to the content of the papers.

During the penalty phase of Gathers's trial, the prosecutor, "(1) commented on the fact that the victim had been a religious man, (2) read a prayer that had been printed on one of the victim's cards, (3) noted that the victim had been a vulnerable man with a history of mental problems which prevented him from holding a job, and (4) pointed to a voter registration card which the victim had been carrying as indicating the victim's belief in his community and his country." Gathers received a death sentence.

Believing that the prosecutor's remarks were inconsistent with *Booth* the South Carolina Supreme Court reversed Gather's death sentence. The court held that those remarks "conveyed the suggestion that the appellant deserved a death sentence because the victim was a religious man and a registered voter."[64] The United States Supreme Court, Justice Brennan writing for a five judge majority, agreed. Allowing such a suggestion, Brennan argued, could result in the imposition of a death sentence " 'because of factors about which the defendant was unaware, and that were irrelevant to the decision to kill.' "[65] As Brennan saw it, the prosecutor's statement was "indistinguishable in any relevant aspect from that in *Booth*."[66]

Justices O'Connor and Scalia both wrote dissenting opinions urging that *Booth* be overruled. O'Connor observed that "I remain persuaded that *Booth* was wrong when decided and am ready to overrule it if the Court would do so...."[67] Failing that she argued that *Gathers* could be distinguished from *Booth*. The key difference, in her view, was that Gathers's case concerned "solely prosecutorial comments about the victim himself."[68] Moreover it seemed odd to her to exclude prosecutorial comment on something which was "introduced into evidence without objection during the guilt phase of the trial."[69]

---

[64] 295 S.C. 476, 484, 369 S.E.2d 140 (1988).

[65] Gathers, 811.

[66] *Id*. Because Justice White agreed that the case was indistinguishable from *Booth* he joined Brennan's opinion.

[67] *Id.*, 813–814.

[68] *Id.*, 814.

[69] *Id.*, 815.

O'Connor suggested that adopting the majority's broad view of *Booth* would enshrine a "rigid Eighth Amendment rule eliminating virtually all consideration of the victim in the penalty phase."[70] She worried that the absence of such consideration meant that the jury in a capital case would inevitably make a "one sided" judgment.[71] In her view the harm caused by a defendant is properly part of "the capital sentencer's moral judgment ... even if the defendant did not specifically intend that harm ...."[72] As she put it, anticipating the facts of *Payne*, "That the victim in this case was a deeply religious and harmless individual who exhibited his care for his community by religious proselytization and political participation in its affairs was relevant to the community's loss at his demise, just as society would view with grief and anger the killing of a mother or father of small children."[73]

Justice Scalia joined O'Connor in denouncing *Booth* and urging that it be overruled. He noted, among other things, "I doubt that overruling *Booth* would ... shake the citizenry's faith in the Court.... In any case, I would think it a violation of my oath to adhere to what I consider a plainly unjustified intrusion upon the democratic process in order that the court might save face."[74] For Scalia, *Booth* exemplified the vices of an activist judiciary and could find no basis in "the common law background that led up to the Eighth Amendment, in any longstanding societal tradition, or in any evidence that present society ... has set its face against considering the harm caused by criminal acts in assessing responsibility."[75] He concluded "we provide far greater reassurance of the rule of law by eliminating than by retaining such a decision."[76]

When, in April, 1990, Payne's case reached the Tennessee Supreme Court on direct appeal *Booth* and *Gathers*, O'Connor and Scalia's wishes notwithstanding, were still binding precedent. Payne presented the Tennessee court with a variety of issues on appeal. Among other things, he argued that the evidence presented in the guilt phase of his trial was not sufficient to support the jury's verdict, that the trial judge erred in admitting evidence of his possession of illegal narcotics and drug paraphernalia, and made errors in admitting other evidence. The court dispensed quickly with all of these claims.

---

[70] *Id.*

[71] *Id.*, 817.

[72] *Id.*, 818.

[73] *Id.*, 821.

[74] *Id.*, 824–825.

[75] *Id.*, 825.

[76] *Id.*

Payne also raised a variety of questions concerning the conduct of the sentencing trial, focusing particularly on the question of whether the "testimony of Nicholas Christopher's grandmother regarding his reaction to the loss of his mother was inflammatory 'victim impact' evidence" barred by *Booth*.[77] The court characterized the judgment in *Booth* as applying only to statements that describe "the personal characteristics of the victims and the emotional impact of the crimes on the family. A second type of victim impact evidence describes the family members opinions and characterizations of the crimes and the defendant."[78] The court distinguished the statements made in Payne's case, characterizing them as follows: "Mrs. Zvalanek's brief answer contains only a matter-of-fact statement that a four-year-old boy misses and cries for his mother and sister. (This case was tried approximately seven months after the crimes were committed). The VIS in *Booth* covered the full range of the two types of irrelevant information described above and was more extensive and inflammatory than the above quoted answer of Nicholas' grandmother."[79]

While the court conceded that even this matter-of-fact statement was "technically irrelevant,"[80] it found that the "statement did not create a constitutionally unacceptable risk of an arbitrary imposition of the death penalty, and was harmless beyond a reasonable doubt."[81] This invocation of the harmless error doctrine later became the device through which the Tennessee Supreme Court disposed of Payne's claims and managed to avoid the reach of *Booth* and *Gathers*.

With respect to the admissibility of the prosecutor's statement, the court acknowledged the relevance of *Gathers*. Yet the court refused to concede its applicability to Payne's case. And, without bothering to distinguish *Gathers*, it rendered its own expansive critique.

> We are of the opinion that the prosecutor's argument is relevant to this defendant's personal responsibility and moral guilt. When a person deliberately picks a butcher knife out of a kitchen drawer and proceeds to stab to death a twenty-eight year old mother, her two and one-half year old daughter and her three and one-half year old son, in the same room, the physical and mental condition of the boy he left for dead is surely relevant in determining his blameworthiness.

---

[77] *State v. Payne*, 791 S.W.2d 10, 23 (1990).

[78] *Id.*, 24.

[79] *Id.*

[80] *Id.*

[81] *Id.*, 24–25.

It is an affront to the civilized members of the human race to say that at sentencing in a capital case, a parade of witnesses may praise the background, character and good deeds of Defendant (as was done in this case), without limitation as to relevancy, but nothing may be said that bears upon the character of, or the harm imposed, upon the victims.[82]

Then, as if recovering and realizing that it was bound by Supreme Court precedent, the Tennessee court again focused on the issue of harmless error.

Finally, we are of the opinion that assuming the argument here violated the Eighth Amendment, as interpreted by the United States Supreme Court, we think it subject to harmless error analysis.... The "personal responsibility", the "moral guilt" and the "blame-worthiness" of the person who committed these crimes, was established by the proof at the guilt phase, to-wit, that inhuman brutality, without reason or explanation was heaped upon three innocent human beings. Once that person's identity was established by the jury's verdict, the death penalty was the only rational punishment available. Thus, the State's argument was harmless beyond a reasonable doubt.

This issue is without merit.[83]

"... The death penalty was the only rational punishment available." With this extraordinary conclusory sentence, the court dispensed with Payne's allegations concerning the unconstitutionality of victim impact evidence. Its lengthy recitation of the facts of the crime provided the underpinnings of this judgment, a judgment seemingly so obvious and powerful that it swept *Booth* and *Gathers* away before it.

The Supreme Court Decision

Payne's writ of certiorari identified three constitutional errors in his case, one involved the introduction of a video tape of the crime scene which it alleged prevented the jury from "making a reasoned, moral decision on whether to impose the death penalty." The second argued that the introduction of the victim impact statement and the prosecutor's statement to the jury violated the Eighth and Fourteenth Amendments, and the third focused on a jury instruction in the penalty phase.[84]

---

[82] *Id.*, 27–28.

[83] *Id.*, 29. This statement seems quite strange since courts have never suggested that any specific set of circumstances requires the death penalty.

[84] See Philip B. Kurland and Gerhard Casper, *Landmark Briefs and Arguments of the Supreme Court of the United States: Constitutional Law 1990 Term Supplement*, Bethesda, Md.: University Publications of America, 1992, 491.

So eager was the Court to re-examine *Booth* and *Gathers* that it called up Payne's case and instructed lawyers for the state and defendant to prepare arguments on an expedited basis. In its order granting review the Court stated that "In addition to the questions presented by the petition, the parties are requested to brief and argue whether *Booth v. Maryland* and *South Carolina v. Gathers* should be overruled."[85]

Amicus briefs, opposing Payne and calling on the Court to overrule *Booth* and *Gathers*, were submitted by the Solicitor General of the United States and by a coalition of members of the United States Congress whose interest in the case was "prompted by the fact that Congress has enacted various pieces of legislation intended to ensure that the impact of the crime on the victim is considered at sentencing, including in capital cases."[86] This coalition included politicians from across the political spectrum, from Newt Gingrich to Barney Frank. They called on the Court to take note of the public's belief that the impact on the victim ought to be considered when sentencing a convicted criminal. As the brief put it, "The public's message is loud and clear."[87]

In addition, the Congressional brief highlighted the import of the victims' rights movement which it equated with "the civil rights movement."[88] The importance of Payne's case to the victims' rights movement was furthered signaled by the amicus participation of Families and Friends of Missing Persons and Violent Crime Victims, the National Victim Center, Parents of Murdered Children, and People Against Child Abuse, Inc. Their brief identified *amici* as "individuals and organizations concerned with promoting victims' rights in the criminal justice system."[89]

Sometime later, when the Supreme Court announced its decision, it became clear that White and Scalia's view in *Booth* had become the majority position in *Payne*. Writing for that majority, Chief Justice Rehnquist admitted that victim impact statements "do not in general reflect on the defendant's 'blameworthiness' ..."[90] However, Rehnquist

---

[85] Quoted in "Court to Review Bar on Statements From Victims' Families," *New York Times* (February 16, 1991), 13. Payne's brief also focused on the Tennessee Supreme Court's harmless error ruling, straightforwardly asserting that the Tennessee court had erroneously concluded that the State had met its burden of proving, beyond a reasonable doubt, that the error of admitting the victim impact statement was harmless. See Kurland, *Landmark Briefs* . . . , 583.

[86] *Id.*, 703.

[87] *Id.*, 706.

[88] *Id.*, 714.

[89] *Id.*, 775. One amicus brief, submitted on behalf of the southern Christian Leadership Conference, was submitted in support of Payne's position.

[90] *Payne*, 819.

contended that punishment need not be limited to wrongs, but could and should be meted out differently depending on the harm that is actually done.[91] "Victim impact evidence," Rehnquist argued, "is simply another form or method of informing the sentencing authority about the specific harm caused by the crime in question...."[92]

Moreover, the state, Rehnquist argued, should be allowed to introduce victim impact evidence to "provide a 'glimpse of the life' which the defendant 'chose to extinguish.' "[93] Doing so would insure that the victim is not a " 'faceless stranger at the penalty phase of the trial,' "[94] and would redress what Rehnquist saw as the "unfairness" which occurred when criminal sentencing focused solely on the life and circumstances of the offender. From anonymity to embodiment, from absence to presence, victim impact evidence becomes a vehicle for resurrecting the dead and allowing them to speak in the trials of their murderers. Giving voice to victims moves them to the center of attention even as it expands the notion of who qualifies as a victim. In Rehnquist's view it presents the jury a fuller picture of the "human cost of the crime of which the defendant stands convicted."[95]

Focusing on that cost by hearing the voice of the victim personalizes death sentencing in just the way revenge personalizes all punishment. In this understanding "the body in pain is the source of a unique ... authority.... The body in pain provides a basis for assuming the authority to assert that a particular action not only did happen, but that the person who did it should be condemned for it and punished."[96] The victim impact statement seeks to move the jury from strangeness to familiarity, overcoming distance, and establishing identification. And identification, in turn, becomes the basis for vengeful action.

Justice O'Connor, in whose opinion White joined, reiterated Scalia's position in *Booth* by noting the existence of a "strong societal consensus" in favor of victim impact statements.[97] Like Scalia, O'Connor wanted the criminal justice system to bend to that consensus and thus turn away from the traditional social contract view in which law resists

---

[91] *Id.*

[92] *Id.*, 825.

[93] *Id.*, 822.

[94] *Id.*, 825.

[95] *Id.*, 827.

[96] Jennifer Culbert, "The Body in *Payne*: The Rhetoric of Victims' Rights and the Predicament of Judgment," Paper presented to the 1995 Annual Meeting of the Law & Society Association, Toronto, Canada, 9–10.

[97] *Payne*, 831.

the clamor of a vengeful public. Moreover, the possibility that passion might triumph over reason need not, in itself, preclude the use of the victim impact statement. That such statements might be "unduly inflammatory" does not require a constitutional bar.[98]

Murder, O'Connor contended, replaying the theme of death and resurrection first developed by Rehnquist, "transforms a living person with hopes, dreams, and fears into a corpse.... The Constitution does not preclude the State from deciding to give some of that back."[99] Victim impact evidence is valuable precisely because it refuses abstraction and impersonality, and insists that punishment respond to real pain. The jury is asked to hear that pain and to avenge it.

Scalia's brief concurrence in *Payne* fully underlines the power of the victims' rights movement as a force in constitutional adjudication. Focusing solely on mitigating evidence while excluding evidence about victim impact would be, in Scalia's view, an "injustice."[100] "*Booth's* stunning *ipse dixit*," Scalia argued, "that a crime's unanticipated consequences must be deemed 'irrelevant' to the sentence conflicts with a public sense of justice keen enough that it has found voice in a nationwide victim's rights' movement."[101]

In Scalia's opinion what is unjust is what conflicts with the public's sense of justice. In this instance Scalia positions himself as the spokesman for the victims' rights movement, and the keenness of public's sense of justice is measured by a political rather than an ethical standard. Finding "voice" is exactly what is at stake in *Payne*, or, more precisely, what is at stake is the question of whose sense of justice will find a voice.

In order to correct the injustice of denying voice to the public's keen sense of justice, Scalia would not only allow victim impact evidence, he would also place limits on the mitigation evidence that is allowed in capital trials. He would direct attention away from the moral blameworthiness of the defendant to the assessment of the harm to the victims, unintentionally transforming the juridical subject into one whose inner life counts for less than his outer actions. "A system arranged in this way," law professor Steven Gey rightly notes,

> would permit sentencers in capital trials to ignore the defendant's character altogether and react solely to the bare facts of the crime and its ancillary consequences. The defendant is viewed in one-dimensional fashion as nothing more than the agent of harm.

---

[98] *Id.*

[99] *Id.*

[100] *Id.*, 741.

[101] *Id.*

Instead of meting out justice in retributive fashion, according to the defendant's moral deserts, Scalia's system avenges a harm by killing the agent of harm. Society's anger is assuaged, even if in traditional retributive terms the punishment is disproportionate to the offense.[102]

While Rehnquist, O'Connor, and Scalia were only too happy to use *Payne* to call into question a substantial part of Court's death penalty jurisprudence, Justice Souter, concurring in the result, tried, albeit in a strained and somewhat convoluted manner, to reconcile the admissibility of victim impact statements in capital cases with existing doctrine. He did so by insisting that the harms which a victim impact statement would bring to the attention of the jury would, in fact, be "foreseeable" by an offender. "While a defendant's anticipation of specific consequences to the victims of his intended act is relevant to sentencing," Souter contended, such *detailed* (emphasis added) foreknowledge does not exhaust the category of morally relevant fact ... Murder has foreseeable consequences. When it happens, it is always to distinct individuals, and after it happens other victims are left . Every defendant knows ... that the life he will take by his homicidal behavior is that of a unique person ... and that the person killed probably has close associates ... who will suffer harms and deprivations from the victim's death.... That foreseeability of the killing's consequences imbues them with direct moral relevance.[103]

Souter tried to personalize the victim by turning the offender into an impersonal repository of stipulated knowledge. Thus for him the harm to the victim's family is a culpable wrong because it is *always* foreseeable. *That* wrong is as blameworthy as the wrong done to the person murdered.

Souter's effort to reconcile victim impact evidence with existing death penalty doctrine proves too much. If every murderer knows, or can foresee, damage to surviving relatives resulting from his act, then there is no need to inform the jury about the nature of such damage since it would not help differentiate murderers who deserve to a death sentence from those who deserve life in prison. If Souter is right, victim impact statements personalize the suffering of the survivors and, at the same time, threaten the focus on defendant blameworthiness and heightened standards of reliability which the Court previously had insisted were central to the constitutional legitimacy of capital punishment.

Justice Stevens's *Payne* dissent points out this consequence of Souter's reasoning. For Stevens the only way to preserve the constitu-

---

[102] Gey, "Justice Scalia's ...," 125–126.

[103] *Payne*, 838.

tional legitimacy of capital punishment is to prohibit the use of victim impact statements. Not surprisingly, throughout his opinion Stevens distinguishes reason from passion, a distinction which, he suggests, the use of victim impact evidence erodes. He argues that though the majority opinion will have "strong political appeal" it has "no proper place in a reasoned judicial opinion."[104] Moreover he insists that unless it can be shown that collateral harm associated with a murder was known in its particularity to the murderer then it is not relevant in determining his blameworthiness or in calculating an appropriate response to the wrong of his act. The use of a victim impact statement is, in his view, unacceptable because it "allows a jury to hold a defendant responsible for a whole array of harms that he could not foresee and for which he is therefore not blameworthy."[105]

Stevens suggests that even in the face of the "political strength of the 'victims' rights' movement . . ." law should not give in.[106] At stake is the viability of what he calls the "retributive rationale" for criminal punishment.[107] Allowing the use of a victim impact statement in capital sentencing will, he warns, be "greeted with enthusiasm by a large number of . . . citizens"[108] yet it "serves no purpose other than to encourage jurors to decide in favor of death rather than life on the basis of their emotions rather than their reason."[109]

Payne did, in fact, open up the legal process and the process through which punishment is imposed in order to satisfy "a public sense of justice" which is equated with the movement for victims' rights.[110] Yet with the exception of Souter, the Justices did not acknowledge the potentially disruptive impact of the urgent call to hear the voice of the victim even as they acted it out in their rhetoric.[111] They responded to

---

[104] *Id.*, 859.

[105] *Id.*, 864.

[106] *Id.*, 867. As Judge Cole put it in *Lodowski v. State*, 490 A.2d 1228, 1277 (Md. 1985) the very purpose of victim input seems to be to allow victims to plead for their "pound of flesh . . ., but the halls of justice should not be the forum by which their cries for vengeance should be heard."

[107] *Payne*, 861.

[108] *Id.*

[109] *Id.*, 857.

[110] *Id.*, 833.

[111] In Kaminer's view the call to hear the voice of the victim "partakes of a popular confusion of law and therapy and the substitution of feelings for facts. But if feelings are facts in a therapists office . . . feelings are prejudices in a court of law. . . . Justice is not a form of therapy, meaning that what is helpful to a particular victim . . . is not necessarily just and what is just may not be therapeutic." See *It's All the Rage*, 84. See also Vivien

the challenge posed by the victims' rights movement by reiterating categories whose very meaning was up-for-grabs.

Payne was thus not simply a triumph for vengeance. Rather it provided an opportunity for victims to participate in an unfamiliar medium of discourse in which grief and rage are joined to rational argument and complex rules of evidence. This is what Justice Marshall identified, in his *Payne* opinion, as the ultimate significance of the case. In his judgment, what was really at stake was the ominous suggestion of "an even more extensive upheaval" in the law, one which "sends a clear signal that scores of established liberties are now ripe for reconsideration."[112] He rightly warned that the element of revenge that the decision in *Payne* signaled could/would not be contained, that it is part and parcel of an indignant, frustrated assault on those who have claimed the role of the victim in today's political discourse—"minorities, women, or the indigent."[113] For Marshall, *Payne* was one major step toward the demise of a conception of law as " 'a source of impersonal and reasoned judgments.' "[114]

The Continuing Legal Struggle

The Supreme Court's 1991 decision ended neither the saga of Pervis Payne himself nor the legal struggle over the admissibility of victim impact statements. In its *Payne* decision the Supreme Court had held only that "if the State chooses to permit the admission of victim impact evidence and prosecutorial argument on that subject, the Eighth Amendment erects no per se bar."[115] This holding left unresolved a variety of questions. As John Blume put it,

> Payne lifted the per se ban on the admissibility of VIE, but what does it permit? .... Payne provides no answers to these and other questions.... Payne's dual reasons for permitting VIE—to offset the defendant's mitigating evidence and to permit the jury to assess the specific harm resulting from the offense—are so vague that it is extraordinarily difficult to determine Payne's scope. One could reasonably argue that Payne sanctions only a very limited victim

---

Berger, "*Payne* and Suffering—A Personal Reflection and a Victim—Centered Critique," 20 *Florida State University Law Review* (1992), 59.

[112] *Payne*, 844.

[113] *Id.*, 856.

[114] *Id.*, 852. What Marshall saw was the connection between criminal justice populism and populism in constitutional interpretation in which "much despised decisions (e.g. *Booth* and *Gathers*) are cast aside if enough political energy is directed at them." e-mail from Jordan Steiker to the author, September 5, 2007.

[115] *Id.*, 827.

impact presentation in order to prevent the victim from being 'faceless.' On the other hand, the enforcement mechanism that the Court chose—whether the evidence is 'so unduly prejudicial that it renders the trial fundamentally unfair'—is so permissive that much more may be tolerable. Thus, the question of how much and what kind of VIE is permissible remains unanswered.... Furthermore, Payne did not address what procedural protections—including notice, pre-admission in in camera hearings, and limiting instructions—are necessary to safeguard a capital defendant's right to a reliable determination of the appropriate penalty.[116]

Determining *Payne's* scope and filling in the details left unaddressed by that decision has kept courts quite busy. They have had to address such questions as: "Are there any substantive restrictions on the types and modes of VIE that the prosecution may present? For example, who may testify about what? What other evidence may the sentencer hear? Are there any procedural safeguards necessary to safeguard a capital defendant's right to a reliable sentencing determination?"[117]

Two cases illustrate some of the ways that courts have dealt with these questions. In *Louisiana v. Bernard*, decided one year after *Payne*, the Louisiana Supreme Court was asked to decide whether prosecutors in that state had to do more than notify the defense of their intention to use victim impact evidence and provide notice of "the exact evidence" that they sought to introduce.[118] The court acknowledged that "Victim impact evidence, by its very nature, is emotionally charged material which involves the risk of injecting arbitrary factors into a capital sentencing hearing."[119] And it framed the question before it as follows:

> Under Payne's holding that the Eighth Amendment does not per se prohibit the use of victim impact evidence, a state statute may authorize the use of such evidence as long as the particular evidence does not result either in a violation of due process by injecting arbitrary factors which render the sentencing hearing fundamentally unfair or in a violation of some provision of the state constitution. The initial inquiry in this case, therefore, is whether Louisiana's capital sentencing statute authorizes the use of victim impact evi-

---

[116] John H. Blume, "Ten Years of Payne: Victim Impact Evidence in Capital Cases," 88 *Cornell Law Review* (2003), 266. As Blume explains, "On the one hand, the Payne majority indicated that there would be no constitutional problem if a State were to permit the prosecution to present a capital sentencing jury with ' "a quick glimpse of the life" ' the defendant took." Thus, the question of how much and what kind of VIE is permissible remains unanswered. See p. 266–267.

[117] *Id.*, 267.

[118] See *Louisiana v. Bernard*, 608 So.2d 966, 967 (1992).

[119] *Id.*, 968.

dence. If so, the next inquiry is whether the statute, as applied in the particular case, is unconstitutional under the federal or state constitution.[120]

Finding that "Evidence of the victim's survivors' opinions about the crime and the murderer is clearly irrelevant to any issue in a capital sentencing hearing,"[121] the court nevertheless held that Louisiana law allowed prosecutors to

> introduce a limited amount of general evidence providing identity to the victim and a limited amount of general evidence demonstrating harm to the victim's survivors.... Informing the jury that the victim had some identity or left some survivors merely states what any person would reasonably expect and can hardly be viewed as injecting an arbitrary factor into a sentencing hearing. But the more detailed the evidence relating to the character of the victim or the harm to the survivors, the less relevant is such evidence to the circumstances of the crime or the character and propensities of the defendant. And the more marginal the relevance of the victim impact evidence, the greater is the risk that an arbitrary factor will be injected into the jury's sentencing deliberations.[122]

Noting the complexity and difficulty that any trial court would face in deciding what kinds of victim impact evidence could be admitted, the court ruled "the defense, upon request, is entitled to notice of the particular victim impact evidence sought to be introduced by the prosecutor and to a pretrial determination of the admissibility of the particular evidence."[123]

Three years after *Bernard,* the Court of Criminal Appeals of Oklahoma confronted similar questions about the limits, if any, on the scope and substance of victim impact evidence in death cases. In *Cargle v. State,* the defendant complained that the prosecutor had been allowed "to present highly emotional, irrelevant evidence to the jury ... (and) that without some guidelines, the evidence becomes nothing more than a 'super aggravator' which negates the narrowing function death penalty procedures are required to provide."[124]

The court resisted the suggestion that after *Payne* " 'the floodgates have opened' and that everything the prosecutor wishes is admissible."[125] Referring to the Oklahoma statutes, the court found that

---

[120] *Id.,* 970.

[121] *Id.*

[122] *Id.,* 971.

[123] *Id.,* 973.

[124] *Cargle v. State,* 909 P.2d 806, 825 (1995).

[125] *Id.,* 826.

victim impact evidence should be restricted to the 'financial, emotional, psychological, and physical effects,' or impact, of the crime
itself on the victim's survivors; as well as some personal characteristics of the victim.... So long as these personal characteristics show
how the loss of the victim will financially, emotionally, psychologically, or physically impact on those affected, it is relevant, as it gives
the jury 'a glimpse of the life' which a defendant 'chose to extinguish' ... However, these personal characteristics should constitute
a 'quick' glimpse ... and its use should be limited to showing how
the victim's death is affecting or might affect the victim's survivors,
and why the victim should not have been killed. Mitigating evidence
offers the fact finder a glimpse of why a defendant is unique and
deserves to live; victim impact evidence should be restricted to those
unique characteristics which define the individual who has died, the
contemporaneous and prospective circumstances surrounding that
death, and how those circumstances have financially, emotionally,
psychologically, and physically impacted on members of the victim's
immediate family.[126]

Applying this standard, the court found that victim impact evidence
that went solely to the emotional impact of a particular murder victim's
death "exceeded the statutory framework of admissible evidence."[127]

Despite the results in these two cases, "few jurisdictions provide any
substantive limits or procedural protections regulating the admission of
VIE and argument. The overwhelming trend is toward the unfettered
admission of a wide array of VIE and arguments."[128] Moreover, as Blume
notes, "due to the increasing power of the victims' rights movement,
almost all jurisdictions with the death penalty have nevertheless taken
advantage of the Supreme Court's relaxation of the constitutional ban
and now authorize VIE and argument. In fact, of the thirty eight states
with the death penalty thirty three allow the use of victim impact
evidence in capital trials.... Most jurisdictions have done so with little
or no reasoned analysis as to why this type of evidence and argument
should be admissible, other than referring to the Payne decision."[129]

While victims groups went about the business of pressuring state
legislatures and judges to allow the broadest possible scope for victim
impact evidence in capital cases, Pervis Payne continued to try to undo
his conviction and death sentence. Thus, in January, 1992 he filed his

---

[126] *Id.*, 828.

[127] *Id.*, 829.

[128] Blume, "Ten Years of Payne ...," 267.

[129] *Id.*, 267–268.

first petition for post-conviction relief in the state trial court. Four years later that court denied post-conviction relief.[130]

On May 31, 2001 the United States District Court for the Western District of Tennessee dismissed most of the claims Payne had previously litigated in the state courts, and several months later decided on five remaining claims. Among these were Payne's claim of ineffective assistance of counsel arising from "the failure of his trial counsel to investigate and present sufficient mitigation evidence at his capital sentencing hearing. In particular, Payne complains about the failure of his trial counsel to interview and present the testimony of numerous character witnesses concerning his character and reputation in the community."[131] With respect to this issue the district court noted that

> After reviewing Payne's additional submission, the Court is unable to conclude that the decision of the Tennessee Court of Criminal Appeals with respect to this claim was contrary to, or an unreasonable application of, clearly established federal law. In particular, Payne has not satisfied his burden of demonstrating prejudice. The character evidence adduced at the post-conviction hearing suggests that Payne was a normal high school student who was interested in music and helpful at his father's church. In light of the horrific nature of the crimes of which Payne was convicted and the fact that one of his victims was a very young child, the Court is not persuaded that a reasonable probability exists that, had the jury only heard more evidence from more witnesses concerning Payne's reputation in the community, the outcome of his sentencing hearing would have been different. Indeed, this Court is unable to speculate about the effect the omitted evidence may have had on the jury. Although evidence that a capital defendant came from a seriously deprived background may create sympathy and put his acts of violence in

---

[130] Payne appealed that denial to the Court of Criminal Appeals of Tennessee. Among the questions he raised were the following: Whether the State failed to disclose exculpatory evidence in violation of *Brady v. Maryland*; Whether the appellant was denied the effective assistance of counsel at trial and on appeal; Whether the appellant was denied his right to be free from cruel and unusual punishment in that the introduction of irrelevant testimony and a color videotape of the crime scene during the sentencing phase caused the jury to arbitrarily impose the death penalty; Whether the appellant was denied his right to confront witnesses against him at the penalty phase of the trial; Whether the appellant was denied his right to due process when the prosecutors engaged in gross misconduct during the sentencing phase of the trial; Whether the trial court erred in denying the appellant's Motion to Suppress or Exclude certain physical evidence and scientific test results; and Whether the trial court properly instructed the jury. See *Payne v. State*, 1998 WL 12670. On each of these questions the court found that "the appellant has failed to prove his allegations by a preponderance of the evidence" and, as a result, affirmed the trial court's denial of post conviction relief.

[131] *Payne v. Bell*, 194 F.Supp.2d 739, 743 (2002).

context, evidence of Payne's stable background may well have had the opposite effect than that intended by defense counsel.[132]

The court also dismissed Payne's claim that the jury's application of Tennessee's "especially heinous, atrocious, or cruel" aggravating circumstance violated the Eighth and Fourteenth Amendments and his allegation that his due process rights were violated by the introduction of a crime-scene videotape during the sentencing phase of his trial.

The district court's decision on Payne's federal habeas claims was affirmed by the United States Court of Appeals for the Sixth Circuit in July, 2005.

Approximately six months after the Sixth Circuit ruling the Tennessee Supreme Court set Payne's execution for April 11, 2007. In the meantime, however, Tennessee had gotten caught up in an escalating national debate about the adequacy of lethal injection as a method of execution. As a result, in February, 2007 Tennessee Governor Phil Bredesen, an avowed supporter of capital punishment, ordered a temporary halt to executions to allow that state's Commissioner of Correction to conduct a comprehensive review of the manner in which death sentences are administered in Tennessee.[133] Two months later the Commissioner sent a revised set of execution protocols to the Governor, and the state sought a new execution date for Payne. Payne opposed that effort claiming that the court should not set a new date because of

---

[132] *Id.*, 743–744. Payne also alleged that there was insufficient evidence to support application of the Tennessee statute's aggravating circumstance that, during the murder of either victim, he created a risk of death to two or more persons other than the murder victim. He argued that since there were two murder victims at the scene of the crime, he could only have created a risk of death to the one other person, namely Nicholas, who survived the attack. The court granted summary judgment on this claim. As the court noted,

> Although there are very few Tennessee decisions that attempt to define the parameters of the 'great risk of death' aggravating circumstance, this Court is unable to conclude that application of that factor under the circumstances in question was 'so arbitrary or capricious as to constitute an independent due process or Eighth Amendment violation.' On the day in question, the record evidence demonstrates that Payne went on a murderous rampage with a butcher knife in a confined space in which three people were present, two of them small children. As a result of Payne's actions, two of those people were killed and the third seriously injured. Payne does not and cannot dispute that his conduct caused a great risk of death to Nicholas Christopher, the surviving victim. Moreover, the totality of Payne's actions while in the Christophers' apartment would seem to fit within the Tennessee Supreme Court's description of 'either multiple murders or threats to several persons at or shortly prior to or shortly after an act of murder upon which the prosecution is based.' The record contains evidence that would permit a rational jury to find the 'great risk of death' aggravating circumstance with respect to both murder victims. *Id.*, 749.

[133] See "Bredesen Issues Executive Order No. 43," at http://www.tennesseeanytime.org/governor/viewArticleContent.do?id=969 & page=2.

continuing litigation in various state and federal courts over lethal injection. The Tennessee Supreme Court denied his motion and set Payne's new execution date for December 12, 2007. That execution was stayed. As of November 2008, Payne remains on Tennessee's death row.

Conclusion

While it is "counter-intuitive to think of a subjective experience like pain as establishing a publicly valid authority," this is precisely what the victims' rights movement has tried to do and what *Payne* has helped them achieve.[134] Today "admission of victim impact evidence appears quite common in death penalty cases."[135] In the world before *Payne*, survivors of murder victims at best could expect to be witnesses in the trials of those who murdered their loved ones; today they are important participants.[136] "In some form or other a victim has a right to speak at sentencing in all fifty states."[137] And, as Blume puts it, "Payne is not going away. VIE is politically popular, and it is difficult to imagine any state or federal court significantly restricting its admissibility. Furthermore, VIE is largely unregulated. Appellate court reversals for admitting VIE or argument are as rare as the proverbial hen's teeth."[138]

Those who pushed for and secured the opportunity to use victim impact statements in capital trials did so in order to extend the idea of the victim to include survivors, those left behind to bear the burden of suffering and grief. In those statements relatives of murder victims describe for the jury, during the sentencing phase of the trial, the effect on them of the death of a loved one, and they present first person accounts of emotional trauma and continuing personal distress.[139] Yet,

---

[134] Culbert, "The Body in *Payne*: . . .," 8.

[135] Mosteller, "Victim Impact Evidence: Hard to Find the Real Rules," 546.

[136] See Douglas Beloof, "Constitutional Implications of Crime Victims as Participants," 88 *Cornell Law Review* (2003), 285.

[137] *Id.*, 286. As Beloof explains, "In examining the constitutionality of participant sentencing recommendations in noncapital cases, no court has ever found a constitutional violation." See 289.

[138] Blume, "Victim Impact Evidence in Capital Cases," 278–279.

[139] Paul Gewirtz, "Victims and Voyeurs: Two Narrative Problems at the Criminal Trial," in *Law's Stories: Narrative and Rhetoric in the Law*, eds. Peter Brooks and Paul Gewirtz. New Haven: Yale University Press, 1996. As Dubber observes, "[I]n the past capital sentencing pitted the defendant against the State. . . . In the new paradigmatic sentencing hearing, the capital defendant now encounters an even more formidable opponent: the person whose death made her eligible for the death penalty, the capital victim." Markus Dubber, "Regulating the Tender Heart When the Axe Is Ready to Strike," 41 *Buffalo Law Review* (1993), 86.

when victims speak in capital trials, public scrutiny invades some of most personal aspects of their lives—the ways they suffer and grieve.

Payne "represents a marked 'sea change' in capital jurisprudence and capital litigation"[140] and signifies that legal norms no longer, if they ever did, adequately express common moral commitments. *Payne* allows the surviving relatives of murder victims to use legal processes in capital cases to express their grief and rage as they, or their surrogates, seek to enlist the loyalty of judges and juries in a quest for revenge. As Richard Burr observes, "victim impact testimony provides a momentary opportunity for survivors to give voice to their loss, be heard, and feel less isolated."[141] The *Payne* case is one key episode in the ongoing effort of victims to turn the quest for justice into a quest of voice and one indicator of their success in getting courts and legislators to equate the absence of the victim's voice as an absence of justice.[142]

---

[140] Blume, "Victim Impact Evidence in Capital Cases," 279.

[141] Richard Burr, "Litigating with Victim Impact Testimony: The Serendipity That Has Come From Payne v. Tennessee," 88 *Cornell Law Review* (2003), 517.

[142] Marianne Constable, "Reflections on Law as a Profession of Words," in *Justice and Power in Sociolegal Studies*, Bryant Garth and Austin Sarat, eds. Evanston: Northwestern University Press, 1998, 26.

9

David Bruck[1]

Simmons v. South Carolina (1994)

No one was surprised when the question came. In death penalty cases, it happens all the time. The jury goes into the jury room to decide whether to sentence someone convicted of murder to death or to life imprisonment. Then (sometimes right away, sometimes after a few hours), there's a knock on the jury room door, and someone inside hands the bailiff a slip of paper with a question for the judge. *If we give him life, what then? Can he get out of prison on parole?*

This time the jury had been deliberating for 90 minutes before it asked. The foreman's note was dated and neatly printed in capital letters:

JUNE 30, 1991

JUDGE ANDERSON:

DOES THE IMPOSITION OF A LIFE SENTENCE CARRY WITH IT THE POSSIBILITY OF PAROLE?

Judge Ralph King Anderson, the presiding judge in the case of *The State of South Carolina v. Jonathan Dale Simmons*, knew what he had to do. The rule laid down by the South Carolina Supreme Court was that he was supposed to avoid answering the question, and to tell the jurors instead to put the issue of parole out of their minds. So Judge Anderson summoned the jury back into the courtroom and, in his oddly formal and repetitive courtroom manner of speaking, read them the answer that the state supreme court had prescribed:

Mr. Foreman, I received the note and I respond as follows: Mr. Foreman and members of the jury, please, please, give me your

---

[1] Clinical Professor of Law, Washington & Lee University School of Law, Lexington, Virginia. The author assisted Jonathan Simmons' lawyers at trial, and served as lead counsel on appeal, in the Supreme Court, and on remand in the South Carolina courts.

attention. You are instructed not to consider parole or parole eligibility in reaching your verdict. Do not consider parole or parole eligibility. That is not a proper issue for your consideration. The terms life imprisonment and death sentence are to be understood in their plain and ordinary meaning. The terms life imprisonment and death sentence are to be understood in their plain and ordinary meaning.

But the jurors were already considering whether Simmons would get out if he wasn't sentenced to death, and so less than 30 minutes later they returned to the courtroom with a unanimous verdict of death. Maybe he didn't exactly deserve it, but at least once he's dead, you *know* he's not getting out.

The real answer to the jury's question would have been simple. The law of South Carolina prohibited someone like Jonathan Simmons from ever being considered for parole, let alone released. So Judge Anderson could have truthfully answered the jury's question with a simple, "No." Why didn't he?

* * *

Five years earlier, in the spring of 1986, the South Carolina legislature was deadlocked over legislation to "get tough" on violent crime. Even though the state already had one of the highest incarceration rates in the world, and no murderer had a chance at parole until he'd served at least 20 years of a life sentence, a new crime victims' organization called CAVE (a near-acronym for Citizens Against Violent Crime) had persuaded many legislators to enact an automatic life-without-parole sentence for any capital murderer who was not sentenced to death. The state House of Representatives approved this change as part of a larger tough-on-crime package, but it ran into opposition in the state Senate.

Now, life-without-parole was a sentence that had never existed in more than 300 years of South Carolina history, and there were (and still are) lots of reasons to oppose it. First, doing away with all possibility of eventual parole mainly affects aged ex-criminals who have long ceased to be much of a threat to anyone. Which leads to the second problem: life without parole is expensive. Prisons have to provide free medical care to inmates, and if the state incarcerates prisoners into their dotage, medical costs rise exponentially. Finally, it's just common sense that the criminal justice system is more likely to make correct decisions about whom to release 20 or 30 years from now if it waits until the 20 or 30 years are up, rather than by settling in advance on a one-size-fits-all answer ("we won't ever release anyone") before the crimes have even been committed, or the criminals identified.

But none of those were the reasons why the South Carolina Senate opposed the House life-without-parole legislation. Rather, the senators

were concerned that life-without parole would prove to be such an
attractive sentencing alternative to juries that they would stop sentencing convicted murderers to death. Prosecutors insisted that providing
juries with a life-without-parole option " 'objectively, over the long haul,'
would do away with the death penalty."[2] State Senator John Drummond
told his colleagues, "[I]f we pass [life without parole], let's close the
death house ... [and] transfer the chair to the state museum." The
problem, Senator Drummond explained, was that "a juror considering
the death penalty will think, 'I can put that person away forever, and my
conscience will be clear.' "[3] In making this point, Drummond was echo-
ing the views of a group of South Carolina law enforcement officials who
asserted in a letter to the legislature that enacting a life-without-parole
sentence "will increase the risk of major crime by encouraging juries to
refrain from applying the existing death penalty."[4] CAVE founder Ray
Rossi, whose career as an anti-crime lobbyist began after his own
daughter was kidnaped, raped and murdered by a group of ex-convicts,
implicitly acknowledged that the prosecutors might be correct in their
assessment of the impact of life without parole on the sentencing
behavior of capital juries, but Rossi argued for adoption of the no-parole
measure all the same:

> "Some prosecutors think they have a better chance of getting the
> death penalty (for a criminal) if the only other option is life (with a
> chance for parole [in] 20 years)," Rossi said. "I'm more concerned
> about the times that we don't get it (the death penalty) and the
> violent criminal is released back on the streets."[5]

Despite Rossi's plea, the prosecutors' argument carried the day in
the Senate, which voted to delete life without parole from the House-
passed anti-crime legislation.[6] The House, however, insisted on its life
without parole provision, and so the crime bill languished in conference
committee. As positions on both sides hardened, House Judiciary Chair
Jean H. Toal, a legislative leader on the crime bill, proposed a way out of
the impasse. Rep. Toal argued that jury decisions in capital cases would
not be affected by the no-parole provision *because trial judges would not
let jurors know about it*. A newspaper report described her position:

---

[2] D. Kern, "Anders argues against life without parole," *The State* (Columbia, S.C.),
March 16, 1986, at 4B.

[3] G. Rigsby, "Senate OKs amended crime bill," *The State* (Columbia, S.C.), March 20,
1986, at 8C.

[4] Associated Press, "Crime bill stalemate continues," *The State* (Columbia, S.C.), May
1, 1986, at 12C (Citizens Against Violent Crime).

[5] D. Kern, "Anders argues against life without parole," *supra*.

[6] 1986 S.C. Senate J. 1071, 1079.

Mrs. Toal said she disagrees with people who say death[sic] without parole would make the death penalty obsolete.

Judges would not permit juries to be told anything about a prisoner's chances for serving life or being paroled, she said.

Ms. Toal said juries would continue to consider a penalty based on the heinous nature of a crime, rather than the possibility of parole.[7]

Eventually, the state legislature agreed to a compromise under which aggravated murders would be punishable by life imprisonment without eligibility for parole for a minimum of 30 years, and sentences of life without possibility of parole would be reserved for murderers with at least one prior conviction for a violent crime.[8]

Representative Toal's prediction that these new limitations on parole eligibility would be concealed from capital sentencing juries proved wrong, at least at first. The year after the legislature adopted the 30–year and life-without-parole provisions, the South Carolina Supreme Court ruled that capital defendants were entitled upon request to a jury instruction concerning the newly-enacted parole restrictions.[9] But a year after that, the legislature elected Representative Toal herself to a seat on the state supreme court, and three years later, the court reversed itself and held that trial judges should not provide jurors with any specific information about parole ineligibility, but should simply direct the jurors to interpret the term life imprisonment "in its ordinary and plain meaning."[10]

It's worth stopping right there to appreciate the raw cynicism of what happened. The unstated premise of the 1986 legislative fight over life without parole was that citizens who serve on South Carolina capital juries knew perfectly well that (until then, at least) a "life" sentence didn't necessarily mean life, and that such jurors actually imposed death sentences to eliminate the risk that convicted murderers would otherwise be returned to society on parole some day. When the abolition of parole was proposed by a citizens' anti-crime lobby, the plan ran into opposition from police, prosecutors and politicians who were so attached to the death penalty that they would rather keep parole for murderers than give up the powerful biasing effect that fear of parole release had

---

[7] D. Kern, "House, Senate deadlocked on crime bill," *The State* (Columbia, S.C.), March 27, 1986, at 1C (emphasis added).

[8] *See* 1986 S.C. Acts 2983, 2990; S.C. Code §§ 16–3–20(A), 24–21–640 (1991 Cum. Supp.).

[9] *State v. Atkins*, 293 S.C. 294, 300–01, 360 S.E.2d 302, 305–06 (1987).

[10] *State v. Torrence*, 305 S.C. 45, 59–60, 406 S.E.2d 315, 320 (1991) (Chandler, J., concurring, for a majority of the court).

on jurors. This reasoning assumed, of course, that the legislature couldn't abolish parole without informing jurors in capital cases of the change. But according to Representative (and later Justice) Toal, the courts could indeed keep the abolition of parole a secret. That way the state could get the best of both worlds: for those murderers not sentenced to death, "life" would finally really mean *life*, but all the while juries would go right on sentencing defendants to death based on their mistaken belief that life imprisonment meant only a relatively few years in jail followed by release on parole. Everyone wins—except, of course, the prisoners sent to their deaths by this game of bait-and-switch, and they don't vote.

* * *

Cynical or not, the South Carolina legislators who voted for life-without-parole only once they were persuaded that sentencing juries would not be told about it were onto something real. Prosecutors and defense attorneys have long understood that capital juries factor in the possibility of early release when deciding whether to sentence defendants to death, and for decades, supreme courts in virtually every death penalty state have been handing down decisions instructing trial judges how to respond when prosecutors slipped references to the possibility of parole into their jury arguments, or when juries interrupted their sentencing deliberations to ask about parole.[11] Moreover, social science research over the past two decades has revealed that the biasing effect of speculation on parole is even more severe and pervasive than lawyers and courts had supposed. Analyzing the results of in-depth post-sentencing interviews with 962 actual capital jurors from 257 trials in 11 states, Northeastern University sociologist Bill Bowers and his colleagues found that jurors almost invariably underestimated the severity of their non-death alternative, guessing wrongly that their real choice was between death and a relatively short stretch in prison—typically around 15 years—followed by release on parole.[12] Since jurors' misconceptions about early release could be expressed numerically (some jurors falsely believe that the defendant was likely to be released after 20 years, while others supposed the correct number was 15 years, or 10), Bowers and his colleagues were able to test for correlations between the precise extent of jurors' misconceptions and their actual sentencing behavior. The findings were chilling. The "myth of early release" exerted great power in the jury room: the more that a given juror underestimated the number

---

[11] *California v. Ramos*, 463 U.S. 992, 1013 n.30 (1983); *id*. at 1026 (Marshall, J., dissenting) (noting overwhelming weight of state court authority against permitting jury consideration of parole release or commutation).

[12] William J. Bowers and Benjamin D. Steiner, *Death By Default: An Empirical Demonstration of False and Forced Choices in Capital Sentencing*, 77 Tex. L. Rev. 605, 648 (1999).

of years that the defendant would have to serve if given a life sentence, the more likely was the juror to believe that the defendant was dangerous (even if the prosecution had not contended that the defendant was dangerous) and should be executed. The degree of underestimation of the meaning of a life sentence also predicted whether a juror would vote for death on the jury's first ballot, and even more so on the last ballot. In other words, the Bowers study found that across the country, in case after case, capital sentencing jurors' ignorance about the actual severity of their life sentence alternative was a powerful force driving them to impose the death penalty. And there was every reason to believe that such jury confusion was just as acute in South Carolina as everywhere else, since a study limited to Capital Jury Project interviews of South Carolina jurors produced essentially identical results.[13]

Moreover, the error always weighed on one side of the scale—that is, on death's side. Jurors almost never assume that life sentences are *more* severe than they really are (a practical impossibility in most states, since by 1993 a large majority of death penalty jurisdictions had abolished parole for life-sentenced murderers). The jury-room myth that Bowers' interviews uncovered was one of *early* release. And the imbalance is inherent in the human condition, because while the unexplained term "life" imprisonment can mean almost anything, jurors don't need instructions from the judge to know that a death sentence, once carried out, is forever.

Since the return of the death penalty at the time of *Gregg v. Georgia* in the 1970s, the Supreme Court had encountered the myth of early release just once, and the result had not been encouraging. In *California v. Ramos*,[14] the Court reached out to reverse a California Supreme Court decision that had invalidated a voter-passed provision, the Briggs Initiative, that required judges to tell capital sentencing juries of the almost entirely theoretical possibility that the governor could commute a murderer's life-without-parole sentence to a parole-eligible term. No matter that no contemporary governor had ever done such a thing, or ever would: the California initiative nevertheless required that juries be told that he *could* do it. And it required that they be told this just before they retired to consider whether to impose the death penalty—or take a chance on whether some future liberal governor would undo the killer's life-without-parole sentence and put him back on the road to freedom.

When *Ramos* arrived at the Supreme Court, it seemed likely that the Court would reject this ham-handed attempt to play on jurors' fears of what were actually very remote possibilities of future release. But by a

---

[13] Theodore Eisenberg & Martin T. Wells, "Deadly Confusion: Juror Instructions in Capital Cases," 79 Cornell L. Rev. 1 (1993).

[14] 463 U.S. 992 (1983).

5–4 vote, the Court overturned the California Supreme Court's invalidation of the Briggs Initiative, and held that introducing the explosive issue of commutation into juries' sentencing deliberations violated neither the Eighth Amendment nor the Due Process Clause. To the defendant's argument that the instruction injected irrelevance and speculation into the sentencing process, Justice O'Connor blandly described the Briggs instruction as "bringing to the jury's attention the possibility that the defendant may be returned to society," and then approved it as "invit[ing] the jury to assess whether the defendant is someone whose probable future behavior makes it undesirable that he be permitted to return to society."[15]

It would be charitable to say that this misses the point. What was so unfair about the Briggs instruction was that in the real world, "the possibility that the defendant may be returned to society" through gubernatorial clemency followed by parole was essentially zero, and so encouraging the jury to debate whether such a return would be "desirable" made as much sense as requiring jurors to debate whether it would "desirable" to assign the convicted murderer to a quad in a co-ed college dorm instead of to a maximum security prison cell. But Justice O'Connor's position had five votes. So for state legislators who wished to help prosecutors exploit the myth of early release, *Ramos* provided some reason to expect that the Supreme Court would not interfere.

* * *

Even without such devices as the Briggs instruction, it's not surprising that the citizens who sit on capital juries greatly underestimate the effect of their life imprisonment option. Decades of tough-on-crime political campaigns and saturation coverage of violent crime have left many Americans with an abiding belief that the criminal justice system is a revolving door staffed by feckless bureaucrats and judges who enjoy nothing more than releasing dangerous criminals at the first opportunity. Indeed, it's this conviction—that law enforcement, corrections and the courts don't really care about protecting ordinary people and their families—that explains the seeming paradox of the death penalty's popular resurgence at a time (the last third of the twentieth century) when Americans increasingly doubted the competence of government to wield far less God-like powers. To citizens who believe that their government habitually fails to protect society from violent criminals, the death penalty is not an assertion of governmental power but a *check* on governmental discretion. Execution settles a murderer's future in a way that everyone can see and understand. It can also never be modified behind closed doors by any parole board, judge or corrections official whose misplaced sympathy for the murderer outweighed society's need

---

[15] 463 U.S. at 1003.

for protection. So the death penalty has become both an example and the ultimate symbol of American crime-control populism: a punishment that strips governmental actors of discretion to be lenient when only severity makes sense. That this punishment also grants to government the authority to extinguish the very existence of American citizens is less salient, because the citizens being executed are presumed to be guilty murderers, while the citizens being protected are law-abiding citizens like us.

Of course, since this very same political dynamic has also led to the near-universal abolition of parole for capital murderers, this transformation of the public's perception of the death penalty from an expression of government power into a limitation on discretionary authority rests entirely on the false belief that state governments still enjoy discretionary authority to release convicted capital murderers. Thus, far from being a minor glitch in the administration of the death penalty system, the myth of early release is, at the end of the twentieth century and the beginning of the twenty-first, a large part of the reason why the American system of capital punishment has endured as long as it has.

And capital punishment is not likely to disappear from American life so long as the myth of early release endures. Severe and bloody criminal punishments, after all, are never simply discarded; rather, they are *replaced* by other punishments. The historical process by which virtually all severe corporal punishments have disappeared from American criminal justice illustrates how this occurs.

Debating the proposed Cruel and Unusual Punishments Clause of the Eighth Amendment on the floor of the First Congress, Rep. Livermore of Pennsylvania thought it self-evident that "villains often deserve whipping, and perhaps having their ears cut off...."[16] The subsequent disappearance of both flogging and mutilation as criminal punishments—a disappearance so complete that such punishments would unquestionably be deemed cruel and unusual today—is the clearest example of how, in rejecting once-common forms of punishment, Americans have established "evolving standards of decency that mark the progress of a maturing society."[17] But these bloody corporal punishments did not simply disappear. Rather, during the course of the nineteenth century, they were replaced. Their replacement was lengthy imprisonment—a practical alternative that scarcely existed in the colonial era.[18] For this process of substitution to have worked as it did, it was essential that the

---

[16] 1 Annals of Cong. 754 (1789), quoted in *Furman v. Georgia*, 408 U.S. 238, 262 (1972) (Brennan, J., concurring).

[17] *Trop v. Dulles*, 356 U.S. 86, 101 (1958).

[18] See Lawrence M. Friedman, *Crime and Punishment in American History*, 74–82 (1993).

decision-maker—whether legislature, judge, or jury—be aware that an alternative to flogging or mutilation had come into existence. Once legislative and sentencing authorities were provided with this alternative, there began an evolutionary process which culminated in the total rejection of the older forms of punishment. But had sentencing authorities been prevented from considering non-corporal punishments (or prevented from even knowing of their existence), flogging and mutilation would surely have persisted as criminal sanctions for much longer than they did.

In much the same way, as state Senator Drummond predicted during South Carolina's 1986 crime bill debate, providing capital sentencing juries with an adequate alternative to the death penalty might well prove part of the evolutionary process by which the state's electric chair would eventually take its place alongside the whipping post and the cat o' nine tails as an outmoded historical curiosity. The question taking shape in 1991 was whether South Carolina—and every other death penalty state—could slow or stop this process by requiring jurors to mete out the death penalty under procedures distorted by the myth of early release.

* * *

When the South Carolina Supreme Court announced in *State v. Torrence* that it had come around to Justice Toal's position against telling jurors that parole had been restricted or (for second-time offenders) abolished entirely, Jonathan Simmons was about to go on trial for his life in the state capital of Columbia. Simmons was a mentally unstable 22–year-old black man who had confessed to a series of break-ins and violent attacks against elderly women, including one against his own grandmother. In another of these burglaries, he had beaten a 79–year-old white woman to death with a toilet lid, and it was this crime for which the state intended to seek the death penalty.

Simmons' capital trial and sentencing would be the first after the South Carolina Supreme Court had overruled the state's truth-in-sentencing rule in *Torrence*. His court-appointed lawyers had already realized that they would have a hard time saving their client's life: if they were prevented from informing the jury that Simmons would never leave prison if sentence to life, their task would probably be impossible. Simmons was mentally ill, he and his siblings gave a horrifying account of a childhood of incestuous sexual abuse, neurological testing showed abnormalities in his brain functioning, and once in jail he'd proven to be a meek and compliant prisoner. But if there was any chance that he'd ever get out of jail and resume his pattern of perverse and frightening assaults, what jury would want to risk giving him a "life" sentence?

The first problem facing his defense team was that Jonathan Simmons wasn't yet ineligible for parole. Under the 1986 legislation, only defendants who had already been convicted of one or more violent crimes were parole-ineligible when sentenced a second time, and while Simmons was facing charges for three additional burglaries involving two sexual assaults, he had not yet been tried for or convicted of any of them. As things stood, the jury that sentenced him for the murder would be sentencing a first offender, and as such a first offender he would not yet fall into the group of violent offenders whose life sentences actually meant life with no chance of parole. So the first thing to do was to get into court and plead guilty to at least one other violent crime.

When criminal defense lawyers try to think up clever strategies, making sure that their clients acquire records for violent convictions just before they go on trial for murder isn't usually the first thing that comes to mind. But there was no doubt that Jonathan Simmons would be serving a sentence of life imprisonment without parole by the time all the cases against him were over, since they all involved violent crimes, he'd already confessed to all of them, and he was sure to be convicted. The only question was a technical one of timing: would he lose any chance of parole *before* the jury on the murder case had to sentence him—in which case he could try to let the jurors know that he could never be released from prison if they spared his life—or after?

In South Carolina, the prosecution has almost complete control over which case gets called for trial when, and in what order.[19] So if prosecutors had wanted to manipulate the order of cases in order ensure that Simmons did not become ineligible for parole until after his murder case was over, they probably could simply have refused to allow him to plead guilty to the other burglaries until he'd been convicted and sentenced on the capital charge. But they didn't. Maybe the state's failure to use its scheduling authority to block his pretrial guilty pleas is explained by the fact that the other offenses occurred in another county: the crimes to which Simmons plead guilty the week before his capital murder trial were the responsibility of a separate prosecutor's office which was more interested in clearing its own docket than helping to manipulate a capital sentencing verdict somewhere else. Or maybe prosecutors assumed that, given the very recent *Torrence* decision from the state supreme court, Simmons would not be allowed to tell the sentencing jury that he was ineligible for parole in any event, so he'd gain nothing by his pretrial guilty pleas to the other crimes. Whatever the state's reason for cooperating, just a few days before his capital murder trial was to start, Jonathan Simmons was brought from Columbia to a courthouse in

---

[19] Andrew M. Siegel, *When Prosecutors Control Criminal Court Dockets: Dispatches on History and Policy from a Land Time Forgot*, 32 Am. J.Crim. L. 325 (2005).

neighboring Lexington County, where two of the burglaries and rapes had occurred, and permitted to plead guilty as charged.

Now Simmons had a violent criminal record, and so if the sentencing jury gave him life imprisonment for the murder, he would have no chance of parole. But that would only help him avoid the death penalty if the jurors knew it. And the *Torrence* decision directed the judge not to tell them, but to say instead only that the jurors were to understand the term "life imprisonment" in its "ordinary and plain meaning."

What is the "ordinary and plain meaning" of life imprisonment?

In South Carolina, parole (or, before that, gubernatorial pardon) had been available for as long as there had been such a sentence as life imprisonment. Until 1977, in fact, a murderer who avoided the electric chair could be paroled after serving only 10 years of his "life" sentence, and many were. In other parts of the country, notorious killers such as Charles Manson and Sirhan Sirhan were coming up for parole every year, and any juror who had been paying the least attention to local or national crime-related news would know that "life imprisonment" carried at least a chance of early release on parole.

But in a legal dispute, what "everyone knows" isn't something that a lawyer can just state as a fact: rather, it has to be proven by evidence. So Simmons' defense counsel asked a professor who ran a program at the University of South Carolina named the Institute for Public Affairs to get some of his graduate students to conduct a telephone public opinion survey about what South Carolinians really did know (or thought they knew) about parole for convicted murderers. The survey was conducted just a few days before the Simmons trial was due to begin and it showed exactly what the defense lawyers expected: almost no one surveyed thought that life imprisonment really meant life, and on average, people in South Carolina believed that a murderer sentenced to life could expect to be released back into society after just over 17 years in prison. Armed with this statewide survey, the defense could now demonstrate that the real "ordinary and plain meaning" of life imprisonment was something far short of the life-without-parole sentence that Jonathan Simmons would actually receive if the jury allowed him to live.

As the trial approached, it still seemed hard to believe that the prosecution would really take advantage of the *Torrence* decision to keep the jury from finding out that Simmons would be locked up for good. Suppose the prosecutor actually believed, as South Carolina law assumed, that every member of every capital sentencing jury understood the term "life imprisonment" to necessarily exclude any chance of parole. In that case, telling the jurors that there was, in fact, no chance of parole wouldn't change anything—so why not tell them? But if the prosecutor knew, as every practicing lawyer and the South Carolina

Senate all did (and as the statewide poll proved) that in reality jurors greatly exaggerated the chances of early release for life-sentenced murderers, then it would take a lot of gall to insist on hiding the truth, and forcing the jury to make a sentencing decision based on ignorance and fear. Surely no one could be *that* cynical.

But as it turned out, Simmons's prosecutor could. Early in the proceedings, he requested and received rulings from Judge Anderson prohibiting defense counsel from asking prospective jurors what they knew, or thought they knew, about parole during the lengthy jury selection process. Then he secured another ruling from the judge that the defense attorneys could not refer in their closing arguments (or anywhere else) to the 1986 no-parole legislation that had foreclosed any chance of parole for Jonathan Simmons. And finally, he prevailed on the judge to refuse the defense request to tell the jury about the no-parole law when he instructed the jury, even though the defense had presented the judge with the results of the statewide public opinion poll that showed that South Carolinians were nearly unanimous in believing (wrongly, in this case) that convicted murderers who received life sentences could expect to be released relatively quickly.

Once the judge refused to give a life-without-parole instruction, the defense had one more last-gasp request. At least, they asked, don't let the prosecution tell the jury that the death penalty is the only way to protect society from future crimes by Jonathan Simmons. It wouldn't be fair to allow such an argument, because the existence of another way to protect society—keeping Simmons locked up for life without hope of parole—was available but was being hidden from the jury. But Judge Anderson refused to limit the prosecutor's closing argument. So when his turn came to tell the jurors why they should sentence Simmons to death, the prosecutor reminded them that even the defense psychologist had acknowledged that Simmons was dangerous, characterized the issue before the jury as "what to do with him now that he is in our midst," and repeatedly described the jury's decision for death as a simple matter of "self-defense."

In instructing the jury, the judge clarified the meaning of a *death sentence,* informing the jury (although no one has asked him to) that it meant death by electrocution. But true to his previous rulings, the judge refused to tell the jury anything about what a *life* sentence meant: when the jury retired to decide whether to sentence Simmons to life or to death, all it knew was that the alternative to the death penalty was something called "life imprisonment."

A member of the trial jury later described in an affidavit what happened in the jury room:

During deliberations at the sentencing part of the trial, members of the jury mentioned the possibility that Mr. Simmons might get out on parole if we gave him a life sentence. Someone actually mentioned the possibility that he could get out on parole and could try to find the members of the jury who had convicted him.

Because of this, I raised the idea of asking the judge whether he could be released on parole if he got a life sentence. The jury felt that we needed to know whether he could be paroled. That is why we asked the question.[20]

The answer the jurors got, of course, was that they were not to consider parole or parole eligibility, and that "[t]he terms life imprisonment and death sentence are to be understood in their plain and ordinary meaning." The juror continued,

The way I interpreted the judge's answer was that he was telling us that we had stepped into an area where we weren't supposed to be, and that we should get back to our places and do our job. I did not understand the judge to be telling us that Mr. Simmons would never be eligible for parole. Rather, I thought he was simply telling us not to concern ourselves with whether he would be released on parole. The problem with that is that we were concerned with whether he could get out on parole. We had seen the pictures and the rest of the evidence about Mr. Simmons' crimes against elderly women, and the solicitor talked about him as if he was a monster. We were naturally worried about whether he could get parole if we gave him a life sentence, and the judge telling us not to be concerned about it didn't change that. We had all heard of cases where people were released on parole after being sent to prison for life, and this was naturally on our minds.

If I had known that under the law of South Carolina Mr. Simmons would never have been eligible for parole if we had given him a life sentence, I would not have voted for the death penalty. I felt that Mr. Simmons had serious mental problems, and so long as he remained in prison for his whole life, there would be a chance for him to be helped and rehabilitated. I don't know for sure whether other members of the jury would have felt the same way, but I believe that there were three or four other jurors who would also have voted for life imprisonment if they had known that there was no possibility of his coming up for parole and being paroled. However, after hearing Judge Anderson's answer to our question, no one had any reason to be confident that Mr. Simmons would not be paroled, and we therefore reached a verdict for the death penalty within a few minutes.

---

[20] Affidavit of Judy C. Wicker, March 25, 1993 (on file with the author).

The jury's sentencing verdict was binding on Judge Anderson, who sentenced Simmons to death moments after the jury came back into the courtroom. Now the case was on appeal to the South Carolina Supreme Court, and as head of the state's appellate public defender office, I moved from my earlier role of helping the trial lawyers make a record to becoming Jonathan Simmons' lead attorney.

The only potentially winning issue to be raised on his behalf was the judge's unfair handling of the parole-ineligibility question—that is, the way that the jury had been left to speculate on what everyone but the jurors knew to be a non-existent risk that he'd be paroled if he wasn't executed. But on that issue, it seemed that the fix was in: the appeal would be to a state supreme court that had eliminated South Carolina's truth-in-sentencing rule just five weeks before the start of Simmons' trial. What was worse, the court was seemingly dominated by a judge who'd assured her fellow legislators five years earlier that if they eliminated parole for life-sentenced murderers, the courts would conceal the change from capital sentencing juries. How could she rule otherwise now without double-crossing the state legislators who'd relied on her legal opinion when they voted for life-without-parole in 1986?

I decided to file a motion to ask Justice Toal to recuse herself from sitting on the Simmons appeal. South Carolina is a small state where most participants in the legal system know each other, so before I filed my motion, I notified the attorney general and then called the Justice on the phone and made an appointment to see her in her chambers at the court. She received me politely and said she would not be offended if I filed a recusal motion. Lots of lawyers did, she said, based on positions she'd taken during her years as a state legislator. But, I protested, this wasn't just a position she'd taken for or against a bill; this concerned a prediction she had made to her fellow legislators that South Carolina would never allow trial judges to tell juries about parole ineligibility, and she'd used that prediction to help break an impasse and get life-without-parole adopted. Surely no one would think that she could now impartially judge whether to go back on her word and require that juries be told about parole ineligibility after all. Well, I could file my motion, she said. I did, the court denied it without comment, and on February 1, 1993, the justices upheld Jonathan Simmons' death sentence by a vote of 4–1.[21] The court's discussion of the parole issue occupies less than two pages, and seemed designed to evade further review by burying the parole claim in the details of Judge Anderson's confusing "plain meaning" response to the jury's question. Rather than flatly rejecting Simmons's claim that he was entitled to inform the jury that he would never be paroled, the court simply declared that "a reasonable juror would have understood

---

[21] *State v. Simmons*, 427 S.E.2d 175 (S.C. 1993).

from the charge given that life imprisonment indeed meant life without parole."[22]

Given the care with which we'd created a trial record to maximize the chances of eventual Supreme Court review, the state supreme court's evasive opinion was discouraging. Rather than squarely presenting an important issue of basic fairness, *Simmons v. South Carolina* would now require the Supreme Court to parse Judge Anderson's instructions to determine whether the constitutional violation complained of had even occurred. Still, there was no alternative but to file the petition for certiorari, and hope that the Supreme Court would take the time to work through the state court's opinion.

The certiorari petition began by recounting how South Carolina legislators had balked at adopting life without parole until they were assured that the courts would conceal the change from capital sentencing juries—and how this assurance came from a legislative leader who later joined the state supreme court and helped ensure that her prediction would come true. The petition then raised two primary claims. First, citing *Beck v. Alabama*,[23] it asserted that South Carolina's refusal to tell the sentencing jury that its "life imprisonment" alternative meant life without parole violated the Eighth Amendment's cruel and unusual punishments clause because it created a needless risk that the jury would impose the death sentence by mistake—specifically, on the basis of a groundless fear that only a death sentence offered any protection against the risk that a dangerous murderer would be allowed to re-enter society. And second, the petition argued that even if the Eighth Amendment did not mandate such a truth-in-sentencing rule in all capital cases, what happened at Simmons's trial violated the due process rule of *Gardner v. Florida*[24] *and Skipper v. South Carolina*,[25] because the court had barred Simmons's most effective response to the prosecution's argument that only his execution could protect society from so dangerous an offender.

In the summer of 1993, eight of the Supreme Court's nine justices (Justice Stevens was the only exception) participated in a "cert pool" arrangement under which only a single law clerk would prepare a detailed summary and recommendation for each petition for writ of

---

[22] 427 S.E.2d at 179.

[23] 447 U.S. 625 (1980) (holding that state law prohibiting jury consideration of any lesser-included offense introduced impermissible arbitrariness into guilt-determining process).

[24] 430 U.S. 349 (1977) (holding that due process forbids imposition of death sentence on basis of information that defendant is not permitted to see or rebut).

[25] 476 U.S. 1, 5 n. 1 (1986) (applying *Gardner* to invalidate death sentence based in part on allegation that defendant was prevented by state law from rebutting).

certiorari. Jonathan Simmons' petition was assigned to a clerk to Justice
Kennedy, Brett Kavanaugh.[26] The South Carolina Supreme Court's ruling that Judge Anderson's instruction adequately conveyed the no-parole
concept to the jury seems to have effectively buried Simmons's constitutional claims as far as Kavanaugh was concerned: while his memo to the
Justices doesn't actually consider whether telling the jury *not to consider*
parole would have the same effect as telling it that *there is no parole*,
Kavanaugh nevertheless thought the South Carolina Supreme Court's
conclusion that the "plain meaning" instruction was substantially equivalent to Simmons's request was reason enough to deny review.[27] Anyway,
Kavanaugh went on, in the past three years the Supreme Court had
denied petitions from at least four Virginia death row inmates who
claimed that the federal constitution entitled them to jury instructions
on Virginia's parole ineligibility rules, and there was little real disagreement among state courts concerning this issue. All in all, Kavanaugh
concluded, neither the record of Simmons's own sentencing nor the issue
he was raising made his case "cert-worthy."

The Court nevertheless granted certiorari to consider both the
Eighth Amendment and Due Process claims.[28] As Simmons's counsel, my
first move was the same as that of any capital defense attorney with a
pending case in the Supreme Court and even an ounce of good judgment:
I wrote to Professor Anthony Amsterdam at New York University School
of Law and asked him what to do next. His stylistic suggestion was to
omit from my brief on the merits the story of Representative/Justice
Toal's successful effort to preserve the myth of early release in South
Carolina capital sentencing: the Court, he advised, would find my focus
on Ms. Toal an *"ad feminam* argument," and wouldn't like it. More
substantively, Tony suggested that I switch both the order and the
emphasis of the two constitutional claims. Ever since *Furman*, the Court
had been more inclined to contract rather than expand the reach of the

---

[26] Kavanaugh later served as Deputy White House Counsel under Alberto Gonzales,
and now holds a life-time appointment as a judge on the United States Court of Appeals for
the D.C. Circuit. His nomination at age 38 by President George W. Bush triggered a bitter
3–year confirmation battle, fueled in part by Democratic resentment over Kavanaugh's
role, while working for Special Prosecutor Kenneth Starr, as the principle author of the
highly explicit "Starr Report" that summarized the case for impeaching President Clinton
in the Monica Lewinsky affair.

[27] Blackmun Papers, *Simmons v. South Carolina* file (hereinafter BP), Preliminary
Memorandum dated September 2, 1993, at 11.

[28] The Court's internal docket sheet reveals that six members of the Court voted to
grant review, with only Chief Justice Rehnquist and Justices Scalia and Thomas voting to
deny. Justice O'Connor would have granted review only as to Simmons' *Gardner* right-of-
rebuttal claim. Lee Epstein, Jeffrey A. Segal, & Harold J. Spaeth, *The Digitial Archive of
the Papers of Justice Harry A. Blackmun* (2007), Docket for Case No. 92–9059, available at:
http://epstein.law.northwestern.edu/research/BlackmunArchive.html.

Eighth Amendment in regulating capital sentencing procedure. No matter how persuasive the claim that a state's wilful refusal to counter the myth of early release violated the Eighth Amendment by creating an intolerable risk of arbitrariness in jury death sentencing, it would be hard to persuade a majority of the Court that such a rule did not expand the Court's Eighth Amendment doctrine. The same was true of the alternative Eighth Amendment theory, which involved the well-established rule that sentencing authorities had to be able to consider and give effect to all mitigating evidence before imposing death as punishment. *Lockett* itself required that the sentencer take into account "any aspect of a defendant's character or record and any of the circumstances of the offense that the defendant proffers as a basis for a sentence less than death."[29] But the unavailability of parole under state law is neither an aspect of the defendant's character or record nor an aspect of his offense. So the *Lockett* rule would require some expansion (which the Court was not inclined to do) before it would encompass a right to the jury instruction that Simmons had sought.

On the other hand, Simmons' due process claim was a narrower one that fit comfortably within existing case law. Whether *all* parole-ineligible defendants were entitled to have their juries instructed that "life means life," surely it was fundamentally unfair for the prosecution to tell jurors that a death sentence was the only way they could incapacitate a dangerous Jonathan Simmons while it simultaneously hid the fact that state law had *already* effectively incapacitated him by eliminating any chance that he would ever be released from prison. Indeed, just seven years earlier, a unanimous Court had applied this due process right-to-reply principle to invalidate another death sentence in *Skipper v. South Carolina*,[30] holding that a state trial court had violated "the elemental due process requirement that a defendant not be sentenced to death 'on the basis of information which he had no opportunity to deny or explain' " when it allowed the prosecution to argue that a defendant's future behavior in prison would be bad while excluding testimony that his past behavior in jail had been good.[31] So it wouldn't be much of a stretch for the Court to apply *Skipper* to the facts of *Simmons*, and rule that once the prosecutor had framed the issue as what to do with Jonathan Simmons "now that he is in our midst" and urged the jury to sentence him to death as a matter of collective "self-defense," the Due Process Clause entitled Simmons to respond by informing the jury that its alternative sentence of life imprisonment would also remove him from society, since it carried no possibility of parole.

---

[29] 438 U.S. 586, 604 (1978).

[30] 476 U.S. 1, 5 n.1 (1986).

[31] *Id.* (quoting *Gardner v. Florida*, 430 U.S. 349, 362 (1977)).

Even this modest objective required that the Court accept Simmons'
factual premises, which were (1) that uninstructed jurors do not believe
that "life imprisonment" actually means life and (2) that telling the jury
to understand the term "life imprisonment" in its "ordinary and plain
meaning" does not keep jurors from assuming that the defendant will
eventually be released on parole if sentenced to life. The state's brief
disputed both contentions, although the first was intuitively plausible,
given that the jury felt the need to ask about parole. As for the second, if
the jurors had begun their deliberations thinking that life imprisonment
probably carried a chance of parole release, Judge Anderson's evasive
instruction to consider the term in its "ordinary and plain meaning" was
just as likely to have confirmed as to have corrected their misconception.

But if the case was to be decided on the narrow ground that
Simmons was denied his right to rebut the state's argument that he was
too dangerous to be allowed to live, such an argument by the state would
have to appear in the record. The state denied that it had raised
"dangerousness" as an issue, and indeed (unlike in Texas and Virginia)
South Carolina's sentencing statute makes no mention of dangerousness
as an aggravating factor. That statute, an almost exact copy of the
Georgia law upheld in *Gregg*, allows the jury to consider all of the
evidence weighing for and against the death penalty once a single
aggravating factor (here, a burglary) was proven. So to see whether the
state has "alleged" dangerousness in any given case, the most logical
place to look is the prosecutor's argument to the jury at the sentencing
hearing. At oral argument, Justice Kennedy grilled the prosecutor (who
had unexpectedly accepted the South Carolina Attorney General's pro
forma offer to argue the case himself) on whether his sentencing argument had relied, at least in part, on Simmons' dangerousness as a reason
for the jury to sentence him to death. To Justice Kennedy at least, the
prosecutor had indeed raised dangerousness when he urged the jury to
view the death penalty in this case as "an act of self-defense," and the
trial court's refusal to tell the jury that Simmons could never be paroled
would have to be evaluated on that basis.

On the petitioner's side, much of the oral argument was given over
to fending off Justice Scalia's suggestions that by requiring a no-parole
instruction here, the Court would be inviting claims that juries should be
told how big inmates' prison cells would be, or whether they would get to
watch television. But after listening to this parrying of skeptical inquiries about what information about sentencing must or must not be
provided to jurors, Justice Souter expressed frustration with the petitioner's argument from a different perspective:

> [Y]ou keep answering these questions in terms of information. Why
> don't you answer the question in terms of *meaning*? [The jury
> wants] to know whether life means life or means something else,

and isn't that a far stronger argument than simply the argument that there are degrees of relevance of extraneous information. This isn't a question about extraneous information; it's a question about meaning, isn't it?

* * *

So why don't you just limit your principle here to saying when there is a legitimate doubt about the meaning of a term which is used in instructing the jury, and which the jury must, in turn, use in sentencing, that term must be defined. Why don't you go to that point and stop?

Of course the real answer to that question was that Justice Souter probably did not have (as in fact he didn't) four more votes for that rationale to reverse Simmons's death sentence. In death penalty cases, the justices know that every new decision will be seized like a lifeline by scores and even hundreds of the condemned. Whatever its intuitive appeal, Justice Souter's proposed constitutional requirement that trial judges eliminate doubt about the meaning of every term that the jury must use in sentencing might well have triggered a cascade of new claims. So when the Court voted in its weekly conference on January 21, 1994, three days after the arguments, there were six votes to reverse Jonathan Simmons' death sentence (with Chief Justice Rehnquist joining Justices Scalia and Thomas in voting to affirm), but a majority concurred only on the relatively narrow holding that the prosecutor's "self-defense" argument had entitled Simmons to respond by informing the jury of the unavailability of parole.

Because the Chief Justice was then in dissent, the power to choose who would write the majority opinion fell to the senior Justice in the majority, Justice Blackmun, and shortly after the conference ended he sent a note to Rehnquist advising, "I shall try my own hand at a majority opinion in this case." The day before, one of Blackmun's law clerks had sent her boss a short memo acknowledging that Simmons' Eighth Amendment argument appeared to lack majority support on the Court, but urging the Justice to press for a broad Due Process ruling, based on the need for "heightened reliability" in capital cases, that could still make this an important case with implications beyond the issue of parole ineligibility.

As it turned out, however, other Justices were already quite aware of Simmons' potential to create a broad new due process "reliability" rubric for evaluating capital sentencing procedures, and were not about to sign on. When Justice Blackmun's initial draft opinion was circulated to the Justices' chambers on May 10, Justice O'Connor noticed that he had included expansive language barring states from "allow[ing] a capital sentencer to predicate its sentence on a misunderstanding of a critically important legal term,"[32] and questioning the right of a state "to conceal accurate legal information from a sentencing jury that reasonably might lead it to impose a sentence less than death."[33] The draft opinion also labored to minimize the significance of the Court's 1983 decision in *Ramos,* suggesting that *Ramos* actually supported the right of capital defendants to put accurate legal information before the jury, rather than (as it actually did) consigning the whole matter to one of state law.[34]

All this was too much for Justice O'Connor, who had written the majority opinion in *Ramos* and viewed that case as upholding the states' general prerogative to either admit or exclude accurate information about early release, as they chose. For Justice O'Connor, Simmons' only valid claim was that he had been unfairly prevented from responding to the prosecutor's future dangerousness argument by informing the jury that he would never be paroled. Three days after receiving Blackmun's draft, she responded with a short note advising that she planned to write a separate concurrence "resting on the narrow ground that due process requires allowing a capital defendant to rebut the State's future dangerousness argument by informing the jury that, if sentenced to life, he would be ineligible for parole."[35] A draft of her concurrence followed a few days later, and as might be expected, it treated *Ramos* more respectfully than had Justice Blackmun. Hoping to secure the fifth vote he needed to convert his draft into a majority opinion of the Court, Blackmun responded with a note assuring O'Connor that he would incorporate her discussion of *Ramos* into his own revised opinion. By then, however, it was too late. Justice O'Connor replied that even Blackmun's revised opinion "sweeps a little too broadly for my comfort, an opinion apparently shared by the Chief Justice," and advised that she intended to file a separate concurrence.[36] Accordingly, when the Court's judgment was finally announced on June 17, 1994, Justice Blackmun's opinion spoke for only a four-member plurality, while Justice O'Connor's

---

[32] BP, May 10, 1994 draft opinion at 7.

[33] *Id.* at 14.

[34] *Id.* at 14–15.

[35] BP, Letter from Justice O'Connor to Justice Blackmun, May 13, 1994.

[36] BP, Letter from Justice O'Connor to Justice Blackmun, May 20, 1994. Judging from a May 20, 1994 letter from Rehnquist to O'Connor, Rehnquist's concern with the Blackmun draft was that it did not seem to limit the due process right to inform the jury of parole ineligibility to cases where the *prosecution* had raised the issue of future dangerousness: in his letter, the Chief Justice expressed his unwillingness to endorse any rule under which a *defendant* could raise the issue of his dangerousness (or, more precisely, his non-dangerousness) and thereby create an entitlement to accurate instructions on his parole ineligibility. BP, Letter from Chief Justice Rehnquist to Justice O'Connor, May 20, 1994.

concurrence garnered three additional votes (including those of Justice Kennedy and Chief Justice Rehnquist) to make up a 7–2 majority to reverse Jonathan Simmons's sentence.

By the time it was filed, Justice Blackmun's opinion (one of his last before his retirement two weeks later) had already been scaled back in an unsuccessful attempt to gain Justice O'Connor's vote, and so like her concurrence, it addressed only Simmons' right-to-respond argument under *Gardner v. Florida*. Under this approach, the truth-in-sentencing right that *Simmons* announced came into existence only when the prosecution made an issue of a non-paroleable defendant's future dangerousness. As Justice Blackmun's opinion summarized the decision, "[t]he State may not create a false dilemma by advancing generalized arguments regarding the defendant's future dangerousness while, at the same time, preventing the jury from learning that the defendant never will be released on parole." But even this limited holding seemed too expansively stated for Justice O'Connor, whose controlling concurrence spelled out some of the circumstances where prosecutors were *still* entitled to conceal the extent to which state law forbade parole in capital cases:

> The decision whether or not to inform the jury of the possibility of early release is generally left to the States. In a State in which parole is available, the Constitution does not require (or preclude) jury consideration of that fact. Likewise, if the prosecution does not argue future dangerousness, the State may appropriately decide that parole is not a proper issue for the jury's consideration even if the only alternative sentence to death is life imprisonment without possibility of parole.

As O'Connor's vote was required to reverse Jonathan Simmons' death sentence, her opinion, with all its hedging and qualification, represented the holding of *Simmons v. South Carolina*. And *Simmons* seemed to offer some encouragement for prosecutors who were still determined to take advantage of jurors' misconceptions about parole release. First, the decision by its terms applied only to defendants who were wholly ineligible for parole. And second, *Simmons'* truth-in-sentencing rule applied only where state law (as in Texas) or the prosecution in a particular case made an issue of the defendant's future dangerousness. Soon prosecutors would be testing the limits of both of these exceptions.

* * *

At the time that Arthur Brown Jr. faced a sentencing jury in Texas, the Texas legislature had limited parole consideration to capital murderers who had already served 35 years of their life sentences. Although Texas law *required* judges to inform juries of defendants' parole eligibility in noncapital jury sentencing proceedings,[37] it prohibited capital defendants from informing the jury of the long term of ineligibility that they would face if the jury did not impose the death penalty. Given that a Texas sentencing jury's primary task is to determine whether the defendant poses a risk of future violence that would constitute a continuing threat to society, Brown asked the trial judge to instruct the jury that in deciding this question, it could take into account that he could not be paroled for at least 35 years. The trial court refused and the ensuing death sentence was upheld by the Texas courts on the ground that Simmons applied only to cases involving life-without-parole. The Supreme Court denied certiorari, despite a concurring statement indicating that four justices agreed with Brown's claim. *Brown v. Texas*, 522 U.S. 940 (1997). Since four votes are enough to grant certiorari, the four justices' concurrence in the denial of certiorari suggests that they lacked the fifth vote needed to extend *Simmons* beyond life-without-parole. A number of Texas legislators understood *Brown* the same way, and in a replay of the 1986 South Carolina debate, the Texas legislature refused until 2005 to pass a life-without-parole alternative to the death penalty at least in part to avert the *Simmons* rule.[38] And as of early 2009, Arthur Brown, Jr., remained on Texas's death row.

By the time of the *Simmons* decision, however, Texas was almost alone in maintaining even a remote possibility of parole for convicted capital murderers. Of the remaining death penalty states, only two besides South Carolina—Virginia and Pennsylvania—required juries to choose between life without parole and death but refused to tell them that life sentences carried no possibility of parole. Perhaps the justices who opted for a narrow ruling rather than the robust Eighth Amendment holding advanced by Justice Souter believed that even *Simmons's* modest corrective nudge would persuade these last outlier states to stop playing games with life-without-parole and just start telling juries the truth. And to be sure, two of the three—South Carolina and Virginia— did eventually take that route.[39]

---

[37] Tex.Code Crim.Proc.Ann., art. 37.07, § 4(a) (Vernon 1997).

[38] Dave Michaels, "House votes to end capital murder parole: Move called victory for victims; death penalty proponents concerned," DALLAS MORNING NEWS 4A (May 25, 2005) (quoting statement by Harris County District Attorney Chuck Rosenthal that passage of life-without-parole sentencing option would be "the first step to ending the death penalty in Texas"). The explanation for Texas's change of heart appears to be its desire to impose life-without-parole sentences on 17–year-old offenders who had just been immunized from the death penalty by the Supreme Court's March, 2005 ruling in *Roper v. Simmons*, 543 U.S. 551. Mike Ward, "High court spares juvenile offenders: Ruling means 72 inmates in U.S., 28 in Texas can't be executed," AUSTIN AMERICAN-STATESMAN (March 2, 2005).

[39] While expressly denying that it was applying *Simmons* or any other federal constitutional rule, the Virginia Supreme Court held in *Yarbrough v. Commonwealth*, 258 Va. 347,

But the myth of early release has proven a hardier weed than *Simmons's* watered-down remedy. As Bowers and Steiner's Capital Jury Project data have shown, even jury instructions about life without parole don't provide much assurance that juries will believe what they have been told: in California, for example, where the jury's non-capital sentencing verdict itself reads "life imprisonment without possibility of parole," only about one-fifth of former trial jurors interviewed by the Capital Jury Project believed that a defendant who received such a sentence would actually spend his whole life in prison.[40]

Moreover, there is very little reason to credit *Simmons's* implicit assumption that the question of dangerousness only enters a capital sentencing jury's deliberation when the prosecutor explicitly places it there.[41] Indeed, in most cases, the bare facts of the murder itself will raise jurors' concerns about whether the defendant would do it again if given the chance. The obvious next question is whether he *will* be given the chance, which is to say, will he be paroled? And it's cruelly ironic that, as in *Simmons* itself, the jury's anxieties about early release are likely to loom especially large in cases where the evidence *in mitigation* involves serious mental illness. Once the defense succeeds in persuading the jury that the defendant would not have committed the crime but for his mental affliction, this understanding will only translate to a life verdict if the jury is given some reasonable assurance that the defendant won't be released to kill again—and there's no need for the prosecutor to drive the point home by arguing it.

That's why *Simmons'* rebuttal rationale, if narrowly construed, has the potential to limit *Simmons* to its facts, and in *Kelly v. South Carolina*,[42] the Court came within a single vote of doing just that. There, a South Carolina prosecutor proved that 17–year-old Billy Kelly had committed a gruesome robbery-murder of a pregnant woman, presented additional evidence that in jail Kelly had cooked up an escape plot included taking a female officer hostage at knife-point, and finally characterized him to the jury as "Bloody Billy" and "the Butcher of

---

366–374, 519 S.E.2d 602, 611–617 (1999), that judges should inform capital sentencing juries in every case—regardless of whether dangerousness was at issue—that "life" meant life without parole. For its part, after South Carolina had experienced two more Supreme Court setbacks on the same issue following *Simmons*, *Shafer v. South Carolina*, 532 U.S. 36 (2001), and *Kelly v. South Carolina*, 534 U.S. 246 (2002), the South Carolina General Assembly amended that state's capital sentencing statute to require life-without-parole instructions in all cases upon request of either the defendant or the prosecution. 2002 S.C. Act No. 278, § 1 (May 28, 2002).

[40] Bowers et al., *supra*, at 650.

[41] *See* John H. Blume, Stephen P. Garvey & Sheri Lynn Johnson, *Future Dangerousness in Capital Cases: Always "At Issue,"* 86 Corn. L. Rev. 397 (2001).

[42] 534 U.S. 246 (2002).

Batesburg." Then, using Justice O'Connor's *Simmons* concurrence as its script,[43] the state persuaded both the trial judge and the South Carolina Supreme Court that no life-without-parole instruction was necessary because the prosecutor had not actually "argued" that the defendant would be dangerous outside of prison.[44] If the Court had affirmed the death sentence in *Kelly*, prosecutors in almost any case could have avoided a *Simmons* no-parole instruction by the simple expedient of *proving* the defendant's dangerousness but then declining to *argue* it. In the event, Justice O'Connor joined a 5–4 majority opinion by Justice Souter that declared the state's evidence and argument sufficient to have triggered the *Simmons* rule. Still, the two justices who had joined Justice O'Connor to form the *Simmons* plurality (Chief Justice Rehnquist and Justice Kennedy) agreed with South Carolina that the prosecutor had, in effect, successfully evaded *Simmons* by this linguistic dodge, and with Justice O'Connor now gone from the Court, it seems likely that today a case like *Kelly* might come out the other way.

To be sure, even before *Kelly*, a solid majority of the Supreme Court had made clear in *Shafer v. South Carolina*,[45] that the rigidity and formalism of the *Simmons* decision were not unlimited. Shortly before 18–year-old Wesley Shafer murdered a convenience store manager during an attempted robbery in the small mill town of Lockhart, S.C., the South Carolina legislature had abolished parole entirely for all violent crimes, leaving life without parole as the only alternative to the death penalty for anyone convicted of a death-eligible murder. Under South Carolina's new no-parole regime, the only circumstance under which a convicted murderer could receive less than life imprisonment without parole was if no aggravating factor was present (that is, only if the death penalty was legally unavailable). Then and only then, the sentencing decision shifted from the jury back to the judge, who could impose anywhere from 30 years to life.

At Wesley Shafer's sentencing, just as at Simmons's, the jury had sent out a written question to the judge during deliberations in a vain effort to find out whether Shafer could be paroled if he received a life sentence. The prosecutor persuaded the judge that he had not actually "argued" that Shafer would be dangerous in the future, and that for this reason *Simmons* entitled the state to conceal from the jury the fact that Shafer could never be paroled. On appeal, however, the South Carolina

---

[43] "[I]f the prosecution does not *argue* future dangerousness, the State may appropriately decide that parole is not a proper issue for the jury's consideration even if the only alternative sentence to death is life imprisonment without possibility of parole." 514 U.S. at 176–77 (O'Connor, J., concurring) (emphasis added).

[44] *State v. Kelly*, 343 S.C. 350, 362, 540 S.E.2d 851, 857 (2001).

[45] 532 U.S. 36 (2001).

Supreme Court by-passed the state's hairsplitting over whether its jury argument had raised Shafer's dangerousness, and instead announced an entirely new rationale for denying a no-parole instruction.[46] Noting that under South Carolina's post-*Simmons* legislation abolishing parole, a convicted murderer could still receive less than life imprisonment if the state failed to prove him eligible for capital punishment by establishing at least one statutory aggravating circumstance, the state supreme court concluded that South Carolina's scheme no longer met *Simmons's* threshold requirement—a jury that is required to choose between life without parole and death. In other words, according to the South Carolina court, the legislature had managed to abolish parole for all convicted capital murders while simultaneously nullifying the effect of *Simmons*; from now on, *Simmons v. South Carolina* no longer applied to South Carolina.

The United States Supreme Court granted certiorari and reversed in an opinion that made short work of the state court's rationale. In her opinion for the Court, Justice Ginsberg pointed out that the availability of a less-than-life sentence for *non*-capital murder had nothing to do with the due process concerns expressed in *Simmons,* and not even the *Simmons* dissenters, Justices Scalia and Thomas, made any effort to defend the spurious distinction by which the South Carolina court had tried to nullify the effect of *Simmons*. On remand, the state Supreme Court applied the subsequent *Kelly* decision to conclude that Shafer's prosecutor had indeed raised the issue of future dangerousness and set the death sentence aside;[47] eventually a new jury, clearly instructed that young Shafer could never be paroled, unanimously sentenced him to life imprisonment instead of death. And by that time, South Carolina's legislature had finally given up and directed trial judges to tell juries the truth about the non-existence of parole in capital cases.[48]

* * *

South Carolina's rear-guard effort to prevent *Simmons* from dispelling the "myth of early release" is just one example of how the *Simmons* Court's decision to craft its new truth-in-sentencing constitutional rule as a right of rebuttal, rather than a general entitlement to dispel jury confusion about sentencing terms, has limited the rule's effect even in cases where the issue was simply one involving parole ineligibility—that is, even in cases involving facts very close to *Simmons* itself. But the timidity of *Simmons* and its progeny may have a broader and more dire consequence.

---

[46] *State v. Shafer*, 340 S.C. 291, 297–300, 531 S.E.2d 524, 527–528 (2000).

[47] *State v. Shafer*, 352 S.C. 191, 573 S.E.2d 796 (2002).

[48] 2002 S.C. Act No. 278, § 1 (May 28, 2002).

The sentencing factor of "future dangerousness" has contributed more than its share of arbitrariness to the American death-selection system ever since the Supreme Court first approved its use in *Jurek v. Texas*.* To begin with, as "dangerousness" becomes salient as a rationale for death sentencing, retributive justice recedes into the background, and with it the sentencer's ability or willingness to take into account mitigating factors such as the offender's background or afflictions. Once you're convinced, as Simmons' prosecutor put it, that imposing the death penalty "will be an act of self-defense "and "a response of society to someone who is a threat," whether that someone actually *deserves* the death penalty begins to seem academic.

Moreover, even accepting that "self-defense" can be a valid justification for the death penalty in some cases, reliably identifying which cases those are has turned out to be beyond human capability. The main problem here is that predictions that any given offender *will* commit serious acts of violence in the future are notoriously unreliable, for the simple reason that most imprisoned murderers don't. False positives— erroneous predictions of future violent behavior—are also the inevitable result of requiring lay jurors to predict a convicted murderer's future behavior immediately after having been inundated with photos, artifacts and testimony depicting what will usually have been the single most violent moment of his life. Compounding the problem in many jurisdictions is the prosecution's use of intuitively plausible but scientifically spurious predictions of dangerousness by "experts"—all with the approval, or at least the tolerance, of the Supreme Court following *Barefoot v. Estelle*.[49]

But much has changed in the field of risk assessment since Supreme Court upheld the blatant quackery of Dr. James Grigson's "100 percent certain" predictions of future violence in *Barefoot*. Today no scientifically literate expert witness would try to assess the risk of violence posed by a given convicted murderer prisoner without taking into account both the setting in which he will be confined—generally a high-security state or federal prison—and the base rate of serious violence in that setting (that is, whether serious violent behavior is common or, as is actually the case in most prison systems, rare). And no such expert would try to predict the prisoner's likely future behavior based on his prior behavior in the free world, or on the facts of his capital crime, since criminological research has failed to uncover any correlation between a murderer's prior record or the facts of his crime and his in-prison behavior.

The rub comes when defendants try to bring all of these modern risk assessment techniques into the courtroom to debunk claims that

---

* 428 U.S. 262 (1976).

[49] 463 U.S. 880 (1983).

only execution can protect society. In many jurisdictions, courts allow or even require juries to make risk assessments of capital defendants, but refuse to allow them to utilize the two most basic tools of risk assessment—consideration of (1) the base rates of violence (2) in the relevant setting (namely life-long high-security imprisonment). Virginia, for example, requires by statute that juries consider whether convicted murderers pose a threat of future violence,[50] but then insists that defendants who wish to rebut this aggravating factor be limited to "individualized" evidence about their own character and record.[51] The practical effect of this rule is that it places off-limits most of the real reasons why any given prisoner is unlikely to commit further violent crimes if his life is spared. Those reasons include the conditions of high security confinement to which the defendant will be subjected, and the counter-intuitive but well-documented fact that very few convicted life term murderers actually do kill or commit other serious violent offenses once sent to prison for life. And absent such information, juries are left to extrapolate from the facts of the crime itself and the defendant's prior record—most or all of which occurred before the defendant was incarcerated.

The difficulty with this is that neither the facts of the murder nor the defendant's prior record actually predict his likely prison behavior, and in any event, the vast majority of convicted murderers cease to commit violent crimes once incarcerated.[52] But Virginia has been able to cite *Simmons v. South Carolina* for the proposition that jurors may be kept from learning any of this. After all, the argument goes, if *Simmons* does not even require state courts to inform jurors (as in *Brown v. Texas*) that a 30–year-old defendant cannot be considered for parole until he is at least 65, surely it does not require that jurors be given much more complex and arguably contingent information such as what his in-prison setting will be,[53] and how low are the rates of serious violence by

---

[50] Va. Code Ann. § 19.2–264.2 (providing as one of two alternative preconditions for imposition of death penalty that prosecution prove a "probability that the defendant would commit criminal acts of violence that would constitute a continuing serious threat to society.")

[51] *Juniper v. Commonwealth*, 271 Va. 362, 626 S.E.2d 383 (2006) (upholding exclusion of expert opinion that defendant would pose a lower risk of future violence in prison than in society on grounds that this opinion was not based on the defendant's personal characteristics or record); *Porter v. Commonwealth*, 661 S.E.2d 415 (Va. 2008) (affirming trial court's refusal to appoint nationally-recognized expert on prison risk assessment of capital murderers on grounds that defense counsel did not adequately show that risk assessment would be based on offender's own prior record, background and crime rather than on research-based "statistical speculation").

[52] *See* Mark D. Cunningham et al., *An Actuarial Model for Assessment of Prison Violence Risk Among Maximum Security Inmates*, Assessment 40 (2005).

[53] *Schmitt v. Kelly*, Slip. op. at 6, 189 Fed.Appx. 257 (4th Cir. 2006).

people just like him in that same setting over time. And so far, Virginia has been able to carry out death sentences imposed by juries whose notions of the likelihood of serious in-prison violence are more likely to have been derived from prison action movies and HBO's *Oz* than from reality. Well over a decade after *Simmons's* "truth in sentencing" decision, states remain free to prevent juries from learning that modern correctional systems have largely solved the problem of inmate violence, and some of them use this latitude to maintain (or at least slow the decline of) death sentencing rates in the first decade of the twenty-first century.

That said, it could have been much worse. Had three more justices joined Scalia and Thomas in viewing Jonathan Simmons's case as another occasion to extol the importance of allowing states to devise their procedures for punishing murderers, what was by 1994 a vestigial practice of deliberately concealing the abolition of parole from sentencing juries might have spread across the country. That is exactly what happened in the aftermath of *Payne v. Tennessee,* which by validating the prosecution's use of "victim-impact" evidence, converted an almost unheard-of practice into a standard feature of capital sentencing proceedings in almost every state. But, however hesitantly, the *Simmons* Court chose to act instead. In so doing, it established a presumption, at least, that when states abolish parole for life-sentenced murderers, capital sentencing juries will learn of the change. In the years since *Simmons* was decided, death sentencing rates have dropped dramatically: while this decline has been uneven and there are a number of likely reasons for it, one of them is surely the fact that, in many cases, properly-instructed juries consider life without parole to be punishment enough.[54] Jonathan Simmons's prosecutor knew the power of appealing to "self-defense against someone who is a threat." Life without parole takes much of that power away, and with it goes the strongest practical reason for choosing death over life.

* * *

Before I left for Washington to argue his case before the Supreme Court, Jonathan Simmons told me that I didn't need to phone him on death row to let him know how the argument went. He said he was willing to appeal because he knew it would help other people on the Row, but he personally did not care whether he lived or died. By the time his case came back before a South Carolina circuit court for resentencing, he seemed determined to do everything he could to get himself resentenced to death. He waived his right to have a new jury empaneled to decide his sentence, and told the resentencing judge that if he was sentenced to life

---

[54] *Baze v. Rees,* 553 U.S. ___, 128 S.Ct. 1520, 1547 (2008) (Stevens, J. concurring).

imprisonment, "I will viciously attack, rape and kill innocent people."[55] In court, he allowed his attorneys to present several days' worth of testimony about his own and his siblings' history of childhood sexual abuse, about his chronic mental illness, and about evidence of brain damage. But when his time came to speak on his own behalf, he delivered a rage-filled diatribe in which he insisted, "I have no remorse."[56] Judge Costa Pleicones was not impressed: he sentenced him to life without parole rather than death, and within a day or two Simmons was moved from his death row cell to another area of the prison where he would undergo an assessment and eventual reassignment.

I went to see him a few days later, and found a different person than the defiant and angry man I'd last seen in the courtroom. Now he seemed shattered, fearful, and grateful for what his defense attorneys had been able to do. And as we talked, it became clear what had happened. Jonathan's diagnoses included Borderline Personality Disorder, a condition often found in adult survivors of childhood sexual abuse that is sometimes described as a disorder of the identity. Whatever the merits of this diagnosis, a disorder of the identity was what I saw before me. The ugliness of Jonathan's behavior in court had not been his own. He had been parroting the instructions and mannerisms of the inmate in the next cell, an articulate middle-class white racist who was then demanding to be executed, and who had apparently been amusing himself by encouraging the pliant and frightened black man next door to do the same. The gestures, the threats, the hate-filled speeches—Jonathan had borrowed them all, along with the trappings of an actual personality, from the inmate one door down. He had even carved KKK into his own skin, as if a black man could join the Klan.

Jonathan's courtroom performance might have been faked, or at least borrowed, but his desperation and fear were real. What had really been motivating Jonathan, I could then see, was his frantic need for everything to remain as it was. He did not want to be re-sentenced to death and he did not want to die. But his fear of death was nothing compared to his fear of being moved from one cell to another. More than anything else, he just did not want to be moved away from his "friend," because once he was alone, he would not have, or be, anything. And sure enough, when he was taken off death row and placed in a new cell block where he did not know anyone, the structure of his personality simply collapsed, leaving a cowering and pathetic man who cringed at everything around him as if he had no skin.

---

[55] Lisa Greene, "Killer Asks Judge to Give Him Death Sentence 'I Have No Remorse,' Simmons Says in Court," THE STATE B1 (Columbia, S.C.) (Dec. 1, 1995).

[56] Id.

Thirteen years later, Jonathan Simmons is in segregation in a high-security prison near Greenville, South Carolina. Wherever he is assigned (he's been moved several times), he becomes convinced that other inmates are related to the woman he murdered and are plotting revenge. His prison files bulge with frantic hand-printed pleas that he is about to be stabbed, poisoned, injected with anthrax. Occasionally the mood of his messages to the prison staff changes ("I Forgive Every Body Forgive Me. Distribute Love and Compassion All Around Me and I Have Been Freed of All My Errors and All Their Consequences.... And I Have Been Swept up in the Wind of Purity"). Almost no one comes to see him; when I do, he wants to talk, rapidly and endlessly, about religious ideas that are swarming in his mind—Hebrew phrases and injunctions, Masonic symbols. The correctional officer who escorts me to see him describes him indulgently, as if he were a difficult but basically harmless mental patient on a locked ward. Which, in a way, he is, except that no one is treating him.

10

By David R. Dow[1]

Bell v. Cone: The Fatal Consequences of Incomplete Failure

Precisely when the downward spiral of Gary Cone's life began is a subject of some importance, and some uncertainty as well. We do know, however, precisely when the proximate beginning of Shipley and Cleopatra Todd's horrific ordeal commenced: on a hot August day in 1980 when Cone robbed a Memphis store of more than $100,000 worth of jewelry and drove off in a car loaded with guns and drugs.[2] A police officer in an unmarked car spotted Cone driving away and gave chase.[3] Cornered, Cone abandoned his car and set off on foot.[4] He shot the officer, B.C. Allen, who survived; he tried to shoot two bystanders, John Douglas Clark and Herschel Dalton, who ran from Cone instead of handing over their car keys.[5] Both had the good fortune of being shot at by Cone after he had run out of ammunition.[6]

Cone escaped. Night fell, with police still on the search. Cone hid in an abandoned building, not far from the home of the Todds.[7] The next morning, Cleopatra Todd, aged 79, rose and went to Sunday church.[8] She

[1] Thanks to the University of Houston Law Foundation for financial support, to Jordan Steiker and John Blume for highly constructive criticism of earlier drafts, to Paul Bottei for discussing the facts and issues of the case, and to Melissa Azadeh for superb research assistance.

[2] Bell v. Cone, 535 U.S. 685, 689 (2002).

[3] *Id.*

[4] *Id.*

[5] Cone v. Bell, 243 F.3d 961, 965 (6th Cir. 2001).

[6] 535 U.S. at 689.

[7] *Id.*

[8] State v. Cone, 665 S.W.2d 87, 90 (Tenn. 1984).

returned home and, with her husband Shipley, aged 93, ate the midday meal that many southerners still call supper.[9] It was their final meal. A few hours later, Gary Cone entered the Todds's home and ended their lives.

No one but Cone knows the exact details of what transpired, but we know enough: that the Todds refused to help him—in Cone's words, that they ceased to "cooperate"—and so Cone beat them to death with a blunt instrument.[10] As the Tennessee court of appeals put it, the Todds were "repeatedly beaten about the head until they died."[11] Their bodies, which were found three days later, were "horribly mutilated and cruelly beaten"[12]—so much so that, at Cone's trial, the judge refused to allow the jury to view photographs of the victims.

But even on the rare occasions when the trial jurors do not see gruesome pictures of the carnage that the murderer has wrought, they hear enough to form mental impressions that are not easily erased. A capital trial in America consists in large part of learning not only what the accused murderer did, but how he did it, and how long it took, and how much the victim (or victims) suffered. It consists of details—details that are deployed to cause the jurors to be outraged or repulsed. Did Cleopatra scream? Did Shipley try to shield her? Did they die alone, or in each other's arms? Murder is an ugly crime, and it is difficult to hear the murderous details and not feel the tug of vengeance. That it why the lawyers who represent capital murder defendants have what is perhaps the most difficult job in all of law. They must try to persuade jurors who have heard the grisly details to spare the life of the man who did it. They must prevail on jurors not to focus narrowly, angrily, and exclusively on the final moments of the victims' lives, but to try to understand as well the entire life of the defendant before them. That was Gary Cone's lawyer's job.

* * *

We also cannot be precisely sure when the downward spiral of John Dice's life began. Dice was the lawyer who represented Gary Cone at trial. Dice was a well-known, and highly regarded, criminal defense lawyer in Tennessee in the early 1980s. He had successfully represented Vietnam veterans, linking their criminal conduct to trauma experienced during combat and to subsequent post-traumatic stress disorder (PTSD). He would eventually adopt a similar strategy in Cone's case. But in

---

[9] *Id.*

[10] State v. Cone, 665 S.W.2d at 91.

[11] *Id.* at 90–91.

[12] *Id.*

Cone's case, the representation was far from successful. Dice's client was convicted and sentenced to death.

By all accounts, Dice took it hard.[13] Following the verdict in the case, Dice would walk around the streets of Memphis, Tennessee, wearing what he said was his old army uniform, talking about his own days as a soldier in Vietnam. The problem is, Dice had never been to Vietnam. He had plummeted into a mental illness of his own. Eventually, the Sixth Circuit deemed him ineffective in connection with his representation of Cone. But the Supreme Court in turn reversed that judgment. Dice himself was not a witness to his vindication. He had killed himself years before.

* * *

When the Supreme Court struck the death penalty down in *Furman v. Georgia*,[14] it did so largely because the Justices perceived that the system was arbitrary. Making sense of *Furman* is no easy matter. Each of the nine Justices wrote his own opinion. In the aggregate, these opinions run to more than 230 pages. The most famous metaphor in the case, if not the most remembered paragraph, was written by Justice Stewart. He said:

> These death sentences are cruel and unusual in the same way that being struck by lightning is cruel and unusual. For, of all the people convicted of rapes and murders in 1967 and 1968, many just as reprehensible as these, the petitioners are among a capriciously selected random handful upon whom the sentence of death has in fact been imposed. . . . I simply conclude that the Eighth and Four-teenth Amendments cannot tolerate the infliction of a sentence of death under legal systems that permit this unique penalty to be so wantonly and so freakishly imposed.[15]

Death sentences were being handed out *not* to the worst criminals who committed the worst crimes, but on the basis of illegitimate or opaque criteria. The Court majority concluded that the death penalty was not being imposed on those murderers who most deserved it. It was being applied randomly, haphazardly, inequitably. This was the problem that the states, in the aftermath of *Furman*, sought to remedy. They enacted procedures designed to channel the jury's sentencing discretion and thereby to insure that the death penalty would be imposed only on the so-called worst of the worst. The core of a capital proceeding, therefore,

---

[13] I am grateful to Paul Bottei, one of Cone's stellar post-conviction lawyers, for talking to me at great length about the personalities of the various actors in Cone's story, including John Dice.

[14] 408 U.S. 238 (1972).

[15] 408 U.S. at 309–10 (Stewart, J., concurring) (footnotes and citations omitted).

is not just whether the defendant committed a murder, but also whether, notwithstanding that he did commit a murder, he is one of the small handful of criminals whose crime warrants death.

To address these two issues, a death penalty trial is actually two trials, each of which is called a stage (or phase). At the first, the jury determines whether it believes that the defendant committed the crime that the state has accused him of. If the jury convicts the defendant of a crime that makes him eligible for death, then the case proceeds to the punishment phase, at which the only question before the jury is whether to sentence the defendant to life or death. The Supreme Court has described the *trial* in a death penalty case (as opposed to the direct appeal or habeas corpus litigation) as the "main event,"[16] and that characterization is undoubtedly apt, yet it is also accurate to say that the main event of the trial itself is typically the punishment phase. Here, the defense offers mitigating evidence: facts that create or support a moral claim that the defendant *ought* not to be executed. In general, these facts fall into two categories: positive and negative mitigating evidence. Positive evidence consists of those facts that reflect well on the inmate: that, for example, he, like Gary Cone, served his country in war; or that he is a loving father and husband; or that he volunteers to help the needy; or that he is a devoted church-goer or Sunday-school teacher. These facts, in other words, are things about the defendant that warrant sparing him from death, because they are laudable characteristics. They give his life some value that the jury ought to preserve. In contrast, negative mitigating evidence consists of those facts that seek to explain how and why the murder came about. We know for example, that most men who batter women had fathers who battered their wives. We know that most men who sexually abuse children were themselves sexually abused. Similarly, we know that murderers on death row have many biographical facts of deprivation in common—they come from homes where they were physically, sexually, or emotionally abused; they come from broken homes and were raised by a parent who abused drugs or alcohol or both. Many are mentally retarded. Many others, like Gary Cone, suffer from mental illness, and many of these men, again like Cone, have their condition exacerbated by drug abuse.

None of these facts excuses the murderer, of course, and the daunting challenge for the defense lawyer is to present these facts in such a way that they are perceived by the jury *not* as an effort to make an excuse for an inexcusable act, but instead as an *explanation* for why our society should hold these men less morally culpable than we would if they had not suffered these fates. The defense lawyer's job is to tell a story using these facts that has but one aim: to persuade the jury that

---

[16] E.g., Wainwright v. Sykes, 433 U.S. 72, 80 (1977).

the man before them who committed a murder is a human being who did a terrible thing, not an inhuman monster who must be euthanized.

In contrast, the prosecution offers aggravating facts: reasons why the state *should* take the murderer's life. As in Cone's case, these aggravating facts often include the lurid details of the crime itself. Because the jurors are human, they have probably cried, and possibly cringed, upon hearing those details.

Some aggravators are more vague than others. In two-thirds of the states with the death penalty, Tennessee included, the jury may impose (or recommend) a death sentence if the jurors believe that the defendant committed a murder that was unusually heinous or vile.[17] Making a comparative assessment of a murder's heinousness is a difficult assignment when the only murder one is familiar with in excruciating detail is the one at issue at the trial where one is a juror. Prosecutors, judges, and even defense lawyers have the advantage—if one may call it that—of knowing about a large universe of murders. Someone who knows the facts of a hundred murders might be able to say that one or five or ten are substantially worse, in some meaningful way, from the rest. (There is even a group of forensic scientists who have embarked on the chimerical task of ranking murders by their depravity.[18]) But the typical juror in a capital trial is familiar with the details of one, and only one, murder.[19] Making a life or death decision is, for a juror, a one-time assignment. For citizens, that might be a good thing, but for purposes of the "unusually heinous" aggravator, it creates a dilemma. There are no sterile or pleasant murders. Photographs of even the most routine murder scene are grisly. Murder victims commonly spill far more blood than seems probable. Every murder is reprehensible and wrong, and capital jurors have no idea whether the murder they grow familiar with over the course of weeks is, comparatively speaking, more heinous or vile than any other.[20]

---

[17] *See* David R. Dow and Mark Dow, eds., Machinery of Death (2002). Richard A. Rosen, The "Especially Heinous" Aggravating Circumstance in Capital Cases—The Standardless Standard, 64 N.C. L. Rev. 941 (1986).

[18] https://depravityscale.org/depscale/.

[19] The reason for this phenomenon is not complicated. Prospective jurors in capital cases are subject to detailed voir dire. Someone who has been on a capital jury where the defendant was either acquitted or sentenced to life rather than death will almost certainly be struck by the prosecution. Likewise, someone who has been on a capital jury where the defendant was convicted and sentenced to death will almost certainly be struck by the defense.

[20] The Supreme Court has considered several vagueness challenges to the "heinous, cruel, atrocious" aggravator. In some cases, the Court found the aggravator unconstitutionally vague. *See* Shell v. Mississippi, 498 U.S. 1, 1 (1990); Maynard v. Cartwright, 486 U.S. 356, 359 (1988); Godfrey v. Georgia, 446 U.S. 420, 422 (1980). In other cases, where the

It is therefore not all that surprising that the jurors in Gary Cone's case characterized the killings of Shipley and Cleopatra Todd as unusually heinous. He did attack two strangers for no apparent reason. He did beat his victims beyond recognition. And although the jurors were not permitted to see the photographs, they did hear the wounds described.[21] Shipley Todd had sixteen wounds. His skull was cracked open. Cleopatra had been struck twenty-two times. Her skull was bashed in as well. Cone had literally beaten their brains out. Both elderly victims had defensive wounds on the back of their hands, likely inflicted as they cowered and tried to shield themselves from the mad onslaught. What juror would not be outraged?

But Cone was not born a murderer. How does someone turn into someone who could do what Gary Cone did? What kind of man beats an elderly couple to death, and for no apparent reason? Cone said he did not remember killing the Todds, but he also said that he had no doubt that he had done so. How does a lawyer try to persuade a jury to spare such a defendant's life? How do you convince a jury who has learned the facts of Shipley and Cleopatra Todd's last minutes that their killer is a human being whom the state ought not to kill?

The defense lawyer's job is steeply uphill, not just because the jurors have spent days listening to the crime's grisly aspects, but because 70 percent of the American public supports the death penalty. And if those odds are not bad enough, the 30 percent who oppose the death penalty are not permitted to sit on a capital jury.[22] The simple reality is that the deck is deeply stacked against the capital defendant. A death penalty lawyer's job at the punishment phase of a capital trial is to persuade men and women who do not personally oppose the death penalty to spare the life of someone who, without provocation or excuse, has taken a human life, often in a brutal and violent way. In this job, there is little margin for error.

In hindsight, it is clear that from the very beginning of the modern death penalty era, the states' response to *Furman* should have dictated

---

Court believed that the state courts had applied a narrowing construction to the factor, its use was upheld. *See Arave*, 507 U.S. at 465; Lewis v. Jeffers, 497 U.S. 764, 780 (1990); Walton v. Arizona, 497 U.S. 639, 652–53 (1990).

Indeed, following the Court's first decision in *Cone*, which is the subject of this essay, the case returned to the Sixth Circuit, which again granted Cone habeas relief, this time on the basis that the "heinous, cruel, atrocious" aggravator in his case was unconstitutionally vague. The Supreme Court reversed the grant of relief. *See* Bell v. Cone (Cone II), 543 U.S. 447 (2005). The case is now before the Court again. See Cone v. Bell, No. 07–1114.

[21] The details of the crime recited in this paragraph come from the state court opinion.

[22] Under Witherspoon v. Illinois, 391 U.S. 510 (1968), someone who is categorically opposed to the death penalty and could never vote to impose it may be disqualified from serving as a juror.

as well the defense strategy in capital cases. If states were going to try to convince jurors that the defendant in front of them was the worst of the worst, then defense lawyers should have been focusing on proving to the jury that their clients, while perhaps guilty of murder, were not in fact among the very worst murderers that ought to be executed. This is not necessarily a new idea—it was exemplified, and arguably reached its apotheosis, with Clarence Darrow's defense of Leopold and Loeb in 1924.[23] But this strategy was rare in Darrow's day, and it remained uncommon for the first half of the modern era. True, not every story is compelling; some murders defy explanation, but a lawyer representing a murderer cannot know her client's background unless she learns it. It took many years, however, for this simple lesson to penetrate the defense culture.[24] For at least a decade and a half following the return of the death penalty in *Gregg v. Georgia*,[25] defense lawyers as a whole continued to believe that the best, and often the only, victory was some form of "not guilty" verdict.[26] They would focus entirely on the first phase of the capital trial, and be entirely unprepared for the second. Eventually defense lawyers learned the lesson, however; and once they did so, the change was cataclysmic. Between 2000 and 2006, death sentences in the United States declined by nearly 60 percent.[27]

Unfortunately for Gary Cone, his trial took place before mitigation was a mainstay of the defense lawyer's arsenal. His lawyer's strategy epitomized the approach to a capital trial that has long since been revealed as unwise and unsound and is therefore increasingly obsolete. Had Cone gone on trial ten or twenty years after he did, the main event of the trial would have been the punishment phase. Cone's jurors would have known the details of his mental illness and how he came to suffer from it. They would have known how this illness affected him and his behavior. They would have learned how it could be controlled in an institutional setting, like a prison. Most of all, they would have learned why these details warranted that they sentence him to life in prison rather than death. But the trial took place too early. Cone's lawyer

---

[23] Darrow's famous closing argument, reportedly twelve hours long, can be found at http://www.law.umkc.edu/faculty/projects/ftrials/leoploeb/darrowclosing.html.

[24] It is also now required. Guidelines promulgated by the American Bar Association require defense counsel to conduct a "thorough investigation of the defendant's background." *See* Wiggins v. Smith, 539 U.S. 510, 522 (2003) (quoting ABA Guidelines); Rompilla v. Beard, 545 U.S. 374, 387 & n. 6 (2005) (same).

[25] 428 U.S. 153 (1976).

[26] Thanks to Tony Amsterdam, Dick Burr, George Kendall, and Jim Marcus for talking with me about the history of death penalty trial litigation, and the emergence of mitigation as a trial focus.

[27] See http://www.nytimes.com/2006/12/15/us/15execute.html.

placed all his eggs in one proverbial basket; he wanted an acquittal. When he did not get it, he had no gas left in the tank.

* * *

Like all criminal defendants, those facing the death penalty are entitled under the Sixth Amendment to be represented by competent counsel. Often they are not. In some jurisdictions, routinely they are not. As a result, the most common complaint that death row inmates raise in their state and federal petitions for writs of habeas corpus are claims of ineffective assistance of counsel. The reason is not that these claims are the easiest to prevail upon, for they are not. The reason is that this constitutional violation occurs with such regularity. Any death row inmate, for example, who went on trial in the era before trial lawyers focused on mitigation will raise a claim that his lawyer was ineffective for not conducting a robust mitigation investigation and presenting a mitigation defense. The inmate may well not prevail—few death row inmates obtain relief any more[28]—but the essence of the claim will probably be truthful.

When an inmate raises a Sixth Amendment claim of ineffective assistance of counsel, he must prove two things: that his lawyer's performance was deficient, and that the deficient performance had consequences, i.e., caused prejudice—meaning that had mistakes not been made, the result of the trial would probably have been different.[29] Meeting either of these prongs is challenging; satisfying both of them is daunting and rare. Under Strickland v. Washington,[30] which established this two-prong test for assessing claims of ineffective assistance of counsel, a lawyer's performance is constitutionally deficient only if the lawyer's conduct fell below objective standards of reasonableness, where the objective standard is set by prevailing professional norms. Ironically, therefore, if everyone is making the same mistake (such as paying inadequate heed to the punishment phase), then it is not unreasonable. Further, if a lawyer's decision can be characterized as a strategic or tactical choice, then it will generally not constitute deficient performance. In other words, a decision can have catastrophic consequences—it can cause massive and manifest prejudice—yet the fact that it caused prejudice will not necessarily mean that it was deficient performance. In short, the lawyer's decision will not be deemed unreasonable if everyone else was doing it, too; further, even if no one else was doing it, the lawyer's decision will not be deemed unreasonable if she made a deliber-

---

[28] David R. Dow and Eric M. Freedman, "The Effects of AEDPA on Justice," in Capital Punishment: The Defining Issues for the Next Generation (2008).

[29] Strickland v. Washington, 466 U.S. 668, 689 (1984). *Wiggins*, supra.

[30] 466 U.S. 668, 687–88.

ate, informed decision to proceed as she did, even if that decision proved catastrophic.

If, despite these barriers, the inmate can nevertheless show that his lawyer's performance was deficient, then he must next show that the precise deficiencies he is complaining about also caused prejudice. Establishing prejudice is even harder than proving deficient performance, for it requires the inmate to show that, but for the lawyer's unprofessional errors, there is a reasonable probability that "the result of the proceeding would have been different."[31] This standard is satisfied when the reviewing court's confidence in the trial's outcome has been undermined. As we have seen, the jury in a typical capital case has been deluged with images and details of a brutal murder; for that reason, establishing prejudice—showing that the result would probably have been different— is difficult precisely because it requires that the appellate court believe that the emotions triggered by those brutal images could somehow be overcome, and that the jury's impulse to exact retribution could have been softened by mercy had the jury only learned some facts that, because of the lawyer's deficient performance, it never heard.

William James says somewhere that the differences among human being are very small, yet very important.[32] A capital murder defendant's life literally depends on the ability of his lawyer to cause the jurors to see the murderer as a broken human being, as a man who has done something inhuman and perhaps even unforgivable, rather than as an inhuman monster. Sometimes the lawyer will focus on his client's mental illness or mental retardation; other times on the abuse his client suffered at the hands of his parents; other times on some trauma, like exposure to combat, that has damaged his client's moral compass. The lawyer's job is to tell a story that explains, not to excuse, because it is not the lawyer's prerogative to excuse—and she probably could not accomplish it even if it were. Explaining, however, is difficult enough. Many jurors are likely to say, "Not everyone with mental illness, or not everyone who was sexually and physically abused by drug-addicted parents, commits murder." That observation, thankfully, is true. And so the job of defense counsel is *not* to argue that cause *necessarily* produces effect, but that *her* client was damaged, that *her* client's culpability was diminished by what he experienced, and that the jury ought to take that into account in assessing his moral blameworthiness. The lawyer's job is to persuade the jury that, notwithstanding the brutal facts of the crime itself, her client is not among the so-called worst of the worst. The

---

[31] 466 U.S. at 694.

[32] William James, The Gospel of Relaxation, in Talks to Teachers of Psychology; and to Students on Some of Life's Ideals 210 (Kessinger Press, 2005).

difference between a lawyer who can do that, and one who cannot, may well be small, but it could hardly be more consequential.

* * *

Had Gary Cone gone on trial a decade after he did, his trial lawyer, steeped in the importance of mitigation, would have identified three strands of Cone's life that needed to be woven together to persuade the jury that Cone's life should be spared: first, the difficult circumstances of his childhood; second, the profoundly altering experience of having served in Vietnam, along with the resultant drug addiction; and third, Cone's desire, as well as his capacity, for self-improvement. (Only the second of these strands was germane to the guilt-phase of the trial, and its relevance even to that phase was limited.)

Gary Cone was the youngest child of Valerie and Zack. Zack was a rigid authoritarian and emotionally abusive.[33] Gary described his own father as a "harsh and unlikeable" man.[34] Because he was not interested in hunting, or other masculine pursuits that appealed to his dad, Gary lived with his grandmother during his senior year of high school.[35] She died shortly after he graduated.[36]

Of his three siblings, Gary was closest to his brother Zach, Jr. and his sister Sue.[37] When Gary was eight or nine, Zach, then fifteen, jumped into a cold lake, suffered cardiac arrest, and died.[38] Young Gary watched as Zach's lifeless body was pulled from the water.[39] By the time of Cone's murderous rampage, everyone he had loved dearly was dead or dying. Zach was only the first. His sister Sue suffered from breast cancer and died ten years after the Todds were murdered.[40] Gary's other sister, Rita, contracted measles at the age of four, and as a result is blind.[41]

After graduating from high school, Cone joined the army in 1966.[42] He was posted to Germany but requested that he be sent to Vietnam,

---

[33] Pyschological Evaluation, Joint Appendix, supra, at pages 90, 96.

[34] The quoted language, as well as the descriptions of Cone's life in and perception of Vietnam, come from Shirley Dicks, From Vietnam to Hell, 13 (1990).

[35] 535 U.S. at 713 n.12.

[36] Id.

[37] Joint appendix, supra, at page 92.

[38] Id. at 92–93.

[39] Id.

[40] Id. at 93.

[41] Id.

[42] 535 U.S. at 708.

and the army obliged.[43] Cone was a supply specialist.[44] Though he did not see much combat, death was all around him.[45] His unit came under repeated mortar fire. There were dead bodies stored in refrigerators adjacent to the food.[46] According to Cone, the tent that served as an emergency room looked like a slaughterhouse. "You could not keep the blood mopped up."[47] He saw women and children who would pretend to befriend the Americans, all the while hiding grenades in their clothes.[48] His sleep was plagued by nightmares in which he would see his friends' heads being blown off by explosions, or witness the Viet Cong cutting children in half.[49] He watched as explosions tore men's arms or legs from their torsos; he saw brains spilling out of cracked skulls.[50] The experience was, he said, "like watching a horror movie."[51] On the night before the murders, while hiding out in a burned-out building, Cone heard helicopters circling overhead and smelled tear gas and, in his mind, he was back in Vietnam, amidst all this carnage, being pursued by the lethal enemy.[52]

I will confess that Cone's hallucination is incomprehensible to me. I've been lucky not to have experienced the circumstances and the brutality that he witnessed. But The New York Times has reported that more than 100 veterans who had no prior criminal records have returned from combat in Iraq or Afghanistan and committed a homicide. I suspect it would not have been incomprehensible to them.

Nearly two decades before the murders, to numb himself to what he was experiencing in Vietnam, Cone began using speed and heroin.[53] He recalled doing fifty-three straight nights of guard duty, looking out from the base perimeter, fueling himself with drugs to stay awake.[54] In 1969, he was awarded the Bronze Star.[55] When Cone was honorably dis-

---

[43] Dicks, supra note 34, at page 13; and Joint Appendix, supra note 29, at page 93.

[44] 535 U.S. at 704–705 (J. Stevens, dissenting).

[45] *Id.*

[46] Dicks, supra at 14–15.

[47] *Id.*

[48] *Id.*

[49] *Id.*

[50] *Id.*

[51] *Id.*

[52] *Id.* at 16.

[53] *Id.* at 14–15.

[54] *Id.*

[55] 535 U.S. at 709.

charged, he had risen to the rank of staff sergeant, and he was addicted to drugs.[56] To tame his memories and his imagination, he started using them in ever greater quantities.

Cone returned home to a country that had turned against the war.[57] He felt abandoned and alone. Still, he had a dream of going to college, and he did.[58] He entered the University of Arkansas and graduated two years later with a bachelor of science degree in business and finance, which he received cum laude.[59] While in college, he met Glenda Cale, and they became engaged.[60] Cone always had money, which led Glenda to believe that he was dealing drugs. In fact, he was getting his cash by robbing gas stations and convenience stores, using the proceeds to finance his own drug habit.[61] All the while, Cone was studying for the law school entrance exam, on which he scored in the 96th percentile.[62] He planned on attending law school at the University of Tulsa. But two months before law classes began, Cone was arrested.[63] He was sentenced to twenty-five years in an Oklahoma prison for armed robbery.[64]

Glenda called off the engagement.[65] Then, while Cone was still in prison, a mental patient from a Nebraska asylum escaped. The escapee raped and murdered Cone's former fiancée.[66] Around the same time, Cone's father died.[67] When Cone emerged from prison, he had no one.

As a convicted felon, Gary would never be able to practice law, yet he was still determined to attend Arkansas Law School.[68] Gary later reported that he intended to stop committing robberies once classes began.[69] He never got to prove it. On August 8, 1980, Gary robbed an Arkansas grocery store, and the next day, he robbed the jewelry store,

---

[56] Id.

[57] Dicks, supra note 34, at page 15.

[58] Joint appendix, supra note 29, at page 94.

[59] Id.

[60] Id.

[61] Id.

[62] State v. Cone, 665 S.W.2d at 91.

[63] Shirley Dicks, supra note 34, at page 15; see also Joint Appendix at page 94.

[64] Dicks, supra, at page 15.

[65] Id.

[66] Id. at page 16; and 535 U.S. at 703 (Stevens J., dissenting).

[67] Dicks, supra, at page 15.

[68] Id. at 16.

[69] Id.

which set off the chain of events that culminated in his brutal murder of the Todds.

There are undoubtedly stories of hardship and deprivation against which Cone's is comparatively mild. Not everyone with an abusive father, dead siblings, a murdered fiancée, suffering from post traumatic stress disorder, with an addiction to methamphetamines that results in drug-induced psychosis, commits murder, much less a double-murder by beating an elderly couple to death. And yet, Gary Cone was, according to all who knew him, one man before Vietnam and another after.

John Dice was far from oblivious to this story. As I have indicated, Dice had successfully defended Vietnam veterans suffering from PTSD. Prior to the commencement of the guilt-innocence phase, he told the jury that four family members (Cone's mother, his sister Susan, and two aunts) would paint a "before and after" portrait of Cone, with Cone's Vietnam experience being the dividing line between the two phases.[70] He said that the sister of Shipley Todd, the older of the two murder victims, had already forgiven Cone, and he teased the jurors by referring to a letter of absolution that she had written Cone, which Dice described as "one of the most loving letters I've ever read in my life."[71] He promised the jury quite a lot. Yet, during the guilt-innocence phase, Dice elected to call only one family member.[72] In total, he presented the testimony of only three witnesses: Cone's mother, who explained how Vietnam had affected her son, and two experts—a clinical psychologist, who explained that Cone suffered from both substance abuse and post traumatic stress disorder; and a neuropharmacologist, who testified that Cone was afflicted with an amphetamine-induced psychosis.[73] (I will discuss this expert testimony at slightly greater length momentarily.) Dice's obvious strategy was to obtain a verdict of not guilty by reason of insanity. Prevailing on a claim of insanity is, however, an exceedingly rare occurrence, and Cone's case was not the exceptional one. The jury found him guilty.[74]

---

[70] 535 U.S. at 713.

[71] *Id.* at 705 (the letter was marked as Trial exhibit 29, but it was never submitted to the jury. It read in part: "Even tho I am still in shock over the tragic death of my dear brother and his wife, I want you to know that you and your family have my prayers and deepest sympathy. I am also praying for Gary. We know he must have been out of his mind to have done the things he did. May God forgive him.").

[72] 535 U.S. at 690.

[73] *Id.*

[74] On attitudes toward PTSD, and mental illness generally, at the time of Cone's trial, see *Cone*, 535 U.S. at 705 (Stevens, J., dissenting) (citing Levin, Defense of the Vietnam Veteran with Post–Traumatic Stress Disorder, 46 Am. Jur. Trials 441 (1991 and Supp. 2001)).

And thus Gary Cone's capital murder trial, like nearly all death penalty trials, came down to the punishment phase—the main event of the main event. Dice, however, was completely unprepared. He had conducted no investigation specifically for use during the punishment phase.[75] His brief opening statement occupies less than 4 pages of a transcript that is 2158 pages in length.[76] He reminded the jury that Cone suffered from drug addition, as the experts at the guilt-innocence phase had testified, but he also asserted—erroneously—that Cone developed this addition as a result of the stress of combat.[77] (In fact, Cone was not in a combat unit.) He had not interviewed any witnesses, and so, not surprisingly, he did not call any witnesses of his own.[78] He did elicit, through cross-examination of a prosecution witness, that Cone had been awarded the Bronze Star; but he did not elaborate on the criteria for the recognition or explain why Cone had received such an honor.[79] He never entered into evidence the letter of forgiveness he had previously referred to. (The letter, moreover, is not all that moving, and does not reflect forgiveness so much as sympathy.) He made no closing statement at all.[80]

The jury found four aggravating circumstances: that Cone had previously been convicted of a felony involving violence or the threat of violence, that he created a risk of death to two or more persons (other than the victim) during the act of murder, that the murder was especially heinous, and that the murder was committed for the purpose of avoiding arrest.[81] The jury found no mitigating factors. It sentenced Cone to death.

Cone had competent and aggressive post-conviction lawyers. They asserted many issues, including the claim that Cone had received ineffective assistance of trial counsel. Often in resolving such a claim, a trial court will conduct a hearing so that the trial lawyer can explain for himself why he did (or did not do) certain things. Was the trial lawyer's behavior consistent with prevailing professional norms? Did the trial lawyer's decision result from a considered tactical judgment, or did it reflect incompetence? Dice had a chance to defend himself and his decisions in the federal habeas corpus proceedings. He explained that his

---

[75] 535 U.S. at 706.

[76] See 535 U.S. at 704–14 (Stevens, J., dissenting) (describing Dice's performance).

[77] Id. at 713; and Dice's Opening Statement at Sentencing, Joint Appendix, supra note 29, at pages 26–27.

[78] Id.

[79] 535 U.S. at 691.

[80] Id.

[81] Id.

objective was to obtain a not guilty verdict, and that once the jury found Cone guilty, he was almost "hopeless."[82] He viewed a death-qualified jury (i.e., a jury from which all those who categorically oppose the death penalty have been removed) as a jury that will automatically sentence a defendant to death once it has convicted him. Dice was asked whether his job was to humanize his client before the jury, to individualize Cone, and his answer was: "That's your view of it as a lawyer, not mine." Then why, he was asked, are death penalty trials even bifurcated—why is there a punishment phase? To which Dice replied, "God only knows." He admitted that there were witnesses in the courtroom—Cone's sister, his aunts, even Cone himself—who could have testified in mitigation, but he gave no reason for not calling them, other than to offer the manifestly incorrect assertion that the substance of their testimony was already part of the record. He also admitted that he did not interview anyone at all from Cone's past, like teachers or classmates, who could have fleshed out the portrait of Cone before his sojourn to Vietnam.[83]

To this day, no one can know for sure whether Dice was already mentally ill at the time of Cone's trial, or whether the ailment developed only later. No one can know what role, if any, the trial and its aftermath played in causing, or exacerbating, his condition. Nevertheless, several years after his infirm defense of Gary Cone, Dice began receiving treatment for a condition characterized by confused thinking, impaired memory, inability to concentrate, paranoia, grandiosity, and inappropriate behavior.[84] He was subsequently declared "mentally incompetent" by his own doctor, and he was disbarred by the Tennessee Bar.[85] Just six months after the evidentiary hearing in the federal habeas corpus proceeding, John Dice killed himself.[86]

* * *

Three and one-half years after Cone murdered the Todds, in January 1984, a man in Texas named Calvin Burdine shot and killed W.T. "Dub" Wise during the course of a robbery. Burdine knew Wise. He had met him in November 1982. The two men started a sexual relationship. Burdine moved into Wise's trailer. Early the following year, in February or March, the relationship ended. Burdine moved out. In April, Burdine,

---

[82] 535 U.S. at 707–10 (quoting the transcript form the state habeas proceeding).

[83] *Id.*

[84] 535 U.S. at 715–716; and Notes from Dr. Hutson's File, Joint Appendix, supra note 29, at page 89.

[85] Anne Gearan, Lawyer Quality at Issue (Capital City Press 2002); and Oral Argument before The Supreme Court, available at: http://www.oyez.org/cases/2000–2009/2001/2001_01_400/argument/.

[86] 535 U.S. at 715–16.

with another man, went back to Wise's trailer, perhaps just to rob (if
Burdine is to be believed), perhaps intending to kill. Either way, Wise
ended up dead, the victim of a brutal murder. His wrists were bound
together with a lamp cord, his ankles tied together with the cord from a
clock-radio. Burdine and his cohort stuffed a pair of socks into Wise's
mouth to serve as a gag, tying it in place with a strip from a bedsheet.
They tried to smother Wise but could not. Wise was wimpering and
crying. They cracked his skull with a lead-filled sap, and Wise lay silent,
bleeding. Using a hunting knife, they stabbed Wise twice, in the back.[87]

Burdine was charged with capital murder. He was represented at
trial by one of the most notoriously inept death penalty lawyers in
history, Joe Frank Cannon. In the course of his career, Cannon represented around a dozen capital murder defendants, and every last one of
them ended up on death row in Texas. Almost all of them ended up
executed, but not Burdine. A decade and a half following Burdine's
conviction, a federal district court ruled that Burdine was entitled to a
new trial.[88] Cannon is now widely known as the infamous sleeping
lawyer, and Burdine is the only one of his clients who had the sheer luck
to win a new trial. Four different witnesses—three jurors and the deputy
clerk of the trial court—testified during an evidentiary hearing that they
had observed Cannon repeatedly dozing off during Burdine's trial.[89]
Another witness, the court coordinator for the trial court, testified that
during Burdine's trial, the prosecutor and he discussed Cannon's ineptitude. The district court concluded that Burdine had not received effective assistance of counsel and therefore granted Burdine's petition for
writ of habeas corpus. The federal judge ruled that Burdine was entitled
to a new trial.

Astonishingly, a panel of the Fifth Circuit reversed. As mentioned
previously, when a death row inmate challenges his conviction or sentence on the basis of ineffective assistance of counsel, he must prove
more than that his lawyer's performance was infirm; he must also show
prejudice. The appellate court accepted that a sleeping lawyer satisfies
the deficient performance prong of the *Strickland* test; however, the
court further reasoned that even if Cannon had in fact slept through
portions of the trial, Burdine had not been able to establish that he had
suffered prejudice as a result. Under this analysis, Burdine would have
to show precisely when Cannon was sleeping, and then show what the

---

[87] The facts come from Burdine v. State, 719 S.W.2d 309 (Tex. Crim. App. 1986).

[88] Burdine v. Johnson, 66 F.Supp.2d 854, 866 (S.D.Tex.1999).

[89] I tell the story of another of Cannon's clients, and about Cannon generally, in David
R. Dow, Executed on a Technicality 1–24 (Beacon Press 2005); the federal district court
decision that contains a summary of the evidence of Cannon's ineffectiveness is Burdine v.
Johnson, 66 F.Supp.2d 854 (S.D. Tex. 1999).

lawyer might have done had he been awake, and then show that had he done those things, the result of the trial would probably have been different.

Subsequently, the Fifth Circuit sitting *en banc* agreed to review the case. (The effect of the court's decision to rehear the appeal meant that the panel's decision was vacated.) By a vote of nine-to-five, the *en banc* court affirmed the district court's decision and ruled that Burdine was entitled to a new trial.[90] Yet the court of appeals recognized that although witnesses had testified that Burdine's counsel was asleep a significant amount of time, Burdine could not show precisely when his lawyer was sleeping, nor could he show that the result would have been different had Cannon been awake. Like the three-judge panel, the Fifth Circuit *en banc* majority believed that, under *Strickland*, despite having been represented by a sleeping lawyer, Burdine could not prevail. Unless he knew exactly when Cannon was sleeping, he could not know what Cannon would have done differently had he been awake, and if he could not know that, he could not establish prejudice. Accordingly, to rule in favor of Burdine, the court of appeals relied on a somewhat different principle. In *United States v. Cronic*,[91] the Supreme Court had ruled that when a habeas petitioner raises a claim of ineffective assistance of counsel, prejudice can be *presumed* where, during a critical stage of trial, counsel is either totally absent or present but prevented from providing effective assistance.[92] Under *Cronic*, it is not necessary to show what would have been different; the lawyer's sheer ineptitude means that the inmate is entitled to a new trial. The *en banc* Fifth Circuit expressed its understanding of *Cronic* as follows:

> We conclude that the Sixth Amendment principle animating *Cronic's* presumption of prejudice is the fundamental idea that a defendant must have the actual assistance of counsel at every critical stage of a criminal proceeding for the court's reliance on the fairness of that proceeding to be justified.[93]

Relying on *Cronic*, rather than *Strickland*, the court of appeals concluded that Burdine's trial was made fundamentally unfair "by the consistent unconsciousness of his counsel."[94] "Unconscious counsel," the

---

[90] Burdine v. Johnson, 262 F.3d 336 (5th Cir. 2001), cert. denied, 535 U.S. 1120 (2002).

[91] 466 U.S. 648 (1984).

[92] 466 U.S. at 659 & n. 25.

[93] 262 F.3d at 345.

[94] 262 F.3d at 341. A significant issue for the *en banc* court, which issue is beyond the scope of this chapter, is whether *Cronic* announced a "new rule," under Teague v. Lane, 489 U.S. 288 (1989), and, if so, whether it was retroactive. The *en banc* court held that the

court opined, "equates to no counsel at all."[95] The court of appeals explained that the *Strickland* test *assumes* that counsel is present, and is therefore exercising "judgment, calculation, and instinct, for better or worse."[96] When that underlying assumption proves unsound, when it is inapplicable in a particular case, then *Strickland* does not apply. *Strickland* sets up a framework under which the appellate court presumes that counsel was exercising his or her best judgment on behalf of the defendant. Where there is some compelling reason to disregard that presumption—such as where a lawyer is sleeping through significant portions of the trial—then the court will presume prejudice, rather than compel the inmate to prove it.

Often in law, death penalty law included, the choice of which principle to apply dictates the outcome of the case. Had the majority of the Fifth Circuit concluded in *Burdine* that *Strickland* was the relevant principle, then Calvin Burdine might still be on death row; indeed, he might have been executed already. But nine of the fourteen judges believed that the *Cronic* rule was the pertinent principle. That principle relieved Burdine from having to show precisely what an awake lawyer might have done differently from a sleeping lawyer, and having to show further how those different things would have caused the jury to sentence him to life rather than death. The court's decision to employ *Cronic* meant that the inmate's lawyer did not need to establish prejudice.

* * *

Burdine's case was egregious as well as notorious. It was suffused with anti-gay rhetoric and lewd innuendo. During closing arguments, for example, the prosecutor said: "Sending a homosexual to the penitentiary certainly isn't a very bad punishment for a homosexual." Burdine's lawyer did not object. His silence was not all that surprising, for attorney Cannon himself seemed homophobic. He had referred during the trial to Burdine's co-defendant as a "tush hog."[97] He called the murder victim a "king homosexual." He used language like "fairies," "queers," and "faggots." Perhaps these scandalous details gave the Fifth Circuit pause. Whatever the explanation, the court of appeals concluded in Burdine's case that there could be no possible reason, aside from ineptitude, for a

---

Cronic rule was not new, and that Burdine could therefore claim its protection. See 262 F.3d at 341–48.

[95] 262 F.3d at 349.

[96] 262 F.3d at 349.

[97] The quoted language can be found in volume 1 of the transcript of the federal habeas proceeding.

lawyer to sleep during a trial. And having decided that, it determined there was no need to inquire specifically into prejudice.

In Cone's case, in contrast, the Supreme Court located excuses, if not justifications, for attorney Dice's desultory performance during the punishment phase. In characterizing Dice's actions as strategic, the Supreme Court, as we will see below, may well have been seizing on a theme identified by Cone's own appellate lawyers. But the conclusion still seems inexplicable in light of *Wiggins v. Smith*,[98] decided just a year after *Cone*. Like Gary Cone, Kevin Wiggins murdered an elderly woman: 77-year-old Florence Lacs. Wiggins was raised by someone whose children should have been taken away from her by the state much sooner than they were. She would leave Wiggins and his siblings at home alone for days at a time. She would not feed them, and they would resort to paint chips and garbage to fill their empty stomachs. She locked the kitchen door to keep them out. She once punished Wiggins by pressing his hand against a hot stove burner—causing an injury that required Wiggins to be hospitalized. At last the state removed Wiggins from his dreadful home and placed him in foster care—and the sons of one of his foster-mothers gang-raped him. He ran away from the foster care program when he was 16, preferring to live on the street. Wiggins later entered the Job Corps program—where he was sexually abused by his supervisor.

Wiggins' case was teeming with so-called negative mitigating evidence. Like Cone's lawyer, Wiggins' counsel promised the jurors a lot. He told them that they would hear the difficult details of Wiggins' life. Despite that assurance, she introduced none of this evidence. In fact, like Cone's lawyer, she introduced no evidence at all of Wiggins' troubled childhood—probably because she was unaware of it. Wiggins's lawyers elected not to have an investigator or social worker construct a social history of their client's life, even though they had funds available for just such an investigation. Like John Dice, Cone's lawyer, Kevin Wiggins' lawyer also conducted no punishment phase investigation. Unlike the *Cone* case, however, the Supreme Court, by a vote of 7-to-2, ruled that Wiggins had received ineffective assistance of counsel, and that he was therefore entitled to a new sentencing trial. The Court ruled that Wiggins' lawyers' decision to present no mitigating evidence on their client's behalf could not be deemed reasonable when they had undertaken no investigation that would be adequate to apprise them of what the mitigating factors actually were. In this respect, *Wiggins* is impossible to distinguish from *Cone*, another case where the lawyer had done nothing to learn what mitigating facts existed, save that Cone's case was decided a year sooner.

---

[98] 539 U.S. 510 (2003).

Wiggins is a decision of great significance, and the lower federal courts have understood it as such. In the years following *Strickland*, the lower federal courts, following the Supreme Court's lead, adopted a highly deferential stance toward trial lawyers. As indicated above, if a lawyer's decision could conceivably be deemed "strategic" or "tactical," it would not satisfy the first (deficient performance) prong of *Strickland*. As the Supreme Court itself phrased it in *Strickland*: "Judicial scrutiny of a counsel's performance must be highly deferential ... [and] every effort [must] be made to eliminate the distorting effects of hindsight."[99] The tendency to defer almost entirely to a trial lawyer's decisions began to soften in *Williams v. Taylor*.[100] In *Williams*, the trial lawyers had argued that they were not ineffective because they had made a strategic choice to focus on the voluntariness of William's putative confessions, rather than develop a punishment-phase case; they claimed, in other words, that their decision to present no mitigating evidence at the punishment phase was strategically sound because it grew out of their decision to concentrate on the evidence of guilt. The Supreme Court rejected this explanation. An uneducated decision is not strategic. In *Wiggins*, the Court observed that *Williams* flowed directly from, and was compelled by, *Strickland*. The majority noted that *Williams* had recognized that a lawyer's performance cannot be justified as tactically sound when the lawyer has not conducted an adequate investigation into his client's background.

In *Williams*, therefore, the Court began to stress the proposition that a lawyer's decision is not tactically sound if it is not based on adequate research. To be entitled to deference, the trial lawyer must actually have learned enough facts to make an informed judgment. For purposes of assessing a lawyer's effectiveness, it can never be prudent to focus exclusively on the guilt phase without at the very least learning what evidence is available for mitigation. Then, in *Wiggins*, the Court said more about the type of investigation that the capital defense lawyer is required to conduct in order for her decisions to be entitled to deference under *Strickland*. Quoting extensively from the ABA Guidelines for the Appointment and Performance of Counsel in Death Penalty Cases, the seven-to-two majority stressed that the lawyer's investigation "should comprise efforts to discover *all reasonably available* mitigating evidence."[101] Relying further on the ABA Guidelines, the Court identified specifically the lawyer's obligation to learn facts relating to her client's medical, educational, and employment history, the client's family back-

---

[99] 466 U.S. at 689.

[100] 529 U.S. 362 (2000).

[101] *Wiggins*, 539 U.S. at 524 (quoting ABA Guideline 11.4.1(C)) (emphasis added by the Court).

ground, and the client's prior correctional experience. Although death penalty lawyers are not required "to investigate *every conceivable* line of mitigating evidence," their decisions will not be entitled to deference unless they make "reasonable professional judgments," and the ABA Guidelines are powerful evidence of what reasonableness means.[102]

When deciding whether the inmate has shown that his lawyer's performance was deficient, the Court compares the actions the lawyer took to the actions a reasonable lawyer would have taken. The exercise has at least the appearance of objectivity. Assessing prejudice is somewhat different, for the Court conducts what is a more normative inquiry:

> [T]o establish prejudice, a defendant must show that there is a reasonable probability that, but for counsel's unprofessional errors, the result of the proceeding would have been different. A reasonable probability is a probability sufficient to undermine confidence in the outcome. *In assessing prejudice, we reweigh the evidence in aggravation against the totality of available mitigating evidence....* Had the jury been able to place [Wiggins'] excruciating life history on the mitigating side of the scale, there is a reasonable probability that at least one juror would have struck a different balance.[103]

The use of the first-person pronoun in the foregoing excerpt is illuminating: The *judges* reweigh the evidence. In deciding whether a juror would have been moved by the mitigating evidence that the trial lawyer neither located nor presented, the judges begin with whether *they* were moved.

Viewed together, *Strickland*, *Williams*, *Wiggins*, and *Cronic* reveal two distinct fault lines in contemporary death penalty jurisprudence when an inmate challenges his lawyer's competence. The first is whether to presume prejudice, or whether the inmate is required to establish it. If the reviewing court views the lawyer's performance as shockingly bad— if the lawyer's ineptitude was spread equally throughout the entirety of the proceeding—then the reviewing court may conclude that the inmate was actually deprived of counsel altogether at a critical stage of the proceeding, and the court will presume prejudice.[104] To be sure, *Cronic*'s "presumption of prejudice" typically rests on a fiction, for the inmate was not *literally* deprived of counsel; the lawyer was there sitting at counsel table, but it was *as if* she were not. Second, in the vast majority of cases, where the lawyer was inept, but not thoroughly and consistently so, then the reviewing court will require the inmate to establish prejudice, under *Strickland*. In these cases, the appellate judges will themselves have to make a judgment about moral culpability; for they

---

[102] 539 U.S. at 533–34.

[103] 539 U.S. at 534–37 (emphasis added) (interior quotations and citations omitted).

[104] 535 U.S. at 695.

must decide whether the evidence that the lawyer did not discover might reasonably have caused a sentient juror to conclude that the defendant should be sentenced to life rather than death. And because there are no ABA Guidelines to direct the assessment of this question of prejudice, whether an inmate wins relief will depend intimately on whether the appellate court judges are moved by his story.

In Cone's case, the Justices were not. Cone's battle to prevail was steeply uphill once the Court concluded that the *Strickland* standard, rather than the *Cronic* rule, applied to the case.[105] The Sixth Circuit had viewed Dice's performance as warranting application of the *Cronic* rule, because, by presenting no punishment phase evidence whatsoever, attorney Dice had failed to subject the state's punishment phase case to "meaningful adversarial testing." He had been no different from Burdine's lawyer. In reversing this judgment, the Supreme Court used Cone's case to transform a narrowly applicable rule into a rule that almost never applies. The Supreme Court stressed that *Cronic* applies only where the trial lawyer *"entirely* fails" to subject state's case to meaningful adversarial testing.[106] The Court itself italicized the word "entirely." And in so doing, it rendered the *Cronic* test almost never germane. For even Burdine's lawyer did not sleep through the entire trial. The Supreme Court, in short, set aside the Sixth Circuit's decision to grant relief to Cone by eviscerating the rule on which the lower court had relied, while simultaneously taking no action in the *Burdine* case notwithstanding that the Fifth Circuit had relied on exactly the same rule.

The difference between *Cronic* and *Strickland*, though characterized by the Court in *Cone* as a difference "not of degree but of kind,"[107] is, in reality, precisely a difference of degree. And the relevant degree of difference is that, in *Cronic*, the reviewing court believes that the defendant lawyer's performance was overwhelmingly dismal, without any significant redeeming aspects, whereas in *Strickland*, the lawyer might have made some colossal errors, but she also did some things right.

* * *

The question that arises, therefore, is this: Why did Cone lose while Burdine and Wiggins won? To say that the difference is that the *Burdine* court relied on *Cronic*, while the *Cone* decision rested on *Strickland*, is only to replace one question with another, for that observation, while true, does not explain why *Cronic* was germane in one case but not the

---

[105] 535 U.S. at 698.

[106] 535 U.S. at 696–97.

[107] 535 U.S. at 696.

other. Moreover, as difficult as it is to reconcile *Cone* and *Burdine*, squaring *Cone* with *Wiggins* is even more challenging. Neither Cone's lawyer nor Wiggins' conducted a punishment phase investigation; neither put on a mitigation case; both devoted their entire effort to the guilt phase of the trial. Why would the same Supreme Court that decided the *Wiggins* case in 2003 say in 2002 that Gary Cone had received constitutionally adequate counsel?

The answer might be that the Court is still finding its way with the *Strickland* test in capital cases. For in contrast to *Wiggins*, *Williams*, and *Rompilla*, where the Court granted relief on *Strickland* claims, it has also over the past few years denied relief (in Schriro v. Landrigan[108]) to another death row inmate, like Cone, whose lawyer presented no punishment phase evidence at all, while also denying relief to a death row inmate whose lawyer conceded his client's guilt without obtaining his client's consent to this risky strategy.[109] Or perhaps the explanation is that although attorney Dice conducted no mitigation investigation whatsoever, he did do some things right, and the Court took note of them. Even Cone's appellate lawyers acknowledged that fact. To be sure, after Cone lost his bid for relief in federal district court, his lawyers appealed to the U.S. Court of Appeals for the Sixth Circuit,[110] and they did claim that Dice had been ineffective.[111] For example, according to the brief, Dice's decision not to say even a single word to try to save Cone's life during closing argument at the punishment phase appears to be the only capital case in modern history where this tactic of silence has been employed. And yet the question of whether Dice was constitutionally ineffective, while front and center in the Supreme Court's decision denying relief, is not central in the papers filed in the court of appeals. Why? The answer, apart from the *Strickland* question of whether Dice's decision to focus on the guilt-innocence phase was indeed strategically sound, is that Cone's appellate lawyers realized that Dice's strategic focus may well have succeeded if only the State of Tennessee had not so egregiously cheated.

---

[108] 550 U.S. 465 (2007).

[109] Florida v. Nixon, 543 U.S. 175 (2004).

[110] I am grateful to Paul Bottei, one of Cone's lawyers, for discussing with me at some length the strategic considerations that went into crafting the appellate argument, and for providing me a number of documents.

[111] The brief is 101 pages long. The claim that John Dice was ineffective for presenting no mitigating evidence appears for the first time, as claim for relief number 5, on page 73 of the brief, and it is not elaborated upon until page 87. The claim of ineffectiveness appears once earlier in the Brief, not as a stand-alone claim, but as a cause argument for why an arguably procedurally-defaulted issue should be addressed. All told, around four pages of the brief are devoted to the argument. The Brief relies entirely on *Strickland* and does not even cite *Cronic*.

Two psychiatric experts testified that Cone committed the murders because he was in a drug-induced psychotic states. A neuropharmacologist (Dr. Jonathan Lipman) testified that Cone had begun using signficant quantities of illegal narcotics since serving in Vietnam. By the time of his murderous spree, Cone had been regularly ingesting large quantities of amphetamines for more than 13 years. He routinely hallucinated and was suffering from chronic amphetamine psychosis that made him incapable of recognizing the wrongfulness of his conduct or conforming his actions to requirements of the law. Similarly, a clinical psychologist (Dr. Matthew Jaremco) testified that the likely explanation for Cone's drug abuse was that he suffered from post-traumatic stress disorder for which he had never received any treatment. The psychologist noted that Cone was remorseful and unquestionably suffering from mental disease at the time of the crime.

The State's response was not to argue that Cone's decision to use drugs was volitional, or that he had done it to himself, or even that drug abuse cannot serve to excuse a homicide. Rather, the State's strategy was to deny the premise of the defense being constructed by attorney Dice. The State's position was that Cone did not use drugs. The prosecution called three witnesses—a Memphis police officer, an FBI agent, and an acquaintance of Cone's—all to say that Cone was not a drug user. In closing argument, the prosecutor, relying on the testimony of these witnesses, scoffed at the claim that Cone used drugs, calling the story a bunch of "baloney."

As it happened, the story was not baloney, and, more important, the prosecutor knew that it was not. The State knew that Cone was a heavy drug user. In its possession prior to trial were documents that detailed Cone's history of drug use. In fact, there was evidence that the same Memphis police officer who testified that Cone did not use drugs had sent a nationwide all-points-bulletin warning that Cone was a heavy drug user. The FBI agent also knew that Cone was a drug user. All of this evidence, which attorney Dice was entitled to receive, was withheld. At Cone's trial, Dice insisted before the jury that the State's witnesses were lying, but he could not prove it. At the evidentiary hearing held years later, Dice testified that this false testimony "totally destroyed our defense."[112] The Sixth Circuit agreed that the State had wrongfully withheld the evidence, but it nonetheless ruled against Cone on procedural grounds.

Yet, like the Fifth Circuit in *Burdine*, the Sixth Circuit in *Cone* did order a new trial. It did so on the basis of *Cronic*—holding that Dice's failure to present any punishment phase case at all meant that Cone

---

[112] Bell v. Cone, 535 U.S. at 705.

"did not have counsel during the sentencing phase of his trial."[113] The court of appeals therefore presumed prejudice. A lawyer who conducts no investigation, interviews no witnesses, calls no witnesses, and does not even bother to plead for his client's life is no different from a sleeping lawyer.

* * *

The State of Tennessee appealed to the Supreme Court from the decision of the Sixth Circuit awarding Cone a new trial on the authority of *Cronic*. The State of Texas appealed to the Supreme Court from the decision of the Fifth Circuit awarding Burdine a new trial on the authority of *Cronic*. Although Calvin Burdine's crime and Gary Cone's were separated by more than three years, their cases reached the Supreme Court at roughly the same time. On March 25, 2002, the Supreme Court issued its ruling in Gary Cone's case. The state court, applying *Strickland* rather than *Cronic*, had ruled that Cone's lawyer's performance was not deficient, and the Supreme Court held that the state court's determination was not unreasonable.[114] Cone lost. Less than three months later, on June 3, 2002, the high Court refused to disturb the decision of the court of appeals in *Burdine*.[115] Burdine won. So while Cone awaits execution, Burdine no longer sits on death row.

* * *

Whatever differences there are between Cone's and Burdine's cases cannot be found in the decisions of the courts of appeals. Both courts realized that, prior to *Wiggins*, it was difficult to satisfy the *Strickland* standard. Confronted, therefore, with appalling facts—a lawyer who slept, a mentally ill lawyer who presented no punishment phase case— both courts of appeals invoked *Cronic*, ruled that the death row inmate had been essentially without counsel, and therefore ordered new trials. But the Supreme Court agreed to review only one of these decisions. Was the Court simply too embarrassed to rule that a state can execute a murderer whose lawyer slept through the trial?

Embarrassment, however, cannot reconcile *Cone* and *Wiggins*. Gary Cone remains on death row because eight Justices on the Supreme Court of the United States concluded that his lawyer's desultory performance

---

[113] 243 F.3d at 979.

[114] Under AEDPA, if a state court has denied relief to a habeas petitioner, a federal court cannot grant relief unless the state court's decision was objectively unreasonable. See 28 U.S.C. § 2254(d). The federal court can believe that the inmate is entitled to relief—i.e., that the state court judgment denying relief is wrong—but that sentiment alone does not authorize the federal court to grant relief unless the state court judgment is not merely wrong, but is also unreasonable. See Williams v. Taylor, 529 U.S. 362 (2000). I discuss AEDPA deference in David R. Dow, Executed on a Technicality 40–41 (2005).

[115] Certiorari was denied in Cockrell v. Burdine, 535 U.S. 1120 (2002).

was enough.[116] Kevin Wiggins got relief because the exact same set of
Justices said that if the lawyer does not conduct an adequate investigation into the defendant's background, then the lawyer's performance will
be deemed deficient, regardless of whether he did some things right. If
one is looking for actual cases to demonstrate that the very arbitrariness
which led the Court in *Furman* to strike the death penalty down still
rampages through the machinery of death, one need not look much
further than *Burdine*, *Cone*, and *Wiggins*.

Gary Cone, Kevin Wiggins, and Calvin Burdine all had lawyers who
did not do nearly enough to save their clients' lives. All three were
sentenced to death by juries that heard nothing about their backgrounds,
because their lawyers did not do what death penalty lawyers are supposed to do. Yet, because an appellate court believed that Burdine had no
counsel at all, and because the Supreme Court was moved by the plight
of Wiggins' personal history, two of the three death sentences were set
aside. To what can we trace such disparity? The three crimes were
similarly brutal. The three murderers are not so different. Even the
lawyers who represented all three were not so dissimilar. The death
penalty today is as arbitrary as it was when the Supreme Court struck it
down a generation ago.[117]

To be sure, there are distinctions among these three cases, yet they
seem contrived, and irrelevant. Cone's lawyer promised much and delivered nothing. Burdine's lawyer likewise delivered nothing, yet he also
promised nothing. Wiggins' lawyer delivered nothing, but he promised
only a little. Cone's lawyer, mentally ill at the time of trial, killed himself
months later. Burdine's lawyer simply slept. Yet Burdine escaped the
sentence of death because his lawyer was comparable to Cronic's lawyer,
and so prejudice was presumed. Wiggins escaped death because seven
Justices, who saw that his lawyer had not acted in accordance with the
ABA Guidelines, were moved by his story, and therefore believed that a
jury, or single juror, would have been, too. Cone alone remains on death
row. Perhaps it is because his lawyer did a smidgen more than the
lawyer who represented Wiggins. He was not quite bad enough. Perhaps
it is because only Justice Stevens was moved by his story. Perhaps it is
because the Supreme Court did not even mention the ABA Guidelines in
his case. These thin distinctions are what separate life from death.

---

[116] Bell v. Cone, 535 U.S. 685 (2002). In June 2008, however, the Supreme Court
agreed to review Cone's case for the third time. Accepting an appeal from Cone's lawyers,
the Court will decide whether the federal court was permitted under AEDPA to consider
evidence that the state courts had not considered relating to the prosecutor's suppression
of exculpatory evidence. See Cone v. Bell, 128 S.Ct. 2961 (cert. granted June 23, 2008).

[117] As I elaborate elsewhere, the arbitrariness results from judicial behavior, not from
juries. Cone's jury sentenced him to death, just as Burdine's did. The arbitrariness that
remains pervasive is attributable to courts, not juries. See Dow, The Last Execution, supra.

11

Scott W. Howe*

Roper v. Simmons: Abolishing the Death Penalty for Juvenile Offenders in the Wake of International Consensus

By early 2005, the United States stood almost alone in the world in refusing to abandon laws permitting the death penalty for juvenile offenders. All other nations, except Somalia, which lacked an organized government, had ratified international conventions that prohibited capital punishment for offenses committed by persons under eighteen.[1] In the United States, however, twenty states allowed the death penalty for persons who committed a death-eligible crime at age seventeen and, in many of those states, at sixteen as well. On March 1, 2005, in *Roper v. Simmons*,[2] the United States Supreme Court declared the execution of offenders who were under eighteen at the time of their crimes to violate the prohibition on cruel and unusual punishments in the Eighth Amendment.[3] The decision overruled *Stanford v. Kentucky*[4] and a companion

---

* My thanks to John Blume, Linda Carter, Ellen Kreitzberg, Celestine McConville and Jetty Maria Howe.

[1] Article 37(a) of the United Nations Convention on the Rights of the Child, adopted before 2005 by all of the countries of the world, except Somalia and the United States, provides in part: "Neither capital punishment nor life imprisonment without possibility of release shall be imposed for offences committed by persons below 18 years of age." The full text of the convention appears at http://www2.ohchr.org/english/law/crc.htm (last visited May 23, 2008). For information on ratifications, see Office of the United Nations High Commissioner for Human Rights, *Status of Ratifications of the Principal International Human Rights Treaties* (June 9, 2004), available at http://www.unhchr.ch/pdf/report.pdf (last visited May 23, 2008).

[2] 543 U.S. 551 (2005).

[3] U.S. Const. amend. VIII ("Excessive bail shall not be required, nor excessive fines imposed, nor cruel and unusual punishments inflicted.").

[4] 492 U.S. 361 (1989).

case, *Wilkins v. Missouri*, decided sixteen years earlier, in which the Court had upheld the juvenile death penalty. The opinion for the five-Justice majority noted changes that had occurred in the world since *Stanford* and, more importantly, changes that had occurred in the Court's Eighth Amendment jurisprudence.[5] The opinion caused a stir both within and outside of the Court because of its lengthy discussion and explicit defense of the relevance of international norms and foreign practices in the application of the Eighth Amendment.

The Murder of Shirley Crook and the Arrest of Christopher Simmons

The murder in the *Simmons* case began with a nighttime burglary and attack against a random victim. On Wednesday evening, September 8, 1993, Shirley Crook went to bed alone in her home near Fenton, Missouri, a town a few miles southwest of St. Louis. Her husband was a truck driver and was out of town on a hauling job. Her daughter and son were grown and lived nearby. According to her sister, Elaine Wild, who spoke with her by telephone at 9:30 p.m., Shirley was happy that evening. She was pleased with some plants that Elaine had brought her in anticipation of her upcoming birthday. Shirley was about to turn forty-seven. But her life was cut short that night by assailants who picked her home to launch a murderous plan.[6]

The authorities first learned of the homicide the following afternoon, when fishermen saw a human body floating in the Merramac River, downstream from a railroad trestle, in Castlewood State Park, sixteen miles from Fenton. At 4:15 p.m., police officers and others arrived and pulled the body from the water. It was of a middle-aged woman. She was nude, except for underwear and boots. Duct tape and a towel covered her head. She was "hog-tied," with her wrists bound behind her back and then to her ankles. There was no identification on her body or nearby, and the officials did not recognize her. After delivering her body to the Medical Examiner's Office, they took her fingerprints, through which they were able to identify her. A short time later, Steve Crook called the local police to report that he had come home that day from a trucking job and was unable to find his wife, Shirley.[7]

---

[5] *See* Jordan Steiker, *United States:* Roper v. Simmons, 4 INT'L J. CON. L. 163, 164–65 (2006).

[6] *See* James Carlson, *Victim's Sister Tries to Live On,* ST. L. POST-DISP., July 24, 2005, at B1.

[7] *See id.;* Roy Malone, *Teens Killed Woman, Got $6, Police Say,* ST. L. POST-DISP., Sept. 11, 1993, at 3B; Missouri v. Simmons, 944 S.W.2d 165, 170 (Mo. 1997).

On Friday, September 10th, police obtained information connecting Christopher Simmons to the murder. Simmons, who was seventeen, lived near Shirley Crook in Fenton. The police found Crook's 1988 Ford Aerostar van parked at the Sunswept Mobile Home Park. A witness also gave the authorities a description that fit Simmons of a young man seen near the van early Thursday morning. On Friday afternoon, police arrested him at his high school and took him to the Fenton police station. After waiving his *Miranda* rights and undergoing about two hours of interrogation, Simmons confessed. He later gave a video-taped statement and participated in a video-taped reenactment of the murder at the crime scene.

Simmons admitted that he committed the crimes with Charles Benjamin, a fifteen-year-old friend. At about 2:00 a.m. on Thursday, September 9th, he and Benjamin, along with another teen who later backed out, met at the home of Brian Moomey, a convicted felon who allowed teens to "hang out" at his home. Simmons previously had announced a plan to commit murder and burglary by breaking into a home, kidnapping a victim and throwing the victim off a bridge. That night, Simmons randomly picked the house of Shirley Crook. He and Benjamin broke in through a window and attacked Shirley Crook in her bed. Upon seeing her face, Simmons recognized Shirley and realized that she would also recognize him from a previous car accident involving both of them. This fact confirmed his resolve to kill her. He and Benjamin beat her up, breaking several of her ribs, tied her up and put duct tape over her face. They forced her into the back of her van and drove to the railroad trestle that spanned the river in Castlewood State Park. Noticing that she had started to untie herself, they tied her more tightly and taped a towel around her head. They walked her out onto the trestle. Simmons then tied her hands to her ankles. Shirley was fully conscious when Simmons pushed her off the trestle into the river below. The two youths took six dollars from her purse before throwing it into the nearby woods. They then drove back to Fenton and abandoned the van in the mobile home park across from the subdivision where Shirley lived.

George McElroy, the Prosecutor for Jefferson County, charged both Simmons and Benjamin with first-degree murder and other offenses. A judge certified Benjamin to face trial as an adult although he was only fifteen. At seventeen, Simmons was automatically charged as an adult under Missouri law. Evidence indicated that the murder involved aggravating factors that made Simmons' death-eligible under the Missouri death-sentencing statute. The murderer appeared to have killed for money and to avoid arrest, and he arguably acted with a depraved mind in that he tortured Shirley Crook before killing her. The death-penalty statute also did not provide a minimum age for eligibility. The question for George McElroy was whether to pursue the death penalty against an offender who was only seventeen.

The History of the Juvenile Death Penalty[8] in the United States

Until near the end of the twentieth century, capital punishment remained a widely authorized but rarely used response to juveniles who had committed capital crimes in the United States. From 1642, when Thomas Graunger, from Plymouth Colony, Massachusetts, became the first, to 2003, when Scott Hain, from Oklahoma, became the last, states executed 366 juvenile offenders, an average of one per year.[9] During the second half of the twentieth century, juvenile executions, although not juvenile death sentences, became limited to offenders who were over sixteen, with the last execution of a fifteen-year-old offender occurring in 1948.[10] Soon after the revision of death-sentencing statutes that followed *Furman v. Georgia*,[11] states also began to abolish the death penalty for all persons who had committed their crimes before age eighteen in a steady progression that continued through the turn of the century. Nonetheless, by 2005, twenty states had not abolished the juvenile death penalty, and twelve of them had juvenile offenders on death row.[12]

Offender Youth as a Mitigating Factor

Prosecutors and capital sentencers, whether judges or juries, have often recognized the youth of an offender as a mitigating factor that weighs against a death sentence. This view has sometimes saved even offenders who are eighteen and older. Perhaps the most famous example

---

[8] In this chapter, "juvenile death penalty" refers to a death sentence for an offender who was below age eighteen at the time of the crime, and "juvenile execution" refers to the execution of such an offender.

[9] *See* Victor Streib, *The Juvenile Death Penalty Today: Death Sentences and Executions for Juvenile Crimes, January 1, 1973–February 28, 2005*, No. 77, p 4 (2005), available at http://www.law.onu.edu/faculty_staff/faculty_profiles/coursematerials/streib/juvdeath. pdf (last updated Oct. 7, 2005)(last visited May 20, 2008).

[10] *See* Victor Streib, Death Penalty for Juveniles 197 (1987) (noting that the last execution of a person for a crime committed before age sixteen was of Irvin Mattio, from Louisiana, who was fifteen at the time of his offense).

[11] 408 U.S. 238 (1972).

[12] *See Roper v. Simmons*, 543 U.S. 551, 579 App. A (2005); Streib, *supra* note 9, at 24–31.

is the 1924 case of Nathan Leopold and Richard Loeb. Sons of two of Chicago's richest families, Leopold and Loeb kidnapped and killed four-teen-year-old Bobby Franks, the son of a wealthy real-estate speculator, merely for the "thrill," after six months of planning. After the arrests, the local prosecutor declared, "I have a hanging case!", and the national press apparently concurred, branding the murder the "Crime of the Century!" Famed attorney Clarence Darrow agreed to represent Leopold and Loeb, but the conventional wisdom remained that they would hang.[13] However, at the sentencing hearing, Darrow presented an elaborate psycho-social defense aimed at showing the abnormal mental development of both defendants. He also offered a twelve-hour summation that constituted "one of the most remarkable legal arguments in the history of advocacy."[14] In the end, Judge John Caverly spared both defendants from death, sentencing them to life plus ninety-nine years in prison. He said that he was moved mostly "by the consideration of the age of the defendants." At the time of the offenses, Leopold and Loeb were nine-teen and eighteen respectively. Judge Caverly noted that Illinois had only executed two persons who were under twenty-one and that he did not want to add to the number. He said that rejection of the death penalty for persons "not of full age" appeared "to be in accordance with the progress of criminal law all over the world and with the dictates of enlightened humanity."[15]

Many factors help explain why some juvenile murderers and rapists, unlike Leopold and Loeb, suffered execution, but three stand out. First, poor legal representation of defendants too often greased the skids to the execution chamber. The United States Supreme Court did not declare a right to counsel in state capital trials until 1932,[16] but even later, the lawyers provided to capital defendants, including juvenile offenders, often lacked zeal.[17] The 1945 case of Willie Francis provides an exam-

---

[13] *See* MAUREEN MCKERNAN, THE AMAZING CRIME AND TRIAL OF LEOPOLD AND LOEB 66, 73–75 (1989); CLARENCE DARROW, THE STORY OF MY LIFE 232 (1932).

[14] *See* Alan M. Dershowitz, *Introduction* to MCKERNAN, *supra* note 13. At the conclusion of the summation, tears reportedly streamed down even the cheeks of Judge Caverly. *See* KEVIN TIERNEY, DARROW: A BIOGRAPHY 341 (1979).

[15] *See* MCKERNAN, *supra* note 13, at 379.

[16] *See* Powell v. Alabama, 287 U.S. 45 (1932).

[17] *See generally* Stephen B. Bright, *Counsel for the Poor: The Death Sentence Not for the Worst Crime but for the Worst Lawyer*, 103 YALE L.J. 1835, 1842, 1844–45, 1855–56 (1994) (asserting that the inadequacy of appointed counsel counts among the major factors contributing to the arbitrary administration of the death penalty). *See also* Justice Ruth Bader Ginsburg, *In Pursuit of the Public Good: Lawyers Who Care*, Lecture at the David A. Clarke School of Law, University of the District of Columbia (April 9, 2001) available at http://www.supremecourtus.gov/publicinfo/speeches/sp_04–09–01a.html (last visited April

ple.[18] Louisiana sentenced Francis, an African–American, to the electric chair for murdering a white pharmacist, Thomas Andrews, during a robbery. Despite "well-founded doubts" about whether Francis was guilty,[19] his appointed lawyers might as well have slept through the trial. They declined to present an opening statement, failed to challenge the state's introduction of purported confessions as coerced, and called no witnesses. The jury took only fifteen minutes to convict and reach a death sentence. The defense lawyers also filed no appeal.[20] These events caused little controversy at the time, and the case would likely have passed into history with minimal notice had the first attempt to electrocute Francis not failed.[21] Reports later indicated that a drunken jailer and inmate trustee had improperly wired the chair. Other lawyers then stepped forward and pursued appeals to the U.S. Supreme Court,[22] trying to stop the execution, an effort that the Court rebuffed in a five-to-four decision.[23] A few weeks later, local authorities returned Francis to the same electric chair and successfully electrocuted him. He was only fifteen at the time of the murder and only eighteen when Louisiana executed him.

As with the use of the death penalty generally, racial bias, in addition to poor defense lawyering, also influenced the use of the juvenile death penalty, especially during the pre-*Furman* era. Willie Francis, for example, was tried before an all-white jury in the Deep South, where overt racism at the time was rampant. Statistical evidence bears out the influence. Of the forty-three juvenile rape cases that

---

29, 2008) ("I have yet to see a death case, among the dozens coming to the Supreme Court on eve of execution petitions, in which the defendant was well represented at trial").

[18] The case of Gary Graham, executed in Texas in 2000, provides another example of a juvenile offender who reportedly received a lackluster defense. *See* Sarah Rimer & Raymond Bonner, *Texas Lawyer's Death Row Record a Concern,* N.Y. Times, June 11, 2000, at 1.

[19] William M. Wiecek, *Felix Frankfurter, Incorporation, and the Willie Francis Case,* 26 J. Sup. Ct. Hist. 53, 55 (2001).

[20] *See id.*; Gilbert King, *The Two Executions of Willie Francis,* Wash. Post, July 19, 2006, at A19; Wiecek, *supra* note 19, at 55.

[21] Witnesses reported that, when the executioner pulled the switch, Francis' body tensed and convulsed, and his lips puffed out as the portable electric chair rocked and slid. Francis yelled, "I am not dying." However, even after a second pull of the switch, Francis did not die. Referring to a hood that had been pulled over his face, he yelled, "Take it off. Let me breathe." Eventually, he was unstrapped from the chair and taken back to his cell. *See Louisiana ex rel. Francis v. Resweber,* 329 U.S. 459, 480 n. 2 (1947) (Burton, J., dissenting); King, *supra* note 20, at A19.

[22] One of the lawyers was J. Skelly Wright, who later became a judge of unusual renown on the United States Court of Appeals for the District of Columbia Circuit.

[23] *See Louisiana ex rel. Francis v. Resweber,* 329 U.S. 459 (1947).

resulted in execution during the pre-*Furman* era, all involved African–American defendants, and all but one involved white victims.[24] In the modern era, the influence of racial bias on the juvenile death penalty surely softened. But twelve of the twenty-two juvenile offenders who were executed between 1973 and 2005 were African–American or Latino, and, in seventeen of the twenty-two cases, the victim or victims were white.[25] Sophisticated statistical studies centered on various states or cities during that period identified a high risk of racial bias in the use of the death penalty generally, and they raise questions about whether a similar risk existed in the use of the juvenile death penalty.[26]

In addition to bad lawyering and racial bias, the very irrationality and impulsiveness associated with youthfulness helped explain why some juvenile offenders suffered execution. The case of Napoleon Beazley, who was executed in 2002, demonstrates the problem. Beazley was the president of his high school senior class in Grapeland, Texas, and was the son of the town's first African–American city council member. In a calculated robbery and murder, he fatally shot sixty-three-year-old John Luttig, and wounded his wife, Bobbie, as they were exiting their car in nearby Tyler. Mr. Luttig was a prominent civic leader in Tyler, and the Luttigs' son, Michael, was a federal court of appeals judge, in fact, one of the most conservative judges in the country. Judge Luttig was a former clerk for Chief Justice Burger and Justice Scalia and on the short list himself for nomination to the Supreme Court during the second Bush administration. For purposes of avoiding the death penalty, Beazley could not have chosen worse victims.[27] Michael Luttig prepared a twenty-nine page victim-impact statement and testified against Beazley at his sentencing trial. Although Beazley was only seventeen, his lawyer also faced problems in urging consideration of Beazley's youth on the sentencing question. First, the law implausibly assumed that jurors could accurately distinguish between immaturity and bad character in assessing juvenile conduct. Second, the law rendered immaturity itself double-edged by allowing sentencers to choose between culpability and future dangerousness in determining the sentence. Assuming the lawyer could

---

[24] *See* STREIB, *supra* note 10, at 60–61. *See also id.* at 59, 61(noting that of the 281 juvenile executions between 1642 and 1986 in which race is known, sixty-nine percent of the offenders were African–American and eighty-nine percent of the victims were white).

[25] *See* Streib, *supra* note 9, at 4, Tab. 1.

[26] For a summary of the studies, see *Scott W. Howe, The Futile Quest for Racial Neutrality in Capital Selection and the Eighth Amendment Argument for Abolition Based on Unconscious Racial Discrimination,* 45 WM. & MARY L. REV. 2083, 2106–2122 (2004).

[27] At least one commentator has suggested that the *Beazley* case involved an appearance that race played a role in the outcome, noting that Mr. Luttig was white and that the jury that determined Beazley's sentence was all-white. *See* Pamela Colloff, *Napoleon's Last Stand,* TEXAS MONTHLY, July, 2002, at 40.

successfully persuade jurors that the deficits of youth, more than bad character, helped explain Beazley's conduct, the prosecutor could still urge jurors to conclude that Beazley's immaturity underscored his continuing dangerousness for several years and on that ground to vote for the death penalty.[28] Thus, evidence of immaturity sometimes did not save juvenile offenders, but, instead, helped the prosecution send them to the execution chamber.

The Foundation for an Eighth Amendment Challenge

The basis for a constitutional challenge to the juvenile death penalty became clear in the decade after the Supreme Court sanctioned the resumption of the death penalty in 1976. The grounding for the challenge arose from the segment of Eighth Amendment jurisprudence known as the proportionality doctrine. Some punishments are inherently cruel and unusual. Amputating limbs and burning at the stake exemplify this class. Proportionality doctrine holds that a punishment can also become cruel and unusual if it is excessive in context. Based on this idea, the Court began exempting certain offenders from death eligibility in the late 1970s.

The first case was *Coker v. Georgia,*[29] where the Court outlawed capital punishment for the aggravated rape of an adult victim "not involving the taking of life." In a decisive plurality opinion, Justice White said that a punishment is "excessive" and unconstitutional if it is grossly disproportionate to the severity of the crime. To resolve the case, he focused, first, on objective evidence of the public's attitude toward the death penalty for aggravated rape, noting that Georgia was the only state that continued to authorize the death penalty for the aggravated rape of an adult victim, that juries in Georgia rarely imposed the death penalty for that offense and that few other countries authorized the death penalty for aggravated rape. Second, he applied the Justices' "own judgment" about excessiveness, emphasizing that, while the personal interests invaded by rape were substantial, they were not equal to the personal interest in life itself. Thus, the Court held that the death penalty for the aggravated rape of an adult victim was cruel and unusual.

---

[28] Death-sentencing statutes not only in Texas but around the country have long allowed capital sentencers to focus on future dangerousness rather than on culpability as the basis for a death sentence, and the Supreme Court has upheld those statutes. *See, e.g., Gregg v. Georgia,* 428 U.S. 153 (1976) (joint opinion of Stewart, J., Powell, J. and Stevens, J.) (upholding Georgia statute that required jurors to identify at least one aggravating factor from a statutory list but that otherwise left the decision to impose a death sentence to their discretion).

[29] 433 U.S. 584 (1977).

In the following decade, the Court also expanded the categorical prohibitions on the death penalty. Only a few months after *Coker*, in *Eberheart v. Georgia*,[30] the Court rejected Georgia's effort to apply the death penalty to a kidnapping where the victim was not killed. In 1982, in *Enmund v. Florida*,[31] the Court also excluded certain minor participants in murders from eligibility for the death penalty.[32] Likewise, in 1986, in *Ford w. Wainwright*,[33] the Court held—although on grounds other than excessiveness—that the Eighth Amendment forbids the execution of a prisoner who is insane. These cases underscored the Court's desire to confine the use of the death penalty to the most deserving criminals.

The *Thompson* and *Stanford* Decisions

Despite calls by the late 1980s for the Justices to exempt all juvenile offenders from the death penalty, the Court initially rejected that position. In 1987, in *Thompson v. Oklahoma*,[34] the Court overturned the death penalty for a fifteen-year-old murderer and cast doubt on whether it would allow any future executions of persons who were under sixteen at the time of their offenses. However, in 1988, in *Stanford v. Kentucky*,[35] and a companion case, *Wilkins v. Missouri*, the Court upheld the death penalty for seventeen-and sixteen-year-old murderers.

Justice O'Connor provided the fifth vote in *Stanford* to allow the death penalty for murders committed by sixteen-and seventeen-year-olds. She wrote a separate opinion but also concurred in much of an opinion authored by Justice Scalia and joined in full by Rehnquist, White and Kennedy, thus providing an opinion of the Court. The majority applied a more demanding test of excessiveness than the Court had applied in cases like *Coker* and *Enmund*. For example, the majority concluded that the number of states that did not permit capital punishment at all was irrelevant to determining the propriety of the death penalty for juveniles. On that view, only fifteen of the thirty-seven states that permitted capital punishment prohibited it for crimes committed

---

[30] 433 U.S. 917 (1977)(per curiam).

[31] 458 U.S. 782 (1982).

[32] The Court subsequently narrowed the exclusion that *Enmund* had drawn. In *Enmund*, the Court had concluded that an accomplice in a felony murder who did not himself kill or intend to kill was not death eligible. *See id.* at 798. However, in *Tison v. Arizona*, 481 U.S. 137, 145 (1987), the Court held that "major participation in the felony committed, combined with reckless indifference to human life" is sufficient to render an accomplice in a felony-murder death eligible.

[33] 477 U.S. 399 (1986).

[34] 487 U.S. 815 (1988).

[35] 492 U.S. 361 (1989).

below age seventeen and only twelve of those thirty-seven states prohibited it for crimes committed below age eighteen. Although Scalia also
rejected the notion that the Court should exercise its own judgment
about the proportionality of the juvenile death penalty, O'Connor disagreed on that point. Nonetheless, she concluded that too many states
allowed capital punishment for offenders over sixteen to conclude that
the Eighth Amendment prohibited it. As a result, in 1989, states had
permission from the Court to impose and enforce death sentences on
sixteen-and seventeen-year-old offenders.

The Simmons Trial and the Path to the U.S. Supreme Court

In October, 1993, George McElroy, the prosecutor in the Christopher Simmons case, announced that he would ask for a death sentence
for Simmons.[36] He told the press that he rarely sought the death penalty
and that Simmons' youth had complicated the decision. But Simmons
was only a few months shy of eighteen when he killed Shirley Crook,[37]
and the murder was atrocious even as murders go. McElroy said that he
wanted to give a jury the option to choose death as the punishment.
Later, McElroy offered Simmons a plea bargain that would have given
him life in prison without parole. Simmons, as it turns out unwisely,
rejected the deal. As a result, McElroy proceeded with his announced
plan to seek a death sentence.

The Trial and Initial Appeals

At Simmons' trial in June, 1994, the prosecutors easily proved that
Simmons was guilty of first-degree murder. They already had won a
first-degree-murder conviction and a jury recommendation of life imprisonment without parole against the fifteen-year-old accomplice, Charles
Benjamin. At Simmons' trial, the prosecutors relied largely on the videos
of Simmons' confession and of his re-enactment of the murder. Witnesses also testified that, during the days before the murder, Simmons
had discussed with friends his desire to commit such a crime. Simmons
had told them that they could get away with it because they were
minors. Brian Moomey also testified that, the day after the murder,
Simmons came to Moomey's trailer and bragged that he had killed a
woman because "the bitch seen my face." Simmons did not take the

---

[36] *See* Roy Malone, *Death Penalty Sought in Case of Woman Tossed Into River*, St. L.
Post-Disp., Oct. 28, 1993, at 3.

[37] Simmons was born on April 26, 1976. *See* Mo. Dept. of Corr., Offender Search,
Christopher L. Simmons, available at https://web.mo.gov/doc/offSearchWeb/searchOffender.
do?docID=990111 & method=getOffender (last visited on May 23, 2008).

stand and called no witnesses. His counsel argued in summation that doubt existed about his guilt. But the jury required only a few hours to find him guilty of first-degree murder.[38]

The sentencing hearing was brief and also seemed to present little difficulty for the jury. It began the morning after the jury found Simmons guilty and lasted only about two hours. The prosecutors called some of Shirley Crook's family members, who provided compelling testimony about the devastation that the murder had wreaked upon their lives. The defense presented evidence that Simmons had no prior convictions and no previous juvenile charges. Also, a few family members and friends testified briefly about their good relationships with him and various considerate acts that he had performed, and they requested mercy on his behalf. In summations, attention also focused on Simmons' age, which the judge had instructed jurors they could consider in mitigation. Defense counsel argued that Simmons' youthful status should make "a huge difference," emphasizing the many state laws that supported a conclusion that persons below eighteen years of age were not fully responsible adults. In response, the prosecutor argued: "Age, he says. Think about age. Seventeen years old. Isn't that scary? Doesn't that scare you? Mitigating? Quite the contrary I submit. Quite the contrary."[39] The jury recommended the death penalty later that same day, after finding that the State had proved three aggravating factors. The judge followed the jury's recommendation.

Simmons lived for years on Missouri's death row at the Potosi Correctional Center, near Ironwood, while the courts reviewed his case. Between 1994 and 2002, new lawyers repeatedly sought a reversal of his conviction and death sentence in state and federal courts. A central claim in the appeals alleged the ineffectiveness of his trial lawyers for failing to present evidence at the sentencing hearing about his background.

One might think that the capital-sentencing decision in *Simmons* had to be flawed given that the jury had almost no evidence about Simmons' life. Surely, most jurors would have wanted to know something about his upbringing and what influences might have led him to commit such a horrible crime. In fact, after the trial, one of the jurors, James Biundo, a professor at Southeast Missouri State University, wrote

---

[38] *See, e.g.,* Leo Fitzmaurice, *Jury Convicts Man in Slaying of Woman Thrown in River*, St. L. Post-Disp., June 17, 1994, at 1C (reporting on the case of Christopher Simmons); Roy Malone, *Jury Convicts Teen in Abduction, Drowning of Fenton Woman*, St. L. Post-Disp., May 19, 1994, at 2B (reporting on the case of Charles Benjamin).

[39] *See Simmons*, 543 U.S. at 557–58.

an article about the case, entitled "Motiveless Malignity," in which he wondered how Christopher Simmons could have gone so wrong.[40]

Evidence that the defense could have presented at the sentencing hearing might have helped jurors answer that question. Simmons' post-conviction lawyers identified witnesses who would have testified about "multifaceted layers of turmoil, abuse, and neglect" that Christopher experienced throughout his life.[41] His parents separated shortly after his birth, and both soon remarried. Christopher lived with his mother and step-father, a severe alcoholic. Physical and emotional abuse at the hands of the step-father pervaded his childhood. For example, once when he was a toddler, the stepfather, too intoxicated to deal with him on a fishing trip, tied him to a tree and left him there alone for hours. The stepfather also took Christopher to a bar when he was only three or four and gave him liquor to intoxicate him for the amusement of other patrons. The step-father regularly beat Christopher, derided him, forced him to perform "slave-labor" and otherwise neglected him. After his half-brothers were born, Christopher was also relegated to live in a basement that reportedly was not fit for animals. His mother was too unstable and fearful of her husband to help. To escape the horror, Christopher abused alcohol and drugs and often ran away, sometimes for weeks on end. As a result of the torment and neglect, he also became mentally disturbed. This evidence might well have helped jurors better understand his pathological thinking and his act of violence—and helped convince some of them to spare him from a death sentence.

The appellate courts, however, rejected Simmons' claims. On the ineffectiveness issue related to mitigating evidence, the Missouri courts concluded that Simmons' trial counsel, after investigating Simmons' history, had decided to focus on positive evidence about him on the view that the evidence of his background might only further alienate the jury. This strategy was not the one that Clarence Darrow had followed in defending Leopold and Loeb. But the test of ineffectiveness was not whether Simmons' lawyers had failed to follow the strategy that Darrow would have chosen—or that almost all highly competent and experienced capital defense lawyers would have pursued—but simply whether they had acted unreasonably under prevailing professional norms. The Missouri courts concluded that they had acted reasonably and, thus, had not

---

[40] *See* James V. Biundo, *Motiveless Malignity: A Case Study of a Capital Murder Through a Juror's Eyes,* AM. ASSOC. OF BEHAVIORAL AND SOC. SCI. J., Fall 1998 (on-line edition), *available at* http://www.eckerd.edu/academics/bes/aabss/perspectives-journal/biundo2.htm (last visited May 21, 2008).

[41] The evidence was described in detail in a petition for a commutation of the death sentence filed by Simmons' lawyers in April, 2002, and available at www.abanet.org/crimjust/juvjus/simmonsclemency.pdf (last visited on May 23, 2008).

provided ineffective assistance.[42] The lower federal courts also rejected Simmons' claims.[43] The United States Supreme Court likewise denied a request for review in October, 2001.[44]

Simmons appeared destined to die soon by lethal injection. After eight years of post-trial litigation, with the review process seemingly exhausted, the state scheduled his execution for May 1, 2002.

Several weeks before the execution date, Simmons' lawyers at the time, Jennifer Herndon,[45] from St. Louis, and Patrick Berrigan, from Kansas City, filed a lengthy petition for a commutation of his death sentence with Missouri Governor Bob Holden.[46] The petition highlighted evidence of Simmons' abusive and chaotic upbringing, substance abuse and schizotypal personality disorder. The petition also urged the governor to consider Simmons' juvenile-offender status. In light of *Stanford*, his previous lawyers had not argued that his age exempted him from a death sentence. But, Herndon and Berrigan contended that the legal landscape had changed and that juvenile executions had become unconstitutional.

Based on Simmons' juvenile offender status, public pressure on Governor Holden to grant a reprieve intensified. Amnesty International officials held a press conference in Jefferson City to protest the execution. Mental health and juvenile justice experts rallied at the Statehouse on Simmons' behalf. The American Bar Association's Juvenile Justice Center established a special web site concerning Simmons' case, opposing the execution. Members of the Youth Ministry Office of the Catholic Church for the Archdiocese of St. Louis organized a letter-writing campaign urging commutation. Many national and international organizations, including the American Bar Association, the Children's Defense Fund, Human Rights Watch, and the NAACP, wrote the governor in support of a reprieve. The governments of several foreign nations, including Mexico and Switzerland, also submitted clemency letters. However, by April 24, 2002, the governor had not acted.

Reconsideration by the Missouri Supreme Court

As the execution date neared, some members of the Missouri Supreme Court became concerned over the prospect of Simmons' execution. Missouri had executed only one juvenile offender in the post-*Furman*

---

[42] *See State v. Simmons*, 944 S.W.2d 165, 183 (Mo. 1997).

[43] *See, e.g., Simmons v. Bowersox*, 235 F.3d 1124 (8th Cir. 2001).

[44] *See Simmons v. Luebbers*, 534 U.S. 924 (2001).

[45] At the time, her name was Jennifer Brewer, but she changed it to Jennifer Herndon before the case proceeded to the U.S. Supreme Court.

[46] *See supra* note 41.

era,[47] and even Heath Wilkins, the juvenile offender whose death sentence from Missouri the U.S. Supreme Court had affirmed in 1989, later secured a reprieve.[48] On April 24, 2002, without a request from either Simmons or the state and without explanation, the Missouri Supreme Court ordered a postponement of the execution until June 5, 2002. Jennifer Herndon stated when questioned by the press that some members of the court might have wanted to wait to see if a pending state bill to raise the minimum age for the death penalty to eighteen would become law.[49]

The bill did not pass, but, on May 2, 2002, Simmons filed a new petition for a writ of habeas corpus with the Missouri Supreme Court, alleging that his death sentence was unconstitutional because he was a juvenile at the time of his crime. On May 28, 2002, the Missouri Supreme Court stayed the June 5th date. The order this time hinted that several members of the court doubted that juvenile executions still complied with the Eighth Amendment. The United States Supreme Court was about to decide *Atkins v. Virginia*,[50] concerning whether the execution of mentally retarded offenders was cruel and unusual. The Missouri Supreme Court stayed Simmons' execution on grounds that the forthcoming decision in *Atkins* might bear on the propriety of executing juvenile offenders. On that same day, Texas executed Napoleon Beazley, after several courts, including the highest court in Texas and the United States Supreme Court, rejected Beazley's claim that juvenile executions violated the Eighth Amendment.[51] The contrast in the treatment of the two cases highlighted the concern within the Missouri Supreme Court over Simmons' death sentence.

On June 22, 2002, the Supreme Court of the United States outlawed the death penalty for mentally retarded offenders by a six-to-three vote in *Atkins*, which gave further life to Simmons' efforts to avoid execution. The stay granted by the Missouri Supreme Court continued, and Simmons' lawyers filed additional pleadings in that court, arguing against

---

[47] Missouri executed Frederick Lashley, a seventeen-year-old offender, on July 28, 1993. *See* Streib, *supra* note 9, at 4.

[48] *See Youngest Ever Sent to Death Row Gets Three Life Sentences*, St. L. Post-Disp., May 22, 1999, at 17 (noting that Wilkins pled guilty to second-degree murder and was sentenced to life imprisonment after securing a reversal in 1995 of his earlier conviction for first-degree murder).

[49] *See* Jeremy Kohler, *High Court Delays Execution That Was Set for May 1; No Explanation is Given; Neither Side Had Sought A Postponement*, St. L. Post-Disp., April 25, 2002, at B1.

[50] 536 U.S. 304 (2002).

[51] *See* Sara Rimer, *In Similar Cases One Inmate is Executed, One Wins Stay*, N.Y. Times, May 29, 2002, at 14.

the legality of executing juveniles under the Missouri constitution and under the Eighth Amendment.[52] They pointed out that the Supreme Court previously had upheld the execution of retarded offenders in *Penry v. Lynaugh*[53] on the very same day that it had upheld the execution of juvenile offenders in *Stanford*. The conclusion in *Atkins* that a societal consensus against the execution of retarded offenders had emerged after 1989 meant that a societal consensus could also have emerged during that period against the execution of juvenile offenders. Also, the methodology employed in *Atkins* for determining proportionality was more favorable to Simmons than the methodology employed by Justice Scalia in *Stanford*. Under the *Atkins* approach, objective evidence arguably revealed a consensus against the juvenile death penalty. Likewise, under *Atkins*, international norms along with recent science regarding the deficits of youth seemed to become relevant to a court's independent judgment about proportionality. Empowered by *Atkins* and this new data, Jennifer Herndon and Patrick Berrigan urged the state high court to vacate Simmons' death sentence.

Recent appointments to the Missouri Supreme Court had changed that court's dynamics in Simmons favor. Democratic governors had appointed four of the seven judges, and three of the four, Michael Wolff, Ronnie White and Richard Teitelman, had previously represented poor people, either in public defender or Legal Aid offices. The fourth, Chief Justice Laura Denvir Stith, came from an activist family with Democratic roots and with many prominent lawyers, including her sister, Kate Stith, a professor at Yale Law School, and her brother-in-law, Jose Cabranes, a federal appellate judge who was on the short list for nomination to the Supreme Court during the Clinton administration. The Prosecutor for St. Louis County reportedly noted, in September, 2002, that prosecutors seeking to maintain death verdicts in the state high court would face "a very, very difficult time."[54]

A reversal of Simmons' death sentence in the Missouri Supreme Court nonetheless was not guaranteed. On the Eighth Amendment question, the holding in *Stanford* was arguably still the law of the land. The majority in *Atkins* had distinguished the recent change in societal views regarding the juvenile death penalty as less dramatic than the change in societal views regarding the propriety of the death penalty for

---

[52] *See* Petitioner's Statement, Brief, and Argument, in State ex rel. Christopher Simmons v. Roper, 112 S.W.3d 397 (Mo.2003) available at http://www.courts.mo.gov/SUP/index.nsf/0/f815b60b1f37baf886256cd3007f104e?OpenDocument (last visited May 23, 2008).

[53] 492 U.S. 302 (1989).

[54] *See* Virginia Young, *Missouri Supreme Court; Is the Balance Shifting to the Left*, St. L. Post-Disp., Sept. 1, 2002, at B1.

retarded offenders.[55] The Missouri court could have avoided the Eighth
Amendment question and effectively foreclosed review by the U.S. Supreme Court by relying on the state constitution. However, at the oral
arguments before the Missouri Supreme Court, in March, 2003, neither
the judges nor the parties pursued the passing reference in Simmons'
written pleadings to the state constitution.[56] The discussion focused
implicitly on whether Simmons' death sentence passed muster under the
Eighth Amendment. On that score, Assistant Attorney General Stephen
Hawke correctly noted that state courts generally cannot override Supreme Court decisions that rest on applications of the federal constitution.[57]

Despite *Stanford*, in August, 2003, the Missouri Supreme Court
reversed Simmons' death sentence, holding that the execution of persons
who were under eighteen at the time of their offenses violated the
Eighth Amendment.[58] The court divided four-to-three, along partisan
lines, with Chief Justice Stith writing the majority opinion. She began by
providing a careful summary of the U.S. Supreme Court's opinions in
Thompson, Stanford, Penry and *Atkins*, noting that the Court's analysis
in *Atkins* more closely resembled the analysis used in a plurality opinion
in *Thompson* than that in Justice Scalia's opinion in *Stanford*. She then
rejected the state's argument that the court was bound by the holding in
Stanford, explaining that the proportionality decisions of the U.S. Supreme Court, including *Stanford*, required a determination as to current
standards of decency rather than those of 1989. Following the analysis in
Atkins, she explained why the majority concluded that a national consensus had developed against the juvenile death penalty. She also provided
an independent analysis about why juvenile offenders did not merit the
death penalty. Based on its conclusion, the court vacated Simmons'
death sentence and re-sentenced him to life imprisonment without
parole.

The ruling sparked anger and frustration in many quarters. Elaine
Wild, Shirley Crook's sister, was distraught and recounted to the press
how the defendants had stomped on Shirley and had beaten her so badly
that they had broken her ribs and jaw. A Republican leader of the
Missouri Senate, Peter Kinder, called the opinion "especially alarming,"

---

[55] *See Atkins*, 536 U.S. at 316 n. 18.

[56] An audio recording of the oral arguments before the Missouri Supreme Court is
available at http://websolutions.learfield.com/deathrow/gestalt/go.cfm?objectid=D75D46F0–
1F63–43D4–87287460AA633B76 (last visited on May 23, 2008, 2008).

[57] *See* Respondent's Statement, Brief and Argument, in State ex rel. Christopher
Simmons v. Roper, 112 S.W.3d 397 (Mo. 2003), available at http://www.courts.mo.gov/SUP/
index.nsf/0/f815b60b1f37baf886256cd3007f104e?OpenDocument (last visited May 23, 2008).

[58] State ex rel. *Simmons v. Roper*, 112 S.W.3d 397 (Mo. 2003).

asserting that it read "like something pulled out of the air." He also warned that the ruling could inspire an effort to unseat one or more of the majority judges. The Republican majority floor leader of the Missouri Senate, Michael Gibbons, accused the court of "stepping into the legislative arena," and asserted that "[p]resuming what the U.S. Supreme Court might do is not its role." Missouri Attorney General, Jeremiah Nixon, said that the court was "overreaching," noting, "It's not generally considered their prerogative to overrule U.S. Supreme Court cases that are based on federal [constitutional] amendments," because "[t]he U.S. Supreme Court is the final arbiter of federal law." He also made clear that he would ask the Supreme Court of the United States to review the decision.[59]

Nixon followed through on his promise, and legal experts predicted that the Court would likely hear the case. The High Court recently had denied review in several cases challenging the juvenile death penalty, which suggested that most of the Justices were not anxious to reconsider *Stanford*.[60] However, the ruling of the Missouri Supreme Court effectively forced the High Court to act. A failure either to confirm or to reject the decision would foster confusion about the validity of the juvenile death penalty in several other states.

In the Supreme Court

On January 26, 2004, the High Court announced that it would hear *Donald P. Roper, Superintendent, Potosi Correctional Center, Petitioner v. Christopher Simmons*, setting the stage for a reconsideration of the permissibility of the juvenile death penalty. The swell of national and international press regarding the Court's decision to grant review made clear that the case carried special significance.

The Briefing Period

For the litigation in the Supreme Court, the parties reinforced their legal teams and, from February through October, 2004, prepared their

---

[59] *See* Virginia Young, *Court Halts Executions for Crimes by Juveniles; Missouri Judges Cite Evolving Standards for Death Penalty,* St. L. Post-Disp., Aug. 27, 2003, at A1; Tim O'Neil, *Missouri High Court Says Ruling Follows Legal Tide,* St. L. Post-Disp., Aug. 31, 2003, at B1.

[60] One of these denials came on October 21, 2002, in the case of Kevin Stanford—whose death sentence the Court had upheld in 1989—after Stanford brought a final appeal in federal habeas review before the Court. *See* In re *Stanford*, 537 U.S. 968 (2002) (denial of petition for writ of habeas corpus). *See also Mullin v. Hain*, 538 U.S. 957 (2003) (vacating stay of execution); In re Napoleon Beazley, 535 U.S. 1094 (2002) (denial of petition for writ of habeas corpus).

written pleadings and oral arguments. James Layton, from the Office of the Attorney General for Missouri, had joined the prosecution group. Layton was an experienced appellate advocate who previously had argued successfully in the Supreme Court.[61] In part because Attorney General Jeremiah Nixon was arguing another case in the Supreme Court only a few days before the scheduled argument in *Simmons*, he concluded that Layton would present the oral argument for the state.[62] To present Simmons' case, his St. Louis lawyer, Jennifer Herndon, obtained the assistance of Seth Waxman and other lawyers at the Washington, D.C., law firm where Waxman was a partner. Waxman had served during the Clinton administration as Solicitor General of the United States, arguing many cases before the Supreme Court.[63] Herndon asked Waxman to guide the preparation of the briefs and present the oral argument for Simmons.

At the outset, commentators predicted that Justices Kennedy and O'Connor would cast the swing votes. Four justices—Stevens, Souter, Ginsburg and Breyer—had already declared, in October 2002, in a dissent from the denial of review of a juvenile death sentence, that "offenses committed by juveniles under the age of [eighteen] do not merit the death penalty."[64] Three other justices—Rehnquist, Scalia and Thomas—seemed unlikely to find an Eighth Amendment violation, given their votes upholding the juvenile death penalty in *Stanford* and their dissent from the holding in *Atkins*. The views of Kennedy and O'Connor were less predictable, because they had voted to uphold the juvenile death penalty in *Stanford* but had voted with the majority in *Atkins*. In light of O'Connor's separate concurrence in *Stanford*, in which she had left open the possibility of a different result later, some predicted that she, rather than Kennedy, was the most likely to provide the fifth vote against the juvenile death penalty.

The Court's decision a few weeks later in another case, however, soon caused close observers to conclude that Kennedy might be Simmons' best hope for a fifth vote. On June 1, 2004, the Court decided a confession case, *Yarborough v. Alvarado*,[65] involving whether a seventeen-year-old murder suspect had been in "custody" during his interro-

---

[61] Layton had argued successfully in *Spencer v. Kemna*, 523 U.S. 1 (1998).

[62] The other case was *Schlup v. Delo*, 513 U.S. 298 (1995), in which the Court heard arguments on October 3, 2004.

[63] A biography of Waxman appears on the web site of the Department of Justice, at www.usdoj.gov/osg/aboutosg/waxmanbio.html (last visited May 23, 2008).

[64] In re Stanford, 537 U.S. 968, 972 (2002) (Stevens, J., joined by Souter, J., Ginsburg, J., and Breyer, J., dissenting from denial of petition for habeas corpus).

[65] 541 U.S. 652 (2004).

gation and, thus, should have received *Miranda* warnings. California courts had not given any special consideration to Alvarado's age in concluding that he was not in custody. Kennedy, for the majority, resolved the case against Alvarado but on grounds related to federal habeas and interrogation law that expressed no view about the functioning of seventeen-year-olds as compared with adults. O'Connor, by contrast, wrote a short concurring opinion in *Alvarado* that focused on that very comparison and that hinted that she was already thinking about *Simmons*. She noted that Alvarado "was almost [eighteen] years old at the time of his interview." She also asserted that such persons "vary widely in their reactions to police questioning, and many can be expected to behave as adults."[66] These statements raised doubts that she would support a categorical rule for purposes of the death penalty that distinguished all persons under eighteen from adults.

Simmons' lawyers pitched their brief to influence O'Connor and, after *Alvarado*, Kennedy in particular. The brief discussed evidence of a societal consensus against juvenile executions. But its opening and most lengthy discussion concerned post-*Stanford* research in developmental psychology and neurology that confirmed the "common sense" view that seventeen-year-olds are biologically and functionally different from adults in ways that render them less culpable. Advances in magnetic resonance imaging during the 1990s revealed that the brains of seventeen-year-olds are not fully developed in the frontal lobe areas, particularly in the prefrontal cortex, which governs reasoned judgment, impulse control and the ability to regulate emotions. Simmons' brief cited more than thirty post-*Stanford* studies confirming that persons under eighteen, as a rule, do not have mature and enduring personalities and lack the capacity of adults for rational judgment, for appreciating future consequences and for exercising self-restraint and resisting the influence of peers. The brief also explained that jurors could not accurately judge the functional maturity of juvenile offenders, especially when the defendant appeared physically mature at trial. A final section of the brief targeted Kennedy's probable interest in international perspectives. Only a year earlier, his majority opinion in *Lawrence v. Texas* had cited the laws of other nations as support for the Court's prohibition of the criminalization of homosexual sodomy.[67] The world-wide consensus that had developed against juvenile executions was far stronger than the international view on the question addressed in *Lawrence*.

Simmons' supporters also arranged for the preparation and filing of more than a dozen friend-of-the-Court briefs, mostly aimed at O'Connor and Kennedy. They came from, among others, the American Medical

---

[66] *Id.* at 669 (O'Connor, J., concurring).

[67] 539 U.S. 558, 576–77 (2003).

Association, the American Psychological Association, the European Union, the Human Rights Committee of the Bar of England and Wales, a number of Nobel Laureates headed by former President Carter, several former U.S. Diplomats, the United States Conference of Catholic Bishops, and the American Bar Association. Several focused on post-*Stanford* scientific research confirming the deficits of seventeen-year-olds regarding their culpability for crimes. Several others spoke primarily to Kennedy, highlighting the almost universal opposition among other nations to the juvenile death penalty.

Missouri's pleadings understandably centered on precedent and arguments about national consensus, but, in light of *Atkins*, this focus was far from sure to retain a majority of the justices. The state's initial brief contended that objective evidence regarding the domestic consensus had not changed substantially since *Stanford* in that only a handful of additional states had abolished the juvenile death penalty and that juries in several states continued at times to render juvenile death verdicts. The state's reply brief responded to Simmons' scientific evidence by hammering on the point made by O'Connor in *Alvarado*, that seventeen-year-olds vary in their behavioral maturity. But, apparently out of concern that these arguments might not hold both O'Connor and Kennedy, arrangements were also made for the preparation and filing of a friend-of-the court brief using a different strategy, by the states of Alabama, Delaware, Oklahoma, Texas, Utah, and Virginia.

The Alabama brief appeared to be a form of scare tactic to convince O'Connor and Kennedy that some murders are so awful that the Court must retain the death penalty as an option regardless of the offender's age. The brief summarized the facts of six terrible cases involving juveniles who were on death row in Alabama. For example, in 1997, Mark Duke, at age sixteen, planned and carried out a gruesome quadruple murder of his father, his father's girlfriend, and the girlfriend's six- and seven-year-old daughters, out of anger at being refused permission to borrow the family truck. Duke committed the crimes with others, primarily Brandon Samra, a nineteen-year-old friend, which underscored that, without the juvenile death penalty, Duke, the ringleader, would escape that sanction, but Samra would face death, despite his lesser role.

The brief also discussed the case of Marcus Pressley, who, during a three-month stretch in 1996, committed eight different robberies involving three murders and three attempted murders. The spree culminated in the robbery of a pawnshop, in which the sixteen-year-old Pressley and his regular accomplice, LeSamuel Gamble, age eighteen, stole guns, jewelry and $2,300 in cash. After Gamble left with the proceeds, Pressley stayed behind to eliminate the witnesses. In cold-blooded fashion, he shot John Burleson and Janice Littleton multiple times, with long pauses in between to clear his jamming gun. As the brief noted, a ruling for Simmons meant that "Gamble—who was eighteen at the time but did not actually kill anyone—would face the death penalty—but Pressley—who at sixteen executed two people with startling coolness—would get a free pass." The facts in Pressley drove home the ability of young defendants to kill in vicious and calculated ways and tested the notion that they should always receive less punishment than adults who received death sentences.

Despite the Alabama examples, the outcome in the most sensational juvenile murder case in the news at the time favored Simmons. That case involved the infamous Beltway sniper, Lee Malvo, whose horrible misdeeds gripped the attention of the nation in October, 2002. At age seventeen, Malvo participated with forty-two-year old John Mohammed in a series of sniper killings that began in the South and ultimately terrorized the residents of Washington, D.C., and the surrounding suburbs in Maryland and Virginia. Malvo was the actual shooter in many of the cases. The terror ended with the arrests of Malvo and Mohammed on October 24, 2002. Legal commentators later speculated that the Supreme Court declined to grant review on the juvenile death penalty during 2003 to allow a jury to resolve Malvo's fate.[68] After a Chesapeake, Virginia, jury chose life imprisonment for Malvo in his first trial in late December, 2003, the case for retaining the juvenile death penalty lost some steam. The rejection of the death penalty, especially by a Southern jury, suggested that the juvenile death penalty had fallen from favor. More importantly, it meant that a ruling in Simmons' favor would not require a reversal of a death sentence for Malvo, who was, in the popular opinion, the poster-child for juvenile executions.

Simmons' case was also coming to the Court in a "social and historical context of a 'crisis in confidence'" in the death penalty generally.[69] Information about the reliability of death sentencing emerged after 1989 that reduced public support for capital punishment. Between 1989 and 2003, based in part on advances in DNA science, seventy-four persons won exoneration after receiving a death sentence.[70] Exonerations in Illinois in particular captured public attention after Governor George Ryan, in February 2000, imposed a moratorium on further executions in the state and later commuted all Illinois death sentences. In addition, a widely publicized study that appeared in June,

---

[68] See Adam Liptak, *Penalty for Young Sniper Could Spur Change in Law*, N.Y. TIMES, Dec. 25, 2003, at 12.

[69] Jeffrey Fagan and Valerie West, *The Decline of the Juvenile Death Penalty: Scientific Evidence of Evolving Norms*, 95 J. CRIM. L. & CRIMINOLOGY 427, 435 (2005)(first published online at www.law.columbia.edu/jdp in 2004).

[70] See Samuel R. Gross et al., *Exonerations in the United States, 1989 Through 2003*, 95 J. CRIM. L. & CRIMINOLOGY 523, 531 (2005).

2000, reported that reviewing courts had reversed two-thirds of all death sentences imposed across the nation from 1973 through 1995.[71] Also, a book about exonerations, *Actual Innocence*, appeared in 2000, causing even conservative columnist George Will to confess to doubts about the death penalty.[72] These developments correlated with less support for the death penalty in public-opinion polls and a decline in death-sentencing rates for both adults and juveniles.[73] One might plausibly have wondered whether this weakened support had influenced the Court to abolish the death penalty for retarded offenders in *Atkins*.[74] Whether any such influence might carry forward in *Simmons* was also a good question.

Oral Argument

The oral argument, held in October, 2004, shed little light on how the Court might rule. Both Layton and Waxman offered strong arguments but did not seem to sway any of the seven Justices with predictable leanings. Attention focused heavily on the comments and questions by O'Connor and Kennedy, but they gave few hints about how they might vote.

Layton began his argument by asserting that the Missouri Supreme Court was wrong to override the holding in *Stanford* and that *Atkins* had not undermined the earlier decision. He contended that the mental ability at issue in *Atkins* was itself a component of culpability, unlike status as a person under eighteen, which he said was a flawed measure of immaturity. This argument prompted an exchange with Scalia, who asked whether retardation was also an imperfect proxy for blameworthiness. Layton responded that the Court, in *Atkins*, had stated that a mentally retarded person was, by definition, not sufficiently culpable to warrant the death penalty. He asserted that the same idea would not be true of all juveniles. "There are seventeen-year-olds who are equally culpable with those who are eighteen, twenty, twenty-five or some other age." Several other justices joined the questioning, but Layton stood his ground, reasserting that "the problem with adopting the ... eighteen-

---

[71] *See* James Liebman, Jeffrey Fagan, Valerie West & Jonathan Lloyd, *Capital Attrition: Error Rates in Capital Cases, 1973–1995*, 78 Tex. L. Rev. 1839 (2000).

[72] *See* Jim Dwyer, Peter Neufeld & Barry Scheck, Actual Innocence: Five Days to Execution and other Dispatches from the Wrongfully Convicted (2000); George Will, *Innocent on Death Row*, Wash. Post, April 6, 2000, at 23.

[73] *See* Fagan & West, *supra* note 69, at 436.

[74] For an argument that changes after 1989 in societal attitudes about the death penalty generally, rather than changes captured by the Court's "evolving standards" doctrine, largely explained the Court's willingness to abolish the death penalty for retarded offenders, see Corinna Barrett Lain, *Deciding Death*, 57 Duke L. J. 1, 35–57 (2007).

year-old line is that it is essentially arbitrary. It's the kind of line that legislators and not courts adopt.''[75]

A few moments later, O'Connor offered her only comments during the proceedings. Layton had responded to a question by Rehnquist regarding whether there was a line forbidding the death penalty before age sixteen by noting that "there's a consensus nationally" to support that line. O'Connor then asked about the Court's obligation to focus on the question of consensus:

Justice O'Connor: Well, but—but there was—it's about the same consensus that existed in the retardation case.

Mr. Layton: Absolutely, that's true if you look at the—the—

Justice O'Connor: And—and so are we somehow required to at least look at that? I mean, the statistics of how many States have approved eighteen years as the line is about the same as those in the retardation case.[76]

Although Layton responded that *Atkins* had presented an "inexorable trend" regarding the mentally retarded that "[w]e don't have . . . here," the remarks by O'Connor raised hopes by Simmons' supporters that she might favor the argument for abolition. If a consensus existed against executing offenders under eighteen that was similar to the consensus against executing retarded offenders, the line established by the Missouri Supreme Court was not arbitrary.

After more questions from several justices on various topics, Kennedy asked Layton a series of questions about the relevance of evidence that other countries had abolished the juvenile death penalty. The exchange began as follows:

Justice Kennedy: Let—let's focus on the word unusual. Forget cruel for the moment, although they're both obviously involved.

We've seen very substantial demonstration that world opinion is—is against this, at least as interpreted by the leaders of the European Union. Does that have a bearing on what's unusual? Suppose it were shown that the United States were one of the very, very few countries that executed juveniles, and that's true. Does that have a bearing on whether or not it's unusual?

Mr. Layton: No more than if we were one of the very few countries that didn't do this. It would bear on the question of unusual. The decision as to the Eighth Amendment should not be based on what

---

[75] *See* Transcript of Oral Argument, Roper v. Simmons, Sup. Ct. No. 03–633 (October 13, 2004), 6–7, available at http://www.supremecourtus.gov/oral_arguments/argument_transcripts/03–633.pdf (last visited on May 23, 2008).

[76] *Id.* at 7.

happens in the rest of the world. It needs to be based on the mores
of—of American society.[77]

Discussion about the role of laws in other countries continued, and,
although Layton maintained that they were irrelevant, Kennedy's questions underscored that he appreciated the strength of international
consensus against the juvenile death penalty. These questions inspired
hope by Simmons' supporters that Kennedy had not already made up his
mind to vote with the conservatives.

When the time came for Waxman to argue for Simmons, he began
by asserting that a consensus against the juvenile death penalty had
developed since *Stanford* and that new scientific evidence had emerged
to support abolition of the juvenile death penalty. These contentions
sparked a series of challenges, mostly from Scalia and Rehnquist. For
example, Scalia asked whether the constitutional calculus used to determine consensus was a "one-way ratchet" that would ever allow the
reinstitution of a juvenile death penalty if the Court were to outlaw it.
He also asked, if the case against the juvenile death penalty were so
clear, "why can't the State legislature take it into account?"[78] Rehnquist
asked several questions about why the scientific evidence discussed in
Simmons' brief had not been presented in the trial court and tested
through cross-examination.[79] These lines of questioning took up much of
Waxman's argument but seemed more aimed at influencing one of the
other undecided justices than at resolving doubts about the right outcome on the part of Scalia or Rehnquist.

Despite the questioning on other issues, Waxman continued to pitch
his argument to Kennedy and O'Connor by returning several times to
the new scientific evidence and why it mattered. He contended that the
evidence provided a neurological explanation for the common sense view
that sixteen and seventeen-year-old murderers were less culpable than
adult murderers. He underscored that this evidence was not available
when the Court decided *Stanford*.[80] He also emphasized that the scientific evidence confirmed the inability to resolve accurately when a seventeen-year-old acted from an enduring bad character or from transient
immaturity. At one point, he noted:

> [A]lthough one could posit that there are sixteen– and seventeen–
> year–olds whose antisocial traits are characterological rather than
> transient, we know it is impossible—we know this from common
> sense and it's been validated by science, of which the Court can take

---

[77] *Id.* at 14.

[78] *Id.* at 24, 31.

[79] *See id.* at 33–34.

[80] *Id.* at 28–29.

note, that it is impossible to know whether the crime that was committed by a sixteen– or seventeen–year–old is a reflection of his true, enduring character or whether it's a manifestation of traits that he exhibited during adolescence.[81]

Repeatedly, Waxman drove home this latter point in an effort to address the state's argument—and the view perhaps suggested by O'Connor in *Alvarado*—that, because some seventeen-year-olds might be mature, the Court should leave the matter for individualized consideration by juries.

Waxman also picked up on Kennedy's questions to Layton about the laws of other countries. He pointed out that the opposition to juvenile executions was not merely among European nations but among all other organized governments in the world. Waxman noted that "we are literally alone in the world even though 110 countries in the world permit capital punishment for one purpose—for one crime or another, and yet every one—every one formally renounces it for juvenile offenders."[82] He contended that, while this information was not "game, set, and match," it helped show the existence of a consensus.

The questioning of Waxman that received the most attention in the press came near the end of the argument, and it did not seem to favor Simmons:

Justice Kennedy: I have—I have one other question I'd like to ask because it's been troubling me and I want your comment.

A number of juveniles run in gangs and a number of the gang members are over eighteen. If we ruled in your favor and this decision was given wide publicity, wouldn't that make sixteen–, seventeen–year–olds subject to being persuaded to be the hit men for the gangs?

Mr. Waxman: Well—

Justice Kennedy: I'm—I'm very concerned about that.

Waxman began to answer, but Kennedy amplified on his concern:

Justice Kennedy: I'm talking about the deterrent value of the existing rule insofar as the sixteen– and seventeen–year–old. If–if we rule against you, then the deterrent remains.

Mr. Waxman: Well, I think—I think, as with the mentally retarded, or in fact, even more than with the mentally retarded, adolescents—the—the role of deterrence has even less to say, precisely because they weigh risks differently and they don't see the future and they are impulsive and they're subject to peer pressure. . . .

---

[81] *Id.* at 38.

[82] *Id.* at 27–28.

Justice Kennedy: Well, there were a number—a number of cases in the Alabama amicus brief, which is chilling reading—and I wish that all the people that sign on to the amicus briefs had at least read that before they sign on to them—indicates that often the seventeen–year–old is the ringleader.[83]

Waxman pointed out again that juveniles were not likely to be deterred by the death penalty, particularly when it was imposed so rarely on them. However, Kennedy's questions left doubts that he was convinced about the propriety of overruling *Stanford*.

After the argument, reporters expressed few predictions about the probable outcome other than to reiterate that the decision seemed to turn on the votes of O'Connor and Kennedy. Several reporters contended that, based on his questions near the end of Waxman's argument, Kennedy seemed less likely to support the ban than O'Connor. However, observers generally concluded that neither of them appeared to lean strongly in either direction.

The Decision: Justice Kennedy's Conversion

When the Court convened on March 1, 2005, Kennedy announced the five-to-four decision, revealing that he had sided with four other justices in concluding that juvenile executions violated the Eighth Amendment.[84] His majority opinion detailed the disturbing facts of Simmons' crime but concluded that execution was unconstitutional for any offense committed by a person who was under eighteen. The opinion provoked a sharply-worded dissent by Scalia, joined by Rehnquist and Thomas. Those three justices strongly disagreed not only with the outcome but with the majority's willingness to jettison the fundamental premises embodied in Scalia's *Stanford* opinion. O'Connor also voted against the ban, because she found the evidence of a national consensus lacking. However, she wrote a separate opinion, disagreeing with major aspects of Scalia's dissenting opinion and favoring much of the methodology employed by Kennedy.

The Objective Evidence of a National Consensus

Kennedy concluded that the evidence of national consensus against juvenile executions was as strong as the evidence that the Court had relied upon in *Atkins*.[85] In both cases, thirty states prohibited the death penalty for the relevant group, including twelve states that rejected the death penalty altogether and eighteen that maintained it but provided an exclusion. The pace of change since 1989 had differed in the two

---

[83] *Id.* at 43–44.

[84] *Roper v. Simmons*, 543 U.S. 551 (2005).

[85] *See id.* at 564–67.

contexts. While sixteen states that permitted the death penalty for retarded persons at the time of *Penry* had prohibited the practice by the time the Court heard *Atkins*, only five states that allowed the juvenile death penalty at the time of *Stanford* had abandoned that practice when the Court heard *Simmons*. But Kennedy said that the same consistency of direction of change existed and that the change regarding the juvenile death penalty carried equal significance in light of the general popularity of recent anticrime legislation and the recent trend toward severely punishing juvenile crime in other respects. Kennedy also noted that, just as executing the mentally retarded had become infrequent after *Penry*, the execution of juvenile offenders had become equally rare. Since *Stanford*, only six states had executed a juvenile offender, and, in the preceding ten years, only Oklahoma, Texas and Virginia had done so. He pointed out that even Kevin Stanford, the petitioner in the *Stanford* case, had received a commutation of his death sentence in 2003 from the governor of Kentucky, who declared, "We ought not be executing people who, legally, were children."[86] Based on this data, Kennedy identified a national consensus against the execution of juvenile offenders.

Kennedy's discussion regarding national consensus rejected the methodology that he had supported in *Stanford* in favor of the Court's approach in *Atkins*. The majority in *Stanford* had refused to count states that had abolished the death penalty altogether as among those opposing juvenile executions. In *Simmons*, Kennedy not only counted them as among those opposed but declared that the *Stanford* majority had been wrong not to do so. Also, the majority in *Stanford* had viewed the small number of juvenile executions in states that allowed them as evidence simply that jurors were commendably careful in imposing death as a punishment on juvenile offenders. In *Simmons*, Kennedy rejected that perspective and viewed the small numbers as aberrations that helped prove the consensus against the practice. These changed perspectives, as much as the changes in the objective evidence, enabled the majority in *Simmons* to find the national consensus that the *Stanford* majority had found lacking.

The Role of the Court's Independent Judgment on Proportionality

Kennedy also asserted the relevance of the Court's "independent judgment" that the juvenile death penalty was excessive. He contended that recent scientific and sociological studies confirmed three broad differences between juveniles and adults that demonstrated that juries could not reliably classify juveniles as among the worst offenders. First, juveniles lack maturity and responsibility and, therefore, act more impulsively and recklessly. Second, juveniles are more vulnerable to negative influences. Finally, juveniles have less well-formed characters and

---

[86] *Id.* at 565 (quoting LEXINGTON HERALD LEADER, Dec. 9, 2003, at B3).

more transitory personalities. These deficits meant that the retributive and deterrent functions of the death penalty applied to juveniles with less force than to adults. At the same time, the deficits enhanced the risk that a capital sentencer would err in assessing a death sentence against a juvenile. Kennedy noted that even expert psychologists in the best of circumstances had difficulty distinguishing "between the juvenile offender whose crime reflects unfortunate yet transient immaturity, and the rare juvenile offender whose crime reflects irreparable corruption."[87] He also noted that, in some cases, a defendant's youth might even be counted against him, and he pointed to the prosecutor's argument at Simmons' trial that Simmons' youth was aggravating rather than mitigating. He said that these conclusions required drawing a categorical line between childhood and adulthood regarding death eligibility and that the best point to draw it was at age eighteen.

Kennedy's discussion regarding "independent judgment" again abandoned the view that he had endorsed in *Stanford* in favor of the Court's position in *Atkins*. Justice Scalia's opinion in *Stanford* had declared independent judgment irrelevant to whether the juvenile death penalty violated the Eighth Amendment. But, in *Atkins*, the Court's independent judgment seemed to play a decisive role in the Court's rejection of the death penalty for retarded offenders.[88] And to at least as great a degree in *Simmons*, Kennedy used the majority's independent judgment, backed by sociological and scientific works, to support the case against juvenile executions.

The Influence of International Norms and Foreign Law

In a final part of his opinion, Kennedy discussed the relevance of international norms and foreign laws against the juvenile death penalty. Although Scalia's opinion in *Stanford* had criticized the practice, the Court, before *Simmons*, had mentioned non-domestic authorities when interpreting the Bill of Rights, not only in *Lawrence v. Texas,* but in many cases involving the cruel and unusual punishment clause, including *Atkins*.[89] However, in *Simmons*, Kennedy devoted much more space

---

[87] *Id.* at 573.

[88] A member of the *Atkins* majority, Justice O'Connor, declared that the Court's independent judgment in *Atkins* was decisive. *See Simmons*, 543 U.S. at 598 (O'Connor, J., dissenting).

[89] *See, e.g., Atkins*, 536 U.S. at 316 n. 1 ("Moreover, within the world community, the imposition of the death penalty for crimes committed by mentally retarded offenders is overwhelmingly disapproved."); *Thompson v. Oklahoma*, 487 U.S. 815, 830–31 (1988) (plurality opinion) ("The conclusion that it would offend civilized standards of decency to execute a person who was less than 16 years old at the time of his or her offense is consistent with the views that have been expressed by respected professional organizations, by other nations that share our Anglo–American heritage, and by leading members of the Western European community."); *Enmund v. Florida*, 458 U.S. 782, 796 n. 22 (1982)

to the subject than the Court had devoted to it in those prior opinions. He emphasized the "stark reality" that the United States was "the only country in the world that continue[d] to give official sanction to the juvenile death penalty."[90] He detailed significant international conventions that prohibited the juvenile death penalty, especially Article 37 of the United Nations Convention on the Rights of the Child, which the United Nations had adopted shortly after *Stanford*, in November, 1989, and which all nations, except the United States and Somalia, had later ratified. He noted that only seven countries other than the United States had executed juvenile offenders after 1990—Iran, Pakistan, Saudi Arabia, Yemen, Nigeria, the Democratic Republic of Congo, and China—and that all of them later either had abolished the juvenile death penalty or had publicly disavowed the practice. In addition, he explained that the United Kingdom, from which our legal heritage emerged, had prohibited the execution of juvenile offenders in 1948, a decade before it prohibited the death penalty altogether. The evidence was convincing that world governments overwhelmingly opposed juvenile executions.

Mixed messages appeared about the degree to which the evidence of international and foreign practices influenced the outcome in *Simmons*. On one hand, Kennedy presented the evidence in a final part of his opinion after already having concluded that the evidence of national consensus and the Court's own judgment required the abolition of the juvenile death penalty. He also twice stated that the international evidence simply provided "confirmation" of the Court's conclusion.[91] On the other hand, the discussion of non-domestic sources seemed too lengthy for evidence that carried no persuasive value. And Kennedy had made no secret in other forums of his belief in the potential for foreign legal practices to sometimes influence the Court. Referring to the European courts, he reportedly told an interviewer shortly after *Simmons* that, "If we are asking the rest of the world to adopt our idea of freedom, it does seem to me that there may be some mutuality there, that other nations and other peoples can define and interpret freedom in a way that's at least instructive to us."[92]

("[T]he doctrine of felony murder has been abolished in England and India, severely restricted in Canada and a number of other Commonwealth countries, and is unknown in continental Europe."); *Coker v. Georgia*, 433 U.S. 584, 596 n. 10 (1977) ("[O]ut of 60 major nations in the world surveyed in 1965, only 3 retained the death penalty for rape where death did not ensue."); *Trop v. Dulles*, 356 U.S. 86, 102–03 (1958)(plurality opinion) ("The civilized nations of the world are in virtual unanimity that statelessness is not to be imposed as punishment for crime.").

[90] *Simmons*, 543 U.S. at 575.

[91] *Id.* at 575, 578.

[92] Jeffrey Toobin, *Swing Shift; How Anthony Kennedy's Passion for Foreign Law Could Change the Supreme Court*, THE NEW YORKER, Sept. 12, 2005, available at http://www.

The Aftermath

As a result of the Court's decision, Christopher Simmons, then twenty-nine, had his sentence permanently modified to life imprisonment without parole, which the Missouri Supreme Court had imposed on him after modifying his death sentence. Having embraced the Christian faith and joined prison ministry programs, Simmons reportedly said, "Thank you very, very much," when told by one of his lawyers of the Supreme Court ruling. Reportedly, he was "eternally grateful" to be allowed to live, although he faced a lifetime in prison. In contrast, Elaine Wild, Shirley Crook's sister, was numb with pain. She told reporters that the ruling "tears my heart out." In the following months, she continued to struggle with the idea that Simmons might experience happiness or peace when he had so cruelly denied the joy of life to Shirley. "He didn't give Shirley a chance. Why should he get a chance?" she asked in despair.[93]

Simmons protected not only Christopher Simmons but all sixteen- and seventeen-year-old offenders across the country who were at risk of execution. Seventy-one juvenile murderers awaiting execution in twelve other states, including twenty-nine in Texas alone, had their sentences reduced to life imprisonment.[94] Trial prosecutors across the country who were seeking the death penalty against juvenile murderers also abandoned those efforts, including the prosecutors in the Lee Malvo cases. The *Simmons* decision thus directly affected scores of defendants and the many other persons connected to their cases.

Simmons also promptly sparked legal challenges to sentences of life imprisonment without parole for juvenile offenders. The Supreme Court has only rarely invalidated non-capital punishments as disproportionate. However, Article 37 of the United Nations Convention on the Rights of the Child, cited by the majority in *Simmons*, prohibits both the death penalty and the sentence of life imprisonment without parole for any person who committed an offense when under eighteen. Likewise, the findings presented in Justice Kennedy's *Simmons* opinion concerning the deficits of youth suggested that life imprisonment without parole, like the death penalty, is cruel and unusual punishment for at least some

---

newyorker.com/archive/2005/09/12/050912fa_fact?printable=true (last visited May 23, 2008) (concluding that Justice Kennedy has become an internationalist during his years on the Court, due in large part to his experience of having lived for several weeks every summer in Salzburg, Austria, where he annually has taught a course to law students on comparative fundamental rights and has participated during four of those summers in a gathering of international judges known as the Salzburg conference).

[93] *See, e.g., Convicted Teen Murderer, Once Sentenced to Die, Grateful for Life in Prison,* LONDON FREE PRESS, Mar. 21, 2005, at D6; Carlson, *supra,* note 6, at B1.

[94] *See* Streib, *supra* note 9, at 11.

young offenders. Spurred by the *Simmons* opinion, attorneys from the Equal Justice Initiative, a non-profit organization in Alabama, challenged the sentences of life imprisonment without parole imposed on numerous offenders in various states for crimes that they had committed when they were only thirteen or fourteen.[95] A study conducted by that organization revealed that, in October, 2007, seventy-three such offenders were serving life imprisonment without parole in the United States. The litigation sought not their immediate release but the invalidation of the prohibition against their eventual consideration for parole. The federal courts will continue to confront questions about the constitutionality of those sentences for juvenile offenders until the Supreme Court takes up the questions.

The *Simmons* decision also fueled efforts in Congress to limit the Supreme Court's use of foreign authorities in determining the meaning of the Constitution. Republicans promoted resolutions in both the House of Representatives and the Senate stating that judicial decisions regarding the U.S. Constitution should not rest on foreign laws, court decisions or government pronouncements, except where those sources bear on the original meaning. Those measures did not receive majority support in either body. However, they revealed the strong opposition of many conservatives to what they saw as a selective use of international norms to support a liberal agenda. Moreover, only a few months later, at the Senate confirmation hearings for Supreme Court nominees John Roberts and Samuel Alito, Republican members of the Senate Judiciary Committee pressed the issue. They elicited statements from Roberts and Alito that the nominees generally did not view current foreign law or international norms as bearing weight in rulings on the meaning of the Constitution.[96]

Academic debate over the Supreme Court's use of international norms and foreign practices in constitutional adjudication also burgeoned after *Simmons*.[97] While the discussion was not new, *Simmons*

---

[95] *See* Adam Liptak, *Lifers as Teenagers, Now Seeking Second Chance*, N.Y. Times, Oct. 17, 2007, at 1.

[96] *See* Confirmation Hearings on the Nomination of John G. Roberts, Jr., to Be Chief Justice of the United States Before the S. Comm. on the Judiciary, 109th Cong. 199–201, 292–93 (2005); Confirmation Hearing on the Nomination of Samuel A. Alito, Jr., to Be an Associate Justice of the Supreme Court of the United States Before the S. Comm. on the Judiciary, 109th Cong. 370–71, 470–72 (2005).

[97] For a small sample, see Youngjae Lee, *International Consensus as Persuasive Authority in the Eighth Amendment*, 156 U. Pa. L. Rev. 63, 66–67 (2007); Frank H. Easterbrook, *Foreign Sources and the American Constitution*, 30 Harv. J. L. & Pub. Pol'y. 223 (2006); Steven G. Calabresi & Stephanie Dotson Zimdahl, *The Supreme Court and Foreign Sources of Law: Two Hundred Years of Practice and the Juvenile Death Penalty*

greatly intensified the debate. One of the central disputed issues concerns whether the Court views international norms and foreign practices as persuasive or merely interesting but of no influential value. Commentators disagree about whether the Court has sometimes accorded these sources meaningful influence. Assuming that, in cases like *Lawrence, Atkins*, and especially *Simmons,* the Court has given them weight, the academic debate has also focused on whether and how these non-domestic sources can support the Court's construction of the Constitution. On this score as well, scholars disagree.[98]

CONCLUSION

The Supreme Court decision in *Roper v. Simmons* to abolish the juvenile death penalty was, in one sense, fortuitous. In staying Christopher Simmons' execution and then rejecting his death sentence under the Eighth Amendment, the Missouri Supreme Court had declined to follow the 1989 decision of the United States Supreme Court upholding the juvenile death penalty in *Stanford v. Kentucky.* Whether courageous or brazen, the state court forced the Supreme Court of the United States to clarify whether *Stanford* was still the law. A majority of the Justices apparently had not been anxious to reconsider *Stanford.* In prohibiting the death penalty for retarded offenders in *Atkins v. Virginia,* in 2002, the Court had distinguished the juvenile death penalty as not implicating a similar societal consensus supporting abolition. Also, after *Atkins,* the Court repeatedly had declined to stay the executions of juvenile offenders to reconsider the holding in *Stanford.* These events suggest that Justice Kennedy, the fifth vote in *Simmons*, had preferred to wait a few years before the Court reconsidered the juvenile death penalty. Forced to choose in *Simmons,* Kennedy chose not to re-approve a practice that continued to lose support within the country and that put the United States at odds with all other governments in the world. But, if the Missouri court had not stopped Simmons execution in May, 2002, the Supreme Court probably would not have stopped it either.

The Court probably would have abolished the juvenile death penalty soon even if it had not been forced to reconsider the issue in *Simmons.* Despite the Court statement in *Atkins* distinguishing the juvenile death penalty from the death penalty for retarded offenders, the objective

---

Decision, 47 WM. & MARY L. REV. 743 (2005); Jeremy Waldron, *Foreign Law and Modern Ius Gentium,* 119 HARV. L. REV. 129 (2005).

[98] *Compare, e.g.,* Robert J. Delahunty & John Yoo, *Against Foreign Law,* 29 HARV. J. L. & PUB. POL'Y,. 291 (2005) ("Foreign and international law cannot be legitimately used in an outcome determinative way to decide questions of constitutional interpretation.") *with* Vicki C. Jackson, *Constitutional Comparisons: Convergence, Resistance, Engagement,* 119 HARV. L. REV. 109 (2005) ("[I]t is Scalia's view ... that is anomalous and properly rejected in *[Simmons]*.").

evidence of societal consensus against the two practices was strikingly similar, and the methodology that the Court employed in *Atkins* undermined the analysis that the majority had employed in *Stanford*. Likewise, between 1989 and 2003, public support for the death penalty diminished,[99] and public opinion about the death penalty seems to influence the Court in ways that death-penalty doctrine does not capture. Between 2002 and 2008, the Court has reversed an unusually large number of death sentences on many different grounds, revealing a Court that is, although no less conservative in composition, more willing than it was in the late 1980s to regulate and restrict the use of the capital sanction.[100] Given also the overwhelming consensus that had developed among other nations against the juvenile death penalty, the country was ready after *Atkins* to accept with relatively little criticism a judicial prohibition on the death penalty for offenses committed by persons under eighteen.

The full significance of the Court's opinion in *Simmons* will only become clear in future decades. Of course, by abolishing the juvenile death penalty, the decision represents another major step in the Court's effort to eliminate excesses in the use of capital punishment. But if the Court seeks to develop a more international perspective in its rulings on the Bill of Rights, the opinion may also become important as the first to provide a lengthy discussion and explicit defense of the relevance of international norms and foreign law. Also, the decision may provide a foundation for an eventual ruling by the Court that life imprisonment without parole for some juvenile offenders violates the Eighth Amendment. Moreover, as Professor Jordan Steiker has noted, the opinion

---

[99] In a dissenting opinion in a recent case, Justice Souter, joined by Justices Stevens, Ginsburg and Breyer, noted the many exonerations of death-row convicts during that period. *See* Kansas v. Marsh, 548 U.S. 163, 207 (2006) (Souter, J., dissenting) ("Today, a new body of fact must be accounted for in deciding what, in practical terms, the Eighth Amendment guarantees should tolerate, for the period starting in 1989 has seen repeated exonerations of convicts under death sentences, in numbers never imagined before the development of DNA tests.").

[100] The number of such decisions is noteworthy, even without considering *Atkins* and *Roper*. For examples, see *Ring v. Arizona*, 536 U.S. 584 (2002) (failure to provide for jury decision at sentencing trial regarding existence of aggravating circumstance); *Banks v. Dretke*, 540 U.S. 668 (2004) (suppression of evidence by government); *Smith v. Texas*, 543 U.S. 37 (2004) (*per curiam*) (inadequate opportunity to give full mitigating effect to mitigating evidence); *Tennard v. Dretke*, 542 U.S. 274 (2004) (same); House v. Bell, 547 U.S. 518 (2006) (ineffective assistance of counsel); *Abdul-Kabir v. Quarterman*, 550 U.S. 233 (2007) (inadequate opportunity to give full mitigating effect to mitigating evidence); Panetti v. Quarterman, 127 S.Ct. 2842 (2007) (insanity at the time of execution); *Snyder v. Louisiana*, 128 S.Ct. 1203 (2008) (racial discrimination in jury selection). By comparison, in the mid-to-late 1980s, when public support for the death penalty was much higher, "[a]cross a variety of doctrinal settings, the Court almost invariably rejected the death penalty claims it considered. . . ." Lain, *supra* note 74, at 41.

provides "a blueprint for judicial abolition of the death penalty in the United States."[101] *Simmons* underscored that the Eighth Amendment can prohibit the death penalty even when forty percent of the states have not abolished it. The opinion also confirmed that the failure or near-failure of states to use the death penalty when legislatively authorized weighs in favor of finding a societal consensus against the sanction. Further, *Simmons* confirmed that the Court's independent judgment is important in deciding whether the death penalty is proportionate, and it made "elite opinion"[102] and, arguably, international norms relevant to the assessment. Judicial abolition of the death penalty as disproportionate punishment for aggravated murder may not be imminent. But if more states follow New Jersey by abolishing the penalty[103] and if execution numbers and death-sentencing rates continue to decline,[104] a future Supreme Court may be ready to reach that conclusion. In the event that happens, *Simmons* provides a template for the decision.

---

[101] Steiker, *supra* note 5, at 171.

[102] *Id.*

[103] See Jeremy Peters, *Corzine Signs Bill Ending Executions, Then Commutes Sentences of 8*, N.Y. TIMES, Dec. 18, 2007, at B3.

[104] After reaching a high of ninety-eight in 1999, annual executions in the U.S. dropped in subsequent years. Only fifty-three executions occurred in the U.S. in 2006, and only forty-two occurred in 2007. *See* Death Penalty Information Center, *Facts About the Death Penalty*, May 16, 2008, available at http://www.deathpenaltyinfo.org/FactSheet.pdf (as visited on May 23, 2008). The annual number of new death sentences also dropped from 326 in 1995 to 110 in 2007. *See id.*

12

Joseph L. Hoffmann

House v. Bell and the Death of Innocence

Introduction

Paul Gregory House was convicted of the 1985 murder of Carolyn Muncey and sentenced to death. For the next two decades, while imprisoned on Tennessee's Death Row, House insisted that he did not commit the crime. He claimed that evidence of his innocence was never introduced at trial because his court-appointed trial lawyer failed to conduct a proper investigation, violating his Sixth Amendment right to the effective assistance of counsel under Strickland v. Washington.[1] He also claimed that the prosecutor kept key exculpatory evidence hidden from the defense, violating his right to due process under *Brady v. Maryland*.[2]

House initially raised both of these constitutional claims in a *pro se* motion for post-conviction relief in the trial court. After the post-conviction motion was denied, however, a new court-appointed lawyer decided not to pursue House's ineffective-assistance and *Brady* claims on appeal.[3] As a result of this procedural default, House thereafter was denied repeatedly, in both state and federal court, the opportunity to obtain a ruling on the merits of his constitutional claims.

In February 1999, House finally got the chance to assert his innocence in court, when a federal district judge agreed to hold an evidentiary hearing in connection with his ineffective-assistance and *Brady* claims. At the hearing, House's federal public defender introduced per-

---

[1] 466 U.S. 668 (1984).

[2] 373 U.S. 83 (1963).

[3] See House v. State, 911 S.W.2d 705 (Tenn. 1995) (finding procedural default based on lawyer's failure to raise claim of ineffectiveness of trial counsel on appeal from denial of post-conviction petition); House v. Bell, 1989 WL 152742 (Tenn. Ct. Crim. App. 1989) (rejecting appeal from denial of post-conviction petition).

suasive new evidence to support House's claim of innocence. Although
both the federal district and appellate courts denied relief, six judges on
the U.S. Court of Appeals for the Sixth Circuit found it "highly probable
that [House] is completely innocent of any wrongdoing whatever,"[4] while
a seventh described himself as "in grave doubt" about House's guilt.[5]
Over the next several years, the New York Times,[6] the National Law
Journal,[7] the Nashville Tennesseean,[8] and 60 Minutes[9] reported extensively on the case, noting the strong likelihood that Carolyn Muncey's
abusive husband, and not House, was the real killer.

On June 12, 2006, a majority of the United States Supreme Court
finally held that, notwithstanding the prior procedural default, House
should no longer be barred from litigating the merits of his claims.[10] The
Court reviewed House's new evidence in detail, and concluded that—
"had the jury heard all the conflicting testimony—it is more likely than
not that no reasonable juror viewing the record as a whole would lack
reasonable doubt [about House's guilt]."[11] The Court held that House's
new evidence so undermined the strength of the prosecution's case
against him that he should be entitled to judicial review of his claims by
a federal habeas corpus court.

Despite the Supreme Court's ruling, however, Paul Gregory House
continued to be imprisoned for more than two additional years. That's
because the Court did not order the State of Tennessee to release House,
nor even to give him a new trial. Instead, the Court merely remanded his
case back to the lower federal courts for further review, where prosecutors and defense attorneys continued to argue about the legal merits of
his constitutional claims. Meanwhile, House's life continued to slip away.
During his prolonged imprisonment, he fell victim to multiple sclerosis,
eventually becoming confined to a wheelchair.

---

[4] House v. Bell, 386 F.3d 668, 708 (6th Cir. *en banc* 2004) (Merritt, J., dissenting).

[5] Id., at 709 (Gilman, J., dissenting).

[6] Adam Liptak, "Seven Dissenters on U.S. Court Cannot Stop an Execution," New
York Times, Oct. 7, 2004.

[7] Brandon L. Garrett & Jason M. Solomon, "Judging Innocence," National Law
Journal, Jan. 1, 2006.

[8] Dwight Lewis, "Did He Kill Her? Doubts, Denial, and a Death Penalty Case,"
Nashville Tennesseean, Oct. 17, 2004; Editorial, "A Troubling Death–Row Case and a
Divided Court," Nashville Tennesseean, Oct. 11, 2004.

[9] CBS News, "Did Husband Kill Carolyn Muncey?," 60 Minutes, Dec. 12, 2004.

[10] House v. Bell, 547 U.S. 518 (2006).

[11] Id., at 554.

The long, convoluted legal saga of *House v. Bell* is a virtual case study in the recurring problem of excessive proceduralism in the American criminal justice system, especially in cases involving the death penalty.[12] The courts did not behave badly in this case—indeed, at every turn, they followed the relevant legal rules carefully and scrupulously. But something is terribly wrong with a criminal justice system that is so focused on protecting the integrity of its own rules and procedures that it cannot manage to find a remedy for an injustice that already has been acknowledged as such by a majority of the United States Supreme Court.

Compelling post-trial claims of innocence, like House's, pose the most excruciating dilemmas. Such claims have the potential to destroy our faith in a legal system that often represents our best hope for achieving a better society. They strike at the heart of the jury system, the foundation of American democracy. They force appellate judges into fact-finding roles with which they may be intensely uncomfortable, and produce conflicts between state and federal courts. They unsettle our notions of finality, creating cognitive dissonance by challenging what we have already accepted as true. The very thought of such an enormous injustice may be so intolerable that almost everyone associated with the legal system—including judges, jurors, prosecutors, police, and even defense attorneys—may prove vulnerable to cognitive biases that prevent them from concluding that a wrongful conviction actually has occurred.

All of this may explain why it is so hard for the courts to remedy an erroneous conviction, but the problem is one that simply must be solved. The case of Paul Gregory House is the kind that gives law, lawyers, and the death penalty a bad name. As one of House's Death Row guards, in late 2007, asked the Rev. Joe Ingle, a minister visiting the prison: "The Supreme Court has said any reasonable juror would find this man innocent, right? Then why is he still here?"[13]

The Crime

In the summer of 1985, 29–year-old Carolyn Muncey lived with her husband, William Hubert Muncey, Jr., also known as "Little Hube," and her two children, 10–year-old Lora and 8–year-old Matthew, in a run-down, four-room backwoods shack in rural Union County, Tennessee, northeast of Knoxville.[14] The Munceys were poor and uneducated, eking

---

[12] See generally Jordan Steiker, Restructuring Post–Conviction Review of Federal Constitutional Claims Raised by State Prisoners: Confronting the New Face of Excessive Proceduralism, 1998 U. Chi. Legal F. 315 (criticizing excessive proceduralism in federal habeas review of state convictions, and proposing solutions to the problem).

[13] Sarah Kelley, "A Vicious Circle," Nashville Scene, Feb. 8, 2007.

[14] The facts of the case have been detailed in numerous court opinions, including House v. Bell, 547 U.S. 518 (2006); House v. Bell, 386 F.3d 668 (6th Cir. *en banc* 2004); and

out a meager living on welfare, food stamps, odd jobs, and handouts from friends. Their home lacked running water, an indoor toilet, and a telephone.

Around 8 PM on July 13, 1985, a Saturday night, Carolyn took her two children across the road to visit with her neighbor, Pamela Luttrell. Carolyn told Luttrell that her husband, "Little Hube," had gone out to dig a grave for a family friend, but had not yet returned. Carolyn said that was OK with her, because she was going to make "Little Hube" take her fishing the next day. The two women talked for an hour or so, and then Carolyn and her children returned home.

Sometime between 9:30 PM and 11 PM, the children were awakened by the sound of a man asking for "Bubbie," another nickname for "Little Hube" that was used primarily by close friends and family members. The children did not see who the man was, but later testified that he had a deep voice that sounded like their grandfather's, William Muncey, Sr. The children heard their mother tell the unidentified man that "Bubbie" was out digging a grave. Sometime later, according to the children, they heard someone telling Carolyn something about their father and a "wreck" down the road, next to a creek. The children heard Carolyn start crying and head down the steps. She never returned.

The children eventually went out looking for their mother. They first tried the Luttrell house, but nobody answered. They also went to the house of another neighbor, Mike Clinton, but he said he had not seen Mrs. Muncey. The children returned home and went back to sleep.

Around 1 AM, "Little Hube" showed up and asked the children where their mother was. Lora told him that she hadn't been around for a while. "Little Hube" took the children over to Pamela Luttrell's house, and went looking for his wife.

At 1:47 AM, "Little Hube" returned to Luttrell's house and used her phone to report Carolyn's disappearance to the local police. "Little Hube" explained to the police chief, Dennis "Dink" Wallace, who answered the call, that he had been out at a dance at the local recreation center, and had returned home to find his wife missing. When Police Chief Wallace arrived at the Muncey home, "Little Hube" said that he believed his wife had been kidnapped. Wallace asked why he would think that, and "Little Hube" replied that he didn't know.

State v. House, 743 S.W.2d 141 (1987). The statement of facts herein was compiled primarily from these court opinions. Some additional details were drawn from the following news accounts of the case: David Murphy, "On the Docket: House v. Bell," Medill News Service, Medill School of Journalism, Northwestern University, posted Sept. 1, 2005, available on-line at http://docket.medill. northwestern.edu/archives/002836.php; Wendell Rawls, Jr., "Innocent on Death Row?," Nashville Scene, Mar. 31, 2005; CBS News, "Did Husband Kill Carolyn Muncey?," 60 Minutes, Dec. 12, 2004.

On the afternoon of the following day, Sunday, July 14, Carolyn Muncey was still missing. Billy Ray Hensley, Carolyn's first cousin and a close friend of "Little Hube," heard about Carolyn's disappearance, and began to look for her. According to Hensley's later trial testimony, around 2 PM, as he was approaching the road where the Munceys lived, he saw a man coming up over an embankment, wiping his hands on a black rag. The man was Paul Gregory House.

House had moved to the area a few months before, after being paroled in Utah after serving four years in prison on a sentence of five years to life for aggravated sexual assault. He was living in a house trailer with his girlfriend, Donna Turner, about two miles from the Muncey home, and was a casual acquaintance of the Munceys. House did not own a car, but he often borrowed Turner's white Plymouth. He did not have a steady job, and spent most of his time hanging around the house trailer watching television and smoking marijuana.

According to Billy Ray Hensley, he saw House coming over the embankment, and also noticed a white Plymouth parked across the road. Hensley proceeded to drive up the road to the Muncey house, then turned around and began to head back the other way. At that point, Hensley saw House driving the opposite direction in the white Plymouth. House flagged Hensley down, explaining that he had heard that Mrs. Muncey was missing and was looking for Mr. Muncey, whom he said was somewhere getting drunk.

Hensley continued to look for Carolyn. Eventually, he wound up at the house of Bill Spivey, where many of Carolyn's friends and relatives were gathering. Hensley told a friend there, Jack Adkins, that his suspicions were aroused by his earlier encounter with House. Hensley and Adkins decided to return to the same stretch of road where Hensley had seen House about an hour before.

After a brief search of the area, Jack Adkins discovered Carolyn Muncey's lifeless body, about 100 yards from the Muncey home, across the road and down an embankment leading toward a creek. She was clothed in a flower-patterned nightgown, and was lying face down in a pile of brush. There was blood on the nightgown, as well as on Carolyn's face and hands. An autopsy revealed that she had died sometime between 9 PM and 11 PM on Saturday night, as the result of a severe injury to her left forehead. The injury was consistent with either a blow from a fist or other instrument, or striking a hard object. The body also showed bruising and signs of strangulation, although strangulation was not the cause of death.

Back at the house of Bill Spivey, Hensley told the county sheriff about his earlier sighting of House near the approximate location where Carolyn Muncey's body was later found. Coincidentally, at about the same time, House drove up to the Spivey house in the white Plymouth, with "Little Hube" sitting in the passenger's seat. The county sheriff asked House to come down to the jail for an interview, which House agreed to do.

During the interview, House told the authorities that he had been inside Donna Turner's house trailer the entire night before. When asked about some scratches on his arms, and a bruise on his right ring finger, House said that the scratches came from Turner's cat, and the bruise from recent construction work.

At first, Donna Turner backed up House's alibi for the night of the murder. But later, after police searched her trailer and found the soiled jeans that House had been wearing that Saturday night, with what the police later described as reddish-brown stains on them, Turner admitted that, at about 10:30 or 10:45 PM, House had gone out. She said that House had returned about an hour later, in a disheveled state, hot and panting, and missing his shirt and shoes. Turner testified that House had told her that, as he was walking on the road near her house trailer, a vehicle pulled up beside him, and somebody inside the vehicle accosted him, calling him names. House had told Turner that, after one of the people in the vehicle tried to grab him, House swung around and "hit something" with his right hand. At that point, House ran off down the bank, throwing off his shirt along the way. House had also claimed that his assailants fired two shots at him.

On Sunday evening, Police Chief Wallace interviewed "Little Hube" Muncey. "Little Hube" reiterated what he had said to Wallace during his prior phone call, namely, that he had spent Saturday evening at the weekly dance at the local recreation center, about a mile and a half from his home. "Little Hube" also admitted that he had left the dance early, to go buy some beer, and he stated that he and his wife had had sexual relations on Saturday morning.

On Tuesday, July 16, the local district attorney, William Paul Phillips, instructed two local law enforcement officers to drive to the Federal Bureau of Investigation in Washington, D.C., with House's jeans, blood samples from the Carolyn Muncey autopsy, and other evidence. In a letter to the FBI, Phillips described the crime as a "sexually motivated attack." The two officers drove through the night, arriving early the next morning. On Wednesday, July 17, initial FBI tests showed human blood on the jeans. House was arrested the same day.

The Trial

House was charged with capital murder.[15] At trial, the state's witnesses included Pamela Luttrell, Billy Ray Hensley, Jack Adkins,

---

[15] This account of the trial was drawn from the opinions of the U.S. Supreme Court in House v. Bell, 547 U.S. 518 (2006), and the U.S. Court of Appeals for the Sixth Circuit in House v. Bell, 386 F.3d 668 (6th Cir. *en banc* 2004).

Lora Muncey, the autopsy physician, the county sheriff, and other law enforcement officers. The key evidence against House, however, consisted of the bloodstains on House's jeans and semen deposits that were found on Mrs. Muncey's nightgown and panties.

An FBI agent testified at trial that the bloodstains on the jeans were Type A (the same blood type shared by House, Carolyn Muncey, and "Little Hube" Muncey). Further testing revealed that the blood contained enzymes and blood serum that would be found in only 6.75% of the population; according to the FBI agent's testimony, the bloodstains were "consistent" with Carolyn Muncey's blood, but could not have come from House.

The same FBI agent testified that the semen came from a person who was a "secretor," meaning that the semen contained blood-type information, a characteristic shared by 80% of the population, including House. The agent testified that the semen on the nightgown came from someone with Type A blood. Although the semen on the panties did not contain all of the blood components that would have been expected from someone with Type A blood, the agent concluded that both of the semen deposits could have come from House. The agent admitted, however, that he did not test "Little Hube" Muncey to see whether he, too, was a "secretor" who could have been the source of the semen.

Among the few witnesses called by the defense was Carolyn Muncey's brother, Ricky Green, who testified that about two weeks before the murder, Carolyn had called him to say that she was afraid of "Little Hube," and wanted to leave him. According to Green, a few years earlier, he had witnessed "Little Hube" return home drunk and strike Carolyn. The defense also called Donna Turner, House's girlfriend, who told the jury that House's shoes were found several months after the crime, in a field near her house trailer, and were delivered to the authorities. The jury never was told, however, that the authorities had tested the shoes but failed to find any trace of blood on them.

In closing argument, the prosecution did not reference the semen deposits, but instead primarily emphasized the bloodstains found on House's jeans. The prosecution noted that "after running many, many, many tests," the FBI agent had concluded that "the blood on the blue jeans was consistent with every characteristic in every respect of the deceased's, Carolyn Muncey's, and that ninety-three percent of the white population would not have that blood type.... He can't tell you one hundred percent for certain that it was her blood. But folks, he can sure give you a pretty good—a pretty good indication."

The defense countered with the observation that the prosecution had completely failed to provide any plausible motive for House "to go over and kill a woman that he barely knew[,] [w]ho was still dressed, still clad in her clothes." In rebuttal, the prosecution explained that "it does not make any difference under God's heaven, what the motive was." Nevertheless, the prosecution suggested, "you may have an idea why he did it":

> "The evidence at the scene which seemed to suggest that he was subjecting this lady to some kind of indignity, why would you get a lady out of her house, late at night, in her night clothes, under the trick that her husband has had a wreck down by the creek? ... Well, it is because either you don't want her to tell what indignities you have subjected her to, or she is unwilling and fights against you, against being subjected to those indignities. In other words, it is either to keep her from telling what you have done to her, or it is that you are trying to get her to do something that she nor any mother on that road would want to do with Mr. House, under those conditions, and you kill her because of her resistance. That is what the evidence at the scene suggests about motive."[16]

After four hours of deliberation, the jury convicted House of murder in the first degree.

The Capital Sentencing Hearing

At sentencing, the prosecution alleged three aggravating circumstances to justify imposition of the death penalty: (1) the murder was committed by a person who previously had been convicted of a felony involving violence or the threat of violence; (2) the murder was especially heinous, atrocious, or cruel in that it involved torture or depravity of mind; and (3) the murder was committed during the course of a rape or kidnapping.[17] The prosecution introduced House's prior Utah conviction for aggravated sexual assault, and his parole, and then rested.

The defense introduced mitigation testimony from House's father and mother, along with evidence that House had attempted suicide after the guilty verdict, explaining in a suicide note to his mother that he was innocent of the crime.

At closing argument, the prosecution claimed that Carolyn Muncey was "decoy[ed] or entic[ed] away from her family, and confin[ed] against her will because you know that as she was being beaten to death." The prosecution also argued that the case "shows strong evidence of attempted sexual molestation of the victim to accompany the taking away and murdering her."

---

[16] House v. Bell, 547 U.S. 518, 531–32 (2006) (quoting from Trial Transcript, State v. House, No. 378 (Crim. Ct. Union County, Tenn.), App. at 106–107).

[17] This account of the sentencing hearing was drawn from the opinion of the U.S. Supreme Court in House v. Bell, 547 U.S. 518 (2006).

The jury unanimously found all three aggravating circumstances, concluded that there were no mitigating circumstances to outweigh the aggravating circumstances, and recommended the death penalty. The judge sentenced House to death.

Post–Trial Review in the State Courts

House's lawyer filed an appeal of House's conviction and death sentence to the Tennessee Supreme Court. The grounds for appeal included the following: (1) four prospective jurors were wrongly excused, upon challenges for cause made by the state, based on their views in opposition to the death penalty; (2) the prosecution violated Tennessee criminal procedure rules by not providing the defense with an adequate and timely opportunity to conduct its own independent tests on the bloodstained jeans; (3) the prosecution improperly commented on the defendant's decision not to testify in his own behalf; (4) the jury instructions improperly shifted the burden of proof to the defense; (5) the trial court failed to suppress the defendant's statements to the police; (6) the prosecution wrongly introduced evidence, at sentencing, about the length of the defendant's Utah prison sentence and the fact that he was out on parole; (7) the jury was allowed to consider guilt-phase evidence during the sentencing phase, even though the prosecution did not move to adopt that evidence for sentencing; (8) the prosecution failed to give proper notice to the defendant about its intention to seek the death penalty; (9) several of the jurors were improperly allowed to go to a lounge and drink alcohol between the guilt and sentencing phases; and (10) various broad-based constitutional challenges to the Tennessee death penalty statute.[18]

On December 14, 1987, in a unanimous 5–0 decision, the Tennessee Supreme Court rejected almost all of the defense claims in short order, either because the court found them to be baseless or because any possible errors were harmless beyond a reasonable doubt. The court gave full consideration to only one of the claims, namely, the claim that the prosecution should have provided the defense with greater access to conduct its own independent tests on the bloodstained jeans. According to the court, however, the prosecution did not "deliberately withh[o]ld" House's jeans from inspection or testing by the defense. Moreover, "[n]o serious question has been raised concerning the reliability of the tests conducted by the F.B.I. or of the results thereof." Finally, any delay in providing the defense with access to the jeans was not produced by "deliberate obstruction" on the part of the prosecution. As a result, the court concluded, "we find no reversible error" in admitting the blood evidence at trial.[19]

---

[18] State v. House, 743 S.W.2d 141 (Tenn.1987).

[19] Id., at 145–146.

Two months after the Tennessee Supreme Court's decision, House returned to the trial court and filed a *pro se* petition for post-conviction relief.[20] In his petition, House argued that his lawyer had rendered constitutionally ineffective assistance of counsel, both at trial and at sentencing. House claimed that his lawyer failed to give him proper advice; to conduct a thorough pre-trial investigation; to file appropriate pretrial motions; to make necessary and timely objections; to conduct appropriate voir dire of prospective jurors; to prepare adequately for trial and sentencing; to object to the jury instructions; and to challenge a biased juror at the sentencing phase of the trial.

The trial court appointed a new lawyer to assist House with his post-conviction petition, and the new lawyer added several new claims to the petition, most notably a new challenge to the jury instructions at trial. At an evidentiary hearing before the same judge who had presided over the trial, the defense did not offer any new evidence, but instead relied solely on the trial transcript. The trial court dismissed the petition.

On appeal from the denial of the petition, House's new lawyer made what can now be described, in retrospect, as the crucial error in the entire case: He raised only the jury-instruction issue, and did not press House's ineffective-assistance-of-counsel claim.[21] The Tennessee Court of Criminal Appeals affirmed the trial court's denial of the petition,[22] and the Tennessee Supreme Court (along with the United States Supreme Court) denied discretionary review.[23]

House, with the help of yet another new lawyer, then filed a second post-conviction petition, renewing the earlier ineffective-assistance claim based on failure to investigate, and seeking investigative and/or expert assistance.[24] The prosecution argued, in response, that the claims raised in House's second petition were barred by Tennessee state law, either because any claims not raised in a prior post-conviction petition are presumptively waived, or because any claims previously determined in connection with a prior post-conviction petition cannot be raised again in a later petition. House contended that any failure to assert his claims

---

[20] The details of House's first post-conviction proceeding are outlined in House v. State, 1989 WL 152742 (Tenn. Ct. Crim. App. 1989).

[21] Id., at p. 2 ("In this appeal, the petitioner complains only about certain jury instructions that were given at his sentencing hearing.").

[22] Id., at p. 11.

[23] House v. State, 1990 Tenn. LEXIS 104 (Tenn. S.Ct. Mar. 5, 1990) (appeal denied); House v. Tennessee, 498 U.S. 912 (1990) (cert. denied).

[24] The details of House's second post-conviction proceeding are outlined in House v. State, 1992 WL 210578, * (Tenn. Cr. Crim. App. 1992).

properly in connection with his first post-conviction petition was the fault of the lawyer who was representing him at that time, which deprived him of a "full and fair hearing" on his claims, and therefore should not serve as a barrier to the filing of a second post-conviction petition. The trial court dismissed the petition, finding it to be procedurally barred.[25]

On appeal, the Court of Criminal Appeals initially affirmed the trial court's dismissal of the petition.[26] But the legal precedent relied upon by the Court of Criminal Appeals subsequently was overturned by the Tennessee Supreme Court, which then remanded House's case back to the Court of Criminal Appeals for further consideration.[27] In March 1994, the Court of Criminal Appeals reversed the dismissal of the petition, concluding that the asserted ineffectiveness of House's first post-conviction counsel could be an "important factor" in determining whether the second petition should be permitted or barred.[28] The court held that House should be provided an opportunity to litigate his ineffective-assistance claim, and that the trial court should consider appointing experts to help him with his claim.

The prosecution appealed to the Tennessee Supreme Court, which granted discretionary review[29] and, in September 1995, reinstated the trial court's dismissal of House's second post-conviction petition.[30] The Tennessee Supreme Court held that the phrase, "full and fair hearing," requires only a fair opportunity to litigate one's claim, and no more than that. Because House was provided such an opportunity at the time of his first post-conviction petition, and was not precluded or prevented from litigating his claim by the actions of the state, he was provided a "full and fair hearing" and therefore was not entitled to raise the same claim in a second post-conviction petition. The Tennessee Supreme Court also held that any possible ineffectiveness on the part of House's first post-conviction counsel was irrelevant, because he enjoyed no constitutional right to have a lawyer at all, at that particular stage of his case, and thus could not assert any right to the effective assistance of counsel. And the court concluded that House could not avoid the effect of his lawyer's

---

[25] Id., at p. 6.

[26] Id., at p. 20.

[27] House v. State, 1993 Tenn. LEXIS 135 (Tenn. S.Ct. Mar. 29, 1993).

[28] House v. State, 1994 WL 97546, at p. 40 (Tenn. Ct. Crim. App.1994).

[29] State v. House, 1994 Tenn. LEXIS 234 (Tenn. S. Ct. Jul. 25, 1994).

[30] House v. State, 911 S.W.2d 705 (Tenn. S.Ct. 1995), cert. denied, 517 U.S. 1193 (1996).

waiver of the ineffective-assistance issue, even if House was not personally aware of that waiver.[31]

The United States District Court

On September 30, 1996, House filed a *pro se* federal habeas corpus
petition, raising numerous claims of ineffective assistance of counsel and
prosecutorial misconduct.[32] The federal district court appointed counsel
for House, and the petition was amended. Although the court found
House's claims to be procedurally defaulted, based on the earlier rulings
by the Tennessee state courts, the district court nevertheless conducted
an evidentiary hearing for the purpose of determining whether House
might fit within the recognized exception to the procedural default
doctrine for a habeas corpus petitioner who can demonstrate "actual
innocence."

The procedural default doctrine in federal habeas corpus derives
from the leading case of *Wainwright v. Sykes*,[33] in which the United
States Supreme Court held that a federal habeas court generally must
decline to review any federal constitutional claims that have been
procedurally defaulted in the state courts, absent a showing of "cause"
for the default and "prejudice" from the asserted error. This doctrine is
based on comity and respect for the state courts, and for state procedural
law. The basic idea is that the federal habeas courts should not serve as
a convenient alternative means for evading, or avoiding, the negative
consequences of a defendant's failure to conform to valid state procedural rules.[34]

The Court has recognized an exception to the procedural default
doctrine, however, in the situation of a habeas corpus petitioner who has
suffered a "miscarriage of justice," meaning that he can make a sufficient showing of "actual innocence."[35] At first, the Court's test for
"miscarriage of justice" seemed to require only that the petitioner
"establish[] that under the probative evidence he has a *colorable* claim of
actual innocence."[36] Later, however, the Court described the exception as

---

[31] Id., at 714.

[32] This account of the proceedings on House's federal habeas corpus petition was taken
from the U.S. Supreme Court's opinion in House v. Bell, 547 U.S. 518 (2006).

[33] 433 U.S. 72 (1977).

[34] See generally John C. Jeffries, Jr. & William J. Stuntz, Ineffective Assistance and
Procedural Default in Federal Habeas Corpus, 57 U. Chi. L. Rev. 679 (1990) (describing
procedural default doctrine and criticizing it on the ground, inter alia, that it punishes the
defendant for the mistakes of his defense lawyer).

[35] Murray v. Carrier, 477 U.S. 478 (1986).

[36] Kuhlmann v. Wilson, 477 U.S. 436, 454 (1986) (plurality opinion) (emphasis added).

limited to "an extraordinary case, where a constitutional violation has *probably* resulted in the conviction of one who is actually innocent."[37] Then, in a series of cases, the Court extended the "miscarriage of justice" exception to capital sentencing, but under an even narrower standard that limited relief to those who could show "by *clear and convincing evidence* that but for constitutional error at his sentencing hearing, *no reasonable juror* would have found him eligible for the death penalty."[38]

Finally, in *Schlup v. Delo*,[39] the Court considered the effect of this new "miscarriage of justice" test, devised for capital sentencing, on the original standard of "actual innocence" for challenges to the guilt-innocence determination. According to *Schlup v. Delo*, in order to get around a procedural default, the petitioner must establish that, in light of his new evidence, "it is *more likely than not* that *no reasonable juror* would have found petitioner guilty beyond a reasonable doubt."[40] The Court described this standard as one that will apply only to the "truly 'extraordinary' "[41] case, in which the new evidence "raise[s] sufficient doubt about [the petitioner's] guilt to undermine confidence in the result of the trial."[42]

In House's case, the evidentiary hearing in district court revealed the following:[43]

(1) The key bloodstain evidence against House was seriously tainted. The four vials of blood taken from Carolyn Muncey at her autopsy were not sealed properly for transport to the FBI Crime Lab. At least one of the vials spilled en route from Tennessee to Washington, DC, potentially contaminating the jeans, which were originally placed in a paper bag but later ended up in a plastic bag with blood on the outside. The jeans were transported to Washington, DC, inside the same cardboard box that contained the unsealed vials of blood. By the time the blood samples eventually were given

---

[37] Murray v. Carrier, supra, 477 U.S., at 496 (emphasis added).

[38] Sawyer v. Whitley, 505 U.S. 333, 350 (1992) (emphasis added), clarifying the exception as previously applied to capital sentencing in Dugger v. Adams, 489 U.S. 401 (1989), and Smith v. Murray, 477 U.S. 527 (1986).

[39] 513 U.S. 298 (1995) (emphasis added).

[40] Id., at 327. The dissent would have insisted on the even more demanding standard of "clear and convincing evidence" that was actually used in Sawyer v. Whitley. Id., at 334 (Rehnquist, C.J., dissenting).

[41] Ibid., quoting McCleskey v. Zant, 499 U.S. 467, 494 (1991).

[42] Schlup v. Delo, supra, 513 U.S., at 317.

[43] These summaries of the evidence introduced at the evidentiary hearing are based on the U.S. Supreme Court's opinion in House v. Bell, 547 U.S. 518 (2006).

to the defense for testing, more than one-fourth of the total amount of blood had disappeared without a trace or explanation. Moreover, a doctor who had consulted for 21 years with the Tennessee Bureau of Investigation testified, at the habeas evidentiary hearing, that the blood on the jeans was much more consistent with the blood in the vials than it was with blood that would have come from a living (or recently deceased) Carolyn Muncey.

(2) DNA testing, which was not available at the time of House's 1985 trial, proved conclusively that the semen found on Carolyn Muncey's nightgown and panties belonged to "Little Hube," not House.

(3) "Little Hube" was widely known to be a violent drunkard who regularly beat his wife.

(4) On the night of the murder, the police chief, Dennis "Dink" Wallace, who was serving as a security guard at the weekly dance at the local recreation center, saw "Little Hube" leave the dance sometime around 10 PM. Wallace did not see "Little Hube" return.

(5) Also on the night of the murder, shortly before 11 PM, two witnesses saw Carolyn Muncey confront her husband, "Little Hube," in the parking lot outside the recreation center. These witnesses saw "Little Hube" grab and strike Carolyn, at which point she abruptly left.

(6) One night, around the time of House's trial, "Little Hube" appeared, drunk and crying, at the home of a neighbor woman, Kathy Parker, who had dated him back when she was 14 years old. According to Parker, "Little Hube" began rambling, and ultimately confessed that he—and not House—had killed Carolyn Muncey. "Little Hube" said that he had been arguing with his wife and had "slapped her," and that she fell and hit her head, killing her. Parker's sister, Penny Letner, confirmed Parker's account of "Little Hube's" drunken confession. Parker also testified that she had gone to the Sheriff's Department, at the time, in an effort to tell the sheriff what she had heard "Little Hube" say, but she was shunted from person to person until she eventually gave up.

Even in light of this new evidence, the district court held that House did not meet the *Schlup v. Delo* standard. The district court found the testimony of the two sisters, Kathy Parker and Penny Letner, not credible; dismissed the DNA testing of the semen as irrelevant to House's conviction for murder, because the prosecution never actually asserted any particular motive for the killing; and concluded that even though the blood samples clearly had spilled within the cardboard box, the spilled blood probably did not end up on the jeans. On February 16,

2000, the district court denied House's habeas petition, and also denied a certificate of appealability. [44]

The United States Court of Appeals

The United States Court of Appeals for the Sixth Circuit granted a certificate of appealability, and House was allowed to appeal the district court's denial of his habeas petition. A three-judge panel of the Sixth Circuit initially affirmed, 2–1, but the panel opinion was withdrawn when the court granted *en banc* review.[45]

In November 2002, a narrow 6–5 majority of the *en banc* Sixth Circuit, after reviewing House's new evidence, concluded that he "presents a strong claim" of "actual innocence."[46] The majority cited and discussed both *Schlup v. Delo* and the Supreme Court's 1993 decision in *Herrera v. Collins*.[47]

Herrera was a Texas Death Row inmate who argued that he should be allowed to pursue federal habeas relief on the ground of "naked innocence." In other words, Herrera argued that, even if no procedural errors occurred during his trial, it is still a violation of the Constitution to execute a man who is factually innocent. The Supreme Court, perhaps surprisingly, could not generate a majority to adopt the premise of Herrera's constitutional argument. Instead, the Court simply assumed, for purposes of the case, that a "truly persuasive demonstration of 'actual innocence' made after trial would render the execution of a defendant unconstitutional, and warrant habeas relief if there were no state avenue open to process such a claim."[48] But the Court ultimately held that, under any plausible legal standard that might be established for such a "naked innocence" claim, Herrera's evidence of innocence was too weak to warrant habeas relief.[49]

Although no subsequent Court decision had identified the governing legal standard for a *Herrera* "naked innocence" claim, the Sixth Circuit concluded that House's new evidence of actual innocence might well satisfy not only the *Schlup v. Delo* standard, but also whatever standard

---

[44] See House v. Bell, 386 F.3d 668, 675 (6th Cir. *en banc* 2004).

[45] House v. Bell, 283 F.3d 737 (6th Cir. 2002), vacated and withdrawn, *en banc* rehearing granted, 283 F.3d 738 (6th Cir. 2002).

[46] House v. Bell, 311 F.3d 767, 768 (6th Cir. *en banc* 2002).

[47] 506 U.S. 390 (1993).

[48] Id., at 417.

[49] Id., at 418–19 ("[C]oming 10 years after petitioner's trial, this showing of innocence falls far short of that which would have to be made in order to trigger the sort of constitutional claim which we have assumed, *arguendo*, to exist.").

might someday be established for the *Herrera* claim. The only remaining issue, under *Herrera*, was whether there were any available alternative avenues for relief that would allow House to litigate his "actual innocence" claim in the state courts. The majority therefore certified a series of state-law questions to the Tennessee Supreme Court, in an effort to obtain further guidance about possible state-court avenues for relief that might still be open to House.[50]

The Tennessee Supreme Court, upon the advice of the Tennessee Attorney General, declined to answer the certified questions, and the case returned to the *en banc* Sixth Circuit.[51] This time around, the court split 8–7, with the majority affirming the denial of House's habeas petition.[52] The majority found House's claims to be procedurally defaulted, and did not find House's new evidence to be sufficiently strong to meet either the *Schlup v. Delo* standard for avoiding the procedural default doctrine, or the (still-unspecified) *Herrera v. Collins* standard for federal habeas corpus relief on a "naked innocence" claim. Six of the seven dissenters concluded that House would meet the *Herrera* test, and should be entitled to immediate release.[53] The seventh dissenter supported at least a new trial.[54]

---

[50] House v. Bell, supra, 311 F.3d, at 777. The three certified questions were:

(1) When the Tennessee Supreme Court finds error in the presentation of an aggravating factor to a jury, and the remaining aggravating factors are disproven by new DNA evidence, does a defendant lose his current eligibility for the death penalty under state law and require a new sentencing hearing?

(2) If under Tennessee law a jury must weigh the aggravating and mitigating circumstances, and the Supreme Court of Tennessee on review then proceeds to consider the reasonableness of the weighing process, does the Court's review process now permit it to remedy any error in the weighing process by the jury in light of newly discovered evidence?

(3) Does Tennessee law require a new trial when newly discovered evidence of actual innocence, a significant part of which is in the form of DNA evidence which *could not be discovered* at the time of trial, creates a serious question or doubt that the defendant is guilty of first degree murder?

[51] House v. Bell, 2003 Tenn. LEXIS 1155 (Tenn. S.Ct. Dec. 1, 2003) ("The Court respectfully declines to answer certified questions.")

[52] House v. Bell, 386 F.3d 668 (6th Cir. *en banc* 2004).

[53] Id., at 686 (Merritt, J., dissenting). ("I regard this as the rare or extraordinary case in which the petitioner through newly discovered evidence has established his actual innocence of both the death sentence and underlying homicide.").

[54] Id., at 709 (Gilman, J., dissenting) ("I am convinced that we are faced with a real-life murder mystery, an authentic 'who-done-it' where the wrong man may be executed. Was Carolyn Muncey killed by her down-the-road neighbor Paul House, or by her husband Hubert Muncey? . . . At the end of the day, I am in grave doubt as to which of the above two suspects murdered Carolyn Muncey.").

The United States Supreme Court

As previously noted, on June 12, 2006, the United States Supreme Court issued its decision on House's appeal from the Sixth Circuit's *en banc* ruling.[55] A narrow, five-Justice majority held that House satisfied the *Schlup v. Delo* standard, and thus should be allowed to litigate his procedurally defaulted ineffective-assistance and *Brady* claims. The Court, in an opinion by Justice Kennedy that was joined by Justices Stevens, Souter, Ginsburg, and Breyer, reviewed the new evidence in detail, and then explained:

> This is not a case of conclusive exoneration. Some aspects of the State's evidence—Lora Muncey's memory of a deep voice, House's bizarre evening walk, his lie to law enforcement, his appearance near the body, and the blood on his pants—still support an inference of guilt. Yet the central forensic proof connecting House to the crime—the blood and the semen—has been called into question, and House has put forward substantial evidence pointing to a different suspect. Accordingly, and although the issue is close, we conclude that this is the rare case where—had the jury heard all the conflicting testimony—it is more likely than not that no reasonable juror viewing the record as a whole would lack reasonable doubt.[56]

The majority also concluded, however, that House's new evidence of innocence was not strong enough to warrant an immediate grant of relief under the still-unspecified *Herrera v. Collins* test for a "naked innocence" claim—nor did it even require any further explication of the *Herrera* test:

> House urges the Court to answer the question left open in *Herrera* and hold not only that freestanding innocence claims are possible but also that he has established one.
>
> We decline to resolve this issue. We conclude here, much as in *Herrera*, that whatever burden a hypothetical freestanding innocence claim would require, this petitioner has not satisfied it. To be sure, House has cast considerable doubt on his guilt—doubt sufficient to satisfy *Schlup*'s gateway standard for obtaining federal review despite a state procedural default. In *Herrera*, however, the Court described the threshold for any hypothetical freestanding innocence claim as "extraordinarily high." 506 U.S. [390,] 417 [(1993)]. The sequence of the Court's decisions in *Herrera* and *Schlup*—first leaving unresolved the status of freestanding claims and then establishing the gateway standard—implies at the least that *Herrera* requires more convincing proof of innocence than

---

[55] House v. Bell, 547 U.S. 518 (2006).

[56] Id., at 553–554.

Schlup. It follows, given the closeness of the *Schlup* question here, that House's showing falls short of the threshold implied in *Herrera.*[57]

Chief Justice Roberts, joined by Justices Scalia and Thomas, concurred in the judgment in part and dissented in part.[58] The Chief Justice agreed with the majority that House could not meet the *Herrera* standard, but argued that—especially given the doubts expressed below about the credibility of Kathy Parker and Penny Letner, and also about the testimony of the TBI doctor—he also could not meet the Schlup v. Delo standard: "Given the District Court's reliability findings, . . . the evidence before us now is not substantially different from that considered by House's jury. I therefore find it more likely than not that in light of this new evidence, at least one juror, acting reasonably, would vote to convict House. The evidence as a whole certainly does not establish that House is actually innocent of the crime of murdering Carolyn Muncey. . . ."[59]

The Court remanded the case to the lower courts for further proceedings.

The End, or Just the Beginning?

One might reasonably assume that, as soon as a majority of the United States Supreme Court concluded that "it is more likely than not that no reasonable juror viewing the record as a whole would lack reasonable doubt," the legal saga of Paul Gregory House would be almost over. But it was far from over.

To review, the Supreme Court majority held that House's new evidence of "actual innocence" was sufficient to meet the *Schlup v. Delo* standard, and thus to get around the *Wainwright v. Sykes* procedural default doctrine, but was *not* strong enough to satisfy the still-unspecified *Herrera v. Collins* test for federal habeas relief on a "naked innocence" claim. House's victory thus meant not his release from Death Row—nor even the clear promise of a new trial—but merely the Court's permission to return to the lower federal habeas courts and begin to litigate the merits of his underlying constitutional claims. In a sense, therefore, House did not win very much at all. Instead, he merely demonstrated a strong likelihood that he *would* win, under the prevailing trial standard of "beyond a reasonable doubt," if he were to receive a

---

[57] Id., at 554–555.

[58] Id., at 555 (Roberts, C.J., concurring in the judgment in part and dissenting in part). Justice Alito, who was new to the Court, did not participate.

[59] Id., at 571–72 (Roberts, C.J., concurring in the judgment in part and dissenting in part).

new trial. But he did not establish that he was, in fact, legally entitled to a new trial. That decision would have to be made in the first instance not by the Court, but by the lower federal courts on remand.

House's two underlying constitutional claims, which in 1996 formed the basis for his federal habeas corpus petition, were: (1) ineffective assistance of counsel,[60] primarily based on the alleged failure of House's trial lawyer fully to investigate the prosecution's evidence against him, and (2) prosecutorial misconduct, primarily based on the prosecutor's alleged failure to reveal potentially material exculpatory evidence to the defense,[61] thus depriving House of a fair trial. The Court's June 2006 decision finally gave House the chance to litigate these two constitutional claims in habeas court, but by no means guaranteed that he ultimately would prevail.

In order for House to succeed on the ineffective assistance claim, and receive a new trial, he would have to convince the lower federal courts that he could satisfy a difficult two-part test: (1) that his trial lawyer committed unprofessional errors, sufficient to constitute constitutionally inadequate performance;[62] and (2) that those errors prejudiced House, meaning that there was a "reasonable probability" that, but for those errors, the outcome of his original trial would have been different.[63]

The Supreme Court's ruling certainly seemed to make the second, prejudice prong of this two-part test a foregone conclusion. If, as the Court held, it was likely that "no reasonable juror" would have been able to find House guilty in view of the new evidence that came to light after his original trial, then it would seem obvious that, if that evidence had been presented at the original trial, there would have been a "reasonable probability" of a different outcome.

The problem for House lay with the first, performance prong of the test. What if the absence of that evidence from House's original trial was not the fault of his defense attorney? What if House's lawyer made reasonable (or at least not unprofessionally unreasonable) strategic choices, in terms of the particular avenues of factual investigation that he decided were worth pursuing, but those choices simply did not turn out very well for House? If so, then the defense lawyer would not be held

---

[60] This claim is based on Strickland v. Washington, 466 U.S. 668 (1984).

[61] This kind of prosecutorial-misconduct claim is based on Brady v. Maryland, 373 U.S. 83 (1963), as later refined and illuminated by United States v. Agurs, 427 U.S. 97 (1976); United States v. Bagley, 473 U.S. 667 (1985); and Kyles v. Whitley, 514 U.S. 419 (1995).

[62] This is the so-called "performance prong" of the two-part test under Strickland v. Washington.

[63] This is the so-called "prejudice prong" of Strickland v. Washington.

constitutionally ineffective, and House's habeas petition would have to be denied.

A similar analysis applied to House's prosecutorial misconduct claim. Under prevailing legal standards, House would be entitled to relief on this claim only if he could show that, at the time of his original trial, the prosecution was in actual or constructive possession of "material" exculpatory evidence that was not turned over to the defense. "Material" means that if the missing evidence had been available at trial, there is a "reasonable probability" that the result would have been different.[64]

Again, the Supreme Court's decision seemed to make the issue of "materiality" a foregone conclusion; if it is likely that, faced with the missing evidence, "no reasonable juror" would have been able to find House guilty, then it would seem obvious that the evidence must be "material." The problem for House lay with the issue of whether that missing evidence was known to the prosecution at the time of the trial. If the prosecution did not actually or constructively possess the missing evidence, then it could not be faulted for the failure to disclose the evidence to the defense, and House's habeas petition likewise would have to be denied.

In short, given well-established legal standards applicable to someone in House's situation, and notwithstanding the Supreme Court's June 2006 holding that "no reasonable juror" could have found House guilty in the face of his new evidence of innocence, there was still a very good chance that House would never receive a new trial. Even though the Court apparently thought it likely that House was an innocent man wrongly sent to Death Row, he would be unable to obtain relief unless he could show that either his own defense lawyer or the prosecutor was somehow responsible for his plight. If neither of the lawyers was at fault, then House—even though likely innocent—would be out of luck.

Post–Trial Claims of Factual Innocence

House v. Bell is symptomatic of a much deeper, and broader, problem in the American criminal justice system. The fundamental problem is that, no matter how hard we may try, and no matter how perfectly we may design and implement our legal rules of criminal procedure, sometimes criminal trials—including capital trials—simply produce erroneous verdicts.[65] Sometimes the evidence that would conclu-

---

[64] See Bagley, supra, 473 U.S., at 682–83. The test for "materiality" under *Brady* doctrine is essentially identical to the test for "prejudice" under Strickland v. Washington.

[65] For an extremely valuable discussion of erroneous convictions in general, see Brandon L. Garrett, Judging Innocence, 108 Colum. L. Rev. 55 (2008). Garrett conducted an extensive empirical study of the first 200 DNA exonerations in the United States,

sively determine who committed the crime doesn't exist, or it is never found. Sometimes witnesses are mistaken, or they lie. Sometimes there's nothing wrong with the evidence at all, but the jury simply makes a poor decision. And these kinds of errors can occur through no substantial fault on the part of any of the major legal actors: the prosecutor, the defense attorney, and the trial judge.

Lawyers, including judges, are members of a distinguished profession that places enormous value on fair procedures. Perhaps it is natural, therefore, that lawyers often put their faith in the belief that perfect procedures can guarantee perfect outcomes. The corollary to this notion, in the context of criminal cases, is that a wrongful conviction must have occurred due to some defect in the procedures that were followed in reaching that result.

A striking example of this kind of lawyerly thinking appears in the *Herrera* case. Justice O'Connor, writing in concurrence, expressed the typical lawyer's faith that perfect procedures can guarantee perfect outcomes:

> [T]he Court has no reason to pass on, and appropriately reserves, the question whether federal courts may entertain convincing claims of actual innocence. That difficult question remains open. If the Constitution's guarantees of fair procedure and the safeguards of clemency and pardon fulfill their historical mission, it may never require resolution at all.

This was a truly remarkable assertion. Justice O'Connor's claim was that—if the criminal justice system's procedural protections, together with the extraordinary remedies of clemency and pardon, operate as they should—habeas courts may never be confronted by the specter of an innocent man facing imminent execution.

---

examining the underlying causes of the errors as well as the various ways that the cases were handled by the legal system. Garrett concluded:

> Unfortunately, courts did not effectively review the unreliable and false evidence that supported these convictions. . . . Exonerees rarely received new trials based on factual claims challenging the evidence supporting their wrongful convictions. Moreover, they often did not even raise factual claims challenging that evidence. No conviction was reversed based on a challenge to an eyewitness identification. None of the exonerees brought federal claims directly challenging forensic evidence, and while half of those who falsely confessed raised claims challenging the confession, none received relief. . . . Prior to obtaining DNA testing, only a handful of exonerees asserted newly discovered evidence of innocence claims and none received a reversal. In short, the appellate and postconviction process did not effectively ferret out innocence.

Id., at 60–61. See also Samuel R. Gross, Kristen Jacoby, Daniel J. Matheson, Nicholas Montgomery, & Sujata Patil, Exonerations in the United States 1989 Through 2003, 95 J. Crim. L. & Criminology 523 (2005) (study of exoneration cases).

Only a few years later, multiple DNA and other exonerations of defendants convicted of capital crimes (including well more than a dozen on Illinois's Death Row[66]) seriously tested Justice O'Connor faith in the system. In July 2001, she delivered a speech to a group of female lawyers in Minnesota, in which she stated, "Serious questions are being raised about whether the death penalty is being fairly administered in this country.... If statistics are any indication, the system may well be allowing some innocent defendants to be executed."[67]

The inescapable truth—too often stubbornly denied by lawyers and judges—is that erroneous criminal trial verdicts sometimes occur for reasons that are independent of inadequate or inadequately enforced legal rules of criminal procedure. Sometimes, police, prosecutors, judges, and juries make erroneous decisions about a defendant's guilt simply because they are fallible, less-than-omniscient human beings.

Moreover, there are reasons to believe that this problem may be even more serious in capital cases than it is in other criminal cases.[68] This is because capital cases involve the most heinous of all crimes, and thus place enormous pressure on the police and prosecutor to identify and convict the murderer. But murder is an inherently difficult crime to solve, because there is no living victim who can testify as to what happened. Sometimes, the prosecution gets lucky, because the murderer leaves behind physical evidence (such as DNA) that can be used to identify him. We do not live in a CSI world, however, and most murder cases can't be solved so easily.

Murder prosecutions often end up relying on the testimony of accomplices or jailhouse snitches—extremely unreliable witnesses, due to the strong motivation to lie to obtain favorable treatment.[69] In the absence of such testimony, the only alternative may be to try to obtain a confession from the defendant, but this can lead to pressure that crosses the line into coercion.[70] In Illinois, these two kinds of suspect evidence were involved in many of the Death Row exonerations that led Governor George Ryan to halt all executions and ultimately, on his last day in

---

[66] See Rob Warden, Illinois Death Penalty Reform: How It Happened, What It Promises, 95 J. Crim. L. & Criminology 381 (2005) (noting 17 exonerations from Illinois's Death Row between 1972 and 2003).

[67] "Justice O'Connor on Executions," New York Times, July 5, 2001.

[68] See Samuel R. Gross, Lost Lives: Miscarriages of Justice in Capital Cases, 61 Law & Contemp. Probs. 125 (1998); Samuel R. Gross, The Risks of Death: Why Erroneous Convictions Are Common in Capital Cases, 44 Buffalo L. Rev. 469 (1996).

[69] See Garrett, supra, at 86–88 (discussing false informant testimony).

[70] See Garrett, supra, at 88–91 (discussing false confessions).

office in January 2003, commute all pending Illinois death sentences.[71] The Illinois legislature has since tried to address these issues through broad procedural reforms, such as pretrial hearings on the reliability of snitch testimony and mandatory videotaping of murder confessions,[72] but such reforms are unlikely to be a perfect solution.[73]

There are rules in every state that allow recently convicted defendants, under certain circumstances, to return to the state courts with newly discovered evidence that might prove their innocence.[74] Such rules, however, cannot eliminate the problem of mistaken convictions, because (1) the rules often are time-limited, with the limits varying widely from state to state, but in many states giving convicted defendants as little as 60 days from the entry of the judgment of conviction to file the necessary motion or petition; (2) the rules generally do not allow for relief if the defendant could have, through "due diligence," discovered the new evidence at the time of the original trial; and (3) the rules generally impose a stringent burden of proof on the defendant, such as requiring "clear and convincing" proof of innocence, or new evidence that "proba-

---

[71] See Rob Warden, Illinois Death Penalty Reform: How It Happened, What It Promises, 95 J. Crim. L. & Criminology 381, 382–83 (2005) (noting that snitch testimony and false confessions were the two most numerous causes of error in the Illinois exoneration cases).

[72] See id., at 383–87:

The most recent bill authorizes judges to bar death sentences in cases resting on the testimony of a single eyewitness, informant, or accomplice, creates a pilot project to test a new eyewitness identification protocol that could cut eyewitness error by as much as half, requires trial judges to hold pretrial hearings on any jailhouse informant testimony offered by prosecutors, establishes an administrative procedure for firing police officers who commit perjury, gives the Illinois Supreme Court authority to set aside death sentences it deems "fundamentally unjust" even if there are no procedural grounds for relief, simplifies jury instructions regarding appropriateness of the death penalty, and creates an independent, sixteen-member Capital Punishment Reform Study Committee to assess the impact and effectiveness of the various reforms and report annually to the General Assembly.

[73] See Warden, supra, at 385 ("As imposing as the package sounds, there is less to some of the measures than meets the eye."); see generally Thomas P. Sullivan, "Proposed Reforms to the Illinois Capital Punishment System: A Status Report: A Co–Chair of the Illinois Governor's Commission on Capital Punishment Reports on the Fate of Various Proposals for Death–Penalty Reform," Illinois Bar Journal, Jan. 2008 (concluding that "while the system is better, there is ample room for improvement"). This may be why executions still have not resumed in Illinois, more than five years after the enactment of the reform legislation. See Editorial, "Our Opinion: Death Penalty Cannot Be Reformed," State Journal–Register, July 7, 2008.

[74] See generally Daniel S. Medwed, Up the River Without a Procedure: Innocent Prisoners and Newly Discovered Non–DNA Evidence in State Courts, 47 Ariz. L. Rev. 655 (2005) (canvassing post-trial remedies in state court for convicted defendants with claims of innocence based on new evidence).

bly would have changed the verdict or sentence." New evidence that
clearly undermines the prosecution's case, but that does not manage to
prove the defendant's innocence under such stringent standards, will not
suffice.

In addition to the above legal restrictions, another important reason
why new-evidence claims almost never succeed is that all legal actors
(including judges and prosecutors), like all human beings, are subject to
well-known cognitive-psychological tendencies such as "confirmation
bias" and "belief perseverance."[75] "Confirmation bias" includes the
phenomenon that, after a person has settled on a particular hypothesis,
he or she will tend to discount evidence that is inconsistent with the
hypothesis, and to overvalue evidence that confirms the hypothesis.
"Belief perseverance" describes the related tendency to resist changing
one's mind, even when new evidence may contradict one's original
beliefs. These cognitive biases, and others, contribute to the overall
problem of "tunnel vision," which arises whenever police, prosecutors,
juries, or judges focus too narrowly on a particular person whom they
believe committed a crime, ignoring exculpatory evidence or alternate
suspects.[76]

Moving beyond the issue of newly discovered evidence, our legal
rules of appellate, state post-conviction, and federal habeas corpus procedure all provide, for the most part, that a convicted criminal defendant
can obtain a new trial (and, ultimately, possibly his release) only if he
can show that a procedural error—meaning a violation of some legal rule
of criminal procedure—was committed in connection with his original
trial.[77] Purely factual errors, of the kind committed by juries, generally
don't count.

---

[75] See generally Keith A. Findley & Michael S. Scott, The Multiple Dimensions of
Tunnel Vision in Criminal Cases, 2006 Wis. L. Rev. 291 (2006) (explaining these and other
cognitive biases that affect legal actors, including judges, in criminal cases, and that—
among other effects—make it difficult for innocent defendants to succeed on new-evidence
claims).

[76] Id., at 292 ("This process leads investigators, prosecutors, judges, and defense
lawyers alike to focus on a particular conclusion and then filter all evidence in a case
through the lens provided by that conclusion."); id., at 309 ("Tunnel vision is the product
of a variety of cognitive distortions that can impede accuracy in what we perceive and in
how we interpret what we perceive. Psychologists analyze tunnel vision as the product of
various cognitive 'biases,' such as confirmation bias, hindsight bias, and outcome bias.
These cognitive biases help explain how and why tunnel vision is so ubiquitous, even
among well-meaning actors in the criminal justice system. . . . ").

[77] See Joseph L. Hoffmann, Substance and Procedure in Capital Cases: Why Federal
Habeas Courts Should Review the Merits of Every Death Sentence, 78 Texas L. Rev. 1771
(2000); see also William J. Stuntz, The Uneasy Relationship Between Criminal Procedure
and Criminal Justice, 107 Yale L.J. 1, 44 (1997) ("It is not only that constitutional law has

Our reluctance to allow appellate judges to reconsider the correctness of a jury verdict may rest on a fairly obvious epistemological base—in some hard cases, we may never really be certain about the truth. The murder of Carolyn Muncey may be just such a case in which the truth may never be known for sure; indeed, one of the Sixth Circuit judges described the case as "a real-life murder mystery, an authentic 'who-done-it.' "[78] Once we acknowledge the inherent limits on our ability to determine the truth, then perhaps leaving the decision about what happened in the hands of the jury, and refusing to allow re-litigation thereafter, is not as unreasonable as it may seem.

Moreover, America's strong predilection to prefer the jury's original verdict to a judicial do-over may also be a product of our deep and abiding faith in the jury system—a faith forged by our turbulent political history, our passion for democracy, and our fundamental fear of over-reaching and oppressive government.[79] Indeed, the willingness of most Americans to accept peacefully almost any verdict rendered by a jury, even when that verdict appears blatantly wrong, is truly remarkable.[80] But that same blind faith in the jury system seemingly blinds us to the reality that juries aren't, and never will be, perfect.

And post-trial judicial review of jury verdicts by federal habeas courts is even more constrained due to the basic principles of American federalism. Allowing a federal district judge to reverse the conviction and sentence of a criminal defendant who has been found guilty by a state-court jury, who has been pronounced guilty and sentenced by a state trial judge, and whose conviction and sentence have been affirmed by the state's highest criminal appellate courts, runs directly counter to the most fundamental notions of shared state-federal sovereignty. Federal courts, for understandable and valid reasons, tend to tread cautiously in such situations.[81]

---

been too loath to regulate substance in the law of capital punishment. The point is that heavy procedural regulation has tended to drive substance away.").

[78] House v. Bell, 386 F.3d 668, 704 (6th Cir. *en banc* 2004) (Gilman, J., dissenting).

[79] As Thomas Jefferson wrote in 1789, in a letter to Thomas Paine: "I consider [trial by jury] as the only anchor ever yet imagined by man, by which a government can be held to the principles of its constitution."

[80] Think, for example, about the most famous criminal trial of the 20th Century: the murder trial of O.J. Simpson. A majority of Americans (notably excluding most Black Americans) believed Simpson to be guilty of the crime, see Alec Gallup & Frank Newport, The Gallup Poll: Public Opinion 2005 (Rowman & Littlefield, 2006), at p. 218 (reporting that 62% of whites, but only 24% of Blacks, disagreed with the jury's verdict), but the jury's acquittal—while widely criticized and even ridiculed—did not lead to any kind of public unrest or other negative social behavior. People simply accepted the verdict as the product of a system that they believed in, even though the result seemed flat wrong.

[81] "Few rulings would be more disruptive of our federal system than to provide for federal habeas review of freestanding claims of actual innocence." Herrera v. Collins, 506 U.S. 390, 401 (1993).

A convicted defendant who persists in claiming to be factually innocent, and who seeks to have his conviction reviewed by an appellate, post-conviction, or federal habeas court, therefore must find some way to convert his claim of factual innocence into the kind of procedural claim that is cognizable in such courts. The two procedural claims that are most obviously available to such a defendant are the same two claims that were asserted by House: (1) ineffective assistance of defense counsel, and (2) prosecutorial misconduct in failing to disclose material exculpatory evidence.[82] These two claims allow such a defendant to convert his claim of factual innocence into the procedural claim that either (1) "I'm innocent, and the jury would have realized that, if only my defense lawyer hadn't been such a screw-up," or (2) "I'm innocent, and the jury would have realized that, if only the prosecutor hadn't hidden the evidence that would have proved my innocence."[83]

But as House's case also demonstrates, ineffective-assistance claims and *Brady* claims can only go so far. These two procedural claims do not really reach all the way down to the substantive merits of the jury's verdict, because they both depend upon a finding that one of the lawyers in the case acted badly, or at least negligently. A defendant who gets convicted at a criminal trial in which both of the lawyers performed reasonably well will be left without a remedy, because the reviewing courts will conclude that the defendant was not denied any of his legal rights.

Moreover, even in those situations where a convicted defendant might be able to sustain an ineffective-assistance or *Brady* claim, that claim will still fail if the defendant's appellate, post-conviction, or federal habeas lawyer (or the defendant himself, if he didn't have a lawyer) makes a procedural mistake in litigating the claim.[84] As in House's case, a convicted defendant whose lawyer procedurally defaults a claim, by not raising it properly in an earlier legal proceeding, generally will be barred from raising the same claim in a later proceeding—unless the claim is so substantially linked to the defendant's factual innocence that he can meet the Schlup v. Delo test.

The bottom line is that our American criminal justice system—even in capital cases, when the defendant's life is literally on the line—is not

---

[82] See generally John H. Blume & Christopher Seeds, Reliability Matters: Reassociating Bagley Materiality, Strickland Prejudice, and Cumulative Harmless Error, 95 J. Crim. L. & Criminology 1153 (2005) (arguing, inter alia, that these two claims are so closely linked that their effects on the outcome should be considered together).

[83] See Joseph L. Hoffmann, Substance and Procedure in Capital Cases: Why Federal Habeas Courts Should Review the Merits of Every Death Sentence, 78 Texas L. Rev. 1771, 1787–88 (2000).

[84] See Wainwright v. Sykes, 433 U.S. 72 (1977).

well-designed to deal with post-trial claims of factual innocence. Our appellate, post-conviction, and federal habeas rules have been written to facilitate post-trial litigation about serious procedural errors that may have occurred before, or during, the defendant's trial. But those same rules tend to discourage, or even preclude, post-trial litigation about the substantive justice of the jury's verdict—in other words, about the defendant's factual guilt or innocence.

This is a fundamental defect in our criminal justice system that needs to be fixed. Perhaps there once was a time when most Americans believed that the system was more or less infallible—or could refuse to acknowledge that it wasn't. But if such a time ever existed, it is long gone, now that we know that, and have witnessed how, DNA evidence can prove a convicted defendant's innocence. The Illinois Death Row exonerations, and the ongoing work of Innocence Projects across the nation, can leave no doubt that the system sometimes makes mistakes— and that those mistakes sometimes put innocent persons behind bars, and even on Death Row.

Whenever, after a criminal trial that results in a conviction, we find ourselves believing—for whatever reason—that an erroneous factual decision has been made by the jury, our criminal justice system must provide some kind of effective means to address, and remedy, that error. In the special context of capital cases, for reasons that should be too obvious to require explanation, the need for a meaningful solution to this problem is paramount. It is simply unacceptable for our appellate, post-conviction, and federal habeas judges—no matter how longstanding and well-established the legal rules of post-trial procedure may be—to be forced to permit a convicted defendant whom they now believe to be, more likely than not, innocent of a capital crime, nevertheless to be executed for committing that crime.

Finding the best solution to this problem, however, will not be easy. For the federalism reasons identified previously, placing the primary responsibility for post-trial substantive review into the hands of federal habeas courts is problematic—although such a suggestion has been made.[85] Yet the state courts do not seem to want this responsibility either. In November 2003, the State of Illinois enacted a special statute, the "Fundamental Justice Amendment,"[86] requiring the Illinois Supreme

---

[85] See Joseph L. Hoffmann, Substance and Procedure in Capital Cases: Why Federal Habeas Courts Should Review the Merits of Every Death Sentence, 78 Texas L. Rev. 1771 (2000).

[86] "(i) Appellate Procedure.

The conviction and sentence of death shall be subject to automatic review by the Supreme Court. Such review shall be in accordance with rules promulgated by the Supreme Court. The Illinois Supreme Court may overturn the death sentence, and order the

Court to review the substantive merits of the conviction and sentence in every capital case. The statute authorized the court to set aside the death sentence, "independent of any procedural grounds for relief," if it found the sentence to be "fundamentally unjust" for any reason— including the factual innocence of the defendant.

In 2006, the Illinois Supreme Court had its first opportunity to make a decision under the new statute. In *People v. Thompson*,[87] the court was faced with a Death Row inmate's claim that his death sentence was "fundamentally unjust" because of his mental illness, lack of prior criminal history, redeeming qualities, and poor health. (The defendant in *Thompson* did not claim that he was factually innocent of the capital crime.) The court, by 5–1, concluded that the new statute did not substantially alter the usual appellate standard of review in capital cases: "Because ... the trier of fact ... has the superior opportunity to assess firsthand the credibility and believability of the witnesses on the stand, we will not lightly overturn the trier of fact's decision."[88] The court rejected the defendant's "fundamental injustice" claim.

Justice McMorrow, alone in dissent, accused the majority of ignoring not only the plain language of the statute, but also the clear legislative intent:

> The fundamental justice determination differs from the traditional appellate review conducted in death penalty cases. . . . [P]rinciples of deference and standards of review do not play a role in the funda- mental justice determination itself—they simply are not relevant.[89]

Justice McMorrow also quoted the legislative co-sponsors of the bill, Senators Cullerton and Dillard, who wrote:

> The [F]undamental [J]ustice [A]mendment ... is ground breaking in scope and conception. . . . [It] authorizes the [Illinois] Supreme Court to engage, in death penalty cases only, in a new and impor- tant kind of appellate review. This new kind of appellate review is designed to be substantive, rather than procedural. . . . The "funda- mental justice" of a death sentence, as applied to a particular case, cannot generally be determined on the basis of legal rules. It is a

---

imposition of imprisonment under Chapter V of the Unified Code of Corrections if the court finds that the death sentence is fundamentally unjust as applied to the particular case. If the Illinois Supreme Court finds that the death sentence is fundamentally unjust as applied to the particular case, independent of any procedural grounds for relief, the Illinois Supreme Court shall issue a written opinion explaining this finding." 720 ILCS 5/9–1(i) (West 2004).

[87] 222 Ill.2d 1, 853 N.E.2d 378 (2006).

[88] Id., at 35, 853 N.E.2d, at 398.

[89] Id., at 61, 853 N.E.2d, at 412 (McMorrow, J., dissenting).

moral issue, not a legal one, and must be based on the facts of the particular case and the moral compass of the decision maker.[90] Justice Fitzgerald wrote separately to agree with Justice McMorrow about the appellate standard of review, although he concurred in the end result because he did not find the defendant's death sentence to be "fundamentally unjust."[91]

The *Thompson* decision illustrates the extent to which appellate judges—especially state judges, who generally must stand for some kind of periodic election or retention vote[92]—are deeply uncomfortable with the kind of substantive appellate review contemplated by the Illinois Fundamental Justice Amendment. As the axiom says, you can lead a horse to water, but you can't make him drink. Without a stronger commitment by the Illinois Supreme Court to fulfill the new responsibility imposed by the statute, the statute cannot possibly achieve its goal.

In the absence of such a solution, perhaps the simplest approach, in a federal habeas case like *House v. Bell*, would be for the Supreme Court to recognize the obvious: Any person who qualifies under the *Schlup v. Delo* standard for avoiding the procedural default doctrine should also qualify, under *Herrera v. Collins*, for federal habeas relief based on "naked innocence." Once the Supreme Court has concluded, as in the *House* case, that "no reasonable juror" would have found the defendant guilty beyond a reasonable doubt, the law should provide a quick and simple path to a remedy—either grant such a defendant a new trial, so that his factual guilt may be re-determined, or else release him forthwith.[93]

The *House* case stands as a stark and tragic example of a legal system that has become so focused on procedures that it has lost all sense of what really matters. Legal procedures are merely a means to an end. The end is substantive justice.

---

[90] Id., at 59–60, 853 N.E.2d at 411–12 (McMorrow, J., dissenting) (quoting J. Cullerton, K. Dillard & P. Baroni, Capital Punishment Reform in Illinois—A Model for the Nation, DCBA Brief, at 10–12 (April 2004)).

[91] Id., at 56, 853 N.E.2d at 409 (Fitzgerald, J., specially concurring) ("This is a great responsibility. Indeed, this court must answer the ultimate question of whether a defendant should receive a death sentence. Because of the seriousness of the issue, and the fact that the decision, in the end, is ours alone to make, our review should be *de novo*.").

[92] See Roy A. Schotland, New Challenges to States' Judicial Selection, 95 Geo. L.J. 1077, 1105 app. 2 (2007) ("Of all state judges (appellate and general-jurisdiction trial courts), 89% ... face the voters in some type of election. Facing contestable elections are 60% ... of our appellate judges ...; facing only retention elections are another 26% [of appellate judges]."); John Blume & Theodore Eisenberg, Judicial Politics, Death Penalty Appeals, and Case Selection: An Empirical Study, 72 S. Cal. L. Rev. 465 (1999).

[93] See Jordan Steiker, Innocence and Federal Habeas, 41 U.C.L.A. L. Rev. 303 (1993).

Epilogue–The Neverending Story

For almost a year and a half after the U.S. Supreme Court's 2006 decision, Paul Gregory House could not even manage to get a hearing on the merits of his constitutional claims in federal court. First, the prosecution raised new procedural objections—different from those that were the subject of the first round of litigation—in an ongoing effort to show that House was not entitled to a hearing on the merits.[94] The U.S. Court of Appeals for the Sixth Circuit took several months to dispose of these procedural issues, and then remanded the case to the U.S. District Court for the Eastern District of Tennessee, where in February 2007 it was assigned to the same judge, the Honorable James H. Jarvis, who had denied House's habeas petition in February 2000. Judge Jarvis then became incapacitated due to serious illness and eventually died.[95] A new judge, the Honorable Harry S. "Sandy" Mattice, Jr., was assigned to the case, but needed some time to get up to speed.

In June 2007, the Attorney General of Tennessee filed a new brief with Judge Mattice, noting the importance of resolving the House case for the good of "the public's confidence in Tennessee's criminal justice system in capital cases."[96] The brief requested that the district court proceed directly to decide the merits of House's federal constitutional claims. Judge Mattice ordered both parties to file written submissions on the merits by August 20, 2007.[97]

Meanwhile, Paul Gregory House's physical condition deteriorated. While on Death Row, House had developed multiple sclerosis, a degenerative and fatal disease made worse by a general lack of available effective medical treatment in prison. Over time, House became confined to a wheelchair, still shackled hand and foot. His memory began to fail, and his ability to carry on a conversation became compromised. Due to his worsening condition, he was moved periodically to a long-term care facility. His supporters desperately sought executive clemency, so that House could enjoy what little time he had left to live, but the odds clearly were not in his favor.[98]

On December 20, 2007, Judge Mattice ordered Paul Gregory House to be released from custody unless a new trial was held within 180

---

[94] See House v. Bell, 466 F.3d 549 (6th Cir. 2006) (asking parties to submit briefs on whether House had exhausted his claims in state court).

[95] See House v. Bell, 2007 WL 4568444 (E.D. Tenn. 2007), at fn. 1.

[96] See Sarah Kelley, "Closer to Freedom: AG Changes Course, Agrees a Federal Judge Should Resolve the Controversial Paul House Case," Nashville Scene, July 19, 2007.

[97] Ibid.

[98] See Associated Press, "Despite Ruling, House Doubts He'll Be Exonerated," Chattanooga Times Free Press, March 27, 2007.

days.[99] More specifically, Judge Mattice found that House was entitled to summary judgment on several of his habeas claims, including (1) the prosecution's failure to notify the defense, at the time of the trial, that Carolyn Muncey's husband had sex with her on the morning of the murder; (2) the prosecution's failure to notify the defense about a Tennessee Bureau of Investigation report that failed to find any blood on House's shoes; (3) the prosecution's failure to notify the defense about the spillage of blood in the box that was used to carry evidence to the FBI laboratory in Washington, DC; and (4) the defense lawyer's constitutional ineffectiveness for failing to call at trial certain witnesses who would have testified as to the abusiveness of the victim's husband, Hubert "Little Hube" Muncey. The order provided that House's conviction and death sentence be vacated unless the prosecution commenced a new trial against him within 180 days[100]

Judge Mattice's decision in favor of House was hailed by some as a victory for justice. But the celebration turned out to be premature. The State of Tennessee appealed the ruling, and asked Judge Mattice to stay his order pending appeal. House's federal public defender, Stephen Kissinger, filed a cross-appeal with respect to a claim of prosecutorial misconduct that had been rejected by Judge Mattice, and also requested an order releasing House from custody pending appeal.

Meanwhile, back in Union County, Tennessee, the same local prosecutor who originally sent House to Death Row back in 1986, District Attorney William Paul Phillips, announced that he planned to refile the murder charge against House. Phillips further stated that, given House's medical condition, he would no longer seek the death penalty, but instead would try to have House sentenced to life imprisonment.

The House case began to proceed, bizarrely, on two separate and parallel judicial tracks. On the federal side, in February 2008, Judge Mattice held a hearing on the state motion for stay and the defense motion for release pending appeal. At the hearing, the state's lawyer, Associate Deputy Attorney General Jennifer Smith, argued that House should not be released pending appeal because he posed a flight risk: "The fact that Mr. House is ill does not eliminate the risk that we would lose this individual and be unable to retry him." Judge Mattice, looking at House slumped in his wheelchair, asked incredulously, "How would that happen, by the way?"[101]

---

[99] House v. Bell, 2007 WL 4568444 (E.D.Tenn.2007).

[100] Id., at pp. 27–28.

[101] Jamie Satterfield, "Judge Will Rule Later on Freedom for Death Row Inmate," Knoxville News Sentinel, Feb. 28, 2008.

On April 7, 2008, Judge Mattice granted both motions, effectively allowing the state to put off retrying House until the disposition of the pending appeal in the Sixth Circuit.[102] Judge Mattice ordered the parties to appear at a hearing in late May to discuss the precise terms of House's release from custody.

On May 5, 2008, the Sixth Circuit—which had accelerated the briefing and oral argument of the cross-appeals—affirmed the grant of habeas relief in a two-page, *per curiam* ruling.[103] At House's request, Judge Mattice agreed to reconsider the stay he had previously granted to the state. On May 29, 2008, the judge decided that the stay should be lifted, and ordered the state to take "affirmative steps to commence and diligently and expeditiously pursue the re-prosecution" of House by no later than June 17, 2008 (which was 180 days after the original grant of habeas relief).[104]

On the state side, the presiding judge in House's Union County murder retrial—a replacement for the originally assigned judge, who had to recuse himself because he had worked for the prosecution during the appeal of House's original conviction—set bail at $500,000. This meant that, notwithstanding Judge Mattice's order of release, House remained in state custody. In June 2008, the judge agreed to reduce bail to $100,000. An anonymous donor stepped forward and posted bond.

On July 2, 2008, nearly 23 years after his arrest for the murder of Carolyn Muncey, Paul Gregory House was released from prison into the custody of his mother. Although he was prohibited from leaving his mother's home, and was subject to 24–hour monitoring, House said, "I feel pretty good. All I am looking forward to is going home and eating some chili verde and pizza. I'm glad to be out. It's been a long time."[105] House's retrial was scheduled for October 14, 2008.

Coda: The Surprise Twist

On July 10, 2008, District Attorney Phillips told the local news media that he planned to ask the presiding judge for permission to conduct new mitochondrial DNA tests on a human hair that had been found clenched in Carolyn Muncey's hand when her lifeless body was found—presumably, a hair belonging to her killer. "If it's not [House's] and not hers and [belongs to] some third party, then we would have to evaluate that along with all the other evidence, and we would determine

---

[102] House v. Bell, 2008 WL 972709 (E.D. Tenn.2008).

[103] House v. Bell, 276 Fed.Appx. 437 (6th Cir.2008).

[104] House v. Bell, 2008 WL 2235235 (E.D. Tenn.2008).

[105] See Rose French, "House Released After 22 Years on Death Row," Chattanooga Times Free Press, July 3, 2008.

if that raised a reasonable doubt.... But if at any time that [hair] or any other evidence raised a reasonable doubt, then we would not prosecute."[106] The judge granted Phillips's request, but because the hair would be destroyed in the process, the judge ordered that the testing be conducted by an independent laboratory. Test results were anticipated within a few weeks.[107]

Just a few days later, House once again was back in federal court. His lawyer filed a new motion with the Sixth Circuit, seeking a ruling that the state should be barred from proceeding with the pending retrial for failure to comply with Judge Mattice's 180–day deadline. The Sixth Circuit heard arguments on the motion, but decided, with one judge dissenting, to remand the case back to the district court for further development of the record.[108]

On September 18, 2008, Judge Mattice held a hearing to determine whether or not the state was in "substantial compliance" with the 180–day deadline. At the hearing, House's lawyer called the prosecutor, District Attorney Phillips, to the witness stand. In response to defense questioning, Phillips dropped a bombshell: The results of the new DNA tests were in, and they showed that the hair in Carolyn Muncey's hand did not belong to Paul Gregory House. Nor did the hair belong to Hubert "Little Hube" Muncey, the victim's abusive husband. Instead, the hair was that of an unidentified third man—an entirely new mystery suspect.[109]

In light of this shocking new DNA evidence, which appeared to exonerate House, his lawyer immediately asked Judge Mattice to bar the retrial: "[The state] continues to prosecute Mr. House when Mr. Phillips knows there is no basis under which he can be convicted." But Judge Mattice denied the defense request, explaining: "There is no authority to allow a federal court to examine evidence in a state criminal case."[110] The judge also found the state to be in "substantial compliance" with the 180–day deadline, and denied House's motion to bar retrial.[111] House's lawyer announced his intention to file yet another appeal with the Sixth Circuit.

---

[106] See Associated Press, "House Case To Get DNA Tests Before His Retrial," Chattanooga Times Free Press, July 10, 2008.

[107] See Associated Press, "Judge Requests Independent Evidence Test in Death Row Case," Chattanooga Times Free Press, July 12, 2008.

[108] House v. Bell, 287 Fed.Appx. 439 (6th Cir. 2008).

[109] See Monica Mercer, "DNA Results Shine New Light on House Trials," Chattanooga Times Free Press, Sept. 19, 2008.

[110] Ibid.

[111] House v. Bell, 2008 WL 4372360 (E.D. Tenn.2008).

Notwithstanding the new DNA evidence and his earlier public statements, District Attorney Phillips persists in the belief that Paul Gregory House is a killer. The new theory of the prosecution's case is that House was with other men on the night of the killing, and that somehow a hair belonging to one of those men made its way into Carolyn Muncey's hand, either by sheer coincidence or because the other man helped to commit the crime. According to Phillips: "We have statements suggesting Mr. House was with other males on the night of Carolyn Muncey's death.... The fact that this hair in her hand was not [House's] or her husband's is consistent with [House] being with other males that night."[112]

District Attorney Phillips, on behalf of the State of Tennessee, still intends to retry House for the murder of Carolyn Muncey. The prosecution still claims to have sufficient proof to convict House, even in light of the new DNA evidence, and even without the seriously tainted blood evidence and the no-longer-inculpatory semen evidence that was so damaging at the original trial. In order to allow time for additional forensic testing of fingernail samples and other fragments of 24–year-old physical evidence, House's retrial has been delayed until March 2009.[113]

If House is convicted of murder a second time, he can be sentenced to life in prison. For all meaningful purposes, however, House's life already has been taken away from him. He already has spent more than two decades in prison—almost all of that time on Death Row—for a horrible, brutal crime that, given all of the evidence, it now seems very likely he did not commit. The long, dark nightmare for Paul Gregory House, which still is not yet over, is really a nightmare for us all.

---

[112] See Jamie Satterfield, "Prosecutor Confirms Hair in Victim's Hand Not House's," Knoxville News Sentinel, Sept. 18, 2008.

[113] See Associated Press, "House Retrial Postponed Until Next Year," Knoxville News Sentinel, Oct. 3, 2008.

Biographies of Contributing Authors

David C. Baldus is the Joseph B. Tye professor of law at the University of Iowa College of Law where among other things he has taught courses on criminal law, capital punishment, and statistical methods for lawyers. He is co-author of two books, STATISTICAL PROOF OF DISCRIMINATION (1980) and EQUAL JUSTICE AND THE DEATH PENALTY: A LEGAL AND EMPIRICAL ANALYSIS (1990), as well as numerous articles on capital punishment. Over the past 25 years, he and George Woodworth, Professor of Statistics and Actuarial Science at the University of Iowa have conducted empirical studies of capital charging and sentencing in Arkansas, Colorado, Georgia, New Jersey, Maryland, Nebraska, and Philadelphia County. Their Georgia research formed the basis of petitioner's claims in *McCleskey v. Kemp* (1987).

In the late 1980's and early 1990's, Professor Baldus served the New Jersey Supreme Court as a special master for proportionality review in death penalty cases. In that capacity, he and Professor Woodworth helped the New Jersey court establish the empirically based system of comparative proportionality review that the court used until the New Jersey legislature abolished capital punishment in 2007. The New Jersey court used its proportionality review database to evaluate individual death sentences for evidence of arbitrariness and to evaluate the state's entire capital charging and sentencing system for evidence of systemic racial discrimination.

Hugo Adam Bedau, Ph.D., Harvard, 1961, is the Austin B. Fletcher Professor of Philosophy, Emeritus, at Tufts University in Medford, Massachusetts. He joined the Tufts faculty in 1966 and retired in 1999. Prior to his appointment at Tufts, he taught at Dartmouth College, Princeton University, and Reed College. He has contributed dozens of scholarly articles to journals and books, and he has written a number of popular essays for several newspapers; he has also edited several volumes dealing with issues in social, political, moral, and legal philosophy. He is best known for his long-standing interest in issues having to do with punishment in general and the death penalty in particular, on which he is a national expert (he has frequently testified against the death penalty before the U.S. Congress and many state legislatures). Professor Bedau is editor of the standard work on capital punishment, *The Death Penalty in America* (1st edition, 1964; 4th edition, 1997), as well as co-editor of *Capital Punishment in the United States* (1976) and *Debating the Death Penalty* (2004). He is the author of *The Courts, the Constitution, and Capital Punishment* (1977), *Death is Different* (1987), and *Killing as Punishment* (2004), and he is co-author of *In Spite of Innocence* (1992). Over the past two decades he has co-authored and co-edited several volumes on critical thinking; he is also the author of *Thinking and Writing About Philosophy* (2nd edition, 2002).

Professor Bedau was elected the Romanell–Phi Beta Kappa Professor of Philosophy in 1994; his Romanell lectures, delivered at Tufts in the spring of 1995, were published by Oxford University Press in 1997, under the title *Making Mortal Choices*. In 1997, Bedau received the August Vollmer Award of the American Society of Criminology. A long-time (and founding) member of the National Coalition Against the Death Penalty, he served many years on its board and two terms as its chairman; he has been an active member of American Civil Liberties Union (ACLU) since the 1950s, and in 2003 he received the Roger Baldwin Award from the ACLU of Massachusetts (on whose board he has also served).

John H. Blume is a Professor of Law at Cornell Law School and the Director of the Cornell Death Penalty Project. Professor Blume teaches Criminal Procedure, Evidence, and several courses related to the death penalty. A 1984 graduate of the Yale Law School, a 1982 graduate of Yale Divinity School, and a 1978 graduate of the University of North Carolina at Chapel Hill, Blume clerked for the Honorable Thomas A. Clark, a judge on the United States Court of Appeals for the Eleventh Circuit. He is also the former Director of the South Carolina Death Penalty Resource Center.

Professor Blume has authored numerous law review articles and book chapters regarding capital punishment, criminal procedure and evidence. Much of his recent scholarship has involved empirical research regarding the administration of capital punishment as well as a variety of topics involving mentally impaired death sentenced inmates. *See, e.g., Killing the Willing: "Volunteers," Suicide and Competency,* 103 Mich. L. Rev. 939 (2005). Professor Blume has argued seven capital cases before the United States Supreme Court—the most recent of which is *Roper v. Weaver,* 550 U.S. 698 (2007)—and he has served as co-counsel or *amicus curiae* counsel in numerous other cases heard by the High Court Additionally, he has represented death sentenced inmates in a number of different jurisdictions at trial, on appeal and in state and federal collateral proceedings.

Jack Boger is Dean and Wade Edwards Distinguished Professor of Law at the University of North Carolina at Chapel Hill, where he has taught constitutional law, education law, and race and poverty law since 1990. Prior to 1990, he served as assistant counsel with the NAACP Legal Defense & Educational Fund, Inc. in New York, where he worked closely with Professor Anthony G. Amsterdam and others from 1978–86 in LDF's capital punishment project. Boger served as a lead counsel in *McCleskey v. Kemp* (1987), which unsuccessfully challenged the application of Georgia's capital statutes on grounds of arbitrariness and racial discrimination in implementation, as well as *Lockhart v. McCree* (1988), which challenged the practice of "death qualification" of capital juries during the guilt-innocence phase. Throughout the *McCleskey* litigation, Boger worked closely with David Baldus and George Woodworth to present statistical studies that lay at the heart of the constitutional challenge. Beginning in 2001 at UNC, Boger assisted Julius L. Chambers to establish a Center for Civil Rights that has challenged the drift toward public school resegregation in the South and the use of zoning devices to exclude poor and non-white residents from the legal boundaries of the municipalities in which they live and work. He is co-editor of two books, *Race, Poverty & American Cities* (1996) with Judith Wegner, and *School Resegregation: Must the South Turn Back?* (2005) with Gary Orfield.

David Bruck is a Clinical Professor of Law at Washington & Lee School of Law, and Director of the Virginia Capital Case Clearinghouse, a law school clinic and resource center for lawyers defending capitally-charged clients throughout Virginia. Bruck began practicing criminal law in South Carolina in 1976, and since 1980 has specialized in defending capitally-charged and death-sentenced inmates at the trial and post-trial stages. His appellate cases include *Simmons v. South Carolina*, 512 U.S. 154 (1994), *Shafer v. South Carolina*, 532 U. S. 36 (2001), and *Kelly v. South Carolina*, 534 U.S. 246 (2002)). Bruck has frequently testified before U.S. Congressional committees on death penalty legislation, and has lectured to lawyers, mental health professionals, and state and federal judges on capital sentencing issues in more than 30 states and U.S. territories. He received the John Minor Wisdom Public Service & Professionalism Award from the ABA Section of Litigation in 1996, and the Significant Contributions to Criminal Justice Award from California Attorneys for Criminal Justice in 2001. He has taught seminars on the law of capital punishment at the University of South Carolina School of Law, was the 1990 Ralph E. Shikes Visiting Fellow at Harvard Law School, and in 2002 served as Scholar in Residence at the Frances Lewis Law Center, Washington & Lee University. He has directed W & L's Virginia Capital Case Clearinghouse since mid–2004.

Deborah W. Denno is the Arthur A. McGivney Professor of Law at Fordham University School of Law. Professor Denno received her B.A. from the University of Virginia, her M.A. from the University of Toronto, and her Ph.D. and J.D. from the University of Pennsylvania, where she was the Managing Editor of the *University of Pennsylvania Law Review*. Prior to joining the Fordham Law faculty in 1991, she clerked for Anthony J. Scirica, now Chief Judge of the Third Circuit Court of Appeals, and worked as an associate at Simpson, Thacher & Bartlett. At Fordham Law School she primarily teaches criminal law, torts, and various seminars on advanced criminal law topics including rape and social science evidence. Professor Denno was a member of the United States Sentencing Commission's Drugs/Violence Task Force, and has visited on the faculties of Columbia Law School and Vanderbilt Law School. She has also been a Visiting Professor of Public and International Affairs at Princeton University's Woodrow Wilson School, a Visiting Senior Fellow at the School of Advanced Study at the University of London, and a British Academy Visiting Professor at the London School of Economics. In 2007, she was selected as one of the *National Law Journal*'s "Fifty Most Influential Women Lawyers in America."

Professor Denno has published on a broad range of topics relating to criminal law, criminal procedure, social sciences and the law, and the death penalty, including the constitutionality of execution methods. She has also initiated cutting-edge examinations of criminal law defenses pertaining to insanity, rape law, gender differences, consciousness, biological and genetic links to crime, drug offenses, jury decision-making, and the impact of lead poisoning. Currently she is working on a book-length project analyzing the neuroscientific correlates of criminal intent and conduct, most particularly the growing scientific evidence on the complexity of human behavior as well as states of conscious and unconscious awareness. Professor Denno was a co-editor of, and contributor to, the Encyclopedia of Crime and Justice (2nd ed. Macmillan, 2002) as well as the author of Biology and Violence: From Birth to Adulthood (Cambridge University Press,1990). For nearly two decades she has written on, and testified as an expert in state and federal courts about, the constitutionality of lethal injection and electrocution. Her experience includes testimony at the trial stage of *Baze v. Rees*, 128 S. Ct. 1520 (2008), where her work was cited in Chief Justice Roberts' plurality opinion and in the concurring opinions of Justices Alito, Stevens, and Breyer.

David R. Dow is the University Distinguished Professor at the University of Houston Law Center as well as the litigation director at the Texas Defender Services. For nearly twenty years, he has represented death-sentenced inmates at all stages of the appellate process, including direct appeal, and state and federal habeas corpus proceedings. He is the author of four books, including MACHINERY OF DEATH (Routledge 2002) and EXECUTED ON A TECHNICALITY (Beacon 2005), and more than one hundred essays and professional articles. His work has also appeared in the New York Times, The Washington Post, The Christian Science Monitor, and The Houston Chronicle, among others.

Joseph L. Hoffmann is the Harry Pratter Professor of Law at Indiana University Maurer School of Law-Bloomington. He is a nationally recognized scholar in the areas of criminal law, criminal procedure, habeas corpus, and the death penalty. He was a founding member of the Capital Jury Project, has taught about the death penalty for more than two decades at the National Judicial College and various state judicial education programs, and recently served as co-reporter for the Massachusetts Governor's Council on Capital Punishment. He has written or co-written numerous articles and book chapters about habeas corpus and the death penalty, including ones published in the Supreme Court Review, Cornell Law Review, Texas Law Review, and N.Y.U. Law Review. In 2002, he drafted the Illinois "Fundamental Justice Amendment," a statute expanding the review powers of the Illinois Supreme Court in capital cases; the proposal was adopted in 2003 and went into effect in 2004. Prior to joining the Indiana faculty, Professor Hoffmann clerked for the Honorable Phyllis A. Kravitch of the U.S. Court of Appeals for the Eleventh Circuit, and for then-Associate Justice William H. Rehnquist of the U.S. Supreme Court.

Scott W. Howe is the Frank L. Williams, Jr. Professor of Criminal Law at Chapman University School of Law. He received his B.A. from the University of Missouri and his J.D. from the University of Michigan. After law school, he worked for five years as a staff attorney for the Public Defender Service for the District of Columbia, defending persons charged with serious crimes, including first degree murder, at all stages of the criminal process. He subsequently served as Deputy Director of the Texas Death Penalty Resource Center, in Austin, Texas, representing inmates under execution warrants on Texas' death row. His representation during this period of death-row inmate Kerry Max Cook is recounted in Mr. Cook's acclaimed memoir, CHASING JUSTICE: MY STORY OF FREEING MYSELF AFTER TWO DECADES ON DEATH ROW FOR A CRIME I DIDN'T COMMIT. Before joining the faculty at Chapman, Professor Howe taught as an adjunct professor at the University of Texas Law School and then was a professor at Western New England College School of Law. He is a co-author of the second edition of UNDERSTANDING CAPITAL PUNISHMENT LAW (LexisNexis 2008) (with L. Carter and E. Kreitzberg).

Sheri Lynn Johnson earned her B.A. from the University of Minnesota in 1975 and her J.D. from Yale in 1979. After working for the Legal Aid Society of New York as a public defender, she began teaching at the Cornell Law School in 1981, where she is currently a Professor of Law and Assistant Director of the Cornell Death Penalty Project. The author of numerous articles and book chapters, Professor Johnson's primary scholarly interests are focused on race and criminal procedure, and, more particularly in recent years, race and capital punishment. Additionally, Professor Johnson has extensive litigation experience in capital cases, and was co-counsel for the death sentenced inmate in several successful Supreme Court cases including *Holmes v. South Carolina*, 547 U.S. 319 (2006), and *Roper v. Weaver*, 550 U.S. 698 (2007).

Charles A. Pulaski, Jr., is a practicing attorney and former law professor at the University of Iowa and at Arizona State University. He was a co-participant with Professor David Baldus and Professor George Woodworth in the empirical studies presented in the *McCleskey v. Kemp* litigation and a co-author of EQUAL JUSTICE AND THE DEATH PENALTY: A LEGAL AND EMPIRICAL ANALYSIS (1990) and a number of related law review articles. In 1985, Professor Pulaski returned to the practice of law with Snell & Wilmer LLP, a regional law firm with offices in Phoenix, Arizona, and six other cities in the west and southwest, including Los Cabos in Mexico. Professor Pulaski is the firm's senior tax partner. His practice is largely concentrated in advising non-profit organizations and in representing businesses and individuals in connection with controversies with the Internal Revenue Service. He has also been active in the Tax Section of the American Bar Association and has served in a number of leadership positions.

Austin Sarat is William Nelson Cromwell Professor of Jurisprudence and Political Science, Five College Fortieth Anniversary Professor, and Senior Advisor to the Dean of Faculty at Amherst College. Professor Sarat is author or editor of more than sixty books including THE KILLING STATE: CAPITAL PUNISHMENT IN LAW, POLITICS, AND CULTURE, WHEN THE STATE KILLS: CAPITAL PUNISHMENT AND THE AMERICAN CONDITION, THE CULTURAL LIVES OF CAPITAL PUNISHMENT: COMPARATIVE PERSPECTIVES, LAW, VIOLENCE, AND THE POSSIBILITY OF JUSTICE, PAIN, DEATH, AND THE LAW, MERCY ON TRIAL: WHAT IT MEANS TO STOP AN EXECUTION, WHEN LAW FAILS: MAKING SENSE OF MISCARRIAGES OF JUSTICE, and CAPITAL PUNISHMENT, 2 Volumes. His most recent book is THE ROAD TO ABOLITION? HE IS CURRENTLY WRITING A BOOK ENTITLED *Hollywood's Law: What Movies do for Democracy*. HE IS EDITOR OF THE JOURNAL *Law, Culture and the Humanities* AND OF *Studies in Law, Politics, and Society*.

Professor Sarat has received numerous prizes and awards including the Harry Kalven Award given by the Law Society Association for "distinguished research on law and society," the Reginald Heber Smith Award given biennially to honor the best scholarship on "the subject of equal access to justice," and the James Boyd White Award from the Association for the Study of Law, Culture, and the Humanities given for distinguished scholarly achievement and "outstanding and innovative" contributions to the humanistic study of law. In May, 2008 Providence College awarded Professor Sarat an honorary degree in recognition of his pioneering work in the development of legal study in the liberal arts and his distinguished scholarship on capital punishment in the United States.

Carol Steiker is the Howard J. and Katherine W. Aibel Professor of Law at Harvard Law School. Professor Steiker attended Harvard–Radcliffe Colleges and Harvard Law School, where she served as president of the Harvard Law Review. After clerking for Judge J. Skelly Wright of the D.C. Circuit Court of Appeals and Justice Thurgood Marshall of the U.S. Supreme Court, she worked as a staff attorney for the Public Defender Service for the District of Columbia, where she represented indigent defendants at all stages of the criminal process. She has been a member of the Harvard Law School faculty since 1992, where she was Associate Dean for Academic Affairs from 1998–2001 and where she currently serves as the Dean's Special Advisor for Public Service. Professor Steiker is the author of numerous scholarly works in the fields of criminal law, criminal procedure, and capital punishment. She recently has joined as co-author the Kadish, Schulhofer & Steiker casebook, CRIMINAL LAW AND ITS PROCESSES (8th ed. 2007), she is the editor of CRIMINAL PROCEDURE STORIES (Foundation 2006), and she served on the Board of Editors of the ENCYCLOPEDIA OF CRIME AND JUSTICE (2nd ed. Macmillan, 2002). In addition to her scholarly work, Professor Steiker has worked on pro bono litigation projects on behalf of indigent criminal defendants and has served as a consultant and an expert witness on issues of criminal justice for non-profit organizations and federal and state legislatures.

Jordan Steiker is the Judge Robert M. Parker Chair in Law and Co–Director of the Capital Punishment Center at the University of Texas School of Law. He served as a law clerk for Honorable Louis Pollak, U.S. District Court (Eastern District of Pennsylvania) and Justice Thurgood Marshall of the United States Supreme Court. He has taught constitutional law, criminal law, and death penalty law at the University of Texas since 1990. His work focuses primarily on the administration of capital punishment in the United States, and he has written extensively on constitutional law, federal habeas corpus, and the death penalty. Professor Steiker has testified before state legislative committees addressing death penalty issues in Texas, including state habeas reform, clemency procedures, sentencing options in capital cases, and the availability of the death penalty for juveniles and persons with mental retardation. He has also litigated extensively on behalf of indigent death-sentenced inmates in state and federal court, including in the U.S. Supreme Court. By way of disclosure, Professor Steiker served as counsel or co-counsel in several of the cases discussed in his chapter (*Tennard v.*

Dretke (2004), *Smith v. Texas* (2004), *Brewer v. Quarterman* (2007), *Abdul-Kabir v. Quarterman* (2007), and *Smith v. Texas* (2007)).

George Woodworth is a Professor of Statistics and Actuarial Science and Professor of Biostatistics at the University of Iowa. He is an elected Fellow of the American Statistical Association. His principal research areas are Statistical Evidence of Discrimination and Biomedical Statistics.

†